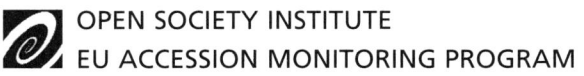

OPEN SOCIETY INSTITUTE
EU ACCESSION MONITORING PROGRAM

D1796493

Monitoring the EU Accession Process:

Corruption and Anti-corruption Policy

2002

Published by

OPEN SOCIETY INSTITUTE

Október 6. u. 12.
H-1051 Budapest
Hungary

400 West 59th Street
New York, NY 10019
USA

EU ACCESSION MONITORING PROGRAM

Október 6. u. 12.
H-1051 Budapest
Hungary

Website
<www.eumap.org>

ISBN: 1-891385-22-4

Library of Congress Cataloging-in-Publication Data.
A CIP catalog record for this book is available upon request.

Copies of the book can be ordered from the EU Accession Monitoring Program
<euaccession@osi.hu>

Printed in Budapest, Hungary, September 2002
Design & Layout by Q.E.D. Publishing

Table of Contents

Acknowledgements

The EU Accession Monitoring Program of the Open Society Institute would like to acknowledge the primary role of the following individuals in researching and drafting these monitoring reports. Final responsibility for the content of the reports rests with the Program.

Bulgaria	Bojko Todorov	*Center for the Study of Democracy/Coalition 2000*
Czech Republic	Quentin Reed	*EU Accession Monitoring Program*
Estonia	Agu Laius	*Jaan Tõnisson Institute/ Transparency International*
	Triin Reinsalu	*Jaan Tõnisson Institute*
Hungary	Elizabeth Barrett	*Oxford University*
Latvia	Inese Voika	*Transparency International*
Lithuania	Aleksandras Dobryninas	*Transparency International*
	Jolanta Piliponyte	*Transparency International*
	Severinas Vaitiekus	*Lithuanian Centre for Human Rights*
Poland	Małgorzata Fuszara	*University of Warsaw*
	Grażyna Kopinska	*Batory Foundation*
	Jacek Kurczewski	*University of Warsaw*
Romania	Oana Mateescu	*Transparency International*
	Adrian Baboi-Stroe	*Transparency International*
Slovakia	Emília Sicáková – Beblavá	*Transparency International*
	Daniela Zemanovicová	*Transparency International*
	Pavel Nechala	*Transparency International*
Slovenia	Matjaž Jager	*University of Ljubljana*

ADVISORY BOARD MEMBERS

Alan Doig	*Liverpool University*
Åse Grodeland	*Norwegian Institute of Urban and Regional Research*
Péter Hack	*former Member of Parliament, Hungary*
Jacek Kurczewski	*University of Warsaw*
Mark Philp	*Oxford University*
Susan Rose-Ackerman	*Yale Law School*
András Sajó	*Central European University*

The EU Accession Monitoring Program developed its methodology for monitoring corruption in close partnership with Transparency International, and wishes to acknowledge the key contribution of TI chapters not only in drafting individual country reports, as noted above, but in sharing their accumulated experience and expertise by commenting on draft reports and organising many of our expert roundtable meetings (see below).

We would also like to thank the following individuals for their invaluable contribution to the reports in the form of research or review and critique of draft reports: Nóra Ábonyi, Jautrite Briede, Oana Cinca, Arista M. Cirtautas, Dennis Cohen, Jim Goldston, Joel Hellman, Janis Ikstens, Valts Kalnins, Franz Kaps, Diana Kurpniece, Puiu Latea, Miklós Marschall, Pauls Raudseps, Peter Sprung, Timothy Waters, János Zolnay

OSI held roundtable meetings in many candidate countries to invite expert critique and commentary on the draft reports from representatives of the Governments, the Commission Delegations, and civil society oganisations and experts. We are grateful to the many participants at those meetings who generously offered their time and expertise. Lists of the meeting participants are available from the EU Accession Monitoring Program (euaccession@osi.hu).

THE EU ACCESSION MONITORING PROGRAM

Rachel Guglielmo	*Program Director*
Quentin Reed	*Program Officer and Editor*
Andrea Gurubi Watterson	*Program Assistant*
Andrea Kiss	*Program Assistant*
Lucie Vidmarova	*Program Assistant*

Preface

The Open Society Institute's **EU Accession Monitoring Program (EUMAP)** was initiated in 2000 to support independent monitoring of the EU accession process by civil society representatives.

In keeping with the broader aims of the Open Society Institute, EUMAP has focused on governmental compliance with the political criteria for EU membership, as defined by the 1993 Copenhagen European Council:

> Membership requires that the candidate country has achieved stability of institutions guaranteeing democracy, human rights, the rule of law and respect for and protection of minorities.

EUMAP reports are elaborated by independent experts from the States being monitored. They are intended to promote responsible and sustainable enlargement by highlighting the significance of the political criteria and the key role of civil society in promoting governmental compliance with those criteria – up to and beyond accession.

In 2001 EUMAP published its first two volumes of monitoring reports, on minority protection and judicial independence in the ten candidate countries of Central and Eastern Europe. In 2002 new and more detailed minority reports (including reports on the five largest EU member States) have been produced, as well as reports on judicial capacity, corruption and – in cooperation with OSI's Network Women's Program/Open Society Foundation Romania – on equal opportunities for women and men in the CEE candidate States.

EUMAP reports on **corruption and anti-corruption policy** point to areas in which corruption appears to be problematic, and assess the efficacy of governmental anti-corruption efforts; they do not attempt to establish levels of corruption or to rank countries according to how corrupt they are.

The EUMAP methodology for monitoring corruption and anti-corruption policy (available at www.eumap.org), was developed by EUMAP with input from Transparency International and an international advisory board. The methodology provides for a broad survey of the legislation and institutions that may serve to prevent or combat corruption, drawing on existing evidence on corruption in each candidate State in conjunction with interviews carried out by country reporters. Although this does not constitute an exhaustive or scientific examination of the specific areas covered, its principle advantage lies in the consistent application of the same methodology to all monitored countries.

First drafts of each report were reviewed by members of the international advisory board and by national roundtables. Roundtables were organised in order to invite comments on the draft from Government officials, civil society organisations, minority representatives, and international organisations. The final reports reproduced in this volume underwent significant revision based on the comments and criticisms received during this process. EUMAP assumes full responsibility for their final content.

Foreword

There is a growing understanding that persistent poverty and the failure of democratic reform are linked to corruption, and to political corruption in particular. In light of the developing consensus in this area – reflected in a growing number of international and national documents addressing anti-corruption efforts – corruption has become a major concern both within the present European Union and among new candidates for membership. The Copenhagen criteria for EU accession and the European Commission's annual Regular Reports evaluating candidate countries clearly reflect this concern.

The recognition that corruption restricts economic and political reform has particularly contributed to the willingness of East European States – in which the process of transition from centralised systems continues – to shape more effective institutional and policy tools with the potential to mitigate corruption.

In addition to the concerns of the international community, the EU, and individual States, the general public has a direct stake in reform. There is evidence that citizens in the candidate countries are well aware of the problem of corruption, and that they believe there is a need for practical anti-corruption measures, even though they may not necessarily agree with the moral criticisms of corruption that are sometimes raised.

However, the efforts taken against corruption in candidate States have often been merely formalistic, and indeed the Union's own expectations about what States have to do to meet the requirements of membership in combating corruption have often been limited to the ratification of conventions, without soliciting more meaningful change. Yet without meaningful and continuing enforcement they will not lead to lasting improvements; indeed, there is even a danger that ineffective measures will undermine the credibility of all anti-corruption efforts.

It is in this regard that monitoring of national and international efforts to combat corruption is important. Governmental and public awareness of corruption and actions to fight it require not only coordination and intellectual guidance, but also independent external monitoring of corruption and anti-corruption policy. Public, independent monitoring and analysis of Government efforts that are intended to curb corruption as part of EU membership not only fulfil a traditional "watchdog" function, but also contribute to a better understanding of the complex social nature of corruption.

Without this understanding and policies based upon it Governments will inevitably fall short in their efforts. In some areas corruption can be effectively tackled by introducing proper administration and supervision; in other areas, such as healthcare, however, there can be no improvement without sector-wide structural reforms. Further, only a vigorous democracy with a free press and committed citizenry can push a society and its political elite towards greater decency. Only if the majority knows what measures are being taken to reduce corruption and how they relate to an honest anti-corruption policy can the electorate evaluate politicians and bureaucracies and push them towards adopting transparent, genuine policies.

In order for the public to exert effective pressure and Governments to respond effectively, unbiased and systematic analysis of current problems is needed. This is the objective of the present project of the Open Society Institute. The methodology of the EU Accession Monitoring Program concentrates on the current structural shortcomings in a number of socio-economic sectors that are of fundamental importance for new or continuing EU membership – that is, those areas that are central to any meaningful understanding of what the Copenhagen political criteria require. As in the other areas the Program monitors, the corruption monitoring component follows a unified methodology that allows the findings to be used comparatively, without the ultimately futile exercise of ranking States and societies in terms of their alleged 'corruptness.'

The country reports and the Overview accompanying them are a promising start to what is, by its nature, a long-term process. Even if all the measures that follow from the findings are implemented, the problem of corruption will not go away. Although technical measures such as conflict of interest rules or public procurement standards play a rightful part in any effective anti-corruption policy, the social complexity of corruption means that one cannot simply rely on measures transferred from current EU member States that have their own specific problems with corruption.

Indeed, one of the Project's principal findings is that the EU itself lacks consistent or comprehensive anti-corruption policies. This in turn has made it more difficult for individual States, whether candidates or current members, to craft solutions that meet their own needs and those that reflect the shared values of the Union.

Of course, we may hope that the former communist countries will develop solutions tailored to their own specific circumstances, and at the same time, as these countries become members of the EU, we may reasonably expect levels of corruption to fall as their markets mature. However, even when societies become more affluent a deliberate political choice must be made to pay the social price of anti-corruption measures, even if that price is ultimately much lower than the social cost of corruption. The present volume is certainly a promising starting point for a social dialogue – both within the candidate countries and the Union as a whole – that can contribute to that choice.

András Sajó
University Professor of Central European University
Member, Hungarian Academy of Sciences

Monitoring the EU Accession Process: Corruption and Anti-corruption Policy

Table of Contents

Corruption and Anti-corruption Policy in the EU Accession Process

1. INTRODUCTION

This Overview and the accompanying country reports assess the extent of corruption in the candidate States of Central and Eastern Europe and the legal and institutional structures and policies with which Governments are seeking to combat it in light of the EU accession process and evolving EU norms and standards.

All EU candidate States have made impressive progress towards establishing (or re-establishing) democracy, the rule of law and a market economy. However, the post-communist transition has been troubled by corruption that has – or is at least perceived to have – persisted or flourished. The European Commission has repeatedly expressed concern at levels of corruption in candidate States, and has made it clear that making progress in the fight against corruption is a task all candidate States have to carry out in order to fulfil the conditions for EU membership.

The focus of the Commission on corruption in the candidate States is justified: there is a clear consensus that corruption undermines both democracy and markets, and post-communist States are especially vulnerable to corruption due to their historical legacy and the nature of transition. However, assessing levels of corruption in candidate States has proven difficult for the Commission, not only because the corruption problems of Central and East European (CEE) States are often different to the corruption problems faced by EU member States, but also because the European Union itself lacks a clear anti-corruption framework. As a result, the European Commission has not established clear benchmarks[1] for candidate States in the area of corruption or anti-corruption policy.

This situation gives rise to several problems. First, in the absence of a comprehensive framework for analysis of the extent, causes and nature of corruption in CEE States, the Commission has assessed corruption on a basis that tends towards a criminal law or "bribocentric" perspective. This perspective misses some of the most important aspects of corruption-related problems in these States, ranging from societal tolerance of corruption to more-or-less deep-rooted traditions of allocating resources on the basis of patronage networks. Second, in a number of cases the effectiveness of the anti-corruption policies the

---

[1] In the sense of a minimum or acceptable standard against which the performance of States can be measured or judged.

Commission has pressed candidates to adopt – in particular the focus on criminal proceedings and control-oriented solutions – has not been demonstrated in other Western liberal democracies.

Third, the Copenhagen mandate allows the Commission to demand anti-corruption policies from candidate States that it is unable to enforce on member States. A clear example of the difference in the Commission's leverage *vis-à-vis* member States and candidates States is provided by the Council of Europe Criminal Law Convention on Corruption. The Commission has consistently pushed candidate States to sign and ratify the Convention. As a result, as of June 2002 eight of the ten candidate States had ratified the Convention, compared to only three out of fifteen member States, giving rise to a justified perception that candidate countries are being held to different standards from those that currently obtain within the EU. In this context, the sluggishness of EU member States in ratifying the 1995 Convention on the Protection of the European Communities' Financial Interests of the Union (see Section 3.2.1) illustrates the limits to the Commission's capacity to implement any EU-wide anti-corruption policy.

These factors have combined to make the integration of anti-corruption goals into the accession framework difficult. Moreover, the primary focus of accession negotiations on harmonisation and implementation of the *acquis communautaire* limits the scope for inclusion of anti-corruption policy: explicit anti-corruption *acquis* is limited, and effective anti-corruption policy covers a broad range of measures and institutional practices, beyond the scope of accession negotiations.

Thus, the scenario that appears to be increasingly likely is that a number of countries with persistent and serious problems of corruption will be admitted to a European Union which lacks an adequate framework for dealing with these problems even in current member States. This scenario is a source of concern for two main reasons. First, while the EU has probably paid less attention to corruption in member States because it has not been perceived as undermining the implementation of the *acquis*, there are increasing signs that corruption in a number of member States represents a significant threat to the quality and functioning of democratic institutions. Second, the extent of corruption in a number of candidate countries may undermine both implementation of the *acquis* and the quality of democratic institutions. Corruption undermines some of the core values to which the Union subscribes, and an unavoidable challenge of the future is to develop mechanisms for promoting effective anti-corruption policy in all the States of an expanded Union.

On the other hand, these observations are mirrored by positive opportunities. While the European Commission itself has had only limited success in this area to date, corruption is being tackled actively by other international organisations, and in particular by the Council of Europe, an organisation that enjoys very close ties to the

EU. The Council has developed a set of broad anti-corruption "Guiding Principles," an active and functioning framework for monitoring adherence to the Principles – the Group of States Against Corruption (GRECO) – and two anti-corruption conventions. The EU has played an important role in pushing candidate States to ratify the conventions, and an important anti-corruption component of the EU accession process has been the joint Council of Europe-EU "OCTOPUS" programme, which has provided advice to candidate States on measures to fight organised crime and corruption.

Moreover, given the much broader scope of the Guiding Principles, the Council would appear to be the obvious candidate to take over the "corruption component" of the EU's Copenhagen criteria, both through the formal adoption of its guidelines by the EU, and by entrusting of the Commission's monitoring role to GRECO. There are clear ways in which the EU could move in this direction (see Section 4). Though GRECO has operated on an essentially voluntary and peer-review basis, the combination of its functioning monitoring mechanism with the more institutionalised leverage of the EU may well be the best way of promoting effective anti-corruption policy.

1.1 Corruption and EU Accession

1.1.1 Corruption and democracy: a key issue for accession

Corruption has consistently been one of the European Union's major concerns in candidate States since its initial 1997 assessment in the "Agenda 2000" report on CEE countries' applications for membership. According to the European Commission's 1998 overall report on progress towards accession by candidate countries,

> The fight against corruption needs to be strengthened further. The efforts undertaken by the candidate countries are not always commensurate with the gravity of the problem. Although a number of countries are putting in place new programs on control and prevention, it is too early to assess the effectiveness of such measures. There is a certain lack of determination to confront the issue and to root out corruption in most of the candidate countries.[2]

The 1999 overall report is more specific about the reasons for corruption:

---

[2] Commission of the European Union, *Composite Paper: Reports on Progress towards Accession by Each of the Candidate Countries*, November 1998, p. 6, available at <http://europa.eu.int/comm/enlargement/report_10_99/>, (last accessed 6 August 2002).

Corruption is widespread… exacerbated by low salaries in the public sector and extensive use of bureaucratic controls in the economy… The authorities lack conviction in the fight against corruption with the result that the anti-corruption programs which have been launched in most countries are having limited results.[3]

According to the November 2000 assessment,

This assessment [from October 1999] remains valid. Corruption, fraud and economic crime are widespread in most candidate countries, leading to a lack of confidence by the citizens and discrediting the reforms. Anti-corruption programs have been undertaken and some progress made, including accession to international instruments in this area, but corruption remains a matter of serious concern.[4]

In 2001 the Commission essentially repeated this assessment, although it acknowledged progress:

This assessment [of corruption as a serious problem] remains largely valid, although several positive developments have taken place. In most countries anti-corruption bodies have been strengthened, and progress has been made in legislation, in such areas as public procurement and public access to information. Encouraging developments in several countries as regards the reform of public administration also contribute to the fight against corruption. Notwithstanding these efforts, corruption, fraud and economic crime remain widespread in many candidate countries, where they contribute to a lack of confidence by the citizens and discredit reforms. Continued, vigorous measures are required to tackle this problem.[5]

These statements are reflected in the Commission's individual Regular Reports on each candidate country's progress towards accession: in November 2001 the Commission in its summary conclusions of the individual country assessments judged that corruption was a "serious" problem or "source of serious concern" in five of the ten Central

---

[3] Commission, *Composite Paper: Reports on Progress towards Accession by Each of the Candidate Countries*, October 1999, p. 12, available at <http://europa.eu.int/comm/enlargement/report_10_99/pdf/en/composite_en.pdf>, (last accessed 6 August 2002).

[4] Commission of the European Union, *Enlargement Strategy Paper: Report on Progress towards Accession by Each of the Candidate Countries*, November 2000, p. 16, <http://europa.eu.int/comm/enlargement/report_11_00/pdf/strat_en.pdf>, (last accessed 6 August 2002).

[5] Commission of the European Union, *Making a Success of Enlargement: Strategy Paper and Report of the European Commission on the Progress towards Accession by Each of the Candidate Countries*, November 2001, p. 7, <http://europa.eu.int/comm/enlargement/report2001/strategy_en.pdf>, (last accessed 6 August 2002).

Eastern European candidate States (Bulgaria, Czech Republic, Poland, Romania and Slovakia), a continuing problem or source of concern in three countries (Hungary, Latvia and Lithuania) and refrained from criticism in only two countries (Estonia and Slovenia). This and the assessment from 2001 cited above suggest that, at least in the eyes of the Commission, corruption remains a serious problem – if not a potential barrier – in relation to EU accession.

1.1.2 EU criteria: the Copenhagen criteria

A clear implication of both the Regular Reports and the Accession Partnerships (see below) is that the political conditions that must be satisfied for countries to enter the EU include demonstrable success in the fight against corruption. The political conditions that candidate countries must fulfil to be eligible for accession were laid down at the Copenhagen European Council in 1993. According to the "Copenhagen criteria," membership requires:

1.   that the candidate country has achieved stability of institutions guaranteeing democracy, the rule of law, human rights, and respect for and protection of minorities;

2.   the existence of a functioning market economy and the capacity to cope with competitive pressures and market forces within the Union; and

3.   that the candidate [has] the ability to take on the obligations of membership, including adherence to the aims of political, economic and monetary union.

In each of these areas corruption is clearly of relevance. Regarding the "political criteria," according to the Commission's own explanation,

> Countries wishing to become members of the EU are expected not just to subscribe to the principles of democracy and the rule of law, but actually to put them into practice in daily life. They also need to ensure the stability of the various institutions that enable public authorities, such as the judiciary, the police, and local government, to function effectively and democracy to be consolidated.[6]

The EU's concern with corruption in candidate States is not surprising. First, corruption has been widely identified as a major problem in post-communist countries,

---

[6]   Commission of the European Union, *The Copenhagen European Council and the 'Copenhagen Criteria'*, <http://europa.eu.int/comm/enlargement>, (last accessed 10 April 2001).

including many of the EU candidate States.[7] Second, there is also a consensus among political scientists that widespread corruption undermines democracy. As one authority on corruption has put it,

> When it is pervasive and uncontrolled, corruption thwarts economic development and undermines political legitimacy. Less pervasive variants result in wasted resources, increased inequity in resource distribution, less political competition, and greater distrust of government. Creating and exploiting opportunities for bribery at high levels of government also increases the cost of government, distorts the allocation of government spending, and may dangerously lower the quality of infrastructure. Even relatively petty or routine corruption can rob government of revenues, distort economic decision-making, and impose negative externalities on society, such as dirtier air and water or unsafe buildings.[8]

Third, there is a widely held assumption in political science and economics that extensive corruption undermines development and the proper functioning of markets.[9] Given the distorting effects on markets that corruption can produce, and given the primary ambition of the EU to create a "single market," tackling corruption seems a central element of the accession process. With respect to the "economic criteria," the EU identifies six conditions as necessary for the existence of a functioning market economy. Three of these conditions are likely to be undermined by corruption, namely that:

- barriers to market entry and exit are absent;

- the legal system, including the regulation of property rights, is in place, and that laws and contracts are enforceable;

- the financial sector is sufficiently developed to channel savings towards investment.[10]

Experience in candidate countries demonstrates how corruption can create barriers to market entry and distort court decisions and the activities of regulators. As the earlier

---

[7] See, e.g., *Anti-corruption in Transition: A Contribution to the Policy Debate,* World Bank, Washington, D.C. 2000, p. 6.

[8] K. A. Elliott, "Corruption as an International Policy Problem," in: A. J. Heidenheimer, M. Johnston (eds.), *Political Corruption: Concepts & Contexts,* Third Edition, Transaction Publishers, New Brunswick, 2002, p. 925.

[9] See for example C. W. Gray and D. Kaufmann, "Corruption and Development," in: *Finance and Development,* March 1998. A number of studies have prevented powerful evidence on the economic and social costs of corruption, mainly focused on less-developed countries; see World Bank, *Anti-corruption in Transition: A Contribution to the Policy Debate,* p. 18.

[10] See <http://europa.eu.int/comm/enlargement/intro/criteria.htm>, (last accessed July 31 2002).

citation shows, the EU has referred to the role of bureaucratic controls as one of the main factors facilitating corruption.

The Union's legal system works under the assumption that Community law will be implemented, observed and enforced by the courts and public administration of member States. Extensive corruption jeopardises the observance, implementation and enforcement of rules (and therefore of the *acquis*) or makes that adoption merely formal – further undermining the status and ultimately the efficacy of laws and rules in general.[11]

1.1.3 The lack of benchmarks

However, despite the suggestive nature of the Copenhagen criteria regarding corruption, neither the reasons for including corruption as an accession issue nor the exact criteria candidate States must fulfil in terms of anti-corruption policy or levels of corruption have been spelled out by the Commission in detail.[12]

Indeed, since 1999 the Commission has expressed the opinion that all candidate States fulfil the political criteria, despite finding at least two countries to be suffering from a very serious – and, in the case of Romania "systemic" – problem of corruption (see Section 3.2.1). The 2001 overall report refers to corruption as a widespread problem in many candidate States and calls for continued, vigorous anti-corruption measures.[13]

There is, however, no indication of either the benchmarks employed to assess corruption levels or the level of progress that would be considered sufficient by the Commission, either in terms of formal anti-corruption policy or in terms of reducing levels of corruption. There is no indication of whether such objectives are feasible in the timescale currently being discussed for accession. Moreover, it seems clear that assessments have not been based on a stable set of coherent criteria (see Section 3.2.).

---

[11] For example, the World Bank classifies corruption in transition countries into two main types: State capture, or illicit provision of gains to public officials to influence the *formation* of laws, regulations, decrees and other Government policies; and administrative corruption, the illicit provision of gains to distort the *implementation* of existing rules, laws and regulations. See World Bank, *Anti-corruption in Transition: A Contribution to the Policy Debate*, pp. xv–xvii (emphasis added).

[12] The inconsistency of the benchmarks used by the Commission in evaluating corruption was highlighted in a paper presented by Andras Sajo in February 2001 at a preparatory meeting for EUMAP reporters. The paper is on file with EUMAP.

[13] Commission, *Making a success of enlargement: Strategy Paper and Report of the European Commission on the progress towards accession by each of the candidate Countries*, p. 7.

The lack of clarity in this area may be partly related to the absence of clearly binding *acquis* in the area of corruption: the only explicit EU conventions relating to corruption, for example, are not yet binding for member States and are not mentioned in connection with corruption in reports on candidate States. For example, as of March 2002 only eight of the 15 member States had completed ratification of the 1995 Convention on the Protection of the European Communities' Financial Interests. There remain serious gaps in member States' ability to control the dispersion of EU funds, as witnessed by the repeated inability of the European Court of Auditors to approve the Community budget without reservations.[14]

Moreover, the EU lacks benchmarks for assessing corruption in member States, and there is little available research or information available for making judgements about the extent to which corruption is more widespread in candidate States than member States, although the limited available evidence does indicate that this is generally the case. However, there are also strong indications that corruption, and especially high-level corruption, is a serious problem in a number of member States, including some of its largest countries – including Germany, France, and Italy – while surveys report that the best candidate countries are less corrupt than the worst EU member States (see Section 2.1).[15]

---

[14] A recent report by the UK National Audit Office noted a 75 percent rise in detected fraud involving EU funds from 1999 to 2000. Most of the rise was due to improved audit mechanisms in the UK; several countries failed to detect any fraud whatsoever. The European Court of Auditors was unable for the seventh year in succession to approve the EU's accounts without qualification; *inter alia* it found that the Commission does not possess complete and reliable information allowing it to distinguish between payments of EU funds made to intermediaries and payments to final recipients. See UK National Audit Office, *Financial Management of the European Union: Annual Report of the European Court of Auditors for the Year 2000*, Report by the Comptroller and Auditor General, HC 859 Session 2001-2, 30 May 2002; P. Waugh, "British watchdog criticises 75 percent rise in European fraud," *The Independent*, 30 May 2002.

[15] See for example S. Theil and C. Dickey, "Europe's dirty secret," *Newsweek*, 29 April 2002.

1.2 Corruption and anti-corruption: the debate

The lack of clear benchmarks against which to measure a country's progress on corruption or anti-corruption policy is not only the result of the lack of an EU anti-corruption framework; it is also related to a more fundamental and ongoing debate on the definition of corruption.[16] This Overview does not attempt to define corruption. However, it attempts to show that corruption cannot be defined or understood simply as violation of formal rules and laws, which is the conception towards which most political scientists move. While we do not propose a definition of corruption that is applicable across all candidate States, and do not attempt to rank countries according to the prevalence of corruption, we attempt to offer a broad understanding of which types of behaviour or phenomena fall under the heading of corruption and are therefore a valid target for anti-corruption policy.

1.2.1 Problems of definition and measurement

The limits of formal rules

Political scientists and corruption researchers have tended to adopt a "public office"-centred conception of corruption, in which corruption is defined or identified as behaviour which

> "deviates from the formal duties of a public role because of private-regarding pecuniary or status gains; or violates rules against the exercise of certain types of private-regarding influence. This includes such behaviour as bribery... nepotism... and misappropriation."[17]

Public office-centred approaches tend to focus on violation of formal rules and laws. However, there are a number of problems with such an approach: for example, elites may devise laws to facilitate corruption, and even in States that attempt to regulate corruption entirely, formal rules and regulations can never entirely cover all actions,

---

[16] The debate centers not only on what constitutes corruption but also on whether definition is possible at all. For example, Frank Anechiarico and James B. Jacobs claim that corruption is a fundamentally subjective concept, and one that changes over time, and therefore cannot be defined in a universally acceptable way. See F. Anechiarico and J. B. Jacobs, *The Pursuit of Absolute Integrity: How Corruption Control Makes Government Ineffective*, University of Chicago Press, Chicago, 1996, pp. 3–5.

[17] A. J. Heidenheimer, M. Johnston and V. LeVine (eds.), *Political Corruption: A Handbook*, Transaction Publishers, New Brunswick, 1989, p. 966.

including many actions that would be widely considered as corrupt.[18] For example, the allocation of private TV licenses by a Government-dominated broadcasting authority in return for systematic political support from the TV station concerned is very difficult to criminalise. In her speech on the occasion of the signing of a Memorandum of Understanding on anti-corruption policy between Hungary and the United Nations in 1999, then Hungarian Minister of Justice Ibolya Dávid acknowledged a need to adopt a broad definition of corruption that went beyond mere compliance with the criminal code:

> [I]t is not enough…to focus…the strategy only on the criminal offences related to corruption; there could be such 'corrupt practices,' which do not constitute a crime according to the letter of the Penal Code…[19]

For these and other reasons, while statistics on criminal convictions may seem to be the only hard-and-fast "true" indicators of corruption, no serious analysis would rely on them to measure the prevalence of corruption in a given State, and certainly would not deduce from a larger number of bribery convictions that corruption is more widespread. The situation in candidate States tends to confirm this argument, as the number of convictions in individual States does not appear to bear much relation to other evidence on the prevalence of corruption. The record in EU member States provides little additional clarity. The number of court proceedings for corruption crimes in Germany, for example, was 1,034 in 1999, which – relative to the size of the country – is broadly similar to figures for a number of candidate countries.[20] However, in the United Kingdom there were almost no convictions in 1999 under the Prevention of Corruption Act or the Public Bodies Corrupt Practices Act, and literally no convictions in Northern Ireland or Scotland.[21]

Survey evidence

The other main source of evidence on levels of corruption is provided by surveys of perception and experience. Surveys are covered in detail in Section 3.1. Public opinion

---

[18] For a discussion of approaches to defining and understanding corruption see M. Philp, "Conceptualizing Political Corruption," in A.J. Heidenheimer and M. Johnston (eds.), *Political Corruption: Concepts and Contexts*, Transaction Publishers, New Brunswick and London, 2002, pp. 41–57.

[19] Speech by Minister of Justice Ibolya Dávid on the occasion of the signing of the Memorandum of Understanding between the UN and the Government of Hungary.

[20] GRECO, *Evaluation Report on Germany*, adopted by GRECO at its 8th Plenary Meeting, Strasbourg, 4-8 March 2002, p. 6. In addition, the number of proceedings has increased dramatically, from 258 in 1994.

[21] GRECO, *Evaluation Report on the United Kingdom*, adopted by GRECO at its 6th Plenary Meeting, Strasbourg, 10-14 September 2001, p. 3.

surveys continue to dominate the field. The principal problem with such indicators is that they are surveys of *perceptions* of corruption rather than corruption itself, and it is questionable whether they can be used as reliable indicators of actual levels of corruption.[22] In particular, perceptions tend to be general, while experience of corruption is particular and specific. Detailed surveys of citizen perceptions and experiences in Ukraine, Bulgaria, Slovakia and the Czech Republic indicate that general perceptions are not a reliable indicator of citizens' real experiences:

> Perceptions of high-level corruption [in post-communist countries] were widespread and irritated citizens everywhere. But although we found that the need to offer presents and bribes to street-level officials was widely discussed by citizens in general terms, it was much less frequent in their reports of personal experience... In their own dealings with officials, corruption was not the only problem... [nor] even the most frequent nor the most annoying feature of their day-to-day interactions with officials in any of our four countries.[23]

Surveys of experience of corruption represent an advance on surveys of perception, although they also face a number of problems such as acquiescence (respondents may give an answer designed to 'please' the interviewer), variations in results depending on the way in which the survey is conducted, and faulty memory.[24]

Institutionalised corruption and patronage

Another problem with narrow conceptions of corruption in all countries is that they do not easily embrace institutionalised corruption such as the acceptance of contributions by political parties in return for public contracts for the donor, where the benefits do not accrue directly to individuals. Moreover, in the CEE region, corruption is often embedded in a historical context of clientelism. Patron-client networks play an important role in all post-communist countries in structuring the relationship between

---

[22] TI itself emphasises the limitations of perception indexes. See J.G. Lambsdorff, *Background Paper to the 2001 Corruption Perceptions Index*, Transparency International and Göttingen University, June 2001, p. 4.
<http://www.transparency.org/cpi/2001/dnld/methodology.pdf>, (last accessed 31 July 2001).

[23] W. L. Miller, A. B. Grodeland and T. Y. Koshechkina, *A Culture of Corruption?: Coping with Government in Post-communist Europe*, Central European University Press, Budapest, 2001, p. 279.

[24] For example, problems related to memory could have affected the results of the World Bank/EBRD Business Environment and Enterprise Performance Survey (see Section 3.1), which asked companies what percentage of annual revenues companies like theirs pay annually in unofficial payments to public officials.

the State, private sector and citizen.[25] Such networks are typically based on a system of inter-temporal exchange of benefits that may be very difficult to measure,[26] and efforts to define or identify corruption become increasingly complex where such systems of exchange operate. Although no effort to deal effectively with corruption in post-communist States can ignore such networks, their complexity raises questions about the feasibility of measuring corruption by any of the methods outlined above.

EU evaluations of candidate States imply that corruption is mostly understood in a narrow sense of bribery according to the criminal law or international conventions. However, the concerns and recommendations expressed by the Commission in its Regular Reports have often been broader in scope, including calls for improvements in frameworks for regulating conflicts of interest,[27] party finance[28] or access to information.[29] Under these circumstances, and given the comments above on the usefulness of criminal statistics, it would appear that the Commission lacks a clear sense of what it means by corruption, and therefore what would constitute successful anti-corruption policy.

1.2.2 Anti-corruption policy: competing approaches

Definitional considerations are further compounded by disagreements over what constitutes good anti-corruption policy. To simplify greatly, approaches to anti-corruption policy may be divided into five main groups:

---

[25] "Clientelism and corruption are different notions. Clientelism is a form of social organization, while corruption is an individual social behavior... that may or may not grow into a mass phenomenon... In the postcommunist context, the two phenomena seem fused at the hip." A. Sajo, "Clientelism and Extortion: Corruption in Transition" (amended version of A. Sajo, "Corruption, Clientelism, and the Future of the Constitutional State in Eastern Europe," *East European Constitutional Review* 1998, Vol. 7, no. 2), p. 2.

[26] For example where a senior public official acts to blunt regulation in a sector where he is later employed by the dominant firm; or where companies agree to fix a public tender in order that a "competitor" wins, in return for that firm helping to collude later to benefit a different company in the same network.

[27] For example Slovenia (2001).

[28] For example Romania (2001).

[29] For example Slovakia (2001), Romania (2001). The introduction of an Act on Public Information in Poland is mentioned as an "important development" in the fight against corruption (2001).

(i) The "criminal and administrative control" approach

In this perspective, corruption is understood in relatively simple terms of bribery; public officials and politicians are viewed as seekers of corrupt opportunities, and anti-corruption policy consists of establishing and enforcing effective criminal law provisions combined with effective formal control mechanisms in the public administration. This appears to be the primary perspective adopted by the European Commission, reflecting the existing European anti-corruption instruments (see Section 2.1.1).

(ii) The "small government" approach

The small government approach shares the basic assumption of the criminal and administrative control approach that officials are essentially corrupt and will make use of any opportunity to enrich themselves. Whereas the "criminal and administrative control" approach seeks to reduce their opportunity to do so by legal-administrative means, the second approach assumes that Government *per se* is the problem. For proponents of this view, anti-corruption policy consists of policies to reduce the role of the State and minimise regulation. The approach of Robert Klitgaard, for whom corruption equals "monopoly plus discretion minus accountability," clearly illustrates the tendency to see the problem of corruption in terms of principal-agent problems,[30] which easily leads to the assumption that minimising the role of Government is the solution.

(iii) The "political economy" perspective

This approach shares with the small government perspective the assumption that corruption arises in conditions where principals are unable to monitor effectively the activities of agents, and appears to share the assumption that officials are primarily self-interest maximisers. However, advocates of such an approach concentrate not on the size of the State but on reform of public programs to increase transparency and accountability and to limit the extent of principal-agent problems.[31] A 1999 statement to the *New York Times* by Daniel Kaufmann is based primarily on this perspective:

> One doesn't fight corruption by fighting corruption, but rather by pursuing macroeconomic stability, marketization, democratisation and other initiatives that alter the environment in which corruption exists.[32]

---

[30] See R. Klitgaard, *Controlling Corruption*, University of California Press, 1991.

[31] The difference between this approach and the small government approach is illustrated by Susan Rose-Ackerman's argument that cutting government spending may in fact increase corruption by increasing scarcity. See S. Rose-Ackerman, *Corruption and Government: Causes, Consequences and Reform*, Cambridge University Press, Cambridge, 1999, p. 41.

[32] S. Schmemann, "What makes nations turn corrupt?: Reformers worry that payoffs and theft may be accepted as normal," *New York Times*, 28 August 1999.

The Commission has sometimes incorporated elements of this perspective into its approach to corruption in candidate States, and in a few countries has commented on the role of State control of licensing and permit procedures in encouraging corruption.[33] However, this approach has not been pursued consistently. Corruption is rarely mentioned under evaluations of compliance with the Copenhagen economic criteria, and it is not clear why concerns over licensing and permits are raised in a few countries and not others.[34]

(iv) The Multi-pronged Strategy/National Integrity System perspective

Recognition that narrowly focused anti-corruption strategies have met with limited success has led several international organisations to widen their anti-corruption policy recommendations. The "National Integrity System" advocated by Transparency International since 1996[35] is an early example of such an approach. The World Bank summarises its own efforts to develop a "multi-pronged strategy for combating corruption" as follows:

> To date, anti-corruption programs have largely focused on measures to address administrative corruption by reforming public administration and public finance management. But with the recognition that the roots of corruption extend far beyond weaknesses in the capacity of government, the repertoire has been gradually expanding to target broader structural relationships... [T]he goals are the same: enhancing State capacity and public sector management, strengthening political accountability, enabling civil society, and increasing economic competition.[36]

Two elements of broader strategies that appear to be of special importance to candidate States are efforts to bring lobbying practices within acceptable bounds and the effort to involve civil society in the anti-corruption project. Lobbying in particular is either potentially or actually a serious corruption problem in most candidate States, as shown by EUMAP's individual country reports. In a few countries, such as Poland and Bulgaria, civic organisations have played a vital role in making corruption and anti-corruption initiatives a domestic as well as an international issue. In other countries, such as Slovenia or the Czech Republic, the role of civil society has been very weak.

---

[33] See e.g Commission of European Union, *2001 Regular Report from the Commission on Bulgaria's Progress towards Accession.*

[34] For example, a new Trade Licensing Act that came into effect in the Czech Republic in April 2000 increased the role of the State in licensing procedures, ostensibly in reaction to EU requirements.

[35] See <http://www.transparency.org/activities/nat_integ_systems/country_studies.html>, (last accessed 5 August 2002).

[36] The World Bank, *Anti-corruption in Transition: A Contribution to the Policy Debate*, p. 39.

The European Commission does not mention lobbying in any of the Regular Reports, and the role of civil society in only two Regular Reports in 2001 (Bulgaria and Lithuania). This may be linked to the fact that both of these areas are the subject of efforts by the Commission to reform governance practices within the Union itself (see Section 2). While this Overview does not aim to condemn all lobbying, it and the accompanying individual country reports show clearly that setting limits on what is to be regarded as acceptable lobbying and implementing measures to prevent lobbying that goes beyond those limits are essential components of tackling corruption in all candidate countries. As the World Bank notes,

> What separates State capture as a form of corruption from conventional forms of political influence, such as lobbying, are the mechanisms by which the private interests interact with the State. State capture occurs through the illicit provision of private gains to public officials via informal, nontransparent, and highly preferential channels of access.[37]

On this perspective, lobbying that takes place through collective organisations (for example industry associations), and in a transparent and public fashion (for example through official consultation processes), is acceptable and even encouraged, whereas covert lobbying by specific interests through *quid pro quo* type relationships with politicians or parties is corrupt and damaging.

(v) Public integrity-based approaches

The approaches to anti-corruption policy outlined above tend to share the assumption that public officials are inherently self-interested, and corruption control is therefore based on making the costs of corruption higher than the benefits to be gained. These anti-corruption strategies tend to emphasise greater democracy and access by citizens to decision-making processes, reduced autonomy and discretion for public officials, improved systems of scrutiny, accountability and repressive sanctions. The focus is on maximising indirect incentives for officials to behave incorruptly, that is, maximising the negative consequences for officials of behaving corruptly.

Another approach to anti-corruption is focused on building public integrity. Such an approach is based on direct incentives – that is, on the assumption that officials can have a positive incentive to behave with integrity rather than only a negative incentive to avoid being caught behaving corruptly – and on the axiom that corruption is best controlled by creating public officials who exercise varying degrees of autonomy for the public good and are more-or-less immune to corrupt opportunities because they define their role in a certain way. Elements of such an approach can be found in the approach adopted by the Polish Civil Service, which is based primarily on education and building civil servant ethics.

---

[37] The World Bank, *Anti-corruption in Transition: A Contribution to the Policy Debate*, p. 3.

A likely advantage of such strategies in post-communist countries is that they appear to address more directly the problem that these countries inherited from the communist regimes: the lack of a clear sense of public responsibilities and a public culture within which officials with integrity would be distinctly recognised. On this perspective, the challenge for candidate countries is to build a civil service and public political culture to change people's expectations – both of themselves and of their public officials.

Public integrity-based strategies also recognise that anti-corruption strategies based on minimising discretion themselves may carry costs. Anti-corruption policies that go too far in limiting discretion may end up denying officials the very discretion they need to make decisions that are in the public interest. In the context of countries in transition, the advisability of trying to maximally limit discretion in States carrying out wide-ranging transitional tasks may be questionable.

Lessons for the EU

The anti-corruption policy measures that the European Commission has tended to recommend to candidate States have been generally oriented towards a control paradigm, with a strong emphasis on ensuring that criminal anti-corruption law is optimal and fully enforced. Such policies may also include the establishment or strengthening of strict conflict of interest provisions, comprehensive asset-monitoring provisions (the violation of which may itself be made a criminal offence),[38] or various agencies engaged in monitoring, supervision and auditing of public administration. Likewise, at least until recently the recommendations of international institutions have tended to focus on reforming civil and criminal law[39] and public administration reforms designed to increase the effectiveness of control mechanisms and accountability of public officials. Although the Commission has attached importance to the adoption of codes of ethics for public officials, it appears to endorse a "top-down" approach to such codes, in which they are imposed from above. Likewise, the approach taken by candidate countries in adopting such codes does not take on board some of the more important lessons learnt in Western countries that have adopted ethical codes: for example, that effective codes are detailed, and need to be developed through a process of consultation with the officials to whom they apply.

Moreover, since the mid-1990's there has been a growing revisionist literature on why conventional approaches to anti-corruption policy may be misplaced. According to some analysts, the pursuit of corruption control at any price may reduce administrative efficiency,

---

[38] This is the case under many US provisions.

[39] Most obviously in the adoption of international anti-corruption conventions such as the 1997 OECD Convention against the Bribing of Foreign Officials in International Business Transactions or the two Council of Europe Civil and Criminal Law Conventions on Corruption.

and moreover may not actually curb levels of corruption.[40] Specifically, a growing plethora of rules, regulations and sanctions backed by proliferating agencies of surveillance and enforcement can produce a situation in which agencies spend as much time dealing with anti-corruption issues as they do performing their basic functions. It may also lead to pathological responses by public servants such as a tendency to "work-to-rule." These analysts conclude that for officials to exercise authority they must have a degree of discretion, at least at higher levels of Government; that "the less we trust [public officials] the less they can do for us and the more diminished is their capacity to rule."[41]

These considerations are of major relevance to the problem of corruption in candidate States. The approach, recommendations and requirements of the European Commission in the arena of anti-corruption policy in candidate States have been focused on elites, top-down anti-corruption strategies pursued with adequate "political will," enforcement of criminal law and establishment of functioning control mechanisms mainly to control the use of EU funds. Indeed, the focus on elites and financial control mechanisms has even increased since 2001 after SIGMA – the joint OECD-EU program of Support for Improvement in Governance and Management in Central and Eastern European Countries – was ordered to reduce its activities in order to focus primarily on financial control and external audit.[42]

The reservations of the anti-corruption "revisionists" about prevailing anti-corruption policy trends may carry considerable weight in the case of post-communist States. In particular, there are good grounds for reservations about relying on repressive solutions and formal control mechanisms in the public administration. Repressive solutions may be undermined by corruption of the institutions that implement them, while administrations that are struggling to perform their own tasks satisfactorily may be particularly ill-equipped to devote resources and staff to expanding internal control mechanisms. In addition:

> Given the sprawling nature of bureaucracy in Eastern Europe, the establishment of more rules and guidelines would threaten to introduce greater inefficiency and more incentives for officials and members of the public to seek to act outside the system. If part of the problem is a lack of

---

[40] The most radical example is provided by Frank Anecharico and James B. Jacobs, who argue persuasively that the "pursuit of absolute integrity" has led to increased bureaucratic inefficiency without reducing levels of corruption in New York City. See F. Anechiarico and J.B. Jacobs, *The Pursuit of Absolute Integrity: How Corruption Control Makes Government Ineffective*, University of Chicago Press, Chicago 1996.

[41] M. Philp, "Corruption Control and the Transfer of Regulatory Frameworks," unpublished paper to World Bank seminar, Warsaw, May 2000, p. 5.

[42] A. M. Cirtautas, "Corruption and the New Ethical Infrastructure of Capitalism," *East European Constitutional Review*, Spring/Summer 2001, p. 83.

respect for State institutions and legal frameworks then more legal barriers cannot be expected to bring benefits.[43]

Finally, the fundamental dilemma for all solutions based on control and ultimately repression is the question of "Who will guard the guards?" In particular, the assumption that establishing formal accountability mechanisms in post-communist countries will further the fight against corruption cannot be taken for granted. The effectiveness of such institutions depends on a wide range of factors, a number of which are dealt with by the Commission (such as the establishment of harmonised financial management systems in public administration as a prerequisite for effective control and audit). In particular, the integrity of senior staff and the readiness of Governments to grant them independence and respect their findings are key issues.

The dangers of generalisation

While these problems do not necessarily undermine the policies encouraged or required by the Commission in candidate States, they suggest that merely transposing a subset of solutions developed in advanced market democracies may not be very effective in States in transition – particularly where the solutions themselves are the subject of controversy even in the West. The approach taken by the Commission also contrasts with wide variation in member State practice. Dealing with corruption is a comprehensive and long-term process, often with country-specific requirements, and the application of reforms with expectations of immediate results may have adverse implications for effective implementation of appropriate reforms.

These considerations lead to further questions concerning whether standards for measuring and combating corruption *should* be entirely universal in transition States, or whether under certain situations it is necessary or even productive to tolerate practices that would be found unacceptable or illegal in consolidated democracies. For example, there are reasons for being cautious about the application of strict conflict of interest regulations forbidding the occupation of "incompatible" functions or restrictions on post-public service employment in transitional States. Although it is clearly desirable that officials are not motivated in their public capacities by their ancillary activities, the immediate introduction of incompatibility provisions may have counterproductive effects in a context where the problem of conflict of interest is poorly understood and where the pool of political and official talent is small. In the worst scenario, by encouraging talented officials to leave the public service it might even reduce efficiency while doing little to limit corruption. At a minimum, it might be more constructive to develop understanding of the concept of conflict of interest through mechanisms based on codes of ethics and case-by-case disclosure requirements.

---

[43] *Oxford Analytica Daily Brief,* 6 November 2001.

2. SOURCES OF EUROPEAN ANTI-CORRUPTION STANDARDS

2.1 The EU anti-corruption framework

The inclusion of corruption as an issue of key importance for EU accession implies that there exists an anti-corruption framework that is already binding on EU member States and to which candidate States must conform. However, in fact no such framework exists, or at least not in a formal sense. The Commission has been in the process of developing a broad "good governance" framework, notably since the publication of the White Paper on Governance in July 2001.[44] The White Paper lays down or reaffirms principles of subsidiarity and in particular the objective of making the policy process more open and transparent. Measures that have emerged since the White Paper include a Code of Conduct for members of the European Parliament and efforts to formulate a code for Commission officials. In light of the dismissal of the Santer Commission in 1999 due to corruption allegations, rumours circulating in early 2002 of another report by the same whistleblower alleging continuing malfeasance at the level of the Commission,[45] his resignation in August 2002 and the suspension of the Commission's former chief accountant,[46] the extent to which the good governance regime is further formalised and institutionalised will be a key indicator of the EU's ability to translate concerns about corruption into concrete anti-corruption measures.

In addition to the above measures, since the early 1990's the EU has adopted several anti-corruption instruments, and in particular conventions on protection of the financial interests of the Community and on the fight against corruption (see below). However, as of mid-2002 neither of these conventions had secured enough ratifications by member States to come into force.

Consequently, the EU anti-corruption framework remains diffuse and largely non-binding. There are probably two main reasons for this. First, the extent and nature of corruption appears to differ widely across member States, reflecting different national

---

[44] Commission of the European Union, *EU Governance: A White Paper*, COM(2001) 428 final, Brussels, 25 July 2001.

[45] D. Cronin, "Whistleblower probe casts doubt over budget sign-off," *European Voice*, 7-13 March 2002.

[46] Paul Van Buitenen, the Commission official whose allegations brought down the Santer Commission in 1999, resigned in August 2002, saying he was "bitterly disappointed" at the failure to improve financial probity since then. Marta Andreasen, the Commission's former chief accountant, was suspended in August 2002 after she voiced repeated criticisms of alleged lax accounting practices in the Commission, comparing the EU's accounting standards to those of Enron. See K. Butler, "Official who exposed lax EU finances is suspended," *The Independent*, 30 August 2002.

traditions and historical legacies. For example, there is a stark contrast between the deeply embedded bureaucratic traditions of rectitude and probity characteristic of the northernmost member States on the one hand, and the more relaxed style of public service characteristic of France or, perhaps to a lesser extent, Germany. This contrast is made clear by a number of topical examples, most notably the departure of Eva Joly, the judge in charge of the investigation into the Elf Aquitaine affair in France.[47] The scandals that have surrounded French President Jacques Chirac[48] or Italian Prime Minister Silvio Berlusconi,[49] along with party financing scandals in Germany,[50] have highlighted the fact that corruption is not a problem for candidate States alone.

Second, to date the Commission has not seen or framed corruption as a concern for the ability of member States to implement EU directives. For this reason it has perceived no immediate need to pressure or criticise existing member States on grounds of corruption. Moreover, the Commission's internal problems of corruption would make it difficult to do so before completing its own internal reform. Finally, even if the Commission did criticise the member States for corruption, they remain powerful enough to oppose any proposed EU directives on how to clean up their polities.

For these reasons, a contradictory situation has emerged. On the one hand, the EU is taking or has taken a number of consequential steps to implement a good governance regime at the level of the EU administration. On the other hand, efforts to extend these steps and promote the "harmonization" of anti-corruption standards and policies across existing member States has been a difficult and fragmentary process. At the same time, the existence of the Copenhagen mandate has enabled the Commission to exert much greater leverage over candidate States to adopt various anti-corruption measures. However, the Commission's authority and bargaining power to demand such harmonisation of candidate States will be lost once they become members.

2.1.1 Direct anti-corruption acquis

Strictly speaking, EU anti-corruption policy falls under the chapter on Justice and Home Affairs. As of September 2002, Community legislation in this area consisted of the following:

---

[47] Norwegian-born Joly left France for her home country in early 2001 amid allegations of political pressure.

[48] See "Bad news for the president," *The Economist*, 9 February 2002; C. Dickey, "Jam Jar Politics," *Newsweek*, 9 April 2002.

[49] See "Is there less than before?" *The Economist*, 16 February 2002.

[50] See "Too much of it," *The Economist*, 6 April 2002.

- The 1995 Convention on the Protection of the European Communities' Financial Interests, which sets forth minimum standards that member States should incorporate into domestic criminal law to deal with fraud against the Community Budget;

- The First and Second Protocols to the above Convention, which stipulate that member States should take effective action to punish bribery that involves EU officials and damage to the Communities' financial interests as understood in the above Convention;

- The 1997 Convention on the Fight against Corruption involving Officials of the European Communities or Officials of the member States of the European Union. The Convention broadens the category of official to which bribery legislation applies to cover the widest possible spectrum of EU employees; establishes standards for defining an official in international anti-corruption prosecutions; and defines both active and passive corruption in the widest possible terms, imposing on member States the duty to ensure that their legislation covers all aspects of this definition;

- The Joint Action on Corruption in the Private Sector. Approved by the EU Council of Ministers in December 1998, this is intended to align national legislation on passive and active corruption in the private sector, the responsibilities of natural persons in this area and penalties and sanctions.[51]

These instruments are focused upon harmonising bribery legislation, extending bribery legislation to cover foreign officials and officials of international organisations, and underlining judicial cooperation in the area of corruption prosecutions. They have not come into force yet for member States: as of March 2002 eight of the 15 member States had fully ratified the 1995 Convention, and the Commission considers it unlikely that all of the ratifications will be completed for some years.[52]

---

[51] Council Joint Action 98/742/JHA, adopted 22 December 1998.

[52] UK National Audit Office, *Annual Report of the Court of Auditors for the Year 2000*, Report by the Comptroller and Auditor General, HC 859 Session 2001–2002, 8 May 2002, p. 27.

2.1.2 "Soft" anti-corruption acquis

In addition to the above anti-corruption instruments, the approach of the EU to corruption in candidate countries includes a number of other international agreements which, once ratified by all member States, will automatically become part of the *acquis*. These are:

- The Council of Europe Criminal Law Convention on Corruption.

- The Council of Europe Civil Law Convention on Corruption.

- The European Convention on Laundering, Search, Seizure and Confiscation of the Proceeds from Crime.

- The OECD Convention on Combating Bribery of Foreign Public Officials.

The Commission explicitly evaluates candidate States on the basis of their signature and ratification of these documents, *inter alia*. These agreements are of a similar nature to the EU instruments mentioned above, although they go further in certain areas. For example, the Criminal Law Convention requires the establishment of liability of legal entities for corruption.

As of June 2002, the record of candidate States in acceding to the Council of Europe conventions was clearly better than the record of EU member States (see Tables 1 and 2), which, as discussed in Section 1, is largely the result of pressure from the European Commission. On the other hand, member States had progressed further in ratifying the OECD Convention (see Table 3).

Table 1: Council of Europe Criminal Law Convention: state of play, June 2002

States	Date of signature	Date of ratification	Date of entry into force	Reservations
CANDIDATE STATES				
Bulgaria	27/01/99	07/11/01	01/07/02	X
Czech Republic	15/10/99	08/09/00	01/07/02	X
Estonia	08/06/00	06/12/01	01/07/02	X
Hungary	26/04/99	22/11/00	01/07/02	X
Latvia	27/01/99	09/02/01	01/07/02	X
Lithuania	27/01/99	08/03/02	01/07/02	
Poland	27/01/99			
Romania	27/01/99			
Slovakia	27/01/99	09/06/00	01/07/02	
Slovenia	07/05/99	12/05/00	01/07/02	X
MEMBER STATES				
Austria	13/10/00			
Belgium	20/04/99			
Denmark	27/01/99	02/08/00	01/07/02	X
Finland	27/01/99			
France	09/09/99			
Germany	27/01/99			
Greece	27/01/99			
Ireland	07/05/99			
Italy	27/01/99			
Luxembourg	27/01/99			
Netherlands	29/06/00	11/04/02	01/08/02	X
Norway	27/01/99			
Portugal	30/04/99	07/05/02	01/09/02	X
Spain				
Sweden	27/01/99			
United Kingdom	27/01/99			

Source: Treaty Office on <http://conventions.coe.int>, (last accessed 5 August 2002).

Table 2: Council of Europe Civil Law Convention: state of play, June 2002

States	Date of signature	Date of ratification	Date of entry into force*
CANDIDATE STATES			
Bulgaria	04/11/99	08/06/00	
Czech Republic	09/11/00		
Estonia	24/01/00	08/12/00	
Hungary			
Latvia			
Lithuania	18/04/02		
Poland	03/04/01		
Romania	04/11/99	23/04/02	
Slovakia	08/06/00		
Slovenia	29/11/01		
MEMBER STATES			
Austria	13/10/00		
Belgium	08/06/00		
Denmark	04/11/99		
Finland	08/06/00	23/10/01	
France	26/11/99		
Germany	04/11/99		
Greece	08/06/00	21/02/02	
Ireland	04/11/99		
Italy	04/11/99		
Luxembourg	04/11/99		
Netherlands			
Norway	04/11/99		
Portugal			
Spain			
Sweden	08/06/00		
United Kingdom	08/06/00		

Note: * The Convention requires 14 ratifications to enter into force

Source: Treaty Office on <http://conventions.coe.int>, (last accessed 5 August 2002).

Table 3: OECD Convention on Bribery of Foreign Public Officials: state of play, June 2002

States	Deposit of instrument of ratification/ acceptance	Date of entry into force	Date of entry into force of implementing legislation**
CANDIDATE STATES			
Bulgaria	22 December 1998	20 February 1999	29 January 1999
Czech Republic	21 January 2000	21 March 2000	9 June 1999
Estonia*			
Hungary	4 December 1998	15 February 1999	1 March 1999
Latvia*			
Lithuania*			
Poland	8 September 2000	7 November 2000	4 February 2001
Romania*			
Slovakia	24 September 1999	23 November 1999	1 November 1999
Slovenia	6 September 2001	5 November 2001	
MEMBER STATES			
Austria	20 May 1999	19 July 1999	1 October 1998
Belgium	27 July 1999	25 September 1999	3 April 1999
Denmark	5 September 2000	4 November 2000	1 May 2000
Finland	10 December 1998	15 February 1999	1 January 1999
France	31 July 2000	29 September 2000	29 September 2000
Germany	10 November 1998	15 February 1999	15 February 2000
Greece	5 February 1999	6 April 1999	1 December 1998
Ireland			
Italy	15 December 2000	13 February 2001	26 October 2000
Luxembourg	21 March 2001	20 May 2001	11 February 2001
Netherlands	12 January 2001	13 March 2001	1 February 2001
Norway	18 December 1998	16 February 1999	1 January 1999
Portugal	23 November 2000	22 January 2001	
Spain	4 January 2000	4 March 2001	2 February 2000
Sweden	8 June 1999	7 August 1999	1 July 1999
United Kingdom	14 December 1998	15 February 1999	

Notes: *Not yet members of the OECD Working Group on Bribery

**This does not mean that countries have fulfilled all the requirements of the Convention. For example, as of June 2002, the Czech Republic still had not introduced liability of legal entities.

Source: <http://www1.oecd.org/daf/nocorruption/annex2.htm>, (last accessed 6 June 2002).

2.1.3 Other provisions indirectly related to corruption

In addition, the accession negotiation process involves the objective of harmonisation of laws in a number of other areas that do not fall under the label of anti-corruption policy *per se*, yet are clearly regarded as of major importance in the fight against corruption. The most important of these are listed below:

- **Public procurement.** The Commission has played a very important role in urging the reform of public procurement procedures in candidate States to comply with Commission directives on procurement. The directives establish threshold values of procurement contracts above which competitive tender proceedings must be used, define situations where restricted tenders or negotiated procedures may be used, and establish general requirements for appeal procedures.[53]

- **Civil service reform.** The Commission has consistently urged candidate States to reform their State administrations under the general objective of "capacity building." There are three main aspects to expected reform: increased staff levels, an increase in professional standards and increased remuneration.

- **State financial control and audit.** The Commission requires candidate States to put in place systems of financial control that will, primarily, provide some assurance that the increasing inflow of EU funds does not go wasted. This includes adopting international State audit standards;[54] establishing effective, independent and *ex ante* internal control systems; and, again, increasing capacity in terms of both staffing and information systems.

- **Judicial reform.** The Commission attaches similar importance to judicial reform in its own right as it does to corruption. The Commission has consistently pushed for reforms that will establish and ensure (i) judicial independence and (ii) efficiency of the court system in processing cases.[55] Both of these objectives are clearly necessary conditions for effectively fighting corruption.

---

[53] European Commission Directives nos. 66/1989, 13/1992, 50/1992, 36/1993, 37/1993, 38/1993, 52/1997, 4/1998.

[54] Lima Declaration of Guidelines on Auditing Precepts, <http://www.intosai.org/2_LIMADe.html>, (last accessed 31 July 2002); INTOSAI (International Organisation of Supreme Audit Institutions) code of Ethics and Auditing Standards, <http://www.intosai.org/2_CodEth_AudStand2001_E.pdf>, (last accessed 31 July 2002).

[55] See *Monitoring the EU Accession Process: Judicial Independence*, Open Society Institute, Budapest 2001; and *Monitoring the EU Accession Process: Judicial Capacity*, Open Society Institute (forthcoming); available at <http://www.eumap.org>.

2.2 The Council of Europe: the Twenty Guiding Principles, GRECO

In addition to the two conventions on corruption, the Council of Europe's Committee of Ministers approved a broad framework of "Twenty Guiding Principles for the Fight Against Corruption" in 1997.[56] Although the principles are not binding for any State, they serve as a potential framework for developing anti-corruption strategies in the broadest sense. The principles encompass not only anti-corruption legislation but also measures to prevent and fight corruption, including promotion of public awareness, independence of the prosecution and judiciary, limitation of immunity for public functionaries, public administration reform (including transparency), codes of conduct for elected representatives, regulation of political party financing, and freedom of the media to seek and publish information.

In 1998 the Council authorised the creation of a Group of States Against Corruption (GRECO) to facilitate international cooperation.[57] GRECO, which had 34 members as of June 2002, organises peer monitoring of fulfilment of the Guiding Principles by member States. The first round of evaluation of GRECO member States' compliance with three of the Guiding Principles is to be completed by the end of 2002.[58]

Despite the fact that GRECO has become the first organisation to systematically evaluate both candidate and member EU States, the European Commission has not mentioned the Twenty Guiding Principles at any point in accession documents or Regular Reports, although it has commented on candidate countries joining GRECO in the Regular Reports.

---

[56] Council of Europe Committee of Ministers Resolution 24 (1997), *On the Twenty Guiding Principles for the Fight Against Corruption*, <http://cm.coe.int/ta/res/1997/97x24.htm>, (last accessed 31 July 2002).

[57] Committee of Ministers, Resolution 7 (1998), 5 May 1998.

[58] The first Evaluation Round has been based on Guiding Principle 3 (the legal status, powers, means of securing evidence, independence and autonomy of those in charge of prevention, investigation, prosecution and adjudication of corruption offences); Guiding Principle 7 (specialisation of persons or bodies in charge of fighting corruption, and means at their disposal); and Guiding Principle 6 (immunity from investigation, prosecution or adjudication of corruption offences). The second Evaluation Round will examine compliance with selected articles of the Criminal Law Convention and six more of the Guiding Principles. For details, see <http://www.greco.coe.int/>, (last accessed 5 August 2002).

3. THE PROBLEM OF CORRUPTION IN CANDIDATE STATES

3.1 Reasons for corruption in candidate States

There appears to be a widespread consensus that corruption in Central and Eastern European countries is a more serious problem than in other countries of the OECD, including existing EU member States (see Section 3.3 below). Although the dividing line between candidate and member States in terms of levels of corruption is not as clear as is often implied, and although corruption in EU member States and within EU institutions is an ongoing problem, both the legacy of communism and the nature of post-communist transition provide powerful reasons why corruption may be expected to be a bigger problem in candidate States than in most member States.

3.1.1 The legacy of communism

Communist systems employed corruption as a means for consolidating power, built economic systems that relied on corruption for their very survival, and – at least in the later stages of their history – ended up as kleptocracies where high-level corruption and embezzlement were the norm. This has left behind a legacy of patterns of behaviour that are not conducive to the establishment of well-functioning democracies or cultures that condemn corruption. In particular, the following patterns may be noted:

(i)   traditions of both high-level grand corruption and low-level petty corruption;

(ii) entrenched mistrust of the State;

(iii) a feeling of legitimacy among the population in circumventing the State ("beating the system");

(iv) widespread clientelism and forms of exchange that run against both formal political and bureaucratic norms;

(v)   corruption in the private sector as a substitute for fair competition.

An important part of the systems that operated under State socialism, even in its milder forms (as in Hungary), was the deeply embedded clientelistic system of exchange that emerged in the absence of effective market, State or other systems of allocation. As noted above, understanding the legacy of these systems is essential in coming to grips with corruption in post-communist States.

Corruption in transition

Post-communist States face a number of factors that combine unfavourably to encourage corruption, while simultaneously rendering corruption control especially difficult. A common denominator of the situation of transition, and a factor that international organisations such as the EU do not always appear willing to recognise, is that while the collapse of the old systems in CEE States removed many types of corruption that were part and parcel of those systems, democratisation and marketisation may create as much corruption, albeit of different types.

Post-communist States inherited bureaucracies that lacked many of the regulatory institutions necessary for a modern State and economy to function, as well as many of the conditions necessary for mechanisms of accountability to function. Their bureaucracies were confronted with an overload of transition tasks – ranging from the privatisation of whole economies to, in some cases, the redrawing of State boundaries – distracting attention from anti-corruption efforts, and making it difficult to ensure the accountability of individual or administrative actions.

Political and economic liberalisation has subjected politicians to a wide range of pressures, many of which are corruptive. Notably, power holders have been placed in a unique position to design fundamental "rules of the game" to facilitate corruption.[59] Civil society, which to varying extents was destroyed or excluded from public life under communist regimes, tends to be weak in transition States and less likely to play a part in fighting corruption.

At the same time, due to economic concentration, the weakness of civil society and the competitive pressures of transition, the private sector is less likely to actively support

---

[59] The recent attempts by the largest Czech political parties to change the electoral system to their own advantage may be an example of the consequences of what Claus Offe labels the problem of "strategy dependence." This hinders what Jon Elster, Claus Offe and Ulrich Preuss term the "vertical" and "horizontal" conditions that are necessary to consolidate democracy. A democracy is *vertically* consolidated if "[T]he... rules according to which political and distributional conflicts are carried out are relatively immune from becoming themselves the object of such conflict." Moreover, *horizontal* differentiation is necessary in terms of "the degree of insulation of institutional spheres from each other and the limited convertibility of status attributes from one sphere to another." J. Elster, C. Offe and U. K. Preuss, *Institutional Design in Post-communist Societies: Rebuilding the Ship at Sea*, Cambridge University Press, 1998, pp. 28–31. The corruption-ridden process of privatising Russia's most lucrative State enterprises in 1994-95, in which a few oligarchs took control of the country's fast energy reserves for nothing in a "loans-for-shares" scheme financed by the State is a prime example.

reforms to limit corruption, even when businesses are highly frustrated by corruption.[60] Finally, in the case of most transition countries a decline in economic welfare – at least in the initial phase of transition – increased both the value of client networks and mistrust in the State. In this environment, corruption has become in many cases a highly politicised and useful weapon in the political struggle, which may in certain circumstances lower the legitimacy of the system more than it harms the legitimacy of individual corrupt politicians.[61]

3.1.2 The dangers of generalisation

While the existence of common factors underlying corruption in post-communist countries is undeniable, it is important to avoid the assumption that corruption in all post-communist countries is the same and therefore requires the same solutions. The major cultural variation among EU member States is not unique. Cultural, historical and other differences among Central and East European countries are also large, and are reflected in differences in the extent and nature of corruption. Corruption in the Czech Republic, for example, is likely to be conditioned not only by the communist legacy but also by the historical legacy of the Habsburg Empire and the bureaucratic tradition it bequeathed, whereas corruption in Poland is thought – at least by many domestic observers – to be underpinned, *inter alia,* by a centuries-old distrust in the State borne of a history of occupation by various external powers. These differences suggest that beyond the establishment of certain basic minimums, there is a need for solutions specific to individual countries; however, to date very little, if any, research has been conducted in this area.

3.2 The EU assessment of corruption in candidate States

Difficulties in measuring corruption deriving from the lack of an agreed-upon definition are exacerbated by the fact that since acts of corruption are usually illicit, the parties involved have an interest in concealing them. The European Commission has acknowledged this difficulty by focusing on anti-corruption policy rather than corruption itself. However, requiring policies without an adequate analysis of the

---

[60] To the extent that this is true then the liberal hope – that private sector actors who acquire wealth through corruption or more-or-less illegal means will later promote a legal State in order to secure their property rights – may be undermined.

[61] The growing support for populist (and even anti-system) parties in Poland is the classic example of such an unfavourable dynamic.

phenomenon at which they are targeted (corruption) invites the criticism that these policies may not address the specific needs of different countries.

In practice the Commission has relied predominantly on evidence gathered by its local EC delegations for its assessment of corruption. The Commission's assessment of anti-corruption policy, on the other hand, is based on a more systematic, although still very general, checklist or set of criteria (see Section 3.2.2).

3.2.1 The assessment of corruption in candidate States

One of the Commission's stated aims in assessing candidate countries' progress towards accession is objectivity. The Commission's 1999 Composite Report notes that,

> [The] process of regular evaluation based on unchanging criteria is the only way to make a fair and balanced assessment of the real capability of each candidate country to meet the Copenhagen criteria.[62]

Clearly, corruption is an area in which objective assessment is comparatively difficult. Indeed, Commission officials state that the Commission does not attempt to measure corruption in candidate States, preferring to concentrate on anti-corruption policy. However, in order to structure its analysis the Commission does make judgements about corruption in candidate countries based on secondary sources, varying from local public opinion surveys to international comparative studies. However, it does not explicitly cite any of the available cross-country evidence, and does not appear to employ a consistent approach across candidate countries when citing survey data. For example, the 2001 Regular Report on Slovakia noted a number of areas where corruption is perceived to be a big problem, which appears to be based on the World Bank's *Diagnostic Surveys* carried out in Slovakia in 1999.[63] However, the same surveys carried out in Romania were not cited in the Commission's assessment of Romania.

The Commission's assessments of the prevalence of corruption (see Tables 4-5), in which the seriousness of corruption in candidate countries is classified according to statements ranging from "relatively limited problem" through "area of concern" to "widespread and systemic" are clearly intuitive. Analysis of the Regular Reports indicates that three main criteria are used to assess corruption. These criteria are discussed below.

---

[62] European Commission, *Composite Paper: Reports on Progress towards Accession by Each of the Candidate Countries,* October 1999, p.10.

[63] European Commission, *2001 Regular Report from the Commission on Slovakia's progress towards Accession,* p. 19.

Table 4: Criteria used to indicate levels of corruption in candidate countries in the *2000 Regular Reports*

Country	Assessment of level of corruption?	Criminal statistics	Public opinion surveys	Reports	Media	Control framework/ regulatory deficiciency	Rumours/ unspecified
Bulgaria	Yes (very serious problem)		X		X	X	X
Czech Republic	Yes (continues to be a problem)	X	X			X	
Estonia	Yes (relatively limited problem)					X	
Hungary	Yes (remains a problem)					X	
Latvia	Yes (serious obstacle to functioning of public administration)					X	
Lithuania	Yes (source of concern)	X				X	
Poland	Yes (environment in which corruption can flourish)	X		X		X	
Romania	Yes (widespread and systemic problem)	X				X	X
Slovakia	Yes (perception that corruption is widespread)		X			X	X
Slovenia	Yes (relatively limited)					X	X

Source: European Commission, *2000 Regular Reports,* available at:
<http://europa.eu.int/comm/enlargement/report2000/>, (last accessed 5 August 2002).

Table 5: Criteria used to indicate levels of corruption in candidate countries in the *2001 Regular Reports*

Country	Assessment of level of corruption?	Criminal statistics	Public Opinion Surveys	Reports	Media	Control framework /regulatory deficiciency	Rumours/ unspecified
Bulgaria	Yes (very serious problem)		X			X	X
Czech Republic	Yes (serious cause for concern)	X	X	X		X	
Estonia	Yes (relatively limited problem)						
Hungary	Yes (continues to be a problem)						X
Latvia	Yes (perceived levels of corruption high)	X				X	X
Lithuania	Yes (area of concern)	X				X	
Poland	Yes (general perception that corruption is widespread)	X				X	X
Romania	Yes (widespread and systemic problem)					X	X
Slovakia	No	X				X	X
Slovenia	Yes (appears to remain relatively limited)					X	X

Source: European Commission, *2001 Regular Reports,* available at: <http://europa.eu.int/comm/enlargement/report2001/>, (last accessed 22 August 2002)

Criminal statistics

A number of Regular Reports cite statistics on criminal prosecutions and convictions for corruption, for example Estonia (1998), Czech Republic (1999, 2000), Poland (1999, 2000) and Latvia (1999, 2000). However, there is some ambiguity in the Commission's interpretation of such statistics. The 2000 Regular Report on Slovenia states that "According to the available statistics and reports, problems of corruption are relatively limited,"[64] indicating that criminal statistics are regarded as indicating actual levels of corruption. However, in most other cases where criminal statistics are mentioned the Commission appears to interpret such statistics as evidence of the strength of the fight against corruption, rather than indicators of the level of corruption itself. For example, the 2000 Regular Report on the Czech Republic cites the limited prosecutions resulting from the country's "Clean Hands" anti-corruption campaign as evidence of the inadequacy of the fight against corruption.

Clearly, there are serious problems in relying on criminal statistics to measure levels of corruption,[65] and the Commission's tendency to interpret the statistics as indicators of the effectiveness of the fight against corruption – where more prosecutions means a more effective fight – has its logic. However, the application of this approach is inconsistent. For example, neither Poland nor Latvia received credit in the 2000 Regular Reports for large increases in the number of convictions for corruption. Similar conviction rates in the Czech Republic and Hungary in 2000 do not prevent corruption being regarded as a more serious problem in the former than in the latter. Although comparison of conviction rates across borders may itself be problematic, this does not appear to be the motivation behind the Commission's differing assessment. In general, no rationale is presented to indicate what might constitute a satisfactory conviction rate, nor is any baseline stated in terms of conviction rates in EU member States that might provide such an indication. Moreover, there are reasons for doubting whether statistics on convictions in member States say anything meaningful about levels of corruption (see Section 2.1).

Public opinion surveys

Three of the November 2000 Regular Reports draw explicitly on the results of public opinion surveys on corruption, while such surveys could also have been used in other country reports (for example, under the heading of "available evidence" in the 2000 Regular Report on Slovenia). The 2000 Bulgaria Report states that according to several

---

[64] Commission, *2000 Regular Report from the Commission on Slovenia's Progress towards Accession,* November 2000, p. 16.

[65] The unreliability of criminal statistics is demonstrated by the 50 percent increase in prosecutions for corruption in Poland in 1999, and the approximate doubling of prosecutions in Latvia in the same period.

surveys, customs, the police and the judiciary are considered to be the most corrupt professions in Bulgaria, though other professions cited as corrupt in the same surveys include university teaching personnel and public sector officials.[66] The 2000 Czech Republic Report cites opinion polls that "show that one in five Czechs assume that corruption pervades many areas of everyday life,"[67] and that the public regards corruption as most widespread in the State administration, followed by the police and intelligence services, healthcare, banking and the political sphere. The 2000 Slovak Report cites a Government survey that found that one-fifth of parties involved in court proceedings experienced corruption.[68]

However, the Commission's approach in this area also lacks clarity. It is not clear to what extent the Commission regards survey results as indicating actual levels of corruption. Moreover, the available detailed cross-country survey evidence, in particular the data from the 1999 *Business Environment and Enterprise Performance Survey* commissioned by the World Bank and European Bank for Reconstruction and Development,[69] does not appear to have been used systematically.

Unspecified evidence

In a number of Regular Reports, the Commission makes statements concerning levels of corruption that are based on evidence that is either specified unclearly – as in the case of Slovenia where "available statistics and reports"[70] are mentioned – or not at all. Unfortunately, this is particularly the case in countries that receive the worst assessments for corruption, such as the 2000 Bulgaria Report, which states that,

> Corruption continues to be a very serious problem in Bulgaria. Whilst it is hard to know its extent, the persistent rumours about corrupt practices at various levels of the administration and the public sector in themselves contribute to tainting the political, economic and social environment.[71]

Likewise, the Romanian and Latvian reports – which appear to rank these two countries along with Bulgaria as the worst candidate countries in terms of corruption,

---

[66] Commission, *2000 Regular Report from the Commission on Bulgaria's Progress towards Accession,* November 2000, p. 17.

[67] Commission, *2000 Regular Report from the Commission on the Czech Republic's Progress towards Accession,* November 2000, p. 21.

[68] Commission, *2000 Regular Report from the Commission on Slovakia's Progress towards Accession,* November 2000, p. 17.

[69] See World Bank, *Anti-corruption in Transition: A Contribution to the Policy Debate.*

[70] Commission, *2000 Regular Report from the Commission on Slovenia's Progress towards Accession,* p. 16.

[71] Commission, *2000 Regular Report from the Commission on Bulgaria's Progress towards Accession,* p. 17.

do not present any specific evidence of corruption. In the 2001 Report on Poland, which the Commission viewed as one of the more corrupt candidate countries, the Commission referred to a "spate of recent prominent allegations" and commented that,

> Irrespective of whether the specific allegations turn out to be true or not, there is a general perception that corruption is widespread. This is damaging both domestically and internationally.[72]

The use of allegations – that may well turn out to be unfounded and a normal part of the political struggle in an election – as evidence to cite a corruption problem that is "damaging internationally" carries the danger of developing into a self-fulfilling prophecy.

Indirect evidence: regulatory deficiencies

In its claims concerning levels of corruption in candidate countries the Commission relies to a significant extent on naming structural regulatory deficiencies in a given sphere. For example, the 2000 Estonia Regular Report emphasised the need to raise police salaries substantially, while stressing under "political criteria" the need to fight corruption in the police. This indicates that corruption is identified as a problem not on the basis of direct evidence of corruption, but of a regulatory shortcoming that might result in corruption: the explanation of an alleged phenomenon is used to identify conditions that suggest but can not prove that the phenomenon exists.[73] Examples of this tendency can be found in almost every Report with the exception of Slovenia, where the apparent adequacy of regulatory institutions (or at least their ongoing reform) appears to be taken as evidence that corruption is a limited problem. Although regulatory deficiencies – as identified by the Commission – may be taken as constituting an aspect of a given institution or system that increases its vulnerability to corruption, this may not always be the case. Likewise, the assumption that the apparent adequacy or reform of regulatory institutions constitutes evidence that corruption is not a serious problem is even more flawed, and would only hold under certain specific conditions. Indeed, EUMAP's report on Slovenia identifies the weakness of enforcement and regulatory bodies as giving rise to possible problems of corruption – the opposite of the Commission's assessment.

The assessment of anti-corruption policy in candidate countries

In terms of both its evaluation of existing anti-corruption policies and actions expected of candidate States in the area of anti-corruption policy, the criteria employed by the

---

[72] Commission, *2000 Regular Report from the Commission on Poland's Progress towards Accession,* p. 21.

[73] Estonia is chosen here as an example since, according to both the *Regular Report* itself and other surveys such as the Transparency CPI, corruption is not a serious problem.

Commission *vis-à-vis* candidate States can be divided into three parts. Officials state that in the preparation of the Regular Reports the Commission follows a "checklist" of six criteria for monitoring corruption:

1. The existence and implementation of anti-corruption policy;

2. Institutional arrangements for implementation and division of tasks among institutions;

3. Codes of conduct for public servants;

4. Training programs for public servants;

5. Cases of corruption in government and public administration, and how the authorities reacted to these cases;

6. Ratification and implementation of the relevant conventions (Council of Europe, OECD).[74]

Analysis of the Regular Reports yields a pattern of comment that is to some extent consistent with this checklist. However, the Commission evaluates or advocates individual policies or the consideration of certain policies in some countries without mentioning them in others.

The criteria implied by the Regular Reports are outlined below.

(i) Criteria that are applied more-or-less consistently across all candidate States.
This category consists of two main elements:

International instruments
The Commission consistently takes into account the extent to which countries have adhered to international anti-corruption instruments: specifically, whether they have signed and ratified the Council of Europe Criminal and Civil Law Conventions on Corruption and the OECD Convention on Combating Bribery of Foreign Public Officials; and whether they have aligned legislation with the requirements of the 1995 Convention on the Protection of the European Communities' Financial Interests and its two anti-corruption protocols, and the 1998 Convention on the fight against corruption involving officials of the European Communities or officials of the member States of the European Union. These requirements appear to provide the basis for the only administrative structures the Commission requires candidate countries to create explicitly under the heading of corruption: efficient anti-fraud services to contribute to the fight

---

[74] Information provided by DG Enlargement Unit, European Commission.

against fraud and corruption, and full cooperation between national authorities and the European Commission, specifically OLAF, the EU's own anti-fraud unit.[75]

Law enforcement

Second, the Commission pursues a consistent policy of urging and assisting the improvement of the institutions of law enforcement. Much of this activity is linked to the existence of the Council of Europe OCTOPUS program, which has consisted of joint seminars of the law enforcement agencies of EU and candidate States. The emphasis of OCTOPUS recommendations has been on increased specialisation of the various organs of enforcement (creation of special anti-corruption departments in the police, investigation organs and judiciary) and improved coordination among them and with other specialised anti-corruption bodies.

The latter direction of policy is linked to a consistent Commission policy of encouraging the development of national anti-corruption strategies. In addition, the Commission consistently urges increased efforts in the fight against corruption in the customs administration.[76]

The application of the above criteria to individual candidate States is summarised in Tables 6 and 7, which draw on the 1999 and 2001 Accession Partnerships.

---

[75] Information provided by DG Enlargement Unit, March 2002.

[76] In this area, however, it appears that the concern with corruption is indirectly motivated by the primary EU concern with smuggling, as little evidence of corruption is presented.

Table 6: Corruption as a commitment under the 1999 Accession Partnerships

Country	Corruption mentioned?	Short-term priorities	Medium-term priorities
Bulgaria	Yes	**JHA:** Upgrade law enforcement bodies and judiciary; National anti-corruption strategy; Ratify European conventions	**IM:** Reinforce fight against corruption in customs administration; JHA; Implement anti-corruption strategy
Czech Republic	Yes	**JHA:** Implement anti-corruption policy (legislation, implementing structures, sufficient qualified staff, institutional cooperation)	**IM:** Continue fight against corruption in customs administration; JHA; Further upgrade law enforcement bodies, continue fight against corruption
Estonia	Yes	**JHA:** Continue fight against corruption: create advanced criminal investigation data system, improve research capacity, improve law enforcement cooperation; Ratify OECD convention	
Hungary	Yes	**JHA:** Ratify European Criminal Law Convention	**JHA:** Further upgrade law enforcement bodies: Continue fight against corruption; Better coordination
Latvia	Yes	**IM:** Continue fight against corruption in customs; **JHA:** Upgrade law enforcement and judicial bodies to continue fight against corruption; Concrete measures to fight corruption, improve coordination; Ratify European and OECD conventions	**JHA:** Implement legislation on corruption and the anti-corruption strategy
Lithuania	Yes	**IM:** Customs: reinforce fight against corruption **JHA:** Upgrade law enforcement bodies and judiciary and improve coordination to continue fight against corruption; Ratify European Criminal Law and OECD conventions; Adopt and start implementing national anti-corruption strategy	**JHA:** Implement streamlined inter-agency structure for fighting corruption
Poland	Yes	**JHA:** Implement anti-corruption and anti-fraud program (particularly customs, police and judiciary); Ratify European Criminal Law and OECD conventions	**JHA:** Further upgrade law enforcement bodies and judiciary and improve coordination
Romania	Yes	**IM:** Customs: apply measures to combat fraud and corruption **JHA:** Upgrade law enforcement bodies and judiciary and improve coordination to continue fight against corruption; Adopt law on prevention and fight against corruption, establish independent anti-corruption department; Ratify European Criminal Law and OECD conventions	
Slovakia	Yes	**JHA:** Ratify European Criminal Law and OECD conventions	**JHA:** Upgrade law enforcement bodies and judiciary; Continue fight against corruption
Slovenia	Yes	**JHA:** Ratify European Criminal Law and OECD conventions	**IM:** Continue fight against corruption in customs **JHA:** Further upgrade law enforcement bodies and improve coordination; Continue fight against corruption

Notes: JHA = Justice and Home Affairs, IM = Internal Market.

Source: 1999 Accession Partnerships, available at:
<http://europa.eu.int/comm/enlargement/report_10_99/acc_partn.htm>, (last accessed 22 August 2002).

Table 7: Corruption as a commitment under the 2001 Accession Partnerships

Country	Corruption mentioned?	Policies
Bulgaria	Yes	PC: URGENT: start implementing national anti-corruption strategy, especially focusing on awareness, prevention and prosecution.
Czech Republic	Yes	PC: Pursue efforts to more effectively fight corruption and economic crime. JHA: Establish framework for better cooperation between law enforcement agencies, especially for fight against economic crime and corruption, further training on organised crime, introduce modern equipment; continue efforts to strengthen customs ethics, combat fraud and corruption.
Estonia	Yes	CU: Continue fight against fraud and corruption in customs, continue to implement ethics policy in customs.
Hungary	Yes	PC: Ensure implementation of anti-corruption strategy.
Latvia	Yes	PC: Complete legal framework for fight against all types of corruption, ensure implementation of legislation and anti-corruption strategy; improve inter-agency and international cooperation.
Lithuania	Yes	PC: Adopt and start implementing anti-corruption strategy, Law on Corruption Prevention and Code of Ethics for Civil Servants; ratify relevant international anti-corruption conventions
Poland	Yes	PC: Implement a comprehensive anti-corruption strategy.
Romania	Yes	PC: Intensify fight against corruption by clarifying competencies of bodies involved in anti-corruption activities, ensuring improved coordination and strengthening implementation capacities; ratifying relevant international conventions; introducing criminal liability of legal persons into criminal law.
Slovakia	Yes	PC: Step up fight against corruption, in particular ensure timely and effective implementation of anti-corruption Action Plans. JHA: Continue efforts to strengthen customs ethics, combat fraud, corruption and economic crime FC: URGENT: Complete legislation for internal financial control, strengthen fight against fraud, step up efforts to ensure correct use, control, monitoring and evaluation of EC pre-accession funding
Slovenia	No	

Notes: PC = Political Criteria, JHA = Justice and Home Affairs, IM = Internal Market, CU = Customs Union, FC = Financial Control.

Source: 2001 Accession Partnerships, available at: <http://europa.eu.int/comm/enlargement/report2001/acc_partn.htm>, (last accessed 5 August 2002).

(ii) Criteria applied inconsistently across candidate States

The second set of criteria consists of legislative provisions that are more-or-less explicitly designed to address corruption, yet are applied by the Commission unevenly across the candidate States. In some cases the Commission urges certain reforms, or mentions or criticises them in the context of a country's existing anti-corruption strategy, yet fails to do so in another State. These include for example:

- Conflict of interest and/or asset monitoring. For example, in 2001 the Commission stated that Slovenia needs to pay more attention to preventing conflict of interest situations in public procurement,[77] yet did not mention the problem in other countries where the problem is also serious (such as the Czech Republic or Poland).

- Political party financing. The Commission noted improvements in the regulations on financing of political parties in Poland (2001) and Lithuania (2000), and called explicitly for a more transparent system of party financing in Romania (2001). The Commission did not mention the passage of similar improvements in Slovak legislation in 2001, and has not stated any criteria for what constitutes a good system.[78]

- A Law on Lobbying is mentioned as an important anti-corruption measure taken in Lithuania in the 2000 Report.[79] However, lobbying is hardly mentioned in any other Report, despite widespread evidence that uncontrolled lobbying is a major source of corruption in candidate States.

- In the 2001 Lithuania report, the Commission explicitly states that "[G]reater involvement of civil society in the fight against corruption should be encouraged." The role of civil society in fighting corruption is not mentioned in other Reports with the exception of Bulgaria. The fact that civil society in Slovakia has played a major role in the emergence of anti-corruption policies, while civil society in Slovenia appears to be so weak in the area of corruption as to play no role at all, has drawn no comment from the Commission.

---

[77] Commission, *2001 Regular Report from the Commission on Slovenia's Progress towards Accession*, p. 18.

[78] This probably reflects the lack of any European standards on political party financing, not to speak of various scandals in party financing in EU countries, notably Germany (see Section 2.1).

[79] Commission, *2000 Regular Report from the Commission on Lithuania's Progress towards Accession*, p. 18.

(iii) "Capacity building"

In addition to its concern with direct anti-corruption policy, a separate major accession criterion applied by the Commission to candidate States is the extent to which they have built sufficient capacity to implement the *acquis*. Indeed, the 2001 overall report indicates that the third set of Copenhagen criteria concerning ability to assume the obligations of membership has now been allocated higher priority:

> The conditions for membership, set out by the Copenhagen European Council in 1993 and further detailed by subsequent European Councils, provide the benchmarks for assessing each candidate's progress. These conditions remain valid today and there is no question of modifying them. In the present phase of the accession process, however, it is necessary to focus as much on the candidates' capacity to implement and enforce the *acquis* as on its transposition into law. For this reason, particular attention is now being given to the candidates' administrative and judicial capacity.[80]

Given the link between corruption and the ability of candidate States to implement the *acquis*, it is not surprising that the EU frequently mentions capacity building in the context of or adjacent to discussions of anti-corruption policy. For example, the citation from the 1999 Composite Report provided earlier identifies low salaries for public employees as one of the two main factors underlying corruption in candidate countries. The two main aspects of capacity building pursued by the Commission are:

- A Civil Service Law that entails proper remuneration, staffing and an adequate control system. The Commission's concern with control systems is primarily related to the need to control the increasing inflow of EU funds into candidate States and the transition to allocation of structural funds. This includes adopting international State audit standards (Lima Declaration and INTOSAI standards); establishing effective, independent and *ex ante* internal control systems; and, again, increasing capacity in terms of both staffing and information systems.

- Enhanced judicial capacity, entailing consolidation of judicial independence, adequate staffing of courts, infrastructure and training.

Although the need to build capacity in the public administration of candidate States is indisputable, the link between the public administration reforms advocated by the Commission and corruption is more controversial. First, the wisdom of giving across-the-board security of tenure and pay raises is questionable to some extent, given that the recipients are to a significant extent the same personnel who appear to be tainted by

---

[80] Commission, *Making a Success of Enlargement: Strategy Paper and Report of the European Commission on the Progress towards Accession by Each of the Candidate Countries*, p. 5.

corruption in the Regular Reports.[81] Second, to the extent that corruption is not simply a question of poorly paid civil servants boosting their salaries but is more deeply rooted in patronage networks, pay raises are unlikely to make a difference. Moreover, the political feasibility of such measures has been questioned by some observers,[82] while the economic feasibility of increasing expenditure on public administration may also be doubtful in many countries.

3.3 Corruption in candidate States: the evidence

3.3.1 The incidence of corruption in candidate States

There is still little comparative research available to provide clear evidence of the extent of corruption in candidate States, and no detailed comprehensive study of corruption in EU member and CEE States that would yield sufficient data to make serious comparisons. Nevertheless, survey evidence suggests that corruption is at a minimum perceived to be a major problem in candidate States. One important survey carried out across candidate countries in November 2001 reported that 73 percent of citizens think that most or almost all public officials are corrupt. The survey found that in Latvia and Lithuania more than nine-tenths of citizens think their government is corrupt, while Slovenia is the only country in which a majority (58 percent) of citizens do not think there is much corruption in Government.[83] Aggregate indicators of 12 international indices of corruption (and other governance variables) calculated by Daniel Kaufmann *et al* suggest that corruption in CEE and the Baltic States is considerably more prevalent than in countries of the OECD.[84] However, the applicability of this comparison to candidate States is less clear as several of them are already OECD members. Also, as the authors themselves admit, the precision with

---

[81] The OECD, for example, explicitly recommended in 2001 that provisions providing for security of tenure be omitted from the Czech Civil Service Act. OECD Economic Surveys: Czech Republic July 2001, p. 164., OECD, Paris, July 2001.

[82] "Given the communist legacy, post-communism tends to be egalitarian, which means that envy is the supreme public virtue. The electorate will never agree to a highly paid civil service, which, in any event, is unaffordable given the sheer size of the State bureaucracy." A. Sajo, "Clientelism and Extortion: Corruption in Transition," (amended version of A. Sajo, "Corruption, Clientelism, and the Future of the Constitutional State in Eastern Europe," *East European Constitutional Review* 1998, Vol. 7, no. 2), p. 10.

[83] New Europe Barometer 2001, Centre for the Study of Public Policy, University of Strathclyde; for details see R. Rose, "Advancing into Europe: Contrasting Goals of Post-Communist Countries," forthcoming in *Nations in Transition 2002*, Freedom House, New York. <http://www.cspp.strath.ac.uk>, last accessed 24 August 2002, p. 11.

[84] See World Bank, *Anti-corruption in Transition: A Contribution to the Policy Debate*, p. xiv.

which the indices measure quality of governance is limited: even with regard to their aggregates of indices of individual components of governance, which the authors argue are more accurate than the individual indices themselves, the authors express the opinion that

> [A]lthough it is possible to robustly identify twenty or so countries with the best and worst governance in the world, it is much more difficult to identify statistically significant differences in governance among the majority of countries.[85]

There are two other main exceptions to the dearth of evidence. These are presented briefly below.

The Transparency International Corruption Perceptions Index

The CPI is constructed from an unweighted average of the available surveys of domestic public opinion on levels of corruption in each country. The index ranges from 0 (most corrupt) to ten (least corrupt). In 2001 the CPI averaged 7.6 for EU member States, ranging from 4.2 for Greece to 9.9 for Finland, but 4.3 for post-communist candidate States, ranging from 2.8 for Romania to 5.6 for Estonia.

Although both the Kaufmann *et al* calculations and the CPI appear to confirm the existence of a broad difference in levels of corruption between member and candidate States, the two regions are not in entirely separate categories with respect to corruption. Italy scores lower in the CPI than Estonia, while Greece scores lower than Estonia, Hungary, Slovenia and Lithuania. Regarding candidate countries themselves, the CPI does not paint an optimistic picture of trends over time, with only two of the ten countries showing improvement over the period 1998-2001. However, it should be taken into account that the CPI exhibits considerable inertia, as the index is based on both present and past surveys, and is therefore in effect a rolling average.

---

[85] D. Kaufmann, A. Kraay and P. Zoido-Lobaton, *Aggregating Governance Indicators*, World Bank Policy Research Paper no. 2195, p. 5.

Table 8: Corruption Perception Index scores and rankings for candidate countries, 1998–2001

	CPI score (ranking)				Trend in ranking
	1998	*1999*	*2000*	*2001*	
Bulgaria	2.9 (66)	3.3 (63)	3.5 (52)	3.9 (47)	Improvement
Czech Republic	4.8 (37)	4.6 (39)	4.3 (42)	3.9 (47)	Decline
Estonia	5.7 (26)	5.7 (27)	5.7 (27)	5.6 (28)	Stable
Hungary	5.0 (33)	5.2 (31)	5.2 (32)	5.3 (31)	Stable
Latvia	2.7 (71)	3.4 (58)	3.4 (57)	3.4 (59)	Stable
Lithuania	NI	3.8 (50)	4.1 (43)	4.8 (38)	Improvement
Poland	4.6 (39)	4.2 (44)	4.1 (43)	4.1 (44)	Stable
Romania	3.0 (61)	3.3 (63)	2.9 (68)	2.8 (69)	Gradual decline
Slovakia	3.9 (47)	3.7 (53)	3.5 (52)	3.7 (51)	Stable
Slovenia	NI	6.0 (25)	5.5 (28)	5.2 (34)	Decline
Number of countries included in index	85	99	90	91	

Notes: Absolute scores are *not comparable* across different years. Rankings are comparable across years to the extent that the sample of countries is unchanging, which is largely the case. "NI" means the country was not included in the index for the given year.

Source: Transparency International, <www.transparency.org>, (last accessed 22 August 2002)

The 1999 EBRD/World Bank Business Environment and Enterprise Performance Survey (BEEPS)

While the indicators outlined above are all constructed from surveys of perceptions of corruption, an important attempt to measure the prevalence of corruption through questions concerning actual experience of corruption has also been made by the EBRD and World Bank in a major survey carried out in 1999 of more than 3,000 enterprise managers in 17 transition countries. Among other things, the survey attempted to measure two main variables:

- **Administrative corruption:** the extent to which companies make informal payments to influence the implementation of formal rules;

- The extent to which companies engage in and are affected by **State capture,** defined as "actions of individuals, groups, or firms both in the public and private sectors to influence the formation of laws, regulations, decrees and other

Government policies to their own advantage as a result of the illicit and non-transparent provision of private benefits to public officials."[86]

Administrative corruption

According to the results of the BEEPS survey, enterprises in candidate States pay on average 2.1 percent of their annual revenues in unofficial payments to public officials (see Table 9). As a percentage of annual profits, the figure would clearly be much higher. Table 10 provides a more detailed view of the proportion of firms in each candidate country that pay various percentages of revenues in bribes.

Table 9: Average percentage of annual revenues paid in unofficial payments to public officials by enterprises in candidate countries

	Bulgaria	Czech Republic	Estonia	Hungary	Lithuania	Poland	Romania	Slovakia	Slovenia	Latvia
Average	2.1	2.5	1.6	1.7	2.8	1.6	3.2	2.5	1.4	1.4
Number of observations	98	97	92	91	75	175	99	80	98	121

Source: BEEPS Interactive Dataset, World Bank, <www.worldbank.org>, (last accessed 22 August 2002).

Table 10: Replies to the question "On average, what percentage of revenues do firms like yours pay in unofficial payments per annum to public officials?" (answers in percent)

Country	0	< 1	1 – 2	2 - 10	10 – 12	13 - 25	> 25
Bulgaria	0	42	32	12	10	3	0
Czech Republic	0	44	18	20	15	2	2
Estonia	0	35	37	28	0	0	0
Hungary	0	61	14	16	8	2	0
Lithuania	0	49	14	24	8	6	0
Poland	0	59	21	14	7	0	0
Romania	3	28	35	23	8	3	1
Slovakia	0	40	21	32	6	2	0
Slovenia	0	54	15	24	5	0	2
Latvia	7	54	19	16	2	0	2

Source: BEEPS Interactive Dataset, World Bank, <www.worldbank.org>, (last accessed 22 August 2002).

---

[86] World Bank, *Anti-corruption in Transition: A Contribution to the Policy Debate*, p. xv.

The question to which the data in Table 10 applies was also asked in a number of EU countries, namely France, Germany, Italy, Portugal, Spain, Sweden and the UK. Although a figure for the average percentage of revenue paid by firms to public officials is not available, the survey nevertheless revealed striking differences. For example, in the EU countries surveyed, on average 84 percent of respondents stated that firms like theirs pay nothing in unofficial payments, a dramatically different result to that shown in Table 10. Likewise, on average 3.5 percent of firms in EU countries stated that companies like theirs pay 2-10 percent of annual revenues in unofficial payments, compared to 20.9 percent of firms in candidate countries. Further, on average 67 percent of companies in the EU countries in the survey said that there are no unofficial payments when firms in their industry do business with the Government, compared to an average of 8.5 percent in candidate countries.[87]

State capture

In order to generate data that might be interpreted as measuring State capture, the BEEPS survey asked enterprise managers whether and to what extent their company is affected by the purchase of various kinds of decision. The summary results for candidate countries are shown in Table 11. In terms of State capture strictly understood according to the World Bank definition, the most interesting overall result is that almost 20 percent of companies on average claim to be affected by corruption in the passage of legislation and in financing of political parties. The figures vary greatly by country however: the percentage of companies affected by the purchase of legislation varies from eight percent in Slovenia to 40 percent in Latvia (see Table 12), while the figure for party finance varies from four percent in Hungary to 42 percent in Bulgaria (see Table 13). The responses of countries concerning court decisions are not clearly indicators of State capture on the World Bank definition, but are nevertheless interesting as they indicate significant problems of corruption in judicial proceedings. The figures on corruption in the passage of presidential decrees and central bank decisions are probably of limited importance in candidate countries, as presidents have limited powers in all the countries and central bank independence is not seriously threatened in any of them.

---

[87] For results of the surveys in EU countries see *The World Business Environment Survey* (WBES) 2000, <http://info.worldbank.org/governance/wbes>, (last accessed 23 July 2002); for results in candidate countries see *The Business Environment and Enterprise Performance Survey* (BEEPS), the transition country component of the WEBS, <http://info.worldbank.org/governance/beeps>, (last accessed 23 July 2002).

Table 11: Indicators of State capture: percentage of firms affected by purchase of/purchase of decisions in…

	Parliamentary legislation	Presidential decrees	Central Bank	Criminal Courts	Commercial Courts	Party finance	Capture Economy Index
Bulgaria	28	26	28	28	19	42	28
Czech Republic	18	11	12	9	9	6	11
Estonia	14	7	8	8	8	17	10
Hungary	12	7	8	5	5	4	7
Latvia	40	49	8	21	26	35	30
Lithuania	15	7	9	11	14	13	11
Poland	13	10	6	12	18	10	12
Romania	22	20	26	14	17	27	21
Slovakia	20	12	37	29	25	20	24
Slovenia	8	5	4	6	6	11	7
Candidate country average	19	14.4	14.6	14.3	14.7	18.5	15.1

Source: J. Hellmann, G. Jones and D. Kaufmann, "Seize the State, Seize the Day: State Capture, Corruption and Influence in Transition," Policy Research Working Paper 2444, World Bank Institute and Office of the Chief Economist, EBRD, September 2000, p. 9.

Table 12: Responses by enterprises to the question "What impact have the following forms of corruption had on your business? Sale of Parliamentary votes to private interests." (percentage of samples)

	No impact	Minor impact	Significant impact	Very significant impact	Number of observations
Bulgaria	62	10	18	10	68
Czech Republic	71	12	14	4	95
Estonia	67	19	9	5	103
Hungary	73	15	7	5	101
Lithuania	77	8	10	6	73
Poland	66	21	8	5	171
Romania	62	16	12	11	76
Slovakia	69	11	17	3	71
Slovenia	80	12	2	6	111
Latvia	30	30	31	9	122

Table 13: Responses by enterprises to the question "What impact have the following forms of corruption had on your business?: Contributions to political parties by private interests." (percentage of samples)

	No impact	Minor impact	Significant impact	Very significant impact	Number of observations
Bulgaria	47	10	22	21	78
Czech Republic	87	8	2	3	89
Estonia	55	29	13	4	108
Hungary	90	7	2	2	108
Lithuania	69	18	7	6	83
Poland	74	16	6	4	172
Romania	59	14	17	10	71
Slovakia	56	24	14	6	84
Slovenia	67	22	6	5	109
Latvia	34	31	24	12	119

Note: numbers may not add up to 100 because of rounding.
Source: BEEPS Interactive Dataset, World Bank, <www.worldbank.org>, (last accessed 22 August 2002).

The problems of generalisation

Although the surveys outlined above provide little evidence that corruption has decreased in candidate countries in recent years, there are several reasons for expressing caution, both about the surveys themselves and about the wisdom of making judgements about whether corruption in general has decreased or increased in a given country. Several of these reasons have been outlined already in Section 1.2.1: in particular, the difference between perceptions and experience, and the limits of understanding corruption only as bribery and informal payments. In particular, the incidence of clientelism as a form of socio-political organisation in post-communist societies has gone almost entirely unassessed.

In addition, much of the survey evidence is based on perceptions of overall corruption in a given country, with little or no sensitivity to the possibility that corruption may, during the same period, have decreased in some areas while increasing in others. While the BEEPS survey is an important step towards greater complexity based on the distinction between administrative corruption and State capture (see above), the size of the samples of firms, which ranged from approximately 70 to 170, raises questions about the extent to which the results are representative of the situation across all firms.

Aside from statistical questions, another difficulty with making judgements about trends in corruption in candidate countries is raised by the situation of economic transition. In particular, a rough distinction may be drawn between "transitional" and "ordinary" corruption. "Transitional corruption" means corruption in one-off processes such as privatisation in particular, and has been widespread in all candidate States. "Ordinary corruption" refers to corruption of activities that are ongoing in any State (such as licensing procedures, company registration or competition regulation). Clearly, statements about trends in corruption in candidate States must be sensitive to this distinction: falls in levels of corruption may reflect the completion of privatisation processes, while increases in corruption may, for example, reflect a rise in the everyday burden on judicial institutions.

GRECO

All of these factors go to underline two main points. First, assessments of corruption in individual countries are of limited use unless they are detailed and institution-specific. Secondly, as EUMAP's individual country reports show, there is a general lack of detailed research on corruption in candidate countries, both in terms of survey research[88] and qualitative analysis of the vulnerability of various institutions to corruption.

On the other hand, analyses of corruption and anti-corruption policy based on the Council of Europe's 20 Guiding Principles have begun to be conducted within the framework of the GRECO evaluation reports. These are still in an initial phase and have not yet begun evaluating countries according to some of the more sensitive Guiding Principles (for example political party finance). Nevertheless, the GRECO reports remain the nearest thing in existence to analysis based on consistent standards, producing evaluations that can be used on a comparative basis, at least in the area of anti-corruption policy.

3.3.2 Loci of corruption

EUMAP's individual country reports confirm many of the findings of the European Commission concerning corruption in candidate countries, notably concerning administrative corruption. However, the reports also contain significant evidence that candidate countries are able to tackle and reduce administrative corruption. In particular, corruption in customs authorities appears to have been cut back significantly in a number of countries, such as the Czech Republic, Latvia and Poland.[89]

---

[88] With a few notable exceptions, such as a large survey carried out by the local branch of Transparency International in Lithuania, the World Bank diagnostic surveys conducted in Slovakia and Romania, and the surveys carried out by Miller *et al* in Slovakia and the Czech Republic and cited above.

[89] The Hungarian branch of Transparency International also regards customs reform as one of the main areas where tangible progress has been made against corruption.

EUMAP reports also echo the Commission in identifying problems in the judiciary and institutions of law enforcement, both in terms of corruption and the ineffectiveness of these institutions in fighting corruption. They highlight problems concerning the independence of the institutions of prosecution, particularly in Poland and Romania. In general, in no candidate country have courts and prosecution offices yet proved to be sufficiently independent or powerful to investigate or prosecute on the basis of suspicions concerning politicians or parties where this does not suit the political establishment.

However, EUMAP country reports differ significantly from the Commission is in the emphasis they place on corruption in a number of other areas, listed below.

State capture

One area to which the Commission has paid little attention has been corruption of the legislative process in candidate countries, an example of what the World Bank defines as "State capture" (see above). EUMAP country reports indicate that uncontrolled lobbying is a serious problem in many candidate countries. A number of countries have taken important steps such as publishing proposed laws on the Internet and soliciting input from civil society. Nonetheless, it appears that in no country is the legislative process designed sufficiently well to limit corrupt influence on the content of legislation by commercial interests, such as through formal consultation processes that include only transparent and inclusive interest associations. In the Czech Republic, for example, the parliamentary process is highly vulnerable to corruption of MPs, and problems of covert lobbying appear to have become systematic over the past decade. Successful lobbying by business interests that have contributed to political parties may have been a problem in Estonia and Lithuania, and is regarded as one of the key problems of corruption in Latvia. In Bulgaria, there exist serious doubts whether the Government's anti-corruption strategy can be successfully implemented against strong countervailing power from entities (such as the customs administration) with an interest in blocking reform.

Political party funding

Corruption through the financing of political parties has been a major problem in most candidate countries. No country has put in place an effective system for limiting corruption, although the transition to generous State funding in the Czech Republic, strict requirements for informing on donations in Estonia (and most recently Latvia), and the allocation of a supervisory role to the Election Commission in Poland are all important steps in the right direction. Otherwise, the extent of the problem varies considerably. At one extreme, in Romania corruption in party financing is systemic and appears to be tied in with a system of contributions by electoral candidates to parties in return for being placed on party candidate lists. Party funding in Bulgaria, Latvia, Poland and Slovakia has been (or is thought to have been) highly corrupt over the past decade. A party financing scandal brought down the Czech Government in 1997, while in the remaining countries there remain serious doubts about the accuracy of party accounts and therefore the links between private interests and parties.

Public procurement

Despite the adoption of progressively more comprehensive public procurement legislation in all candidate countries, corruption in public procurement remains a serious and widespread problem in most if not all candidate countries. Although procurement legislation has done much to stamp out more blatant forms of corruption based on avoidance of tender requirements, both contracting authorities and tendering companies have adapted easily to the new conditions. Bribes of 10-20 percent of contract value were cited as typical in a number of countries, including the Czech Republic, Hungary, Latvia, Lithuania, Poland and Romania. In Bulgaria and Slovakia procurement appears to be a hotbed of corruption, while in Estonia and Slovenia inadequacies in the framework for supervising procurement give rise to doubts about the integrity of procurement processes.

Public administration

EUMAP country reports confirm widespread perceptions that corruption is a serious problem in public administration, underpinned, *inter alia,* by a failure to reform vulnerable areas such a licensing procedures, failure to root out patronage in appointments, the absence of effective procedures for appealing against or investigating administrative decisions, and failure to prevent widespread conflicts of interest.

Although the country reports have not focused specifically on local government, it became apparent during the course of EUMAP research that corruption at local government level is a particularly serious problem in a number of countries. Indeed, in Estonia corruption in local government emerged consistently as the most pressing problem, underpinned by close ties between local businesses and officials and the inability of a number of important regulatory institutions to operate effectively at the local government level. Given the apparently relatively low levels of corruption in general in Estonia, the problem of local government corruption appears likely to be an important problem area in other candidate countries.

Citizen awareness and redress

In candidate countries, citizen awareness of corruption is both overblown and under informed. Corruption has been a prominent political issue in most candidate countries, with the exception of Estonia and Slovenia. However, the character of citizen awareness has not been of a type that encourages consistent pressure on elites to behave non-corruptly or to pursue consistent and effective anti-corruption policy. Instead, a pattern has emerged in a number of countries – although to differing degrees – in which corruption and sleaze in general become one of the most important weapons in the armoury of those vying for power. The consequence of this is elections where corruption is used to topple Governments and as a promise of a cleaner future, but post-election anti-corruption drives lack competence or real political will, or even worse are used mainly to attack or undermine political opponents. This phenomenon has been most apparent in Poland, where elections in 2001 were fought mainly on the issue of corruption, while the resulting government has done little to pursue any consistent anti-corruption policy or behave differently to its predecessors. Even where Governments have come to power with a sincere objective of putting in place lasting anti-corruption policy, the very prominence of corruption as a political issue tends to hinder the creation of the cross-party consensus that is necessary in order to put through some of the most important reforms (for example to limit corruption in the legislative process).

In a few countries civil society organisations have played a vital role in formulating anti-corruption policy and maintaining a degree of consistent pressure on Governments to implement it, notably in Bulgaria and Latvia. Nevertheless, there remains a general lack of effective procedures for citizens to appeal against administrative decisions, and of efforts to educate citizens as to their rights *vis-à-vis* the State. In contacts with the public administration, citizens who are aware of their rights and how and to whom they may turn for redress may play a major role in reducing everyday corruption, even in countries with corruption problems as severe as Bulgaria, for example.[90]

Media independence

Although the media has played an extremely important role in raising awareness of corruption in candidate States, a number of important barriers to effective investigative journalism remain. In Romania draconian provisions remain on the statute books that undermine freedom of speech, while less worrying but nevertheless problematic laws remain on the books in Bulgaria and Poland. A more serious problem across almost all candidate States remains a widespread failure to guarantee the independence of public broadcasting: in most countries political control or influence is exercised over public television through the broadcasting regulator or financial pressure.

---

[90] One local analyst in Sofia expressed the opinion that citizens who are aware of their formal rights can deal with the Bulgarian public officials without having to resort to corruption. Interview with Ruslan Stefanov, Project Director, Economic Policy Institute, Sofia, 8 February 2002.

Table 14: Corruption: main problem areas identified by EUMAP country reports and European Commission in 2001

Country	Main problems identified in EUMAP report, 2001	Main problems identified in 2001 Regular Report
Bulgaria	Customs Political party funding Local Government Judiciary	Judiciary Enforcement of existing anti-corruption law Burdensome licensing and permit procedures
Czech Republic	Formal implementation of anti-corruption strategy Uncontrolled lobbying Public procurement	No civil service law Public procurement
Estonia	Weak law enforcement Ineffectiveness of anti-corruption institutions Local Government Public procurement	Police (petty corruption) Customs
Hungary	Political party patronage Independence of prosecution Public procurement Media independence	Non-specific
Latvia	Poor coordination of anti-corruption institutions Uncontrolled lobbying Political party funding Public procurement	Public administration Lack of coordination
Lithuania	Lack of reliable information Political party funding	Public administration Need to approve National Anti-corruption Strategy
Poland	Lack of will to produce anti-corruption strategy Off-budget agencies Independence of prosecution Corruption as a populist political issue	Public perceptions of corruption Lack of coherent approach, coordination and resources
Romania	Judiciary, prosecution and police Party finance Parliament: immunities Political party funding Legal provisions against media	Lack of secondary legislation to follow anti-corruption law Non-functioning anti-corruption agency Party finance
Slovakia	Tolerance of corruption Failure to implement anti-corruption strategy Judiciary Public administration Health and education	Judiciary Anti-corruption strategy not yet implemented
Slovenia	Lack of anti-corruption strategy Conflict of interest, clientelist networks Weak law enforcement Local government Public procurement Weak civil society	Conflict of interest

3.4 Anti-corruption policy in candidate States

3.4.1 The evidence

A number of trends in anti-corruption policy in candidate States emerge from the evidence presented in EUMAP's country reports. An overarching theme is a lack of political will to tackle corruption.[91] The evidence for this is widespread, including the inability of candidate States to achieve cross-party consensus on anti-corruption policy,[92] the unwillingness of executive authorities to grant sufficient independence to anti-corruption prosecutors,[93] and tendencies to fulfil the easier components of national anti-corruption strategies or to fulfil anti-corruption policies in formal terms but without genuine implementation.[94] An apparent exception to these reservations appears to be Lithuania, which has formulated one of the most comprehensive and sophisticated anti-corruption strategies in the region, put in place a number of very important legislative measures that are being increasingly well enforced, and above all created the only truly independent anti-corruption agency among all candidate States.

Where Governments have put in place anti-corruption strategies, these have been oriented by design or in implementation towards repression and a criminal law-based approach, and have been directed primarily towards low-level corruption rather than high-level corruption. This has been most clearly the case in Romania, but is characteristic of the implementation of most anti-corruption strategies, where efforts to tighten provisions of criminal law or tackle administrative corruption tend to be passed much more easily than for example, stricter conflict of interest provisions for high-level officials or provisions to regulate lobbying or stricter party financing provisions. Again, a notable, if partial, exception is Lithuania; Estonia has also put in place more comprehensive legislation than other candidate countries, although the extent to which the legislation has been implemented is questionable.

The repressive bias of most current anti-corruption strategies in candidate countries itself reflects the fact that such strategies have been in a number of cases overly "top-down;" that is, created at elite level with little or no incorporation of business, civil society and lower level officials. Although such an approach may yield results in

---

[91] This is due at least in part to the incentives facing power holders in post-communist countries. See Section 3.

[92] This has been a particularly severe problem in Poland, but has also clearly hindered anti-corruption policy in Bulgaria, the Czech Republic and Slovakia, for example.

[93] This appears to be a particularly visible problem in Poland and Romania, although EUMAP findings are not sufficiently detailed to conclude that it is not equally serious in certain other States.

[94] This has been noticeable in the Czech Republic and Slovakia, for example.

reducing administrative corruption, it suffers from major drawbacks by failing to build lasting societal pressure against corruption, and failing to incorporate the officials who are the targets of policy into the policy-making process, thereby losing an important opportunity to gain their support.[95]

In fact, these general tendencies in the anti-corruption strategies of candidate States are formally consistent with the requirements of the European Commission, and allow local elites to satisfy accession requirements such as the signature and ratification of international conventions, while in reality making little real progress against corruption or in formulating promising anti-corruption policies. Given the character of accession negotiations as a dialogue between the Commission and candidate Governments, this is difficult to avoid. Nevertheless, it inevitably raises questions about the feasibility of tackling high-level corruption through a process in which the Commission relies for both policy initiation and implementation on the very elites who can be expected to undermine anti-corruption policy.

3.4.2 The impact of the accession process on anti-corruption policy

The EU accession process has had a major impact on legal and institutional frameworks that are involved in the fight against corruption. Commission pressure has led to important legislative changes, especially in the areas of public procurement legislation, criminal and civil procedure, anti-corruption legislation, and civil service legal frameworks. The relative clarity of the EU approach in the area of enforcement of criminal law has led to important changes in candidate States, such as increased coordination between the various organs of enforcement, training of law enforcement officials and EU-assisted reform of the judiciary. The progress achieved in the Czech Republic in increasing the effectiveness of enforcement bodies and the courts in tackling corruption and economic crime has been to a large extent made possible by EU assistance, for example.

However, even in the area of anti-corruption policy narrowly-conceived, as above, the Commission has lacked the mandate or any standard of EU best practice in the areas of criminal investigation and proceedings that would allow it to pressure candidate States

---

[95] The most obvious example of this has been the adoption by a number of candidate countries of civil service codes of ethics. These have generally been adopted at government level without consultation with the officials to whom the codes will apply.

to take steps to ensure the freedom of institutions of prosecution enforcement from improper influence, for example in Poland and Romania.[96]

Moreover, the influence of the Commission on the development in candidate States of policies that would effectively limit corruption has been limited for a number of reasons. First, as Section 2.1 showed, the Union itself lacks a broadly based anti-corruption framework. Second, as noted above, the top-down elite focus of Commission influence in this area prevents attempts to encourage on a systematic basis more broadly conceived strategies, beyond supporting initiatives that Governments have already expressed their willingness to adopt. Again, this is perhaps inevitable in the area of anti-corruption policy, if the Commission is not to risk coming into open conflict with corrupt Governments. The absence of any Commission pressure on candidate States to deal with problems of corruption of legislative processes stands out in this area.

Third, in a number of policy areas the EU standards that exist are not directed primarily at preventing corruption. For example, the primary objective of Commission directives on public procurement is to encourage a single market in procurement, and the anti-corruption effects of procurement legislation are secondary.[97] Likewise, the pressure exerted by the Commission on candidate countries to carry out civil service reform is not motivated primarily by a desire to limit corruption but by the need to put in place a professional public administration capable of implementing the *acquis*.

In itself, the broader focus of such Commission directives is a good thing. Corruption is not the only, and probably not the most, important problem facing public administrations in Central and Eastern Europe, and this fact should be taken into account when designing reforms. However, this underlines the importance of underlining the positive aspects of such reforms for candidate Governments and officials, rather than emphasising their "negative" impact on corruption. As mentioned earlier (see Section 1.2.2), the best way of fighting corruption may often be not to fight against corruption but to pursue other primary policy objectives whose fulfilment reduces corruption as a side-effect.

EU assistance for anti-corruption policy

Although the European Commission wants candidate States to deal with corruption, in practice the support offered for anti-corruption policies has been organised in an uncoordinated fashion. PHARE projects related to anti-corruption policy are created on an *ad hoc* basis, often relying on consultancy contracts with private firms; there is no centralised pool of resources or official EU expertise, nor any system of twinning or secondment organised on a systematic and planned basis.

---

[96] For example, the chief prosecutor in France is the Minister for Public Prosecutions.

[97] See for example European Commission, *Public Procurement in the European Union*, Commission Communication, COM (98) 143, 11 March 1998.

4. CORRUPTION AND THE ACCESSION PROCESS: OPTIONS FOR THE FUTURE

Corruption is an issue of major importance for candidate States, primarily as a barrier to consolidation of their own democracies and market economies. Anti-corruption policy has also been made one of the most important requirements for EU accession. However, the approach of the European Commission to corruption in candidate States has not always prompted the development of anti-corruption policies appropriate to the problems that exist. Likewise, it has not been made sufficiently clear to candidate countries what benchmarks they must fulfil (or are supposed to have fulfilled) in terms of anti-corruption policy in order to satisfy the accession criteria.

This may no longer be of immediate relevance for the eight candidate countries that are likely to be invited into the Union in the near future. However, it remains of immediate relevance in the case of Bulgaria and Romania – the two countries that will not be invited to join the EU in the initial enlargement, and that appear to suffer from the most severe problems of corruption. Clearly it is of relevance to countries that are at an earlier stage of talks with the EU, but are expected to join eventually (for example the Western Balkan countries). In reality, it is also of relevance for the countries that will be invited to join. Corruption is not only an "EU accession issue," but a problem that is of concern for candidate countries as a phenomenon that to varying extents undermines the quality of their democracies and perhaps their economic development as well.

Moreover, corruption in candidate States should also remain a concern for the Commission itself. The coming accession wave heightens the concern that the European Union itself lacks a clear anti-corruption framework. Currently, the framework is limited to conventions that are narrowly focused, not ratified by a large proportion of member States[98] and therefore not yet in force. The mandate of the Commission to raise issues of corruption in candidate States was artificially widened by the Copenhagen mandate, which has allowed the Commission to require candidate countries to carry out reforms and policies that it does not have the mandate to impose on existing member States. However, the Copenhagen mandate will cease to exist once candidates are invited to join the Union, despite the fact that problems of corruption remain serious in most of the countries expected to be invited to join in the near future. In this situation, attention must be refocused on tackling corruption through clarified standards and strengthened mechanisms for the EU as a whole.

---

[98] The failure of the majority of member States to ratify the 1995 Convention on Protection of the European Communities' Financial Interests is one example, as is Italy's unwillingness to join GRECO.

A useful starting point for analysis of future options for the EU in the area of anti-corruption policy is the observation that the Union lags behind several other international organisations in terms of the creation of anti-corruption instruments and mechanisms. In the absence of any real EU anti-corruption framework, this raises urgent questions concerning how the EU will tackle corruption in member States after accession. This problem may become acute if, as much of the available evidence suggests, administrative corruption is much more widespread in candidate States than in the vast majority of member States, which could undermine implementation of the *acquis* and the distribution of Union funds. However, it is also a problem in EU member States, where corruption may be becoming an increasingly important issue. Even if corruption does not directly undermine implementation of the *acquis*, it undermines the core democratic values the Union seeks to represent, not to speak of the integrity of the single market.

Given the observations made in this Overview concerning the lack of quality information and research on corruption, and the inevitably long-term nature of effective anti-corruption policy, there appear to be two primary areas in which the EU needs to find solutions. Firstly, there is a need for much more research on corruption in both current EU member and candidate States to identify the real loci and causes of corruption on a sector-specific basis. Such research might be carried out directly under the auspices of the Commission itself, but – given the limited formal mandate of the Commission in the area of corruption – is at present more likely to come from other international organisations such as the World Bank, EBRD, OECD, and civil society organisations. Second, the EU clearly lacks a framework of anti-corruption standards or a mechanism for monitoring adherence to such a framework.

In this situation, the clear way forward for the EU is to forge deeper links with the Council of Europe in this area. As outlined in Section 2.2, the Council of Europe has approved a number of key anti-corruption documents, in particular the two anti-corruption conventions and the Twenty Guiding Principles, and a separate organisation of States against corruption, GRECO. GRECO organises monitoring of adherence to the Principles (and the Conventions as they come into force). The strengths of this framework in particular are that:

- The Principles are embedded in a framework that is flexible and allows for national variation: adherence or approximation to the Guiding Principles does not necessarily mean exactly the same policies and priorities in every State.

- The Principles are amenable to development on the basis of dialogue between a community of equals.

- GRECO has established a functioning evaluation process based on peer review and dialogue with Governments of member States, and the review process incorporates in evaluation teams representatives of Western and Eastern European States on an equal basis.

Although formal links between the EU and Council of Europe are generally minimal, in the area of anti-corruption policy there are clear opportunities that the EU could pursue to increase the influence of the Council's anti-corruption framework within the EU. Under Article 5 of the Statute of GRECO, the European Community may be invited to participate in the work of GRECO in a manner to be defined by the resolution establishing such participation.[99] Second, the requirement imposed on candidate States to sign the Council of Europe anti-corruption conventions, and the membership in GRECO of almost all member States, together constitute strong moral – if not legal – fulcra for pushing all member States to ratify the conventions. Moreover, the Criminal Law Convention entered into force in July 2002, and entities that that have ratified it are automatically obliged to become members of GRECO and thereby become subject to monitoring of their adherence to the Guiding Principles. The combination of these factors provides a clear route by which both candidate and member States can be incorporated into a functioning framework for monitoring corruption and anti-corruption policy.

5. RECOMMENDATIONS

On the basis of the arguments presented in this Overview and the findings of its individual country reports, EUMAP addresses the following recommendations to candidate States and the EU regarding anti-corruption policy.

5.1 Recommendations to candidate States

The following recommendations apply to candidate States generally. See individual country reports for additional country-specific recommendations.[100]

1. Strive for cross-party consensus on the development and implementation of anti-corruption policy; to facilitate this, label as "anti-corruption policy" only those policies whose *primary* aim is to reduce corruption;

---

[99] Statute of the GRECO, Appendix to Resolution (99) 5, Article 5.
<http://www.greco.coe.int>, (last accessed 31 July 2002).

[100] The fact that the number of recommendations differs slightly from one country to another does not signify that countries with more recommendations have more to do.

2. Sponsor more detailed research on corruption to increase knowledge of the prevalence and nature of corruption in specific areas, as a precondition for designing effective anti-corruption policy;

3. Sponsor education and public awareness initiatives on corruption to make citizens aware of their rights and encourage the development of a culture more resistant to corruption;

4. Take steps to ensure that prosecutors are free from undue influences;

5. Reform legislative processes to restrict "State capture" by changing parliamentary procedures to make corruption more difficult, and by extending reforms to include compulsory and transparent consultation with interest associations;

6. Phase out patronage in public service appointments in a realistic and systematic way;

7. Carry out an "Audit of Public Administration" and of licensing and permit procedures to identify sources of corruption, and implement recommendations;

8. Reform administrative procedures to provide citizens with real redress, and establish appeal procedures that would allow courts to influence the substance of decisions;

9. Pursue measures designed to avoid abuse of conflicts of interest – to create an anti-conflict of interest culture of disclosure and case-by-case "self-disqualification," rather than basing conflict of interest provisions primarily on incompatibility provisions;

10. Devise Codes of Ethics in public administration through a consultative process that enables officials to regard such codes as their own rather than as imposed from above;

11. In the context of decentralisation of powers to local governments, ensure that the existing competent authorities (particularly the supreme audit institution and the public procurement authority) are able to audit and control local government;

12. Reform party funding rules to prevent corruption in a number of different ways, such as: setting expenditure limits, providing sufficient State funding to allow financing of election campaigns without heavy reliance on sponsors, and entrusting monitoring to institutions likely to enjoy advantages in terms of independence (such as the Election Commission);

13. Pay more attention in public procurement reform to measures designed to ensure the integrity of public procurement officers, rather than designing procedures that can be circumvented anyway and hamstring good officials;

14. Ensure independence of broadcasting regulators as much as possible, most likely through provisions defining strictly which organisations have the right of representation in the regulator.

5.2. Recommendations to the EU

1. Sponsor comparative research on corruption in candidate States and member States;

2. Join GRECO;

3. Use the Community's membership of GRECO to provide the Community with the mandate to:

   - carry out research on specific areas of corruption (such as party finance) in which it has so far lacked a mandate; and

   - increase pressure on member States to complete ratifications of the Council of Europe anti-corruption conventions, and on the remaining non-members of GRECO to become members, thereby leading to a situation in which all candidate and member States are evaluated on the basis of the Council of Europe's Twenty Guiding Principles for the Fight Against Corruption.

Corruption and Anti-corruption Policy in Bulgaria

Table of Contents

OPEN SOCIETY INSTITUTE 2002

Corruption and Anti-corruption Policy in Bulgaria

EXECUTIVE SUMMARY

Corruption is widespread in most areas of Bulgarian public life. The most affected areas include the customs administration, public procurement, political party finance and possibly the judiciary. Privatisation has suffered from endemic corruption in the past, but may have improved. While public attention has focused on corruption of ministers and senior officials, for ordinary citizens corruption appears to be most widespread in dealing with customs, the health system and the police, and corruption in the local branches of an over-centralised State administration presents a particularly serious problem. The existence of a large grey economy, extensive smuggling networks and active (although perhaps weakened) organised crime groups has both exacerbated the problem of corruption and made fighting it more difficult.

Corruption and anti-corruption policy have been major political issues since 1997, when a new Government came to power on a platform that included the fight against corruption as one of its main priorities. The Government took important steps to limit the influence of organised crime on the economy. The subsequent Government approved a National Anti-corruption Strategy in October 2001, based not only on repression but also prevention and civil society involvement. Both the Government and civil society organisations have played a very active role in putting corruption at the top of the public agenda and formulating the national anti-corruption policy.

Although a number of important laws have been passed – notably on freedom of information – some reforms (for example public administration reform) have been ineffective, and the coordination of anti-corruption efforts has been poor until recently. Moreover, the National Anti-corruption Strategy remains focused on low-level corruption, and virtually no progress has been made towards fighting corruption at the level of Government, the Parliament (National Assembly) and in political parties. Most worrying, there are doubts over whether the Government can pursue reforms in areas where powerful vested interests are opposed, such as customs.

The EU accession process has been one of the most important influences on the development of anti-corruption policy, and anti-corruption is clearly recognised by the Government as a condition for both EU and NATO accession. Pressure from the

European Commission was instrumental in encouraging the Government to produce the National Strategy, and anti-corruption policy has been an important part of the *Accession Partnerships*. The Commission has provided increasing assistance for the development of anti-corruption policy.

Bulgaria has made important progress in approximating national anti-corruption legislation to the requirements of international anti-corruption instruments. Further changes required to fulfil the requirements of the Council of Europe Criminal Law Convention are in the process of legislative approval. The definition of a public official remains unclear.

There is minimal regulation in the area of conflict of interest in Bulgaria, with only limited provisions for ministers and almost none for MPs. Since 2000 senior officials have been subject to duties to submit declarations of assets and income, but supervision and enforcement is inadequate and there are no sanctions for violation.

State financial control has undergone major reforms in recent years, including new legislation on the National Audit Office (NAO) and on State Internal Financial Control. Although the NAO is independent, the impact of its findings is almost zero and its record in providing information to the public is mixed. On the other hand, considerable resources have been invested in the institutions to implement internal financial control, and the EU has praised the Government's success in putting in place mechanisms to distribute pre-accession funds.

There are no specialised anti-corruption agencies in Bulgaria, with the exception of a unit to fight organised crime at the Ministry of Interior. Moreover, there are no specialised units for fighting corruption within the prosecution offices or courts. Progress has been made towards the establishment of an Ombudsman.

Bulgaria has passed important laws to reform the public administration, including a Civil Service Act. Despite this, the impact of the reforms has been largely cosmetic, and the civil service remains overly politicised. In addition, mechanisms for redress against administrative actions are burdensome and ineffective. The only regulation of conflict of interest in the executive branch and civil service are vague provisions in the civil servants' Code of Conduct, and the Code of Conduct itself is of little value. There are no provisions for monitoring the assets of officials below the level of minister. As of early 2002, a number of investigations of former senior officials and ministers were under way, especially related to privatisation.

The Parliament does not function as an effective anti-corruption mechanism. Parliament does not scrutinise public finances effectively or initiate anti-corruption legislation, and two anti-corruption committees were abolished in 2001 after proving to be entirely ineffective. Regulation of conflict of interest and lobbying is minimal or non-existent, and immunity provisions are extensive, creating an environment highly susceptible to corruption. There are serious concerns that Parliament may be effectively under the control of vested interests with an interest in blocking anti-corruption policy.

The judiciary is widely regarded as highly corrupt both by public opinion and foreign observers, and there is some specific evidence of corruption. However, corruption may not be a bigger problem than executive interference and neglect of the needs of the judicial branch. The Government has initiated a programme of judicial reform; however, certain of the proposed reforms may undermine judicial independence.

Political party finance is an extremely weakly regulated area. Liberal rules on donations, a non-transparent system for determining State subsidies and the virtual absence of supervision probably underpin widespread illegal funding and corruption, although direct evidence of corruption is scarce.

Likewise, regulation of public procurement remains weak, despite significant legislative progress. In particular, procedures for supervision and redress are highly ineffective, contributing to a system of contract allocation that has allowed widespread collusion and probably major high-level corruption. Attempts at further reform recently faltered.

Bulgaria suffers from serious problems of corruption in a number of public services. The Customs Administration appears to be more seriously affected by corruption than any other public institution, and was identified by the Government as the number one priority in the fight against corruption. However, recent events indicate that the Government may not be strong enough to overcome the influence of groups with a vested interest in the *status quo*. Licences and permits remain major barriers to doing business, due to the number required, control of allocation by unaccountable local offices of central Government and arbitrary criteria. However, the Government is in the process of carrying out important licensing reforms.

The legal environment for the media is generally favourable, and has received an important boost with the passage of an Act on Access to Public Information. However, the effectiveness of the new Act may be counteracted by other laws and regulations that have been recently adopted. The independence of public broadcasting remains an important concern, as political influence appears to rule out any investigative role.

1. INTRODUCTION

1.1 The data and perceptions

Although there are few criminal convictions for corruption, corruption remains widespread in most areas of Bulgarian public life and the public regards corruption as one of the most serious problems facing the country. The most affected areas include the customs administration, public procurement, political party finance and possibly the judiciary. Privatisation has suffered from endemic corruption in the past, but may have improved. While public attention has focused on corruption of ministers and senior officials – particular in the privatisation process – ordinary citizens appear to experience most corruption dealing with customs officers, doctors and the police. Corruption in the local offices of the over-centralised State administration has been identified as a particularly serious problem. Corruption is underpinned, *inter alia,* by a large grey economy and the existence of active organised crime networks, especially in the area of smuggling.

Criminal proceedings

Criminal statistics are unreliable in Bulgaria: although the courts are supposed to provide the Ministry of Justice with the statistics, not all do so or do so consistently.[1] According to the National Statistical Institute[2] there were 45 convictions for bribery-related cases in 2000. Tables 1 and 2 show data on corruption related offences provided by the police for 1998-1999.[3]

Table 1: Corruption related offences registered in Bulgaria, 1998–1999

	1998	*1999*
Bribery	95	114
Malfeasances in office	2,489	2,376
Tax offences	112	220

Source: Ministry of Justice

---

[1] As the Commission of the European Union noted in its *2000 Regular Report,* "It is difficult to obtain concrete information on how the judicial system is dealing with corruption cases." Currently proposed amendments to the Judicial System Act would give the Ministry of Justice greater powers to obtain statistics.

[2] *Standart,* 30 May 2001.

[3] *Bulgaria's Progress towards EU Membership in 2000 – the NGO's Perspective,* conference proceedings of the European Institute, Sofia, 31 January 2001, pp. 37–38.

Table 2: Cases of acceptance of a bribe by public officials, 1997–2001

Year	Number of convictions	Acquittals
1997	26	3
1998	21	4
1999	25	2
2000	21	1

Source: Ministry of Justice

These statistics appear more likely to indicate a lack of enforcement than low levels of bribery.

Perceptions

While Bulgaria's ranking in the Transparency International Corruption Perception Index has improved considerably, from 67th place in 1998 to 47th place in 2001, the share of the public that ranks corruption among the three most serious problems facing the country has risen from 36 percent in 1999 to 45 percent in October 2001.[4] Moreover, the perception that corruption is widespread has grown and people have become less optimistic about the prospects of eradicating it. A survey conducted in October 2001 indicated the following:[5]

- Six percent of respondents said that during their contacts with the public sector, officials asked them directly for cash in all or most cases, while 17 percent said this happened in isolated cases.

- Fifteen percent of respondents said that officials showed that they expected cash or a benefit in all or most cases, while 20 percent said this happened in isolated cases.

- Twenty percent of respondents said they had given cash to officials in the previous year (and six percent in "all or most cases"), and similar percentages had given officials gifts.

- Seventy-six percent of respondents believed that most or all public officials are involved in corruption, and the same percentage believed that to solve a problem one is rather or very likely to have to give cash or other benefits to an official.

---

[4] Coalition 2000, *2001 Corruption Report,* p. 61.

[5] Survey data provided by Vitosha Research.

Thirteen percent of respondents regarded it as admissible for a minister to solve a problem for someone and accept a gift in return, while six percent thought it admissible to accept cash

The findings of international organisations tend to support the public assessment. According to a UNDP *Report on Anti-corruption Initiatives in Bulgaria*, published in January 2002,

> The lack of transparency and accountability and effective internal and external oversight in the Bulgarian system of state administration reinforces and shelters corrupt activity, thereby contributing to economic stagnation, high rates of poverty and widespread corruption.[6]

Corruption at higher levels is also a principal concern for international investors. According to the *Country Commercial Guide* of the Central and Eastern Europe Business Information Centre,

> Although the Bulgarian Government has achieved some successes in the fight against organised crime and corruption, many observers believe that corruption and political influence in business decision-making continue to be significant problems in Bulgaria's investment climate. The problems range from the demand for petty bribes for government licences and permits to nontransparent privatisation's of major state enterprises.[7]

1.2 Main loci of corruption

According to surveys from January 2002 (see Table 3) the Bulgarian public perceives the most corrupt institutions to be the customs administration, senior politicians, and Parliament and occupations linked to the judicial system. Perceptions of MPs and ministers have worsened noticeably. Surveys of experience with corruption indicate that bribery is most common among customs officers, doctors, police officers, higher education staff and judicial staff and judges (see Table 4).

---

[6] D. A. Bilak, *Report of the Evaluation Mission on Anti-corruption Initiatives in Bulgaria,* review commissioned and funded by the Bulgaria Country Office of the United Nations Development Programme, p. 3.

[7] Central and Eastern Europe Business Information Centre, *Bulgaria Country Commercial Guide FY 2002,* p. 7. The same report notes, however, that, "[R]ecent business surveys indicate that foreign investors consider bureaucratic impediments to be a considerably larger problem than corruption," (p. 75).

Table 3: Opinion of the Bulgarian public concerning the incidence of corruption in specific groups

	Relative quota of the answers "almost all are corrupted" and "most of them are corrupted"						
	February 1999	April 1999	Sept. 1999	January 2000	April 2000	Sept. 2000	January 2002
Customs officers	73.3	73,2	75.2	77.0	78.6	75.2	74.15
Members of Parliament	39.0	37.7	42.6	45.0	55.1	51.7	47.78
Ministers	39.1	35.3	43.9	45.3	53.4	55.0	45.34
Police officers	51.5	49.2	55.8	51.9	50.5	54.3	47.00
Prosecutors	48.5	50.0	50.8	46.3	54.4	51.3	55.35
Judges	49.5	50.8	50.7	48.5	56.0	50.1	55.00
Lawyers	55.5	55.4	55.6	54.8	51.9	52.9	55.53
Tax officers	47.1	45.2	56.4	53.9	51.0	53.7	51.26
Ministry officials	42.5	41.9	48.2	47.9	55.1	49.7	47.08
Business people	49.5	47.6	48.3	48.5	51.4	42.3	
Investigators	43.6	41.8	44.9	41.0	48.0	43.8	48.04
Political parties and coalition leaders	40.5	31.1	42.7	37.5	45.0	43.8	
Administrative officers in the judiciary	42.0	40.5	49.7	42.0	45.2	40.2	41.17
Municipal officials	44.3	39.6	48.8	45.0	46.5	41.6	39.34
Bankers	-	-	-	20.9	38.8	33.5	
Local political leaders	34.0	27.5	38.2	31.7	36.4	36.8	
Municipal counsellors	31.2	26.4	34.7	32.5	35.2	32.1	31.77
Doctors	56.9	46.0	47.3	42.5	40.9	43.6	
University officers or professors	29,5	28.5	35.7	29.4	29.3	28.1	27.68
Representatives of NGOs	16.3	11.5	20.9	16.2	18.2	23.9	
Journalists	12.7	12.0	14.3	10.6	14.1	13.9	12.27
Teachers	12.6	8.4	11.5	9.5	8.2	10.9	9.75

Source: Coalition 2000.

Table 4: Percentage of respondents experiencing requests for bribes from officials

Type of official	January 2000	April 2000	Sept. 2000	January 2001	October 2001	January 2002	May 2002
Customs officer	19.8	29.1	15.8	22.7	18.4	18.55	25.5
Doctor	20.0	18.6	22.1	6.1	22.3	17.96	20.2
Police officer	23.4	19.5	24.0	18.9	18.5	19.9	15.2
University professor or official	10.1	12.6	13.9	13.2	8.8	14.29	12.0
Administrative staff from the judicial system	18.5	10.4	11.5	13.3	11.3	9.38	11.0
Judge	6.9	7.7	9.1	5.8	6.8	7.8	10.7
Businessman	13.7	11.9	9.7	11.6	13.4	10.77	9.4
Ministry official	3.2	3.7	7.0	8.9	5.6	4.92	9.3
Prosecutor	5.9	4.7	7.8	7.2	0.8	4.07	8.5
Criminal investigator	6.1	8.4	6.0	5.5	6.0	4.27	8.2
Banker	8.1	1.8	2.9	4.1	4.1	4.07	5.6
Municipal official	11.3	11.7	10.3	11.2	11.3	9.96	5.5
Tax official	8.4	7.8	8.3	6.4	9.1	5.29	3.8
Member of Parliament	1.9	4.5	6.4	4.2	2.1	2.08	3.5
Teacher	4.9	3.0	5.5	3.7	6.1	3.6	3.1
Municipal Council member	6.7	5.6	3.2	2.1	1.4	2.05	2.7

Source: Corruption Indexes of Coalition 2000, May 2000, <www.online.bg/vr/crl/corr_ind_05E.htm>, (last accessed 23 July 2002).

Privatisation

The privatisation process has been regarded as highly corrupt, and many investigations of former senior officials and politicians have concerned allegedly corrupt privatisation deals (see Section 3.6). In October 2001, the Deputy Prosecutor General requested the investigation of over 200 suspicious privatisation cases, including those of the national airline carrier Balkan Airlines and the Plama oil refinery. The current Government has moved to reduce the number of "worker-management buy-outs," which was considered a major source of corruption whereby the Government appointed its preferred managers and then sold companies to them.

Corruption in public administration

The problem of corruption in customs is widely acknowledged and has been confirmed by expert analyses (see Section 8.2). Although the perception of endemic corruption in the courts and prosecution system is shared by a significant number of expert observers, the extent of corruption is in fact unclear (see Section 5.2). Networks of political party patronage, nepotism and clientelism are deeply entrenched, and influence staffing decisions for senior administrative posts and managerial positions in State enterprises.

Political party finance

Political party finance is an extremely weakly regulated area. Liberal rules on donations, a non-transparent system for determining State subsidies and the virtual absence of supervision probably underpin widespread illegal funding and corruption, although direct evidence of corruption is scarce.

Public procurement

Likewise, regulation of public procurement remains weak, despite significant legislative progress. In particular, procedures for supervision and redress are highly ineffective, contributing to a system of contract allocation that has allowed widespread collusion and probably major high-level corruption. Attempts at further reform recently faltered.

Local government

Corruption at the level of local public administration is a problem of particular. According to the UNDP *Report on Anti-corruption Initiatives in Bulgaria,* these problems are rooted in an anachronistic, centralised system. As a result, around 90 percent of public budgets are determined at the central level, and a wide range of public services are provided not by local governments and agencies appointed by and accountable to local citizens, but by local offices of central institutions. For example, gaining a construction permit requires signatures from four such institutions: the safety inspectorate (Ministry of Labour), fire inspectorate (Ministry of Interior), health inspectorate and sanitation inspectorate (Ministry of Health), all of which routinely require bribes for their approvals; the total amount necessary to obtain a permit may reach as high as €2,000.[8]

One recent study[9] identified the following areas of local public administration as especially prone to corruption: municipal procurement; licensing of economic and trade activities; renting and tenders for reconstruction of municipal sites; tenders for

---

[8] OSI Roundtable Discussion, Sofia, 8 February 2002. *Explanatory note: OSI held a roundtable meeting to invite critique of the present Report in draft form. Experts present included representatives of the Government, international organisations, and civil society organisations. References to this meeting should not be understood as an endorsement of any particular point of view by any one participant.*

[9] Study carried out by the NGO Coalition 2000 as part of a project to establish Centres for Information Services in five municipalities.

privatisation of municipal property and supplying of municipal premises with fuel and consumables

Organised crime and State capture

Since 1997, the Bulgarian Government appears to have made significant progress in breaking the links between the State and economic groups that operated outside or on the edge of the law. Key steps in this respect include the re-licensing of insurance companies launched in 1997, and the refusal of the Bulgarian National Bank in 2001 to provide banking licences to the former owners and founders of two banks that went bankrupt in 1996 (First Private Bank and Orthodox Bank).

Nevertheless, the continuing power of entrenched interests with an overriding interest in preventing effective anti-corruption policy is still strong. The resignation of the Director of the Customs Agency in February 2002 amid politically motivated attacks on a contract with a British consultancy company to help clean up the customs administration appears to indicate the continuing power of strong lobbies against anti-corruption reform in this area at least.

1.3 Government anti-corruption policy

Corruption and anti-corruption policy have been major political issues since 1997, when a new Government came to power on a platform that included the fight against corruption as one of its main priorities. The Government took important steps to limit the influence of organised crime on the economy. A number of important laws were passed, in particular the Acts on: Administration, Administrative Services to Natural and Legal Persons, Civil Servants, Asset Disclosure by Persons Occupying Senior Positions in the State, and Access to Public Information, as well as amendments to the Criminal Code. However, some reforms have been ineffective, particularly public administration reform (see Section 3.1) and asset disclosure provisions (see Section 2.3). The coordination of anti-corruption efforts has been poor, at least until recently, and the National Anti-corruption Strategy approved by the Government in October 2001 was the first attempt to place anti-corruption efforts within a systematic framework. However, the National Anti-corruption Strategy remains focused on low-level corruption, and virtually no progress has been made towards fighting corruption at the level of Government, the Parliament and in political parties. Most worrying, there are doubts over whether the Government can pursue reforms in areas where powerful vested interests are opposed, such as customs.

The National Anti-corruption Strategy

The Government adopted a National Anti-corruption Strategy in October 2001, supplementing the National Strategy for Combating Crime adopted in 1998. The strategy was divided into the following main headings:

1. Guaranteeing transparency in the work of the public administration

2. Improvement of financial and fiscal control

3. Anti-corruption reform in the Customs Agency

4. Anti-corruption measures in the Ministry of Interior

5. Combating corruption at local government level

6. Anti-corruption measure in the financing of political parties

7. Reform of the judiciary and criminal legislation

8. Cooperation between Government, NGOs and the media

The Strategy itself is a short and very general five-page document. However, the Government supplemented it with an action plan for implementation, which lists a number of more specific measures with deadlines for implementation. An Implementation Commission was created at the end of 2001, chaired by the Minister of Justice.

The action plan elaborates the strategy, with the notable exception that reform of political party financing is missing entirely. On the other hand, it dedicates an additional section to reducing corruption in the economic sector and liberalising the conditions for private business development (see Section 8.6). Table 5 shows some selected measures from the plan.

Table 5: Selected measures in the National Anti-corruption Strategy

Measure	Deadline	Fulfilled?
Review of public administration reform strategy in order to elaborate a new strategy	30.6.2002	Implementation plan adopted
Amend Act on Administration to inter alia distinguish political from career positions	28.2.2002	Partially implemented by amendments in force since 23.11.2001
Implement project to introduce "one-stop shop" system of service provision	30.12.2002	Ongoing project funded by DFID (UK) and implemented by KPMG
Amend Act on Letters, Signals, Complaints and Petitions to improve exercise of rights to redress	30.7.2002	No progress
Introduce register of property status of tax officials	30.12.2002	No progress
Set up Interdepartmental Coordination Council at Ministry of Interior	30.12.2001	Completed
Draft amendments to Penal Code to harmonise with international conventions (bribery of foreign officials, trade in influence, restrict immunity provisions, bribery in private sector)	30.7.2002	Draft law in Parliament
Draft Act on restriction/removal of MPs immunity	28.2.2002	No progress
Develop system of case distribution among magistrates excluding based on objective criteria	31.12.2002	Implementation plan adopted
Reform of licensing arrangements: transfer to registration/notification for economic activities, transfer specific licensing to professional organisations	March 2002 (development), 30.12.2003 (implement)	Working group established

Source: Programme for the Implementation of the Anti-corruption Strategy, draft version, February 2002.

Implementation of the strategy is still at a very early stage, with most of the deadlines not yet reached. Important measures that appear to be on track are reform of licensing procedures (see Section 8.6) and amendments to criminal law. However, there has been little progress on more politically sensitive measures, particularly changes that would start to limit the opportunities for abuse of power and political corruption at the highest level – for example the restriction of immunity for MPs or measures to reform party financing rules (see Section 6).

As of May 2002, however, the ability of the Government to continue its progress on anti-corruption measures appeared somewhat doubtful. For example:

- In accordance with the plan, in March 2002 the Parliament passed a proposed new Act on Privatisation and Post-Privatisation Control, which would exclude the method of negotiations with selected bidders. However, the President vetoed the Act.

- The resignation of the customs Director mentioned above took place in the context of strong pressure from the opposition.

On the other hand, one of the most important anti-corruption figures appointed by the Government, the Secretary General of the Ministry of Interior, enjoyed the highest ever approval rating for a public figure.

The role of civil society

A key role has been played in the development of the anti-corruption debate by Coalition 2000, a group of civil society organisations set up in 1998 as an anti-corruption initiative. The coalition has worked to facilitate cooperation between the Government, NGOs and other institutions in the area of anti-corruption policy, and currently operates a Corruption Monitoring System through regular public opinion surveys. Coalition 2000 drafted an Anti-corruption Action Plan for Bulgaria which was endorsed by the first Coalition 2000 Policy Forum in November 1998, attended by over 150 government officials, business leaders, NGOs and international organisations. The National Anti-corruption Strategy itself is largely based on the Action Plan.

Local municipalities and the local NGO partners of Coalition 2000 have also set up "public-private councils" in a number of cities, including Smolian, Varna, Vratza, Pleven, Plovdiv, and Pazardzhik, to generate and support local anti-corruption initiatives and achieve coordination of anti-corruption activities between municipal and regional levels.

In addition, the NGO Access to Public Information has played a very important role in lobbying for the adoption of the Act on Access to Public Information (see Section 9.2), educating officials on the Act and facilitating appeals by citizens.

1.4 The impact of the EU Accession Process

The Bulgarian Government has explicitly cited EU accession as one of the most important reasons for the adoption of its national anti-corruption policy. The preamble to the National Anti-corruption Strategy states that, "Efforts to introduce up-to-date international standards of transparency and publicity... are a significant prerequisite for... guaranteeing membership in the EU and NATO..."[10]

The European Commission has registered increasing concern about corruption in Bulgaria. The *2000 Regular Report* noted that, "Corruption continues to be a very serious problem in Bulgaria,"[11] on the basis of "persistent rumours" and the assertion that "allegations of corruption are rife,"[12] there was no analysis of the causes of corruption or reference to existing national and international studies. The *2001 Regular Report* adopted a more precise approach, referring to existing surveys and identifying some areas of particular concern. Despite acknowledgement of some new anti-corruption measures, notably the anti-corruption strategy (described below), the Commission expressed continuing concern: "Whilst there have been some improvements since last year, in particular in the legal framework, corruption continues to be a very serious problem in Bulgaria."[13]

Anti-corruption policy was first incorporated into Bulgaria's EU accession agenda in the *1999 Accession Partnership.* The *Partnership* addressed corruption within the justice and home affairs section, and set as the most important short-term priority the adoption of a comprehensive Government anti-corruption strategy, to be implemented by the end of 2000.[14] Subsequently, the Commission criticised the previous Government for having failed to implement this provision. The present Government fulfilled the priority in October 2001 (see Section 1.3).

A medium-term priority of the *1999 Accession Partnership* was the implementation of an anti-corruption strategy; in the *2001 Accession Partnership* this became a priority "in need of particularly urgent action,"[15] as did the completion of the legal framework for external audit. A new Act on the National Audit Office came into force in December 2001 (see Section 2.4).

---

[10] *National Anti-corruption Strategy,* p. 1.

[11] Commission of the European Union, *2000 Regular Report from the Commission on Bulgaria's Progress towards Accession,* p. 17.

[12] Commission, *2000 Regular Report,* pp.17-18.

[13] *Commission, 2001 Regular Report,* p. 19.

[14] *2001 Accession Partnership,* p. 6.

[15] *2001 Accession Partnership,* p. 6.

EU assistance

The European Union has not provided any assistance to Bulgaria explicitly for the development of the anti-corruption strategy. However, the 2001 PHARE programme includes the projects listed in Table 6, which are indirectly related to corruption prevention. In addition, two large assistance projects for anti-corruption policy at the ministries of Justice and Interior are expected to be announced during the summer of 2002.

Table 6: Selected PHARE projects, 2001 (support in €000)

Project Code	Objectives and projects	Total Phare support	Institutions building	Investment
0103.02	Implementing civil service reform	2,400	1,800	0,600
0103.03	Recruitment and training strategy for the judiciary	2,000	2,000	-
0103.05	Strengthening the national customs agency	1,300	1,300	-
0103.07	Combating money laundering	1,200	1,200	-
0103.09	Improving the management of EU funds	1,800	1,590	0,210

Source: PHARE 2001, Bulgaria National Programme

NATO accession

As for neighbouring Romania, the prospect of entering NATO has become a much more important issue after the events of 11 September in New York. The Alliance has given clear signals that the two countries could be invited to join at the November 2002 summit in Prague, and at the same time has stated or given signals that one of the main obstacles to accession is corruption. In March 2002, the US *charge d'affaires* in Sofia, Roderick Moore, stated that,

> The closer the date that Bulgaria becomes an ally with the U.S., the more we insist on the fight against corruption, because this is a factor that could run in the whole partnership between us.[16]

As the former UDF Government had made EU and NATO membership top priorities, the UDF's strong opposition to the current Government of National Movement

---

[16] "Bulgarian Deputy Prosecutor-General admits to problems in fight against corruption," RFE/RL Newsline, 28 March 2002.

Simeon II and the Movement for Rights and Freedoms appears to have been softened somewhat by the sudden prospect of early membership in NATO. [17]

Other international initiatives

Bulgaria participates in the monitoring procedures in the framework of the OECD Working Group on Bribery in International Business Transactions and GRECO, is a member of the Stability Pact for Southeast Europe (which launched an Anti-corruption Initiative in February 2000) and has also played an important role in the Southeast Europe Legal Development Initiative (SELDI), of which the Bulgarian policy institute, the Centre for the Study of Democracy, was a co-founder.

2. INSTITUTIONS AND LEGISLATION

Bulgaria has made important progress in approximating national anti-corruption legislation to the requirements of international anti-corruption instruments, although further changes will be needed for full compatibility. There is minimal regulation in the area of conflict of interest in Bulgaria. State financial control has undergone major reforms in recent years, including new legislation on the National Audit Office and on State Internal Financial Control, although the impact of the NAO's findings is minimal. There are no specialised anti-corruption agencies. Progress has been made towards the establishment of an Ombudsman.

2.1 Anti-corruption legislation

Bulgarian anti-corruption legislation has developed significantly in recent years, and is compatible with most international standards. Bribery is made an offence by the Bulgarian Criminal Code in the following ways:

- Acceptance of a bribe by a public official[18] in order for the official to perform or not perform his/her duties is punishable by one to six years' imprisonment. If the bribe is received in return for violation of official duties the penalty is up to eight years. Public officials can be sentenced to 10-30 years and have their

---

[17] See e.g., U. Buechsenschuetz, "T-SO opposition in Bulgaria," RFE/RL Newsline, 3 April 2002.

[18] Criminal Code, Article 301.

property confiscated if the bribe is particularly large (as defined by court practice). Passive bribery of foreign public officials is not yet covered.

- Offering or giving a bribe to a public official[19] (including foreign public officials) is subject to up to six years imprisonment, or seven years in the case of violation of official duties.

- A person who acts as a mediator in the process of giving or receiving a bribe[20] is subject to up to three years imprisonment.

In addition, there are several articles in the Criminal Code grouped under the title of Malfeasances. For example:

- An official who uses his or her official position to acquire unlawful benefit for him or herself or for another is subject to imprisonment for up to three years.

- An official who violates or fails to fulfil official duties, or exceeds his or her powers or rights for the purpose of acquiring a benefit for himself/herself or for another, or to cause damage to another, from which significant harmful consequences may result, may be punished by up to five years imprisonment, deprivation of the right to hold a certain State or public office, and/or corrective labour. If there are major harmful consequences or the perpetrator occupies a senior official position the penalty rises to up to eight years, and for particularly grave cases from three to ten years.

- Penalties for the above crimes may be even higher in certain cases, such as if they are connected with privatisation or management of state property.

- An official who refuses or delays the issue of a permit beyond the terms provided by law may be punished by up to three years imprisonment, fined up to €255,000 and deprived of the right to perform certain official activities.

- An official who consciously allows a subordinate to commit a crime related to his/her office or work is subject to the same sanctions as the individual who committed the crime.

The sanctions for a number of the anti-corruption provisions are very severe compared to sanctions in OECD countries, and could paradoxically deter courts from passing guilty verdicts in corruption cases.

Trading in influence does not receive sanctions under criminal law, nor is the threshold at which a benefit is considered a bribe specified. In order to harmonise Bulgarian law

---

[19] Criminal Code, Article 304.
[20] Criminal Code, Article 305a.

with international obligations and particularly the Council of Europe's Criminal Law Convention, these areas need to be regulated, along with the inclusion of requesting and accepting non-material benefits under bribery provisions. In addition, the definition of a public official is not entirely clear under current Bulgarian law. For example, it is disputable whether an MP or municipal councillor can be prosecuted for passive bribery under the present Criminal Code.

As of July 2002, amendments to the Criminal Code had passed first reading in Parliament. The amendments would broaden the definition to include foreign public official and criminalise acceptance of bribes by foreign officials, criminalise bribery in the private sector, include non-material benefits as possible types of bribe, criminalise trading in influence and increase the sanctions for bribery of magistrates (judges, prosecutors and investigators).

2.2 Conflict of interest legislation

Conflict of interest in individual areas are covered separately in Sections 3.3 and 4.3.

2.3 Asset declaration and monitoring

In May 2000, the Act on Property Disclosure by Persons Occupying Senior Positions in the State came into effect, introducing significant changes to a previously unregulated area. Civil servants occupying senior official positions (MPs, President and Vice-president, ministers, Constitutional Court judges, senior magistrates, district governors, etc.) are now obliged to submit declarations of their assets by 31 May each year. The declaration must include all income and property acquired during the previous year, and also the income and property of spouses and children under 18 years of age.

The register of asset declarations is held by the President of the National Audit Office. The law has also defined the group of persons entitled to have access to the data contained in that register and lays down the procedure for obtaining access.

The disclosure of compliance or failure to comply with the rules is expected to entail strong moral sanctions. The National Audit Office published such a list of those who failed to submit declarations in 2000 on their website, but has not yet done the same for 2001. Nevertheless, the need for effective monitoring of compliance, as well as for sanctions against those who breach its provisions, is illustrated by the fact that as per mid-July 2001, 90 persons (including MPs from the outgoing Parliament as well as magistrates and deputy ministers) had failed to file declarations.

2.4 Control and audit

The National Audit Office

The auditing of public finances is performed by the National Audit Office (hereinafter NAO). The NAO reports to the Parliament. According to surveys the Bulgarian public believes the NAO to be one of the least corrupt institutions.[21] The NAO audits the use of central budget and off-budget funds, management of State debt, privatisation, and the financial statements of local governments, as well as other accounts if provided by law (principally the financial activities of political parties).

The President and ten members of the NAO are elected for nine years by the Parliament, which may also dismiss them under the following circumstances: upon their own written request; in case they are incapable to perform their duties for more than six months; if they have been convicted for a crime; in case of a court-imposed deprivation of the right to hold office; due to incompatibility of his or her mandate occurring after the appointment; or in case of death.[22]

Neither the President nor NAO members may have been members of the Government or heads of administrative agencies during the three years prior to their appointment, nor may their spouses, siblings or any other close relatives. The President and members may not perform other paid activities with the exception of scientific work or teaching.[23]

The NAO performs audits according to an annual programme adopted by the NAO and presented to the Parliament.

In December 2001, a new Act on the National Audit Office came into force, which adopted international audit standards and laid out a broader set of anti-corruption measures, including the following:

- The audit competencies of the NAO were broadened to include the budget of the State Social Insurance Fund, the National Health Insurance Company and the financial resources from funds and programmes of the European Union, including their management by the respective authorities and end users.

- All audit reports are to be made public after they are approved by the NAO.

- The law specifies more clearly the procedures for reporting to the Parliament, and provides for regulation of cooperation between the NAO, the State internal financial control authorities, the tax and customs administrations, the authorities for

---

[21] Coalition 2000, *Beyond Anti-corruption Rhetoric: Coalition Building and Monitoring*, forthcoming.

[22] Act on the National Audit Office, Article 9.

[23] Act on the National Audit Office, Article 10.

collection of State receivables, the financial intelligence authorities and the courts. The specific forms of cooperation are to be specified by joint agreements, which had not been reached as of May 2002.

The NAO also holds the register of declarations of assets submitted by public officials (see Section 2.3). The chairperson presents the audit reports carried out by the NAO to the Parliament, and once a year, upon approval by Parliament, an annual report is published in the *Official Gazette*. However, the record of the NAO in providing information on political party finances and officials' asset declarations is poor (see Section 9.2).

The NAO may submit recommendations to the audited authorities and, if these are not followed, it may send a report to the Parliament, the Council of Ministers or the Municipal Councils, depending to which institution the audited authority is subordinate. However, there is no institutionalised mechanism for cooperation with Parliament or the Government, and most NAO reports are ignored.

The NAO does not perform an enforcement role. When it uncovers criminal violations of the law, it sends the materials to the Prosecutor's Office or to the superior institution responsible for imposing administrative or other liability. Violations of the Public Procurement Act are reported to the Ministry of Finance.

The NAO has adopted 11 Auditing and Reporting Standards, as well as a Code of Conduct for auditors.[24]

Internal control and audit

An Act on State Internal Financial Control was adopted in 2000 and came into force on 1 January 2001. The Act lays down a modern system of financial control ranging from preliminary internal control to external control by the NAO, and created an Agency for Internal Financial Control to supervise implementation of the law. The Agency is staffed by around 1,500 employees.

In its *2001 Regular Report,* the European Commission noted these changes without criticism, and in addition commented that Bulgaria's SAPARD agency for distributing pre-accession funds was the first in any candidate country to be accredited by the Commission.[25] On the other hand, in June 2001 the European Parliament noted in an opinion produced for the Committee on Foreign Affairs, Human Rights, Common Security and Defence Policy that,

---

[24] Cited in: *Corruption In Transition: The Bulgarian Experience,* A Report by the Bulgarian Anti-corruption Working Group to the Partners in Transition II Conference, Sofia, September 2001.

[25] Commission, *2001 Regular Report,* p. 90.

[It] is surprised… at the absence of a genuine anti-fraud system and takes the view that setting up such a system would lend even more credibility to the efforts already made by Bulgaria.[26]

2.5 Anti-corruption agencies

There are no special anti-corruption agencies in Bulgaria, with the exception of the National Service for Combating Organised Crime at the Ministry of Interior. Neither Prosecution offices nor courts have specialised units or teams for fighting corruption.

The Bureau of Financial Intelligence

In 1998, the Bureau of Financial Intelligence was established as the main agency for implementing the Act on Measures against Money Laundering. The Act was amended again in 2001 in order to harmonise the legislation with the Directive of the Council of the European Community on prevention of the use of the financial system for money laundering. In June 2000, an evaluation team from the Council of Europe Select Committee of Experts on the Evaluation of Anti-money Laundering Measures published a report on Bulgaria that identified some positive results in the implementation of the law, in particular, the uncovering of a major money laundering channel in 1999. However, the report recommended further widening the circle of institutions subject to the provisions of the law, and the introduction of administrative and financial liability for legal entities.[27]

2.6 Ombudsman

At the time of writing there was no national ombudsman. However, work on the establishment of this position has been in progress since 1998, and as of July 2002, a draft law was in preparation. The institution of the ombudsman is expected to have an effect on anti-corruption efforts by providing redress against administrative abuses.

Meanwhile, the Centre for the Study of Democracy and the Centre for Social Practices have launched experimental projects for introducing the positions of civic observer and

---

[26] Opinion of the Committee on Budgetary Control for the Committee on Foreign Affairs, Human Rights, Common Security and Defence Policy on Bulgaria's application for membership of the European Union and progress in the negotiations (COM[2000]701 – C5-0601/2000 – 1997/2179 [COS]), 26 June 2001, p. 5.

[27] European Committee on Crime Problems, Select Committee of Experts on the Evaluation of Anti-money Laundering Measures, *First Mutual Evaluation Report on Bulgaria*, Strasbourg, June 2000.

public mediator in several municipalities. In May 2001, the Sofia Municipal Council appointed an ombudsman for Sofia under the title of Public Mediator; there are also local ombudsman offices established in other Bulgarian cities either on the initiative of the local municipality or under an agreement between the municipality and local civic organisations. They act as *de facto* ombudsman offices processing complaints and issuing recommendations. The experience of their work allowed a provision on establishing local level ombudsman offices to be included in one of the draft acts considered by the Parliament.

3. EXECUTIVE BRANCH AND CIVIL SERVICE

Although Bulgaria has passed very important legislation to reform its public administration, including a Civil Service Act, the impact of reform so far has been limited. Mechanisms for redress against administrative actions are burdensome and ineffective. The only regulation of conflict of interest in the executive branch and civil service are vague provisions in the civil servants' Code of Conduct, and the Code of Conduct itself is of little value. Provisions on asset declarations only apply to the most senior official, while supervision and sanctions for violation are inadequate. Corruption of senior officials has become an the subject of increasing media focus, and as of early 2002, a number of investigations of former senior officials and ministers were under way, especially related to privatisation.

3.1 Structure and legislative framework

Although a number of laws have been passed to reform the Public administration in recent years, to date the Government has not succeeded in establishing the legal framework for a professional and independent civil service. Bulgarian public administration remains highly over-centralised, which results in citizens at the local level being confronted by unaccountable and highly corrupt local offices of central Government.

The December 1998 Act on Administration lays down in detail the structure of the administration, the distribution of powers between different bodies of the executive, and the rules and structures of its work.[28] The Act established common rules for the internal organisation of the administrative structures of the executive bodies. The Rules

---

[28] Act on Administration no. 130/1998, in force since 6 December.1998; the Act has been amended many times since, most recently in November 2001.

of Organisation and Procedure for administrative structures, most of which were adopted in 2000, as well as their subsequent amendments, outline the concrete functions, tasks, and responsibilities of administrative units.

The Civil Service Act lays down the requirements for acquiring the status of civil servant, recruitment procedures and rules governing termination of employment.[29] It defines as civil servants all employees of the Council of Ministers, ministries and other central administrative structure, and district and municipal administrations. Technical staff, members of political cabinets (which can include up to ten members in a ministry), deputy regional governors and deputy mayors are exempted, however – an omission criticised by NGOs, which claim that this undermines bureaucratic continuity and preserves the tradition of political appointments.

Although amendments to the Act on Administration adopted in November 2001 mandated stricter provisions to regulate the division between political and non-political appointments, according to a January 2002 UNDP *Report on Anti-corruption Initiatives in Bulgaria,* "[E]ven under the new civil service law, civil servants are dependent on political masters and senior bureaucrats to gain promotion."[30]

The Civil Service Act also created the State Administrative Commission (SAC) to supervise adherence to the Act. The SAC supervises the hiring of civil servants and arbitrates in labour disputes. The Commission, which was established in August 2000, consists of five members appointed by the Council of Ministers upon a proposal by the Prime Minister. However, as the UNDP *Report on Anti-corruption Initiatives in Bulgaria* notes, the Commission's role is restricted to protecting the social and employment rights of civil servants; it does not play any role in ensuring that hiring, firing and promotion are free from political interference, nor does it have any mandate to play a direct role in combating corruption.[31]

In the area of training, an Institute for Public Administration and European Integration was established in 2000 to train civil servants. In November 2001 the Institute organised a round table of senior civil servants to discuss corruption and measures to combat it in the public administration, and is now offering a training course on "Preventing corruption – risks and challenges to the public administration."

---

[29] Civil Service Act no. 67/1999, in force since August 1999; the Act has been amended five times since, most recently in April 2002.

[30] D. A. Bilak, *Report of the Evaluation Mission,* p. 18.

[31] D. A. Bilak, *Report of the Evaluation Mission,* p. 19.

3.2 Administrative procedure and redress

The 1999 Act on Administrative Services for Natural and Legal Persons sets forth general procedures for the provision of administrative services. Specifically, the Act stipulates a deadline of three working days following the submission of the request for the provision of an administrative service. When the service requires an administrative decision, the deadline is seven days. If provision of a service is denied, reasons must be provided within three days. However, the Act also states that procedures for providing administrative services are governed by the specific Rules of Organisation and Procedure of each administrative body, while problems not covered by these rules are to be dealt with in "internal regulations approved by the competent administrative secretary," which are not public.

The 1989 Act on State Liability for Damages Inflicted on Citizens, and the Act on Administrative Procedure lay down rules for redress and claiming damages. Citizens may file a complaint against an administrative act to the body that carried out the act, with the right to appeal to the superior administrative body and finally to a court. If the act is annulled by the respective administrative body or by the court, citizens may also apply for damages to a court, either at their place of residence or at the place of damage. When damages are claimed as a result of an act whose defects are so serious that it cannot be considered valid, no previous annulment of the act is required. Claimants pay court costs if the claim is overruled in whole or in part. The Supreme Administrative Court is the final arbiter of appeals.

In practice, these provisions do not enable citizens to effectively defend their rights *vis-à-vis* public bodies. Rules concerning administrative procedure, appeals and redress are scattered across several acts, legal procedures are slow and complicated, and implementation is undermined by the fact that the very institution that is accused of carrying out a damaging act is charged with explaining to claimants their rights and complaint procedures. According to the UNDP, the existence of various rules and deadlines for procedure and appeals makes it very difficult for citizens to seek redress.[32] There are no known cases in which the law has been used to obtain compensation for acts involving corruption. In order to provide one of the basic conditions for effective redress, all rules concerning administrative procedure, appeals and redress should be codified in a single act.

---

[32] D. A. Bilak, *Report of the Evaluation Mission,* pp. 19-20.

3.3 Conflict of interest and asset monitoring

There are no rules on conflict of interest at the executive branch level, with the exception of some vague provisions in the Code of Conduct for Civil Servants (see Section 4.2). Apart from the ineffective Act on Asset Disclosure by Persons Occupying Senior Positions in the State (see Section 2.3), which does not apply to officials below the level of minister, there are no provisions for monitoring officials' assets.

3.4 Internal control mechanisms

The Civil Service Act provides for the establishment of a seven-member Disciplinary Board in each unit of public administration to hear disciplinary cases and impose disciplinary penalties ranging from reduction in rank for a period of six months to one year to dismissal. In practice, many administrative units have fewer than seven civil servants and are therefore unable to form such disciplinary councils.

3.5 Interaction with the public

The Code of Conduct for Civil Servants, approved by the Minister of State Administration on 29 December 2000, outlines the fundamental principles and rules of ethical behaviour for civil servants in their interactions with citizens, in the performance of their professional duties, and in their private and public lives. However, the Code is vague, does not provide clear rules on conflicts of interest and imposes a duty of loyalty to the organisation, which may encourage the withholding of public information and provides a clear disincentive to whistleblowing – a situation which is exacerbated by the absence of mechanisms or legal provisions to protect whistleblowers. There are no mechanisms for observing or enforcing the Code. In practice, the Code contributes little to increased transparency and accountability in the civil service.

The most positive step taken in regulating the relationship between officials and citizens was the Act on Access to Public Information, which came into force in July 2000 (see Section 9.2).

3.6 Corruption

As the figures in Section 1.1 show, there have been very few convictions of Bulgarian public officials for corruption. However, in the past few years the executive branch has been increasingly the focus of media allegations of corruption. As of January 2002, 34 senior public officials or former public officials were under investigation or had been charged, including nine former ministers. The more important cases are summarised below:[33]

- Former Executive Director of the Privatisation Agency Zahari Zheliazkov was fired in November 2000 and subsequently charged in connection with the privatisation of Incoms Telecom Holding, which was cancelled in February 2001 amid accusations of corruption. Zheliazkov was under criminal investigation in connection with the privatisation of several other companies, including Balkan Airlines.

- Former Deputy Prime Minister and Minister of Industry Alexander Bozhkov was charged in three cases: the first in connection with the sale of an optical technology company for a very low price in 1998 (a deal he signed without receiving the opinion of the Privatisation Agency); the second in connection with the privatisation of a publishing company; and the third for allegedly exceeding his powers by signing an inflated issue of compensatory bonds to an individual. Then Deputy Minister of Industry Marin Marinov was also charged for his activities in connection with the liquidation of an electronics company.

- Former Minister of Health and Director of the National Health Insurance Company Ilko Semerdzhiev was charged in connection with a contract signed for the State insurer for an integrated information system with the US company AremiSoft, allegedly in violation of numerous provisions of the Public Procurement Act.

- In April 2000, former Minister of Interior Bogomil Bonev alleged that then PM Ivan Kostov had withheld from prosecution offices a number of materials pointing to corruption within the ruling Government coalition and by senior officials. At the same time, four of Kostov's advisors became embroiled in corruption scandals and were removed, one due to revelations that his company located at a border checkpoint was used for smuggling cigarettes.

The number of scandals affecting the most senior officials may be related to an important characteristic of executive decision-making in Bulgaria: the very high degree of discretionary decision-making power retained at the highest ministerial level. A British Embassy official commenting on the process for foreign investors to gain licensing and concessions, noted, that, "It's all about ringing up ministers, no-one below the minister can take decisions."[34] While this might be a way of limiting lower

---

[33] "Who is hounded for what," *Sega,* 25 January 2002.

[34] Interview with Dennis Leith, First Secretary (Commercial/Economic), British Trade Partners, British Embassy, Sofia, 7 February 2002.

level corruption, it is also to some extent both a cause and consequence of high-level corruption.

To date, no scandals have hit top officials in the present SNM Government, despite the efforts of the opposition UDF to create a scandal around the Government's decision to hire a British customs consultancy company without a public tender – which appear more politically motivated than grounded in actual malpractice (see Section 8.2).

4. LEGISLATURE

The Bulgarian Parliament does not function as an effective anti-corruption mechanism, and is itself highly vulnerable to corruption. Parliament does not scrutinise public finances effectively or initiate anti-corruption legislation, and two anti-corruption committees were abolished in 2001 after proving to be entirely ineffective. Regulation of conflict of interest and lobbying is minimal or non-existent, and immunity provisions are extensive. There are serious concerns that Parliament may be effectively influenced or controlled of vested interests with an interest in blocking anti-corruption policy, for example in the area of customs reform.

4.1 Elections

Bulgarian elections are free and fair. Elections are organised and supervised by three sets of electoral commissions: a Central Election Commission, regional electoral commissions and sectional/local electoral commissions. The CEC is appointed no later than 60 days before elections by the President, following consultations with parliamentary caucuses, and its composition reflects the relative strength of different parties; no party or coalition may have a majority.

The only scandal to date concerning the conduct of elections broke when a member of the CEC during the November 2001 presidential elections attacked the Commission's choice of a company to calculate the election results (see Section 7.3).

4.2 Budget and control mechanisms

Although the State budget is subject to approval by the Parliament, there are a significant number of categories of public expenditure that do not require legislative approval. In the 2001 budget, there were 21 extra-budgetary accounts.[35] The number and types of these funds is decided by the Government.

Both the State budget and the accounts of extra-budgetary funds are audited by the National Audit Office. As described in Section 2.4, audit by the NAO does not provide sufficient scrutiny, partly due to the lack of a mechanism by which the Parliament would enforce its findings.

Until April 2001, the Parliament had two specialised committees dealing with corruption issues: The Committee for Countering Corruption and Organised Crime and the Committee for Legal Issues and Anti-corruption Legislation. The former was invested with investigative powers to deal with complaints on corruption-related issues but remained inactive despite receiving around 1,000 letters during its existence, while the latter dealt with legislative reform in the area of anti-corruption. Both were abolished after the 2001 elections, having contributed very little to either investigation or legislation.[36] The Parliament constituted after the June 2001 elections does not have a specialised anti-corruption committee.

4.3 Conflict of interest and asset monitoring

Regulation of both conflict of interest and asset supervision is inadequate, and the holding of external business interests by MPs appears to be widespread.

Existing regulations of conflict of interest are minimal. A general conflict of interest provision in the Internal Regulations of the Parliament prohibits individual members

---

[35] These were: Unemployment and vocational training with the Ministry of Labor and Social Policy; Environmental Protection Fund; Social Integration Fund; "13 Centuries of Bulgaria" charity fund; National Compensation Fund for Housing Savings; Television and Radio Fund; Extra-budgetary account of the National Assembly; Fund for Safety and Storage of Nuclear Waste; Fund for Decommissioning of Nuclear Power Plants; Special Account for the Proceeds of Municipal Privatisation; Fund to meet the costs of Privatisation of Municipal Property; Special Municipal Fund for Investment and long-term Acquisition of Assets; Municipal Environmental Protection Fund; Housing Construction Fund for all agencies funded through the State budget; Municipal Social Protection Fund; Municipal Fund for Compensation of Former Owners of Confiscated Agricultural Land; Ministry of Finance National Fund established by memorandum of understanding between Bulgaria and the European Commission; Ministry of Finance Fund to cover the costs of concessions; Central Government Fund to cover the costs of privatisation; State Agricultural Fund; Municipal Forestry Fund.

[36] For example, the Committee for Countering Corruption and Organised Crime received several thousand letters from citizens about corruption, mostly in local government, but took no action.

from carrying out "activities which are contrary to the status of Members of Parliament."[37] MPs may not be paid for external work under an employment contract, but may receive honoraria for *ad hoc* work. In addition, they may not be members of the boards of commercial entities or use their position to earn money from commercial advertising. When introducing or debating a draft law, MPs are obliged to declare any relevant financial or other commercial interests. These provisions are subject to monitoring through an annual declaration submitted to the Committee on Budget and Finance. These regulations are very vague; for example, there is no definition of what might be "contrary to the status" of an MP. Moreover, in practice the Committee does not monitor adherence to the provisions. Many MPs have continued to operate as lawyers, including the former Speaker of the Parliament.

In addition to the provisions of the Act on Property Disclosure by Persons Occupying Senior Positions in the State (see Section 2.3), under the Internal Rules MPs must notify the same Committee of any gifts or other material benefits received by members "in their capacity as an MP" exceeding a value higher than 20 percent of their base monthly salary. Again, the Committee does not monitor these declarations.

Lobbying of MPs is entirely unregulated. Although specific evidence is thin, one respected analyst believes that one of the main problems facing both the current and former Governments is uncontrolled lobbying:

> [L]egislators do not work in the interests of the State, but act as lobbyists for business interests or even on behalf of business groups linked to organised crime, which flourishes under a fragile, powerless Government.[38]

The National Anti-corruption Strategy calls for the Government to initiate the adoption of legislation to regulate lobbying, but no practical measures have been undertaken yet.

4.4 Immunity

Members of the Parliament enjoy complete immunity from criminal prosecution, which may only be lifted with the consent of the Parliament. Members of the Parliament may not be held criminally liable for their opinions or votes in the Parliament. A Member of the Parliament is immune from detention or criminal prosecution except in the case of grave crimes, when a warrant from the Parliament is required.

---

[37] Internal Regulations of the Parliament, Article 102.

[38] Cited in: U. Buechsenschuetz, "T-SO opposition in Bulgaria," RFE/RL Newsline, 3 April 2002.

There are no statistics available on the number of applications for lifting immunity or how many have been refused. According to the press, up to November 2001 three MPs had had their immunity removed, out of five requests.[39] One of the denied requests was a potential minor corruption case.

In practice, immunity provisions serve to shield MPs from criminal responsibility. For example, a criminal investigation into alleged abuse of office against Major-General Brigadier Asparuhov, the former Director of the National Intelligence Service, was dismissed after he was elected to the Parliament in the 2001 elections. The Constitutional Court stated that the case should be stopped for the period of his Parliament mandate.[40]

4.5 Corruption

There are no known cases of sitting MPs being charged for corruption-related offences. In October 2000, the Prosecutor General's Office charged former MP Julia Berberjan and her husband of tax evasion in relation to her acquisition of two hectares of municipal land in Sofia. According to the press, in January another MP was being investigated for his former activities as a director of an industrial plant.[41]

5. JUDICIARY

The judiciary is widely regarded as highly corrupt both by public opinion and foreign observers. However, although there is some indirect evidence that corruption may be a serious problem, a bigger problem may be executive interference and straightforward neglect of the needs of the judicial branch. Although the Government has initiated a programme of judicial reform, some of the proposed reforms may undermine judicial independence.

---

[39] *Dnevnik,* daily, 27 November 2001.

[40] "Who is investigated for what," *Sega,* 25 January 2002.

[41] "Who is investigated for what," *Sega,* 25 January 2002.

5.1 Legislative framework

The judiciary suffers most from an absence of political commitment to judicial independence, reflected in substantial executive interference in the operation of the Supreme Judicial Council.[42] Other problems which hamper the effective functioning of the judiciary include a severe lack of funds, very slow court proceedings for both civil and criminal cases,[43] insufficient publicity and transparency, shortages of qualified staff, inadequate training, outdated paper-based filing systems, and lack of coordination between judges, prosecutors and investigators.

The Bulgarian judiciary encompasses the court system, prosecution offices and investigators. Judges, prosecutors and investigators are commonly referred to as the magistracy.[44] As with members of the Parliament, magistrates enjoy immunity from prosecution for all but serious crimes with more than a five year sentence. Magistrates may be stripped of their immunity only by the Supreme Judicial Council. As the European Commission noted in its *2001 Regular Report,* requests to the Supreme Judicial Council to lift immunity are rare.[45] A proposal to limit magistrates' immunity was rejected by the Parliament in February 2001 but was being considered again by the Government in March 2002.

Judges are generally banned from carrying on any commercial activities, with the exception of scientific and teaching activities. The Bulgarian Judges Association has produced a set of guidelines for judges, but these rules are voluntary and apply only to the members of the Association. The Association of Prosecutors has not produced any ethical standards, and there are no written standards of conduct for investigators. As of early 2002, a Code of Ethics for magistrates was under development.

Members of the two Supreme Courts are subject to general requirements to disclose income and assets (see Section 2.3), although there are no legal consequences attached to the declarations. There is no such requirement for judges at lower levels.

The SJC has the clear constitutional responsibility and right to supervise and discipline all employees of the judicial branch. The Chairperson of each court is responsible for

---

[42] For a detailed account of the judicial legal framework in Bulgaria, see EU Accession Monitoring Program, *Monitoring the EU Accession Process: Judicial Independence in Bulgaria,* Open Society Institute, Budapest 2001, pp. 72–108, <http://www.eumap.org>, (last accessed 27 August 2002). See also Sections 3.6 and 5.2.

[43] The average case takes three to five years to complete, and in perhaps as many as 70 percent of civil cases the ruling is not enforced until an administrative judge intervenes, which has taken up to seven years in extreme cases.

[44] Constitution of the Republic of Bulgaria, Article 117 (1).

[45] Commission, *2001 Regular Report,* p. 17.

reporting disciplinary matters to the SJC, where she believes the offence is serious enough to warrant disciplinary measures. However, in the absence of guidelines or administrative review from either the SJC or Ministry of Justice this procedure is very rarely pursued. The European Commission noted in its *2001 Regular Report* that,

> [W]hilst the Supreme Judicial Council has quite wide administrative responsibilities for the operation of the court system, it does not have the necessary administrative capacity to exercise them. Its secretariat is insufficiently staffed for this role.[46]

Amendments to the Judiciary Act passed in 1998 empowered the Minister of Justice and the heads of units within the judiciary (i.e. chairpersons of courts and of prosecution and investigation offices) to institute disciplinary proceedings against all magistrates. However, in practice the likelihood of such proceedings resulting in the removal of immunity are minimal.

According to the *2000 Regular Report,* "very little has been done to upgrade the judiciary, which remains weak."[47] Although the *2001 Regular Report* acknowledges progress made with a new Strategy for Judicial Reform adopted in October 2001, it concludes that,

> While there have been developments in some areas, there is as yet no reason to change the overall assessment made last year that further efforts are needed for the judicial system to become strong, effective and professional and able to guarantee full respect for the rule of law as well as effective participation in the internal market.[48]

One of the consequences of the problems described above appears to be the failure of the judicial system to bring any senior officials to justice for corruption: none of the cases involving former or deputy ministers mentioned in Section 3.6, or a number of other cases involving similarly ranked officials, have resulted in conviction.

5.2 Corruption

The judiciary has been subject to widespread criticism since the beginning of transition and enjoys very little public confidence. According to surveys, the judiciary is perceived

---

[46] Commission, *2001 Regular Report,* p. 18.

[47] Commission, *2000 Regular Report,* p. 23.

[48] Commission, *2001 Regular Report,* p. 19.

to be the fourth most corrupt institution in Bulgaria (see Section 1.2). Western embassy officials share the opinion that the judiciary is highly corrupt.[49]

This perception may have been sharpened by cases such as a January 2002 decision by the Supreme Court in a drug-related case. The case began in 1997 when police anti-mafia units raided a synthetic drugs laboratory and seized 313 kg of drugs. The Court ruled that there was insufficient evidence that the drugs were intended for sale, acquitted one of the suspects and gave a one year suspended sentence to the other.

In another case that raised concerns of political interference, a Sofia City Court Judge refused to register the National Movement Simeon II (NMS II) as a political party a month before the June 2001 Parliament elections. The Supreme Court subsequently confirmed the decision. NSM II was forced to participate in the elections as a coalition, and was not registered as a party until April 2002.

The CEEBIC *Report on the Bulgarian Business Environment* warns that "some courts and law enforcement officers may be susceptible to influence (political or economic)."[50] The January 2002 UNDP *Report on Anti-corruption Initiatives in Bulgaria,* however, urges caution in making across-the-board judgements about judicial corruption, noting that,

> [T]he perception of a corrupt judiciary may not be as clear-cut as the public perceives. There is a strong case to be made that judges are not perpetrators of the problem, but victims themselves. This is a view held not just by judges, but also by senior law enforcement officials.[51]

The UNDP report indicates that the lack of political commitment to an independent judiciary combined with a failure to reform judicial procedures adequately leaves many judges "at the mercy of unscrupulous political and administrative authorities."[52] This is exacerbated by the miserable level of funding allocated to the judiciary: less than one percent of GDP, compared to a European norm of three to four percent.[53] The failure of the prosecution and court system to perform its role adequately (including by carrying through corruption cases) may be as much the result of pressure on judges as corruption.

---

[49] Interview with officials from British Embassy, Sofia, 6 February 2002: Dennis Leith (First Secretary, Trade Partners UK); Christine Winterburn (Second Secretary); Peter Petrov (Political Officer).

[50] CEEBICnet, *Bulgaria Country Commercial Guide FY 2002,* p. 71.

[51] D. A. Bilak, *Report of the Evaluation Mission,* p. 19.

[52] D. A. Bilak, *Report of the Evaluation Mission,* p. 20.

[53] D. A. Bilak, *Report of the Evaluation Mission,* p. 20.

6. POLITICAL PARTY FINANCE

The funding of Bulgarian political parties is extremely weakly regulated. Liberal rules on donations, a non-transparent system for determining State subsidies and the virtual absence of supervision probably underpin widespread illegal funding and corruption, although direct evidence of corruption is scarce.

6.1 Legislative framework

Although major progress has been made towards putting a framework in place to regulate the financing of Bulgarian political parties, to date these efforts do not appear sufficient to make a significant difference, and serious loopholes in financing rules remain, accompanied by entirely ineffective supervision.

The funding of political parties has only been legally regulated since a new Act on Political Parties came into force in March 2001. Under the Act,

- Parties may not carry out commercial activities or own shares in entities carrying out commercial activities;

- Parties are allowed to receive anonymous donations up to a total annual maximum of 25 percent of their annual State subsidy (see below), or 25 percent of the minimum annual subsidy in the case of parties that do not receive any subsidy. This was retained in the law despite a Presidential veto.

- Parties are not allowed to receive donations from one individual or legal entity if such donations exceed €15,000 in total.

- Parties are not allowed to receive donations from firms with more than 50 percent State or municipal ownership, or by firms and organisations carrying out a State or municipal contract.

- Parties are not allowed to receive donations from foreign governments or foreign State-owned firms and organisations.

Political parties are entitled to subsidies from the State budget. Parties represented in the Parliament receive an amount proportionate to the number of votes they received in the previous elections, as do parties that are not in the Parliament but received at least one percent of the total vote. The overall amount for political party subsidies is determined annually in the act on the State budget, and divided by the amount of votes to yield the contribution to each party. Curiously, the President of the National Audit Office told the press that the total State subsidy for political parties in the 2002 budget is €2.295m to be distributed among the qualifying parties by a ratio of one Leva

(€0,51) to one vote, although the 2002 State budget does not contain any item clearly corresponding to this. Under this formula, the present governing party would receive €918,000.

6.2 Control and supervision

Parties are obliged to submit to the National Audit Office a financial report of income and expenditures by 15 March each year. The NAO must decide within six months whether the report is in accordance with the law. However, there is no legal duty to make the reports or any related information public, and the NAO has failed to reply to requests for parties' reports. The only sanction imposed on parties for failing to submit financial reports is a one-year subsidy cut. This probably provides little incentive for parties to submit reports, especially if – as is widely suspected – they rely heavily on covert forms of finance.

6.3 Party finance in practice

There is a widespread feeling that a large proportion of corruption and practices connected with corruption – ranging from nepotism to the establishment of monopolies, shady privatisation deals, political interference in the judiciary, and rampant smuggling – have been connected with political party financing. Although the total absence of regulation of financing until recently provided strong reasons for such a belief, the evidence on party financing in practice is extremely thin – a fact which is itself partly the result of lax regulation and supervision. An MP from the Movement for Rights and Freedoms (MRF), a political party supported predominantly by ethnic Turks and currently represented in Government, accused one of its leaders in October 2001 of pocketing approximately €433,333 in party income. He was excluded from the Parliament party caucus, but continued to sit as an independent MP. There has long been suspicion that smuggling groups contribute to political parties.[54]

A survey carried out in January 2001 found that 51 percent of companies expected illegal financing of parties to remain on the same level over the next three years, while 22 percent expected it to decrease significantly and 17 percent to increase significantly.[55]

---

[54] Interview with Alexenia Dimitrova, reporter, *24 chassa*, daily, Sofia, 8 February 2002.

[55] Vitosha Research and Centre for Economic Development, *Global Competitiveness Survey*, January 2001, cited in: Coalition 2000, *Corruption Assessment Report 2001*, p. 20.

7. PUBLIC PROCUREMENT

The legal framework for public procurement has seen massive improvements in the past few years. However, procedures for supervision of and redress against procurement decisions remain ineffective, contributing to a system of contract allocation that has allowed widespread collusion and probably major high-level corruption. The effectiveness of the new system in practice is doubtful without further reform, but attempts at further reform recently faltered.

7.1 Legislative framework

The first Act on Government and Municipal Procurement was passed in 1997, and since then procurement legislation has developed rapidly. The latest version of the Act in effect since January 2002[56] provides for a relatively advanced procurement framework. Further amendments were in preparation in the first half of 2002, supported by a PHARE programme, to complete the harmonisation of public procurement legislation with the *acquis* and strengthen the institutional capacity, structures and procedures of the Public Procurement Office and agency procurement units.

Contracts over the following threshold values are subject to the Act: €306,000 for construction works, €25,500 for purchase of goods, and €15,300 for purchase of services. As a general rule, procurement must be carried out by open tender, and contracts may not be split in order to circumvent these thresholds.

Contracts may be allocated by a restricted tender (closed bidding procedure) involving bidders invited by the principal after a pre-qualification process, if, in view of the specific character of the subject of procurement, it is only capable of being performed by a limited number of contractors, or the subject of procurement is of a complex technical nature that requires successive technical or technological specifications to be defined in the course of contract performance.

Contracts may be allocated by direct negotiation procedure (similar to sole sourcing), where the principal negotiates with one or several selected persons, under a number of conditions. The most important of these are where:

- There is a need for accident of disaster prevention or relief, a threat to human health and life, or considerable damage or loss of property.

---

[56] Public Procurement Act, *State Gazette,* no. 97, 28 November 2000, effective 1 January 2001.

- The subject of procurement concerns supplemental supply by an existing contractor not later than one year after the award of the main contract, and provided a number of further conditions are met, such as when purchase from a different contractor might result in incompatibility or technical differences in operation, and that the total value of the supplemental contract does not exceed 30 percent of the original contract.

- Similar rules apply if the subject of procurement concerns a recurrence of service or supply of supplemental service or construction works by an existing contractor not later than one year after the award of the main contract, and the original contract was awarded by open or restricted tender and invitation to bid set out the likelihood of supplemental procurement or construction works.

- The open or closed tender procedure has been terminated due to lack of bidders, failure of any bidder to conform to tender requirements, the top three ranking participants successively refuse to close a contract, or the grounds on which the original tender was issued change for unforeseeable reasons.

The principal may award a tender by direct negotiation with the permission of the Public Procurement Agency in cases in which:

- The procurement may only be implemented by a specific entity.

- It is objectively impossible to meet the deadlines for conducting an open or restricted tender.

- The tender concerns out-of-warranty servicing or spare parts for machines, facilities or complex equipment.

The Act contains a number of other important standard provisions, for example prohibiting additions to a contract unless circumstances arise that could not have been foreseen at the time the contract was signed, and which render the contract prejudicial to the legitimate interests of one of the parties.

Tender proceedings must be conducted by a special committee appointed by the head official of the authority. Committee members are subject to conflict of interest provisions forbidding any involvement or interest in the tender (for example, specifying the requirement of sealed bids, strict rules for opening bids, and the right of any bidder or applicant to bid to be present at the opening of bids).

Agencies subject to the Act must submit annually to the *Official Gazette* information about their procurement plans for the coming year by 1 March. A Register for Public Procurement was set up in 2001, which must contain information on all procurement contracts regulated by the Act. A recently adopted Act on Electronic Signature and

Electronic Documents in force since October 2001 has created one of the preconditions for introducing online public procurement.[57]

The Public Procurement Office was created in 2001. It is appointed by the Council of Ministers and subordinate to the Ministry of Public Administration. The Office has a wide range of responsibilities, from drafting new legislation, issuing methodological instructions, issuing mandatory instructions if it detects violations of the law, monitoring the performance of public procurement contracts, to keeping the Public Procurement Register.

7.2 Review and audit

Procedures for complaints and review of public procurement decisions are covered only very briefly in the Public Procurement Act. Under the Act, any participant in a public procurement procedure may file a complaint under the Act on Administrative Procedure. This effectively means that redress can be sought only through the courts, and raises the same concerns about redress covered in Section 3.2. The Act further states that review of its application shall be exercised by the National Audit Office and the State Internal Financial Control Agency. The Chairperson of the Public Procurement Office may request the SIFCA to review particular procurements.

Again, given the stage of development of financial control in general, and the weakness of current regulations on administrative procedure, the effectiveness of this framework in limiting abuses during public procurement procedures is questionable. One of three proposed amendments to the Act submitted at the end of 2001 would have established an independent Public Procurement Agency to oversee procurement. The Agency would have received information on each appeal, although it would not have been given powers to decide appeals. The amendments would also have introduced other improvements to the Act, for example the duty of contracting authorities to explain to bidders its choice of winner, and a prohibition on arbitrary changes to tender conditions. However, the proposals were rejected in March 2002 by the Parliament's Economic Committee.

Another weakness of the Public Procurement Act concerns the leniency of the sanctions it imposes for violations of its provisions. The most serious sanction is for failure to conduct a procurement procedure when it should have been conducted, which is subject to a fine of €510 to €2,550. Agencies that award contracts by direct negotiation without due reason are punishable by a fine of €510 to €1,530. There is no provision for the annulment of contracts awarded in violation of the Public Procurement Act.

---

[57] See <http://www.csd.bg/publications/law/law_e.htm>, (last accessed 27 August 2002).

7.3 Corruption

Corruption has been a serious problem in procurement, partly due to the absence of any law until 1997. The law remains widely criticised, even after amendments to the 1997 Act, and in a January 2001 survey, half of companies surveyed stated that additional payments and bribes are necessary to win public contracts and obtain licences.[58]

In particular, improvements in the law may not have done anything to deter widespread collusion. According to the Chief Financial Officer of an international organisation with offices in Sofia, rampant collusion raises the price of every contract the organisation issues by around 20 percent on average.

One big corruption scandal surfaced in November 2000 when Jeilan, a Turkish construction company, claimed it provided €58.8m in bribes, some to senior Government officials, to secure large construction contracts, such as one making it the primary contractor for the Gorna Arda water cascade project in an inter-governmental agreement with Turkey. The company went public with the allegations when the Government decided to cancel the contract because the company went into bankruptcy proceedings.[59]

During the November 2001 presidential elections, the Central Electoral Commission had to terminate its contract with a private company that had been commissioned to process the election results after it emerged that the company lacked the technical capacity to carry out the task.[60] A representative of the Civic Initiative for Free and Fair Elections publicly expressed suspicion that members of the CEC took bribes from the company.[61]

IT companies have also registered strong complaints about contracts for software through the Bulgarian Association for Information Technologies, which recently detailed allegedly "flagrant" violations of the procurement law by the Parliament and ministries of Finance, Agriculture and Public Health.[62]

---

[58] Vitosha Research and Centre for Economic Development, *Global Competitiveness Survey,* January 2001; cited in: Coalition 2000, *Corruption Assessment Report 2001,* p. 47.

[59] G. Alexandrova, "Cok Selam, Jeilan," *Kapital,* 13 November 2000.

[60] *Sega,* 13 November 2001.

[61] *Troud,* 16 November 2001.

[62] *Standart,* 11 July 2001.

8. PUBLIC SERVICES

Bulgaria suffers from serious problems of corruption in a number of public services. The Bulgarian Customs Administration appears to be more seriously affected by corruption than any other public institution, and was identified by the Government as the number one priority in the fight against corruption. However, there are indications that the Government may be unable to push through meaningful reform against the influence of groups with a vested interest in the *status quo.* Licences and permits remain major barriers to doing business, although the Government is in the process of carrying out important licensing reforms.

8.1 Police

The Bulgarian police is regarded as the one of the most corrupt institutions in Bulgaria according to surveys (see Section 1.2), and bribery in the traffic police is a particularly prominent area of concern.[63] Bulgarian law enforcement agencies have recently started to develop internal control departments to deal with corruption, *inter alia,* but these are still *ad hoc* in nature and there is no coordinated strategy. The current Government appointed a widely respected former police chief as Secretary General at the Ministry of Interior, one of whose tasks is to devise a strategy to fight corruption in the police. In 2001, the Ministry made serious efforts to adopt a number of anti-corruption priorities as part of the National Anti-corruption Strategy. Most particularly, within its Inspectorate the Ministry has established a special unit on internal corruption monitoring and prevention. The Ministry has also prepared a Draft Code for the Ethical Behaviour of Police Officers with references to anti-corruption.

8.2 Customs

Smuggling, which was already institutionalised by the secret services under the Communist regime, has become even more pervasive in response to the sharp rise in demand for imported goods after 1989. As a result, the Bulgarian customs service has been subject to more corruption pressure than any other sphere of public administration

---

[63] One editorial in an English-language weekly recently referred to alleged widespread bribes of €5-10 to avoid tickets from traffic police; see "Corruption 101," *Sofia Echo,* 31 August 2001.

during the past decade.[64] In addition, as in neighbouring Romania, the Yugoslav embargo led to massive and highly profitable illegal exports of oil and other products during the 1990's,[65] facilitated by the active or passive acquiescence of senior Government officials. The symbiosis between corruption and smuggling has become endemic through criminal interactions between smugglers and civil servants at virtually all levels, according to one report published in 2000.[66] Illegal imports fuel a grey economy that amounts to as much as 35 percent of GDP,[67] and according to statements to the media in 2001 by the highly respected former Director of the Customs Agency, goods worth some €1.08b are smuggled into Bulgaria every year – an amount equivalent to roughly one-quarter of the annual State budget.[68]

Measures taken under previous governments to combat corruption in the customs agency were largely ineffective. According to the General Customs Directorate (now the Customs Agency), between October 1997 and October 1999, 102 customs officers were fired on account of "proven grave offences" against customs legislation.[69] One 2000 report calculated that 86 percent of foreign cigarettes imported into Bulgaria in 1998 were imported illegally,[70] one of the authors of this report recently estimated the percentage at 90 percent in 2001. On the other hand, illegal imports of high-quality alcoholic spirits fell from nearly 100 percent to 20-30 percent, as a result of changes to the law mandating that duties be determined on the basis of alcohol content, rather than on declared value as previously.

The Government has identified improving the customs administration as one of its top priorities in the fight against corruption, and this constitutes part of the Anti-corruption Strategy. In August 2001 it appointed Emil Dimitrov, a former auditor of the Ministry of Finance, as Director of the Customs Agency; under the previous

---

[64] For information on smuggling channels and their origins in Bulgaria, see material by Centre for Study on Democracy, available at
<http://www.csd.bg/publications/corrup_1_e_cont.htm>, (last accessed 27 August 2002).

[65] Neicho Neev, former Deputy Prime Minister in Luben Berov's 1993-4 cabinet, was being investigated in January 2002 in connection with criminal violations of the Yugoslav embargo and suspicion of large scale corruption deals.

[66] See Centre for the study of Democracy, *Corruption and Trafficking: Monitoring and Prevention,* Centre for the Study of Democracy, Sofia 2000.

[67] Centre for the Study of Democracy, *Corruption and Trafficking: Monitoring and Prevention,* p. 35.

[68] *Troud,* 22 August 2001.

[69] Centre for the Study of Democracy, *Corruption and Trafficking: Monitoring and Prevention,* p. 17.

[70] Centre for the Study of Democracy, *Corruption and Trafficking: Monitoring and Prevention,* p. 43.

Government, Mr Dimitrov wrote a damning report on the customs administration and was forced to resign. It has also established an Internal Control Department within the Customs Agency, and announced new investigative powers for customs officers. A number of dismissals of customs officers have already taken place. For example, in November 2001 Dimitrov announced he would dismiss the head of the regional customs agency in Rousse and replace other customs officials there, because of confirmation that money had been collected in Rousse for bribes for a high-ranking official in the Customs Agency in Sofia.[71] Also in November, the Agency opened a 24-hour hotline to facilitate reporting of corruption.

Part of the Government's plan was to obtain advice on customs reform from Western experts; Finance Minister Milen Velchev even suggested that customs activities might be outsourced to foreign companies.[72] In fact, in November, the Government announced a contract with the British consultancy firm Crown Agents for advice on customs reform. However, the contract provoked a strong reaction from the opposition UDF (the previous governing party). In March 2002, four months after the announcement of the contract, the UDF presented a request to the Prosecutor General to investigate the contract, and a petition for the creation of a parliamentary investigative committee. In the wake of these events, Dimitrov presented his resignation.

The UDF's opposition has been widely interpreted to have been motivated by the danger posed to its members by investigations of customs violations that took place under the former Government. The situation was clouded further when Dimitrov also declared his opposition to the contract – which was awarded without a public tender – and declared after his resignation that he was offered €306,000 a year not to interfere with the Crown Agents deal.[73]

Under these circumstances, it appears that the anti-corruption drive in the Government's top priority area may have lost momentum, and the prospects for reforming customs and breaking the links between powerful smuggling groups and smuggling channels involving customs officials are uncertain.

8.3 Tax collection

There have been no major allegations in the media of corruption in the tax administration. Victimisation surveys indicate that the tax authorities have become less

---

[71] I. Vatahov, "Customs bribes alleged in Rousse," *Sofia Echo,* 9 November 2001.

[72] I. Vatahov, "Customs to be foreign-run?" *Sofia Echo,* 3 August 2001.

[73] I. Vatahov, "Dimitrov attacks Crown Agents contract," *Sofia Echo,* 22 March 2002.

of a source of corrupt pressure over time. Nevertheless, the public still ranks tax officials among the top ten most corrupt public services in the country.[74]

8.4 Health

According to survey results almost half the population believe most or almost all doctors are corrupt (see Section 1.1). Results of victimisation surveys of the general public in May 2002 indicated an increase in perceptions of corruption pressure in healthcare, with doctors ranked lower only than customs officers as the public officials exerting the strongest pressure to obtain bribes.[75] The January 2002 UNDP *Report on Anti-corruption Initiatives in Bulgaria* cites perceptions by local citizens that hospitals and doctors are very corrupt as a result of their subordination to the Ministry of Health and lack of accountability at the local level.[76] One area that has attracted particular attention with regard to corruption has been funeral services.[77]

The Government has acknowledged the problems of corruption in this area – in July 2002, the Minister of Health gave an interview admitting corruption in the health care system (*Standart*, daily, 11 July 2002). Remarkably, however, despite the social sensitivity of this public service there have been almost no anti-corruption policies formulated by the Government in this area. Health care is not even identified one of the target areas in the Government's anti-corruption strategy adopted in October 2001.

Doctors are subject to the bribery provisions of the criminal code. There have been a few prosecutions but – according to available evidence – only one conviction, which resulted in a suspended sentence.

8.5 Education

According to surveys from May 2002, educational staff rank fourth among officials in terms of their tendency to pursue bribes, although the scores in that survey indicated a slight improvement. According to media articles, the most widespread forms of corruption in higher education are linked to pressure on students to purchase learning

---

[74] Corruption Indexes of Coalition 2000, May 2002, <http://www.online.bg/vr/crl/corr_ind_05E.htm>, (last accessed 27 August 2002).

[75] Corruption Indexes of Coalition 2000, May 2002, <http://www.online.bg/vr/crl/corr_ind_05E.htm>, (last accessed 27 August 2002).

[76] D. A. Bilak, *Report of the Evaluation Mission*, p. 12.

[77] "Corruption 101," *Sofia Echo*, 31 August 2001.

materials from certain publishers only and the "purchase" of exams.[78] According to information provided to the Ministry of Education by the National Audit Office, corruption persists due to low penalties for offenders.

Although the Government has acknowledged the existence of corruption problems, education is not explicitly identified as a target area in the Government's anti-corruption strategy.

8.6 Licensing and regulation

Licences and permits remain a major barrier to doing business in Bulgaria. The system of licensing regimes is non-transparent; estimates of the number of regimes in existence vary between 450 and 526, and State authorities may create licensing regimes by ordinance and maintain them even when the law enabling the ordinance is cancelled.[79]

> [One of t]he main impediments to medium-term economic prospects include excessive administrative requirements for entrepreneurs... Recent business surveys indicate that licensing and administrative requirements impose a heavy burden on the private sector, particularly small businesses.[80]

The UNDP *Report on Anti-corruption Initiatives in Bulgaria* supports this opinion, noting that around 30 documents are required from different institutions in order to start a small business.[81] Corruption is believed to be widespread at various stages in this process, such as securing permission from safety inspectorates.[82]

The previous Government carried out a review of licensing regimes and eliminated or simplified 121 licensing regimes in 2000. In 2001, both the old and new Governments promised to carry out major reviews of licensing regimes. By early 2002, the Government appeared to have carried out the necessary analysis of existing regimes to do this.[83] The Government has set up an inter-ministerial working group on licences and registration regulation and, in May 2002, announcing that it will repeal 74 and simplify procedures for another 120 licences. As of June 2002, this commitment had not been fulfilled.

---

[78] *Sega*, daily, 19 April 2002, editorial.

[79] Coalition 2000, *Corruption Report 2001*, p. 48.

[80] CEEBICnet, *Bulgaria Country Commercial Guide FY 2002*, p. 7.

[81] D. A. Bilak, *Report of the Evaluation Mission*, p. 13.

[82] Interview with Alexenia Dimitrova, reporter, *24 chassa*, daily, Sofia, 8 February 2002.

[83] Interview with Ruslan Stefanov, Project Director, Economic Policy Institute, Sofia, 8 February 2002.

9. ROLE OF THE MEDIA

The legal environment for the media is generally favourable, although a few provisions may discourage freedom of speech. The media received an important boost with the passage of an Act on Access to Public Information in 2000. However, the effectiveness of the new Act may be counteracted by other laws and regulations that have been recently adopted. The independence of public broadcasting remains an important concern: political influence appears to rule out any investigative role, and has been singled out by the Council of Europe as a problem.

9.1 Press freedom

The Bulgarian Constitution guarantees freedom of expression and press freedom.[84] However, several legal provisions directly discourage investigative journalism. Specifically, the Criminal Code allows the imposition of a fine up to €16,000 for publicly insulting a public official,[85] and there have been several instances of fines being imposed on journalists.

Although under Bulgarian law journalists may have the right to preserve the confidentiality of sources, in some instances authorities have sought to force disclosure. For example, *24 chassa* (the second largest Bulgarian daily) published a story about alleged non-payment of rent to the Sofia municipality by an NGO run by the wife of the then Chairman of the Parliament (*24 chassa,* 24 May 2000). In a poll of journalists run by Coalition 2000 performed the following week, the story was voted as the top corruption story of the week. The wife of the Speaker filed suit against *24 chassa,* and the court ordered Coalition to reveal the names of the journalists who participated in the poll. Up to May 2002, the court had taken no further action.[86]

9.2 Access to information

Access to information has improved very significantly since the passage of a Freedom of Information Act in 2000, helped by the Access to Public Information Programme, a

---

[84] Bulgarian Constitution, Articles 40–41.

[85] Criminal Code, Article 148.

[86] *24 chassa,* daily, 24 May 2000.

strong civil society foundation.[87] Access, however, remains difficult in many cases, and could be compromised by other changes in laws and regulations that have been passed recently.

Under the 2000 Access to Public Information Act (APIA) all Government bodies, public law subjects and legal entities financed from the consolidated State budget are obliged to provide public information on request within 14 days. Public information is defined as any information related to public life and which enables citizens to make their own judgements about the activities of persons to whom the Act applies. The meaning of "information related to public life" has so far been interpreted relatively broadly in the small number of cases that have been heard by courts.

The Act lists a number of exceptions, including internal preparatory documents, State or other secrets protected by law and documents affecting third-party interests (such as the rights and reputations of third parties and commercial secrets) in particular. Access to public information may not be used "against national security, public order, health and morality." Although APIA gives the administration discretion only in deciding on internal preparatory documents, many officials still interpret all exemptions widely. For example, the Ministry of Finance refused journalists' requests to reveal whether certain Bulgarian MP's paid taxes on a real-estate deal on the grounds that the information is an "official secret."

The newly adopted (in April 2002) Protection of Classified Information Act (PCIA) further regulates the exemptions of the access to public information. PCIA gives definitions of State secret and official secrets:

- A State secret is classified information which is included on the List of Information Classified as State Secret (Schedule 1 to this Act – list of 64 categories) and unauthorised access to which would jeopardise or harm the interests of the Republic of Bulgaria relating to national security, defence, foreign policy or the protection of the order established by the Constitution.

- An official secret is classified information produced or stored by the State authorities or by the authorities of local self-government which does not constitute a State secret and unauthorised access to which would affect adversely the interests of the State or would prejudice another interest protected by law.

The only discretion that officials have is in deciding if certain information can be classified as an official secret, i.e. they can decide whether or not its disclosure would

---

[87] Access to Information Programme Foundation was the leading organisation in the public debate for the adoption of the Access to Public Information Act.
See <http://www.aip-bg.org/discuss.htm>, (last accessed 27 August 2002).

prejudice another interest protected by law. In that case the Protection of Classified Information Act (PCIA) provides for a "harm test."

Citizens may appeal against a refusal to provide information to the institution that refused to grant information, and thereafter to the courts. This appeal is also filed through the institution, which thereby gets another chance to grant access before forwarding the appeal. Up until April 2002, Access to Information Programme Foundation registered 716 refusals to provide information under the law. Most refusals were without grounds (173 cases), but reasons provided were on the grounds of an instruction from a superior (111), because the matter is not within the particular official's discretion (78 cases) or on the grounds that it is an administrative secret (51). The largest number of refusals came from territorial branches of central Government bodies (189), followed by local administration (101), central Government bodies (68), courts (67), and legal entities (57). As of April 2002, AIP was assisting in 27 appeals, only one of which involved a journalist. As of March 2002, an appeal by a journalist against the refusal of the Government to provide minutes of a Cabinet meeting was awaiting a hearing by the Supreme Administrative Court.

The Act on Access to Public Information has made an important difference to access to information in practice. Important cases in which access has been secured under the Act include requests for full copies of privatisation contracts and the release of an NAO report on disbursement of EU funds. According to journalists, the Act has had a big impact, and access to information is improving.[88] An important role in educating citizens about their rights under the Act and in assisting applications for information and appeals against refusals has been played by the Access to Information Programme (AIP).[89]

According to the AIP, it remains difficult to obtain information, especially from central Government institutions and when concerning financial and budget problems. The Ministry of Finance's Agency for Internal Financial Control defines its audits reports as secret, while the National Audit Office has failed to reply to requests for political party financial reports, MPs asset declarations and other audit reports.

Public officials are not encouraged to reveal public information. The duty to provide information is not mentioned in the Code of Ethics for civil servants adopted in 2000, which also introduces the concept of "internal information," a term vaguely defined as official discretion that might potentially be used to limit access to information.

---

[88] Interview with Alexenia Dimitrova, reporter, *24 chassa*, daily, Sofia, 8 February 2002.

[89] See, e.g., the website of Access to Information Programme Foundation, <http://www.aip-bg.org>, (last accessed 27 August 2002).

Moreover, the Code includes the duty of officials to be loyal to their institutions, which could also clash with freedom of information provisions.[90]

A new Act on Personal Data Protection that came into effect in January 2002 may also create problems through a provision that defines data created during the exercise of duties within a public institution as personal.[91] It is too early to tell whether this provision will be used to deny access to public information.

9.3 Broadcasting regulation

The Bulgarian National Television (Channel I) and Bulgarian National Radio are defined as "national public TV and radio operators."[92] Their property is State-owned[93] and their budget requirements are met by the State.[94]

Licensing and supervision

The regulatory framework for broadcasting appears to have been subject to mainly political considerations. Under the Act on National Radio and Television, the Council on Electronic Media appoints the Director-Generals of Bulgarian National Television and Bulgarian National Radio and approves the compositions of their boards. The Council consists of nine members: five appointed by Parliament and four by the President. There are no provisions regarding nomination of candidates, and they are essentially political appointees. Council members are elected for six years.[95]

In practice, the Council has reflected the balance of political power in the Parliament and Presidency rather than acting as an independent regulator. However, the appointment in early 2000 by the Council of an unpopular but politically acceptable Director-General of National Radio led to a strike by radio employees, the withdrawal of the appointment and the resignation of the Chairman of the Council.

In 2001, the Government prepared amendments to the Act, which would impose an obligation on the public media to guarantee the pluralism of views presented. However,

---

[90] Interview with Gergana Jouleva, Executive Director, Access to Information Programme, 8 February 2002.

[91] Act on Personal Data Protection, Article 2.

[92] Act on Radio and Television, in force from 24 November 1998, last amended 9 November 2001, Article 7.

[93] Act on Radio and Television, Article 42.2.

[94] Act on Radio and Television, Article 70.

[95] Act on Radio and Television, Article 29.

the proposal would not tackle the problem of political influence over the Council, and has been criticised on this basis by the Council of Europe, according to which,

> Specific regulations are need[ed] in order to prevent improper influence of the Government on the media regulation bodies which should be appointed in a democratic and transparent manner.[96]

9.4 Corruption in the media

Corruption in the media itself is a significant concern, ranging from the restriction of coverage of official State visits abroad to a limited number of journalists whose costs are paid by the State, to standard problems of hidden advertising. Journalists view a widespread media campaign against the contract between the Government and Crown Agents (see Section 8.2) as an example of "publication by order" and of the strength of the anti-reform customs lobby.[97]

9.5 Media and corruption

The media, and the press in particular, have played an important role in bringing the issue of corruption to the centre of public debate. Although investigative journalism is not well developed, the press has brought numerous cases of high-level corruption to the public's attention. For example, as a result of disclosure by *Sega* of unlawful property transactions between the municipality of Sofia and the family of Julia Berberyan, a former MP from the then ruling UDF coalition, Berberyan was obliged to settle due taxes and was under criminal investigation in early 2002 (see Section 4.5).

10. RECOMMENDATIONS

The following recommendations have been highlighted as particularly important to Bulgaria. For additional recommendations applicable to candidate States generally, please see Part 5 of the Overview report.

1. Redouble efforts to reform the Customs Administration, if necessary by outsourcing to a foreign administrator.

---

[96] Cited in: *Banker*, 6 October 2001.

[97] OSI Roundtable Discussion, Sofia, 7 February 2002.

2. Complete administrative reform to define responsibilities, decentralise functions to local government and provide effective redress to citizens against administrative decisions.

3. Implement measures to prevent uncontrolled lobbying, especially reform of party funding.

4. Pursue judicial reform based not only on anti-corruption measures but also on commitment to judicial independence and provision of adequate resources.

5. Introduce independent supervision of public procurement and effective sanctions for violation of procurement regulations.

Corruption and Anti-corruption Policy in the Czech Republic

Table of Contents

OPEN SOCIETY INSTITUTE 2002

Corruption and Anti-corruption Policy in the Czech Republic

EXECUTIVE SUMMARY

Available indicators of corruption, ranging from opinion surveys and expert indices to estimates by organs of criminal investigation, suggest that corruption is a serious problem in the Czech Republic, and, more worryingly, that it may be increasing. From the evidence collected for this report, the areas that appear to be seriously affected by corruption are the State administration, the legislative process, judicial system and public procurement. Political party finance appears to have receded as a corruption hot spot since the scandals of the late 1990's. Although the Czech Republic is not ranked as a country seriously affected by "State capture," corruption of the legislative process appears to be an increasingly serious problem, encouraged by uncontrolled lobbying, MPs' immunity and inadequate conflict of interest regulations. The dynamics of corruption have been shaped in very important ways by the nature of Czech privatisation and its consequences.

Since 1998, the Government has placed anti-corruption policy high on its agenda, and has formulated a comprehensive national anti-corruption strategy. A number of the tasks in the strategy have been fulfilled, in particular, changes in criminal law and procedure, increased specialisation of anti-corruption enforcement bodies and changes to political party funding regulation. However, a number of the more important measures have not been fulfilled, such as changes to provisions on conflict of interest or parliamentary immunity, and the strategy has suffered from a lack of publicity. Moreover, the Government increasingly sets a bad example itself, particularly in public procurement. Until the June 2002 elections, the balance of political power favoured an unspoken agreement between the two main political parties to maintain silence on suspected corruption in each other's ranks, and there has been a lack of political consensus to create effective anti-corruption policy.

The EU accession process has been of major importance in influencing Czech anti-corruption policy since 1997. The Commission has identified corruption as one of the country's main institutional problems, and has consistently urged improvements in anti-corruption policy. These factors have contributed both to the creation of sufficient will to produce a national anti-corruption strategy and to reforms of institutions investigating and prosecuting corruption, for which the Commission has provided significant direct assistance.

Czech bribery legislation is largely compliant with the requirements of international conventions, with the exception of the Council of Europe Civil Law Convention on Corruption. Amendments in preparation as of June 2002 were expected to include criminalisation of bribery in the private sector. A general Act on Conflict of Interest and Asset and Income Declarations exists, but applies only to a narrow range of functionaries, contains no sanctions for violation and is often not observed. The framework for State financial control and audit remains inadequate, with legislation to establish an integrated system only passed in July 2001. However, the Supreme Audit Office has played an important role in uncovering malpractice, while its findings have been implemented with increasing efficiency. The main anti-corruption agency in place is the Department for Revealing Corruption and Serious Economic Criminality, which has played an important role in a number of investigations, although its degree of independence is a possible source of concern. Specialised police, prosecution and court departments have been created and appear to have improved the quality of investigation significantly. The Office of the Ombudsman was established in 2000, but has not dealt with any corruption cases.

There is very little direct evidence of corruption in the Czech public administration, and there are almost no convictions or employees of the State administration for bribery. There have been a number of scandals concerning ministers, but almost no criminal cases and no convictions. To date, the legal framework for public administration has been largely inadequate, failing to regulate conflict of interest or discourage patronage and nepotism. However, a new Civil Service Act will improve the legal framework significantly in both these areas. Procedures for appealing against administrative decisions do not appear to provide citizens with effective redress. A Code of Ethics came into effect in 2001, but is vague and largely repeats provisions already stated elsewhere.

Until recently, a number of significant categories of public expenditure were excluded from the State budget, although recent reforms have ended this situation. Parliament has not functioned as an effective anti-corruption mechanism, and is itself highly vulnerable to corruption, especially through unregulated lobbying. Immunity provisions effectively protect deputies from prosecution for corruption, and Parliament recently rejected proposed reforms in this area.

The Czech judiciary has undergone major reforms since 1999, including new Acts on Courts and Judges and far-reaching changes in court and criminal procedures. There is very little direct evidence of corruption of judges; however, there is a widespread belief that corruption is a serious problem in commercial proceedings and in business registration.

Corruption in political party financing has been one of the most prominent issues in Czech politics, with a number of important scandals in the late 1990's – one of which was the immediate reason for the collapse of the Klaus Government in 1997. Since then, funding rules have been changed to provide parties with sufficient State funding, and evidence of covert funding or corruption is now minimal.

Corruption of public procurement appears to be a serious problem. Despite relatively advanced legislation, supervision and monitoring of procurement is ineffective. Moreover, the Government has increasingly set a bad example, allocating a number of major contracts without tenders.

There are significant problems of corruption in a number of Czech public services, in particular the healthcare system. Anti-corruption mechanisms in the police and customs administration have improved considerably in recent years.

Freedom of speech is guaranteed, although there are isolated cases of the State using other legal provisions to attempt to deter journalists, including a major scandal that broke in July 2002. A Freedom of Information Act came into effect in 2000, although its impact on access to information in practice may have been limited. Broadcasting regulation has suffered from problems of political interference in the activities of public media, which led to the adoption of an improved legal framework in 2001. Licensing policy for private broadcasters has been subject to major problems, and the activities of the Broadcasting Council have resulted in a foreign investor winning an arbitration case against the Czech State. The Czech media has been very active in uncovering corruption, and initiated the downfall of the Government in 1997.

1 INTRODUCTION

1.1 The data and perceptions

According to available indicators of corruption, ranging from opinion surveys and expert indices to estimates by organs of criminal investigation, corruption is a serious problem in the Czech Republic. Perhaps more worrying, the same indicators suggest that, if anything, corruption may be increasing.

Table 1 below shows the number of convictions under the main anti-corruption paragraphs between 1993 and 2000.

Table 1: Numbers of convictions under selected paragraphs of the Criminal Code, 1993–2000

Paragraph	1993	1994	1995	1996	1997	1998	1999	2000	2001
160: Accepting a bribe	6	18	23	24	34	20	19	49	28
161: Bribery	47	68	88	111	98	88	88	68	83
162: Indirect bribery	0	3	1	2	1	1	3	1	3
158: Abuse of power by a public official	18	86	78	79	69	100	85	100	99

Source: Ministry of Justice of the Czech Republic.

While the number of prosecutions remains stable, the Service for Revealing Corruption and Serious Economic Criminality (a special police unit, see Section 2.5), believes that the incidence of corruption has been growing, both in quantitative terms and, even more worryingly, in terms of the seriousness of cases, especially with regard to corruption among public officials.[1]

International survey evidence

The Czech Republic's performance in the Transparency International Corruption Perception Index has worsened in recent years, with scores of 4.8 in 1998 (37th place), 4.6 in 1999 (39th place), 4.3 in 2000 (42nd place out of 90 countries) and 3.9 in 2001 (47th place) out of 91 countries.

The EBRD/World Bank *1999 Business Environment and Enterprise Performance Survey* found that Czech companies report paying on average around 2.5 percent of annual

---

[1] Czech Ministry of Interior, *Zpráva o korupci v ČR a o plnění harmonogramu opatření Vládního programu boje proti korupci* [Report on Corruption in the CR and on the Following of the Schedule of the Government's Programme of Fight against Corruption], Ministry of Interior, January 2001, p. 5. (approved by Czech Government Resolution no. 144, 14 February 2001).

revenue on administrative corruption (bribes to influence the implementation of existing rules), compared to 1.6–1.7 percent in Poland and Hungary.

The same survey found that 11 percent of Czech firms reported they are affected by "State capture," the illicit influencing of formation of laws, regulations, decrees and other policies. The figures for Poland and Hungary were about 12 percent and six percent respectively.

Domestic surveys

The Institute for Public Opinion Research has consistently found that corruption and economic criminality is regarded as a very urgent problem by a higher percentage of respondents (80 percent in October 2000) than any other problem, although according to a survey carried out by GfK-Praha[2] in 1999, only one-fifth of respondents would report an act of corruption to the police. According to the same survey, 26 percent of respondents regarded corruption as a "necessary part of life." Both this and other surveys[3] have found that around 20 percent of citizens admit to giving bribes occasionally, although four-fifths of this group reported giving only small gratuities. One quarter of respondents said State officials had requested a bribe from them in the past three years.

According to the most recent public opinion research, carried out by SC&C in April 2002, 49 percent of respondents believed that corruption had increased in the previous four years.[4]

1.2 Main loci of corruption

The areas most affected by corruption appear to be the State administration, legislative process, judicial system and public procurement. Political party finance was the subject of major scandals in the second half of the 1990's, and since appears to have receded as a corruption hot spot with the reform of funding rules. Corruption of the legislative process appears to be an increasingly serious problem, encouraged by uncontrolled lobbying, MPs' immunity and inadequate conflict of interest regulations.

The main dynamics of corruption, (particularly the way in which corruption has impacted the political sphere), have been strongly conditioned by the nature of

---

[2] GfK-Praha, *Korupční klima v České republice v roce 1999* [Corruption Climate in the Czech Republic in 1999], Transparency International Czech Republic, September 1999.

[3] E.g., Sofres-Factum, *Názory české veřejnosti na korupci* [Opinion of the Czech Public on Corruption], September 1998.

[4] *Lidové noviny* daily, 25 April 2002.

economic transformation. In particular, the process of privatisation through vouchers and/or sales to Czech entities without sufficient capital created an economy dominated by investment funds and a State-controlled banking system that provided loans on non-market criteria. The result in both cases was widespread asset stripping, both of funds and privatised companies, with the tacit or active acquiescence of State officials. In this whole process corruption was prevalent – during privatisation decisions, the allocation of bank loans and, probably, the creation of legislation to regulate investment funds.[5]

The consequence of this situation for the Government that came to power in 1998 was the need to renationalise a number of large companies, together with a costly process of cleaning up the banking sector. The institutions in charge of administering bad assets and restructuring and selling companies – in particular the Czech Consolidation Agency – also constitute a new locus of corruption, in which the Agency has sold a number of debts without publishing the list of debts, for a tiny percentage of nominal value, and to a consultancy firm that then profited by selling the debts for a higher price (but still a fraction of nominal value) effectively to the original debtors themselves. In this way the original debtors can get rid of their own debt, while the State loses to the extent that it sells debt for a lower than market price.[6] In addition, the bankruptcy process that has occurred in a number of companies as a result of the restructuring process has evidently been prone to corruption.

GfK also carried out a general survey of perceptions of corruption among Czech citizens in 1999 and 2000 (mentioned above), which also asked citizens in which area they believed corruption to be most widespread. The results are shown in Table 2 below, and show that public administration, the police, courts, and healthcare are regarded as most affected by corruption.

---

[5] See, e.g., Q. Reed, "Corruption in Czech Privatisation: Dangers and Policy Implications of 'Neoliberal' Privatisation," paper to Princeton University-Central European University Joint Conference on Corruption, 30 October–6 November 1999.

[6] T. Spurný, "Loupež století u konce," [The Robbery of the Century Has Ended] *Respekt*, weekly, 3 June 2002.

Table 2: Percentage of respondents believing corruption to be "most widespread" in selected areas, 1998–1999

Area	1998	1999
Public administration	31	23
Police	9	24
Judiciary	15	16
Healthcare	15	12
Services	9	4
Army	0	4
Education	2	2
Hotel and restaurant trade	2	1
Don't know	15	16

Source: GfK-Praha.

A survey by the Centre for Public Opinion Research carried out in April 2001 found that respondents ranked political parties as the most corrupt institutions in the Czech Republic (with an average score of 4.02 on a scale where five is most corrupt), followed by central State administration (3.7), banks (3.7) and the police (3.6). According to the newest survey by SC&C mentioned earlier, 47 percent of respondents believed corruption is most widespread in the State administration, followed by the police (14 percent), healthcare (nine percent), national politics (four percent) and local politics (three percent).[7]

The evidence and testimony collected for this report tends to confirm the worrying perceptions of corruption in the judiciary, particularly at the commercial courts. In addition, other areas seriously affected by corruption are public contracts and the legislative process in Parliament. Party finance appears to have ceased to be a hot spot of corruption as a result of changes in regulations that have made State subsidies the main source of funds.

1.3 Government anti-corruption policy

Anti-corruption policy has become, at least formally, one of the main priorities of Government policy since 1998. Since then, the Government formulated a comprehensive national anti-corruption strategy, a number of components of which have been fulfilled, for example changes in criminal law and procedure, increased

---

[7] *Lidové noviny*, daily, 25 April 2002.

specialisation of anti-corruption enforcement bodies, and changes to political party funding regulation. However, a number of the more important measures have not been fulfilled, such as changes to provisions on conflict of interest or parliamentary immunity, and the strategy has suffered from a lack of publicity. Moreover, the Government increasingly sets a bad example itself, particularly in public procurement. Until the June 2002 elections, the balance of political power favoured an unspoken agreement between the two main political parties to maintain silence on suspected corruption in each other's ranks, and there has been a lack of political consensus to create effective anti-corruption policy.

The first move towards active anti-corruption policy was a Government decision in October 1997 to develop a strategy of "offensive methods" for fighting corruption in the civil service.[8] This initiative provided the basis for what subsequently grew into the National Fight Against Corruption (see below).

"Clean Hands"

The Social Democratic Party won the 1998 elections on a promise to implement a "Clean Hands" anti-corruption campaign. The new Government established an inter-ministerial Committee for the Protection of the Economic Interests of the Czech Republic in September 1998 to coordinate anti-corruption policy, supported by a Coordinative and Analytical Commission headed by a special Minister without Portfolio. The Commission was informed directly by the inspection bodies of individual ministries, re-examined old investigation files, and also took initiatives from the public.

Although the official objective of the campaign was to "create an environment acceptable for both foreign and domestic investors and recover the credibility of the State in the eyes of its own citizens,"[9] it suffered from suspicions that it was vulnerable to politically motivated decisions, and ended in May 2000. Until then it submitted 107 initiatives for investigation to bureaus of investigation. At the end of 2000, 48 cases were being investigated, with specific bribery charges filed in 17 cases.[10]

---

[8] Czech Government Resolution no. 673, 29 October 1997.

[9] *Analysis of Activities Conducted by the Committee for the Protection of the Czech Republic's Economic Interests and Its Coordination and Analytical Group,* Report of Minister without Portfolio Jaroslav Bašta, approved by the Government on 15 March 2000.

[10] Czech Ministry of Interior, *Zpráva o korupci v ČR,* p. 7.

The Government Programme for the Fight against Corruption

In February 1999, the Czech Government took a key step in anti-corruption policy by approving the Government Programme for the Fight against Corruption,[11] a more-or-less comprehensive strategy embracing not only measures to make prosecution more effective, but also a wider set of measures to prevent corruption and raise public awareness. However, the Government made almost no effort to publicise the Programme. The contents of the Programme are summarised in Table 3.

Table 3: Selected measures in the Government Programme for the Fight against Corruption

Type of measure	Description	Deadline for implementation	Implementation as of January 2001
A. Legislative measures	1. Define police powers to combat corruption, provide institutional support for police.	30.6.1999	No
	2. Define independence of tax authorities, improve power to check accuracy of tax statements, authorise inspectors to acquire a statement on origin of income, introduce clear duty to notify and cooperate with police of suspected criminal acts, increase remuneration for "vulnerable" officials.	30.6.2000	No
	3. Allow legal entities acting in the interests of competitors and consumers to file suit against corrupt and unfair competition, allow prosecution of corruption and unfair competition that has an impact abroad.	31.12.1999	Partially
	4. Arrange accession to the OECD anti-bribery Convention.	31.12.1999	Partially
	5. Define failure to notify and act to prevent corruption as criminal acts, lengthen statute of limitations for bribery, and consider defining bribery in unfair competition as a criminal act.	31.12.1999	No/partially
	6. Reform criminal code to speed up and simplify pre-court proceedings, consider introduction of offensive anti-corruption methods (e.g. agent provocateur).	31.12.1999	No/partially
	7. Propose law on protection of witnesses and court experts.	31.12.1999	Partially
	8. Support an Act on Freedom of Information.	31.12.1999	Yes
	9. Reform law to make political party financing more transparent: increase sanctions for	31.12.1999	Yes

---

[11] *Vládní program boje proti korupci*, Czech Government Resolution no. 125, 17 February 1999.

	violation of law, restrict contributions by foreign subjects, State maximum annual membership contribution.		
	10. Support amendment to Czech Constitution to restrict immunity of MPs and Senators.	31.12.1999	No
	11. Amend conflict of interest law to widen circle of persons regulated, provide for checking of asset declarations, and introduce real sanctions for violation of law.	30.9.2000	No
	12. Consider widening powers of State prosecutors to supervise civil court and administrative proceedings, ensure that specialised teams of prosecutors at regional level have responsibility for supervising investigation of serious economic criminality and corruption and if necessary carrying out such investigations themselves.	30.6.1999	No (except special teams)/partially
	13. Reform of administrative proceedings and administrative disciplinary proceedings in such a way as to maximise transparency, State deadlines where possible, consider allowing faster proceedings for higher payments, prepare a register of disciplinary proceedings.	31.12.1999	No/partially
	14. Amend Act on State Audit to define State control system, its elements and responsibilities, define central institution responsible for unified audit system, increase sanctions for not acting on the basis of audit conclusions.	28.2.2000	Yes/partially
B. Organisational measures	1. Individual ministries to indicate sources and forms of corruption in their arena of responsibility, analyse and propose anti-corruption mechanisms. Provide conditions for citizens to be informed about rights and duties in dealing with the administration. Propose, implement and assess technical anti-corruption measures.	on-going/ annually	Yes (?)
	2. Draft agreements between the police and auditing and control (especially tax) institutions to improve co-operation.	30.9.1999	Yes
	3. Provide a report on every revealed or publicly presented case of corruption after completion of criminal proceedings.	on-going	No (problematic legally)
	4. Establish a contact and consultation centre for victims of corruption.	31.12.1999	No
	5. Set aside within individual State institutions an office to which the public can file complaints and initiatives, enable direct communication with employees of the office.	As soon as possible	Yes (?)

	6. Carry out regular internal audits, hold directors responsible for violation of regulations.	on-going, control annually	Yes (?)
	7. Support all forms of corruption research.	on-going	Partially (police)
	8. Support activities of NGOs that are active in the fight against corruption; agree forms, methods and scope of co-operation.	on-going, control annually 30.6	Yes
	9. Audited institutions to inform the Government within 60 days of publication of Supreme Audit Office audit reports on corrective measures taken, corrective measures to be assessed within 6 months.	on-going	Yes
C. Other	Prepare a national training project on corruption prevention for civil servants.	30.6.1999	Partially (?)
	Support anti-corruption education in schools, produce civilian anti-corruption handbook.	30.6.1999	Yes (?)

Notes: Entries in the column on implementation are based on the *Report on Corruption and Fulfilment of Measures in the Government Programme for the Fight against Corruption*, issued in January 2001. Fulfilment of legislative measures is judged not only according to whether a proposal was submitted but whether it also became law. "No" indicates that a proposal either had not been submitted or had been rejected by Parliament; "Partially" indicates that a proposal was going through the legislative process at the time of evaluation. Question marks indicate either that not enough information is provided by the Report to evaluate whether a measure had been fulfilled, or that there are reasons for doubting fulfilment.

Up to early 2002, the Programme had only been fulfilled partially. Despite early setbacks, the Government succeeded in pushing through the planned laws for its justice reform programme, including fundamental changes to criminal procedure that were included in the anti-corruption strategy (see Section 5.1) and changes to political party funding regulation (see Section 6.1). However, a number of very important commitments, such as changes to parliamentary immunities and conflict of interest regulations, had been rejected.

More importantly, the Programme has suffered from a lack of cross-party consensus on anti-corruption policy and the failure of the Government to illustrate a commitment to integrity. Several ministers have been the subject of scandals, and the resignation in early 2001 of the Minister of Finance – who had been a force for transparency in the Government – was a warning sign. In addition, the Government's increasing use of its power to allocate major contracts without public tenders (see Section 7.2) indicates scant respect for principles of transparency. The January 2001 assessment approved by the Government stated explicitly that,

> One of the main reasons why anti-corruption policy appears unsuccessful is that the implementation of the programme by the State administration has not been accompanied by adequate changes in the political environment... whose leaders have not created a minimal common anti-corruption programme of an

integrating nature. The formulation of such a programme should form the basis of anti-corruption activities… in the immediate future, for the success of the fight against corruption is threatened in the absence of clearly declared political support.[12]

Further, in order to stay in office, the minority Social Democratic (ČSSD) Government relied on an "Opposition Agreement" with the main opposition party, the Civic Democratic Party (ODS) of former Prime Minister Václav Klaus. Under the Agreement, the ODS agreed not to initiate or participate in a vote of no confidence, in return for parliamentary positions and policy influence. An important consequence of the agreement was the near silence of the two parties on corruption in each other's ranks. According to an opinion survey carried out by GfK in 1999, 62 percent of respondents believed that the Government did not have a real interest in fighting corruption.

Although a February 2001 Government Resolution charged the ministers of Interior and Justice with initiating a public discussion with representatives of political parties and civil society in order to formulate a minimal common anti-corruption programme, there is no evidence that the resolution was implemented and the Government made no effort to publicise it.[13] The only specific result of the new move was the establishment in March 2001 of a Senate Subcommittee for Corruption, which has been almost entirely inactive.

After the June 2002 elections, a more standard coalition Government has emerged, one of whose main programme components is the fight against corruption. As of July 2002, the details of this had not yet been published.

1.4 The impact of the EU Accession Process

The EU accession process has had a very important influence on Czech anti-corruption policy. In 1997, the Commission identified corruption as one of the country's main institutional problems, and has consistently urged improvements in anti-corruption policy. This gave added momentum to the effort to formulate a national anti-corruption strategy. The Commission has provided significant direct assistance for reforms of institutions investigating and prosecuting corruption.

One of the most important motors of anti-corruption policy in the Czech Republic since 1997 has been pressure from the European Union. In its *1997 Opinion on the*

---

[12] Czech Ministry of Interior, *Zpráva o korupci v ČR*, p. 43.

[13] Information about the proposed Anti-corruption Agreement was only discovered in the course of conducting research for this report.

Czech Application for Membership, the Commission listed the impact of institutional corruption as one of three "main institutional problems,"[14] and noted that corruption may be increasing.[15] The *1998 Regular Report* criticised the Government for not mentioning corruption in its National Programme for the Adoption of the *Acquis*,[16] and the *1999 Regular Report*, while acknowledging that fighting corruption was a priority of the Government, noted that, "An effective policy has not yet been developed,"[17] and concluded that although the Czech Republic fulfils the Copenhagen political criteria, further efforts should be made in three main areas, one of which was an effective policy to combat economic crime and corruption.[18]

The *2000 Regular Report* judged that "little progress can be reported" in the fight against fraud and corruption,[19] and that Czech law is not yet aligned with the *acquis* on criminalisation of corruption in the private sector. Under its global assessment of progress in Justice and Home Affairs the Commission concludes that, "[T]wo years after the launch of the 'Clean Hands' campaign the results obtained in the fight against organised crime, corruption and economic crime remain inadequate. Greater enforcement capacity is required and there is still a lack of qualified staff and inter-institutional cooperation in the area… insufficient progress has been made in addressing this priority."[20]

The *1999 Accession Partnership* between the EU and Czech Republic includes a number of policies of direct or indirect relevance to corruption that are listed as short-term priorities (for completion or substantial implementation by the end of 2000): implementation of policy on organised crime and corruption and ratification of the OECD Bribery Convention and the Council of Europe Criminal Law Convention; strengthening capacities to deal with money laundering, adoption and implementation of a programme for reform of the State administration, completion and implementation of the legislative framework for internal and external financial control; and beginning implementation of a programme to reform the judiciary.

Although it noted "some important steps," the *2001 Regular Report* remained of the opinion that,

---

[14] Commission of the European Union, *Agenda 2000 – Commission Opinion on the Czech Republic's Application for Membership of the European Union*, DOC/97/17, July 1997, p. 96.

[15] Commission, *Agenda 2000*, p. 108.

[16] Commission, *1998 Regular Report from the Commission on the Czech Republic's Progress towards Accession*, p. 45.

[17] Commission, *1999 Regular Report*, p. 13.

[18] Commission, *1999 Regular Report*, p. 76.

[19] Commission, *2000 Regular Report*, p. 88.

[20] Commission, *2000 Regular Report*, p. 106.

> [C]orruption and economic crime (fraud, money laundering, institutional theft and the phenomenon of "tunnelling" or asset stripping) remain a serious cause for concern… surveys of public opinion show a consistent increase in the perception of corruption and economic crime. Concern is greatest as regards the State administration, the police and intelligence services, healthcare, banking and the political sphere.[21]

In terms of anti-corruption policy, many of the measures implemented by the Czech Government have been strongly influenced by EU pressure. For example, Czech Ministry of Justice officials believe the current Government's justice reform programme would never have emerged at all without pressure from Brussels, and that without such assistance they would never have obtained sufficient funding in these areas.[22] The EU has provided crucial assistance for judicial reform, including the following PHARE assistance programmes:

- 1998–1999: €1.2m to finance investment in computers for courts.

- 2000: €300,000 on a twinning project to train State prosecutors.

- 2000: €800,000 on a twinning project (with France) to gain knowledge on how to establish a Judicial Academy; €1.2m on investment in equipment for the academy.

- 2001: €6m approved to help build an information system connecting courts and prosecutors.

In 1998, experts participating in the OCTOPUS project, a common project of the European Union and Council of Europe to exchange information with transition countries on methods to fight organised crime, recommended concentrating forces in the fight against corruption and building cooperation between various investigation units.

After the Government's "Clean Hands" policy foundered largely on lack of cooperation between different institutions (see above), this philosophy became an important motor of reform. In April 2000, an order of the Attorney-General established special teams of prosecutors at the higher prosecution offices in Prague and Olomouc to supervise investigations of serious financial criminality. Following Government resolutions passed in the summer of 2000, a special Department for the Investigation of Corruption and Serious Economic Criminality was formed with a supporting analytical team, divided between the higher and Supreme Offices of Investigation in Prague, Brno and Ostrava. The job of the investigation team is to investigate cases submitted to it by the police Department for Revealing Corruption and Serious Economic Criminality (see Section 2.5).

---

[21] Commission, *2001 Regular Report*, p. 20.

[22] Interview with Josef Baxa, Deputy Minister of Justice, Prague, 25 April 2001.

According to officers at the Department and to Ministry of Interior officials,[23] cooperation with ÚOK, the Ministry of Finance Financial Analytical Unit, the Attorney General's Office and the tax authorities has already yielded results. The team took over 45 cases left over from the "Clean Hands" effort (see above). Fifteen investigations had been completed by mid-May 2001, in which €410m in damages were identified. The Department was prosecuting 75 people and had recovered around €11.7m. Moreover, officials said that improved cooperation with the courts had yielded faster proceedings even in the absence of justice reform.

The Czech Republic became a member of GRECO in February 2002, and an evaluation visit was expected to be scheduled at some time in 2002.

2. INSTITUTIONS AND LEGISLATION

Czech bribery legislation is largely compliant with the requirements of international conventions. A general law on conflict of interest and asset and income declarations exists, but its content and implementation are both inadequate. The framework for State financial control and audit remains inadequate, although recent legislation has established the basis for an integrated system, and the findings of the Supreme Audit Office have been used with increasing efficiency. The main Czech anti-corruption agency – the Department for Revealing Corruption and Serious Economic Criminality – has played an important role in a number of investigations, although its independence from political interference is not secure. Since 1999 specialised police, prosecution and court departments have been created and appear to have improved the quality of investigation significantly. The Office of the Ombudsman was established in 2000, but has not dealt with any corruption cases.

2.1 Anti-corruption legislation

The Criminal Code criminalises the following acts if committed by any citizen:

- acceptance of a bribe (paragraph 160);
- active bribery (paragraph 161);

---

[23] Interviews with Milan Šiška, Chief of the Department for the Investigation of Corruption and Serious Economic Criminality; Michal Mazel, Head of the Security Policy Department, Ministry of Interior.

- indirect bribery: requesting/accepting or offering a bribe as a reward for influencing a public official.

Bribery provisions apply to influences on any actions connected with matters that are of public interest. The above acts are punishable by two to eight years' imprisonment, and the punishments were increased in 1999. Sentences for bribery are higher for public officials than other citizens; the eight-year maximum sentence may be imposed on public officials who accept bribes with the intention of obtaining considerable benefits for themselves or another person.

Under an effective repentance provision (paragraph 163), criminal liability is cancelled if the perpetrator offers or promises a bribe only because it was demanded, and informs the police voluntarily and without delay.

Until 1999, the Criminal Code did not define the concept of a bribe, and it was often difficult to distinguish a bribe from a commission. Amendments to the Criminal Code passed in 1999[24] defined a bribe as "an unauthorised benefit consisting in direct material enrichment or other advantage which is obtained by the bribed person or another person with his/her agreement, and to which s/he has no right" – thereby widening the scope of bribery provisions beyond public officials alone. The same amendments also increased penalties for bribery and extended the bribery provisions to apply to foreign public officials. Although existing legislation allows prosecution of private sector bribery where this can be shown to be of clear damage to matters of general public interest, the Czech Criminal Code does not yet explicitly criminalise bribery in the private sector; however, this is expected to be included in amendments under preparation.

Other relevant paragraphs in the Criminal Code are Abuse of Information in Commercial Activity (paragraph 128),[25] Machinations in Public Tenders and Public Auctions (paragraphs 128a-c) (giving to one competitor or participant in a public tender or auction priority or more advantageous conditions at the expense of other competitors, with the intention of furnishing benefit to oneself or another), and in particular, Abuse of Power by a Public Official (paragraph 158). The latter paragraph is the most important apart from normal bribery provisions and is punishable by between six months and three years' imprisonment or a prohibition of certain activities, and by

---

[24] Act no. 69/1999.

[25] This paragraph prohibits the use by an individual of "hitherto non-publicly available information... gained by reason of his employment, profession, position or function, and the publication of which would considerably influence decision-making in a commercial relation, to deliberately furnish disadvantage to himself or another...," or to use such information to instigate a contract between business entities that damages one or more of them. The penalty for violation ranges from a fine to 12 years' imprisonment.

three to ten years' imprisonment if the perpetrator secures major benefit or it causes especially serious consequences.[26]

The Czech Republic has not yet ratified the Council of Europe Civil Law Convention on Corruption.

2.2 Conflict of interest and asset declaration

Both conflict of interest and the duty to declare interests and assets are regulated by the 1992 Act on Several Measures Connected with Protection of the Public Interest and Incompatibility of Functions (hereinafter Conflict of Interest Act).[27] The Act applies to "public functionaries:" MPs, Senators, members of the Government and heads of central administrative bodies. The law defines conflict of interest somewhat curiously as:

> behaviour or neglect by a public functionary which threatens trust in his or her objectivity, or where a public functionary abuses his or her position to gain unauthorised benefit for self or another individual or legal entity.

This definition appears to confuse conflict of interest as such with its potential consequences.

The most important provisions of the Act are as follows:

- Public functionaries may not, *inter alia,* deal with the State in a commercial capacity for themselves or other entities.

- Members of the Government and heads of central administrative organs may not carry out any business activities, be members of the statutory organs of business entities (unless explicitly authorised by another law) or earn money from employment or in a service capacity apart from their official function.

- Where public functionaries participate in the proceedings of a State or constitutional organ, they must declare their relationship or the relationship of their partner or husband/wife, children, brothers and sister to the matter if the outcome of the proceedings could lead to personal benefit for any of these persons.

---

[26] Article 89, paragraph 9, of the Criminal Code defines a public official as "[A]n elected functionary or other responsible employee of an organ of State administration and self-administration, of a court or other State organ, or a member of the Armed Forces or armed unit, as far as s/he shares in the fulfilment of the tasks of society and at the same time uses authority which was entrusted to him in the framework of responsibility for the fulfilment of these tasks. The criminal responsibility and protection of a public official require that the criminal act was committed in connection with his authority and responsibility."

[27] Act no. 238/1992, as amended by Acts nos. 287/1995 and 228/1997.

- MPs, Senators, ministers and heads of central administrative bodies must declare, *inter alia,* if they or their husbands/wives carry on any business activities apart from administration of their own property, if they are members of the statutory organs of any business entity or are employed in any capacity apart from their official function.

All public functionaries must submit a declaration of:

- any income and other material benefits received during the calendar year by the end of June of the following year;

- any immovable property that they or their wife/husband acquired in the previous year.

MPs submit declarations to the Chairman of the Senate and Senators and ministers to the Chairman of the Chamber of Deputies; the declaration is held by the Mandate and Immunity Committee of the respective chamber. Any citizen may examine the declarations on written request.

On the initiative of at least ten MPs or five senators, the relevant Mandate and Immunity Committee checks the authenticity of the functionary's income and asset declaration. If a three-fifths majority of the Committee so decides, the Committee issues a statement to the effect that the functionary violated his or her duty and why. The statement is read publicly by the chairman of the same chamber as the Committee.

The law contains no other sanctions for violation of the law, relying on the effects of publicity, and in practice has proved to be entirely ineffective. No requests have ever been filed to either parliamentary chamber to check the declarations submitted by public functionaries.[28] A summary of declarations sent to the Senate by MPs, members of the Government and heads of central administrative organs is shown in Table 4. Given that some form of declaration is compulsory for all these categories of functionary, and that the Chamber of Deputies alone has 200 MPs, compliance with even formal requirements of the law is very poor.

---

[28] Answers from Chamber of Deputies, April 2001, and Senate, July 2001.

Table 4: Declarations submitted to the Senate by MPs, ministers and heads of central administrative bodies, 1997–2000

| Year | Total number of declarations filed | Types of declaration | | | |
		Negative*	Declaration of activities	Declaration of income and gifts	Declarations of assets
1997	105	28	50	32	5
1998	120	34	32	67	14
1999	120	37	36	61	20
2000	135	45	35	65	26

Note: "Negative" means that the functionary submitted a blank form or a letter declaring that s/he had nothing to declare

Source: Mandate and Immunity Committee, Senate of the Czech Republic.

That said, the media has used the law to put pressure on officials. Minister of Regional Development in the ČSSD Government Petr Lachnit came under considerable media pressure for not ceasing his business activities after joining the Government in March 2000 and subsequently took actions to comply with the law.[29]

A limited amendment to the Act forbidding MPs and Senators from receiving payments as members of the statutory organs of companies where the State owns a stake was passed in 2001. However, the Act's greatest problem is the fact that it does not explicitly forbid MPs and Senators from participating in any business activities.

2.3 Control and audit

Supreme Audit Office

Auditing of public expenditure is carried out by the Supreme Audit Office (hereinafter SAO), which was established in 1993. The President and Vice-President are proposed by the President of the Republic and confirmed by Parliament for a nine-year term, while the other 13 members are elected for life and by the opposite process. Members may only be removed by Parliament on grounds of criminal conviction, gross misconduct or following disciplinary proceedings.

Disciplinary proceedings are carried out against an individual member on the proposal of a Senator or MP by a disciplinary senate composed of the SAO President and two

---

[29] J. Kubík and S. Slonková, "Ministr Lachnit stále podniká" [Minister Lachnit is still in business], *Mladá fronta Dnes*, 29 July 2000.

Supreme Court judges. Disciplinary proceedings appear to be the only potential threat to the SAO's independence (see Section 4.5).

The SAO[30] is responsible for monitoring all the main State budget accounts, submitting a report on the Government's quarterly budget report and an opinion on the final budgetary statement. The SAO selects subjects to audit on the basis of proposals from the Parliament, Government or on the basis of its own previous findings. However, neither Parliament nor Government may mandate audits, and in practice the Office chooses the vast majority of its audits. According to the International Monetary Fund, the standard of auditing is high.[31] Reports are published in a quarterly bulletin and are also available on the Internet.

Until 1998, Governments "took note of" SAO audit findings without imposing any sanctions or measures. However, since 1998, the Government has improved follow-up on audits: it produces a resolution on the basis of every audit report, requires specific corrective measures and checks fulfilment after six months. According to SAO officials, cooperation with the Government has improved greatly. Officials would like to see the Government apply the most effective method of sanctioning violations – the withdrawal of State subsidies from the organisation in question.

In 2000, an SAO auditor was prosecuted for accepting a €100,000 bribe to alter an audit report. Court proceedings had not been completed in March 2002. The proceedings were actively supported by the SAO leadership.

Internal control

A major problem for the Czech State administration remains its inadequate system of internal control. The biggest problem faced by the SAO in its audits of State bodies is the lack of effective internal control mechanisms. As the *1999 Regular Report* notes, internal control departments lack functional independence and unified instructions and methodology from the Ministry of Finance.[32] The passage of a legislative framework in this area was a priority of the *1999 Accession Partnership*,[33] and in July 2001 Parliament

---

[30] The following information on the SAO audit of the State budget was obtained from Václav Peřich, Vice-President of the SAO.

[31] IMF, *Report on the Observance of Standards,* Chapter IV.

[32] Commission, *1999 Regular Report,* p. 57.

[33] Commission, *2000 Regular Report,* p. 97.

passed an Act on Financial Control in the Public Administration. The law is one of the conditions for EU entry and for the allocation of structural funds.[34]

2.4 Anti-corruption agencies

In addition to the specialised anti-corruption bodies mentioned in Section 1.4, the following units deal directly or indirectly with corruption.

The Department for Revealing Corruption and Serious Economic Criminality (ÚOK)

This Department was established in 1991 (its name has changed twice), and is responsible for carrying out preliminary investigation and surveillance activities to furnish other investigation bodies with information. It employs about 130 people in the whole of the Czech Republic and has the same powers as the criminal police. Although ÚOK played an important role in the conviction of the head of the Centre for Voucher Privatisation in 1994, it has historically suffered from inter-agency rivalry. Moreover, its independence came into question when Prime Minister Miloš Zeman publicly attacked the unit at the same time as it was allegedly examining the ruling ČSSD party's financing activities. The Department may not possess sufficient autonomy to pursue corruption cases involving high-level politicians.

In addition, according to press reports the police established a special department ("Department 15") in 2001 with the task of investigating possible crimes committed by influential Czech public personalities. The Department investigates possible illegal conduct by cabinet members, parliamentary deputies, judges and members of the Czech National Bank board.[35]

The Financial Analytical Unit

In 1996, an Act on Several Measures against the Legalisation of Proceeds from Criminal Activity[36] was passed, and in July 1996, a Financial Analytical Unit was formed at the Ministry of Finance to monitor suspicious transactions on the basis of

---

[34] "Sněmovna přijala zákon o finanční kontrole ve veřejné správě" [Parliament approves Act on Financial Control in the Public Administration], ČTK [Czech Press Agency], 12 July 2001. The effect of the Act in practice will depend on the necessary accompanying rules that must be issued by the Ministry of Finance, and on the effectiveness of provisions in the Act stating that employees carrying out control activities in public institutions must not be influenced by any factors other than the Act.

[35] "Czech police set up special department on VIP crime," RFE/RL Newsline, 30 July 2002.

[36] Act no. 61/1996.

notification by financial institutions. The Act was amended in 1998 and 2000[37] to increase the Department's access to information (most notable in the May 2000 amendment, which gives tax authorities the duty to provide information to the FAU) and State more clearly the duty of institutions to report suspicious transactions. According to officials at the Unit, the Act is now fully compatible with the European Convention. In 2000, the Unit filed 104 notifications of suspected criminal activity to the police on the basis of 1910 notifications from institutions (mostly banks).

However, the *2000 Regular Report* was sharply critical of enforcement capacity and particularly the continuing existence of anonymous bank accounts.[38] In February 2002, the Chamber of Deputies passed an act that would phase out anonymous bank accounts, a subject of long-running disputes with the European Union.

2.5 Ombudsman

The Czech ombudsman was established by law in 1999,[39] and the first ombudsman was elected in December 2000. According to the law, the ombudsman function is to "protect people against behaviour by State institutions that violates the law, principles of a democratic legal State and good administration, and against their inactivity."

The ombudsman and deputy ombudsman are elected for a six-year period by the Chamber of Deputies from candidates proposed by the Senate and President of the Republic. The ombudsman accepts complaints from citizens concerning the following institutions:

- ministries and other national administrative organs and their subordinate organs;
- the Czech National Bank;
- the Council for Radio and Television Broadcasting;
- district offices and municipalities in the exercise of tasks of the State administration;
- the Czech Police (with the exception of investigative organs);
- the Army;
- the Prison Service;

---

[37] Acts nos. 15/1998 and 159/2000.

[38] Commission, *2000 Regular Report*, p. 49.

[39] Act no. 349/1999.

- any institution where people are held against their will, including special institutions for young people and medical treatment;

- public health insurance companies;

- judicial organs in their exercise of functions of State administration.

Anonymous complaints are not admissible to the ombudsman.

The ombudsman may enter any institution it investigates without warning, demand documents, written answers to questions and proof in a deadline it states. Institutions must reply to the ombudsman explaining what corrective measures were taken within 30 days of the ombudsman's report. If the institution fails to do so, or the ombudsman believes the measures are insufficient, or the institution failed to provide information according to the law, the ombudsman informs the superior institution or the Government, and may inform the public.

As of March 2002, the ombudsman had 85 employees. The Office received 5,996 complaints in 2001, and dealt with 3,139 in the same year. In 32 cases, the Office found fundamental mistakes, not one of which concerned corruption; however, according to ombudsman officials, several initiatives of the Office concerning organisations falling under the competence of the Ministry of Interior have resulted in measures that make corruption more difficult.

3. EXECUTIVE BRANCH AND CIVIL SERVICE

Evidence of corruption in the Czech public administration is limited, with virtually no convictions or employees of the State administration for bribery. There have been a number of scandals concerning ministers, but almost no criminal cases and no convictions. The legal framework for public administration is largely inadequate, failing to regulate conflict of interest or discourage patronage and nepotism. However, a new Civil Service Act will improve the legal framework significantly in both these areas. Procedures for appealing against administrative decisions do not provide citizens with effective redress. A Code of Ethics came into effect in 2001, but is vague and largely repeats provisions already stated elsewhere.

3.1 Structure and legislative framework

Employment relations between public officials and the organisations that employ them are based entirely on the Czech Labour Code and there are no legal instruments to guarantee the stability or independence of the civil service. Employees of State organs can be hired and fired like any other employee, competitive procedures are not mandatory, and there are no rules to prevent nepotism or any other criteria in recruitment. Politicisation has long been regarded as a problem, as changes of minister or department heads are often accompanied by widespread changes of subordinates.

A short-term priority of the *1999 Accession Partnership* was the passage of a Civil Service Act. The *2001 Regular Report* criticises the failure of Parliament to achieve the necessary consensus on civil service reform, noting that, "The adoption of the Civil Service Act remains a precondition for establishing an independent, professional, stable and accountable public administration."[40]

In April 2002, Parliament finally passed a Civil Service Act. Under its provisions, most of which will take effect from January 2004, the Act defines public service as a special employment relation, and lays down a clear career structure. However, Parliament deleted from the original proposal security of tenure for civil servants, although officials will have the right to five months severance pay if they are dismissed. In accompanying documents to the original proposal the Government intended to raise salaries by around 40 percent on average after the law goes into effect.

3.2 Administrative procedure and redress

Under the 1967 Code of Administrative Procedure,[41] administrative decisions must be carried out within 30 days, or 60 days in more complicated cases. The deadline can be renewed at official discretion. Citizens may appeal administrative decisions to the same organ that issued the original decision within 15 days, although the appeal deadline is in practice 30 days and can be extended if there is good reason. If the appeal is fully or partially rejected, it is then dealt with by the superior administrative organ, generally the minister.

Administrative judiciary

Appeal decisions of administrative bodies may be appealed to a court under the rules of administrative judicial proceedings. At the time of writing, administrative courts had not yet been created; appeals are handled by special departments of ordinary courts. However, a new Code of Administrative Procedure passed in early 2002 lays down the structure and rules of the administrative judiciary, and in January 2003, the Supreme Administrative Court will begin functioning.

---

[40] Commission, *2001 Regular Report*, p. 17.

[41] Act no. 71/1967.

Courts can only judge the formal legality of an administrative decision, not its substance, and may only cancel the decision or return it to the same administrative organ to be decided again.

Complaints

Under the Czech Constitution, any citizen has the right to file a complaint, organs of the State administration have the duty to reply and no citizen may be sanctioned in any way for filing a complaint. Parliament passed a new Act on Complaints in July 2001, which lays down procedures and deadlines for dealing with complaints. However, the Act contains no sanctions for violations and was not submitted as part of a broader reform of administrative proceedings. The Ministry of Interior proposed a new Code of Administrative Procedure in 2001, which was rejected by the Chamber of Deputies in early 2002.

As a result, the main mechanism for administrative redress remains the ombudsman (see Section 2.6).

3.3 Conflict of interest and asset monitoring

The Czech Conflict of Interest Act (see Section 3.2.2) does not apply to officials below the rank of minister or head of a central administrative body. Under the Labour Code, employees of organs of the State administration have a general duty to act and decide objectively, avoid behaviour that could lead to a conflict between public and personal interests and not accept gifts in connection with performance of duties. In addition, officials may not be members of the managerial or controlling organs of business entities, unless they are delegated there by the employer and receive no payment; and may not engage in business activities only with the prior written agreement of the employer. Officials who do not engage in business activities or secondary employment are entitled to a 25 percent salary premium, although this provision does not appear to be used at all.[42]

The Labour Code allows employers to include in employment contracts clauses forbidding employees for a maximum of one year after leaving the employment from carrying out any activity that was the subject of the original employer's business or could be in competition with it. The clause is virtually useless as there are very few cases where the activities of a private firm fulfil these conditions.

---

[42] When the author of this report worked at the SAO for a year, this provision was never mentioned.

The effectiveness of the Labour Code in regulating conflict of interest appears to be minimal. According to the Ministry of Industry and Trade, which has no rules regulating conflict of interest apart from the Labour Code, in the whole history of the ministry, only four officials have been terminated as a result of conflicts of interest.

Some State institutions include conflict of interest provisions in internal employment rules, although these do not go beyond other existing provisions. The Ministry of Finance refused to provide a copy of its employment rules on the basis that is not a public document and stated that the rules impose the same duties as the Labour Code. According to the Ministry (the largest ministry) no employee has ever been removed for reasons of conflict of interest or abuse of power.[43]

Under the Civil Service Act, civil servants will be prohibited from earning any income apart from their official salary, and senior officials will be prohibited for two years from doing business or working in a sphere in which they held responsibilities as an official.

3.4 Internal control mechanisms

There is no legal protection for whistleblowers in the Czech Republic, and disclosure is strongly discouraged by the absence of protection from dismissal.

3.5 Interaction with the public

The Code of Ethics

In March 2001, the Czech Government approved a Code of Ethics for Employees of the State Administration, which is vague and largely repeats the provisions of the Labour Code.[44] Every ministry and District Office must acquaint its employees with

---

[43] Information from Press Department, Ministry of Finance, 17 May 2001.

[44] Czech Government Resolution no. 270/2001, 21 March 2001. Under the Code, officials should:

- decide objectively on the basis of facts and without unnecessary delays;
- avoid any occurrence of conflict of interest, where private interests include any advantage for his/her family, relatives or close persons, or individuals or legal entities with which s/he has or has had commercial or political relations;
- carry on any political or public activities that could undermine trust in his/her objectivity;
- not accept any gifts or advantages that could even be seen to undermine trust in objectivity or be payment for work that is his/her duty.

the Code, and the Ministry of Interior was to produce a guide to the Code for citizens. The Ministry of Interior has its own Code of Ethics.

Until very recently there existed no specific mechanisms in the State administration for citizens to register complaints about corruption. However, the Government's anti-corruption strategy includes a commitment to establish a Contact and Advisory Centre for Victims of Corruption and for every ministry to establish an organ where citizens can register complaints and initiatives. The Ministry of Interior established an Anti-corruption Commission in September 1999, including telephone and e-mail links where citizens can register complaints (including anonymously). The Ministry allocated €150,000 for a non-governmental organisation to establish a Contact and Advisory Centre, but withdrew the money due to lack of interest.

3.6 Corruption

Under the 1998-2002 Government no explicit cases of criminal corruption emerged in the executive. Minister of Finance Ivo Svoboda was sacked in 1999 after the police began investigating him for suspected fraud. In May 2002, he was charged with fraud together with his former business partner and subordinate at the Ministry.[45] A number of other scandals uncovered by the media have cast doubt on the integrity of high-ranking officials, although not necessarily indicating corruption *per se*. The most famous of these was the "Lead Affair," in which Government employees prepared compromising materials on a political ČSSD party rival of Prime Minister Miloš Zeman (see Section 9).[46]

The other most important affair was a contract between the Ministry of Foreign Affairs and a private company to rent a Ministry building ("Český dům Moskva") in Moscow on terms disadvantageous to the State. In November 2001, the Senate Foreign Affairs Committee condemned the agreement and chastised Minister Jan Kavan for not providing information on the role of a prominent lawyer who represented parties on both sides of the transaction.[47]

---

[45] S. Slonková, "Policisté zatkli bývalého ministra financí Svobodu" [Police arrest former finance minister Svoboda], *Mladá fronta Dnes*, 24 November 1999; "Former Czech finance minister charged," RFE/RL Newsline, vol. 6, no. 96, part II, 23 May 2002.

[46] The affair was named "Lead" because the document in question was code-named "Olovo" (*lead* in Czech) – since the initials of the target politician, then-Vice Chairwoman of the Social Democratic Party, Petra Buzková, correspond to the letters for lead in the Periodic Table (pb).

[47] J. Kubík and S. Slonková, "Český dům: svou roli má i Kavanova náměstkyně" [The Czech House: Also Kavan's Deputy has a part], *Mladá fronta Dnes*, 24 April 2001; Resolution no. 95 of the Committee for Foreign Affairs, Defence and Security, 21 November 2001.

The State's reaction to these cases was to attempt to sweep them under the carpet or even punish the journalists who uncovered them, most notably in the case of the "Lead Affair" (see Section 9).[48] However, in July 2002 the Český dům affair took on a new dimension when one of the General Secretaries of the Ministry of Foreign Affairs, who had left the Ministry as a result of the affair, was arrested and charged with planning the murder of the main journalist who had investigated the affair. The initial stages of the investigation appeared to indicate widespread corruption in the allocation of public contracts by the Ministry.[49]

The public's assessment of the Zeman Government with respect to corruption worsened steadily through its term of office. According to research conducted by GfK, the proportion of respondents believing that the Zeman Government had spread the greatest share of corruption of all Czech Governments rose from three percent in 1999 to 39 percent in May 2001, making it the Government with the worst rating.[50]

As Table 5 shows, the number of employees of the State administration convicted for the most important corruption-related paragraphs of the Criminal Code is extremely low, with zero convictions for bribery in recent years. This is in spite of the fact that in surveys the State is ranked as the most corrupt sphere of public life (see Section 1.1).

Table 5: Convictions of employees of the State administration for selected criminal acts, 1998–2000

Criminal act	1998	1999	2000
Abuse of power by a public official	9	29	22
Acceptance of a bribe	0	2	0
Bribery	1	0	0
Indirect bribery	1	0	0

Source: Czech Ministry of Interior, Zpráva o korupci v ČR a o plnění harmonogramu opatření Vládního programmeu boje proti korupci, January 2001, p. 3.

"Consultancy" services

The relative ineffectiveness of justice organs in detecting and prosecuting bribery in the Czech State administration may reflect the relative sophistication of corruption

---

[48] See, e.g., "Aféry sociální demokracie a jejich aktéři" [Affairs of the Social Democracy and their actors], *Mladá fronta Dnes*, 5 November 1999.

[49] J. Grohová, "Policie zkoumá korupci z doby ministra Kavana" [Police investigate corruption from the period of Minister Kavan], *Mladá fronta Dnes*, 25 July 2002.

[50] GfK-Praha, "Žijeme v korupčním státě!, říká polovina obyvatel ČR" [We live in a corrupt State!, as claims half of the Czech Republic's inhabitants], press release, <http://www.gfk.cz/download324_cj_int.doc>, (last accessed 24 May 2002).

mechanisms. According to anonymous testimony from several firms that have gained subsidies from various ministries a common corruption channel is one whereby State officials refer applicants for subsidies to consultancy firms to which they have links.

4. LEGISLATURE

Until recently, a number of significant categories of public expenditure were excluded from the State budget, although recent reforms have ended this situation. Parliament has not functioned as an effective anti-corruption mechanism. Moreover, although there is almost no direct evidence of corruption among MPs, Parliament itself is highly vulnerable to corruption, especially through unregulated lobbying, while conflict of interest provisions are inadequate. Immunity provisions effectively protect deputies from prosecution for corruption, and Parliament recently rejected proposed reforms in this area.

4.1 Elections

According to all international organisations that have assessed the Czech Republic on democratic criteria, parliamentary elections are free and fair.[51] Elections are supervised by a permanent State Election Commission, and regional election commissions composed of citizens delegated by all subjects standing for election. The State Election Commission is chaired by the Minister of Interior, and its members are representatives of various ministries and State institutions appointed by the Government on the Minister's proposal

4.2 Budget and control mechanisms

The State budget is subject to approval by the Chamber of Deputies. However, in a number of respects, parliamentary scrutiny of public finances is (or until recently has been) inadequate:[52]

- There has been no statute preventing the Government from changing the budget after its approval by Parliament or missing targets. For example the Government

---

[51] See, e.g., Commission, *Agenda 2000*, p. 14.

[52] This section draws heavily on World Bank, *Czech Republic – Toward EU Accession*, World Bank, October 1999, Chapter 3; International Monetary Fund, *Report on the Observance of Standards and Codes, Czech Republic*, July 2000, Chapter IV.

exceeded the approved deficit for 2000 by around one-quarter or €333m, and as of July 2002 was expected to exceed the planned deficit for 2002 by around 50 percent.

- State guarantees have been approved by the Government without any need for parliamentary approval, and have grown rapidly as hidden subsidies without democratic scrutiny. According to the World Bank, risk-adjusted guarantees outstanding grew from €200m in 1995 to €3.6b in 1998, and this figure has continued to grow at least at the same rate since then, as the Zeman Government has been faced with tasks such as cleaning up the banking sector. Although direct corruption has never been proven in the allocation of guarantees, former Minister of Finance Ivan Kočárník came under scrutiny for his approval of a €133m guarantee for Česká spořitelna, the largest Czech savings bank, and for allegedly approving a similar type of guarantee for Česká pojišťovna, the largest insurance company.[53] Parliament refused to lift Kočárník's immunity from prosecution in connection with the former case.

- Third, major items of public expenditure have remained outside the official budget, most importantly the funding of Konsolidační banka (Consolidation bank - the State hospital bank for administering non-performing assets), but also the Agricultural Guarantee Support Fund or National Property Fund. Parliament approves the accounts of such funds only *ex post*.

The result of these factors was a so-called "hidden deficit" in public finances, amounting to around five percent of GDP in 1997 and 1998. The current Government has made significant steps to make public finances more transparent. Since 1998, for example, the Ministry of Finance has published information on all outstanding State guarantees, while the accounts of Konsolidační banka have been included in the State budget since 2000. Nevertheless, the European Union urged fiscal reform in the *2000 Regular Report*, noting that:

> A strong commitment to fiscal transparency is needed to stop the proliferation of off-budget deficits and contingent liabilities, which could endanger macroeconomic sustainability in the medium term... Most worryingly, this situation continues to deteriorate.[54]

In January 2001, a new Act on Budget Rules came into effect, under which the Chamber of Deputies must approve State guarantees, and the Government may exceed the approved spending by a maximum of six percent of total planned expenditure plus approved expenditure. In June 2001, the Chamber of Deputies took the unprecedented

---

[53] Q. Reed, "Shareholders say Pojišťovna fixed its books," *Prague Business Journal*, 8 November 1998.

[54] Commission, *2000 Regular Report*, p. 32.

step of voting not to accept the Government's final budgetary statement for 2000. However, the vote has no direct consequences for the Government.

Investigation committees

The Chamber of Deputies may form an investigation committee for a specific purpose on the vote of a majority of MPs. This has rarely happened. The main case in recent years was a committee set up to investigate the role of the State in the collapse and takeover of the then third largest Czech bank, Investiční a poštovní banka (Investition and Post Bank; IPB), in 2000. In reality, the committee was used by a number of its members with close ties to the bank to pursue their own political agenda, and played no role in clarifying events objectively.

4.3 Conflict of interest and asset monitoring

As Section 2.2 has shown, conflict of interest regulation for MPs and Senators is largely inadequate. Moreover, there is no regulation of parliamentary lobbying. Parliamentary procedure is highly vulnerable to lobbying pressure: MPs can submit proposed changes to laws individually after the first reading of legislation. There is no mechanism for filtering such proposals, which are then voted on by the Chamber as a whole during the second reading. According to experienced MPs, the effect of uncontrolled lobbying on the legislative process has become more serious over time.[55] Recent cases in which lobbying behind the scenes is regarded as the main influence on Parliament's decision on important laws include the passage of legislation to abolish duty-free shops in 2001, the passage of a Lotteries Act in 1998 and of a Hunting Act in 2001.

4.4 Immunity

Czech MPs enjoy immunity from prosecution not only for actions carried out in connection with the exercise of their mandate, but also for ordinary transgressions of the law or criminal acts. If the police wish to prosecute an MP or Senator, they must request that the relevant chamber remove the Parliamentarian's immunity. If the chamber refuses, then immunity in relation to the matter in question will last for life.

Under the National Programme for the Fight Against Corruption, in 1999 the Government submitted a proposal to narrow parliamentary immunity only to prosecution for actions directly related to the exercise of an MP's mandate. The Chamber of Deputies rejected the proposal in September 1999.

---

[55] OSI Roundtable Discussion, Prague, 25 March 2002.

4.5 Corruption

There have been no criminal cases of corruption of MPs or Senators in the past three years. However, a 1997 SAO audit of the Chamber of Deputies revealed serious violations of the law and poor management of public money,[56] involving, *inter alia*, repeated awarding of contracts for construction and maintenance of Parliament buildings to the same company without proper tender procedures. Another audit carried out in 1998 revealed similar (although less serious) problems in the Senate, which used the same firm for construction contracts. The audits received widespread media attention.

The consequences of the audit findings were diametrically different in the two cases. The Chamber of Deputies rejected the audit findings aggressively, and on the initiative of one MP disciplinary proceedings were conducted against the SAO College Member who was in charge of the audit. The proceedings found that he did not break any rules and no sanctions were imposed on him. The Chamber of Deputies carried out no other corrective action except for the issuance of an order by the Head of the Office of the Chamber of Deputies concerning the use of public money in the Chamber, from budget approval to internal audit of vulnerable areas. In the case of the Senate, the Head of the Office of the Senate and several other staff were removed, and the Senate made radical improvements in its system for managing public tenders, outsourcing its tenders to a professional consulting firm.

5. JUDICIARY[57]

The Czech judiciary has undergone major reforms since 1999, when the Zeman Government began an ambitious programme of judicial reform. However, although parts of the reform programme can be expected to reduce corruption in the judiciary, there is a strong resistance among Czech judges to admitting the existence of corruption problems, although the taboo has been increasingly broken recently. Further, reforms have not yet gone far enough in dealing with corruption in commercial court proceedings and business registration.

---

[56] Nejvyšší kontrolní úřad [SAO], Kontrolní závěr 97/1997 [Audition Control], approved October 1998.

[57] Information for this section was gathered with the help of interviews with Josef Baxa, Deputy Minister of Justice (25 April 2001), and Pavel Šamal, Supreme Court judge (9 May 2001).

5.1 Legislative framework

The legislative framework for the Czech judiciary is largely described in the OSI *2001 Report on Judicial Independence*, which criticised the relative lack of independence of Czech judges and the lack of self-administration.[58]

Regarding corruption, the Act on Courts and Judges,[59] in force as of March 2002, prohibits judges from behaviour that threatens to undermine their objectivity or independence. According to the Criminal Code, a judge is disqualified from participating in criminal proceedings if there are no reasons to the contrary stemming from conflict of interest or other reasons for bias, specifically if the judge's relationship to the matter of the proceedings, the participants or to another organ active in criminal proceedings makes it impossible to decide objectively.[60]

Judges may not perform any other work or business activity. The Union of Judges also publishes a Code of Ethics, which reflects the same considerations, and the new Act on Judges and Courts provides for a binding Code of Ethics.

Judges enjoy similar immunity from prosecution as Parliamentarians. However, the Minister of Justice, the chairman of any court or the police may submit an initiative for disciplinary proceedings against any judge. Disciplinary proceedings, which are not public, are carried out by a Disciplinary Senate of the High Court, which can propose various disciplinary measures depending on the seriousness of the offence. The Senate may propose that a judge be removed from office, although this is subject to the approval of the Supreme Court. Statistics indicate that disciplinary proceedings are on the increase (see Table 6 below).

Table 6: Disciplinary proceedings against Czech judges, 1999–2001

Year	1999	2000	2001 Jan-May
Number of disciplinary proceedings	29	31	17
Number of proposals by Minister of Justice for removal or transfer of judge	6	11	3

---

[58] EU Accession Monitoring Program, *Monitoring the EU Accession Process: Judicial Independence*, Open Society Institute, Budapest, 2001, pp. 109–146, available at <www.eumap.org>.

[59] Act no. 335/1991.

[60] Act no. 141/1961, paragraph 30.

Disciplinary proceedings according to initiator

Year	1999	2000	2001
Minister of Justice	2	2	12
Chairman of court	22	20	5
Police	5	9	0

Source: Mladá fronta Dnes, 7 June 2001.

Judicial reform

A new Act on Courts and Judges that is due to come into effect shortly contains a number of provisions that are, *inter alia,* designed to prevent corruption. The Act states strict standards of behaviour, including for example the duty of a judge not to behave in such a way as to cast doubt on objectivity or independence, even in private life. Second, the Act establishes three councils (for civil, criminal and administrative law) to assess judges' expert suitability to carry out their functions, and in particular a 60-month probation period after which judges receive appointment for life on the basis of a council assessment. The latter in particular provoked bitter opposition among many judges.

In addition to the new Act, fundamental changes to the Criminal Procedure Code (2001) and amendments to the Act on State Representatives [prosecutors] (2000) have been passed which should make criminal proceedings more efficient. In particular, they have abolished the office of "investigator" and concentrated proceedings under the control of prosecutors – thereby ending time-consuming dual collections of evidence in the preliminary investigation and prosecution stages.

5.2 Corruption

There has only been one conviction of a Czech judge for bribery, in which a local judge offered a bribe to a State prosecutor to propose a lower sentence in a criminal case. The judge was convicted and given a suspended sentence. The Chairman of the Senate of the Regional Court in Ostrava was charged with bribery and abuse of power in 1997 but committed suicide.

Corruption has been a serious problem at the Commercial Register, with bribes to speed up company registration and changes in capital widely regarded as common practice. Although judges and Ministry of Justice officials complain that there is no specific evidence to prove the existence of such practices, the testimony of a number of business people and commercial lawyers suggests that commercial registers are seriously affected by corruption. For instance, according to one commercial lawyer with extensive experience of company registration, bribes for court officials and judges are mediated by a number of middlemen, normally hired by lawyers on behalf of clients.

In addition, the vulnerability of commercial court proceedings to corruption has been highlighted by the increasing importance of bankruptcy proceedings in recent years, which have grown rapidly in importance since 1998 as a number of large Czech companies have gone into bankruptcy. Suspicions of corruption have emerged in several large bankruptcy cases.[61] Circumstantial evidence and the testimony of senior Western consultants involved in bankruptcy proceedings indicate that such proceedings are highly vulnerable to corrupt alliances between bankruptcy administrators (receivers) and commercial court judges. In particular, the qualification requirements for receivers are lax and courts themselves suffer from a lack of judges sufficiently qualified in commercial matters.

In 2000, the Prague Commercial Court launched its own anti-corruption programme with the aim of preventing speed payments being made to judges. The programme is based on abolishing personal contact between the two sides, for example allocating judges to particular cases randomly, and allowing face-to-face meetings of judges and applicants for company registration only in the presence of a court guard. In addition, the new Commercial Code that came into effect in January 2001 introduced 15-day deadlines for registering companies and changes in the register. Although investors have the impression that the situation with registration has improved, the same is not clear for securing changes in registration. Moreover, the new deadlines are not effective; there are no sanctions for failing to meet the deadlines and appeals concerning delays are subject to a two-month deadline.

6. POLITICAL PARTY FINANCE

Following a series of major scandals in the late 1990's, the funding of Czech political parties has undergone important changes, notably major increases in State subsidies. These changes appear to have lessened parties' dependence on illicit sources of income, and there is now little evidence of covert funding or corruption.

---

[61] In particular, a decision in 2000 by a judge of the Brno Regional Commercial Court to declare bankruptcy on Kralovopolska, a large engineering company, came under scrutiny due to alleged interests of the bankruptcy receiver in real estate owned by the company, and the lack of grounds for the decision. The decision was later reversed and the judge dismissed.

6.1 Legislative framework

Under the Act on Political Parties, parties are allowed four main sources of income: membership contributions (a tiny proportion of total income), donations, loans and State subsidies. Party finance has undergone significant development since 1997, when a scandal involving disguised donations from a company that bought the country's second-largest steel works led to the collapse of the Government. A number of previous scandals involved both loans to parties[62] and suspicious donations. Since that period, parties have withdrawn from borrowing money from banks, and State contributions to parties have become the most important source of income for parties.

Until recently, Czech law allowed virtually unlimited donations to political parties, not only from private entities but even from those in which the State itself holds an interest, although donations from the latter were prohibited by a Government directive in 1998. The only limitation on donations was a duty to state the source of every donation exceeding €3,333.

Under the Act on Political Parties, since amendments passed in July 2000:[63]

- donations exceeding €1,667 may only be provided via a written donation voucher, which must be submitted to the tax authorities before the money is transferred;

- parties may not receive donations from the State or entities where the State owns more than a ten percent stake, municipalities, regional governments, foreign legal entities with the exception of political parties and foundations or foreign individuals (with the exception of permanent residents in the Czech Republic);

- a party may receive a maximum of €1.3m in total donations annually;

- the identities of all donors must be published irrespective of the size of the donation;

- parties must submit detailed annual reports, including a breakdown of spending;

- if a party violates rules on donations, it must return the relevant donation to the donor, or to the State if the donor cannot be identified. Moreover, the party must also pay a fine equal to double the relevant donation;

---

[62] For example the Civic Democratic Alliance borrowed €1.7m from a bank that was subject to criminal investigation (and as of May 2002 had still not paid it back), while the Civic Democratic Party borrowed a similar amount from State-controlled Investiční a poštovní banka (Investition and Post Bank; IPB). See Q. Reed, *Political Corruption, Privatisation and Control*, Chapter 6.

[63] P. Černý and B. Clough, *Innovation and Transparency in Political Party Financing in the Czech Republic*, forthcoming paper, Transparency International Czech Republic; Czech Ministry of Interior, *Zpráva o korupci v ČR*, p. 21.

- annual party membership contributions may not exceed €1,667.

Under the 1991 Act on Political Parties and Movements, as amended in 1995,[64] parties winning three percent of the vote in elections to the Chamber of Deputies received a "regular contribution" of €100,000 per year, plus €3.333 for every further 0.1 percent of the vote up to a maximum of €166,667. In addition, parties received a €16,667 annual "mandate contribution" for every Deputy and Senator elected.

The 1995 Electoral Act[65] contains a third contribution for election costs: parties that gain at least three percent of votes in elections to the Chamber of Deputies receive €3 per vote.

The Act passed in 2000 doubled the regular contribution: parties winning three percent of the vote receive €200,000, rising to a maximum of €333,330 for parties that win five percent. The same passage, however, withdrew the regular contribution from parties that exceed the three percent threshold but not the five percent threshold necessary to enter the Chamber of Deputies. At the same time, the amendment raised the mandate contribution to €33,330 per Deputy and Senator. However, in February 2001, the Constitutional Court ruled the latter provision as unconstitutional,[66] mainly on the grounds that the Czech Constitution dictates that parties be "separated from the State." In May 2001, the Chamber of Deputies approved a mandate contribution of €30,000.

Finally, in addition to these contributions, under the 2000 amendment parties also receive a €8,333 annual mandate contribution for every deputy elected to regional assemblies and the Prague City Assembly.

---

[64] Act no. 424/1991, as amended by Act no. 296/1995, paragraph 20.

[65] Act no. 247/1995, paragraph 85.

[66] Constitutional Court proceedings 53/2000, decision 27 February 2001.

Table 7: State contributions to political parties (€m), 1998–2001

Party	1998	1999	2000	2001 (Jan-June)
Czech Social Democratic Party	7.5	1.8	1.8	1.45
Civic Democratic Party	6.8	1.7	1.7	1.7
Christian Democratic Union-Czechoslovak People's Party	2.3	0.7	0.7	0.8
Communist Party of Bohemia and Moravia	2.9	0.6	0.6	1
Freedom Union	1.8	0.5	0.5	0.6
Civic Democratic Alliance	0.31	0.1	0.1	0.15
Democratic Union[1]	0.02	0.02	0.3	0.07
TOTAL STATE CONTRIBUTIONS[2]	21.63	5.42	5.7	5.77

Notes:

[1] On the basis of a Constitutional Court decision, the Democratic Union received €260.000 in State contributions for the 1998 elections in 2000.

[2] Total contributions exceed the individual party contributions due to contributions to the Republican Party, which have not been listed due to complicated legal disputes that distort the State contribution, and the Pensioner's Party, which won enough votes in the 1998 elections to receive funding but not enough to be represented in either chamber.

Source: Ministry of Finance of the Czech Republic.

6.2 Control and supervision

Supervision of party accounts and financing is generally inadequate. Under the 1994 version of the Act on Political Parties, parties had to submit annual financial reports to Parliament and the SAO. However, in 1995 the Supreme Court ruled supervision by the SAO to be unconstitutional, which left only publicity as the sanction for violation of the law or other problems in financing. Any citizen may visit the Parliamentary Budget Committee and read parties' annual reports.

The amendments to financing rules passed in 2000 did not introduce any changes to the system of scrutiny of party accounts, and continued to rely on the existing system of public access. According to a recent paper by Transparency International Czech Republic on Czech party financing, "The Act… still leave[s] ample room for parties to elaborate tales on the transparency of their finances. This is mainly due to limited auditing functions and controlling mechanisms of party financial reports."[67]

---

[67] P. Černý and B. Clough, *Innovation and Transparency*, [page ref. not yet available].

6.3 Party finance in practice

From the mid-to-late 1990's, all parties in the right-wing coalition that ruled from 1992 to 1997 were hit by financing scandals (see Section 6.1). After the collapse of the Klaus Government and victory of the Social Democrats (ČSSD) in the 1998 elections, the ČSSD itself was subject to a few revelations: for example, in 1999 it emerged that one of the figures associated with the largest investment fund fraud in Czech history was also one of the party's biggest donors in 1998.[68]

The only corruption case with major implications for important political elites or parties that ended in court in the last three years was the prosecution of former vice-chairman of the ODS Libor Novák for the party's failure to pay taxes on donations, which the party split into smaller amounts and declared as donations from non-existent donors. The case ended in an acquittal.[69] One of the results of the ODS financing scandal was the departure of a number of party politicians and the formation of the Freedom Union, one of whose main claims is to be the most transparent party in the country in terms of finance.[70]

The scandals of the 1990's appear to have left their mark on public perceptions of parties. According to research by the Centre for Public Opinion Research carried out in April 2001, political parties were evaluated as the most corrupt institutions in the country (see Section 1.2).

7. PUBLIC PROCUREMENT

Czech public procurement legislation is relatively advanced, with the major exception of provisions allowing the Government to allocate contracts without a tender. However, the absence of effective monitoring and supervision has allowed a situation in which corruption continues to be widespread.

7.1 Legislative framework

Public procurement in the Czech Republic is regulated by the Act on Public Contracts.[71] The Act applies to all State organisations and legal entities established by

---

[68] Q. Reed, *Corruption in Czech privatization,* p. 19.

[69] S. Slonková, J. Kubík, "ODS nedostala trest za podvod," *Mladá fronta Dnes,* 29 November 2000.

[70] The party publishes its accounts and a register of donors on the Internet, and introduced the written donor agreement system before it became law.

[71] Act no. 199/1994 on Public Contracts, as amended by Acts nos. 148/1996, 93/1998 and 28/2000.

the State that receive funds from the State budget, utilities, companies that carry out exploration for oil or other fuels, airport and harbour administrators, health insurance companies and any contract wholly or partly financed from public funds.

The Act states the following duties with respect to public contracts of different sizes:

- Contracts with a value over €166,670 must be allocated on the basis of an open public tender.

- For contracts whose value is between €33,330 and €166,665, the organ may carry out the competition by selecting at least five entities to compete. This method may also be used for larger contracts under certain special conditions, for example if the Government decides the contract is fulfilling urgent needs.

- For contracts between €16,670 and €33,330, the winner may be chosen from offers submitted by at least three selected participants.

- Contracts with a value lower than €16,670 may be closed without a tender.

- Contracts can be closed on the basis of an invitation to one party if the Government so decides or under certain special conditions.

Public contracts are carried out by a commission appointed by the head of the contracting authority. Commission members may not have any relationship to a bidder. However, there is no mechanism for supervising this provision, nor any system for monitoring assets, incomes or lifestyles of members of tender commissions. For most State organisations, the tender commission usually consists of the same group of people for all tenders. If a contract exceeds €6.7m in value, then the commission is appointed by the minister or head of organ, and must include representatives of the Ministry of Finance and two other ministries; if the size of the contract exceeds €30m, the Government appoints the commission.

All calls for public tenders must be published in the *Commercial Bulletin,* and, since amendments to the Act passed in 2000, on a central Government website.[72] The results of tenders must be communicated to all participants in the final bidding, although there is no duty to publish the results in any universally available media.

Tender documents must state the criteria for choosing the winner, with weights attached to each criterion. However, the law still does not state exactly what is meant by weighting criteria, which leaves considerable discretion in the hands of officials picking the winner. Moreover, the law does not clearly prevent public institutions from setting tender criteria

---

[72] See <http://www.centralni-adresa.cz/cadr/index.htm>, (last accessed 23 August 2002).

that effectively exclude all but one possible winner, which is a common mechanism of corruption in procurement.[73]

A major problem in regulation of public tenders is that there is no restriction on subsequent increases in price or changes in the work being carried out. Rather, these are matters for agreement between supplier and investor. The SAO regularly finds large and in most cases unjustifiable price increases for contracts.[74]

According to the Tender Act, a public contract allocated in violation of this Act is invalid, as are changes in the contract that violate the conditions of a public tender. However, this provision is virtually impossible to apply as contracts are only audited *ex post*.

A potentially important provision included in the most recent amendment to the Act on Public Contracts states that any company, one of whose employees, owners or members of statutory organs has been convicted of a criminal offence in connection with a public contract, is to be disqualified from participation in public tenders by the Office for the Protection of Economic Competition (the organ that supervises public tenders) for a maximum of five years.

However, given the minimal number of such convictions (See Table 1), the effect of this provision is questionable. There is no formal system for blacklisting companies who have carried out public tenders poorly.

7.2 Review and audit

Any participant in tender proceedings may appeal any part of a tender proceeding, first to the same organ that issued the tender, and then to its superior. If this is unsuccessful the participant may appeal to a court. Participants may also submit an initiative to the Office for the Protection of Economic Competition (Competition Office), which is responsible for supervising adherence to the Act on Public Contracts. The Office may on its own initiative be present in tender proceedings or investigate the public tender proceedings before the contract is awarded. In practice, the Office is not sufficiently equipped to handle the workload of supervision (it had a staff of around 20 dealing with procurement issues in 2001); moreover, where it intervenes, it tends to deal with the form rather than substance of tenders.[75]

---

[73] A glaring example of this was a recent tender issued by a regional governor to purchase cars, in which the tender conditions were specified so as to make only one car qualify. See also J. Ciglerová, "Hejtman vypsal svéráznou soutěž na své auto" [Regional governor runs curious tender for car], *Lidové noviny*, daily, 23 April 2001.

[74] Interview with Josef Pohl, Member of SAO College, 17 May 2001.

[75] Interview with Josef Pohl, Member of SAO College, 17 May 2001.

An unfortunate aspect of the public tender framework is that the regulatory framework is as likely to harm both honest bidders and honest tender issuers as it is to reveal corruption. When appeals take place, they typically delay tenders for 6-12 months.

The SAO plays the most important role in auditing public tenders, and has consistently produced serious findings in this area. A large percentage of audit findings relate to problems involved in the preparation of tenders (see below), and according to the SAO are very often the result of insufficiently qualified personnel. The result of this is that in many cases vague tenders are issued, without a clear description of the work that is required; this alone may result from corruption, and itself facilitates corruption during the rest of the tender.

7.3 Corruption

Again, there is virtually no evidence of wrongdoing in Czech public tenders in terms of criminal proceedings, with only two convictions since 1996 for machinations in public tenders. However, this underlines only the ineffectiveness of the monitoring framework, and there are a number of reasons for serious concern with the framework for public contracts in general.

According to SAO officials, the loopholes in the law, absence of qualification requirements to issue a public tender and lack of qualified personnel allow widespread corruption.

Second, the 1998-2002 Government directly set a bad example in public tenders by making excessive use of its power to grant exemptions from the duty to hold a tender. In 2001, these included a contract to build a highway to Northern Moravia, a contract awarded to Český Telecom to build a telecommunications network for the State administration and a contract for the advisors on privatisation of the energy industry.[76] The *2001 Regular Report* explicitly stated the need to tighten the law to limit fast-track procedures and exclude the possibility of "arbitrary government decisions."[77]

According to an SAO analysis of its own audit findings, between 1995 and 2000 the most important problems in public procurement were:

- Failure to issue tenders properly (36 percent of all audit findings). Failure to define tender requirements exactly resulted in subsequent increases in costs of up to 300 percent, while the division of contracts into smaller parts in order to avoid tender requirements was also common.

---

[76] M. Pražák, "Vláda obchází výběrová řízení" [Government avoids tenders], *Mladá fronta Dnes*, 23 March 2001.

[77] Commission, *2001 Regular Report*, p. 45.

- Abuse of the exceptions in the law allowing public institutions to carry out tenders by inviting a limited number of parties (33 percent of audit findings).

- Failure to maintain sufficient evidence on tender proceedings and to issue and publish tender results.

- Using sole sourcing on the basis of provisions in the law that allow follow-up contracts to be allocated without a tender (eight percent of all findings).[78]

- Not awarding contracts to the party submitting the best bid (four percent).

- Conceptual problems (four percent).

- Mutual relations between organisations issuing a tender and participants in the tender (two percent).

With regard to criteria, as already mentioned, the law leaves wide space for tender issuers to choose criteria they like, and there is little scope for restricting maximum use of this provision. In addition to all of the problems mentioned, the practice of fixing tenders through collusion is generally felt to be widespread in the absence of effective control mechanisms.

The Ministry of Defence has been the subject of more scandals relating to procurement than any other State institution. In 1996-1997, a major scandal broke over a tender for an army information system, including allegations of a €1.7m bribe to the Christian Democratic Union-Czechoslovak People's Party,[79] and there have been a series of army contracts in which the army purchased faulty parts or parts it did not need.[80]

---

[78] For example, the company that carried out reconstruction of the Czech Chamber of Deputies building was also hired without a tender to carry out future maintenance and repair (see Section 2.4).

[79] Q. Reed, "IT tender still raises hackles," *Prague Business Journal,* 19 December 1997. Other major tenders surrounded by suspicion include a project to modernize the country's T-72 tanks, see "Slova o zmanipulování a korupci padala již na začátku projektu" [Words on manipulation and corruption were heard already at upon launching of the project], *Mladá fronta Dnes,* 9 March 1999.

[80] J. Gazdík and M. Mocek, "Vetchý přiznal své chyby" [Vetchy admits mistakes], *Mladá fronta Dnes,* 5 April 2001. One of the most serious cases was when the Ministry of Defence signed a €16.7m contract without a public tender to purchase parachutes from a firm that did not legally exist; according to the Register of Industrial Ownership the inventor of the parachute was also an employee of the Ministry department responsible for the purchase. The parachutes turned out to be unsafe (resulting in the death of one soldier), and, at the time of writing, the Ministry was attempting to withdraw from the contract and get its money back. See J. Gazdík, "Ministr Tvrdík: Došly nám padáky, pomozte" [Minister Tvrdík: Help, we're out of parachutes], *Mladá fronta Dnes,* 29 May 2001.

Another major contract that led to widespread speculation was a tender held by the Government to select a supplier of Western supersonic fighter aircraft, which raised serious doubts of the Government's commitment to fighting corruption. In January 2001, the Government issued a tender for the purchase of between 24 and 36 Western fighter aircrafts, despite clear signals from NATO that such a purchase should not be a priority. In May 2001, shortly before the deadline for submission of bids, four of the five bidders withdrew from the tender, leaving only a consortium of BAE Systems and Saab in the tender. The other contenders left partly on the grounds that the tender was not transparent and was rigged in favour of the consortium.[81] In early 2002, the Government awarded the contract to the consortium.

The most recent scandal concerning public contracts broke after the arrest of the former General Secretary of the Ministry of Foreign Affairs for the alleged attempted contract murder of an investigative journalist that wrote extensively about him (see Section 9.1). The investigation of the scandal led to revelations of widespread corruption in the allocation of contracts by the Ministry between 1998 and 2002.[82]

8. PUBLIC SERVICES

There are significant problems of corruption in a number of Czech public services, in particular the healthcare system, allocation of permits and business registration. Although corruption in the police and customs administration have been long regarded as important problems, improvements in anti-corruption mechanisms and other reforms provide room for optimism in both areas.

8.1 Police

As the statistics in Table 8 show, convictions for corruption in the police are minimal. Statistics on police criminal activity are only available up to mid-1999.

---

[81] Economist Intelligence Unit, *Business Operations Report Czech Republic*, 2nd quarter 2001, p. 22. For example, one of the tender conditions was that bids be submitted in Czech and denominated in the Czech Crown, against US rules for foreign military sales.

[82] See for example "Černínský palác se otřásl v základech" [Cernin palace (Ministry of Foreign Affairs building) shaken to the foundations], *Mladá fronta Dnes,* 27 July 2002.

Table 8: Criminal convictions of police, 1996–1999

Criminal act	1996	1997	1998	1999 (Jan-June)
Abuse of power by a public official	140	86	109	84
Bribery (all forms)	10	11	10	3
Fraud	25	36	12	16
Other	199	154	242	90
Total	374	287	373	193

Source: Ministry of Interior, Problematika nezákonného jednání policistů [The Problematics of the Unlawful Behaviour of Policemen], p. 5.

The figures for convictions for corruption are, again, small and do not reflect public perceptions of police corruption. According to research carried out by GfK for a research project on corruption in the police in 1999, 24 percent of the public believed that corruption is more widespread in the police than in any other group institution, exceeding even the State administration.[83] The police surveyed in the research believed that most opportunities for corruption are in the foreign police and traffic police, the latter being regarded as the most financially lucrative.[84]

Control mechanisms

The police organisation includes internal control and complaints departments at central, regional and local police units, which are responsible for investigating evidence of criminal activity among the police and processing complaints from the public. The decentralised nature of this control system results in a situation where individual police essentially supervise their own colleagues. In 1999, these departments received 2,597 public complaints, of which 21 percent were found to be justified. Thirty-eight cases were submitted to the investigation organs and 127 to the Ministry of Interior Inspectorate.[85]

In addition, the Inspectorate of the Ministry of Interior exercises external control over the police. The Inspectorate is staffed by police and is responsible directly to the Minister of Interior. It relies largely on information supplied by police control departments and its employees' networks of contacts. According to a 1999 Ministry of

---

[83] GfK-Praha and Transparency International Czech Republic, "Korupce v Policii ČR" [Corruption in the Czech police], March 2000.

[84] Cited in: Ministry of Interior of the Czech Republic, *Zpráva o korupci v ČR*, p. 12.

[85] Ministry of Interior, *Problematika nezákonného jednání policistů, analýza a návrh řešení* [The Problematics of the Unlawful Acts of Members of the Police Force – Analysis and Suggested Solution], 1999, p. 9.

Interior report on police criminality, the Inspectorate was significantly understaffed, and co-ordination between the Inspectorate, local police departments and investigatory organs was "absolutely unsatisfactory."[86] However, since that time the staff of the Inspectorate has roughly doubled according to Ministry officials, and the Ministry is considering increasing independence of supervision by staffing the Inspectorate with employees who are not police.[87]

8.2 Customs

The Customs Inspectorate regards corruption as a significant problem within the customs administration. In 2000, the Inspectorate submitted to the police 56 cases of suspected abuse of power and a number of cases of bribery. For example, in 1999 a lawyer from the Brno Customs Office was charged with allegedly accepting a bribe of €13,333 in return for allowing a company to pay lower duties on imported goods.

Czech customs legislation has been simplified considerably, partly in an effort to reduce the opportunities for corruption. According to officials from the Customs Service Inspectorate, customs legislation is harmonised with EU directives, and in 2001 proposed amendments were under discussion to achieve full compatibility. The Customs Service was in 2001 the only customs authority in EU candidate countries to be a signatory on EU agreements on adopting a common transit regime (New Computerised Transit System), which will simplify customs procedures considerably and reduce the scope for corruption.

The employment conditions of customs officers are regulated by the same law as the police.[88] The Customs Inspectorate is subordinate to the Director General of the Customs Service. Unlike the Inspectorate of the Ministry of Interior, the Inspectorate does not have the status of an organ of criminal investigation, and can only file criminal notifications to the police in order to initiate criminal proceedings.

In December 1998, the Inspectorate approved a comprehensive Integrity Action Plan divided into 12 areas: minimisation of administrative regulations, transparency, automation of customs procedures, personnel policy (including rotation of staff), management responsibility, control mechanisms, morality and organisational culture, recruitment procedures to minimise the likelihood of recruiting corruptible staff, a Code of Ethics and Behaviour, expert training, increased pay and communication with

---

[86] Ministry of Interior, *Problematika nezákonného jednání policistů*, p. 12–13.

[87] Interview with Michal Mazel, Head of the Security Department, Ministry of Interior, 6 April 2001.

[88] Police Act no. 186/1992.

exporters and importers. The Code of Ethics was approved in 2001, and an anonymous phone link was established to facilitate complaints. One of the major obstacles to effective anti-corruption policy in the customs service is that it is very difficult to implement staff rotation due to very high geographical immobility.

The Customs Administration participated in early 2002 in an EU anti-corruption project entitled "Ensuring Integrity," in partnership with the German and Dutch customs authorities.

8.3 Tax collection

Corruption in tax assessment does not appear to be a major problem area for companies. According to the SAO, much more serious problems exist in the area of control by the tax authorities of value-added tax, where fraudulent schemes organised by complicated chains of companies (and sometimes aided by corrupt local tax officials) cause massive losses to the State budget.[89]

8.4 Health

Since 1989, not one case of corruption has been proven in the Czech healthcare system.[90] However, surveys show that around 15 percent of the population believe corruption is most widespread in healthcare (see Section 1.2), ranking the sector better only than the State administration and police (and judiciary in one year according to GfK).

A major problem facing efforts to analyse or deal with corruption in the healthcare system is a pure lack of detailed research on what is in practice a highly complicated issue. For example, informal payments are often the result of underfunding, and although illegal in many cases are used to fund the activities of hospitals and not channelled into private pockets. The rights of patients are inadequate in the health service, as are complaint mechanisms, which have no guarantee of recourse.[91]

---

[89] SAO officials estimate that non-payments of VAT total approximately € 2b annually, an amount equal to approximately ten percent of total tax revenues.

[90] Only one case was dealt with in court, where the head nurse of a medical centre for the permanently ill was charged with accepting bribes to place patients in the centre. The case ended in acquittal.

[91] P. Háva, "Je naše zdravotnictví transparentní?" [Is Our Healthcare Transparent?], unpublished summary of a seminar organised by Transparency International Czech Republic, 5 October 2000.

8.5 Education

According to surveys, between two and six percent of survey respondents believe corruption is most widespread in the education system (8.5 percent in a most recent but smaller telephone survey by SC&C).[92] There is almost no evidence on corruption, with the important and worrying exception of a major scandal that broke in June 1999 surrounding admission procedures for the prestigious Legal Faculty of Prague's Charles University. The scandal began with anonymous notifications to the press that the exam papers were widely available for money before the exams, and the allegations were subsequently confirmed by other witnesses. A police investigation was halted for lack of evidence. However, former students at the Faculty confirm that bribery to gain admission has been widespread.

8.6 Licensing and regulation

In the area of trade licenses and business registration, criteria are generally clear. Business registration is widely regarded as an area troubled by corruption (see Section 5.2).

Trade licenses, which are issued by the Trade License Department of the relevant local council, appear to be a relatively unproblematic area. However, amendments to the Trade License Act, passed in 1999, introduced more stringent conditions for many occupations, which has increased incentives for applicants to circumvent the law.[93]

Construction permits are more problematic. Permits are issued by the Building Department of the local municipal authority. The planning process is extraordinarily complicated and usually takes 8-14 months for a business development permit; for example, investors must secure written approval from around 60 different local authorities ranging from hygiene and sanitation to air traffic authorities.[94] There is wide room for discretion in the process.

The Office for the Protection of Economic Competition

Although not explicitly an anti-corruption agency, the Czech Office for the Protection of Economic Competition (ÚOHS) is the most important State institution of market regulation and a potentially major source of corrupt pressure. The *2000 Regular Report*

---

[92] *Lidové noviny*, daily, 25 April 2002.

[93] For example, to operate a riding stable the holder of the trade license must hold a certificate of higher education, a requirement that in theory would put most stables out of business.

[94] Economist Intelligence Unit, *Business Operations Report Czech Republic*, 2nd quarter 1999, pp. 50–51.

identified "effective application and enforcement of anti-trust rules" as the "main challenge" facing the Czech Republic in competition regulation.[95]

There have been reasons for concern over the ÚOHS's competence in the past. The staffing of the upper positions of the Office on a political party basis was standard practice, at least until an amendment to the Act approved in September 2000 banned the Chairman of the Office from being a member of a political party.[96] The Office's real separation from political institutions was called into question somewhat by its approval in June 2000 of State aid to cover losses at Investiční a poštovní banka (Investition and Post Bank) on the same day as the aid itself was approved by the Government. In the private sector, the Office found itself in the spotlight over a long-running merger battle in the brewing industry between 1997 and 1999, in which it issued several conflicting decisions under alternating lobbying pressures. However, in the past year the Office has made decisions that indicate a more independent approach, for example ruling that State aid provided to the country's largest steel works was illegal.

9. ROLE OF THE MEDIA

The Czech press is free, although there have been isolated cases of the State using legal provisions to attempt to deter journalists. A Freedom of Information Act came into effect in 2000, although its impact on access to information in practice may have been limited. Broadcasting regulation has suffered from some problems of political interference in the activities of public media, although an improved legal framework was adopted in 2001. Licensing policy for private broadcasters has been subject to major problems, and the activities of the Broadcasting Council have resulted in a foreign investor winning an arbitration case against the Czech State. The Czech media has been active in uncovering corruption, and initiated the downfall of the Government in 1997.

9.1 Freedom of speech

Freedom of speech is guaranteed according to the Czech Constitution, and reiterated in the 2000 Press Act.[97] The right to publish may be restricted only under circumstances

---

[95] Commission, *2000 Regular Report*, p. 52.

[96] Economist Intelligence Unit, *Business Operations Report Czech Republic*, 2nd quarter 1999, Chapter 3.

[97] 2000 Press Act, paragraph 5.

stated by law and if doing so is necessary to protect the rights and freedoms of others, State security, public safety or public health and morality.

The Press Act also contains provisions under which individuals have a right to the correction of untrue information published about them.[98] More controversially, publications have a duty to publish a reply by individuals and legal entities to statements published in the press that, even if true, impinge on their honour, dignity or privacy. However, despite the fears of some publishers, this has not proved to be a stick that the Government uses to weaken the media.

There are no legal restrictions on coverage of corruption cases. Moreover, libel law is weak and does not deter journalists from seeking out corruption. Journalists have been put under pressure through different laws, however. A key case was the exposure by daily *Mladá fronta Dnes* of a plan organised in the Office of Prime Minister to discredit a political rival. Although the case resulted in the prosecution of one of Zeman's advisors, the police also decided to prosecute the journalists who broke the story for not revealing their source at the Office of the Government, on grounds that the person who gave them the document committed slander and should therefore be prosecuted. In March 2001, the Prague City Prosecution Office set a welcome precedent by halting criminal proceedings.

In another case, a former TV reporter was charged in 2000 for revealing State secrets after filming a documentary alleging that the former Chief of the Military Intelligence Service (now Director of the Security Information Service, the Czech intelligence service) helped a friend avoid prosecution for drunk driving by informing the police in a letter (untruthfully) that the man was an intelligence officer. The director had classified the letter as "Strictly Secret." The journalist faced a sentence of up to eight years if found guilty. Although the court dismissed the case in June 2001, it did not do so on grounds of press freedom. Moreover, the State Prosecutor appealed the decision.[99]

In July 2002, a much more worrying case emerged when the police arrested and charged the former General Secretary of the Ministry of Foreign Affairs with renting a contract killer to murder an investigative journalist who has covered, *inter alia*, the case of Czech House (see Section 3.6).[100] Ironically, the former official (who resigned as a result of the Czech House scandal) was originally hired by Minister Jan Kavan to

---

[98] Act no. 46/2000, Article 12.

[99] J. Unger, "Soud osvobodil novináře Smrčka" [The Court dismissed journalist Smrček], *Mladá fronta Dnes,* 16 June 2001; J. Unger, "Smrček půjde opět k soudu" [Smrček to face the Court again], *Mladá fronta Dnes,* 20 July 2001.

[100] "Vrah měl zabít novinářku" [A killer was to assassinate an investigative woman-journalist], *Mladá fronta Dnes,* 23 July 2002.

implement the "Clean Hands" campaign at the Ministry. If confirmed, the case would be unique among EU candidate countries.

9.2 Access to information

The Czech Act on Free Access to Information[101] (Freedom of Information Act), which came into force on 1 January 2000 has established citizen rights to public information that were previously stated only in general terms in the Constitution. The Act applies to all State organs (such as the Government, Parliament and ministries), organs of regional and local government and self-administration, and public institutions that manage public money. The only information excepted from the law are State secrets, information that is protected under the Act on Protection of Personal Data and commercial secrets. However, the Act prohibits information concerning the use of public funds from being classified as a commercial secret.

Since the Act came into force, the Government has issued an instruction to organs falling under the law in September 2000 to harmonise procedures for provision of information.

At the time of writing it is still too early to judge accurately whether the Act has made a radical difference to access to information. All ministries have established procedures for fulfilling their duties under the law, and it appears that the more flagrant cases of withholding information that used to occur before the law came into effect[102] are no longer possible. Although there have been isolated cases of institutions charging excessive amounts for information, this does not appear to be common.[103]

On the other hand, State institutions also appear to have learned to obey the letter of the law without providing information requested, for example by using every possible mistake in the information request to avoid replying. Moreover, it is unclear whether the government instruction is effective: for example, despite an explicit provision in the instruction stating that internal employment rules of State organisations cannot be withheld, the Ministry of Finance refused to supply a copy of its rules for the purposes of this report.

Finally, the definition of "commercial secrecy" remains ambiguous, and a number of institutions have attempted to define themselves as being outside the scope of the law, for example the National Property Fund.[104] In 2000 the Government refused to

---

[101] Act no. 106/1999.

[102] For example, the withholding by ministries of recipients of State subsidies.

[103] The Government instruction states that charges may not exceed the real costs of obtaining the information.

[104] This was confirmed by a decision of the Prague City Court in September 2000.

provide information on subsidies to companies such as a major steelworks by setting up special mechanisms for allocating funds.

9.3 Broadcasting regulation

Broadcasting media are licensed and regulated by the Broadcasting Council, elected by the Chamber of Deputies. Two main private stations exist (plus one new station established recently), but inadequate regulation by the Broadcasting Council (also elected by Parliament) has resulted in opaque ownership structures and suspicions that both stations are controlled by the same entity. A battle has been raging since 1999 over the larger of the two, TV Nova, after the company owning the broadcasting license (CET 21) broke off ties with the service company (CNTS) operating the station and took full control of the station. CNTS was controlled by a foreign investor (Central Media Enterprises). CME sued the Czech Government for failing to protect its investment, *inter alia,* on the basis that CET 21s withdrawal from the agreement was allegedly facilitated by a change in the wording of the broadcasting license in 1997. At the end of 2001 a Stockholm arbitration court decided that the Czech State did indeed violate its duty, and as of July 2002 negotiations on compensation were continuing. As of May 2002, the General Director of Nova and main protagonist against CME, Vladimír Železný, was under investigation for allegedly damaging creditors. Former Prime Minister and Chairman of the Civic Democratic Party Václav Klaus openly expressed support for Železný.[105]

Czech Television and Czech Radio are regulated by councils also elected by the Chamber of Deputies. A major crisis broke at Czech Television in December 2000 after employees reacted to what they perceived as political interference culminating in the appointment of a new director. The appointment, carried out by a Council dominated by the ODS and ČSSD, led to a revolt by TV staff and mass public protests. The eventual result was an amendment to the Act on Czech Television. In response to a situation where the Council of Czech Television was elected on a party basis – facilitating political influence on the public media – the law was amended to create a council elected by the Chamber of Deputies from representatives proposed by civic organisations.

---

[105] Klaus stated in response to questions about his support for Železný that, "When someone is good to me, I am good to him." V. Žák, "Drahá televize Nova" [Good old TV Nova], *Listy* 1, 2002, p. 18.

9.4 Corruption in the media

There is little evidence of direct corruption of journalists in the Czech Republic, although article buying by PR agencies was much discussed in 1997–1998. The Czech PR industry is one of the best regulated in the region, with an association and a Code of Ethics.

9.5 Media and corruption

The Czech media has played a key role in exposing corruption and related issues since the mid-1990's, in cases ranging from its exposure of party sponsors as false (see Section 6) to exposing the failure of a minister in the current Government to adhere to the provisions of the Conflict of Interest Act. The media played a dominant role in the collapse of the Klaus Government in 1997, and has uncovered numerous scandals under the Zeman Government. The poor relationship between the media and Zeman himself bears witness to the success of the media in putting the Government under pressure. In the run-up to the 2002 elections, for example, *Mladá fronta Dnes* has published an extensive series of articles examining the property and lifestyle of prominent party politicians.[106]

10. RECOMMENDATIONS

The following recommendations have been highlighted as particularly important to the Czech Republic. For additional recommendations applicable to candidate States generally, please see Part 5 of the Overview report.

1. Carry out an analysis of the risk of corruption in the legislative process, particularly in Parliament, and carry out reforms based on the findings.

2. Pay special attention to the risks of corruption stemming from post-privatisation processes of bankruptcy and debt management.

---

[106] See, e.g., *Mladá fronta Dnes*, "Zbohatli v politice?" [Grown rich in politics?], 3 April 2002.

Corruption and Anti-corruption Policy
in Estonia

Table of Contents

Corruption and Anti-corruption Policy in Estonia

EXECUTIVE SUMMARY

Estonia is widely regarded as the least corrupt – or among the least corrupt – of the EU candidate States. While this report tends to confirm the perception that corruption is a relatively limited problem among senior officials and politicians, survey evidence indicates significant corruption problems in a number of areas. According to public opinion the most corrupt functionaries are political leaders and police officers, while the Estonian authorities regard local government and the Customs Board and border guard as the main loci of corruption. Corruption may be a particularly important problem at local government level, where the main institutions with a role in fighting corruption appear not to have much impact. An area that is little discussed or researched is organised crime, which anecdotal evidence and Estonia's geographical situation indicate is an important local phenomenon.

Estonia has made major progress towards putting in place a comprehensive anti-corruption framework, ranging from bribery laws, through provisions on conflict of interest and asset declarations to freedom of information legislation. The accompanying institutions for fighting corruption have mostly been established. However, there is no coordinated anti-corruption strategy, although the Government has taken important steps towards formulating one. Moreover, there are some doubts concerning the effectiveness of enforcement and implementation. In particular, several important institutions with roles in fighting corruption appear not to fulfil this role as effectively as they might, notably the Parliament (Rigiikogu) Anti-corruption Committee and the Public Procurement Office.

The European Commission has not identified corruption as an important problem and has exerted little pressure on Estonia in the area of anti-corruption policy. However, the Commission has provided some assistance to the fight against corruption and financial crime.

Anti-corruption legislation is very advanced by transition country standards. Estonia is the only country in the region to define corruption separately as a distinct crime under criminal law, and was one of the first countries to ratify the Council of Europe Civil Law Convention on Corruption. Minor changes to bribery legislation to widen criminal liability of legal entities and foreign officials will be necessary to fulfil all international conventions.

The Anti-corruption Act lays down comprehensive rules on conflict of interest, and imposes duties on public functionaries to submit declarations of assets and income. There is little evidence of violation of these provisions. However, the system for monitoring adherence to them, particularly the operation of the Parliamentary Anti-corruption Committee, does not appear to be effective.

Estonia has made considerable progress towards establishing an integrated system of State financial control, with legislation fully compatible with EU requirements. However, the effectiveness of control and audit concerning corruption does not appear to have been very effective to date, especially at local government level.

The security police has been the agency responsible for coordinating anti-corruption policy and investigating most cases of corruption. The agency appears to have carried out its investigative role well, although the removal from its competence of investigation of corruption cases at local government level raises concerns about the ability of the regular police to take over this function. The Legal Chancellor performs the functions of an ombudsman, although corruption is not a central priority.

There is very little evidence of corruption among executive officials and civil servants, while the resignation of a former Prime Minister indicates that corruption control mechanisms work relatively well at the highest level. The legal framework for the public administration is advanced, with a Civil Service Act in force since 1996 and Public Administration Reform Programme approved in April 2001. However, reform of local government, where there is a need to reduce the number of units of government, has not progressed significantly. The legal framework governing procedures for appealing against administrative decisions has only been completed since January 2002. A Civil Service Code of Ethics exists, although its effectiveness is doubtful. The implementation of conflict of interest and asset declaration provisions remains a concern in this area, however.

The State budget approved by Parliament includes all public revenue and expenditure, although the effectiveness of audit of public expenditure has in the past been blunted by the lack of formal cooperation between the State Audit Office and Parliament. Although there is some evidence of lobbying by business interests that contributed to political parties, survey research indicates that "capture" of parliamentary votes is not a serious problem. The ineffectiveness of supervision of conflict of interest and asset declarations by the Parliamentary (Riigikogu) Anti-corruption Committee makes assessment of this area difficult.

The judiciary is independent, and recent legislation will consolidate this situation further. The effectiveness of the courts in prosecuting corruption cases is subject to some concerns, including a lack of specialisation, a short statute of limitations for some corruption offences and the apparent leniency of the courts towards those convicted of corruption. International monitoring has drawn attention to a lack of professionalism of courts and prosecution offices in this area, while recent changes to criminal procedure have restricted the competence of the security police to investigate corruption cases. There is almost no evidence of corruption in the courts or prosecution offices.

Regulation of political party funding has undergone major changes with the passage of a new act in 1999. The act introduced relatively strict restrictions on donations and disclosure requirements. However, there is no institutional supervision of party accounts and there are proposals to increase the maximum permitted cash donations. In practice, parties can probably evade the new funding rules fairly easily, and there is some evidence that corruption in political party funding has been a significant problem.

The public procurement process appears to be particularly vulnerable to corruption. Although a fairly advanced legal framework is in place, monitoring of procurement and resolution of complaints is inadequate. In particular, the Public Procurement Office appears to be vulnerable to political interference and is not sufficiently staffed to inspect procurement or check complaints. Although there appear to have been no criminal prosecutions for corruption in public procurement, local observers believe tender fixing is common, and corruption in procurement at local government level is believed to be more-or-less widespread.

There is little evidence of corruption in public services such as health and education. However, the European Commission has drawn attention to the need to fight corruption in the police and customs administration, while GRECO expressed concern at the vulnerability of the customs authorities to corruption and organised crime. Business registration and licensing do not appear to be troubled significantly by corruption.

The Estonian media is free, despite some limited evidence of the use of libel and defamation provisions to deter journalists. Freedom of Information legislation is in place, although its impact on access to information may be subject to doubt. Although the printed press has been increasingly active in exposing corruption, the broadcasting media have played little part in exposing corruption. This is, however, more likely due to lack of financial resources than direct political interference.

1. INTRODUCTION

1.1 The data and perceptions

According to international surveys Estonia is the least corrupt – or among the least corrupt – among EU candidate States. Nevertheless, domestic surveys indicate significant corruption problems. According to public opinion surveys of perception, the most corrupt functionaries are political leaders and police officers, while the authorities regard local government and the Customs Board and border guard as the main loci of corruption. For a number of reasons, corruption may be a particularly important problem at local government level.

Table 1 shows the number of convictions from 1998 to 2001 for the main corruption-related criminal acts. Moreover, the punishments given to perpetrators tend to be very lenient: of 58 convicted for the main corruption offences in 2001, 45 received suspended sentences, while only seven received prison sentences.[1] GRECO expressed the opinion in its 2001 evaluation of anti-corruption policy in Estonia that,

> Despite impressive anti-corruption legislation in Estonia and dedicated police and prosecutors, the GET (GRECO Evaluation Team) considered that the results of corruption investigations and prosecutions are not impressive.[2]

Table 1: Convictions for corrupt acts, 1998–2001

Criminal act	1998	1999	2000	2001
Accepting a bribe	31	12	17	17
Giving a bribe	8	6	24	18
Arranging a bribe	2	1	2	1
Misuse of official position	12	8	7	8
Abuse of authority	14	10	6	8
Unlawful acceptance of remuneration	[??]	[??]	[??]	0
Corrupt act	N/A	N/A	0	6
Failure to submit declaration of economic interests/presentation of false evidence	2	0	0	0

Source: Ministry of Justice, GRECO, *Evaluation Report on Estonia*, adopted by GRECO at the 6th Plenary Meeting, Strasbourg, 10-14 September 2001.

---

[1] Ministry of Justice statistics.

[2] GRECO, *Evaluation Report on Estonia*, adopted by GRECO at the 6th Plenary Meeting, Strasbourg, 10-14 September 2001, p. 24.

Surveys

According to the Transparency International Corruption Perception Index, Estonia is the least corrupt of all CEE countries, with an index of 5.7 in 1997 and 2000 (27th place) and 5.6 in 2001 (28th place).[3] The World Bank makes a similar assessment based on its *1999 Business Environment and Enterprise Performance Survey*, concluding that the average level of corruption is relatively low when compared to other CEE countries: 84 percent of companies surveyed said that companies like theirs pay less than five percent of annual revenues in bribes, while none said companies pay more than 20 percent. However, when broken down, the World Bank results do not give such a positive picture, and in a number of important categories, corruption appears to be as big a problem for Estonian companies as for those in other CEE countries, for example in the area of political party financing (see Section 6.3). The World Bank concluded in 2000 that, "[T]he average level of corruption in Estonia is relatively low when compared to other CEE countries, although relatively high with regard to political corruption."[4]

According to a domestic survey carried out by the Jaan Tõnisson Institute and Saar Poll in 2001,[5] the proportion of Estonians having had experience of corruption has fallen since 1998: 84 percent of respondents said they had never had any experience with corruption, a sharp increase from 69 percent in a similar survey from 1998, while ten percent said they had. However, 42 percent thought that most officials are corrupt and 12 percent that almost all are. The percentage of respondents considering most or all politicians to be corrupt increased since 1998 from 19 to 25 percent.[6]

1.2 Main loci of corruption

According to popular belief, political leaders and police force officials are the most corrupt public functionaries in Estonia.[7] However, the evidence on corruption in these spheres is not strong. While a number of high-profile scandals (not all of which have

---

[3] Transparency International, *Annual Report 2000*, available at <http//www.transparency.org>, (last accessed, 28 August 2002).

[4] World Bank, *Anti-corruption in Transition: A Contribution to the Policy Debate*, World Bank, 2000, p. 13.

[5] Jaan Tõnisson Institute, "Public Opinion Poll About Corruption," Tallinn 2001.

[6] Although these results appear to be somewhat contradictory, they might consistently reflect the real situation to the extent that corruption of a type that is not experienced directly by citizens (for example, corruption in political party financing) has increased.

[7] Ministry of Internal Affairs, "Survey of Victims," Tallinn 1995.

confirmed individual wrongdoing) may have underpinned the public perception,[8] there is an impression among journalists that senior officials take their responsibilities seriously and are sufficiently motivated by national interests not to let corruption interfere with processes that are perceived to be key to national interest, in particular accession to the EU and NATO.[9] In the central State administration, the Ministry of Economy may be a possible weak spot in terms of corruption (see Section 3.6). Although it is one of the smallest ministries, it retains important powers: for example, the Public Procurement Office is subordinate to it.

Among experts on corruption and officials involved in anti-corruption efforts, there is a strong feeling that the biggest corruption problems lie at the level of Estonia's 247 local governments, which, while gaining wide autonomy, have also become progressively less subject to external supervision (see below).[10] In addition, according to the opinions expressed by officials to GRECO, the other main affected area is the border guard and Customs Board, a major issue in a country where 70 percent of State revenues come from customs and excise duties.[11]

In 1995-2001 the Security Police initiated and forwarded to the court 147 criminal cases concerning malfeasance, of which 118 were tried. In these cases 206 persons were accused and 165 convicted. Suspended sentences were handed down in 112 cases, fines in 34 cases, and 19 people were imprisoned. The accused included local mayors, junior police officers and a number of customs officials and border guards.[12]

---

[8] For example, the Prime Minister was forced to resign in 1997 as a result of a scandal involving his previous position as the Mayor of Tallinn; the current Prime Minister was previously the Governor of the Central Bank when several million dollars disappeared, although he was cleared of any personal wrongdoing; the Mayor of Tallinn (a possible future candidate for Prime Minister) was once expelled from office for abuse of power.

[9] Conversation with Rafael Behr, *Financial Times* correspondent for the Baltic States, 23 July 2002.

[10] OSI Roundtable Discussion, Tallinn, 14 March 2002. *Explanatory note: OSI held a roundtable meeting in Tallinn to invite critique of the present report in draft form. Experts present included representatives of the government and civil society organisations.*

[11] GRECO, *Evaluation Report on Estonia,* p. 6.

[12] GRECO, *Evaluation Report on Estonia,* p. 8.

Table 2: Percentage of respondents having experienced corruption in selected areas

Area/action	Percentage of respondents experiencing corruption in the last three years
Recruitment, keeping one's job	16
Bribery or gift for better medical care	13
Bribery requested but not provided	9
Composing and registering documents	8
Public works	6
Bribing employment bureau official to be offered better job	5
Registering land	2
Getting residency permit	2
Obtaining information about restitution of property	2
Bribing doctors in public health service	1

Source: Jaan Tõnisson Institute, "Public Opinion Poll About Corruption," Tallinn 2001.

The most famous recent corruption case was the conviction in 2001 of the former Chairman of the Board of the Maapank bank for misuse of funds from a State foundation. In 1996 the official concerned worked as the Chairman of the Board and shareholder of the Virumaa Kommertspank and at the same time served as a Board Member of the Agricultural American Foreign Aid Foundation. He was convicted of corruption in 2001 and sentenced to 18 months' imprisonment, specifically in connection with the transfer of €1.9m of Foundation money to Maapank.[13] Another major case, although not involving a court conviction, was the resignation of the former Prime Minister after revelations concerning allocation of apartments when he was previously Mayor of Tallinn (see below and Section 9.5).

Corruption in local government

Some of the most important corruption problems appear to arise at the level of the country's 247 municipalities, where strong local networks tying business to administration combine with poor control and external supervision. There is a general impression among agencies involved in fighting corruption that local government is literally out of control in this respect.[14]

---

[13] The money was used to boost Maapank's own equity, enabling it to satisfy Central Bank requirements. Information provided by the Jaan Tõnisson Institute.

[14] OSI Roundtable Discussion, Tallinn, 14 March 2002.

The only control mechanism at the parish and town level is a three-member auditing commission appointed by the local council and consisting of its own members. Commission members often lack any qualifications for such activities, and the Tallinn City Council is the only municipality employing a specialised control department.

A striking development concerning control of local government is the *de facto* removal of external control mechanisms. Under amendments to the Code of Criminal Procedure that came into effect in July 2000, pre-trial investigations of corruption cases involving municipal officials no longer fall under the jurisdiction of the security police, which is the only institution that explicitly fights against corruption.[15] Although the State Audit Office checks the use of State budget funds by local government, it does not audit local government as such, and the extension of its competence to cover this area was only under discussion at the time of writing. Moreover, there is a general feeling that the local press does not play a role in exposing corruption.[16]

According to local audit officials,[17] corruption in local government has been concentrated in the following areas:

Restitution/privatisation of property and land. Corruption has varied from bribery to obtain property from municipalities to schemes by which officials obtain property themselves.

Dealing in town property. A number of suspicions and scandals broke during Tiit Vähi's term as Prime Minister, culminating in a scandal that led to his resignation. The case related to his previous position as Mayor of Tallinn and the unauthorised sale of apartments rented by Tallinn city officials. Vähi resigned under public pressure and did not run in the next elections to the Parliament.

Rental contracts that have been favourable to tenants but damaging to the municipality have been relatively common. For example, in 1995 a complex of buildings in Old Tallinn was rented to a private company for 25 years by an order of the municipal government. An audit by the commission established by the Tallinn City Council later found that the tenant did not fulfil obligations to renovate the property and rented the property at a price 15 times the rent paid to the municipality (which alone caused

---

[15] Although this change was motivated primarily by efforts to distribute tasks more rationally between the security and regular police, its impact on anti-corruption activities may be negative. Previously, the security Police had begun initiating several cases against municipal officials.

[16] GRECO, *Evaluation Report on Estonia*, p. 20.

[17] Interviews with the Head of the Controlling Department of the Tallinn Town Council, Toomas Johanson, and a Senior Auditor, Leho Rehemäe; audits by the Tallinn Town Council and broader research carried out by Mr. Rehemäe.

€101,333 damage to the municipality). The whole situation was made possible due to a total absence of control over rental contracts and procedures.

In another case, Tallinn city sold Tallinn Central Market to individuals connected to the market's governing body for half its market value. The share of stock could have been €1.583–2.216m, but was reduced to €760,000–950,000.

Public procurements. Ordering construction projects and other services from companies involving town officials or related persons appears to be common. For example, between 1996 and 1999 a municipal official of the Haaberst district of Tallinn ordered construction plans from his own firm. In April 2001, the Deputy Mayor of Tallinn was investigated for allegedly allocating contracts to a firm owned by his son.[18]

Abuse of study visits. Study visits by local officials to foreign countries have often turned out to be expensive pleasure trips. For example, the Mayor of Võru sent four members of the town government for a week to a seminar in Morocco, exceeding the budget for the trip by 300 percent. The town council of Võru forced the Mayor and his assistant to resign.

According to the opinion of one experienced Estonian business journalist, Tallinn City Council is the most corrupt unit of public administration, with many shady deals, real estate privatisations and public contracts (particularly construction contracts) awarded without tenders.[19]

Organised crime

One area that is relevant to corruption in Estonia but has been almost entirely unresearched is organised crime. GRECO expressed concern that the authorities did not seem sufficiently aware of the danger posed by organised crime in a country that is a natural transit route for smuggling, expressing the opinion that, "[T]he absence of visible links between corruption in Estonia and (cross-border) organised crime might be an illusion," and recommending intensified research to check the existence of such links.[20] Foreign journalists are of the opinion that organised crime is well established, and appears to enjoy a degree of impunity from enforcement authorities.[21]

---

[18] "Deputy mayor faces corruption charges," *Ceturtdiena*, 19 April 2001.

[19] Interview with Anvar Samost, Chief Economic Editor, Baltic News Service, Tallinn, 15 March 2002.

[20] GRECO, *Evaluation Report on Estonia*, p. 23.

[21] Conversation with Rafael Behr, *Financial Times* correspondent for the Baltic States, 23 July 2002.

1.3 Government anti-corruption policy

Estonia has made major progress towards putting in place a comprehensive anti-corruption framework and the accompanying institutions for fighting corruption. However, there is no coordinated anti-corruption strategy, although the Government has recently taken steps towards formulating one. As other sections of this report indicate, there are some doubts concerning the effectiveness of enforcement and implementation of anti-corruption policy by several of the institutions with roles in fighting corruption.

As of August 2002, the Government did not possess an explicit national anti-corruption strategy. However, various agencies have developed specific anti-corruption strategies, such as the Ministry of Internal Affairs and Customs Board. Otherwise, Estonia is advanced in the arena of legislation: bribery legislation is already largely compatible with EU and other international requirements, and Estonia was the third country to ratify the Council of Europe Civil Law Convention on Corruption in October 2001. The country was the first among candidate countries to adopt an explicit Anti-corruption Act in 1995,[22] which provides the legal basis for prevention and prosecution of corruption, including definitions of a public official and corruption, comprehensive provisions on conflicts of interest and asset declarations and the establishment of a Parliamentary Anti-corruption Committee. An important breakthrough also took place when the Parliament passed the Act on Public Information in November 2000.

The National Strategy for Crime Prevention, adopted in July 2000[23] and lasting until 2003, contains some priorities for the fight against corruption to be implemented by the security police. These priorities include: setting up or improving the work of internal control units in Government offices; exposing cases of corruption in the law enforcement system, larger local government units and ministries connected with smuggling illegal arms, alcohol, fuel, drugs and radioactive material, the illegal issue of residency and citizenship documents; fighting corruption related to public procurement and large State investments; and exposing persons involved in money laundering and identifying their involvement in corruption cases.

The most important anti-corruption measure adopted by the previous Government was a regulation approved in October 2000 that mandated the creation of internal audit bodies and procedures in all State institutions (see Section 2.4).[24]

---

[22] Anti-corruption Act, *State Gazette* I/1999, 16, 276.

[23] Estonian National Programme for the Adoption of the Acquis 2001, Part III, Chapter 24; <http://www.eib.ee/english>, (last accessed 31 July 2002).

[24] Government Regulation no. 329, General Procedures for Internal Audit in Power Authorities and State Institutions within Their Administrative Area and Additional Requirements Set for Internal Auditors, 18 October 2000.

However, these measures do not amount to a comprehensive anti-corruption strategy. Estonia has not come under pressure from the European Commission to develop such a strategy. Yet, the evaluation carried out by GRECO in 2001 contained a number of important criticisms of the anti-corruption framework, in particular noting the lack of involvement by bodies that normally would play an important role in fighting corruption, notably the State Audit Office and the Public Procurement Office, and the poor functioning of the Parliamentary Anti-corruption Committee.[25]

Largely in response to the GRECO report, the Crime Prevention Council proposed a joint committee to draft an Anti-corruption Strategy. The expert committee was formed in June by Government decision.[26]

Role of civil society

Cooperation between the State and NGOs in the preparation of anti-corruption legislation and between public authorities and civil society groups in monitoring implementation of this legislation has been relatively weak. However, civil society organisations are slowly taking on a more significant role in anti-corruption efforts[27] and are undertaking a number of activities to complement governmental efforts. The most active NGO in this area is the Jaan Tõnisson Institute, which formed a Corruption Analysis Centre in February 2000 and also hosts the Estonian branch of Transparency International (TI). In 1998, the Institute launched a project on corruption beginning with the first joint roundtable discussion with all State institutions involved, as a result of which Parliament amended the Anti-corruption Act. In April 2002 the General Assembly of the Roundtable of Estonian Non-profit organisations adopted a Code of Ethics.[28]

1.4 The impact of the EU Accession Process

The European Commission has not identified corruption as an important problem in Estonia and anti-corruption policy has not been a significant component of Accession Partnerships or other recommended measures. The Commission has provided some assistance to the fight against corruption and financial crime.

The Commission's *2000 Regular Report on Estonia's Progress towards Accession* devotes only one paragraph explicitly to corruption, beginning with the observation that,

---

[25] GRECO, *Evaluation Report on Estonia,* p. 33.

[26] OSI Roundtable Discussion, Tallinn, 14 March 2002.

[27] For example, the Jaan Tõnisson Institute has established a Corruption Analysis Centre which constitutes the executive structure of Estonia's Transparency International affiliate.

[28] For details see <http://www.emy.ee>, (last accessed 28 August 2002).

> Corruption is a relatively limited problem in Estonia. Only isolated cases can be reported, mainly in the local administrations where business and officials are more closely interconnected.[29]

The Report noted considerable progress in adopting international instruments, and urged only extra attention to fighting corruption in the police and customs administration. The *2001 Regular Report* continues on a similar note, praising further progress and urging in addition only continuing attention to the capacity to enforce compliance with anti-corruption legislation at the local government level.[30] The Accession Partnerships contain minimal references to corruption, especially those from 2001.

From January to May 2002, a project entitled "Fight Against Economic and Financial Crime" was carried out as part of the Netherlands pre-accession aid "PSO 2000" programme. The main emphasis of the project was to improve the ability of law enforcement agencies to fight economic crime and corruption and also to focus on prevention. In October and November 2001, two integrity courses were held for 30 officials from the Ministry of Finance, Customs Board, Security Police Board, Tax Board and Central Criminal Police. In October 2001 and February 2002, the program also trained seven officials from the Security Police Board, Police Board, Tax Board, Customs Board and State Prosecutors Office. An internal integrity survey was carried out in the Security Police Board.

Estonia has also participated in the OCTOPUS programme (1999-2000) against organised crime and corruption, a joint programme of the European Commission and Council of Europe. Some preliminary steps have been taken in order to prepare cooperation with OLAF, the EU's anti-fraud body.

2. INSTITUTIONS AND LEGISLATION

Anti-corruption legislation is very advanced by transition country standards. In addition to standard provisions on bribery and other explicit acts of corruption, the Anti-corruption Act lays down comprehensive rules on conflict of interest, and imposes duties on public functionaries to submit declarations of assets and income; the system for monitoring adherence to them, however, does not appear to be operate effectively. Estonia has made major progress towards establishing an integrated system of State financial control, although doubts remain concerning the effect of control and audit on corruption. The main anti-corruption agency is the security police, which appears to

---

[29] Commission, *2000 Regular Report*, p. 17.

[30] Commission, *2001 Regular Report*, p. 19.

have carried out its investigative role well, although the removal from its competence of investigation of corruption cases at local government level raises concerns about anti-corruption mechanisms at that level. The Legal Chancellor performs the functions of an ombudsman, although corruption is not a central priority.

2.1 Anti-corruption legislation

The Anti-corruption Act

The 1995 Anti-corruption Act, which was amended in 1999, provides the legal foundation for the prevention of corruption and prosecution of corrupt officials.

A corrupt act is defined in the Criminal Code but not in the new Penal Code, which is replacing the Criminal Code and will probably come into effect in Autumn 2002. No special definition for a "corrupt act" is considered necessary, since other forms of official misconduct established by the Penal Code can cover the concept.

The Anti-corruption Act provides the legal basis for the prevention of corruption and the prosecution of officials involved in corruption. The Act lays down three sets of provisions designed to prevent corruption, which apply to a long list of officials including MPs, the President of the Republic, ministers, judges, prosecutors, police, the Auditor General and chief auditors of the State Audit Office, county governors, members of local councils, mayors and members of local governments, notaries, members of statutory organs of companies in which the State or local government participates, heads of State agencies administered by Government agencies and bankruptcy receivers. The Act defines a corrupt act as "the use of official position for self-serving purposes by an official who makes undue or unlawful decisions or performs such acts, or fails to make lawful decisions or perform such acts,"[31] and prohibits officials from committing such acts or entering into relationships with persons involving a risk of corruption or receiving income (widely defined as any benefit) from corrupt acts.

In addition, the Act restricts employment, activities and certain types of actions in order to prevent conflict of interest situations, and establishes a framework under which the same circle of officials are duty-bound to submit declarations of economic interests (see Section 2.2 below).

---

[31] Anti-corruption Act, Chapter 1, Article 5 (1).

Bribery

The Criminal Code[32] criminalises the giving, request and acceptance of both bribes (in return for an illegal act or omission) and gratuities (in return for a lawful act or omission) by or to a variety of persons. Such persons are those who have an official position in an agency, enterprise or organisation, based on any form of ownership, who perform functions that are administrative, supervisory, managerial, operational or relating to the organisation of the movement of tangible assets or who serve as representatives of State authority, assigned by the State or owner. Penalties range from a fine to five years' imprisonment in the case of gratuities, and from a fine to ten years' imprisonment in the case of bribery. Two paragraphs explicitly extend the scope of bribery to foreign officials.

Persons to whom these provisions apply are bound by law to notify an immediate superior or the head of the agency in writing of any offer, giving or acceptance of a bribe, which becomes known to him or her. Failure to do so constitutes grounds for dismissal.

In order to fulfil the international conventions not yet ratified, some minor changes in bribery legislation are required to widen the criminal liability of legal persons and officials of foreign countries and international organisations.

2.2 Conflict of interest and asset declarations

The Anti-corruption Act sets out two groups of rules designed to prevent conflict of interest situations and abuse of such situations.

Restrictions on employment and activities to prevent or correct conflict of interest situations[33]

An official may not:

- hold a second job with a workload higher and at a time different than permitted by the immediate superior, if such employment damages the reputation of the position or office, or if the official's duties involve supervision over the other employer;

- be a member of the directing or supervisory body of a company, except as the representative of the State, local government or public legal entity in a company with the participation of the State, local government or legal person in public law;

---

[32] Criminal Code, Chapter 8, sections 164-165.

[33] Anti-corruption Act, Chapter 3.

- be the director of a branch of a foreign company;

- be employed in an office where an immediate superior or directly monitoring official is a close relative or close relative by marriage;

- be a member of a public legal entity and, at the same time, the directing or supervisory body of another legal person directly monitored by the first legal entity;

- be a member of the directing or supervisory body of a company with State or local government holding within three years after resignation from the public service.

Officials are also prohibited from self-dealing (concluding transactions with themselves on behalf of the agencies in which they work), concluding transactions of a similar nature or involving a conflict of interest and may not authorise subordinates to perform such transactions on their behalf.[34] Conflict of interest occurs if officials, in the course of their employment, are required to make a decision or participate in the making of a decision which significantly influences their own economic interests, or those of close relatives (including by marriage) or legal persons with whom they have a relationship.[35] For example, if a family relationship creates a risk of corruption, the official's superior, employer or appointment body shall be promptly notified in writing by the official who must also apply to be relocated, for the other party to move to another position, for transactions to be entrusted to another person or take other steps to terminate the risk of corruption.

Failure to give notification of a relationship involving the risk of corruption is subject to a fine of 50 to 100 days' salary or up to one year's imprisonment.

Asset declarations

The same officials to whom the above provisions apply are obliged to submit declarations of economic interests every year one month after expiry of the term for submission of income tax returns or within one month after the date of commencement of employment. The declaration must contain data on immovable assets (including assets in joint ownership), vehicles, shares, other securities and dividends, bank accounts, taxable income, debts exceeding six months' salary in value and extra income exceeding ten percent of the previous six months salary. If assets change by more than 30 percent or €6,333, a new declaration must be submitted within one month. Altogether, about 15,000 politicians and officials present such declarations.

---

[34] Anti-corruption Act, Chapter 24 (1-2)

[35] Anti-corruption Act, para. 25/1.

Declarations are submitted to and held by the head of the institution. The holder of the declaration may inspect it on his or her own initiative and is obliged to do so in case of suspicion of corruption. The declarations of high-ranking officials, including MPs, President of the Republic, ministers and secretaries general, Auditor General, Chief Public Prosecutor, judges and county governors, are submitted to the Parliamentary Anti-corruption Committee and published in the *State Gazette*. Since April 2001 the wages of high-level civil servants and members of the boards and supervisory councils of State-owned enterprises have been freely available on the Internet.

Failure to submit asset declarations or submission of an inaccurate declaration is a criminal offence.

The record of public officials' and politicians' adherence to the conflict of interest and asset declaration provisions is covered individually in specific sections of this report. The information submitted in asset declarations does not include assets of any relatives (with the exception of jointly-owned property), underlining their largely formal nature.

The record of the Parliamentary Anti-corruption Committee in scrutinising declarations has received severe criticism. GRECO noted that it was unable to meet with any members of the Committee, and that, according to those whom its team questioned, the Committee:

> [L]acked methodology and means to check the faithfulness of declarations, conducted purely formal revisions, made no analysis of collected data and had never contributed to the disclosure of any corruption case.[36]

Accordingly, GRECO urgently recommended the strengthening of control over declarations and monitoring of conflicts of interest.[37]

On the other hand, officials say that the declarations do play a preventative role, since the mere fact of having to declare income and assets creates the possibility that the declaration could be checked at some point.[38] For example, as of June 2002 a scandal was in progress concerning a loan declared in 2000 by an MP and leader of the largest political party, which was used to buy a house in Tallinn. In 2002 the MP declared that he no longer had the loan, but appeared unable to explain satisfactorily the source of funds used to pay the debt in response to journalistic enquiries.

---

[36] GRECO, *Evaluation Report on Estonia,* p. 15.

[37] GRECO, *Evaluation Report on Estonia,* p. 30.

[38] Interview with Paavo Paal, lawyer, Ministry of Defence, Tallinn, 31 May 2002.

2.4 Control and audit

Estonia has made considerable progress in the past two years towards establishing an audit system for the public sector, and legislation concerning financial control is entirely compatible with EU requirements. Amendments to the Government of the Republic Act that came into effect in July 2000 established the legal framework for a three-tier system, based on the State Audit Office, the Financial Control Department of the Ministry of Finance and internal financial control and audit departments. Although the establishment of the new system has been in progress, the effectiveness of both external and internal control in fighting corruption has so far been limited.

State Audit Office

The State Audit Office (SAO), in existence since 1990, is the supreme audit institution for the public sector. The Parliament appoints the Auditor General for a five-year term on the proposal of the President, and may dismiss the Auditor General only when divested of legal capacity, if criminal charges are brought or death occurs.

The Auditor General determines the SAO audit plan. The Office conducts financial audits, performance audits and compliance/regularity audits. It has wide competence to audit all activities involving the use of public funds, including the activities of all companies where the State owns more than a 50 percent stake, use of all public subsidies, public procurement's compliance with the law, monitoring of contract fulfilment and disbursement of EU funds. The major exception to this is that the SAO is not competent to audit local government activities.

Under the latest version of the State Audit Act, in effect since March 2002, the SAO's proposals for corrective measures in audited bodies are subject to compulsory review by the corresponding directing body of the agency, enterprise or other organisation, local government, ministry or other Government agency. The SAO shall be notified of the measures implemented within one month after receipt of the corresponding decision or proposal. According to SAO officials, the Office follows up to check implementation of its recommendations after one month and six months, and if audit findings were very serious, repeats the audit a year later.

The SAO submits to Parliament its opinion on the State budget implementation report and on the draft State budget. Until the new Act came into effect there were no formal mechanisms by which Parliament received or dealt with SAO reports, which diminished their impact. According to one SAO official, the impact of reports has been insufficient.[39] Under the new Act, the Office sends reports to the Parliamentary

---

[39] Interview with Mare Haljak, Audit Manager, Operational Risk Department, State Audit Office, 13 March 2002.

Finance Committee, which is responsible for supervising the SAO's activities. Audit reports are also available on the SAO's website.

Despite the SAO's wide powers, adequate budget resources and young enthusiastic staff, GRECO also levelled considerable criticism at its role in fighting corruption. In particular, it noted that the SAO does not feel a part of the fight against corruption and even seems to reject the idea of playing such a role. GRECO noted that both the SAO and the Financial Control Department of the Ministry of Finance rely mostly on information provided by the internal control of bodies of audited organisations. If true, doubts about the effectiveness of external audit must be raised, since internal control and audit are only in the process of being developed (see below). The inability of the SAO to audit local governments was also a source of concern, given the indications that local government is seriously affected by corruption. GRECO noted in particular that, "Neither the activities of the Financial Inspectorate [Financial Control Department of the Ministry of Finance] nor those of the SAO are likely to lead to repressive measures for misuse of public funds as none of these bodies considers itself responsible for initiating financial investigations."[40] That said, the new Act on the State Audit Office explicitly establishes the duty of the SAO to forward information on violations of law to the enforcement authorities. Moreover, in the past year the SAO has initiated criminal cases against senior officials, including the Director of the Estonian Traffic Insurance Foundation, who was convicted of corruption and misuse of official position and had to return more than €1.203m to the State funds.

Internal control

Amendments to the Government of the Republic Act in effect from June 2000, along with secondary legislation passed by the Government in October 2000, imposed a duty on heads of Government and State agencies to implement an internal audit system in all agencies. A person responsible for the internal audit is to be appointed in each agency, and if necessary a corresponding structural unit subordinated to the head of the agency. Prior to the passage of the Act the Ministry of Finance composed guiding material based on IIA standards entitled *Good Practice in Internal Audit* in May 2000.

According to statistics issued by the Ministry of Finance, the formation of internal audit units has been successfully completed, although at the time of writing they were not yet fully functional. The State Audit Office is responsible for providing methodological guidance to State agencies, State enterprises and other State organisations on the conduct of internal audits. As of early 2002, it is impossible to judge the effectiveness of internal control and audit, and this will be a key area to be monitored. This is particularly true in local government, where the almost total absence

---

[40] GRECO, *Evaluation Report on Estonia,* p. 29.

of effective control, combined with extensive autonomy and financial power, appears to have exacerbated corruption. According to the security police, the majority of the corruption cases taken to court in 2000 were the result of ineffective internal control systems in governmental institutions.[41]

2.5 Anti-corruption agencies

The only agency that explicitly specialises in investigating corruption is the Security Police Board, which is responsible for coordinating implementation of the anti-corruption components of the Government's anti-crime policy (see Section 1.3). The security police appears to perform its anti-corruption role well within the limits of its powers; for example, in 1998 it uncovered a major tax fraud involving organised bribery of customs inspectors, and in early 2002 was proceeding with a case involving well-established bribery practices in the Motor Vehicle Registration Centre.

In line with the concerns raised in this report concerning corruption in local government is the fact that after amendments to the Criminal Procedure Code that came into effect in July 2000, pre-trial investigations of corruption cases involving municipal officials are no longer within the jurisdiction of the security police. Notwithstanding the ongoing establishment of internal audit bodies (see Section 2.4), this indicates that control of corruption at the local government level may be negligible.

The Financial Intelligence Service

With the passage of the Money Laundering Prevention Act in July 1999, money laundering became a criminal offence. The Financial Intelligence Service (hereafter FIU) was created on 1 July 1999 to combat money laundering. By the end of 2000, the FIU had filed 452 suspicious and unusual transactions, and filed 1,829 during 2001.[42] Criminal proceedings were started in four cases, and one conviction resulted. By the end of 2001, a total of €35.5m had been identified as proceeds from criminal activities.

The FIU has received 28 requests from other countries for assistance. In two cases, one in cooperation with the German authorities and one with the Norwegian authorities, criminals were caught with the help of the Estonian FIU.

---

[41] GRECO, Evaluation Report on Estonia, p. 7.

[42] Figures provided by Ministry of Internal Affairs, Internal Security Policy Department.

2.6 Ombudsman

The function of ombudsman is performed by the Legal Chancellor, a position established by the Constitution and now regulated according to the 1999 Legal Chancellor Act. The Legal Chancellor is appointed by Parliament for seven years on the proposal of the President of the Republic. The office's main function is to review legislation for conformity with the Constitution and other laws, but also to investigate the activities of State agencies on the initiative of other institutions, organisations or individuals who believe their constitutional rights and freedoms have been endangered.

The Chancellor has the power to demand information, documents and explanations from agencies it investigates, and to call witnesses. It may propose corrective measures to inspected institutions that are not legally binding, but may not initiate criminal proceedings. According to officials from the Legal Chancellery, the office must forward cases involving corruption to enforcement bodies, but corruption does not seem to be a central concern. In 2001 the Office received 1,516 petitions, concerning mainly the rights of prisoners (111), police activities (95), property reform (84) and national minorities (78).

3. EXECUTIVE BRANCH AND CIVIL SERVICE

There is very little evidence of corruption among executive officials and civil servants. Corruption does not appear to be a major problem at the highest level, and the resignation of a former Prime Minister as a result of a corruption scandal indicates that corruption control mechanisms work relatively well. The legal framework for the public administration is advanced, with a Civil Service Act in force since 1996 and a Public Administration Reform Program approved in April 2001. The legal framework governing procedures for appealing against administrative decisions was completed in January 2002. However, reform of local government, where there is an urgent need to reduce the number of local government units, has not progressed far. A Civil Service Code of Ethics exists, although its effectiveness is doubtful. Concerns exist regarding the effectiveness of conflict of interest and asset declaration provisions.

3.1 Structure and legislative framework

The most important acts regulating the behaviour of the executive and the civil service are the Civil Service Act, Anti-corruption Act, and the Government of the Republic Act. The Public Service Act entered into force on 1 January 1996. The Act applies to both central and local government. The civil service has some 20,000 members in central Government, and 4,000 in local government.

Estonia passed a Public Service Act in 1995 and, along with the other acts described earlier, has ensured that, as the European Commission notes, "The integrity of civil servants has long been a requirement of Estonian legislation."[43] All Government officials, executive officers and advisers must be recruited by public competition with the main exceptions of: officials of the Chancellery of the Parliament, Office of the President of the Republic, Office of the Legal Chancellor, Supreme Court and State Audit Office, officials appointed to office by the Government, and advisers to the Prime Minister and ministers and officials appointed by the Prime Minister. Persons who are in a close relationship with an official who has control over the position in question, or who have been punished for an act of corruption under administrative or criminal procedure, may not be employed.

In its *2000 Regular Report*, in which the European Commission was otherwise critical of public administration reform, the Commission judged that, "Overall, Estonia's civil servants continue to perform their tasks in an impartial and politically neutral way."[44] Estonia established an EU training strategy for civil servants, first approved in May 1997 and updated in April 1999. At the beginning of 2000 an implementation plan for the strategy was worked out as part of a PHARE programme.

3.2 Administrative procedure and redress

Until 2002, appeals against administrative decisions and actions could be filed only to the courts. Appeals could (and still can) be filed against activities, omissions or delays by agencies and officials, either directly to an administrative court or through a county or city court, which will immediately forward the action to an administrative court.[45] In 2001, four specialised administrative courts of first instance were established and all changes were aimed at increasing specialisation of judges in the area of administrative law. By the end of 2001 administrative courts were sufficiently equipped that three judges were able to hear complicated cases, which is expected to improve the quality of

---

[43] Commission, *2001 Regular Report*, p. 19.

[44] Commission, *2000 Regular Report*, p. 14.

[45] Code of Administrative Court Procedure, *State Gazette* I/1999.

judgements.[46] Since 1999 the same court has decided claims for damages suffered as a result of administrative acts.[47]

Amendments to the Code of Administrative Court Procedure that came into force in January 2002 now allow parties to dispute an administrative decision at the level of a higher administrative body, as a non-compulsory alternative to administrative court procedure. The disputed administrative decision can nevertheless be later appealed to an administrative court. The scope of decisions by administrative courts was also widened, allowing them to decide on the substance as well as the formal legality of administrative decisions. The new Code also concentrates rules of administrative procedure, making it easier for citizens to understand and use.

3.3 Conflict of interest and asset monitoring

Conflict of interest and asset monitoring provisions are covered in Section 3.2.2. Problems of officials having ancillary business interests or corrupt contacts with business interests appear to be much more serious at local government level than in the central State administration.

3.4 Interaction with the public

With the adoption of the Anti-corruption Act, the Public Service Code of Ethics was incorporated as an amendment to the Public Service Act. However, the Code is brief and vague, and was not prepared in consultation with the officials it is supposed to affect.

The provisions of the Code are listed below:

1. An official is a citizen in the service of the people.

2. The activities of an official shall be based on respect for the Constitution of the Republic of Estonia provided for in the oath of office.

3. An official shall adhere, in his or her activities, to the legally expressed will of politicians who have received a mandate from the citizens.

4. Public authority shall be exercised solely in the public interest.

---

[46] NPAA's *Regular Reports*, see <http://www.eib.ee/pages.php/02030102>, (last accessed 28 August 2002).

[47] Before the Code of Administrative Court Procedure was amended in 1999, claims for damages had to be submitted to a civil court after a ruling by a administrative court.

5. Public authority shall always be exercised pursuant to the law.

6. The exercise of public authority shall always involve liability.

7. The exercise of public authority is, as a rule, a public activity.

8. An official shall be prepared to make unpopular decisions in the public interest.

9. A person exercising public authority shall endeavour to achieve as broad a participation of citizens in the exercise of authority as possible.

10. An official shall always, in his or her activities, subject departmental interests to public interest.

11. An official shall be politically impartial in his or her activities.

12. An official shall make decisions based on public and generally understandable criteria.

13. An official shall avoid creating a situation which arouses or may arouse suspicion with regard to his or her impartiality or objectivity in considering matters under suspicion.

14. An official shall treat property entrusted to him or her economically, expediently and prudently.

15. An official shall use information, which becomes known to him or her through official duties solely in the public interest.

16. A person exercising public authority is characterised by honesty and respect for the public and co-employees.

17. An official shall be polite and helpful when communicating with people.

18. An official shall be respectable, responsible and conscientious.

19. An official shall do his or her best in the public service by constant individual development.

20. An official shall facilitate the dissemination of the above principles in every way.

There are no mechanisms for protecting whistleblowers in the civil service, or any overall law regulating complaints.

3.5 Corruption

There have been a number of successful prosecutions of corrupt senior officials in the past three years. The last example that attracted wide publicity occurred when two top officials from the Ministry of Finance were prosecuted for corruption in the Autumn of 2000 in connection with a car that was purchased for the Ministry at a special discount and then sold to an official for the same price. Two officials were convicted, one for corruption and the other for misuse of official position. In August 2002 the press reported that the governing council of the Estonian Culture Endowment fired its director, who confessed to gambling away between 6.5 million and 8 million kroons (approximately €415,256–512,315) of the endowment's funds between 1999 and 2002. As of August 2002 the former official was being held by the security police and investigated for abuse of office and theft while in office.[48]

Surveys of public perceptions indicate that political leaders are the most corrupt people in Estonia, followed by top civil servants (see Section 1.2). However, this perception was not confirmed by the research carried out for this report, and may rather reflect the fact that the activities of politicians and top civil servants receive the most attention from the media. Investigative journalists generally perceive corruption in the central State administration level to be within reasonable limits, although there are cases of corruption at senior levels.[49]

On the other hand, the ineffectiveness of the framework for monitoring conflict of interest and officials' assets leaves room for doubt concerning how much is known about potential malpractice among officials at all levels. Moreover, there is some evidence and indication that corruption may be a problem, particularly in the Ministry of Economy, described by one business editor in Tallinn as "the one very weak part of the State."[50] After the privatisation of the bulk of the economy, the Ministry lost many of its functions, but still controls the Public Procurement Office and regulation of the energy market. There have been a number of cases of "parachuting" by officials from the Ministry to companies towards whom the same officials previously behaved favourably in their official capacity.[51] A scandal in 2001 surrounding railways privatisation provided strong evidence of irregular practices at the Ministry. However, these examples do not even begin to address problems of political interference in the activities of the Public Procurement Office (see Section 7.3).

As previous sections of this report have already emphasised, among ordinary officials, those in local government appear most affected by corruption (see Section 1.2).

---

[48] RFE/RL Newsline, vol. 6, no. 155, part II, 19 August 2002.

[49] Interview with Tiina Jõgeda, journalist, *Eesti Ekspress*, 10 April 2001.

[50] Interview with Anvar Samost, Chief Economic Editor, Baltic News Service, Tallinn, 15 March 2002.

[51] Interview with Anvar Samost, Chief Economic Editor, Baltic News Service, Tallinn, 15 March 2002.

4. LEGISLATURE

The State budget approved by Parliament includes all public revenue and expenditure. The effectiveness of audit of public expenditure has in the past been blunted by the lack of formal cooperation between the State Audit Office and Parliament, although new legislation should lead to improvements in this area. There is no evidence of corruption of MPs, and survey research indicates that "capture" of parliamentary votes is not a serious problem. However, there is some evidence of lobbying by business interests that contributed to political parties. The ineffectiveness of supervision of conflict of interest and asset declarations by the Parliamentary Anti-corruption Committee makes assessment of this area difficult.

4.1 Elections

Elections are free and fair, and there have been no indications or even allegations of irregularities. Parliamentary elections are organised and supervised by an independent Electoral Commission. The Commission is composed of two judges appointed by the Chairman of the Supreme Court, one by a first instance court, one by the Court of Appeal, one by the Legal Chancellor (ombudsman) from his advisers, one by the Auditor General, one by the Director of the Chancellery of the Parliament from his officials, one from the officials of the State Chancellery (the office of the Government of the Republic) and one prosecutor appointed by the Chief Prosecutor. There are also electoral commissions in every district appointed by local councils.

4.2 Budget and control mechanisms

The State budget includes all State income and expenditure. As Section 2.4 described, the main control institution for the State budget is the State Audit Office, and the lack of formal cooperation with Parliament has blunted the impact of its reports in the past. The impact of amendments to the Act on the State Audit Office (see Section 2.4) on this situation remains to be seen.

4.3 Conflict of interest and asset monitoring

Conflict of interest and asset monitoring provisions are covered in Section 3.2. The Anti-corruption Committee is responsible for monitoring whether the information submitted in the declarations of the economic interests of, *inter alia*, MPs is correct and whether the restrictions on employment and activities of members are observed. There have been no publicised cases of breaches of conflict of interest rules by parliamentarians. However, this appears more likely to be the result of the fact that the Committee does not function effectively than a reflection of clean behaviour by members.

Although conflict of interest provisions are fairly comprehensive, there are no specific provisions to regulate lobbying in the Parliament.

4.4 Immunity

Under the Constitution, criminal charges may be brought against MPs only on the proposal of the Legal Chancellor, and with the consent of the majority of MPs. The Legal Chancellor also enjoys immunity, which can only be lifted on proposal of the President of the Republic and the consent of the majority of MPs. Since 1990, only two such cases involving MPs have arisen, one involving alleged abuse of parliamentary powers as a bank employee and another involving misconduct with foreign currencies by the former President of the Bank of Estonia. Immunity was lifted in both cases and both were acquitted.

4.5 Corruption

Local observers have made references to lobbying that appears to have gone beyond mere persuasion, for example by alcohol producers. However, there have been no scandals involving corruption of MPs. According to the World Bank/EBRD 1999 survey, Estonia appears to be among the EU candidate countries least affected by the purchase of parliamentary votes.[52]

5. JUDICIARY

The judiciary is independent, a situation that will be reinforced by recent legislation. The effectiveness of the courts in prosecuting corruption cases is subject to some doubts: courts and prosecution offices lack specialised departments for dealing with

---

[52] Sixty-seven percent of companies responded that the sale of parliamentary votes had no impact on their activities; 19 percent said it had a "minor impact," nine percent that it had a "significant impact" and five percent a "very significant impact". See The World Bank, *Business Environment and Enterprise Performance Survey*, <http://info.worldbank.org/governance/beeps>, (last accessed 28 August 2002).

corruption, the statute of limitations for some corruption offences may be too short, and the apparent leniency of the courts towards those convicted of corruption may encourage a climate of tolerance towards corruption. International monitoring has drawn attention to a lack of professionalism of courts and prosecution offices, while recent changes to criminal procedure have restricted the competence of the security police to investigate corruption cases. There is almost no evidence of corruption in the courts or prosecution offices.

5.1 Legislative framework

Judicial appointment and independence

Judges are appointed for life, and the rules for removal are not perceived as threatening to judicial independence.[53] Since Estonia became independent there have been no discussions or suspicions voiced about political appointments of judges or politically influenced court rulings. Judges are subject to standard exclusion rules in cases where they might be biased, and are subject to the provisions of the Anti-corruption Act, including restrictions on activities and the duty to submit asset declarations. Again, monitoring of this area by the Parliament is, by all accounts, inadequate.

All court decisions are public and available, as are trial proceedings, and journalists are generally granted access to information from case files.

Recent amendments to the Courts Act regulate the organisation of courts and judicial service in more detail, introduce guarantees of budgetary independence, increase judges' salaries and increase the extent of judges' self-governance by establishing a Court Administration Advisory Council.[54]

Public Prosecutor's Office

Public prosecutors are appointed by the Minister of Justice through competitive selection, and may be dismissed only on reaching retirement age or as a result of disciplinary action. The public prosecutor lies midway between the model in which prosecutors are an

---

[53] EU Accession Monitoring Program, *Monitoring the EU Accession: Judicial Independence*, Open Society Institute, Budapest 2001, pp. 150–184.

[54] The Council will be comprised of the Chief Justice of the Supreme Court, five judges elected by the judges' assembly two MPs, an attorney, the Chief Public Prosecutor or a State Prosecutor appointed by him and the Legal Chancellor or a representative appointed by him. The council will approve the structure of courts, the number of judges in a court, appointment and pre-term release of court chairpersons, the number of lay judges, and the number of judge candidates. It will also give its opinion on candidates for Supreme Court judges and budgeting principles.

independent part of the judiciary and the second model in which prosecutors are part of the executive, subordinate to the Ministry of Justice. The prosecutor is an administrative official who has independence as broad as that of a judge.

A new draft Code of Criminal Procedure would make the prosecutor the head of pre-trial investigation, which is expected to increase the efficiency of proceedings. The influence of this change on corruption prosecutions is difficult to gauge, as the security police have played the main role in pre-trial investigations and specialisation of prosecutors in the fight against corruption is still limited. The Tallinn Public Prosecutor's Office includes a special unit dealing with economic crime, as well as with corruption. In 2000, the department sent around 50 cases to court, most of which concerned giving and accepting bribes. Other city and county prosecution offices are small and lack specialisation. GRECO cited the doubts of "well-informed Estonian practitioners" concerning:

> [T]he lack of reliability of the repressive system when it comes to the sanctioning of unlawful public operations… The reason for this would be the lack of professionalism… of judicial authorities and the prosecution.[55]

GRECO cited in particular railways privatisation as an area where prosecution authorities appeared ineffective (see Section 7.3).

In addition to the lack of specialisation, there are two other concerns regarding the judicial and prosecution system. First, the statute of limitations for corruption offences is only two years, running up to the moment a case is given to court. Moreover, the new Penal Code that will probably enter into force in Autumn 2002, sets the period as lasting until the first court decision. Although many corruption crimes probably also involve offences with a limitation of five years, the two-year statute of limitation appears very short and could threaten proceedings, especially of crimes as complicated to investigate and try as corruption crimes typically are.

Second, the very lenient sentences applied to those convicted of corruption offences (see Section 1.1) suggest that the courts do not help to make corruption a high-cost, low-benefit activity. For example, of 54 convictions for "offences in office" handled by the security police between 1995 and 1999, only five defendants were imprisoned.[56]

---

[55] GRECO, *Evaluation Report on Estonia*, p. 12.

[56] Cited in: GRECO, *Evaluation Report on Estonia*, pp. 24–25.

5.2 Corruption

There have been only three prosecutions of judges for corruption offences since 1995 (two of them in 2002), all of which resulted in acquittal. Otherwise, there is no evidence of corruption in the courts system.

Moreover, according to a public opinion poll conducted in October 2000, 45 percent of the population expressed trust in the courts, a relatively high figure for the region and similar to the trust rating enjoyed by the media.[57] Among the population, the Government and Parliament had much lower ratings than the courts, while the President of the Republic had a much higher rating. According to the Ministry of Justice of the Republic, there has not been a survey on how people view the effectiveness of the courts on limiting corruption.

There is no empirical evidence of corruption in prosecutor offices. However, the press recently reported alleged connections between a candidate for assistant prosecutor and organised crime.[58] The candidate was appointed as an assistant prosecutor in February 2001 although his brother-in-law was rumoured to have links to organised crime.

6. POLITICAL PARTY FINANCE

Regulation of political party funding has undergone major changes as the result of the passage of a new law in 1999 which established many of the important elements of a transparent and regulated system. However, the absence of any institutional supervision of party accounts enables parties to evade the provisions with relative ease. Moreover, opposition to regulation has been reflected in recent proposals to increase the maximum permitted cash donations. There is some evidence that corruption in political party funding has been a significant problem.

6.1 Legislative framework

Until 1999, the financing of political parties was, as one of the main experts on the country's party finance puts it, "a complete mess."[59] At that time, it was not clear

---

[57] ES Turu-Uuringute, public opinion poll, October 2000.

[58] T. Ploom, A. Plekksepp, K. Muuli, "Raski raske elu," *Postimees,* 12 October 2000.

[59] Interview with Daimar Liiv, Praxis Centre for Policy Studies, 13 March 2002.

whether political parties were even required to produce accounts, and companies could finance political parties to an unlimited extent.

The most important provisions of the Act as amended in 1999 are the following:

- Anonymous donations are forbidden, and must be turned over to the State budget within one week. Donations through third parties are also prohibited.

- A number of entities may not provide donations to parties, including in particular: Government or State agencies, local governments or agencies, public legal entities, non-profit associations or foundations in which the State is a member, entities that have received support directly or indirectly from the State, local governments or public legal entities.

- Donations in cash are only permitted up to a value of €63. Banks may only deposit funds in bank accounts, about which they must provide full information in reports.

- Parties must publish accounts every quarter according to the Accounting Act, including the sources of all funds, all donations and the identities of all donors. Donations are defined widely to include non-monetary gifts and support for activities (the difference between the market price of a service provided to a party and the price for which it is actually provided).

- During election campaigns, parties must publish similar accounts every week.

The 1999 Act also introduced State subsidies for parties. Under the Act, political parties represented in the Parliament have the right to subsidies allocated from the State budget in proportion to the number of seats they won in the last elections. The Parliament decides the total State subsidy each year, which in 2001 was €1.267m. Parties that receive less than the five percent threshold necessary for entering the Parliament, or are successful in local elections but not at central level, receive no subsidy.

The 1999 Act contains no restrictions of party expenditures.

Since the new Act came into effect there has been general discussion of the possibility of prohibiting private contributions altogether. Yet a more specific proposal that was under discussion in Parliament in March 2002 would be a step in the opposite direction: the proposal would raise the threshold for permitting cash donations from €63 to €630.

6.2 Control and supervision

Under the new provisions, parties must provide complete accounts including the information mentioned above to the Register of Non-Profit Associations and Foundations, where it must be available to the public free of charge. The 1999 Act does not, however, contain any provisions regarding supervision or audit of political party accounts, which raises doubts over the enforceability of the seemingly strict financing rules. A sign of the difficulty in achieving Parliament's passage of the new Act is the fact that a provision creating a special committee to check party accounts had to be withdrawn from the originally proposed amendments, as did criminal sanctions for violations of the financing rules.

6.3 Party finance in practice

The results of the World Bank/EBRD *1999 Business Environment and Enterprise Performance Survey* indicated that corruption in political party financing is a significant problem, and an exception to the country's favourable image in other areas. Seventeen percent of respondents said that private contributions to political parties had a significant or very significant impact on their business, which places Estonia in a worse position than all candidate countries except Bulgaria, Romania, Slovakia and Latvia.[60] A number of major companies have tended to make donations to all important parties, including oil companies, alcohol producers and breweries. In 1997, the Pro Patria Union pushed through favourable excise taxes on beer and the Reform Party is widely regarded as closely tied to big business and the financial sector. Evidence is very scarce, however, since parties did not have to publish the names of donors before the new Act came into effect.

Disguising donations as contributions from members appears to have been a widespread practice. Prior to the elections of 1999, a €6,333 lump sum provided to the Estonian People's Union was deposited gradually in 1,000 kroon (€63.3) units as a series of donations from a number of party members, including the Chairman of the Parliamentary Anti-corruption Commission. The Central Party collected no money in membership contributions in 1999, but suddenly collected €31,670 in 2000 and €6,340 in 2001. In 1999, the Chairman of the Estonian United People's Party donated €9,500 to the party, equal to two-thirds of his income in the previous year.[61] According to press reports from July 2002, the Reform Party is suspected of having disguised

---

[60] See <http://www.worldbank/org/wbi/governance/beepsinteractive.htm>, (last accessed 15 May 2002).

[61] Jaan Tõnisson Institute, Archive Collection of Articles, Tallinn 2001.

donations from unknown sponsors as contributions from party candidates in the 1999 municipal elections. A State prosecutor was cited as saying that the party could not be sued due to the vague wording of the party financing law, and pointed out that there are no sanctions for violation of the law anyway.[62]

Although the new legal provisions on party finance might be expected to somewhat improve the situation, the absence of provisions for monitoring appears to preserve parties' capacity to easily violate or get around the law. According to a number of Estonian observers, parties have implemented the letter but not the intent of the law. Many ways of getting around the law still exist, including the practice described above of disguising donations under the guise of public collections or membership contributions, or using shell companies to channel funds from real donors.[63]

7. PUBLIC PROCUREMENT

Public procurement appears to be particularly vulnerable to corruption. Although a relatively advanced legal framework is in place, monitoring of procurement and resolution of complaints is inadequate, and the Public Procurement Office appears to be vulnerable to political interference. Local observers believe tender fixing is common, and corruption in procurement at local government level may be a serious problem.

7.1 Legislative framework

Public procurement is regulated by the 1995 Public Procurement Act, which has since been amended four times. The most important amendments came into effect in April 2001 and were motivated mainly by the need to harmonise the law with EU directives.

The PPA does not apply to a number of procurements, including cases when:

- adherence to the Act would result in the disclosure of a State secret;

- procurement involves water, electricity, gas, thermal energy, cable distribution and telecommunications services, if such services can only be supplied by one person;

---

[62] "Parties guilty of breaking financing regulations," ETA, 4 March 2002.

[63] Comments at OSI Roundtable Discussion, Tallinn, 14 March 2002; interview with Anvar Samost, Chief Economic Editor, Baltic News Service, Tallinn, 15 March 2002.

- procurement involves weapons, ammunition, battle equipment and related training equipment.[64]

Contracts for goods or services with a value of less than €6,340 are not subject to any tender requirements (€31,670 for construction work, contracts for draft legislation or contracts between utilities companies and penal institutions). Contracts with a value of over €12,670 must be allocated by open tender, or by restricted tender or negotiated procedure (sole sourcing) under certain conditions:

- A restricted tender may be used for example when "the contracting authority has approved objective selection criteria for the tenderers, and… it is economically expedient to verify the qualifications of applicants before submission of the tender documents."[65]

- A negotiated procedure with prior publication of tender notice may be used under certain conditions, particularly if all bids in an open or restricted tender were rejected, if it is not possible to estimate the value of the procurement or the specific terms and conditions in advance.

- A negotiated procedure without prior publication of a tender notice, in other words classic sole sourcing, may be used under certain typical conditions under which such a procedure is allowed. For example, if for unforeseeable events, rapid completion of the procurement is necessary to save lives or prevent substantial damage to property or if the procurement is supplementary to a previous tender and only one contractor can provide compatible goods or services.

The PPA forbids dividing contracts into smaller parts, although its officials admit this is very difficult to monitor and the Act is not sufficiently clear to allow the Office to intervene in questionable cases.[66] The PPO also regards the conditions under which sole sourcing can be used as rather wide, particularly a provision that allows sole sourcing for works or services that were not included in the initial public procurement, have become necessary due to unforeseen circumstances, cannot be separated from the initial procurement and do not exceed 50 percent of the value of the initial procurement. According to PPO officials, the Office has had many conflicts with authorities wanting to use sole sourcing.[67]

---

[64] Public Procurement Act, Article 4.

[65] Public Procurement Act, Article 55 (1).

[66] Interview with Tom Annikve, Deputy Director General, Public Procurement Office, Tallinn, 13 March 2002.

[67] Public Procurement Act, Article 57 (3). Interview with Tom Annikve, Deputy Director General, Public Procurement Office, Tallinn, 13 March 2002.

Procuring entities may organise tenders as they see fit; in other words, they may allow proceedings to be run by one individual, by a commission or even hire external experts. Bidders have the right to be present at the opening of bids.

The PPA contains provisions designed to prevent nepotism and conflicts of interest: neither representatives of the authority conducting a tender nor external experts hired to carry out tender procedures may be persons who have been in contact with the supplier that could give rise to suspicion about their objectivity. Officials dealing with public procurements are also subject to the conflict of interest and asset monitoring provisions of the Anti-corruption Act.

Public procurement regulations are available to the public. All tender notices and procurement decisions are entered into the State procurement register on the Internet, and in the case of very important contracts are advertised in the press.

7.2 Review and audit

Under the PPA, the Public Procurement Office *inter alia* exercises State supervision to verify compliance of procurements with the law, implements a public procurement information system, organises the State register of public procurements, and reviews protests against procurement decisions. The Minister of Economy appoints the Head of the PPO.

Participants in public procurement proceedings may protest procurement decisions to the Public Procurement Office, and may appeal at the same time to an administrative court. Upon receiving a complaint, the PPO must suspend the tendering procedure until the resolution of the protest. Complaints must be filed "within seven days after the date the person becomes or should have become aware of the violation of rights or damage to the interests of the person, but not after the contracting authority has accepted the successful tender."[68] This appears to prevent bidders from complaining to the Office about violations discovered after the completion of the tender. Review of protests is carried out by the PPO, which may annul tenders on the basis of a well-founded protest or its own inspection protests. Decisions of the Office may also be appealed to an administrative court.

As far as supervision and inspection of contracting authorities is concerned, the capacity of the PPO is very limited. As of March 2002, the Office only had three people to carry out this task (including checking protests). Moreover, although the Office can impose fines of up to €31,670 for violations of the PPA, it can only do so

---

[68] Public Procurement Act, Article 62 (2).

against legal entities and not State agencies, municipalities or local government agencies.

The State Audit Office is also competent to audit public procurements *post hoc*, and has begun to concentrate on procurement specifically in 2002. However, the SAO only audits the use of funds in procurement, not adherence to procedures.

7.3 Corruption

There have been no important successful criminal investigations into corruption in public procurement. However, the lack of any evidence on corruption indicates inadequate supervision rather than the absence of any corruption, especially given the defects in the system for monitoring procurement outlined above.

Moreover, both the GRECO evaluation[69] and evidence collected for this report indicate that the Public Procurement Office has been subject to political interference and lacks force when contracting agencies ignore it. The most important case concerns the privatisation of Estonian Railways, where the PPO tried to annul the tender for the adviser for the privatisation,[70] but the Minister of Economy ignored the Office and went ahead. The Minister later resigned despite strong support from the Government, although his resignation may not have been connected with the privatisation.[71] According to PPO officials, the case was one of several in which the Minister attempted to influence PPO decisions.[72] GRECO also cited testimony indicating that the allocation of public contracts in return for donations to political parties may be common.[73]

According to a number of Estonian officials, most problems with public procurement are not the result of the law, but of the strength of personal networks and the fact that "everybody knows everybody," resulting in widespread collusion.[74] According to local observers, the formulation of tenders to suit only one party is quite common; for example, a tender organised by the Ministry of Defence and in progress in early 2002

---

[69] GRECO, *Evaluation Report on Estonia,* p. 18.

[70] The tender was won by Gibbs Ltd, although the adviser's offer was more than three times more expensive than that of PriceWaterhouseCoopers.

[71] For details, see articles: "Minister charged with shady privatization," *Ceturtdiena,* 29 March 2001; "Financing pulled from under railway deal," *Ceturtdiena,* 2 August 2001.

[72] OSI Roundtable Discussion, Tallinn, 14 March 2002.

[73] GRECO, *Evaluation Report on Estonia,* p. 18.

[74] OSI Roundtable Discussion, Tallinn, 14 March 2002; interview with Mare Haljak, Audit Manager, Operational Risk Department, State Audit Office, Tallinn, 13 March 2002.

to purchase boots for the army allegedly contained requirements that meant only one Finnish company could win. PPO officials also regard tailor-made tenders as the main problem, and regard procurement at the local government level as particularly devoid of control.[75]

8. PUBLIC SERVICES

Although there is very little evidence of corruption in public services such as health and education, the European Commission has drawn attention to the need to fight corruption in the police and customs administration, and GRECO has expressed concern at the vulnerability of the customs authorities to corruption and organised crime. Business registration and licensing do not appear to be troubled significantly by corruption.

8.1 Police

There have been no major cases of corruption initiated against the police. In the last few years approximately ten traffic policemen have been dismissed for bribery in connection with violations of traffic regulations. Five corruption cases were investigated in 1998, seven in 1999, four in 2000 and 13 in 2001.[76]

According to the State Police Board, there have been a number of criminal cases involving higher police officers who were convicted for official misconduct, for example two chief constables. In March 2002 Võru County Court convicted a senior officer in the Põlva district of intentional misuse of official position and repeated acceptance of bribes. He was sentenced to nine months' imprisonment.

Citizen trust in the police is relatively high, and rising. According to the *2000 International Crime Victim Survey*, 51 percent of Estonians found the police to be rather or very professional, a rise from 17 percent in 1993. According to a survey carried out by the Estonian Conjuncture Institute in January 2000, 60 percent of respondents said the police do a good or very good job.[77]

---

[75] Interview with Tom Annikve, Deputy Director General, Public Procurement Office, Tallinn, 13 March 2002.

[76] These cases are mainly reported in local government offices where business and officials are more closely interconnected.

[77] For Estonian Police statistics, see <http://www.pol.ee/politseistatistika/politseistatistika.htm>, (last accessed 28 August 2002).

The conditions under which the police work are relatively favourable from the point of view of susceptibility to corruption. The minimum police salary is around 25 percent less than the national average wage, but one of the highest in the public sector. A Disciplinary Unit of the Police Department is subordinated directly to the General Director of the Police. Complaints about police activities may be filed to the Legal Chancellor, the Internal Control Department of the Ministry of Internal Affairs, the Public Prosecutor's Office, the courts and the security police.[78] The latter institution investigates allegations or suspicions of corruption. Perhaps most important, the security police – the main body responsible for investigating corruption – is functionally independent of the police.

8.2 Customs

The Estonian Customs Board is the only specific sector for which the European Commission has stated a need to concentrate on the fight against corruption.[79] Estonia has adopted several new acts to harmonise customs legislation with EU customs procedures. The Customs Board has taken a number of important anti-corruption measures, in particular the establishment of an Internal Control Department to conduct financial audits and monitor compliance with the Anti-corruption Act, and an Investigation Division and five investigation units to participate in the investigation of corruption cases. In addition, several changes in procedures have been introduced to make corruption more difficult, including the compulsory presence of two officers ("four eyes control"), division of tasks, rotation of staff and a six-month probation period for new officers.

These measures appear to have worked to some extent, with some 50 officers prosecuted for corruption offences in recent years. Despite this, GRECO expressed concern about a seeming lack of awareness of the danger of organised crime given Estonia's position as a transit route for smuggled goods, a danger illustrated by a major fuel tax fraud uncovered by the security police in 1998 involving bribery of customs inspectors by an organised crime group.[80] In addition, the lack of coordination between the Customs Board and the border guard was also criticised, including disparate salaries.

---

[78] See <http://www.kapo.ee>, (last accessed 28 August 2002).

[79] Commission, *2001 Regular Report*, p. 35.

[80] GRECO, *Evaluation Report on Estonia*, p. 22.

8.3 Licensing and regulation

Corruption in licensing and regulation appears to be a limited phenomenon. Business registration seems relatively clean, partly because registration is not carried out by courts but by the Commercial Register. Registration can take up to a month. There are occasional rumours of clerks being bribed to speed up registration and one bribery case was prosecuted in 2001.[81] There may be reason for concern over the functioning of the Competition Board, responsible for monitoring compliance with the Competition Act. The Board appears to be a largely nominal institution that has so far failed to move against anti-competitive behaviour, for example price-fixing by milk producers in 2000.[82]

9. ROLE OF THE MEDIA

The Estonian media is free, although there is some evidence of the use of libel and defamation provisions to deter journalists. Freedom of information legislation is in place, although its impact on access to information may have been uneven. The broadcasting media have played little part in exposing corruption, probably more due to lack of financial resources than direct political interference. Investigative journalism has been relatively underdeveloped, at least until recently, but the printed press has become increasingly active in exposing corruption.

9.1 Freedom of speech

The Constitution enshrines the principle of freedom of expression and forbids censorship. The legal environment for the media is liberal; for example, no licence or permission is required to set up a printed publication. There is no general press law, although there have been attempts to write one. There are a decreasing number of media outlets, and Scandinavian media companies control much of the national media.

Libel and defamation provisions have been used on occasion to deter journalists. The new Penal Code, which has been passed by Parliament but is not yet in effect, has abolished libel and defamation provisions after strong lobbying by the media. The Estonian Newspaper Association also successfully campaigned for the abolition in the

---

[81] Interview with Anvar Samost, Chief Economic Editor, Baltic News Service, Tallinn, 15 March 2002.

[82] Interview with Anvar Samost, Chief Economic Editor, Baltic News Service, Tallinn, 15 March 2002.

draft law of a proposed two-tier set of punitive measures on libel, offering special protection for high officials.

The Estonian press has been affected significantly by the case of Enno Tammer, a journalist who was found guilty in 1996 of the criminal offence of degrading the honour and dignity of a politician's wife. Tammer subsequently took the case to the European Court of Human Rights, which upheld the verdict of the Estonian court. The Estonian Newspaper Association has information about cases in which reporters have withdrawn their statements or retracted a story after having been warned of a "Tammer scenario."

9.2 Access to information

A major breakthrough in access to public information was achieved when a new Act on Public Information came into effect in March 2001. Although the Constitution declares that public information must be freely available, media activities have been hampered by arbitrary access to information.

The Act defines information that must be disclosed by public authorities in a digital document register, including contracts into which the agency enters. Requests for information must be complied with promptly and no later than five days from the request, although the deadline may be extended by up to 15 days if the request requires further specification or if searching for identification of the information is time-consuming. Information is provided for free with the optional exception of restricted charges for copying. The Act specifies a long list of information that must be disclosed, including draft legal acts and regulations, assets and budgetary funds that have been transferred to legal entities established by the State or local government.

The Data Protection Inspectorate is responsible for supervising compliance with the Act. As of June 2002, the DTI had received 21 complaints, but was not able to provide any statistics on its decisions.

The Act requires State and municipal bodies to keep a webpage with information about their activities. Public libraries all over the country will have the task of opening public Internet access points and providing advice to citizens who want access to public information.

Although the duties given to authorities under the Act are extensive, journalists give mixed accounts of access to information in practice. According to the business editor of the main local wire service, officials often arbitrarily appeal to exceptions in the Act in order to withhold information, or charge fees exceeding the costs of copying, and quality of access varies considerably among ministries.[83] According to the local correspondent of a major international newspaper, the authorities are much more advanced than neighbouring Latvia or Lithuania in terms of access to public officials and provision of information, although a lack of professionalism among local journalists and an unwillingness to "wash dirty laundry" in public may result in a lack of effectiveness in investigative journalism.

9.3 Broadcasting regulation

Broadcasting is governed by the 1994 Broadcasting Act, which lays down procedures for the allocation of licenses and the regulatory framework for public service television and radio.

Estonian TV and Radio are the public broadcasting stations. They are regulated by a Broadcasting Council appointed by the Parliament. On the proposal of the Parliament's Cultural Affairs Committee, Parliament appoints five MPs and four outside experts to the Council. The Council is therefore dominated by politicians; whenever the Government changes, the Chairman of the Council is also changed. Despite this, journalists perceive that direct political interference in public broadcasting has been less of a problem than financial difficulties that restrict their ability to carry out investigative journalism, while GRECO also cited financial constraints and the dependence of public media on direct State funding as a possible "obstacle to objectiveness and criticism."[84]

9.4 Corruption in the media

According to journalists, corruption is not a systematic problem in the print media. Pressure from private companies through advertising also does not appear to be a major problem except at the local level.

9.5 Media and corruption

In practice, neither public nor private TV stations cover corruption at all. Until recently, as GRECO noted, "investigative journalism as such" was not developed and it

---

[83] Interview with Anvar Samost, Chief Economic Editor, Baltic News Service, Tallinn, 15 March 2002.

[84] GRECO, *Evaluation Report on Estonia*, p. 20.

was not the media that uncovered corruption cases.[85] However, there have been exceptions, and as a result of journalists' disclosures of scandals, senior officials and a number of mayors have been forced to resign. Indeed, the Prime Minister, Tiit Vähi, was forced to resign in 1997 after the media revealed a complex scheme by which he bought State apartments cheaply for himself and his family in Tallinn, in cooperation with the Mayor of Central Tallinn District Jüri Ott.

Corruption has been covered to an increasing extent as investigative skills have grown. For example, in the last two years, the media devoted extensive space to the privatisation of Estonian Railways and corruption in the issuance of driving licences, and revealed that it is possible to register documents in the Commercial Register faster with bribes.[86] Corruption is very rarely reported in the local press.

10. RECOMMENDATIONS

The following recommendations have been highlighted as particularly important to Estonia. For additional recommendations applicable to candidate States generally, please see Part 5 of the Overview report.

1. Carry out a review of the activities of the Parliamentary Anti-corruption Committee.

2. Review the adequacy of control of local government activities.

3. Establish an institutional mechanism for monitoring and supervising party finances.

4. Review the independence of the Public Procurement Office, and strengthen its capacity to monitor and impose sanctions.

---

[85] GRECO, *Evaluation Report on Estonia,* p. 20.

[86] Comments from OSI Roundtable Discussion, Tallinn, 14 March 2002.

Corruption and Anti-corruption Policy in Hungary

Table of Contents

Corruption and anti-corruption policy in Hungary

Executive summary

Hungary has been perceived as one of the least corrupt post-communist states on various international measures. Official statistics show more convictions in Hungary than in other candidate countries, although this probably indicates more effective enforcement rather than more corruption. Domestic surveys of perception indicate widespread corruption in healthcare in particular, followed by traffic police, customs and central State administration. This report identifies three negative trends under the 1998–2002 Government of Viktor Orbán, notably diminishing accountability and openness, increasing politicisation of appointments to key institutions and a tendency to violate the spirit if not the letter of public procurement regulations. While many of these developments are not direct evidence of corruption, reduced openness and weaker accountability mean that corruption has become harder rather than easier to monitor and that individuals may face fewer disincentives to engage in corruption.

In the period since 1998, the Hungarian Government has introduced a number of changes to anti-corruption legislation that meet international criteria, and adopted a resolution on anti-corruption strategy in March 2001. The measures adopted under the Orbán Government seek to prevent opportunities for corruption in the civil service and punish more strictly particular types of corrupt acts. The legislation has had some positive effects, particularly at the lower level. However, at the same time the Government has neglected to create a more transparent overall environment in which corruption is less likely to occur.

The European Commission has identified corruption and organised crime as one of the main institutional problems facing Hungary, and has recently focused on public procurement in particular. The Commission has not provided financial support to anti-corruption policy specifically.

Anti-corruption legislation in Hungary is advanced, and the country has ratified all international conventions on corruption with the exception of the Council of Europe Civil Law Convention on Corruption. There is no general law on conflict of interest or asset declarations, but individual laws exist for the executive, civil service, MPs, judges and prosecutors. Hungary has made significant progress towards establishing an integrated system of State financial control, although the Commission has identified a number of areas where further progress is required. Three parliamentary ombudsmen exist and have been independent and critical, although their findings are not always respected.

Civil service reform has been in progress since 1994. However, the legal framework has not prevented continuing political appointments, and candidates with strong connections to FIDESZ-MPP, the governing party from 1998 to 2002, were increasingly appointed as heads of various governmental bodies, State-owned companies and quasi-governmental organisations. Procedures for appealing against administrative decisions are in place. Conflict of interest provisions forbid civil servants from holding executive positions in private companies, but not from being employed by them. Since 2001 civil servants and senior functionaries have had to submit declarations of interests, income and assets. However, there are still gaps in the conflict of interest provisions, while the asset declaration provisions rely on a dysfunctional procedure for submitting complaints, and there are no sanctions for submitting false information. A Code of Ethics for civil servants was under preparation as of May 2002.

The openness and accountability of the executive has diminished since 1998: access to information has been increasingly restricted, especially in the area of public procurement. Evidence of corruption is sporadic, although there have been several important scandals in recent years involving ministers, and particularly the allocation of public contracts through the Hungarian Development Bank.

Parliament's role in scrutinising the executive has been undermined since 1998 in several ways, notably through the introduction of a two-year State budget (a practice to be ended from 2003), and reductions in plenary sessions and time for parliamentary questions. MPs are subject to limited conflict of interest provisions and must declare business interests, income and assets. However, the mechanisms for scrutinising assets are weak, there are no sanctions for providing false information, and the provisions do not appear to command much respect among MPs. Immunity provisions for MPs have been increasingly undermined in a way that threatens parliamentary debate, through increased defamation and civil law suits against MPs. There is little direct evidence of corruption of MPs.

Hungary has made major progress in putting in place the legal framework for a truly independent judiciary. However, the Government's commitment to judicial independence has been suspect, and there have been indications that some court and prosecution decisions have been politically influenced. In particular, the resignation and replacement of the Prosecutor-General in 2000 has raised concerns about the independence of the institutions responsible for investigating corruption.

There is significant evidence that covert funding of political parties is widespread. Although funding regulations are relatively strict, supervision of party funding is largely formal and State subsidies are regarded as insufficient. The use of Government advertising to promote the governing party appeared to be a particular problem prior to the 2002 elections.

Public procurement has been subject to increasing criticism in recent years. The Government has extensively made use of the Hungarian Development Bank to allocate major contracts – in particular massive public investment in the motorway construction programme – thereby avoiding public tenders. While acknowledging that procurement legislation is largely aligned with EU directives, the European Commission has strongly criticised this practice. In general, while mechanisms of supervision of procurement are relatively well established, corruption appears to remain widespread.

Corruption is an important problem in a number of Hungarian public services, in particular healthcare and the allocation of licenses and permits. Corruption in the police has been regarded as widespread, particularly in the traffic police, although recent reforms may have improved the situation. The Customs and Finance Guard has been carrying out important reforms *inter alia* to reduce corruption. As far as the tax authorities are concerned, their extensive powers and discretion may be an important source of corruption. Corruption does not appear to be such an important problem in the education system.

Although press freedom is guaranteed, there are a number of serious concerns related to the ability of the media to perform its watchdog role. Freedom of information legislation is in place, but access to information in practice is problematic, and vague provisions on State secrets may have been used to intimidate journalists. Regulation of public broadcasting has been put in doubt by the dominance on boards of trustees by appointees from the governing party, while personnel policy at Hungarian Television has been strongly motivated by political criteria, and the allocation of private broadcasting licences has given rise to concerns about political influence. Between 1998 and 2002 the Government made concerted efforts to support the right-wing press, and foreign journalists have come under pressure after criticising the Government.

1. INTRODUCTION

Hungary is ranked as one of the least corrupt EU candidate countries on various international measures. Domestic surveys of perceptions indicate widespread corruption in healthcare in particular, followed by traffic police, customs and central State administration. This report identifies three negative trends under the 1998–2002 Government of Viktor Orbán, notably diminishing accountability and openness, increasing politicisation of appointments to key institutions and a tendency to violate the spirit if not the letter of public procurement regulations. While not direct evidence of corruption, these developments have contributed to an environment that may be more vulnerable to corruption.

1.1 The data and perceptions

Statistics show the number of persons convicted for bribery and trafficking in influence to be fairly stable over recent years (see table below).

Year	Number of detected crimes of bribery and trafficking in influence	Number of persons convicted for bribery and trafficking in influence
1998	902	274
1999	609	289
2000	650	274
2001	836	not available

Source: Ministry of Justice.

However, such data are a notoriously poor guide to the actual level of corruption since they depend on factors such as the efficiency of the penal system. Other measurement methods rely heavily on the perceptions of respondents to surveys.

International surveys

Hungary has generally performed well in international surveys of corruption, especially relative to other transition countries. Transparency International's Corruption Perception Index (CPI) ranked Hungary 31st out of 91 countries in 2001, with a score of 5.3 (on a scale where ten is least corrupt and 0 most corrupt). This marks Hungary out as a regional leader, less corrupt than all other Central and East European transition countries covered in the survey except Estonia. Hungary's score has remained stable: 5.2 in 1997, 5.0 in 1998 and 5.2 in 1999 and 2000.

According to the EBRD/World Bank's *1999 Business Environment and Enterprise Performance Survey,* 32 percent of firms in Hungary report paying "irregular payments to get things done" frequently, mostly or always.[1] Procedures to obtain licences and permits are identified as the area where unofficial payments are most frequent and highest, with around 25 percent of respondents reporting a need to make a payment sometimes, frequently, mostly or always. Eight percent of firms reported that they have to pay to influence the content of new laws, decrees and regulations. More than one-third of firms reported paying unofficial payments to public officials equivalent to one to 25 percent of revenues on average per year.[2]

Domestic surveys

There have been no surveys of citizens' experience of corruption in Hungary. The Government commissioned the Gallup market research agency to carry out a number of surveys of perceptions of corruption from December 1999 to autumn 2000, within the framework of the Global Programme against Corruption. Gallup's nationwide survey of the public in April 2000 (n=1839) found that payment of bribes is rife in the public services, particularly healthcare and the traffic police, and in local government authorities with responsibility for issuing permits and licences. Surveys conducted by another Hungarian research institute, Tárki, found that 81 percent of adults think it is necessary to break "the rules" to be successful, and 93 percent think that those who break the rules need not face judicial consequences.

Gallup's focus groups with judges, mayors and business people in this period produced the following conclusions about the general situation:[3]

- Since 1990, "business interests have encroached upon politics. Attempts at separating the two spheres have failed so far. This is one of the main sources of large-scale corruption in the country."

- Implementation of laws is weak: "even if the laws are consistent, institutions are not strong enough, and not dedicated enough, to implement the laws." Moreover, "better law enforcement itself would not suffice. Even the best laws cannot be enforced if the economic and social conditions that would enable the citizens to observe the laws are not given."

- The "over-bureaucratised legal system and public administration" is a "hotbed of corruption" and radical deregulation a priority. Participants felt that reforms were proceeding too slowly since they were not in the interests of the ruling elite.

---

[1] See <http://info.worldbank.org/beeps/>, (last accessed 15 August 2002).

[2] 29.4 percent of respondent firms report paying one to ten percent of revenues on average per year and 9.8 percent pay 10–25 percent.

[3] See <http://www.gallup.hu/Gallup/monitor/en/gsurveys/010120_focus.html>, (last accessed 15 August 2002).

- The ruling elite sets a bad example for the rest of the population by ignoring laws and court rulings and failing to resign after being found guilty of corruption.

- While privatisation had previously been the main area of high-level corruption, public tenders and the allocation of positions in the public administration are now becoming key loci of corruption.

In interviews with the managers of 520 small and medium-sized companies (hereinafter SMEs) in Budapest, Gallup found that the business operations of one-third of enterprises are significantly hindered by corruption and those of another one-third moderately hindered. Thirty-two percent of the SMEs reported receiving offers or requests for bribes.[4]

1.2 Main loci of corruption

The main institutions associated with corruption, according to the sources consulted in preparation of this report, are the healthcare system (see Section 8.4), the traffic police (Section 8.1), and the civil service (Section 3). These findings tally with the perceptions of respondents in a 2000 Gallup survey on public institutions cited in Table 2.[5]

---

[4] <http://www.gallup.hu/Gallup/monitor/en/gsurveys/010129_business.html>, (last accessed 15 August 2002).

[5] <http://www.gallup.hu/Gallup/monitor/en/gsurveys/010119_pubinst.html>, (last accessed 15 August 2002).

Table 2: Public perceptions of the incidence of corruption in public institutions[6]

	Total	Budapest	county town	other town	village, farmstead
Hospital doctors	77	78	78	81	72
Hospital nurses	62	74	60	56	59
General practitioners	59	72	50	56	59
Children's doctors	58	68	52	56	58
Traffic Police officers	39	53	35	33	37
Police – Traffic Police Authority	28	36	25	25	27
Customs and Excise Authority	28	23	30	28	29
Ministries	20	14	18	18	25
Police – other branches	19	24	13	18	20
Market Supervision Authority	18	25	19	12	17
Bank Credit Departments	16	14	11	18	19
Traffic Supervision Authority	16	17	15	16	16
Public Grounds Supervision Authority	14	24	16	10	11
State Public Health and Medical Officer Service	14	18	13	13	12
Consumer Protection Authority	13	14	11	16	13
Courts	13	8	8	14	17
Municipality – Technical Department	13	19	14	13	9
Public notaries	13	13	10	15	13
Inland Revenue Office	13	15	10	12	13
National Health Insurance Fund	11	10	9	11	12
Court of Registration	11	8	8	12	13
Municipality – Property Department	10	13	12	11	8
Municipality – Social Department	10	14	10	10	9
Land Registry	10	11	9	10	11
Municipality – Housing Management	10	20	7	7	8
Social Security Office	9	10	9	7	9
Municipality – Client Relations	7	7	8	6	7
Municipality – Education Department	6	4	5	7	6
Municipality – other	6	3	6	5	7

Source: Gallup Hungary.

---

[6] The numbers represent the percentage of given segments of the population that believed corruption of the groups listed in the left-hand column to be "typical" or "highly typical."

Gallup's April 2000 nationwide survey shows that, depending on the department, six to 13 percent of participants thought that local authorities were corrupt. However, Gallup's survey of over 400 local authority employees in five municipalities revealed that 78 percent of respondents believed that "informal, unwritten rules" operate in at least 80 percent of municipal proceedings, and that gratuities are paid in one-fifth of proceedings within the authorities' mandate.[7]

In addition, two activities which are associated with high levels of corruption are public procurement (Section 7) and the issue of licences (Section 8.6). A Gallup survey of 520 SMEs supports this (see Table 3).[8]

Table 3: Percentage of respondents (from SMEs) rating corruption levels as "high"

	Percentage of "high" answers from companies surveyed
State investments	53
Public procurement	53
Obtaining technical (MOT) papers for a vehicle	46
Obtaining municipal permits	41
Obtaining business licenses	38
Customs clearance of goods	37
Obtaining goods and services from the Government	36
Environmental protection regulations and their fulfilment	30
Residence and work permits	26
Obtaining goods and services from private companies	20
Work safety regulations	18
Health care regulations	17
Court / legal cases	13

Source: Gallup Hungary.

In addition, public procurement has been identified as an area of concern by a number of international organisations, as discussed in Section 7.

---

[7] <http://www.gallup.hu/Gallup/monitor/en/gsurveys/010122_municip.html>, (last accessed 15 August 2002).

[8] <http://www.gallup.hu/Gallup/monitor/en/gsurveys/010129_business.html>, (last accessed 15 August 2002).

1.3 Government anti-corruption policy

Hungary volunteered to be a test case in the UN Global Programme against Corruption in 1999. A Memorandum of Understanding signed by Hungary and the relevant UN organisations in June 1999 set out six aims. These amounted to the design and execution of an assessment of corruption, followed by evaluation, analysis and discussion at an international seminar. The Government adopted a resolution on its anti-corruption strategy in March 2001.[9] The strategy identifies some circumstances that facilitate corruption and resolves to examine ways in which the scope for corruption can be reduced, primarily by altering the law. The measures adopted between 1998 and 2002 have sought to prevent opportunities for corruption in the civil service and punish more strictly particular corrupt acts.

The Government has made good progress in implementing its strategy. Of 14 measures identified as requiring legislative tasks, nine have been acted upon.[10] The changes include amendments to the Public Procurement Act, a new act requiring public servants to submit property declarations and an increase in the penalties for bribery. Parliament has also adopted Act no. 83/2001 on combating terrorism and tightening provisions on money laundering. An important complement to the strategy is the Government's 2001 decision to substantially increase the salaries of public officials and law enforcement officials.

These measures may have had some positive effects, particularly at the lower level of public administration. However, the strategy's recommendation to improve monitoring of the sources of donations to political parties has not yet led to action. A Board against Corruption proposed in the strategy, with members to be invited by the Minister of Justice, Minister of Interior and the Minister leading the Prime Minister's Office, is expected to be established in 2002.[11]

The anti-corruption strategy is an important contribution and will help to exert pressure on the employees of public institutions and members of the public to conform to the law. Critics of the strategy have argued, however, that it concentrates on corruption in the private sector and public services, while failing to address high-level political corruption, and that it takes a rather conservative approach designed largely to address EU concerns. The Ministry of Justice initially consulted with the Hungarian

---

[9] Government Resolution no. 1023/2001.

[10] Interview with Dr Zoltán Márki, Assistant Secretary of State, Ministry of Justice, 21 December 2001.

[11] According to Dr Márki.

chapter of Transparency International, but did not include it in the drafting process.[12] In particular, the Government has neglected the need to create a more transparent environment in which corruption would be less likely to occur, as individual sections of this report illustrate.

1.4 The impact of the EU Accession Process

The European Union has consistently noted the prevalence of corruption in Hungary as a problem. The *1997 Opinion on Hungary's Application for Membership* identified "the impact of organised crime on the state, including some corruption" as one of the main institutional problems. It recommended strengthening the system for training judges and commented that efforts to combat corruption needed to be made more effective. In 1998, the Commission noted that, "Hungary continues to be confronted with corruption problems."[13] In 1999, corruption was identified as one of two problems Hungary faced in meeting the Copenhagen political criteria.[14] The report noted that the number of recorded cases of corruption had increased by four percent over the previous year. In 2000, the Commission found that, "despite a number of important measures taken to fight corruption, this remains a problem and renewed efforts should be made to address this issue." In 2001, the Commission described "a continuous negative background of corruption which could undermine the trust of the citizens in the democratic institutions."[15]

Public procurement was first identified as an area of concern in the *1999 Accession Partnership,* Hungary having been commended the previous year for its transparent application of public procurement rules. Even in 1999, the recommendations focused on harmonisation with the *acquis communautaire* and the abolition of national preferences, rather than on corruption. The *2000 Regular Report* criticised public procurement practice more heavily, focusing on the area of motorway construction. The Commission found that, "the Hungarian authorities have not applied the normal public procurement procedures required under national law," but instead negotiate

---

[12] According to the comments of TI Hungary's President at OSI Roundtable Discussion, Budapest, 3 April 2002. *Explanatory note: OSI held a roundtable meeting to invite critique of the present Report in draft form. Experts present included representatives of the Government, international organisations, and civil society organisations. References to this meeting should not be understood as an endorsement of any particular point of view by any one participant.*

[13] Commission of the European Union, 1998 *Regular Report from the Commission on Hungary's Progress towards Accession,* pp. 9 and 45.

[14] Commission, *1999 Regular Report,* p. 76.

[15] Commission, *2001 Regular Report,* p. 19.

with a small number of companies, "suggesting a lack of transparency and giving the impression of corruption."[16] This problem had not been resolved by 2001, when the Commission stated its disapproval more forcefully:

> A particular effort is needed to ensure transparency of public procurement at all levels, including at lower levels of Government, and in all sectors, in particular as regards major public infrastructure works such as road construction. The *acquis* does not allow for the circumvention of basic procurement principles, including the obligation to tender, by the manner in which contracts are structured or by delegating the implementation of public works to nominally private but state-controlled agencies.[17]

Regarding the judiciary, the Commission noted in 1998 that new legislation had consolidated the separation of the judiciary from the executive and improved training for judges.[18] The *1999 Regular Report* highlighted successful efforts to implement the 1997 judicial reform. The *2001 Regular Report* noted modernisation of the Court Information System and an improvement in overall efficiency of court procedures, but found that the courts were still overburdened. The Commission also found that funding for the judiciary had declined, "contrary to what would be needed in the light of the increased number of judges and their increasing tasks."[19]

Overall, the Commission has tended to focus on the implementation and efficacy of governmental anti-corruption measures, rather than areas of corruption outside such strategies:

Year of Report	Anti-corruption achievements noted by the Commission
1998	The introduction of stricter rules for economic crimes. Adoption of laws on the conduct of senior officials and on public procurement.
1999	Amendment of Penal Code to allow stricter punishment of corruption. Establishment of anti-corruption units at the national headquarters of the police and at regional border guard directorates. Conclusion of anti-corruption cooperation agreement between Hungarian and Romanian border guards. Review of legislation underway to identify "loopholes which provide potential for corruption." Agreement on cross-border crime and corruption with South-East Europe Cooperation Initiative.
2000	Training for police and border guards designed to help them recognise and avoid situations of corruption and additional staff recruited for internal police anti-corruption unit. New conflict-of-interest legislation for local government representatives. Ratification of the Council of Europe Criminal Law Convention on Corruption.
2001	Government approved anti-corruption strategy containing modifications to existing laws and recommending a new law on lobbying. High-ranking civil servants and their families required to make property declarations. MPs obliged to make asset declarations annually. New police unit created to combat bribery of officers on street duty.

---

[16] Commission, *2000 Regular Report*, p. 28.

[17] Commission, *2001 Regular Report*, p. 42.

[18] Commission, *1998 Regular Report*, p. 9.

[19] Commission, *2001 Regular Report*, p. 17.

The European Commission has not provided financial support specifically for anti-corruption activities. However, a new multi-country anti-fraud programme is to be set up by mid-2002, for which Hungary will receive €1m from the PHARE budget. This aims to strengthen capacity to fight against fraud, enhance cooperation and coordination activities and improve the exchange of information about frauds and irregularities affecting the financial interest of the European Community. The EU has helped Hungary strengthen administrative capacity and develop the administration through its twinning scheme under the PHARE financial assistance programme.

The most important international influence on anti-corruption policy in Hungary has been the United Nations (see Section 1.3). Hungary is a member of the Group of States against Corruption (GRECO), organised under the auspices of the Council of Europe. GRECO carried out a first evaluation of Hungary in October 2001, but the report had not been published as of July 2002.

2. INSTITUTIONS AND LEGISLATION

Anti-corruption legislation in Hungary is advanced, and the country has ratified all international conventions on corruption with the exception of the Council of Europe Civil Law Convention on Corruption. There is no general law on conflict of interest or asset declarations. Hungary has made significant progress towards establishing an integrated system of state financial control, although further progress is necessary in a number of areas. There are no specialised anti-corruption bodies. Three parliamentary ombudsmen exist and have been independent and critical, but their competencies have recently been limited and their findings are not always respected.

2.1 Anti-corruption legislation

Act no. 4/1978 of the (many times amended) Hungarian Criminal Code specifies that:

> [C]orrupt practices (accepting bribes) are committed by an official who asks for or accepts advantage or a promise thereof in relation to his or her official activities, or makes an agreement with a person asking or offering such advantage.

Changes to the Criminal Code in recent years have sought to deter bribery among public officials in three ways, by:

- increasing the applicable penalty for senior officials from zero to five years to two to eight years imprisonment, while non-senior officials can be imprisoned for one to five years (Article 250);

- obligating official persons to report corruption if they meet it in their work (omitting to do so is defined as a criminal act in Article 255/B); and

- granting immunity to one party to a bribery if s/he subsequently reports the act, turns in the received undue favour and discloses the circumstances (Article 255/A).

Penalties for the person offering the bribe are slightly lower (up to three years imprisonment). They apply to bribery of both national and foreign officials.

The law also defines as criminal acts:

- "Trafficking in influence," which is committed by a person who, purporting to influence an official, asks for or accepts an advantage for himself or for another person. The penalty is imprisonment for one to five years, rising to two to eight years if the perpetrator claims to or gives an impression of bribing an official or if he or she attempts to pass for an official person.

- "Persecution of a Conveyor of an Announcement of Public Concern," defined as "taking a disadvantageous measure against the announcer because of an announcement of public concern," is punishable with imprisonment of up to two years, labour in the public interest, or a fine (Article 257). Hungary is unusual among Central and East European States in offering this protection for "whistleblowers."

Hungary has ratified all international conventions on corruption with the exception of the Council of Europe Civil Law Convention on Corruption, which it had not signed as of June 2002. According to the Ministry of Justice, it plans to do so in 2002.[20]

2.2 Conflict of interest and asset declarations

There is no general law on conflict of interest, but regulations exist in the relevant acts concerning the status of judges,[21] auditors,[22] civil servants,[23] ministers,[24] MPs[25] and

---

[20] Email from Ákos Kara, 20 March 2002.

[21] Act no. 67/1997 on The Legal Status and Revenues of Judges, Articles 22–24.

[22] Act no. 38/1989 on The State Audit Office, Article 10.

[23] Act no. 23/1992 on The Legal Status of Civil Servants, Articles 21–22.

[24] Act no. 79/1997 on The Legal Status and Liability of Members of Government and State Secretaries, Articles 3–4.

[25] Act no. 55/1990 on The Legal Status of Members of Parliament, Articles 9–23.

prosecutors,[26] outlined in subsequent sections of this report. Parliamentarians, and, since 2001, civil servants, are required by law to submit declarations of their assets (see Sections 4.3 and 3.3 respectively).

2.3 Control and audit

The State Audit Office

The State Audit Office (hereinafter SAO) is the main State financial and economic supervisory organ, governed by Act no. 38/1989 on the State Audit Office. It is responsible to Parliament, which approves its annual budget, organisational structure and staffing. The President is elected by a two-thirds majority of Parliament for a twelve-year term, ensuring a high degree of independence. Salaries of SAO staff are around 80 percent higher than those of other civil servants.

The SAO annually audits the closing of the State budget, the pension fund and healthcare fund and 3,200 local government branches. Every two years, the SAO audits political parties' accounts, the National News Agency, the Privatisation Agency, the Hungarian National Bank and others. The SAO has wide-ranging powers to investigate, and can request access to business secrets and bank secrets. However, it has no power to impose corrective measures and its recommendations are sometimes ignored. The SAO presents an annual report of audits to Parliament, which is also published and on which the parliamentary Audit Committee gives an opinion. Around 60 percent of the SAO's capacity is generally occupied with compulsory audits, while the allocation of other resources and the choice of additional subjects for investigation is subject to the SAO President's discretion.[27] Parliament cannot mandate audits but can make suggestions to the SAO President.

The European Commission has noted that the SAO meets the basic requirements for efficient functioning, although it noted that improvements should be made in follow-up by Parliament on the Office's findings.[28]

The Government Control Office

The Government Control Office (hereinafter GCO)[29] audits Government expenditure financed from the central budget and the State funds, reporting directly to the

---

[26] Act no. 80/1994 on The Prosecutorial Service Relation and the Data Handling by the Prosecution, Articles 35–40.

[27] The allocation of resources is not defined by law.

[28] Commission, *2001 Regular Report,* p. 93.

[29] Established by Government Decree no. 61/1999 (IV.21) on The Supervision, Tasks and Jurisdiction of the Government Control Office.

Government and operating on the basis of a Government decree. The GCO is supervised by the Minister heading the Prime Minister's Office and its President is appointed by the Prime Minister. The GCO is mainly concerned with performance audits, intended to assess whether "value-for-money" has been achieved in public spending. The GCO seeks to prioritise its subjects according to risk analysis.[30]

On average, around 30 percent of audits performed by the GCO are done on the special request of the Prime Minister. This makes the GCO vulnerable to being used for political purposes. In the first six months of 2001, all of the capacity of the GCO was used for assignments requested by the Prime Minister, who ordered several investigations into the work of the Ministry of Agriculture and Rural Development following corruption allegations concerning the ministry and its head (a Smallholders MP).[31]

The GCO also monitors the implementation of international aid programmes, in particular those deriving from EU funding schemes. The EU may request that the GCO carry out such an investigation, but the GCO is not obliged to do so. The GCO reports its findings to the Prime Minister if required or otherwise to Government meetings through the permanent secretaries of the ministries concerned, who sometimes seek to change or influence the report.[32] To date, the Government has always approved the GCO's reports, thereby turning its recommendations into Government decisions. Permanent secretaries must submit an action plan of corrective measures within 30 days of a report's approval. Deadlines for implementation are not always set, reducing the effectiveness of any checks on implementation.

Internal control

According to the European Commission, Hungary has made "significant steps" in the development of legislation on internal financial control and audit, and has set up the necessary internal control and external audit bodies. However, the *2001 Regular Report* noted that internal audit units are understaffed and inadequately prepared for their

---

[30] According to Dr Péter Janza, the following signs alert the GCO to a need to investigate further:

- where ministries pay large sums of money to organs outside the Government;
- where a State Secretary has significant discretionary rights to overrule a regulation;
- bodies where there is a long chain of command between the decision-maker and implementer, as with the police;
- where organisations have accumulated high levels of debt.

[31] Interview with Dr Péter Janza, Vice-President of the Government Control Office, 20 December 2001.

[32] According to Dr Janza.

future role, and that the functional independence of internal auditors should be guaranteed and developed.[33]

2.4 Anti-corruption agencies

Investigation of corrupt practices is primarily the role of the Police and the Prosecutor's Office. Act no. 126/2000 set up a Coordination Centre against Organised Crime, subordinated to the Government and controlled through the Ministry of Interior. It does not undertake investigative work but rather performs a coordinating role among other investigatory bodies concerned with detecting crimes specified in the aforementioned law, including bribery and money-laundering.

2.5 Ombudsman

There are three parliamentary ombudsmen, covering civil and political rights, national and ethnic minorities, and data protection (and freedom of information). They are elected for six years by a two-thirds majority of Parliament. The ombudsmen are charged with investigating violations of constitutional rights and can initiate measures to remedy any violations. They can request any relevant data for inspection. The ombudsmen are responsible exclusively to Parliament, to which they report annually, while their opinions and recommendations are also made public. In March 2001, the Constitutional Court ruled that the ombudsmen's power to review the activities of governmental branches, juridical agencies (except courts) and other extra judicial bodies of conflict resolution is unconstitutional. Ombudsmen thus do not now have jurisdiction over Parliament, procurators, tribunals and organisations of commercial arbitration, public notaries or mediating bodies for consumer protection. These limitations came into effect in December 2001.

The ombudsmen are seen as independent and willing to make critical statements, but their statements are not always acted upon and sometimes meet hostility from governing politicians. For example, although László Majtényi, former data protection and freedom of information ombudsmen, in 1999 suggested that the decision not to record Government sessions violated the constitutional right to access public information, the Government did not reverse the decision.

---

[33] Commission, *2001 Regular Report,* p. 93.

3. EXECUTIVE BRANCH AND CIVIL SERVICE

Civil service reform has been in progress in Hungary since 1994. However, the legal framework has not prevented continuing political appointments. Procedures for appealing against administrative decisions are in place. Conflict of interest provisions forbid civil servants from holding ancillary executive positions, but not from external employment. Since 2001 civil servants and senior functionaries have had to submit declarations of interests, income and assets, but the provisions are undermined by a badly designed procedure for submitting complaints, and there are no sanctions for submitting false information. A Code of Ethics for civil servants was under preparation as of May 2002. The openness and accountability of the executive has diminished since 1998, as access to information has been increasingly restricted. Evidence of corruption in the executive branch is sporadic, although there have been several important scandals in recent years.

3.1 Structure and legislative framework

There is no single uniform law on institutions with executive power, but fundamental legal regulations are set out in the Constitution and the procedural rules of Government. The role of the civil service is established in the 1992 Act on the Legal Status of Public Servants.[34] Reform of the Public Administration has been underway since 1994. According to the OECD, since the change of Government in 1998, "[T]he principles of devolution and decentralisation have been applied more widely and the strategic functions of the ministries have been strengthened."[35]

Ministers are political appointees. They have two under-secretaries reporting to them: one a political appointee, the other, the administrative State Secretary, a civil servant. Competitive selection of civil servants is compulsory only for heads of department in the Prime Minister's Office, ministries (with the exception of the Ministry of Foreign Affairs) and central bodies of public administration subordinated directly to the Government. The Governments of both Antall (1990–1994) and Horn (1994–1998) replaced around 50 percent of civil servants in the highest ranks.[36] Following the 1998 elections, 11 of the 13 administrative State Secretaries were replaced.

Reforms in 2001 included steps to make the civil service a more appealing "lifelong career" option, including a substantial salary increase (60-70 percent for employees with

---

[34] Act no. 23/1992.

[35] OECD, *Issues and Developments in Public Management: Hungary 2000,* OECD, 2001.

[36] *HVG,* 8 August 1998.

higher education qualifications and 40-45 percent for those with secondary qualifications, to be implemented over four years) and better training provision, particularly in foreign languages. These improved benefits may help to ensure the independence of civil servants, although salaries remain low relative to the private sector.

A new elite of top civil servants was established in March 2002, entitled to higher salaries and appointed for a five-year term that cannot be ceased prematurely. The Prime Minister decided which individuals were awarded this status, with no legal possibility for appeal. The opposition contended that the Government's aim was to install politically loyal civil servants.[37]

3.2 Administrative procedure and redress

The main rules on administrative proceedings are laid down in Act no. 4/1957 on the General Rules of Administrative Procedure. Article 15 states that decisions must be made within 30 days of the submission of a petition or the date of launching an *ex officio* procedure. Shorter deadlines can be set by statute, but the deadline can be extended only by force of law or governmental decree. An appeal can be made to the second-instance administrative organ within 15 days of the delivery of the decision. However, if the Government or a member of the Government issued the first instance decision, there is no appeal procedure and further complaints must be pursued in the courts. Article 72 (1) guarantees judicial review concerning the final, binding administrative decision brought on the case. An applicant can submit a petition only after exhausting the appeal process, within 30 days of the delivery of the final administrative decision and exclusively on the grounds of claiming a violation of law.

3.3 Conflict of interest and asset monitoring

According to Act no. 23/1992 on the Legal Status of Civil Servants, a civil servant cannot hold office in a political party and may not undertake a public appearance on behalf of or in the interest of a political party apart from participation in general or local elections as a candidate; or an executive of a commercial enterprise or member of the supervisory board except if the commercial enterprise is majority-owned by a local authority or public entity or is in State property permanently. A civil servant cannot be a member of the body of representatives of the local government that functions in the area of competence

---

[37] See report of opposition question to Prime Minister's Office given in "Government installs own top civil servants before election – Liberals," Hungarian TV2 satellite service, 27 November 2001, as reported by BBC Monitoring.

of the agency of public administration employing him. There are no restrictions on the jobs a civil servant can hold before or after leaving the civil service.

The provisions on involvement with political parties appear contradictory, with civil servants allowed to stand for election but prevented from taking a public political stance (at least outside the campaign period). Civil servants starting a political career may be vulnerable to an adverse interpretation of the law. In January 2002, the head of the Budapest Public Services Office was fired after declaring that he would stand as a candidate in the 2002 elections. Allowing civil servants to sit on the boards of State companies also risks conflicts of interest. There are currently no rules on accepting gifts, but the forthcoming Code of Ethics is expected to prohibit the acceptance of gifts where this could sway a decision.

Ministers, parliamentary under-secretaries, public service under-secretaries, deputy under-secretaries and senior public servants are required to submit asset declarations annually to the Control Office of the Public Service (hereinafter COPS), established in 2001. Heads of department and all employees junior to them are required to make declarations every two years. Declarations must also be submitted for spouses or common-law partners and children.

COPS collected the first batch of property declarations in October 2001, relating to assets held at the end of 2000, and a second batch in March 2002, relating to declarations for the year 2001. Property declarations are private, seen only by the employee and their employer, and handled anonymously by COPS. If an inexplicable difference is found between declarations made in consecutive years, and a complaint is made, COPS can investigate. It conducts its supervisory procedure over a maximum six-month period, during which it can hear witnesses and request documents from many sources, including banks, brokers and the Land Registry. However, its request will be denied if the information sought represents a bank or tax secret. In such a situation, COPS reports that a negative response was received, but cannot investigate further. After six months, COPS concludes that the enrichment of the public servant either can, or cannot, be explained by legal means. This conclusion is forwarded to the person who initiated the investigation, generally the superior of the employee under investigation, who can then take appropriate action – this might include expelling the public servant or initiating a criminal procedure or tax investigation.

Although the new provisions strengthen the legal basis for monitoring and punishing corruption in the civil service, there are some important deficiencies:

- Investigations are initiated only if COPS receives a complaint. While sifting every declaration would clearly be impossible given the sheer volume of declarations submitted, this means that the main benefit is through encouraging self-regulation. Vast scope for irregularities to be overlooked remains.

- The procedure for submitting complaints is asymmetric. Public servants may submit complaints only about staff junior to them, not their superiors. For example, ministers can only be investigated on the request of the Prime Minister. Members of the public can make complaints, but only if they are willing to provide their name and address.

- There are no penalties for submitting false information.

3.4 Internal control mechanisms

The ministries have internal audit departments, which are overseen by the GCO.

3.5 Interaction with the public

There are currently no guidelines for interaction with the public. A Code of Ethics is being drawn up and is expected to be available in 2002.[38]

3.6 Corruption

The Government has shown an increased tendency towards closed decision-making and reluctance to countenance external monitoring or criticism. Freedom House has noted "attempts by the executive branch of Government to limit control over its activities" and, as a result, "the increasing irrelevance of formal democratic institutions."[39] This attitude is also reflected in the response to EU monitoring. Following the publication of the *2001 Regular Report,* Prime Minister Viktor Orbán said that Hungary must

> … grit its teeth and suffer [as] others assess its performance in reports if it wants to join the EU. We do not write country reports and therefore it is not entirely clear to us why others have an insurmountable yearning to make assessments on us.[40]

The main string of corruption scandals in the executive in recent years concerns the activities of former Minister of Agriculture and Rural Development, József Torgyán. In autumn 2000, Torgyán was at the centre of allegations that his asset declarations did

---

[38] Interview with Réka Tóth, Department of Civil Service, Ministry of Interior.

[39] See chapter on Hungary (by Zoltán Miklósi), in: *Nations in Transit,* Freedom House, 2001.

[40] Radio Free Europe/Radio Liberty Newsline, vol. 5, no. 217, part II, 15 November 2001.

not include the estimated €410,000 costs of a new villa which he was building in Budapest. His official salary as a minister was around €1,230 per month. The opposition demanded that the parliamentary Immunity Committee launch an investigation on conflict of interest and gain access to the non-public part of Torgyán's asset declaration. Around the same time, the media revealed that the ministry headed by Torgyán had spent large amounts on irregular activities, including several trips to the Far East.[41] Finally, in early 2001, the daily newspaper *Népszava* published tape recordings in which a businessmen discussed a €12,300 bribe which was, allegedly, to be delivered to Torgyán's son, Attila, in exchange for which he was to mediate with his father concerning a €168,100 contract from the Ministry of Agriculture. Shortly afterwards, Torgyán resigned from the cabinet. The investigations against his son were closed owing to absence of crime, but the other suspects were charged with official trading in influence.[42]

Reports of corruption in areas of the civil service in regular contact with the public, such as offices issuing licences and permits, is common. For example, in late August 2001, a corruption scandal emerged involving the allocation of immigration permits by the Budapest Metropolitan District Governor's Office. Allegedly, several foreigners who had attempted unsuccessfully over a period of months to obtain immigration permits paid sums of €820-2,050 to a company which would mediate with the office. Within one or two days, in some cases hours, those involved were issued with permits. The investigators suspected that the owner of the company, having deducted a commission rate, transferred the money to high-ranking officials in the agency.[43]

4. LEGISLATURE

Although all public expenditure is included in the State budget, Parliament's role in scrutinising the executive has been undermined since 1998 in several ways. MPs are subject to limited conflict of interest provisions and must declare business interests, income and assets. However, the mechanisms for scrutinising assets are weak, there are no sanctions for providing false information, and the provisions do not appear to be observed sufficiently. Increasingly common defamation and civil law suits against MPs may have undermined the ability of MPs to scrutinise senior officials sufficiently. There is little direct evidence of corruption of MPs.

---

[41] In February 2002, the Prosecutor General's Office submitted charges against Torgyán's deputy, Béla Szabadi, for damages to the Ministry in this regard (see Section 4.5).

[42] *Népszabadság,* 5 February 2002 and 13 February 2002; *Magyar Hírlap,* 30 March 2002.

[43] *HVG,* 1 September 2001.

4.1 Elections

Elections are monitored by the Electoral Commission, comprising one delegate from each political party large enough to have a nationwide party list, plus five non-party "expert" members who have a relevant professional background. The party representatives are nominated by their parties and appointed by the Interior Minister. Prior to the 1994 and 1998 elections, the expert representatives were agreed upon by consensus in the Parliament and formally appointed by the Interior Minister. In late 2001, however, the Interior Minister rejected all of the candidates nominated by opposition parties – some of whom had been supported by both Left and Right in previous election years – and appointed five experts nominated by the governing parties. This cast serious doubt on the impartiality of the Commission. The Interior Minister declined to explain to the press why he had rejected all of the opposition nominees[44] and at the same time announced that the party representatives on the committee would not be decided until mid-March, the latest date possible. Thus, until three weeks before the elections, the five Government-nominated experts were the only members of the Commission. The Organization for Security and Co-operation in Europe expressed concern over this practice after the first round of the elections.[45]

4.2 Budget and control mechanisms

All public expenditure is included in the State budget. However, the introduction of a two-year budget in September 2000 means that governmental plans for expenditures and revenues are subject to less scrutiny. The Government still reports to Parliament at the end of each year on the execution of the budget, but this is after the fact, making objections somewhat meaningless. The SAO President finds that the two-year budgeting has had no implications for the annual audit of the budget.[46] Hungary will return to a one-year budget in 2003.

Some local analysts argue that the Government has adopted a practice of underestimating inflation when it makes its budget projections. The Government forecast six to seven percent inflation for 2000 and five to seven percent for 2001, whereas inflation turned out at 9.8 percent and 9.2 percent respectively. In this way,

---

[44] Of those appointed, the opposition claims that four out of five have clear links to the right-wing parties in Government; see commentary by Mária Kórodi, "SZDSZ MP," in *Magyar Hírlap,* 18 December 2001.

[45] OSCE Office for Democratic Institutions and Human Rights, *Preliminary Statement,* Budapest, 8 April 2002.

[46] Interview with Árpád Kovács, President, State Audit Office, 12 December 2001.

surplus revenue (of €820m and €1.148b respectively) was earned, and this money was spent without the normal degree of parliamentary scrutiny.[47] The Ministry of Finance argues that such discrepancies arise because the budget is planned – and hence forecasts made – several months prior to its announcement.[48] Nevertheless, the IMF has argued that, "the practice of allowing the Government to conduct additional spending from higher-than-forecast revenues should be ceased."[49]

Parliament's ability to control public spending is also curtailed by the Government practice of conducting some areas of public procurement – primarily road construction and other public works – through the State-owned Hungarian Development Bank (see Section 7.3). This part of expenditure is thereby excluded from the budget and Parliament cannot check how much is spent or in what manner. The amount involved is significant – e.g., the road-building programme commenced under the current Government is worth €2.460b (around five percent of GDP). Scrutiny relies on two sources, both after the fact: the annual report of the Hungarian Development Bank is made available to the Minister of Finance, who can be called upon to answer questions in Parliament; and the bank can be audited by the SAO.

Parliamentary questions

Following a change to the Rules of the House in 1999, supported by a two-thirds majority of MPs present, plenary sessions of Parliament are held every third week rather than every week. Although the Government argues that this improves efficiency, the change has significantly reduced opportunities to scrutinise the executive:

---

[47] Parliament votes to approve the spending of surplus revenues as part of the final accounts; but this tends to be a formality subject to less scrutiny than the rest of the budget. At the end of 2000, the Government carried surplus tax revenues of €307.5m over to 2001 using its deposit account, thereby deciding itself on spending. The SAO found this an inappropriate use of the deposit account. See János Eörsi, "Fiscal transparency and the parliamentary control of the budget," *Üvegzseb*, March 2002.

[48] Letter from the Ministry of Finance Department of Budgetary and Fiscal Policies, 30 April 2002.

[49] "Hungary needs to improve fiscal transparency, IMF says," *Interfax Hungary Weekly Business Report*, 19 June 2001.

- The total time devoted to interpellations declined from 90 minutes per week to 180 minutes every third week and that for questions from 60 minutes per week to 60 minutes every third week.[50]

- Ministers, who have the right to postpone answering a question twice, can now delay their answer for six weeks – past the point at which it was relevant or in the public eye. The lack of continuity also inhibits deep scrutiny.

The opposition objected to the change and referred the decision to the Constitutional Court. Although the Court ruled that the lack of regulation of the frequency of plenary sessions in the Rules of the House is unconstitutional, Parliament has been unable to muster two-thirds support for a new regulation.

Investigatory committees

Parliament can set up special investigatory committees, pursuant to the request of 78 MPs. However, the item must first be put on the agenda, on which the whole chamber votes. Opposition requests to set up investigatory committees have in the 1998-2001 period repeatedly been defeated at this stage. Since 1998, 25 investigatory committees have been proposed but only the four suggested by the governing parties have been established. In 1994-8, seven investigatory committees were set up, six on the proposal of the opposition.

4.3 Conflict of interest and asset monitoring

A Member of Parliament cannot simultaneously serve as President of the Republic, a member of the Constitutional Court, an ombudsman, President, Deputy President or an auditor of the SAO, or as a judge, prosecutor, civil servant, member of the armed forces, police or other institution responsible for law enforcement. A Member of Parliament may not sit on the board of State-owned companies. It is legal for an MP to

---

[50] The difference between an interpellation and a question lies in the pattern of response required. In the case of questions, once an addressee has responded, the MP asking the question does not have the right to reply nor does the Parliament vote on approval of the response. In the case of an interpellation, the MP who submitted the question has the right to reply to the response, and if he does not accept the response, Parliament must approve the response. If Parliament rejects the response, it is sent to a committee for further consideration and approval.

own or work for a private-sector company, even one that bids for public procurement contracts, but such activities must be reported in the asset declaration.[51]

According to Article 19 of Act no. 55/1990, MPs must make a declaration to the Speaker of Parliament on their assets, income and business interest. Declarations must also be provided for the MP's spouse or "life partner living together with them in the same household" and children. The declarations of MPs are public, but those of spouses and children can be accessed only by the parliamentary Committee on Immunity, Conflict of Interest and Mandates, in a proceeding related to the MP's asset declaration. MPs who do not submit their declarations can be denied their rights as an MP and have their honorarium withheld.

The declarations consist of five major parts:

A: Asset declaration:

   I. Real estate

   II. High-value moveables (motor vehicles; protected works of art; other moveables which either per piece or as a collection exceed the sum of six monthly MP's basic honoraria; savings in stocks or other investments, savings deposits; cash exceeding the sum of six monthly basic honoraria; invoices or pecuniary claims exceeding the sum of six monthly basic honoraria; other more valuable assets if their total value exceeds sum of six monthly basic honoraria)

   III. Debts (public debts, debts against financial institutions or against private persons)

   IV. Other announcements

B: Income Declaration (any incomes subject to taxation outside the MP's honorarium)

C: Business interest declaration (business interest or leading executive position on companies)

D: Statement on allocations or things provided for *per gratis* usage to the MP necessary to carry out his/her work or closely related to that, from the Parliament, or from his/her faction, or from any foundation supporting the legislative work

E: Statement on the gifts received in relation to the mandate of the MP or any free allocation which does not fall under part D

---

[51] According to Act no. 55/1990, Article 18, on the Legal Status of Members of Parliament, MPs must report to Parliament the following: labour relations, shares or membership in or position on the supervisory board of a company, cooperative, public-service organisation; membership or leading executive position in social organisations, public organisations; and any activity or contractual relation which provides regular income, or such occasional income which exceeds the amount of the monthly MP's honorarium.

In 2001, following a corruption scandal involving the former Minister of Agriculture (see Section 3.6), the law was changed to require MPs to make asset declarations on an annual basis, rather than at the beginning and end of each term.[52]

Several weaknesses remain:

- Parliamentarians can avoid scrutiny by transferring assets to relatives or friends not required to make asset declarations.

- The mechanisms for checking the truth of asset declarations are weak. After the scandal involving the Agriculture Minister, the Government set up a special committee to investigate unusual increases in MPs' assets over the last ten years. This bypassed the permanent Conflict of Interest Committee, on which the political parties are represented proportionally. The special committee hired experts and collected information about the assets declared by MPs in 1994 and 1998. The opposition did not take part, arguing that the committee had been set up in an unconstitutional manner, ignoring provisions in the Rules of the House for dealing with such occurrences.[53]

- The law does not prescribe sanctions if information given in property declarations is found to be false.

- Ministers have damaged the credibility of the system through their own comments. The former Agriculture Minister claimed that revealing the full extent of his assets would have highlighted his wealth unnecessarily and made him a target for burglars. The Political State Secretary of the Defence Ministry stated that he simply did not wish to reveal the source of his assets.

4.4 Immunity

Article 20 (3) of the Hungarian Constitution declares that MPs enjoy immunity as specified in Act no. 55/1990 on the Legal Status of Members of Parliament. Articles 4-7 state that MPs can be subject to criminal or misdemeanour proceedings or any criminal procedural coercive measures only with the prior assent of Parliament. The

---

[52] Act no. 103/2001, effective 24 December 2001.

[53] The opposition feared that the committee, with its governing-party majority, would turn into a witch-hunt against opposition deputies. The special committee failed to investigate some high-profile cases where the assets of governing party MPs had significantly increased over recent years – for example, the case of the Political State Secretary of the Defence Ministry, whose assets increased by €246,000 between property declarations (equivalent to around 25 years of an MP's average salary).

procedure for lifting immunity can be initiated exclusively by the Prosecutor-General and is subject to parliamentary approval.

MPs and former MPs cannot be held responsible for their votes in Parliament or statements on facts or opinions expressed in the course of the exercise of their mandate. This immunity, however, does not apply for infringement of State secrets, libel, defamation and civil law liability, and litigation against MPs appears to be increasingly common. The 1990–1994 Parliament discussed 44 immunity cases, the 1994–1998 Parliament 51 cases, while between 1998 and 2001, 82 immunity cases have been discussed by Parliament, the majority concerning defamation issues.[54] Where the MP's immunity is not lifted and criminal proceedings cannot be launched, the legal basis for such cases is the Civil Code's protection of a person's good reputation and "personality rights."

In June 2000, László Pallag, chairman of a parliamentary committee investigating an oil-related affair, announced the testimony of a witness which connected the Minister of Interior, Sándor Pinter, and former Finance Minister, Ivan Szabó, with certain crimes. Pinter and Szabó subsequently sued Pallag for violating their personality rights. The final binding decision established the violation and awarded Pinter €5,125 and Szabó €2,050 as non-pecuniary damages, to be paid by Pallag. The Supreme Court upheld the decision and ruled that an MP cannot be exempt from this liability even if he made such an announcement in his official capacity.[55] According to a leading constitutional lawyer, Gábor Halmai, a recent string of judicial decisions in such cases severely impedes the discussion of public affairs in Parliament.[56]

4.5 Corruption

Two MPs were subject to criminal investigation at the time of writing.

Zoltán Székely, a former member of the Smallholders Party and former chair of the Public Procurement Committee in Parliament, faces criminal indictment for alleged bribery in connection with a public procurement application and an environmental protection investment.[57] Prosecutorial investigators caught Székely accepting a bag containing €82,000 from a businessman. The authorities consider the act to be a bribe, while Székely argues that it was a "provocation and a trap," since he expected the bag to contain documents.[58]

---

[54] *Népszabadság,* 31 December 2001.

[55] *Népszabadság,* 20 September 2001 and 31 December 2001.

[56] *HVG,* 9 March 2002.

[57] *Népszabadság,* 24 January 2002.

[58] *Népszabadság,* 9 February 2002.

Béla Szabadi, former member of the Smallholders parliamentary group and then State Secretary at the Ministry of Agriculture, was put under house arrest in 2001. The Central Prosecutorial Investigation Office submitted an indictment against him and three other persons to the Metropolitan Court at the beginning of 2002. Szabadi is charged with several counts of misappropriation (largely related to the ministry's high expenditure on foreign travel), two counts of embezzlement, fraud, and as an instigator in connection with the forgery of a private document.[59] The affair has been highly politicised, with Szabadi telling a parliamentary committee that the Prime Minister had been fully aware of the way in which the Agriculture Ministry was spending its money.

Péter Medgyessy, Prime Minister since May 2002, was put at the centre of allegations prior to the election campaign. In December 2001, police launched an investigation against "unknown suspects," after newspaper reports about the activities of Medgyessy's private company (Medgyessy Consulting Kft.). The reports alleged that the firm received €110,000 from a company named Gresco in 1998 for successfully convincing Socialist representatives in the local government of Budapest's fifth district to support plans related to the sale and utilisation of the Gresham Palace.[60] Medgyessy argued that the activity was a simple and legal case of lobbying. Following two extensions of the deadline, the police ceased the investigation in May 2002, finding that no crime had been committed. Medgyessy also won a civil case against the two newspapers which broke the story, *Magyar Nemzet* and *Magyar Demokrata,* with the newspapers obliged to publish corrections of their false statements.[61]

5. JUDICIARY

Although the legal framework for a truly independent judiciary is in place in Hungary, the Government has shown weak commitment to judicial independence. The resignation and replacement of the Prosecutor-General in 2000 raised concerns about the independence of the institutions responsible for investigating corruption, and there have been indications that some court and prosecutorial decisions have been politically influenced.

---

[59] *Népszabadság,* 2 February 2002.

[60] The information surfaced after a burglary at the firm's office, two days after Medgyessy announced that he would stand as the Hungarian Socialist Party's candidate for Prime Minister. Two weeks after the burglary, the documents were anonymously delivered to the press.

[61] *Magyar Hírlap,* 23 March 2002.

5.1 Legislative framework

The legislative framework for the Hungarian judiciary is examined in detail in the 2001 OSI *Report on Judicial Independence*.[62] While the report acknowledged that the country had made very significant steps towards creating a truly independent judiciary, a number of serious reservations were also levelled, in particular at the 1998–2002 Government's commitment to judicial independence.

Constitutional and legislative guarantees of judicial independence are well established, and have been boosted by the 1997 institutional reforms and increases in salaries over recent years. However, other factors may have jeopardised judicial independence:[63]

- During the three-year probationary period, judges may be vulnerable to political influence.

- Pay increases are in some cases linked to evaluations of "performance," which may create distortionary incentive structures.[64]

- Working conditions remain poor and judges are overburdened.

Several developments in recent years further threaten judicial independence:

- Delayed establishment of appeals courts known as "boards of justice," which are required by the Constitution and were to be established as part of the reforms initiated in 1997.

- Extension of the lustration law to the judiciary, potentially undermining long-serving judges.

- Executive control of the judiciary budget, and notably the Government's repeated curtailments of the National Council of Justice's budget proposals (in contrast to improved financing for the Public Prosecutor's service).[65]

---

[62] EU Accession Monitoring Program, *Monitoring the EU Accession Process: Judicial Independence,* Open Society Institute, Budapest 2001, pp. 185–223, available at <http://www.eumap.org>.

[63] See chapter on Hungary in: Open Society Institute, *Monitoring the EU Accession Process: Judicial Independence,* Budapest 2001, pp. 185–225.

[64] Performance is evaluated according to a set of criteria established in Act no. 67/1997 and based on at least fifty cases which the judge has presided over. Judges may be awarded honorary titles after six years of outstanding service, with a financial bonus attached.

[65] *Monitoring the EU Accession Process: Judicial Independence,* p. 189. Also, in April 2001, the Board of the Hungarian Judicial Association reported that it was "striking" that the proportion of budgetary expenditures assuring the operating conditions of courts within the State budget had decreased. See *HVG,* 5 January 2002.

In December 2001, the National Association of Prosecutors, Hungarian Bar Association and Budapest Bar Association published a declaration endorsed by prominent signatories, stating that the independence of the judiciary was under threat because members of the legislature, executive and media make public comments on cases before and after decisions. The heads of two of the associations also criticised the fact that members of Parliament are allowed simultaneously to practise law. Following the declaration, András Hegedűs, Chief Prosecutor of Budaörs, was dismissed from his post.

Judges are subject to standard conflict of interest provisions, and must also submit asset declarations every third year, which are collected and monitored by the National Council of Justice.

Some commentators have noted with concern that in recent years Supreme Court decisions frequently have deviated significantly from the decisions of lower courts. For example, in a case concerning the construction of a proposed fourth metro line in Budapest, the first four judicial decisions ruled in favour of the Municipality of Budapest, headed by an opposition mayor, whilst the Supreme Court, owing to a "change of legal conception," ruled in favour of the Government.[66]

5.2 Corruption

In general, the 1997 reforms, which sought to improve judicial independence through a combination of organisational changes and increases in salaries, are thought to have reduced corruption in the judiciary. There have been no proven cases of explicit corruption in recent years. However, the judiciary has become increasingly vulnerable to political influence. The appointment of a former FIDESZ-MPP candidate, Péter Polt, as Prosecutor-General has prompted concern about judicial independence.

Since Polt's appointment, the Prosecutor's Office has handed down some controversial decisions on corruption cases involving Government members. In November 2001, two serious criminal cases linked to senior members of FIDESZ-MPP were closed after almost three years of investigation owing to lack of evidence. One of the cases involved allegations of tax fraud, bankruptcy crime and forgery of public documents. Csaba Schlecht, then treasurer of FIDESZ-MPP, sold 17 companies – some of them allegedly set up by Viktor Orbán and other members of FIDESZ in the early 1990s – to two

---

[66] *HVG,* 5 January 2002. András Sajó, a Professor of law at the Central European University, commented in the article cited that, "[I]t is not fortunate in a political case to change the legal practice, especially if the changed standpoint makes possible those legal conclusions which are pleasant for the ear of the Government... In a political case the judgement... must be conservative. Otherwise the charge is inevitable: the judge complied with *external factors.*"

foreigners who later claimed that they had no knowledge of the sale.[67] Some of these companies had huge tax arrears (amounting to a total of €410,000 according to some reports) and other debts, and some had allegedly been used to channel funds to firms that provided campaign services to FIDESZ.[68] However, charges of tax fraud and bankruptcy crime could be made only with regard to one, Centum. The Budapest Prosecutor's Office closed the proceedings in November 2001, arguing that no crime could be established as the companies had no assets of their own (indirectly implying that the companies had been established solely for the purpose of tax fraud). The Budapest Prosecutor's Office later rejected all complaints submitted against the police decision to close the investigation.[69]

The second case involved Attila Várhegyi, chairman of the FIDESZ-MPP Executive Board, former Political State Secretary at the Ministry of National Cultural Heritage and Mayor of Szolnok. Several charges were filed against Várhegyi in 1998, including deliberate bribery of a senior official (allegedly concerning fictitious invoices related to Várhegyi's campaign for the mayoralty) and misappropriation related to a real estate purchase contract apparently on disadvantageous terms for the municipality and allegedly ignoring the intentions of the municipality and statutes.[70] In November 2001, the Prosecutor's Office reduced his charges to a single act (neglectful abuse of funds) and two days later the first instance court found him guilty and fined him €1,230. The court acquitted Várhegyi from bribery charges related to campaign financing, stating that although formally bribery was performed, "danger to society" could not be established and hence a crime could not be established.[71] After this decision, which is being appealed, Várhegyi resigned from his post at the ministry, but retained his party position.

Some local commentators argue that the timing of cases is also politically influenced. Both of the above cases were finally cleared, following several years' delay, just a few months before the general election. A case concerning the "Tocsik Affair," the biggest scandal of the previous administration, was tried a month before the election.

---

[67] *Budapest Business Journal,* 26 November 2001.

[68] *Budapest Business Journal,* 26 November 2001.

[69] *Népszabadság,* 22 September 2001 and 30 October 2001.

[70] *Népszabadság,* 9 February 2002.

[71] *Népszabadság,* 10 November 2001.

6. POLITICAL PARTY FINANCE

There is significant evidence that covert funding of political parties and corruption has been an important problem in Hungary. Although funding regulations are relatively strict, supervision of party funding is largely formal and insufficient, while subsidies to political parties from the State appear to be insufficient to dampen incentives to seek financing on a *quid pro quo* basis. The use of Government advertising to promote the governing party appeared to be a particular problem prior to the 2002 elections.

6.1 Legislative framework

Under Act no. 33/1989 on the Operation and Financial Management of Political Parties (several times amended), parties may receive income from donations, membership contributions and the State budget, as well as earnings from their assets and companies:

- Donations can be accepted from any source except foreign Governments, State enterprises, foundations supported by the State and anonymous donors.

- All donations from legal entities and companies which are not legal entities must be declared in the party's balance sheet.

- Any donation above €2,050 from a Hungarian national must be declared and the identity of the donor made public. From a foreign national, contributions exceeding €410 must be detailed. Individual donors contributing less than these amounts must make their identity known to the party.

- Income originating from a company established by the party must also be declared.

- Most of the parties' declared income comes from the State budget. Of the total State subsidy, 75 percent is allocated among parties that received more than one percent of votes cast in the last general election, proportional to the share of the vote received, and the remaining amount is distributed equally among parties in Parliament. The operating costs of parliamentary caucuses are financed from the budget of Parliament.

- Election campaigns are financed from the parties' ordinary budgets; no separate support from the State is received. The law sets a quota on the amount which can be spent during the campaign at €4,100 per candidate.

- Parties are allowed to establish their own companies.

All of the MPs interviewed for this report regarded the State financing for political parties as inadequate. Parties thus rely on their own assets (e.g., the sale of party headquarters, and in the case of the MSZP, considerable assets left from the Communist period) and donations. Some donations are made "in kind" rather than in cash. This encourages clientelism, with parties perceiving a need to "re-pay" favours granted by supportive firms. Parties also use associated foundations to channel money from anonymous donors and avoid reporting on expenditure.[72]

6.2 Control and supervision

Parties submit reports on their financial situation every year, which are published in the *Official Gazette – Magyar Közlöny*. The SAO audits the accounts of parties receiving funds from the State budget every two years and monitors election costs and campaign spending every four years. The SAO's President identifies the monitoring of campaign financing as the biggest problem facing his organisation. Two important items are missing from the law: a definition of the start-date of a campaign; and the type of materials which qualify as campaign costs. This prevents the SAO from effectively monitoring campaign financing, while no sanctions are applied if the amount is exceeded. The SAO can work only on the declarations of campaign spending that the parties make and has no capacity to check whether they are truthful. The SAO's recommendations to modify the law and end this ambiguity have been ignored or rejected by Parliament.[73]

6.3 Party finance in practice

The SAO sometimes finds examples of mismanagement or irregularities in the accounts of political parties. The penalty is a fine equivalent to the amount involved in the irregularity. The SAO President says that the party itself is usually found to operate correctly, but that at the "outskirts" one may find friendly companies and supporters with "grey or black money."[74]

One irregularity in the State financing of parties occurred in 2001. The Christian Democratic National Party sued the State for failing to pay it the amount it was due. The Ministry of Finance claimed that it would not pay since the party had split since

---

[72] Zsolt Enyedi, "Party Funding in Hungary," paper produced for Constitutional and Legal Policy Unit, Budapest, forthcoming 2002.

[73] Two-thirds support is required to alter the law on political parties.

[74] Interview with Dr Árpád Kovács, 12 December 2001.

the elections. The Christian Democrats won the case. The leader of the Christian Democrats claimed that the Government had ceased financing in order to impede the party's participation in the election, since it targets core FIDESZ-MPP supporters.[75]

Smaller parties complain that State support is barely enough to finance operating costs. Such parties clearly have great difficulty attracting funds from elsewhere, whilst the larger parties either have significant assets (e.g., the MSZP has considerable assets left from the Communist era) or are in a stronger position to attract funding. FIDESZ-MPP suggested doubling the maximum campaign spending per candidate ahead of the 2002 general elections. This drew protests from smaller parties. However, the current ceiling was set prior to the 1997 general election.

The limits on campaign financing in any case appear academic, given that the SAO cannot monitor spending or make pronouncements on whether the official limit has been exceeded. It also appears that the parties have little regard for obeying the rule. One FIDESZ-MPP MP admitted that, in order to meet the limit, "the parties take into consideration only those expenses which are in strict connection with the campaign," ignoring, for example, the extra wages of new employees taken on for the campaign period.[76] Campaign assistants can also be paid through foundations close to the parties, whose finances are not subject to scrutiny.

Another controversial issue concerns the boundary between Government and party campaigning. The OSCE noted that Government advertising increased markedly in the weeks preceding the 2002 elections.[77] The overlap between Government and party campaigning may indeed stretch much farther back. In 1999, the then Government set up a new Country Image Centre (CIC), responsible for promoting Hungary, to which it allocated a large amount of public money – €53.3m – over three years. The CIC focused largely on promoting Hungary to the Hungarian population, and the content of its materials often praised Government activities. For example, in December 2001, the CIC began to take out weekly full-page advertisements (at a cost of €155,500 per week) in daily newspapers for a *Parliamentary Report*. The report was not, in fact, produced by Parliament and its content openly criticised the policies of the previous MSZP-SZDSZ Government.

The media has also speculated about political bias in the Country Image Centre's awarding of contracts. Two companies, Happy End and Ezüsthajó Kft, won 90 percent of the contracts awarded by the CIC, amounting to more than €41m.[78] Happy End

---

[75] "A KDNP egyelőre nem jelenti fel a pénzügyminisztert" ("The Christian Democrat Party will not sue the finance minister yet"), *Index,* 12 January 2002.

[76] Interview with FIDESZ-MPP MP, 9 January 2002.

[77] OSCE/ODIHR, *Preliminary Statement,* Budapest, 8 April 2002.

[78] *Magyar Hírlap,* 12 December 2001.

was founded by András Wermer, the communications adviser to the Prime Minister, and Csaba Káel, formerly a member of the FIDESZ-MPP campaign team (which was organised by Wermer). The company has not published an annual report since 1998. Ezüsthajó subcontracts much of its work to Well Done Kft, the directors of which are András Wermer and Csaba Káel. Happy End has also used Well Done Kft as a subcontractor. These examples reveal that companies closely linked to the governing party have had great success in obtaining public contracts. Despite the losing bidders in some cases expressing doubts about the fairness of tender procedures, no case of corruption has been proven. However, in late May 2002, the Prosecutor-General's Office announced that several contracts between Happy End and the Prime Minister's Office were illegal, owing to public procurement procedures having been bypassed.[79]

One of the major corruption scandals under the 1994–1998 Government was linked to party financing. In January 1996, the State privatisation and holding company, ÁPV, hired lawyer Márta Tocsik to negotiate with local governments regarding the compensation which ÁPV owed them after privatising real estate in the municipalities' ownership.[80] A public scandal broke out over the fee paid to Tocsik, which, at ten percent of the money she saved ÁPV, amounted to €3,296,400. The first instance court found no irregularity here, since Tocsik had saved ÁPV more than €41m. However, the findings of a parliamentary investigatory committee led to the launch of several other criminal and civil procedures. In particular, some information from Tocsik's testimony was leaked, in which she stated that László Boldvai, treasurer of the then governing MSZP, and György Budai, a businessman close to the SZDSZ party in coalition with MSZP, had asked that 50 percent of her fee should be transferred to companies named by them. Indeed, Tocsik did transfer €943,000 to Boldvai and €471,500 to firms controlled by Budai. This raised suspicions that Tocsik's contract was part of a party financing deal.[81]

The civil procedure launched by the Prosecutor-General's Office ended in the first instance with a ruling for Tocsik and ÁPV.[82] However, the criminal procedure has thus far resulted in a series of contradictory decisions. The first decision by the Metropolitan Court of Budapest, in 1999, acquitted Tocsik and the officials of ÁPV, but convicted Boldvai, Budai and another businessman of influence peddling.[83] The convicted defendants and the prosecutors appealed and, in 2000, the Supreme Court sent the

---

[79] *Népszava*, 31 May 2002.

[80] *East European Constitutional Review*, vol. 8, Winter/Spring 1999, p. 17.

[81] *Népszabadság*, 19 March 2002, and *East European Constitutional Review*, vol. 8, Winter/Spring 1999.

[82] *HVG*, 14 July 2001.

[83] *Népszabadság*, 19 March 2002.

case back for a new procedure. In March 2002, the Metropolitan Court sentenced Tocsik to four years imprisonment as an accomplice related to misappropriation, confiscating €2.6m. The ÁPV officials were also convicted for various charges of misappropriation and neglectful handling of affairs, and the businessman was convicted of forgery. However, Boldvai and Budai were acquitted from blackmail charges.[84] The case has been appealed again.

7. PUBLIC PROCUREMENT

Public procurement in Hungary has become an increasing source of concern in recent years. Although procurement legislation is relatively advanced, the Government has taken advantage of loopholes to avoid public tenders by using the Hungarian Development Bank to allocate major contracts, in particular massive public investment in the motorway construction programme. The European Commission has strongly criticised this practice. Although mechanisms of supervision of procurement are relatively well established, corruption still appears to be generally widespread.

7.1 Legislative framework

Public procurement is regulated by the Act no. 40/1995 on Public Procurement, amended in 1999 and 2001. The act applies to contracting entities defined as bodies financed by public resources or governed by public entities, as well as organisations – public or private utilities – which are in an exclusive or special position in the market granted by the State or municipality and provide public services. There is no code of ethics for public procurement officers.

Procurements of goods, works and services come under the scope of the Act if their value equals or exceeds the "public procurement value threshold." This amount is set in the annual State budget. For 2001–2002 the amounts are:

- for procurements of goods, €73,800;

- for public works, €147,600;

- for services, €36,900; and

- for works in respect of the obligation of pre-qualification, €984,000.

---

[84] *Népszabadság,* 19 March 2002 and 20 March 2002.

Specific procedural rules apply for some areas, including the procurement of military equipment and procurements involving national security.

There are three main types of public procurement procedure:

- **Open**. All interested persons may submit bids. A pre-qualification procedure can be used in some cases, e.g., where a works procurement equals or exceeds the value threshold.

- **Restricted**. The number of bidders can be restricted if the nature of the public procurement means that only a limited number of bidders are capable of fulfilling the contract, or if at least five qualified bidders are suitable.

- **Negotiated**. The number of bidders is highly restricted. This applies in cases precisely determined by law, for example, if one of the above procedures was unsuccessful, owing to technical reasons, or for reasons of extreme urgency. It usually applies where competition is limited. Participants are not bound by their bids in the course of this procedure.

The open procedure is used most commonly, as shown in the Table 4.

Table 4: Breakdown of public contracts by method of allocation, 1995–2000

	Open		*Restricted*		*Negotiated*	
Period	*number*	*share*	*number*	*share*	*number*	*share*
Nov 95 – Dec 96	2252	69.5 percent	194	6 percent	795	24.5 percent
1997	2778	64 percent	241	6 percent	1319	30 percent
1998	2789	62 percent	159	4 percent	1533	34 percent
1999	2361	61 percent	103	3 percent	1364	36 percent
2000	2828	76.2 percent	85	2.3 percent	797	21.5 percent

Source: Ministry of Justice.

However, in the first nine months of 2001, although 70 percent of tenders were awarded by open bidding, these tenders accounted for only 42 percent of all public procurement spending, or €709.3m.[85]

The law allows social and economic criteria to be used in the evaluation procedure, which seek to: improve possibilities for SMEs; ensure environmental protection; develop

---

[85] "Hungarian Public Procurement News Ltd.," *Interfax Hungary Daily Business Report,* vol. 3, no. 192, 5 October 2001.

underdeveloped regions; and enhance employment. Only one criterion can be utilised in any one tender and it is to be applied according to guidelines set out in the law.

Modifications to the Act in 1999 introduced stricter rules for the evaluation of bids, such that contracting authorities are required to state in advance not only the criteria they will use for selection of the winner, but also the weights they attach to each and how scores are allocated. Nevertheless, in November 2000, the Political and Legislative Committee of the American Chamber of Commerce in Hungary still felt that:

> [T]he possibility of allocating many points to intangible or subjective criteria can result in an unduly high consideration of these intangibles and the corresponding unduly low consideration of price. It is very difficult, if not next to impossible, to contest an award where the majority of the points are granted for elements other than price. By allocating the majority of points to such elements, the subjective evaluation of these elements results in the award being granted to the bidder to whom the owner wishes to award the tender rather than to the best offer.[86]

The Ministry of Justice in 2001 proposed a series of further modifications to the Act to eliminate some of the remaining possibilities for corruption[87] as well as advancing the Act's harmonisation with the *acquis*. However, the Government decided to include modifications to the bill in a package of amendments to other Acts, omitting the more far-reaching recommendations. The Ministry hopes to see more amendments to the Act in 2002. In preparation, it will commission a survey of those involved in public procurement, in an effort to observe and appraise problems observed in legal practice.[88] Other proposed modifications would increase penalties for non-contractual fulfilment of contracts. The practice of splitting up procurements – so as to circumvent the law by generating several procurements below the value threshold – is prohibited in the 1995 Act, while the 1999 modifications sought to tighten control in this respect.

The 1995 Act includes "preferential rules" for local companies, which can be used in the pre-qualification procedure and in evaluating bids. If the domestic value added in a proposal represents more than 50 percent of the total value, that proposal can be considered as equivalent to cheaper proposals, provided that the price differential is not more than ten percent. This is in line with Hungary's obligations under its Europe Agreement, and a 1997 survey by the Ministry of Justice found that the rule was not often applied. The Ministry and the European Commission have recommended that

---

[86] American Chamber of Commerce in Hungary, Position Paper in Relation to the Transparency in the Public Procurement Process, 6 November 2000.

[87] Government Resolution no. 1023/2001 on the Governmental Strategy against Corruption.

[88] Interview with Dr. Anita Németh, European Communities Law Department, Ministry of Justice, 14 December 2001.

the preferential rules be deleted from the Act, but this appears to be politically difficult.[89]

7.2 Review and audit

The Public Procurement Council comprises 19 members representing central Government agencies, contracting authorities and bidders. It is responsible to Parliament and oversees the application of procurement rules as well as initiating legislative amendments. It also provides information and training, and publishes the notices for procurement procedures. Members of the Public Procurement Council are subject to incompatibility rules.

Within the Public Procurement Council, a Procurement Arbitration Committee is responsible for providing legal remedy in issues of dispute or violations of the Public Procurement Act. The procedure can be initiated by the Council, by anyone with an interest in the tender, or by one of ten other organisations with a relevant mandate, e.g., the SAO and the GCO. The Committee comprises 18 commissioners appointed by the Council. If it detects violations of the law, the Committee can apply various sanctions, including requiring a certain tender condition to be met, imposing fines and prohibiting the bidder from taking part in any public procurement procedure for five years. The 1999 amendments made it compulsory for fines to be imposed if a violation is uncovered during the review procedure.

In 2000, 700 cases (around 20 percent of public procurement procedures) were submitted to the Committee for legal remedy, and infringements of the law were found in 277 cases. The most common problem was that the winner was found not to be the highest bidder. In 68 cases, determination of the invalidity of bids was found to be flawed, and in 24 cases a problem was found where the negotiated procedure had been invoked for reasons of extreme urgency. Eighty-eight of the problem cases concerned negotiated procedures, of which there were only 797 in 2000.

The cost of initiating the review procedure was increased in 2002, from €123 to €615. The move was intended to take into account inflation, since the cost had not been increased since 1995, but may also have the effect of preventing some unnecessary reviews being launched. There is no appeal against the Committee's decision, but companies can seek judicial review by claiming that their right or legal interest has been violated. They must submit a petition within 15 days of the delivery of the Committee's decision. The decision of the first-instance court can be appealed to a second-instance court, but no further.

---

[89] Interview with Dr Anita Németh, Ministry of Justice, 14 December 2001.

7.3 Corruption

The SAO finds a lot of mistakes in the tender procedures, and the SAO President argues that local government has an interest in avoiding the public procurement procedure since the process is so long.[90] The GCO, by contrast, is of the opinion that strong control in public procurement is effective at deterring irregularities. In general, the GCO finds that bribes and misconduct are not characteristic of central Government, but more so of local government.[91]

László Tunyogi, whose firm runs a weekly publication about public procurement in Hungary, notes three problems:

- Relations between contractors and subcontractors are barely supervised. Thus, "main" contractors (winning bidders) often pay subcontractors a fraction of the money received for the contract, resulting in substandard work. Moreover, companies which might otherwise be excluded from the process (for example due to bankruptcy or misconduct during public procurement in the past five years) can indirectly become involved.[92]

- There is little to stop contractors from changing the terms of the contract once it is signed, since fulfilment is not checked.

- Where companies are required to meet "pre-qualification" conditions in order to participate in a tender, the persons carrying out the pre-qualification assessment are often the same as those organising the tender.

Interviews for this report also revealed anecdotal evidence that firms pay bribes equal to 10-20 percent of the bidding price to the persons awarding the contract. Accusations of favouritism in the awarding of public contracts are regularly reported in the press. They include speculation that the stone mine owned by Győző Orbán, father of the fromer Prime Minister, owes its success in winning public contracts to political links. In January 2002, the owner of a competitor firm, Mészkő és Dolomit Kft., claimed that he had not been treated fairly by tendering and licensing agencies and announced that he was forced to close down his business.

One scandal in 2001 involved the Chairman of the parliamentary Public Procurement Committee, who was caught by police whilst apparently taking a bribe from a businessman in exchange for a public contract (see also Section 4.5).

---

[90] Interview with Dr Árpád Kovács, 12 December 2001.

[91] Interview with Dr Péter Janza, 20 December 2001.

[92] Interview with Dr László Tunyogi, Hungarian Public Procurement News Exchange, 7 January 2002.

A private security firm has been at the centre of allegations that it is favoured by the Government because of close connections to FIDESZ-MPP members. The company, Defend, was established by a former secret service officer with links to the governing party and has grown rapidly. In 2001, the company's top ten clients were all State organs, amounting to €180.4m worth of business.[93]

Off-budget public procurement

A serious cause for concern is the fact that certain important areas of public expenditure circumvent the public procurement law if channelled through nominally private but State-controlled agencies. The highest-profile example is that of motorway construction. State expenditure on motorway construction is conducted off-budget, through the State-owned Hungarian Development Bank (HDB). The activities of the HDB are bank secrets, while the bank does not need legislative approval for spending projects and is not required to use open tender procedures. The Prime Minister and Finance Minister appoint all executives and members of the supervisory board. Since 1 January 2002, the bank has been required by law to report on its activities quarterly.

In July 2000, a contract was signed between the National Motorway Company and contractors for the construction of a new 60-kilometre section in North East Hungary at a cost of €279.5m. The HDB was the main Government funding agent and the contract was not put out to tender. The Office for Economic Competition expressed its view, in 2000 and 2001, that the decision not to put motorway contracts out to tender is anti-competitive. The IMF also criticised the practice: "[T]he circuitous flow of funds through (state privatisation agency) APV and the MFB [Hungarian Development Bank] should be discontinued… The practice of allowing Government, through government resolution, to conduct additional policy spending… should be discontinued."[94]

Two of the main companies that have won contracts from the National Motorway Company are rumoured to have had no prior experience of road building. In September 2001, the Hungarian Motorway Construction Consortium launched charges of bribery against unknown suspects in connection with reconstruction work on the M7 motorway. They alleged that one subcontractor had concluded a deal with the contractor whereby it would pay over half of the money earned in return for receiving the commission.[95]

---

[93] *HVG*, 12 January 2002.

[94] IMF, *Report on the Observance of Standards and Codes – Hungary* (section on Fiscal Transparency), 18 April 2001.

[95] *HVG*, 29 March 2002.

Following a 2001 change in the law regarding the types of companies which can be privatised, the HDB has also been used to carry out the privatisation of agricultural companies, without reference to the privatisation law. Shares in the agricultural companies were first transferred to the HDB and then sold on without an open tender.

Criticism of the Government's use of the HDB intensified in May 2001 when a number of changes were made to the law regarding the bank, on the initiative of the Government. Before the new legislation was approved, the HDB was regulated by Chapter 31 of the 1996 Credit Bank Act. Under the new Act, the State covers any loss in the capital of the bank, and can act as guarantor for loans granted and bonds issued by the HDB, as well as any liabilities for third parties which the bank undertakes. A legislative proposal which would have required an annual audit of the HDB by the SAO was rejected in Parliament. The GCO is not mandated to supervise spending on motorway construction, since it is not implemented through the State budget. The GCO is authorised to control how State guarantees are drawn, hence if the Hungarian Development Bank were to seek to draw upon a Government guarantee, the GCO might become involved to control this procedure – but only at the Government's request.

The new MSZP government announced in July 2002 that it intends to use public procurement procedures – and open tenders – for awarding road-building contracts from August. However, a restricted rather than an open procedure was initially chosen for the first tender issued by the new Government, in July, with four companies invited to submit bids. One company, which had won the majority of contracts under the previous Government, notably was not invited to participate. Under pressure from the media, the tender was annulled and an open tender subsequently launched.[96]

8. PUBLIC SERVICES

Corruption appears to be an important problem in a number of Hungarian public services, especially in healthcare and probably in the allocation of licenses and permits. Corruption in the traffic police – an area pinpointed by surveys – may have been reduced by recent reforms. The Customs and Finance Guard has been carrying out important reforms, *inter alia,* to reduce corruption. The extensive powers and discretion of the tax authorities may be an important source of corruption. Corruption in education does not appear to be an important problem.

---

[96] MTI EcoNews, 25 July 2002.

8.1 Police

According to Gallup's research, perceptions of corruption in the police vary according to the branch. The traffic police are widely seen to be the most corrupt, followed by other departments in contact with the public. A 2000 Gallup survey in 1999 found that, of those who had been stopped by policemen because of a driving-related offence, 27 percent did not pay a fine although they had committed the offence, while 14 percent paid but did not receive a ticket or receipt. The Association of Police Research carried out a comprehensive survey of corruption in 2000, through interviews and discussions with police personnel. The report found that traffic police accepting bribes and investigators collecting bribes from small businesses were prevalent forms of corruption. Policing of white-collar crime, tax fraud and evasion and drugs also offer significant opportunities for corruption. Bribes and sexual favours are used within the police force to gain promotion or good jobs (sometimes the most "lucrative" ones, such as a particular traffic policing shift).[97]

A number of recent measures aim at reducing corruption:

- Police are no longer allowed to impose on-the-spot fines. This aims to curb the practice of traffic police taking bribes. Any exchange of money witnessed on the street is now suspicious.

- Immunity is offered to one party in a bribe if he reports it within a certain period. Thus policemen accepting bribes face a greater risk of being caught.

- Since January 2000, policemen have worn name badges so that citizens can identify them more easily.

- Police training programmes include an element in which officers are asked to consider possible instances of corruption and think about how they would respond.[98]

Bribe-taking among the traffic police is thought to have decreased as a result of some of these measures. However, since salaries are low, police may be easily tempted by bribes, which significantly augment their regular income. Overall, Dr Benke of the Association of Police Research assesses that "a considerable proportion of police time and effort is devoted to corrupt money collection instead of maintenance of order."

---

[97] Association of Police Research, *Küzdelem a rendőri korrupció ellen* (The Battle Against Police Corruption), 2000.

[98] Interview with Dr Miklós Benke, Association of Police Research, 7 January 2002.

8.2 Customs

Gallup found in 2000 that 28 percent of those surveyed considered the customs and border guards to be corrupt[99] and that 37 percent of SMEs surveyed expected to face corruption when seeking clearance for goods.[100] In 2000, a Central Investigation Office with a staff of 130 was set up at the Customs and Finance Guard. It is empowered to carry out nationwide investigations. The Customs and Finance Guard was reorganised and a decentralised risk analysis system introduced. Hungary also began to prepare the customs service for EU accession by transposing the Customs Information System Convention.

8.3 Tax collection

Although the legal framework is fairly sound, with a general prohibition of tax evasion and many specific laws, anecdotal evidence suggests that tax evasion is extremely common. Regular practices include failure to register employees, trade in false expenses, and channelling income into offshore accounts.[101]

In 1998, the Government introduced a law establishing a criminal investigation division within the tax authorities, authorised to undertake secret searches and open mail as part of its investigations. In addition, the law incorporated provisions of the section of the Act on the Police which deal with secret surveillance. When the bill was debated, the opposition claimed that this law could only be passed by a two-thirds majority of Parliament, since surveillance laws normally required this procedure. The law was passed by 61.8 percent of the votes. The opposition Association of Free Democrats then brought a challenge in the Constitutional Court, which later ruled unconstitutional various provisions of the law relating to secret surveillance. The Court annulled the law in July 2001,[102] but it will remain in force until the end of 2002.

The extensive investigatory powers of the tax authorities may themselves be a source of political pressure and corruption. As described by one newspaper recently, "at any time, a squad of investigators from the National Tax Office (APEH) can appear in your office for a 'random' check of your books going back a half-decade, with the obvious intent of not leaving without money for the state and a commission for

---

[99] See <http://www.gallup.hu/Gallup/monitor/en/gsurveys/010119_pubinst.html>, (last accessed 15 August 2002).

[100] See <http://www.gallup.hu/Gallup/monitor/en/gsurveys/010129_business.html>, (last accessed 15 August 2002).

[101] A change in the law from January 2002 seeks to close this loophole.

[102] Decision no. 31/2001.

themselves."[103] The tax authorities also have some discretionary power to forgive debts or defer payment if payment would make impossible the economic activity of a private entrepreneur, legal person or other entity, or at the person's request, taking into account his or her income, assets and social conditions.[104]

8.4 Health

In the April 2000 Gallup survey, 77 percent of respondents thought it was "typical" or "highly typical" to give a gratuity or tip to hospital doctors. More than half of the population believe that if they want proper service in a healthcare institution they will probably have to pay a tip or gratuity. This finding is significant given that 62 percent of respondents actually visited a healthcare institution in 1999. The amounts involved are considerable – of those who made a payment, 52 percent paid an average of €36 – although anecdotal evidence suggests that an informal "means testing" occurs, with elderly and poorer patients expected to pay less.

Public procurement in the healthcare system may be prone to corruption, owing to a rather anti-competitive system regarding the procurement of pharmaceuticals. Some companies signed long-term contracts to supply hospitals before the 1995 public procurement law came into force. Moreover, the three associations of pharmaceutical companies which dominate the market engage in price-fixing. The Office for Economic Competition appears to play the greatest role in supervising their conduct.[105]

8.5 Education

Corruption occurs in higher education, with some students gaining admission to university or good exam results through paying bribes. This is very difficult to measure and is not mentioned in any of the surveys of the public consulted for this report. However, anecdotal evidence suggests that it is not a common occurrence.

---

[103] "Nine years on, and still the enemy," *Budapest Business Journal,* 2 December 2001.

[104] According to Act no. 91/1990 on the Order of Taxation.

[105] In 2000, the Competition Council, the main decision-making body of the Office for Economic Competition, stated that an agreement among three pharmaceutical associations to recommend that their members make identical price increases constituted indirect price fixing and violated the Competition Act. See *Annual Report on Competition Law and Policy Developments in Hungary January–December 2000.*

8.6 Licensing and regulation

A Gallup 2000 survey found that ten percent of respondents thought it necessary to pay bribes to municipalities concerned with property, land registry and housing.[106] However, Gallup's survey of SMEs found much higher perceived levels of corruption, with 46 percent regarding corruption as high in the area of obtaining technical papers for a vehicle, 41 percent for obtaining municipal permits, 38 percent for obtaining business licences, 30 percent for fulfilling environmental regulations, and 26 percent for obtaining residence and work permits.

9. ROLE OF THE MEDIA

Press freedom is guaranteed in Hungary. However, access to information is problematic despite the existence of freedom of information legislation, and vague provisions on State secrets may have been used to intimidate journalists. Regulation of public broadcasting has been put in doubt by the recent dominance on television and radio boards of trustees by nominees of the governing party, while personnel policy at Hungarian Television indicates strong political interference. Likewise, the allocation of private broadcasting licences has given rise to concerns about political influence. Between 1998 and 2002 the Government made concerted efforts to support the right-wing press, and foreign journalists have come under pressure after criticising the Government.

9.1 Press freedom

According to Article 61 of the Hungarian Constitution, "everyone has the right to freely express his opinion and furthermore to access and distribute information of public interest." The Civil Code provides for "protection of reputation" by granting a right of rectification to someone who is damaged by an untrue fact or by a true fact used in a distorted or negative light. The Criminal Code prohibits insulting statements. These laws do not significantly hinder the freedom of the press to criticise Government officials. In 1994, the Constitutional Court ruled that Article 232 of the Criminal Code – on libel – is unconstitutional because the public's right to criticise Government officials or other

---

[106] See <http://www.gallup.hu/Gallup/monitor/en/gsurveys/010119_pubinst.html>, (last accessed 15 August 2002).

politicians must be protected to a greater extent than its right to criticise private citizens.[107] Nevertheless, it is common for politicians to launch libel suits against journalists.

In May 2000, on the proposal of a Smallholders MP, Parliament extended the law on lustration to include leading journalists and editors of the press, broadcast and online media. This creates a new source of political pressure on journalists. In addition, members of the governing parties have sought to introduce other laws which would curtail the freedom of the press to criticise politicians or government activities:

- *Lex Pokol,* proposed in summer 1999, would have provided those offended by articles expressing "socially unfavourable opinions" with a right to respond through the same media outlet. The bill was not passed.

- In September 2000, the Government introduced a bill such that, "those who... publicly spread unreal facts or real facts in an unrealistic way that may provoke worry or disorder among a great number of people, commit a crime and are punishable with up to three years of imprisonment." The bill was not passed.

- In May 2001, Parliament passed *Lex Répássy,* giving those whose "private rights are offended" by an *opinion* article the right to reply in the same media. Publications transgressing the law were required to pay a penalty, of an unspecified amount, to the State. After protests from the opposition and journalists associations, the President of the Republic sent the law to the Constitutional Court. The Court ruled that the law was unconstitutional, but only in the sense that the extent of the reply and the fine were not defined. According to the Hungarian Press Freedom Centre, the ruling avoided the main issue, while paving the way for a slightly modified version of the law to be passed in future.[108]

9.2 Access to information

Article 19 of Act no. 63/1992 on the Protection of Personal Data and Disclosure of Data of Public Interest grants access to public information. The authorities must decide on whether to grant access within 15 days of an application, and in the event of a rejection, must notify the applicant of the reasons within eight days. The authorities may charge expenses to communicating data of public interest. Applicants may apply to the courts if an application is refused. The Data Protection Ombudsman's 2000 report noted that most cases seeking to uphold freedom of information were raised by journalists, politicians (typically from the opposition) and environmentalists, with the

---

[107] Decision no. 36/1994, Article VI.24.

[108] Telephone interview with Judit Bayer, lawyer, Hungarian Press Freedom Centre, 23 January 2002.

involvement of society at large falling behind "both international standards and what the conditions would permit here in Hungary."[109]

The law provides for secrets to be classified as such through a procedure according to Act no. 65/1995 on State Secrets and Official Secrets. The classifier can mark data as secret if it belongs to a list of categories contained in the annex of the Act and if the classifier can establish that publication before the expiry of validity and unauthorised acquisition or use would without doubt damage or jeopardise the interests of Hungary related to a number of areas. However, it is common practice for the Government to claim that documents which have not undergone this procedure are nonetheless secret. One editor noted that, "despite there being quite a good law, there is a lot of closed information. An official at a ministry will say that something is 'operational' or closed and it is difficult for us to check."[110] Freedom House echoes this sentiment,[111] while Gallup's research among journalists in 1999 also found that, "too large a number of documents are classified" and that, "Individual, business and state secrets are overprotected."[112]

In addition, the law does not clearly state who is obliged to keep a secret, leading to difficulties in interpreting the law when, for example, a journalist prints a "secret" which was originally leaked by a Government official. In June 1999, László Juszt, the editor of weekly magazine *Kriminális,* was charged with revealing State secrets. *Kriminális* had published documents that disputed claims made by FIDESZ-MPP that the previous Government had engaged in illegal spying on FIDESZ-MPP party members when the party was in opposition. The published documents contained information that there was no proof of such a claim. Police searched Juszt's home, held him in custody for seven hours, searched the offices of *Kriminális* and confiscated the computer equipment, effectively closing down the magazine. Following Juszt's arrest, Hungarian TV terminated its contract with him. The Budapest Prosecutor's Office dropped the charges against Juszt, stating that the reporter had broken no law. As reported in the *World Press Freedom Review* of 1999, "this prompted a startling chain of legal events:"

> The case was then picked up by the Hungarian Chief Prosecutor, supported by the Metropolitan Police Commissioner; then dropped by the Deputy Chief Prosecutor; picked up again by the Chief Prosecutor; dropped again by the Budapest Chief Prosecutor; and then picked up by the Minister without Portfolio for Secret Services László Kövér. But the application was finally

---

[109] See <http://www/obh/Hungary/adatved/indexek/besz/index.htm>, (last accessed 15 August 2002).

[110] Interview with Ilona Kiss, editor, *Beszélő* magazine, 7 January 2002.

[111] Freedom House, *Nations in Transit,* 2001.

[112] See <http://www.gallup.hu>, (last accessed 15 August 2002).

closed down by the Hungarian Chief Prosecutor and the Juszt affair was thus closed for once and for all.[113]

The Data Protection Ombudsman noted in his recommendation on the case that two of the documents published by Juszt had never been classified, another had been classified by an unauthorised person and the fourth document contained no information that would fall into any one of the state secret categories listed in the annex to the Secrets Act.

9.3 Broadcasting regulation

Three of the five national television channels are State-owned. In 1998, research by the National Radio and Television Board (NRTB) found that the parties of the governing coalition were over-represented in broadcasts, with their activities accounting for around 80 percent of all news coverage.

The law seeks to provide balance in State broadcasting through vesting supervisory powers in Boards of Trustees – or Presidia – to which both the Government and opposition make appointments. By law, half of the eight party-appointed members are to be proposed by the Government and half by the opposition parties in Parliament. However, since 1998, when the previous Presidium for Hungarian Television was dissolved, only the four members appointed by the governing parties sat on the board. The opposition was unable to appoint its members because the three opposition parties submitted five nominees altogether for the four positions. This occurred because the extreme right-wing Hungarian Justice and Life Party (MIÉP) requested two of the four opposition seats, despite having only 14 seats in Parliament, and refused to back down. The SZDSZ nominated one candidate and the MSZP, by far the largest opposition party, two. The Government argued that no opposition nominees should be appointed until the three parties had reached a consensus on the four trustees they wished, collectively, to appoint. The Presidium was subsequently appointed comprising only four members, all Government nominees. The two main opposition parties' suggestion that Parliament should select the four opposition members from the five nominees was rejected.

Both the Court of Registration and the Prosecutor-General found the incomplete Presidium to be illegitimate, but the Supreme Court allowed the move and the Constitutional Court

---

[113] *Hungary – World Press Freedom Review,* 1999, available at
<http://www.freemedia.at/wpfr/hungary/htm>, (last accessed 15 August 2002).

argued that it was not a constitutional issue.[114] Györgyi Kálmán, then Prosecutor-General, published his view that the Presidium was illegitimate; this statement was deemed to be of no legal relevance by the Speaker of the House, János Áder. The same process occurred when the presidia of the national radio broadcaster and the State-owned satellite channel, Duna TV, expired – partial presidia comprising only Government nominees were appointed. Following the change of Government after the April 2002 elections, new boards of trustees have been appointed, with the proper political balance.

The National Radio and Television Board regulates the broadcast media and allocates licences for television channels and radio broadcasting frequencies. Political parties appoint its members, with one member per parliamentary party and voting rights weighted according to parliamentary representation. The Board publishes tenders for licences and a procedure is laid out according to which bids are allocated a score.

9.4 Corruption in the media

Rather than explicit evidence of corruption in the media, Hungary has seen creeping political influence on the media. The State has few opportunities to exert influence on the press through ownership, since most of it is in private ownership, much of it foreign-owned. However, the former Government made a concerted effort to support the rightwing and conservative press:

- The Orbán Government heavily favoured right-wing papers when placing State advertising: in particular, the daily *Magyar Nemzet.*

- State-owned Postabank's decision in 1998 to cease financial support to two left/liberal magazines and deny their editorial boards the right to use the same titles caused one of the journals to close down.

- *Magyar Nemzet*'s ideological stance has shifted further to the right, following a merger in 2000 with the radical right *Napi Magyarország* under the name *Magyar Nemzet.* The merger took place after Postabank sold *Magyar Nemzet* to the MAHIR company, which also owned *Napi Magyarország.* Many journalists from the original *Magyar Nemzet* were dismissed, leaving those from the more radical paper in the majority on the new title. Local analysts argue that the paper has become much more extremist as a result, while leaving right-wing readers without a choice of newspapers. The MAHIR company is closely linked to FIDESZ-MPP.

---

[114] The Constitutional Court might have ruled that the regulation on the appointment of the Presidium was unconstitutional in that it failed to prevent a situation in which a board lacking opposition nominees was appointed. Instead, the Court in effect blamed the political parties for failing to reach a consensus.

- In 2000, officials from the Ministry of Defence and Ministry of Environment revealed that their ministries had provided significant financial support to *Kis Újság*, a newspaper closely tied to the Smallholders Party (then part of the governing coalition).

Under the Orbán Government, appointments favoured candidates with connections to the Government or from the right wing. In October 1998, senior news staff at Hungarian Television were removed and replaced. In autumn 1999, the President of Hungarian Television fired hundreds of journalists, apparently because the company was making huge losses. However, at the same time, new journalists loyal to the Government were appointed. By summer 2001, the President of Hungarian Radio was Katalin Kondor, a journalist known for making weekly interviews with the Prime Minister,[115] and the President of Hungarian Television Károly Mendreczky, formerly a FIDESZ-MPP candidate in the 1998 municipal elections.[116]

The NRTB has been criticised for failing to stick to its procurement procedures. Some local analysts argue that practical considerations such as the burden of work make it impossible to keep the rules, while others allege that political considerations influence the evaluation of tenders.

Although a large proportion of the broadcast media is in direct State control and apparently under Government influence, the two private television channels attract higher viewing figures. These channels may also be vulnerable to political influence. One of them, TV2, is in financial trouble; a bid to buy some of its equity was recently made, by one of the primary contractors on the national motorway construction programme. The other private channel won its licence in peculiar conditions. When the runner-up, Iris, took the National Radio and Television Board to court over its decision to give the licence to RTL Klub, it won the case. The NRTB was expected subsequently to withdraw RTL's licence and pay significant compensation to RTL and Iris. However, it did neither. It allowed RTL to retain its licence and the head of Iris was later appointed as a presenter at one of the state-run channels. RTL Klub might thus be vulnerable to pressure from the NRTB, to which it owes a debt for enabling it to continue broadcasting.

9.5 Media and corruption

According to journalists participating in Gallup's 1999–2000 research, the conditions in which investigative journalism might flourish do not exist in Hungary. Neither

---

[115] Kondor has argued that Hungarian Radio should be the "loyal opposition" of the Government. See interview in: *HVG*, 25 August 2000.

[116] See M. Sükösd & P. Bajomi-Lázár (eds.), *Reinventing Media*, Central European University Press, Budapest 2002.

owners nor editors are willing to devote the resources needed to support investigative journalism, while journalists felt that they would risk their job security if they revealed controversial evidence, or be threatened by the mafia or political parties. They suggested that some topics, such as the mafia, are taboo. In addition, journalists felt that, even where they publish incriminating material or evidence, there is a "chronic lack of follow-up" by courts and district attorneys.

Journalistic skills and culture are weak, with many journalists unaware of their legal rights to gain access to information, while the practice of submitting interviews for "correction" before publication is common.[117]

Foreign journalists have in the past two years come under pressure after criticising the Government. On several occasions, foreign journalists have been attacked and quoted out of context in *Magyar Nemzet,* and on Hungarian State radio and television. In January 2002, *Magyar Nemzet* ran an article listing the names and publications of foreign journalists, along with a "ranking" of how favourable their writing was to the Government. This provoked some journalists to protest through the Hungarian International Press Association, by sending a letter to the Foreign Minister. The letter detailed instances of verbal attacks and commented:

> We have become alarmed by the persistence of reports which are unpleasant, vindictive, and sink far below the standards of civilised discourse which we expect. As you will notice, the places where they have appeared are in media organs and programmes normally noted for their support for the Hungarian Government.

10. RECOMMENDATIONS

The following recommendations have been highlighted as particularly important to Hungary. For additional recommendations applicable to candidate States generally, please see Part 5 of the Overview report.

1. Ensure that all public expenditure is subject to thorough scrutiny, particularly the activities of the Hungarian Development Bank.

2. Consider increases in State funding for political parties to enable them to run campaigns without resorting to illegal funding.

3. Uphold the freedom of the media by ensuring that both Government and opposition are represented on television and radio boards of trustees.

---

[117] Interview with Éva Vajda, OSI Media Program, 10 January 2002.

Corruption and Anti-corruption Policy in Latvia

Table of Contents

Corruption and Anti-corruption Policy in Latvia

EXECUTIVE SUMMARY

Corruption is ranked as a major problem in Latvia on the basis of indicators used by international organisations. These evaluations spotlight concerns about the influence of private interests on the legislative process; the World Bank's concept of "State capture" is often used by Latvian corruption experts to describe what is perceived as the country's main corruption problem. The evidence collected for this report indicates that illicit lobbying and similar practices are indeed serious problems in Latvia, although this may reflect to some extent the greater attention paid to these phenomena in Latvia than in many other candidate countries.

Latvia has been one of the most active CEE countries in combating corruption, at least on a formal basis. Latvia was the first to seek assistance for anti-corruption policy from the World Bank in 1996, and since then has carried out a number of important reforms designed to improve governance and prevent corruption, including an annually updated Corruption Prevention Programme. These efforts have been given a new boost with the recent establishment of a Corruption Prevention Bureau, which is expected to take over a number of important anti-corruption tasks and coordinate anti-corruption policy. Fulfilment of the Corruption Prevention Programme has been relatively complete. Civil society organisations have played an important part in both the development and implementation of anti-corruption policy.

The EU accession process has provided constant pressure to improve anti-corruption policy, and has resulted in extensive assistance creation and implementation. Latvia's national strategy for EU accession states explicitly the need to fight corruption as a condition for accession, and a number of important anti-corruption policy measures have been the direct result of EU pressure or assistance.

Latvian bribery legislation is relatively advanced, with the exception that legal entities are not yet criminally liable for acts of corruption. Latvia boasts quite extensive legal provisions that regulate conflict of interest and mandate compulsory declarations of assets and income by public officials. However, to date the impact of the provisions has been limited due to inadequate supervision and enforcement, although the media has used the law to expose and put pressure on officials. Recent amendments to the law can be expected to improve supervision considerably.

Latvia is in the process of putting in place an integrated State financial control framework. The State Audit Office enjoys independence and wide competencies, although its findings are not sufficiently used. An internal audit system established in 2000 is in the process of implementation, and the European Commission has expressed satisfaction with progress in this area.

Although Latvia possesses a number of institutions directly involved in the fight against corruption, lack of coordination between them appears to be a serious problem. The recent creation of a new Anti-corruption Bureau to coordinate anti-corruption strategy is a very important step towards improving this situation. The effectiveness of the Bureau will be a key measure of Latvia's ability to implement anti-corruption policy. Proposals to establish an ombudsman are currently under discussion.

The Government has identified public administration as one of the most important sources of corruption, and most of the anti-corruption programme is directed towards fighting corruption in this area. Since 2000, the civil service has undergone important developments, with a new law and development strategy. Procedures for appealing against administrative decisions have tended to be ineffective to date, although a new Code of Administrative Procedure is expected to come into effect in 2003, which should improve citizen redress. Taken together, these changes may be expected to create an environment more resistant to corruption.

Until recently, parliamentary scrutiny of public finances was undermined by the existence of a number of off-budget agencies, while the allocation of State guarantees by the Government appears to have been non-transparent. While there have been almost no cases of MPs prosecuted for corruption, there is evidence (or at least testimony) that "State capture" – that is capture of the legislative process by business interests – is a problem.

The Latvian judiciary suffers from serious problems of lack of independence, funding, and lack of capacity, resulting in endemic court delays. Access to information on court decisions remains an important problem, although guaranteeing this is a component of the Government's anti-corruption strategy. Surveys indicate that a significant proportion of citizens that come into contact with the courts may have faced problems of corruption. Although a judicial reform programme is underway, the strength of political commitment to effective reform remains uncertain.

Political party funding has been weakly regulated until recently. However, new funding regulations approved in June 2002 have put in place a much more transparent system. Nevertheless, the continuing absence of any State funding leaves parties vulnerable to corruption and there is evidence that corruption is an important problem. The effectiveness of the new Corruption Prevention Bureau in inspecting party financial reports under the new provisions will be an important test of its impact.

Public procurement is rated as one of the country's most corrupt spheres. Although a Public Procurement Act has been in force since 1997, the Act contains provisions that allow contracting authorities to avoid tenders relatively easily, and the system of supervision and redress has not functioned effectively. A new procurement law in force since January 2002 has improved the legal framework considerably. However, the capacity of the monitoring agency remains a concern, and there are still effectively no sanctions for violations of procurement regulations.

Corruption appears to be more or less widespread in a number of public services. According to surveys of perception, the police (specifically the traffic police) and customs authorities are regarded as more corrupt than any other institutions. However, reforms of both institutions have either led to improvements or can be expected to do so. While there is some evidence of corruption in tax administration, important reforms have been implemented, although wide discretion to award tax breaks creates an environment vulnerable to corruption. Surveys indicate that unofficial contributions are more widespread in the healthcare system than in any area except the traffic police, although the proportion of such payments that is corrupt is not clear. Corruption in business licensing does not appear to be a problem, while corruption in other areas of business regulation appears to be limited. In the latter areas significant potential for successful anti-corruption reform has been demonstrated.

The Latvian press is free. Although Latvia was the first among EU candidate countries to pass freedom of information legislation, the impact of the law has not been clear to date. Broadcasting regulation appears to be relatively free of political manipulation. Corruption in the media is not regarded as a major problem, although there is some indirect evidence of phenomena such as hidden advertising. The media has played an important role in monitoring corruption, especially adherence to the Corruption Prevention Act.

)UCTION

data and perceptions

riminal proceedings for corruption-related crimes are shown in Table 1. The
onvictions appear to be small even by the standards of EU candidate countries
(see Table 1).

Table 1: Crimes registered and criminal convictions for corruption, 1996–2001

Criminal offence	1996		1997		1998		1999		2000		2001		
CC 164, CL 320: Acceptance of Bribes	63	24	32	40	74	12	43	23	34	5	553	46	11
CC 165, CL 323: Giving of Bribes	17	6	12	7	17	5	15	9	9	6	12	9	6
CC 164.1, CL 322: Intermediation in Bribery	3	1	0	0	5	0	3	0	2	0	5	5	0
CL 321: Misappropriation of a Bribe	-	-	-	-	0	-	1	0	1	0	2	2	1
CL 198: Unauthorised Receipt of Financial Benefits	-	-	-	-	0	-	2	0	0	4	1	1	0
CL 199: Commercial Bribery	-	-	-	-	0	-	0	0	0	0	1	1	0
CC 162.1, Article 317: Exceeding of Official Authority	95	6	75	11	3	23	38	11	42	9	34	11	2
CC 162, 318: Abuse of Official Status	105	11	79	15	78	12	46	12	54	4	56	32	3
CL 319: Failure to Act by a State Official	-	-	-	-	0	-	3	0	13	4	27	24	2
CL 196: Use of and Exceeding Authorisation in Bad Faith	-	-	-	-	0	-	5	0	16	0	102	85	0
CC 167.2: Failure to Disclose Conflict of Interest Situations	0	0	0	0	0	0	0	0	0	0	0	0	0
CC 162.5, 325: Violation of Restrictions Imposed on Officials CL 326: Unlawful Participation in Property Transactions	0	0	3	0	4	0		0	2	0	1	1	1

☐ Registered crimes   ☐ Sentenced persons

Source: Latvian Ministry of Justice.
Note: For all years, the right hand column indicates convictions; the left-hand column indicates
registered crimes. For 2001, the 1st column is registered crimes; the 2nd column is charges filed; and
the 3rd column is convictions.

Survey evidence suggests that corruption is a much more serious problem. The Transparency International Corruption Perception Index has given Latvia a score of 3.4 (where 0 means most corrupt and ten least corrupt) since 1999, ranking it between 57th and 59th place – the worst position for any candidate country except Bulgaria and Romania.[1]

The EBRD/World Bank's *1999 Business Environment and Enterprise Performance Survey* (BEEPS) indicated that Latvia was relatively unaffected by administrative corruption (1.4 percent of annual revenue spent on unofficial payments by companies compared to a 2.2 percent regional average).[2] According to previous a large diagnostic survey on corruption carried out by the World Bank in 1998, 37 percent of firms and 13 percent of households reported having made unofficial payments.[3]

On the other hand, according to the BEEPS survey Latvia suffered from a serious problem of "State capture," with the highest "capture economy index" of any EU candidate country (30 compared to a candidate country average of 16). Forty percent of Latvian firms reported that their business was significantly or very significantly affected by the sale of parliamentary votes.[4] These survey results indicate that firms perceive the legislative process to be influenced by corruption, more than in any other candidate country with the arguable exception of Bulgaria and Romania. According to the 1998 World Bank report:

> [E]conomic power in Latvia has become concentrated in a small number of conglomerates. Business and political interests have become intertwined in a complex and non-transparent way, and businesses are increasingly active in political parties. Excessive concentration of economic power, due in part to weak enforcement of competition legislation, drains efficiency from the economy and presents the risk that Latvia could become prone to high-level corruption.[5]

According to the *2000 Latvia Human Development Report* by UNDP, the political decision-making process is characterised by informal processes that take place outside official structures, in which private actors with interests in legislative results have

---

[1] See <http://www.transparency.org>, (last accessed 2 September 2002).

[2] World Bank, *Corruption Prevention in Transition Economies, A Contribution to Debate,* World Bank 2001.

[3] J. Anderson, *Corruption in Latvia: Survey Evidence,* World Bank, report prepared for Corruption Prevention Council, December 1998, p. 12.

[4] J. Helman, G. Jones, D. Kaufmann, "Seize the State, Seize the Day: State Capture, Corruption, and Influence in Transition," Policy Research Working Paper 2444, World Bank Institute and EBRD, September 2000.

[5] J. Anderson, *Corruption in Latvia,* p. 22.

considerable hidden influence.[6] According to the report, "There is lack of openness in the work of state institutions, and civil servants tend to rely on a rather closed circle of potential agents in public policy.[7] According to research published by the UNDP in 2001, 79 percent of the public trust the Parliament and the Government "very little or not at all."[8]

A survey conducted among enterprises by the Latvian Development Agency in 1999 found that 23 percent of businesses regarded corruption as one of the three greatest barriers to economic development, and in 2001, corruption was listed as the second biggest obstacle after excessive bureaucracy. However, when asked to rank the seriousness of petty administrative corruption as a barrier to doing daily business, this proved to be the least of five concerns.[9]

1.2 Main loci of corruption

The World Bank as well as domestic surveys found that the institutions seen as most corrupt are the customs administration, followed by the traffic police and the State telephone monopoly *Lattelekom* (see Table 2). The high ranking of *Lattelekom* may be an example of perceptions lagging behind reality; perceptions of the company are conditioned by memories of the past, when it was necessary to pay a bribe to get a telephone connection, and may also be influenced by disputes between the Government and the company over fulfilment of its obligations under the 1994 privatisation contract.

---

[6] UNDP, *2000 Latvia Human Development Report,* draft concept paper, pp. 64–65. The Report presents a model that it states is common in Latvia, according to which:

- A private person advocates legislation via political contacts in the executive, often secured in advance through contributions to a political party.
- After consultation, lawyers make a proposal to be adopted by the Government, and the minister who is contacted by the interested entity ensures the bill is passed in the Government.
- The bill is reviewed in the Parliament and political "agents" ensure it is passed in the form desired. Ordinary MPs are not fully informed and trust the party leadership. Public administration implements the bill, and "agents" ensure smooth implementation.

[7] UNDP, *2000 Latvia Human Development Report,* p. 66.

[8] N. Coleman, "Latvia's anti-corruption efforts tripped up," AFP, Riga, 24 July 2002.

[9] *2001 Survey on the Business Environment,* <http://www.lda.gov.lv>, (last accessed 25 April 2001).

Table 2: Views on the six most dishonest institutions: surveys by the World Bank and Delna (the Latvian chapter of Transparency International)

Survey carried out by Delna in 1999	Survey carried out by WB in 1998
1. Customs (most dishonest)	1. Customs (most dishonest)
2. Traffic Police	2. Traffic Police
3. *Lattelekom*	3. *Lattelekom*
4. Privatisation Agency	4. Government
5. State Real Estate Agency	5. Parliament
6. *Latvenergo*	6. Police
7. Courts	7. Courts

Graph 1 shows the results of a survey of experience of corruption commissioned by Delna (the Latvian Chapter of Transparency International) in 1999, according to which only one to five percent of respondents had encountered corruption in most State and municipal institutions, while 45-75 percent of the population consider these same institutions dishonest.[10] This discrepancy might result from the fact that only a limited number of citizens actually come into contact with these institutions. Much higher levels of corruption were reported regarding the traffic police and healthcare institutions. Interestingly, despite its ranking as the second most corrupt institution in terms of the proportion of respondents having made unofficial payments there, healthcare enjoyed one of the highest rankings in terms of honesty, suggesting that in Latvia as in other candidate countries, many payments made in healthcare systems are not regarded by the population as bribes, or at least are not negatively perceived.

---

[10] TI Latvia, *Face of Corruption in Latvia,* Latvia, 2000.

**Graph 1: Perceived dishonesty of institutions and personal bribing experience.
Percent from all respondents.**

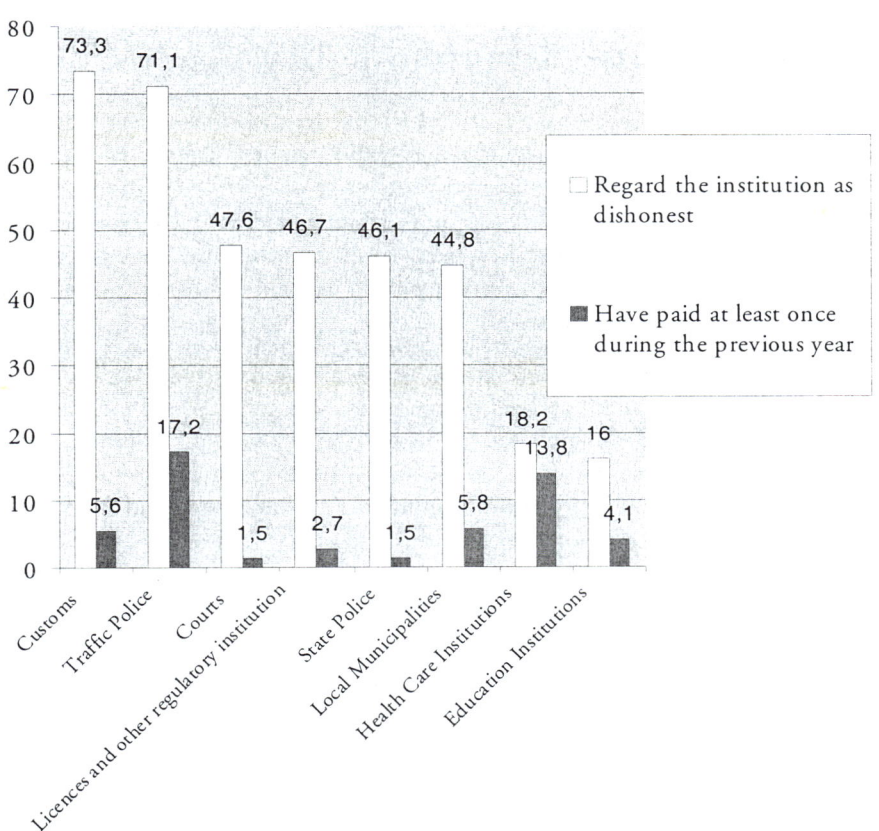

Source: "Face of Corruption in Latvia", *Delna* (TI Latvia), 1999

The Government's Corruption Prevention Strategy lists the following areas as "least protected against corruption:" customs, traffic police, judiciary, local government, privatisation, public procurement, tax collection, State supervisory institutions and the appointment of public officials.[11]

From the evidence presented in this report, it is difficult to make a clear assessment of the prevalence of administrative corruption, given the current implementation of fundamental civil service reforms. Public procurement appears to be seriously affected

---

[11] Government of Latvia, "Corruption Prevention Programme," September 2001, p. 3.

by corruption, especially at the local government level. The weakness of regulation of political party funding raises worries about this area, and the available evidence is consistent with Latvia's poor ranking on measures of "State capture."

1.3 Government anti-corruption policy

The Government began to develop a substantial anti-corruption policy when it established the Corruption Prevention Council in 1997, chaired by the Minister of Justice and consisting of representatives from a wide range of State institutions as well as civil society.[12] Early in 2000, the work of the Council was strengthened by a Secretariat with a director, lawyer and PR officer. In 2000-2001, the Secretariat took the leading role in coordinating anti-corruption policy, while the Council served only as a consultative body on important matters.

The Council adopted a Corruption Prevention Programme in 1998 based on the objectives of prevention, prosecution and enforcement, and education. The Programme is updated every six months and contains both short-term and long-term objectives. The Corruption Prevention Programme for 2001 consists of three main elements.[13] A preventive element aims at improving the functioning of the court system, administrative and competition procedures, issuing of licences and transparency. It also states the need to reform further the system of political party finance. Under the enforcement section, the programme identifies the need to establish an Audit Centre and improve anti-corruption mechanisms in customs and the State Revenue Service. The objectives of the educational element are training civil servants in new, more transparent administrative procedures and in ethics, raising public's awareness of citizens' rights and trying to involve ordinary citizens in the fight against corruption.

Among the key measures the Government has taken to fight corruption in recent years are:

- Government workshops and nation-wide conferences to formulate an effective Corruption Prevention Programme in 1997–1999;

---

[12] There were 16 members of the Council: the Minister of Justice (Chair of the Council); Minister of Interior (Deputy Chair); Director-General of State Revenue Service; Prosecutor-General; Auditor-General; Governor of the Bank of Latvia; a representative of the Economic Police; Director of the Bureau of Public Administration Reform; Director of the School of Public Administration Reform; Chairperson of the Competition Council; representatives of the Ministries of Justice, Finance, and Internal Affairs; a representative of Transparency International Latvia; a representative of the National Radio and Television Council; and a representative of Latvian Lawyers' Association. The Statutes and Programme of the Council are approved by the Cabinet of Ministers.

[13] Taken from GRECO, *Evaluation Report on Latvia*, p. 5.

- surveys of households, business and officials conducted in 1998 with assistance from the World Bank;

- the Act on Public Access to Information, passed in 1998;

- the 2002 Act on Conflict of Interest of Public Officials (see Section 2.2);

- the Act on the Corruption Prevention Bureau, passed in April 2002;

- amendments to political party finance regulations, passed in June 2002 (see Section 6.2);

Anti-corruption policies have clearly success in a number of areas, for example in the customs administration (see Section 8.2) and strikingly in the Traffic Security Department (see Section 8.3). However, progress against high-level corruption and "State capture" is less clear, and the political will of the Government to fight corruption is doubtful. Corruption experts and other observers have perceived the Corruption Prevention Council as ineffective and the Government as lacking sufficient political will to pass effective anti-corruption legislation,[14] although the pace of legislative change in 2001-2002 does not support the latter view. A particularly severe problem affecting implementation of the Government's anti-corruption policy has been the dispersal of responsibility among various institutions, in particular among those responsible for investigating corruption (see Section 2.5).

Reflecting these reservations, in April 2002, Parliament passed a bill establishing a Corruption Prevention Bureau as the central institution coordinating the fight against corruption. The Bureau was intended to start functioning in July 2002. The new Bureau has the authority to draft legislation on corruption prevention, control its implementation, examine the asset and income declarations of public functionaries, and sanction officials for violations of the Anti-corruption Act. The head of the Bureau is appointed (for a five-year term) and removed by Parliament on the proposal of the Government. However, foreign experts have expressed some concerns and reservations about the legal framework establishing the Bureau, and an open competition to select a person to head it had run into problems as of July 2002 (see Section 2.4).

Some of the more important components of the version of the Corruption Prevention Programme approved in May 2001 are presented in Table 3, including deadlines for fulfilment. The record on fulfilment of the chosen measures appears to be relatively good, especially when taken together with the recent creation of the Corruption Prevention Bureau as a much-needed coordinating body. However, the goals to introduce whistleblower protection and to devote more attention to educating the public have not been met.

---

[14] OSI Roundtable Discussion, Riga, 10 April 2002.

Table 3: Selected measures in the Corruption Prevention Strategy, May 2001

Measure	Deadline for implementation	Fulfilment as of June 2002
Draft new Anti-corruption Act	October 2001	Yes
Develop legal basis for Anti-corruption bureau	October 2001	Yes
Submit draft political party financing law	June 2001	Yes (but not yet approved)
Draft new Code of Criminal Procedure	October 2001	Yes (pending in the Parliament)
Sign OECD Convention and Council of Europe Civil Law Convention	December 2001	No
Draft law to protect whistleblowers, include protection measures for whistleblowers in Labour Code and Code of Administrative Procedure	December 2001	No
Introduce uniform administrative procedures allowing appeal against decisions of State and municipal officials	December 2001	Yes (law enters into force 2003)
Strengthen internal audit: inter alia, develop proposals for action of internal auditors on detection of fraud and corruption		Yes (ongoing EU project)
Introduce Principles of Conduct of Civil Servants, prepare brochure	August 2001	Yes
Publish all tenders and procurement decisions on the Internet	September 2001	Yes
Restructure Central Criminal Police Department to prevent duplication of functions in detecting and investigating corruption	June 2001	Yes
Implement methodology for checking legitimacy of officials' income and increasing role of heads of institutions in controlling officials' asset declarations	December 2001	Yes
Provide public access to court sentences in electronic form	December 2001	No, ongoing EU PHARE project as of 2002
Provisions of brochures and information materials on citizens' rights and other issues	December 2001	Yes

Source: Corruption Prevention Programme, May 2001, Delna (TI Latvia).

Role of civil society

Latvia boasts an active community of NGOs dealing with corruption issues. Moreover, the Government is one of the most progressive in the region in its approach to NGOs. Professional NGOs work closely with State institutions in all spheres, and there are around 30 different advisory and policy-setting councils with representatives from civil society.[15] In the Spring of 2001, the Cabinet adopted an instruction on how to conduct consultations with NGOs on draft legislation.

New planned legislation on NGOs is expected to further strengthen the role of civil society. Under the draft proposal, NGOs may be awarded the status of a "public good organisation" according to strict criteria.[16]

An example of active participation by NGOs in anti-corruption policy was an Integrity Pact signed in 2001 between the Latvian Privatisation Agency and Delna/Transparency International Latvia. The Pact granted TI Latvia experts full access to all documentation and meetings concerning the privatisation of the Latvian Shipping Company, and applied a no-bribery commitment to all parties involved in the privatisation. TI concluded that all procedures and rules were followed, and that there was no evidence of corruption.

The Foreign Investors' Council representing 15 major investors has established regular channels of dialogue with the Government. Since 2000 corruption has been one of the issues discussed, and in 2002 the Council and the Government established a working group on procurement.

1.4 The impact of the EU accession process

The fight against corruption has been stated as one of the main requirements for accession under the political criteria in the European Commission *Regular Reports*. In 1998, the Commission noted that corruption is an important problem, but acknowledged measures taken under the new anti-corruption strategy.[17] In 1999, corruption was regarded as a serious problem, with a "much greater effort needed" to combat it.[18] In 2000, corruption had become, according to the Commission, "a serious obstacle to the proper and efficient functioning of the public administration in

---

[15] TI Latvia, *Civil Society Participation and Councils in Latvia, draft report*, Latvia 2001.

[16] *NGO Legislation,* NGO centre home page, <http://www.ngo.org.lv>, (last accessed 10 May 2001). The purpose of the new legislation is mainly to prevent the establishment of NGOs merely to obtain tax advantages.

[17] European Commission, *1998 Regular Report from the Commission on Latvia's Progress towards Accession*, p. 9.

[18] Commission, *1999 Regular Report*, p. 13.

Latvia."[19] The *2001 Regular Report* continued to acknowledge commitment to anti-corruption policy, but judged that measures taken "have not yet translated into concrete results on a broad scale" and that "further sustained efforts" are needed.[20]

The National Programme for Integration into the European Union includes anti-corruption policy as a priority. Moreover, the Government Corruption Prevention Strategy states explicitly that:

> The development of... [anti-corruption] policy and its implementation are also necessary for... Latvia to successfully integrate into the European Union and to ensure compatibility of its administrative activities with the requirements set forth for a democratic and legal state.[21]

A number of institutions have mentioned the EU as the main driving force for changes in the public administration, especially in terms of civil administration, procurement and internal audit.

Latvia was subject to an evaluation by GRECO in September 2001. The *Evaluation Report on Latvia,* published in May 2002, acknowledged that the seriousness of the corruption problem appears to be recognised at the highest level,[22] but levelled considerable criticism at the lack of coordination and effectiveness of institutions investigating and prosecuting corruption (see Section 2.5).

EU assistance

A PHARE programme on Anti-corruption Training, Legislation and Education was among the first EU anti-corruption projects in the accession countries. The project ran for 18 months from 2000 to 2001 and provided assistance in drafting some important anti-corruption laws, training prosecutors, the police force and investigative journalists and organising various public awareness campaigns.[23]

A project on corruption prevention in the courts system began in 2002, aimed at supporting the Government's anti-corruption programme regarding reform of the judicial system and improving transparency in the courts system, in particular by guaranteeing public access to court decisions (see Section 5.1).

---

[19] Commission, *2000 Regular Report,* p. 18.

[20] Commission, *2001 Regular Report,* p. 20.

[21] Government of Latvia, "Corruption Prevention Programme," September 2001, p. 1.

[22] GRECO, *Evaluation Report on Latvia,* adopted by GRECO at the 9th Plenary Meeting, Strasbourg, 13-17 May 2002, p. 2, <http://www.greco.coe.int>, (last accessed 2 September 2002).

[23] For information on the projects and criticism, see *Draft Report on Implementation of PHARE Anti-corruption Project,* TI Latvia, Latvia 2002.

Several twinning programmes have been established.[24] Since November 2001, the State Audit Office has been participating in a twinning project with the UK National Audit Office. This project is part of a broad EU project "Budget and Financial Management" involving Internal Audit, Procurement Supervision Bureau and the Ministry of State Reform. The Swedish National Police Board (NPB) is responsible for implementing a twinning project on "Preventing, Combating and Reducing [of] Organised Crime in Latvia," with components addressing money laundering and corruption.

NATO accession

In addition to the EU accession process, the prospect of NATO accession has also become a potentially important influence on Latvian efforts to tackle corruption. In advance of the NATO Summit in Prague in November 2002, NATO chief George Robertson stressed the importance of stepping up anti-corruption efforts during a visit to Latvia in early 2002, stating that, "The quality of the legal system and the robustness of anti-corruption measures are of enormous importance to NATO countries and to your application."[25]

2. INSTITUTIONS AND LEGISLATION

Latvian bribery legislation is relatively advanced, with the exception that legal entities are not criminally liable for corruption.

2.1 Anti-corruption legislation

Under Latvian Criminal Law, last amended in April 2002, sanctions are imposed on the following actions:

- Active bribery (Article 323) – defined as the provision of valuable property or benefits of a financial or other nature to a State official in order that s/he uses official position to perform or fail to perform acts in the interest of the giver of the bribe – is punishable by up to six years' imprisonment, or by 5-12 years' if

---

[24] PHARE, *2000 Annual Report,*
<http://europa.eu.int/comm/enlargement/pas/phare/pdf/phare2000.pdf>, (last accessed 25 April 2002).

[25] Cited in: N. Coleman, "Latvia's anti-corruption efforts tripped up," AFP, Riga, 24 July 2002.

the offence is committed repeatedly or by a State official.[26] The wording of the law permits prosecution for offering a bribe, although it is unclear whether the courts clearly interpret offering a bribe as covered by the provision.

- Passive bribery (Article 320) – intentionally accepting valuable property or benefits of a material or other nature in return for using one's official position to perform or fail to perform an act in the interests of the giver of the bribe – is punishable by up to eight years' imprisonment, from 3-10 years if the offence is committed repeatedly or on a large scale, and by 8-15 years if a bribe is extorted by a group of persons pursuant to prior agreement or by a State official holding a position of authority.

- Both active and passive bribery in the private sector are criminalised (Articles 199 and 198 respectively).

- The Criminal Law also sanctions indirect bribery (Article 322), misappropriation of a bribe (Article 321), exceeding official authority (Article 317), using official position in bad faith (Article 318), failure to act by a State official (Article 319), violation of restrictions placed on State officials (Article 325) and unlawful participation in property transactions (Article 326).

Latvian law does not allow legal entities to be held criminally liable for corruption, although legislation to establish such liability passed the initial stage of preparation at Government level in May 2002.

2.2 Conflict of interest legislation and asset declaration and monitoring

Latvia boasts quite extensive legal provisions that regulate conflict of interest and mandate compulsory declarations of assets and income by public officials. However, to date the impact of the provisions has been limited due to inadequate supervision and enforcement, although the media has used the law to expose and put pressure on officials. Recent amendments to the law can be expected to improve supervision considerably.

Conflict of interest and asset declarations are regulated by the 1995 Corruption Prevention Act and the 2002 Act on Conflict of Interest of Public Officials, which establish conflict of interest and asset monitoring provisions for public officials. The provisions apply to the highest officials of the country, such as the President, MPs, all

---

[26] GRECO, *Evaluation Report on Latvia,* p. 3.

ministers and parliamentary Secretaries. In addition, the law is rendered applicable to the following public officials:

- persons appointed, elected or approved to a position or performing work (on a permanent or temporary basis) at a public or municipal institution if, upon performing official or professional duties in compliance with legal acts, the said persons have the right to formulate or issue administrative acts independently or as a member of a collegiate decision-making body, or to prepare and take other decisions related to individual rights, or have the right to perform oversight, control, investigation or penal functions or to dispose of the public or municipal property or financial resources, or who draft normative acts or develop policy or a development strategy for an industry or coordinate the operation of an industry;

- persons who are otherwise authorised to perform public functions at a public or municipal institution or at any other institution outside public administration (for example, auditors, members of the Physicians' Association, the Chamber of Crafts or any other non-governmental organisation authorised by the law to perform public functions).

As of January 2001, there were 40,302 State officials according to this definition.[27] Under the Act, it is prohibited for a public official to prepare or adopt decisions with respect to:

- themselves and their relatives;

- questions whose resolution affects or may affect the material or other personal interests of the relevant official or their relatives;

- natural or legal persons from whom the relevant official or their relatives obtain income of any kind, except income from capital in companies in which s/he owns less than one percent of the share capital; or

- enterprises in which the relevant official or their relatives are members of the administration or audit institutions or own more than one percent of the capital.

Persons occupying the positions mentioned above may not own companies or more than a one percent share of capital in companies that receive State procurement contracts, State financial resources, State-guaranteed loans or State privatisation fund resources, unless these are awarded as a result of a public tender or open competition.

All public officials are prohibited from accepting any gifts or other material benefits (except diplomatic gifts and gifts which are presented to the official during official or

---

[27] *VID Korupcijas novēršanas kontroles daļas P Ā R S K A T S par valsts amatpersonu deklarāciju pārbaužu rezultātiem 2001.gadā* [Report on Control of the State Official Declarations in 2001].

work visits abroad and on national holidays), and are prohibited from working with any kind of advertising or having their name used in an advertising context, except where this is part of their duties. Officials may not carry on work outside their position with the exception of offices in voluntary, political or religious organisations or trade unions, or as a teacher, scientist, doctor or artist.

The Corruption Prevention Department of the State Revenue Service (SRS) has punished more than 100 officials a year, but the fines are insignificant (between EUR 8 and EUR 150).[28] A few officials have had to resign in order to avoid conflicts of interest. The head of the SRS acknowledges that the department lacks sufficient staff to monitor adequately or respond to all notifications concerning officials.

Moreover, the activities of the SRS have been undermined on several occasions by opposition from senior officials. For example, the SRS decided that a trip to Spain, taken by a number of Riga City Council deputies and paid for by a Spanish company that develops traffic regulation systems, violated the provisions on accepting gifts and material benefits.[29] However, the Chairman of the City Council defended the deputies on the grounds that the private company's financing of the trip saved public money. In August 2002 a Latvian daily petitioned the Corruption Prevention Council to investigate a possible conflict of interest involving the Latvian Prime Minister, who reportedly spent part of his summer vacation on a yacht owned by a Latvian company that benefited from more than six million LATS (10,246,305 EURO) in tax relief granted by the government. The case raised concerns over the ability of the Council to investigate such a case, given that the Prime Minister is also Chairman of the Council.[30]

In an even more high-profile case, the President of the Bank of Latvia announced in August 2001 his attention to establish and chair a new political party, and opened a bank account to accept donations as a fee for holding the position of Chairman. The Prosecutor General's Office examined the case but concluded that it did not violate provisions prohibiting acceptance of gifts because the agreement with the bank specified that the President would not receive the funds until he stepped down from his official position.[31]

Under the same Act, public officials as defined above must submit annual declarations of assets and income to the Corruption Prevention Department of the SRS. Declarations must contain information on all property (real estate, cars, land, etc.), money in banks

---

[28] Information provided by SRS, July 2002.

[29] V. Kalniņš, "Latvia's Anti-corruption Policy: Problems and Perspectives," unpublished paper, 2002. The group of deputies included the Chairman of the Transportation Department.

[30] RFE/RL Newsline, vol. 6, no. 155, part II, 19 August 2002.

[31] V. Kalniņš, "Latvia's Anti-corruption Policy: Problems and Perspectives," unpublished paper, 2002.

and in cash, loans and credits given, and ownership of shares and involvement in any other official organisation, such as NGOs and private interest groups.

All declarations are public and some are published in the official bulletin *Latvjas Vestnesis* annually. In 2000, the Department checked 931 declarations (five percent of the total). Additional information was requested from 108 officials, plus 47 concerning information about relatives. Additional information was required in seven cases under the Act on the Income Tax to check the legality of income. Nine cases were passed to law enforcement institutions, and 287 administrative cases were raised either for being late or not delivering declaration.

Although the Corruption Prevention Department is armed with a paragraph of the Criminal Act that places sanctions on the provision of false information, in practice it has been ineffective. It has no powers to check declarations against bank accounts and other financial assets and has effectively relied on officials to disclose their assets fully.

Public attention has been raised by the phenomenon of political party appointees to the boards of State-owned enterprises,[32] who were not classified as State officials under the Corruption Prevention Act until May 2002. As a result of scandals involving such officials, the new Conflict of Interest Act includes this category of appointees in the definition of public officials, meaning they must also submit income and asset declarations.

The system for monitoring declarations is not effective due to overload and inadequate formal checks of declarations. The new Act is expected to improve this situation, transferring initial monitoring roles to the heads of individual State institutions.

On the other hand, the media has continued to investigate how officials obey the Corruption Prevention Act. In several cases journalists have discovered luxurious houses owned by prosecutors, judges, or heads of State institutions, but none of the cases have led to charges or sanctions against the officials involved. This is largely due to the fact that officials were not obliged to prove the legality of their income until the legal changes in May 2002, and also a result of the passivity of law enforcement institutions.

In addition to the new Conflict of Interest Act, a new draft law was under discussion in the Parliament in early 2002 which would require all citizens to declare their monetary assets over €8,000 and gold and antiques worth more than €16,000. The draft law was expected to be approved by the Parliament in June 2002. However, the proposal has been criticised for its cost and the fact that low trust in the State will reduce the probability of citizens submitting declarations.

---

[32] Party declarations 2001, <http://www.lursfot.lv>, (last accessed 28 April 2001).

2.3 Control and audit

Latvia is in the process of putting in place an integrated State financial control framework. The State Audit Office enjoys independence and wide competencies, although its findings are not sufficiently used. Since 2000 an internal audit system has been in the process of being implemented, and the European Commission has expressed satisfaction with progress in this area.

The State Audit Office

The State Audit Office (SAO) was set up in 1993 to audit the use of State and local budget funds. The Auditor-General is appointed by Parliament for a term of seven years, the longest term of any official appointed by Parliament. The current Auditor-General is serving his second term. The SAO enjoys considerable independence, although the Auditor-General has expressed worries about the dependency of the SAO on the Government regarding budget allocations.[33]

The SAO may audit State and municipal organisations and officials, State and municipal enterprises, and any other institution, organisation, enterprise, or NGO which disposes of State or municipal funds. Since 2001, the SAO is also responsible for reviewing the annual reports of 27 State and 578 municipal institutions.[34] The SAO does not have the authority to audit Parliament.

Following suggestions provided by SIGMA experts in 1999, in May 2002 the Act on the SAO was amended to allow the audit of the use of EU funds down to the level of final recipients.[35]

The SAO Council determines the Office's audit plan. The Council consists of the Auditor-General and five other auditors. The members of the Council are recommended by the Auditor-General and are also elected by Parliament for the term of seven years.

In 2001, the SAO completed 248 audits (the same number as in 2000). The Office referred 30 cases to law enforcement bodies in 2001, an increase from 17 in 2000. The SAO imposed fines for illegal transactions totalling €7,023m in 2000 and €586,064 in 2001.[36]

---

[33] "Stressing necessity to grant independence of SAO budget in the law," LETA news agency, 23 March 2002.

[34] State Audit Office, *2000 Annual Report;* see <http://www.lrvk.gov.lv/htmls/english/engindex.htm>, (last accessed 20 April 2002).

[35] "Discuss Implementation of International Recommendations," LETA news agency, 22 May 2002.

[36] SAO Annual Report 2001, <http://www.lrvk.gov.lv/htmls/gadapati/gada2001/gada2001_a6.html>, (last accessed 5 August 2002).

SAO findings are rarely used to impose corrective measures on audited institutions, and cooperation between the Office and other State and law enforcement institutions has been relatively poor.

An EU twinning project began in 2001 to give SAO officials training in anti-corruption and other skills. The project will finish in 2003.

Internal control

Latvia is currently in the process of developing an internal financial control system for the public sector, following the enactment of Cabinet Regulations on Internal Audit in 1999 and Ministry of Finance decrees on methodology for performing joint internal audits in 2001. Internal audit units have been established in most authorities, while the Ministry of Finance has been developing the capacity of a new Internal Audit Unit. The EU *2001 Regular Report* appeared to be largely satisfied with the development of internal financial control.

2.4 Anti-corruption agencies

There are a number of more-or-less specialised agencies responsible for investigating and prosecuting corruption. However, the division of responsibilities between them is very poor. The creation of the Corruption Prevention Bureau is intended, *inter alia,* to introduce coordination of anti-corruption efforts.

The main anti-corruption agencies are partly covered in Section 1.3. A number of different agencies and units are involved in the fight against corruption. The main ones are:

- Security Police
- Bureau for Combating Organised Crime and Corruption
- Economic Police Bureau
- Constitutional Protection Bureau
- Inquiry Board of the State Police
- Internal Security Department and Inquiry Board of the Financial Police Board, SRS

Until recently, the Bureau for Combating Organised Crime and Corruption was officially regarded as the principal coordinating institution for investigation and operational activities in the fight against organised crime and corruption. Centralised receipt, storage, processing and distribution of information provided by the institutions involved in the fight against corruption has been realised by the Information Centre of the Ministry of Interior.

However, an important problem in the institutional set up for the fight against corruption appears to be poor coordination and unclear division of responsibilities. In many cases, anti-corruption institutions have not investigated corruption in the belief that another institution would do it, resulting in no action at all. The GRECO *Evaluation Report* published in May 2002 notes that there is a range of policing institutions involved in fighting corruption, and that:

> [T]heir efforts are frankly segmented and disjointed and that there is an obvious lack of direction and co-ordination... These bodies are failing to produce the results expected by society. During the visit, the GET [Greco Evaluation Team] was told by a member of the Economic Police that "there is a need to make clear who is (has to do) what."[37]

One of the objectives in setting up the new Corruption Prevention Bureau is to take over primary responsibility for preliminary investigations into corruption from the existing units, although other law enforcement institutions will not be restricted from investigating corruption cases within their competencies. Under the Act establishing the Bureau, it will coordinate the fight against public sector corruption, with powers to review cases of administrative offences and to investigate cases of deliberate delays in submitting income declarations, exceeding official authority and misuse of power, bribery and the other criminal acts listed in Section 2.1. The Bureau will also be the main institution for checking officials' income and asset declarations. Finally, it will also be responsible for monitoring the adherence of political parties to party funding regulations. The Bureau is expected to have a staff of at least 100, and will be made up of a central apparatus and regional departments.

As of July 2002, the process of making the Bureau operational had run into problems, after the top candidate to head the Bureau – currently the Deputy Director of the Security Police – was disqualified on grounds of suspected conflict of interest related to a firm that stores and destroys contraband seized by police and customs officers.[38] In addition, a team of US experts who evaluated the legislation establishing the Bureau has criticised the subordination of the Bureau to the Ministry of Justice, and the insufficient resources committed to the Bureau, given the responsibilities it is expected to perform. The team was also of the opinion that the Bureau's mandate is not broad enough to allow it to obtain

---

[37] GRECO, *Evaluation Report on Latvia*, p. 21.

[38] The controversy surrounds an expensive Mercedes used by the official's wife, which she was alleged to be using on loan from the firm; the official said the car was being rented. N. Coleman, "Latvia's anti-corruption efforts tripped up," AFP Riga, 24 July 2002.

information and investigate all corruption cases, as there are no mechanisms for it to enforce cooperation or require information from other institutions.[39]

Money laundering

The Office for the Prevention of Laundering Proceeds from Criminal Activity was created in 1998 after the passage of the Act on Prevention of Laundering of Proceeds derived from Criminal Activity in March 1998. The Office operates under the supervision of the General Prosecutor's Office, and employed 13 staff in September 2001.[40] As of mid-2001, there had been only two convictions for money laundering. The European Commission noted in the *2001 Regular Report* that, although the number of reports submitted to the Office quadrupled to 4,014 in 2000, there had been no corresponding increase in its capacity; perhaps as a result, only 40 of the reports were forwarded to the General Prosecutor's Office, and only 30 criminal cases were initiated.[41] A special unit for investigating money laundering was established in the Board of the Finance Police at the SRS in June 2001.

2.5 Ombudsman

There is as yet no ombudsman in Latvia, though a National Human Rights Office (LNHRO) was established in 1994. In 2000, the LNHRO reviewed 775 applications and gave 4,012 oral consultations. The ability of the Office to deal with corruption cases is very limited, as it can only deal with cases where human rights have been violated. Moreover, its recommendations are not legally binding. As of July 2002, a draft law to establish an ombudsman was being prepared under the auspices of the President's Office, and was expected to be submitted to Parliament after the October 2002 elections.

3. EXECUTIVE BRANCH AND CIVIL SERVICE

The Government has identified the country's public administration as one of the major sources of corruption, noting in the introduction to the Corruption Prevention Strategy

---

[39] The information was conducted on the basis of an agreement to assist Latvia in the development of its anti-corruption policy. Information provided by Gale E. Rogers, Rule of Law Coordinator, Embassy Riga.

[40] GRECO, *Evaluation Report on Latvia,* p. 4.

[41] Commission, *2001 Regular Report,* pp. 49–50.

that, "[The] institutional system of public administration is a mess."[42] Since 2000, however, the civil service has undergone important developments, with a new law and development strategy. These changes may be expected to create a considerably more corruption-resistant environment. Procedures for appealing against administrative decisions have been largely ineffective to date, although a new Code of Administrative Procedure expected to come into effect in 2003 should improve citizen redress. The EU accession process and assistance have been among the most important reasons for these changes. While there have been a number of important cases of corruption in the public service, the evidence on corruption is insufficient to make a clear assessment.

3.1 Structure and legislative framework

Civil service reform in the 1990's was largely unsuccessful. State institutions increasingly employed non-civil servants due to greater flexibility in salaries and employment conditions, resulting in a dramatic fall in the number of civil servants from around 40,000 in the mid-1990s to only 6,000 in December 2000.

A new Civil Service Act was passed in 2000 and came into effect in 2001. Under the Act, civil servants may be hired only on the basis of an open competition run by a specially formed commission, and may be dismissed only under specific circumstances defined in the law.

Under the new Act, since 2001, the Civil Service Administration (CSA) has been responsible for:

- preparation of civil service regulations, analysis and forecasting of civil service development;
- disciplinary supervision, investigation of disciplinary cases and consideration of appeals against disciplinary sanctions;
- development of personnel management;
- examination of civil servant candidates and civil servants;
- information and education of public administration employees;
- coordination of implementation of EU norms.

Since the Act came into force, the number of civil servants has increased substantially. As of December 2001 64 percent of public administration employees had civil servant

---

[42] Government of Latvia, *Corruption Prevention Strategy*, May 2001, p. 2.

status.[43] A survey carried out by the CSA in 2000 showed that 65 percent of officials valued stability as one of the most important elements of a job.

3.2 Administrative procedure and redress

The deadline for administrative decisions is 15 days, or a maximum of 30 days in complicated cases. Many State institutions have established shorter deadlines in internal rules, for example the Passport Authority. Citizens may appeal administrative decisions under special regulations approved by the Cabinet.[44] Under the 1997 Act on the Procedure for Reviewing Applications, Complaints and Proposals citizens may submit complaints against administrative actions. The head of the institution concerned must deal with the complaint or claim within 15 days (30 days in complicated cases). Under the new Civil Service Act, the CSA reviews complaints rejected by civil service authorities, and complaints may subsequently be appealed to the courts. The CSA may initiate disciplinary proceedings against civil servants as a result of its findings. Prior to the introduction of the new system, complaints were reviewed by the head of the respective institution and were usually rejected. It is too early to judge whether the new system works better in practice. Appeals against municipalities are submitted directly to the courts.

A new Code of Administrative Procedure that will come into effect in 2003 provides for special administrative courts to deal with appeals.

3.3 Conflict of interest and asset monitoring

The legislative framework for conflict of interest regulation and asset monitoring is covered in Section 3.2. All civil servants are subject to these provisions, and the new act makes heads of civil service agencies responsible for collecting annual income and asset declarations and monitoring possible conflicts of interests of civil servants.

The media has revealed conflicts of interest concerning senior officials on a number of occasions. For example, in 2001, the Minister of Defence went on a business trip to Great Britain with his wife, paid for by BAE Systems, which is participating in the tender for purchasing long-range radars.[45] The Minister defended himself on the

---

[43] Annual Report of the Civil Service Administration (CSA) 2001, <http://www.vcp.gov.lv/faili/cdlv/informz/2001parskats.htm>, (last accessed 5 August 2002).

[44] Cabinet of Ministers Regulation no. 154.

[45] "Kristovskis says visit to British company BAE Systems was a working visit," LETA news agency, 25 May 2001.

grounds that the trip was a working visit. Recently, allegations have centred on the Latvian Prime Minister himself (see Section 2.2).

The Anti-corruption Act provided the media with material for one of the first major scandals in Latvia. In 1997, newspapers published more than 100 articles about officials who violated the provisions of the act that prohibit officials from having positions in private companies.[46] The media has also written about conflicts of interest in many ministries, such as the Ministry of the Interior and the Ministry of Foreign Affairs.

In particular, the media has followed the interests of local government officials, especially in Riga. In November 2000, the press reported that the house of the executive director of the Riga City Council was being renovated by a company that was previously awarded a contract to work on repairs of the National Opera. The director denied any private connection in this case.[47] In May 2001, the SRS, which is responsible for reviewing income and asset declarations of State officials, fined the head of the real estate department of Riga City Council €140 for not reporting her position as a director of a private enterprise and a member of the board of an insurance company.

3.4 Internal control mechanisms

In 2000, 156 disciplinary cases were initiated against civil servants and 143 fines imposed.[48] Most cases involved non-fulfilment of duties (102 cases and 94 fines), but there were also cases of illegal use of public office (12 cases and 11 fines). The State institution most affected was the Ministry of Agriculture, with 87 cases and 85 fines.

There is no legal protection for whistleblowers, and job security remains insufficient to encourage disclosure of officials' misconduct.[49]

---

[46] Ingrīda Puce, "Corruption Issue in Agenda Setting and Role of Media," university degree paper.

[47] Aiva Bārbale, "Riga city Executive Director Grinbergs is building big," 28 November 2000, on file with EUMAP reporter.

[48] Data provided by The Civil Service Administration.

[49] For example, one Ministry of Finance official related a case where a special ministerial commission was choosing a bank to handle the Ministry's money. According to the official, the Minister came to the commission and instructed it to award the account to a bank on whose board he previously sat. "But you either obey Minister or you will not have a job the next day," the official said.

3.5 Interaction with the public

A Code of Conduct for Civil servants entered into force in January 2001. The Code includes principles of conduct in relations between civil servants and society and in conflict of interest situations. The Civil Service Administration (CSA) has also produced a special report on ethics, which provides a theoretical background and discusses practical issues of implementation.

The Government has taken important steps to increase transparency. The Government website provides the agenda of all meetings of the Cabinet and subordinate legislative bodies (for example the Committee of the Cabinet of Ministers, or meetings of State Secretaries) and most documents prepared for those meetings. An Internet portal for all State institutions began functioning in April 2002. In February 2002, the Government approved a bill that would allow representatives of NGOs to attend meetings of State secretaries, which are the first step in the process by which the Government approves legislation.[50] One of the main priorities of the CSA is an information campaign to clarify for citizens their rights and provide information to public administration employees.

3.6 Corruption

According to the UNDP's *2000 Latvia Human Development Report,* 91 percent of citizens held very negative perceptions of public officials, six percent very positive and eight percent neutral.[51] Officials were evaluated as more corrupt than any other type of public functionary.

However, the EBRD/World Bank's *1999 Business Environment and Enterprise Performance Survey* indicates that administrative corruption is a comparatively minor problem (see Section 1). The CSA *Annual Report* cites the results of a citizen survey indicating that 12 percent of respondents encountered corruption in a State institution, while 55 percent were not satisfied with access to information and 58 percent encountered excessive bureaucracy (such as being sent from place to place).

One of the largest and most well-documented scandals was the so-called "three million" scandal, which broke in 1997 over the settlement of a €17.3m guarantee granted by State energy monopoly Latvernego to Banka Baltija. Latvernego reached an agreement whereby it sold the debt to a Lichtenstein-based company, in a deal that resulted in the disappearance of three million Lats (€5.2m). Charges against two board managers of

---

[50] "Views of NGOs in the Meeting of State Secretaries will represent NGO centre," LETA news agency, 19 February 2002.

[51] UNDP, *2000 Latvia Human Development Report,* p. 34.

Latvenergo (State officials) and one attorney were filed, and a special parliamentary investigation commission was formed. However, nothing happened until 2002, and failure to prosecute the case has played an important role in undermining perceptions of law enforcement and the political elite.[52]

The case also had ramifications in the Parliament (Saeima), where the Chairman of the parliamentary commission investigating the case was prosecuted for holding a credit card paid for by an off-shore company (see Section 4.5). In May 2002, indictments were finally filed against the President and two directors of Latvernego, and a representative of the Lichtenstein company. According to the Prosecutor's Office, the case will to go to court in late 2002.

In November 2001, a director of the Environmental Inspection Bureau was caught accepting a bribe of €2,000 from a Latvian company in return for a promise to allocate to the company a contract for an international project.[53] Another case raised by the media charged the Director-General of the Government Real Estate Agency with awarding luxurious apartments in the centre of Riga illegally to agency colleagues and celebrities. The Director-General was dismissed, a criminal investigation began and the Prosecutors' Office initiated a procedure to return the apartments to the State.[54]

Corruption in privatisation has attracted extensive media attention, and surveys have shown that the Privatisation Agency is perceived as the fourth most corrupt institution. In 2000, a member of the Board of the Privatisation Agency was caught receiving a €16,000 bribe in order to secure the briber the purchase of a house in a resort town. He was denounced by the leadership of the Agency and prosecuted. However, the court decided that the official had not committed bribery but misuse of public position, as there was no evidence of the payment serving his private interest.[55]

In May 2002 court proceedings began against a lawyer charged with the murder of an official who worked in the Privatisation Agency in 2000. Among the evidence collected, €183,600 was found in the official's safe, and prosecutors suspected that he sold rights to administer insolvent and bankrupt enterprises to the lawyer.[56]

---

[52] J. Domburs and I. Voika, "Kas nozaga trīs miljonus?" [Who stole 3 million?], *NIP birojs*, Riga 1998.

[53] "Director of the Environment Inspection arrested and charged for bribery," LETA news agency, 22 November 2001. The Ministry of Environment and Regional Development informed the public that the particular person did not actually have direct influence on the decision process she had promised to influence.

[54] TI Latvia, *Watchdogs*, draft report on the "The Watchdog 2001" project, 2001.

[55] TI Latvia, *Watchdogs*.

[56] "In June the Court will start hearing on the murder of LAP official Skadina," LETA news agency, 22 May 2002.

The media also reported on suspected corruption in the privatisation of Latvian Shipping. However, Transparency International Latvia's monitoring of the privatisation did not reveal any evidence of corruption or illegality in the process.[57]

Recent corruption cases indicate that individual citizens have become more willing to report corruption to the police, an impression shared by the recent GRECO evaluation.[58]

One particularly worrying form of corruption reported by the World Bank was the practice of bribes being paid to secure jobs as public officials.[59] Such practices are likely to have been reduced greatly by the civil service reforms outlined in Section 3.1.

4. LEGISLATURE

Until recently, parliamentary scrutiny of public finances was undermined by the existence of a number of off-budget agencies, while the allocation of State guarantees by the Government appears to have been non-transparent. While there have been almost no cases of MPs prosecuted for corruption, there is evidence or at least testimony that "State capture," that is capture of the legislative process by business interests, is a problem.

4.1 Elections

Elections are regulated and supervised by the Central Election Committee (CEC). The Chairman of the Commission is appointed by Parliament for a term of five years. There have not been any attempts to remove the chairman, and elections are considered free and fair.[60]

---

[57] Fith Rating Agency, *Latvia Report 2001,* p. 3.

[58] GRECO, *Evaluation Report on Latvia,* p. 20.

[59] J. Anderson, *Corruption in Latvia,* p. 7.

[60] The last external observers' mission of OSCE visited Latvia during the parliamentary elections in 1995. The CEC dealt with two complaints at the last municipal elections in March 2000, and in two municipalities elections were repeated.

4.2 Budget and control mechanisms

Although the State budget is subject to parliamentary approval, until recently the transparency of public finances was undermined by a number of off-budget funds, largely a result of the fact that agencies under ministry management were not included in the State budget accounts. The IMF commented in March 2001 that:

> [T]he proliferation of agencies in recent years in Latvia, without adequate criteria to define their functions or limit their operations, has had a contrary result in some instances and has made budgetary control more difficult.[61]

The SAO has identified off-budget agencies as one of the most significantly corruption-prone areas.[62] In addition, the situation surrounding State guarantees was non-transparent. For example, in 2000, the Government proposed a €14.9m guarantee for a distillery company without informing Parliament or the public. In 2001, the director of the company was assassinated. He was a close business colleague of the former Prime Minister Andris Skele, now an MP and Chairman of the People's Party. The Ministry of Finance did not approve the guarantee.

New budgetary rules approved in 2001 have made important changes to the State budget, providing for the abolition of off-budget funds. The 2001 State Budget Act included the maximum limits of the deficit at the end of 2001, as well as budgets of some agencies that were not previously included and a list of the State guarantees given during 2001.[63]

4.3 Conflict of interest and asset monitoring

Conflict of interest and asset monitoring provisions are discussed in Section 2.2. According to the recent evaluation by GRECO *Evaluation Report,* a Parliamentary Code of Ethics was under preparation.[64]

---

[61] International Monetary Fund, *Report on the Observance of Standards and Codes (ROSC) – Latvia,* March 2001.

[62] GRECO, *Evaluation Report on Latvia,* p. 17.

[63] Act on the State Budget, 30 November 2000, <http://www.fm.gov.lv>, (last accessed 30 April 2001).

[64] GRECO, *Evaluation Report Report on Latvia,* p. 5.

4.4 Immunity

MPs may not be arrested, prosecuted, detained or have their property searched without the prior consent of the Parliament. While GRECO regarded the extent of immunity as acceptable, it noted the absence (and recommended the creation of) clear guidelines for when immunity should be lifted.[65]

In some cases immunity has been lifted in order to allow sanctions to be imposed for petty offences, such as speeding or submitting late or incorrect income and asset declarations. The willingness of MPs to vote for removing immunity in such cases has increased in the past three to four years. In June 2002, Parliament lifted immunity from an MP who had been investigated for suspected violation of political party funding rules.[66] There have been some other allegations of politicians building luxurious houses. In these cases the Prosecutor's Office has investigated the matter, but has not found sufficient evidence to request removal of immunity.[67]

4.5 Corruption

There have been almost no cases of MPs being prosecuted for corruption-related offences. In 1998, the head of a special parliamentary commission investigating a controversial deal involving the energy monopoly Latvenergo (see Section 3.6) was charged in connection with use of credit cards billed to an account from which he was receiving around €1,880 per month. The MP denied the charges and was elected to Parliament. At the time of writing, the prosecutor's office was still investigating the case, which – again – appears to illustrate the weakness of the office in investigating economic crime.[68] In 2000, another MP came under investigation in connection with services provided to Latvernego by his law firm.

Latvia's reputation for "State capture," whereby laws and rules are illegitimately influenced by private interests, is related directly to powerful lobbying interests. According to one investigative journalist, companies that wish to influence legislation use a network of PR firms with connections to politicians and political parties, which systematically mediate payoffs to parties and individuals. No cases of such activities have been proven,

---

[65] GRECO, *Evaluation Report Report on Latvia,* p. 25.

[66] The MP was suspected of accepting for his political party and then misappropriating €25,000 in cash from an oil transit company. See "Saeima agrees to start criminal procedures against Burvis," LETA news agency, 13 June 2002.

[67] Information provided by Delna (Transparency International Latvia).

[68] TI Latvia, *Watchdogs.*

but the passage of a number of laws has raised suspicion. Examples include the passage in 2001 of restrictive legislation on pharmacies or the approval of lower taxes for free ports, regarded as the result of strong influence by business interests in the free port of Ventspils, one of the largest transit ports in Europe.[69] The ties between politicians and local business interests in Ventspils, such as Ventspils Nafta (Ventspils Oil), are regarded as one of the main examples of the phenomenon of "State capture."

5. JUDICIARY

The judiciary suffers from serious problems of lack of independence, underfunding and lack of capacity, resulting in endemic court delays. Access to information on court decisions is an important problem, although guaranteeing this is a component of the Government's anti-corruption strategy. Surveys indicate that a significant proportion of citizens that come into contact with the courts have faced problems of corruption. Although a judicial reform programme is underway, there appears to be a persistent lack of political commitment to effective reform.

5.1 Legislative framework

The legal and institutional framework of the judiciary is described in detail in a 2001 OSI monitoring report, which criticised excessive interference by the Ministry of Justice in judicial affairs – including direct intervention in individual cases and very low levels of enforcement of court decisions – and referred to a general perception of widespread corruption in the judiciary.[70]

Although trials are generally public and court verdicts are officially public documents, access to court judgements is very poor: in practice presiding judges have not been willing to provide verdicts to third persons after announcing them verbally in the court room.[71] Since 1996, judgements of the Supreme Court and, since 1998, judgements of the regional courts have been published in an annual publication. The 2002 PHARE project on

---

[69] Interview with Anita Brauna, journalist, Riga, 11 April 2002.

[70] EU Accession Monitoring Program, *Monitoring the EU Accession Process: Judicial Independence,* Open Society Institute, 2001, pp. 225–265., available at <www.eumap.org>.

[71] During research on access to information, TI Latvia was denied verdicts in various courts. However, the courts provided the documents when told the reason for the request, and the problem of secrecy appears to be largely a problem of habit.

corruption prevention in the courts system has provided a set of recommendations for active publication of court cases on the Internet.

5.2 Corruption

Poor administration, poor access to information and delays in courts, especially, underpin public perceptions of relatively high corruption in Latvian courts. Forty-eight percent of respondents in surveys regarded courts as dishonest institutions, and only 16 percent regarded them as honest.[72] Although 83 percent of respondents said they had never made any additional payments at courts, only nine percent of respondents had come into contact with the courts, indicating that the proportion of those that came into contact into court who made additional payments may be considerable. A survey by TI Latvia indicated that 1-2 percent of the population have faced problems of corruption in courts. Citizens rate the courts better than the police, municipalities and other institutions in ranking corrupt institutions. Public opinion surveys show that there is more dissatisfaction with court delays (39 percent) than with quality of proceedings (29 percent).[73]

Since 1991, there has been only one case of judicial corruption, when a district court judge was caught receiving a €900 bribe in 1997. In May 2001, a Supreme Court judge was dismissed from her position for violating court procedures. Three judges were dismissed by the Disciplinary Board – a body composed of judges – in 2001. One case concerned abuse of position by a judge in Riga in connection with annulment of marriages.

Court delays are one of the main possible sources of corruption in the judicial system, especially in commercial civil court proceedings in Riga. Civil court proceedings take 12-18 months on average. In a court in Riga, it takes two years to handle criminal cases without any detainees and six months for cases with detainees. According to judges and lawyers, it is too easy to postpone cases, and there are no rules governing how judges should allocate cases to free spaces in their calendar.

The current Minister of Justice has set court reform as a top priority.[74] A programme of judicial reform currently underway envisages the creation of a Judiciary Agency to take responsibility for administrative and financial management of the courts away from the Ministry of Justice in 2003. Several multilateral and bilateral projects (EU, UNDP, the Swedish Government) are devoted to helping with State reform, in particular an EU

---

[72] TI Latvia, *Face of Corruption in Latvia, Riga,* 2000.

[73] TI Latvia, *Face of Corruption in Latvia, Riga,* 2000.

[74] Government Declaration, 2000, <http://www.mk.gov.lv>, (last accessed 30 April 2001).

PHARE project running from October 2001 on "Prevention of Corruption within the Court System." The main objective of this project is the publication of all court decisions, but this may take several years, since many district court verdicts do not exist in electronic form. Other planned reforms include the introduction of compulsory random procedures for assignment of cases, the creation of a Penalty Registry[75] and the introduction of courses on professional ethics and access to information at the Judicial Training Centre.

a) On the other hand, judges largely blame the Government for the problems of the judiciary. In May 2002, the President of the Latvian Judges' Association reacted to critical remarks addressed to the judiciary by President Vaira Vike-Freiberga by classifying them as symptomatic of the Government's neglect of the judiciary, in particular its lack of funding.[76]

6. POLITICAL PARTY FINANCE

Political party funding has been weakly regulated until recently. However, new funding regulations approved in June 2002 have put in place a much more transparent system. Nevertheless, the absence of any State funding leaves parties vulnerable to corruption and there is evidence that corruption is widespread. The effectiveness of the new Corruption Prevention Bureau in inspecting party financial reports under the new provisions will be an important test of its impact.

6.1 Legislative framework

Under the Act on Financing of Political Parties, parties may receive income from membership dues, donations and profits from business activities. The main provisions of the Act in force until June 2002 are as follows:

• Parties may not receive donations from enterprises where the State or a municipality holds 50 percent of shares or more, from State or municipal institutions, from religious organisations, from stateless persons or foreign or anonymous entities.

• A single donor may not contribute more than €45,000 in any one year.

---

[75] Corruption Prevention Programme of the Government of Latvia, 2001.

[76] Interview with Ivars Bickovics, President of the Latvian Judges' Association, Latvian State Radio, 27 May 2002.

- Parties may not establish foundations for financing purposes.

- If an anonymous donation is received, it has to be transferred to a separate fund controlled by the Ministry of Justice, which subsequently redistributes the donations to all registered parties.

Under amendments to the Act that came into force in June 2002,

- Any one entity may donate a maximum of €17,347 to a political party in any one year;

- All donations over €173 must be provided through a bank account, and all other donations must be delivered to party offices in person;

- All donations must be submitted directly, and no third parties may be involved;

- Parties must publish every donation and its source on the Internet within five days of receiving it, declare all donors and expenditures before and after elections and provide more details of expenditures in their reports.

Until 2002 parties have received no direct financial assistance from the State. A Government proposal for funding of parties from the State budget was prepared in January 2001 but was not discussed in Parliament. Instead, parties initiated amendments to introduce limited State funding, which were among the amendments approved in June 2002. Under the new provisions all parties receiving at least three percent of votes will receive an amount equal to 0.1 percent of the minimum salary per vote, which in 2002 would mean €1 per vote. Discussion of more substantial State funding is expected to take place after the October 2002 elections.

6.2 Control and supervision

Under the provisions in force until June 2002, all parties were required by law to submit their annual financial declarations to the Ministry of Justice, and failure to do so could result in disbanding of the party. Since 2001, declarations of political parties have been available online free of charge at <http://www.lursoft.lv>, (last accessed 30 August 2002).

Under the June 2002 amendments, parties will now submit their financial declarations to the Central Election Commission, which will be responsible for monitoring them. This is a positive development, given the independence and professionalism of CEC staff. In addition, party financial reports are also to be submitted to the Corruption Prevention Bureau, which may inspect party accounts. The Bureau may impose a fine of up to €17,347 for violation of the law.

6.3 Party finance in practice

Table 4 shows the breakdown of political party income between 1995 and 1999.

Table 4: Breakdown of political party income, 1995–1999, in percent

	1995	1996	1997	1998	1999
Donations	89.5	78.4	91.2	83.5	88.5
Private persons	47.1	21.2	32.1	49.3	65.8
Corporations	52.9	78.8	67.9	50.7	34.2
Membership dues	2.2	20.5	7.1	3.2	9.0
Entrepreneurship	5.5	0.04	0.5	0.3	0.4
Other	2.8	1.1	1.2	12.9	2.1
Total (percent)	100	100	100	100	100
Total, in €'000	1945	841.4	950.7	5251	1113

Source: J. Ikstens, *Political party financing and reducing corruption in Latvia: analysis of alternative solutions,* Soros Foundation Latvia, 2001, p. 9.

Donations

On average, more than four-fifths of party funds come from donations. Major political parties, which have or have had parliamentary representation, appear to rely heavily on large contributions. On average, large donations (more than €5,500) make up 80 percent of corporate contributions and donations of more than €1,100 cover almost 75 percent of income from private donations. According to the figures, donations from individuals have grown over time, which contradicts growing dissatisfaction with politicians and political parties. Yet, nine out of 11 parties admit disguising corporate contributions as private donations.

Since 1998, parties have begun taking out bank loans to fund campaigns. Annual declarations indicate that these loans are often interest-free.

Analysing data across parties and over time, two groups emerge as major contributors: financial institutions (banks and insurance companies), and companies engaged in transportation of oil and chemical products. The latter are believed to be particularly influential, and are increasingly being rivalled by the food industry, which has been the third most important financial contributor since 1998. Representatives of two parties admitted accepting donations from companies which have received contracts or licenses from State or municipal agencies controlled by representatives of the respective party.

Eight out of 11 parties admitted that potential sponsors frequently put forward suggestions or even demands of political or economic character, and most admitted that they "occasionally" yielded to such demands. Three representatives conceded that at times their parties had to give up their ideological principles in order to satisfy their financial supporters.

There was only one corruption scandal covered by the press at the 1998 elections. The media reported that the Latvian Social Democratic Workers Party (LSDSP) pledged that specific donor-supported candidates would be placed higher on its ticket, practically guaranteeing them election.[77] Although the party officially denied the allegations, other party members confirmed them off the record. The case did not receive wide press coverage and was not followed up.

In 2002, prosecutors began investigating another case involving the LSDSP. The head of the party publicly accused an MP of accepting €25,000 from an oil transit company for the party, and then spending it himself. In June 2002 Parliament met a request from the State Prosecutor and lifted the MP's immunity (see Section 4.4).

In March 2002, after parties submitted their annual reports, a TV programme investigated the parties' donors.[78] The programme found that the largest donors to the People's Party (which won the most seats in the 1998 elections) were companies without official addresses and which could be contacted only by mobile phone. One of the party's donors turned out to be a company suspected of involvement in organised smuggling. Under media pressure, the party announced that it would give the dubious donations to a children's home. The same programme then found that the LSDSP had received donations from various suspicious donors: one company had been investigated for tax evasion, one was bankrupt and one company was registered in the name of a person who claimed to have no knowledge of the company.

Expenditure

According to an expert on Latvian party financing,[79] most major parties do not declare a significant share of campaign expenses. On average, parties are thought to fail to declare approximately 5-15 percent of their total campaign budget, although some are believed to leave more than half of their expenditure undeclared.

---

[77] "LSDSP promised top positions on ticket for financial support for its election campaign," LETA news agency, 1 March 2001; see <http://www.leta2000.com>, (last accessed 2 September 2002).

[78] *Tadi esam,* (weekly documentary), Latvian State TV, April 2002.

[79] Interview with Janis Ikstens, political scientist, expert on party financing, 21 April 2001.

7. Public Procurement[80]

Public procurement is rated as one of the country's most corrupt spheres. Although a Public Procurement Act has been in force since 1996, the Act contains provisions that allow contracting authorities to avoid tenders relatively easily, and the system of supervision and redress has not functioned effectively. A new procurement act in force since January 2002 has improved the legal framework considerably, although there are still effectively no sanctions for violations of procurement regulations.

7.1 Legislative framework

Until January 2002, public procurement was regulated by the 1996 Act on State and Local Government Procurement. The Act applied to all procurement financed fully or partially from public funds. A new Act on Public Procurement for the Needs of State or Local Governments was passed in July 2001 and came into effect in January 2002. The new Act is intended explicitly to harmonise procurement legislation with EU directives.

Under the previous legislation, competitive tendering had to be applied to contracts exceeding €17,000 in the case of supply of goods or services, and €85,000 for construction works projects. The 2001 Act reduced the threshold to €8,500 for goods and services and kept the same threshold for construction works. As of July 2002, legislation was under discussion in Parliament to raise the threshold for goods and services contracts to €17,000. Sole sourcing may be used under the following circumstances:

- it is possible to purchase the goods or receive services only from one supplier and there are no justifiable alternatives or substitutes;

- the goods or services are needed urgently for unforeseeable circumstances, therefore involvement in a tendering procedure is impossible or unjustified;

- insurmountable circumstances or an emergency situation have arisen, which make it impossible to use other procurement methods due to time pressure;

- the contracting authority, at whose disposal there are already goods, equipment or technology purchased from a supplier, determines that an additional supply has to be purchased from the same supplier for reasons of standardisation, or to ensure technical compatibility with goods, equipment and technology already purchased, regarding the effectiveness of the initial purchase in satisfying the

---

[80] On-line resources on procurement in Latvia in English can be found at <http://www.fm.gov.lv/80Sabiepirk/80Sabiepirk_a.htm>, (last accessed 3 September 2002).

needs of the Government contracting authority. The value of the additional purchase must be "limited," although no exact threshold is stated;

- the contracting authority is looking for an opportunity to enter into a contract in order to conduct research, an experiment, training or improvement which requires the purchase of a prototype.

These conditions leave considerable space for authorities to abuse the sole sourcing provision. The Act also states that members of procurement commissions shall be held civilly and criminally liable for violations of the tender provisions.

Information on upcoming public tenders and invitations to bid are published in the *Latvijas Vestnesis (Official Gazette)* and on the website of the Public Procurement Monitoring Agency, giving adequate access to information. The Ministry of Finance must place tender notices on the Internet within two working days after its receipt. Under the 1996 Act, procurement was non-transparent in practice: although information could be obtained on which company was awarded a contract, often the size of the winning offer was not public. Under the new Act, general information on both the winning and losing bids is available.

For procurements by tendering or competition methods, contracting authorities must establish a commission of at least three people. For construction procurements, the commission must comprise at least five people, one of whom should be an authorised construction representative, usually a civil engineer. Procurement commissions employ widely varying practices: many comprise eight people or more, and because the law does not state the functions of commissions clearly, many contracting authorities form commissions both to write the bidding documents and to evaluate bids, whereas others form commissions only for bid evaluation. Commission members are often untrained in procurement.[81]

Statistical data show that in 99.5 percent of cases, procurement contracts are awarded using the simplest two methods – one bidder or a questionnaire on prices.[82] This probably accounts for 30-40 percent of total finances spent through procurement.

The 1996 Act did not mandate economy and efficiency in the use of public funds, require contracting authorities to conduct bid openings in public or open bids immediately after the submission deadline, or include any procedure for debarring bidders for fraudulent or corrupt activity. The 2001 Act has introduced all of these provisions.

---

[81] World Bank, *Final Country Procurement Assessment Report,* vol. I, Europe and Central Asia Region, January 2001, p. 5.

[82] Data from the Ministry of Finance, 1999.

7.2 Review and audit

The main body for supervising procurement and reviewing complaints is the Procurement Monitoring Bureau (PMB). The Director of the PMB is appointed by the State Secretary of the Minister of Finance. Under the 1996 Act, the Bureau (then called the Public Procurement Monitoring Department) was a ministry department with no powers, while complaints and appeals submitted against procurement processes did not result in the halting of procedures while the complaint was being processed. Under the new Act, participants in tender proceedings may submit complaints to the PMB during tender procedures or within ten days of a tender decision. On receipt of the complaint the tender procedure must be halted for 30 days, the deadline within which appeals must be dealt with. Participants may also appeal thereafter to the courts.

According to the World Bank, the Department under the old legislation was ineffective and lacked autonomy to carry out its role.[83] The Department employed only six staff in 2001 and could barely handle appeals, let alone carry out systematic monitoring of procurement. Although appeals procedures have been considerably improved by the new legislation, the law still contains no sanctions for violation of procurement regulations. Although violations might be sanctioned by standard fines for violations of administrative law, there is no institution responsible for imposing fines and none have ever been issued.

The State Audit Office may audit procurements, and did so in 25 cases in 1999 (nine percent of all audits it carried out in that year). These cases constituted four percent of the total €876.40m in public procurements that year. The Office also suffers from lack of capacity and training to audit a sufficient proportion of procurements adequately. However, the Office has identified a number of regular and serious violations of procurement regulations, in particular that:

- contracts are awarded for works or for the supply of goods or services without tendering or competition or the lowest bid is rejected without justification;

- the number of bidders is limited without reason;

- procurement commissions include persons who represent the interests of both contracting authority and supplier;

- the sums indicated in bidding documents are exceeded.[84]

---

[83] World Bank, *Final Country Procurement Assessment Report,* p. 7.

[84] Republic of Latvia State Comptroller's Office, *2000 Annual Report* (State and Municipal Procurement). Cited in: V. Kalniņš, "Latvia's Anti-corruption Policy: Problems and Prospects," unpublished paper, 2002.

In most cases, officials are not sanctioned for such violations, a fact which appears to indicate significant potential corruption. The Office does not have the authority to suspend procurement processes while the actual circumstances or facts discovered in a complaint are investigated.[85]

7.3 Corruption

There have been no criminal investigations of breaches of procurement procedures.

In 1998, the media exposed a Ministry of Transportation tender for construction traffic signs, in which the tender documentation was written in such a way that only one Latvian company with business relations with officials of the Ministry qualified for the tender.[86] According to the reports, an Estonian company could do the same job for half the price. No action was taken as a result of the scandal.

The press has on a number of occasions raised suspicions of corruption in the allocation of contracts for construction works by the Riga City Council. For example, a tender to build a bridge was issued in 2000. Documentation was provided to seven tendering parties, but bids were only submitted by four, one of whom subsequently withdrew its bid. The Council's Procurement Commission awarded the contract to a company whose offer was regarded by the media as clearly not the best.[87] The State Audit Office found a number of violations of procurement regulations. Competing bidders then appealed to a district court, which agreed that the award of the contract was illegal. However, the Riga City Court overturned the verdict.[88]

According to an investigative journalist who covers procurement issues, collusion both among bidders and between bidders and authorities is common. For example, agreements with authorities in which the bidder promises not to appeal a tender in return for a contract in the future are common. According to the same journalist, companies say that a bribe of 10-20 percent of the contract's value is normal, most of which is channelled to political parties.[89]

---

[85] State Auditors' Office, *1999 Annual Report;* see <http://www.lrvk.gov.lv/htmls/english/engindex.htm>, (last accessed 30 April 2001).

[86] Articles in *Diena* newspaper by Ingus Bērziņš, Jānis Domburs, *NIP birojs,* September 1998, <http://www.lursfot.lv>, (last accessed 30 April 2001).

[87] Interview with journalist Anita Brauna, *Diena,* Riga, 11 April 2002.

[88] V. Kalniņš, "Latvia's Anti-corruption Policy: Problems and Prospects," unpublished paper, 2002.

[89] Interview with journalist Anita Brauna, *Diena,* Riga, 11 April 2002.

An online discussion on public procurement organised by Delna in June 2001 indicated serious corruption problems in procurement. The discussion include the following contributions:

- "I am dealing with such issues and can say one thing – access to information will not change anything. There are many legal ways to grant the deal to a particular enterprise. We are corrupted and we have to start thinking about cleaning up the highest levels. Members of Parliament are poor and they need to live from something. State policy is directed towards corruption."

- "You can offer goods even at dumping prices, and you still will not [win any contract], because a commission has its own people and companies to whom they have to award [contracts] in turn."

- "My job is to produce tender documents for my boss for a certain winner, so all activities concerning information access are only a show."[90]

8. PUBLIC SERVICES

Corruption in the police (specifically the traffic police) and customs authorities have been regarded in perception surveys as more widespread than in any other institutions. However, reforms in both institutions have either led to improvements or can be expected to do so. Unofficial payments in the healthcare system appear to be more widespread than in any other area except the traffic police, although many payments may not in fact be bribes. There is some evidence of corruption in tax authorities, although important reforms have been implemented and public satisfaction has risen. Corruption in business licensing does not appear to be a problem, while corruption in other areas of business regulation appears to be limited. In the latter areas significant potential for successful anti-corruption reforms has been demonstrated.

8.1 Police

In the first nine months of 2001, seven police officers were arrested by the Bureau for Combating Organised Crime and Corruption, compared to five in 2000.[91] Corruption

---

[90] *Versions*, <http://www.delfi.lv> discussions, <http://www.delfi.lv/archive/index.php?id=1387012&categoryID=898102&ndate=05.06.2001&sID=5>, (last accessed 5 May 2001).

[91] GRECO, *Evaluation Report on Latvia*, p. 9.

appears to be a much more serious problem in the police than these figures suggest, however. As Section 1.2 shows, the traffic police is regarded as the second most corrupt institutions in Latvia. This may be expected to change somewhat as police have been unable to levy on-the-spot cash fines since 2000. A major case of police corruption emerged in November 2001 when the Deputy Chief of the Economic Police was arrested in the act of receiving a bribe of €6,250. The Deputy was the highest police official ever detained for corruption, and was trying to stop the investigation of a smuggling and tax evasion case.[92] According to press reports, several other senior police officers have been hit by accusations in 2001 and 2002, including the head of the Economic Police, whose wife made expensive real estate purchases.[93]

In every police unit, one officer is responsible for investigating complaints from the public. If individuals are not satisfied with the response, they may appeal to a higher police officer, the Security Police and ultimately the Minister of the Interior. According to GRECO, increased attention is being devoted to gathering operative information on and investigating corruption among police officers. Within the police, responsibility for investigation of corruption lies mainly with the Human Resource Inspection, which is subordinate directly to the Chief of State Police.

8.2 Customs

Seven customs officials were arrested by the Bureau for Combating Organised Crime and Corruption in 2000, while three were arrested in the first nine months of 2001.[94] Customs is regarded in surveys as the most corrupt institution in Latvia (see Section 1.2). However, there has been a broad improvement in all aspects of customs procedures and clearance in recent years. Changes introduced include: simplified declarations for certain types of movements of goods; the introduction of a system of electronic declaration of goods (although full implementation is hindered by the absence of a law on electronic signatures); more precise delineation of duties and authorities of customs officers; and a cooperation scheme with the Border Guard. In addition, specific anti-corruption measures have been introduced, notably rotation of staff. Graph 2 shows an improvement between 1999 and 2001 in companies' perceptions of the consistency of treatment by customs authorities.

---

[92] Galzons, "Two high officials arrested for bribing," *Diena,* 20 November 2001.

[93] N. Coleman, "Latvia's anti-corruption efforts tripped up," AFP, Riga, 24 July 2002.

[94] GRECO, *Evaluation Report on Latvia,* p. 9.

Graph 2: Perceptions of consistency of shipments at the same border points and at different border points, 1999–2001

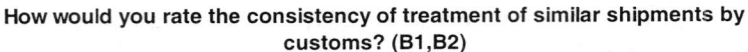

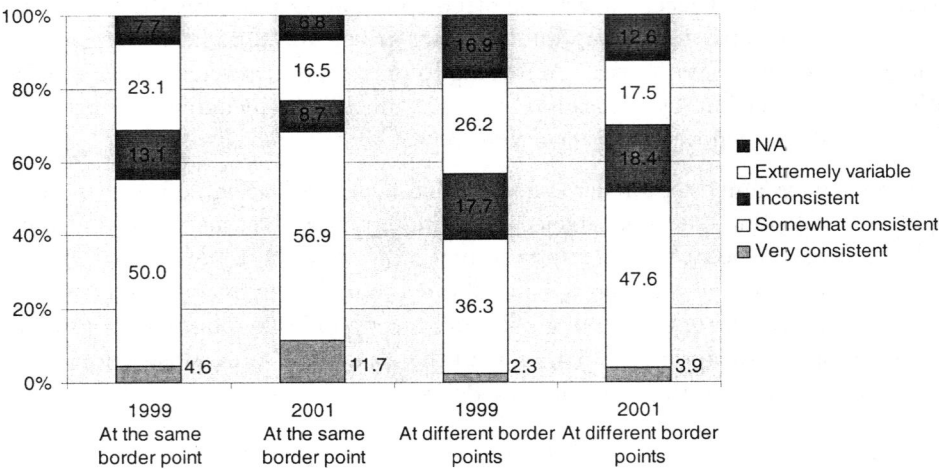

How would you rate the consistency of treatment of similar shipments by customs? (B1,B2)

Source: *1999* and *2001 Surveys on the Business Environment in Latvia,* available at <http://www.lda.gov.lv/images/2001anal_for_internet.doc>, (last accessed 22 July 2002).

8.3 Tax

Although direct evidence on corruption in the State Revenue Service is very limited, the tax authorities are regarded in surveys as the most difficult of inspectorates for clients to deal with. However, the situation has been improving. In 2001, 26 percent of respondents to a survey of the business environment found tax inspectorates "somewhat unhelpful and difficult," compared to 38 percent in 1999.[95]

Nevertheless, the "grey economy" is estimated at between 25 and 40 percent of GDP, and VAT fraud in particular is regarded as a major problem.[96] An "Islands of Integrity" project run by TI Latvia in cooperation with the Latvian Merchants' Association indicated that SRS inspectors are often threatening to impose large fines for minor tax

---

[95] 2001 Survey on the Business Environment in Latvia, <http://www.lda.gov.lv/images/2001anal_for_internet.doc>, (last accessed 22 July 2002).

[96] Press Release, SRS, 17.01.2001, <http://www.vid.gov.lv/2vidinf/show.asp?id=259>, (last accessed 22 July 2002).

violations in order to extort bribes. The tax authorities and local authorities appear to have considerable discretion to provide tax breaks to selected companies. For example, in 2002 Riga City forgave €2 million tax debt for a company operating in Riga port; the company's shareholders included a member of one of the governing political parties and businessmen that had sponsored a number of political parties in recent years.[97]

The State Revenue Service has been implementing important reforms to fight corruption, based on a Modernisation Strategy for the SRS adopted in 1999.[98] Measures include the establishment of an Appeals Department in January 2000, the provision of extensive information on tax regulations and procedures on the SRS website and the opening of 17 modern client centres.

8.4 Healthcare

According to surveys unofficial payments appear to be more widespread in the healthcare system than in any other area with the exception of the traffic police: in 2000 14 percent of respondents said they had made unofficial payments to doctors compared to 17 percent in the case of the traffic police.[99] However, it is not clear what proportion of unofficial contributions are bribes that are necessary to receive treatment: according to a survey carried out by the Baltic Institute of Social Studies 47 percent of patients had given something to doctors; most of those gave flowers and sweets, while only 31 percent gave money.[100] Moreover, along with education the healthcare system is one of the most trusted institution in Latvia.

On the other hand, regional focus groups organised by TI Latvia in September 2001 identified admission to hospitals and special treatment (especially operations) as the most corrupt areas, with bribes starting from €150. Anecdotal evidence indicates at least isolated cases of aggravated corruption. For example, in July 2002 a medical care quality control inspectorate found that a patient died after emergency surgery was denied without reason, and the case was being investigated after relatives claimed bribes had been demanded.[101]

---

[97] "Social Democrats want explanation of tax relief to the company of Kehris and Indriksons," *NRA* daily, 22 March 2002.

[98] Modernisation Strategy 1999-2003, State Revenue Service of Latvia, <http://www.vid.gov.lv/search./document.asp?src=1parvid/docs/19.htm>, (last accessed 22 July 2002).

[99] *Face of Corruption in Latvia,* TI Latvia, 2000

[100] I. Peņķe, "Evaluation of the Latvian Health Care System," unpublished presentation, The Baltic Institute of Social Studies, 2002, p. 23.

[101] "Death of patient at Stradins' hospital due to ungrounded delay of emergency surgery," LETA, 26 July 2002.

Corruption in healthcare is encouraged by a lack of consensus on what constitutes bribery in the health system, along with a funding system whereby hospitals are allocated lump sums with no conditions on how it is to be used.

Reform of the healthcare system has been identified as a priority of the Government's anti-corruption strategy. As of July 2002 the OECD was conducting a survey on request of the Government, and will submit recommendations on reforms to curb corruption.

8.5 Licensing and regulation

Business registration and regulation do not appear to be particularly severe problems. One of the areas where considerable progress has been made in fighting corruption has been in licensing processes. The most striking example of this has been the reform of the Traffic Security Department, the authority responsible for vehicle licensing, running driving tests and issuing driving licences. The Department is a State-owned joint-stock company, and through the 1990s was notorious for endemic bribery. A newly-appointed director carried out a comprehensive reform plan in 1999, involving simplification of application procedures, increasing and rotating staff, linking together all branches of the department electronically, introducing official extra fees for attractive licence plates, computer-generated written tests to prevent the sale of test papers, computer-selected examiners and driving test routes and manoeuvres and driving tests carried out in the presence of the instructor as well as the examiner.

Combined with a purge that has left almost none of the staff that worked in the Department ten years ago, the effect of these measures has been to virtually eradicate corruption. The only potential worry stemming from the changes is the fact that many of the staff sacked for suspicion of corruption have moved to positions in the police or customs; some have even been elected as MPs.[102] The example of the Department has not been applied in other agencies such as the Land Registry or passport authorities.

Business registration

Business registration is another activity that appears to be remarkably clean. Businesses surveyed by the Latvian Development Agency give the Register an unambiguously positive evaluation (see Graph 3). Rather than being administered by the courts as in a number of other candidate States – a solution that appears to be vulnerable to corruption – the Enterprise Register is an independent agency. Registration of a company costs between €35-450, depending on the type of company, while amendments to the register cost from €3-6.25. Registration takes between one day and

---

[102] Comments from OSI Roundtable Discussion, Riga, 10 April 2002.

two weeks, and to register quickly costs more (twice the normal charge to be registered in three days, four times to be registered in one day).

In addition, accessing information in the Companies Register is easy. The register is administered by a private company (Lursoft), which provides a searchable database of companies, annual reports, balance sheets, founders and officials.[103]

Graph 3: Satisfaction with procedures relating to enterprise registration or registering changes in corporate documents in Latvia

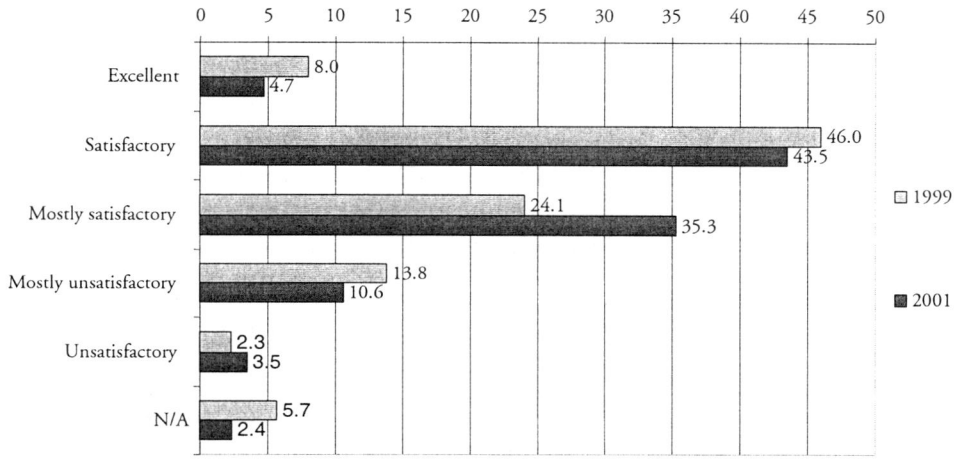

Source: Latvian Development Agency, *2001 Survey on the Business Environment in Latvia,* <http://www.lda.gov.lv/images/2001anal_for_internet.doc>, (last accessed 20 April 2002).

---

[103] <http://www.ur.gov.lv>, (last accessed 2 September 2002).

9. ROLE OF THE MEDIA

The Latvian press is free. Although Latvia was the first among EU candidate countries to pass freedom of information legislation, the impact of the law is uncertain to date. Broadcasting regulation appears to be relatively free of political manipulation. Corruption in the media is not regarded as a major problem, although there is some indirect evidence of phenomena such as hidden advertising. The media has played an important role in monitoring corruption, especially adherence to the Corruption Prevention Act.

9.1 Freedom of speech

Freedom of the press is guaranteed by the Constitution and the 1990 Act on the Press and other Mass Media.[104] The climate for journalists is generally free of restrictions. The Ministry of Justice issues licenses to print media publications, and there have been no cases of barriers to establishment except in the case of attempts to establish extremist publications. Barriers to a free and independent media are largely of a financial nature.[105]

The Press Act grants media organisations the legal right to protect the identity of sources. However, journalists are obliged to disclose a source on request of either a court or a prosecutor. A proposal submitted by an MP in 2000 to remove the provision was rejected.

Cases of libel and defamation are rather rare. Those in power do not often use these provisions against journalists, as court procedures are slow and court decisions appear to have favoured the interests of the press over the interests of those suing.

In 1998, the State Real Estate Agency sued an independent office of investigative journalism for not paying office rent. Journalists had published a series of articles about corruption in the leadership of the agency, which later led to a dismissal of the director and a criminal investigation against him. At the same time, the journalism office was renting space in a house owned by the Estate Agency. The court froze all accounts of the media organisation, and they were forced to establish a new enterprise in order to conduct their daily business. The case was later won by the journalists. This case is not typical, however.

---

[104] Howard Jarvis, *2000 World Press Freedom Review*,
<http://www.freemedia.at/wpfr/latvia.htm>, (last accessed 30 April 2001).

[105] IJNet, *Latvia: Press Overview*, <http://www.ijnet.org/Profile/CEENIS/Latvia/media.html>, (last accessed 30 April 2001).

Interference by publishers and media owners in the editorial activities of journalists can be a problem, as no publications have internal rules to define editorial freedom or the relationship between advertising and editorial departments.[106]

9.2 Access to information

Latvia was one of the first countries in the region to pass a Freedom of Information Act in October 1998.[107] The Act gives any individual the right to access information from State administrative and local government institutions. Authorities must reply to requests for information within 15 days.

The Act lays down exceptions to the right of access. "Restricted information" is defined as information that:

- has been granted such status by law;

- is intended and specified for internal use by an institution;

- concerns trade secrets;

- concerns the private life of natural persons; or

- is related to certifications, examinations, submitted projects, invitations to tender and other assessment processes of a similar nature.

Authorities may not charge for information with the exception of the actual cost of copies. The author of information or the manager of an institution has the right to apply to information the status of restricted access, but must indicate the justification for doing so provided under the Act or by other acts. In August 1999, the Government adopted Procedures Governing the Release of Information at the Disposal of National Administrative Institutions.

Applicants may appeal refusals to provide information to the superior of the institution concerned, and thereafter to the courts.

Research carried out by Delna (TI Latvia) in October 1999[108] indicated that the impact of the Act had been disappointing at that time. Participants in the research sent

---

[106] Results of Information Access and Media Relationship project carried out by the Independent Bureau of Research and Information, 1995–1997.

[107] The Constitution also gives citizen the right to address questions to State or local government institutions and to receive a materially responsive reply.

[108] TI Latvia, *2000 Annual Report,* <http://www.delna.lv>, (last accessed 2 September 2002).

requests to 300 institutions for information accessible under the law, and obtained the following results:

- When requests were submitted in writing, a response was received in approximately 80 percent of cases, but three-quarters of the responses were negative.

- After a repeated request (usually submitted with legal arguments) satisfactory answers were provided in approximately 50 percent of cases.

- The courts were found to be the least accessible institutions, with only one of district courts providing information on case decisions.

- The research revealed widespread ignorance of the Act among State institutions, while arbitrary classifications of information as confidential were routine.

On the other hand, representatives of Delna believe that in the four years since the Act came into force, general acceptance by public institutions of their duty to provide information has increased, though State institutions are generally more ready to provide information than municipal institutions.

The main problem remaining in this area is a lack of systematic implementation of the Act across all State institutions. From January 2002 one official at the Data Protection Inspectorate has been responsible for overseeing practical implementation of the Act.

9.3 Broadcasting regulation

The licensing and functioning of Latvian television and radio is regulated by the National Television and Radio Board. All parties in Parliament appoint the nine-member Board for a term of four years, but any political party can have no more than three representatives on the Board. The terms of individual members expire alternately, ensuring relative continuity. The structure of the Board has not created any problems with impartiality, despite the highly political nature of the appointment process. Several times in recent years members of parties in the governing coalition failed to be appointed, reflecting a struggle for power within the Government.

The legal status of State broadcasting (Latvian Radio and Television) has not yet been solved, and both institutions are financed directly from the State budget. The Board has prepared draft laws to introduce licence payments for TV and radio, turning them into public broadcasting companies, but the proposal was rejected by the Parliament, as it is generally an unpopular move.

Public TV and Radio are generally regarded as relatively independent. For example, during the municipal elections, both public radio and TV, especially news programmes, were considered to be free from political bias. The recent competition for a new director for National TV (see Section 6.4) was regarded as highly transparent, despite coming elections.

9.4 Corruption in the media

In the Spring of 2001, several newspapers signed up to a new Code of Ethics, adding to four or five already-existing codes in other media. The codes include avoidance of conflicts of interest.[109] However, research performed during the municipal election campaign by TI Latvia, the Soros Foundation Latvia and the National TV and Radio Board showed that several newspapers and TV stations did not follow rules of fair reporting, and particularly, noted a problem of "hidden advertising" on television.[110]

A major corruption scandal broke concerning the Director General of National TV in early 2002 after he signed agreements at the end of 2001 selling most of the stations' advertising time to a private media company for half its market value. The National TV and Radio Board dismissed him as a result.

The legal status, owners, subsidiaries, annual reports and balance sheets are available online from the Lursoft company at <http://www.lursoft.lv>, (last accessed 2 September 2002). The Lursoft Company also provides a list of the biggest media publishers, by number of publications. Latvia is one of the most progressive countries in Europe concerning access to information on media ownership: the database is searchable together with the Enterprise Register, making it possible to monitor the other business interests of individuals involved in the media.

9.5 Media and corruption

According to the *1998 World Press Freedom Review,* journalists "have begun to build a tradition of effective investigative journalism," forcing a number of officials with political or financial responsibilities to resign as a result of exposure of *(inter alia)* corruption.[111] However, the same review noted two years later that, "... Latvian journalists are still unprofessional in their approach to work."[112] A UNDP report on

---

[109] UNDP, *2000 Latvia Human Development Report,* p. 81.

[110] N. Ločmele, R. Berugs, *Slēptās reklāmas monitorings* [Monitoring of Hidden Advertising], TI Latvia, SFL, 2000.

[111] Rozitis, J. Ojars, *1998 World Press Freedom Review,*
<http://www.freemedia.at/archive97/latvia.htm>, (last accessed 30 April 2001).

[112] *2000 World Press Freedom Review.*

the political decision-making process stated that, "Media have a significant impact to formation of public policy, but there is still a lack of editorial independence and too little dependence on the readers and viewers."[113]

The mass media has played a major role in keeping corruption on the political agenda, especially since the Corruption Prevention Act came into effect in 1996. In 1997, media attention to corruption reached its peak, focusing particularly on breaches of the conflict of interest provisions of the new law (see Section 2.2). More than half of the newspaper articles that addressed corruption in 1996-1998 focused on breaches of the Corruption Prevention Act (see Table 5).[114] The biggest dailies continued covering corruption issues also after these scandals, and played an important part in underpinning perceptions of relatively high corruption.

Table 5: Corruption-related articles in the printed press by subject, 1996–1998

Topics	Total	Diena	NRA	Vakara Ziņas	Lauku Avīze	Panorama Latvii
Violation of the Corruption Prevention Act	247	135	70	23	11	7
Corruption cases among State officials	174	86	75	9	3	1
Biggest cases of mismanagement of State property	122	39	69	14	-	-
Corruption scandals abroad	18	15	-	-	-	3
Corruption Prevention Act	75	39	31	3	2	-
Corruption as a social and political issue	86	47	19	11	5	4
Topics indirectly related to corruption	27	7	17	1	2	-

Source: Delna (TI Latvia).

In 1999 and 2000, there were approximately 2-5 articles a day in the press mentioning corruption, according to Lursoft. Media attention has succeeded in stopping some projects, all by the Riga City Council. For example, media attention resulted in a criminal investigation into the director of the Riga Development Agency,[115] although this took two years.

---

[113] UNDP, *2000 Latvia Human Development Report,* p. 45.

[114] *Corruption Issue in Agenda Setting and Role of Media,* Delna, 1999, p. 13.

[115] TI Latvia, *Watchdogs,* p. 4.

10. RECOMMENDATIONS

The following recommendations have been highlighted as particularly important to Latvia. For additional recommendations applicable to candidate States generally, please see Part 5 of the Overview report.

1. Improve coordination of the activities of agencies fighting corruption, and ensure the Corruption Prevention Bureau enjoys the independence and resources necessary to carry out its extensive tasks.

2. Carry out an analysis of lobbying and "State capture" to determine the real extent of the problem, and introduce policy measures based on the analysis.

3. Implement meaningful judicial reform to ensure judicial independence, capacity and access to information.

4. Introduce standardised procedures for responding to requests filed under the Freedom of Information Act and impose these on institutions to which the Act applies.

Corruption and Anti-corruption Policy in Lithuania

Table of Contents

Corruption and Anti-corruption Policy in Lithuania

EXECUTIVE SUMMARY

As other international organisations have noted, the relative absence of reliable information, statistics or research represents a significant obstacle to investigation of levels of corruption in Lithuania. Surveys indicate that administrative corruption is a relatively serious problem. Although World Bank surveys indicate that "State capture" and high-level political corruption are relatively minor problems compared to other candidate countries, the public maintains high perceptions of political corruption at the levels of Government and Parliament. According to surveys the public regards the customs administration and law enforcement bodies as the most corrupt institutions, and experiences corruption most in contacts with the traffic police and in the healthcare system. Perceptions of corruption in the tax inspectorate, customs and public procurement are also high.

Since the early 1990s, Lithuania has put in place most of the components of an anti-corruption legislative framework, including comprehensive bribery legislation, conflict of interest and asset declaration provisions. Since 1997-98 in particular, there has been intensive progress on the anti-corruption front, especially through the creation of the Special Investigation Service in 1997 (the only truly independent anti-corruption agency in candidate countries), and the approval of a comprehensive National Anti-corruption Strategy in January 2002.

The concerns of the European Commission about corruption in Lithuania have been very important in the development of Lithuanian anti-corruption policy. The Commission has provided extensive assistance for the development of anti-corruption policy, especially for the development of the National Anti-corruption Strategy. Most of the important international anti-corruption conventions have either been ratified or are scheduled for ratification in the near future.

Although Lithuanian bribery legislation is not yet fully in line with the requirements of international conventions, legislation has been passed that will fill the remaining gaps – criminalising trading in influence, extending liability for bribery to legal entities and extending bribery provisions to cover foreign officials – when a new Code of Criminal Procedure comes into effect.

Lithuania has advanced and comprehensive legislation in place on conflict of interest, and provisions on declaration of assets and income that are so comprehensive that they theoretically apply to the entire population. Conflict of interest legislation is based on a case-by-case approach mandating avoidance and declaration of conflict of interest situations, rather than incompatibility provisions. Enforcement and implementation of the provisions has improved steadily since they were passed in 1997, and have been instrumental in the resignation of several ministers. An act to regulate lobbying is also in place, although its effectiveness is questionable.

A system of State financial control is in the process of being implemented, reflecting EU requirements. The effectiveness of the system in practice, in particular whether Parliament will use the findings of the State Control effectively, is impossible to judge at such an early stage of implementation.

Lithuania is alone among EU candidate countries in possessing a truly independent anti-corruption agency, the Special Investigation Service. Created in 1997, the SIS was granted full independence through a new Act in May 2000, and has detained a relatively high number of public officials.. Its activities may be hampered by unclear division of responsibilities between prosecutors and police, and poor quality of police investigations, however. Lithuania also established parliamentary ombudsmen in 1994.

The Lithuanian executive and civil service has undergone fundamental reform, partly due to the requirements of EU accession. Since the passage of the 1999 Civil Service Act, the Civil Service has been largely depoliticised. Administrative law provides citizens with channels for appealing against both the legality and substance of official actions, although citizens remain generally unaware of their rights. Civil servants are subject to restrictions on ancillary activities. A Code of Ethics is expected to be approved by the end of 2002, although its effectiveness may be limited by lack of consultation during its preparation. There is limited protection for whistleblowers. According to surveys administrative corruption is a serious problem; although specific evidence is limited, the most serious indications concern corruption in local government.

A number of public funds are not subject to scrutiny by the Lithuanian Parliament (Seimas), and are largely non-transparent, while the ability of the Parliament to use the findings of the State Control under a new Act on State Control remains to be seen. MPs are subject to conflict of interest provisions, and enforcement of these provisions and duties to declare assets and income has improved steadily. Immunity provisions currently in force may hamper investigation of criminal activities by MPs. Although only one MP has ever been convicted, public trust in the Parliament is extremely low.

Although the Lithuanian judiciary is independent in law and in practice, it is regarded as one of the most corrupt institutions, although there are signs that criminal proceedings against corrupt judges may be becoming more effective. An increasing backlog of cases increases the vulnerability of the system to corruption, while there is a lack of public control over both courts and prosecutors.

Lithuania has put in place a relatively advanced legal framework to regulate political party funding, including some State funding. However, State subsidies account for only a very small proportion of total party income, the formal nature of supervision of party finances allows parties to evade the legal provisions relatively easily, and party expenditures are believed to be significantly higher than officially declared. There is evidence of strong ties between parties and business groups, and the Special Investigation Service views corruption in party financing as a problem requiring further reform.

A relatively advanced system regulating public procurement exists in Lithuania. However, significant loopholes remain, provisions allowing for single source procurement are not sufficiently regulated, and there are no provisions to encourage ethics among procurement officials to blacklist corrupt companies. The system for appealing against procurement decisions is flawed, especially through the bearing of costs of appeals by the appealing parties. Corruption is regarded as a serious problem by the Special Investigation Service and the large majority of surveyed companies.

Corruption in several public services is a serious problem, particularly in the traffic police, customs department and the healthcare system. However, important steps have been taken to reduce corruption, particularly in the customs department. Business registration does not appear to be troubled seriously by corruption.

Lithuania enjoys one of the most liberal legal frameworks for the media in Europe, underpinned by deep cultural opposition to any interference in press freedom. Freedom of information legislation is in place, although its provisions have not yet been implemented adequately. While the media has been reasonably active in uncovering corruption, public broadcasting remains subject to strong political influence.

1. INTRODUCTION

Evidence on corruption in Lithuania suffers from a lack of clear criminal statistics and, at least until recently, research. Surveys indicate that administrative corruption is a relatively serious problem, but that "State capture" and high-level political corruption is a relatively minor problem compared to other candidate countries.

1.1 The data and perceptions

Criminal statistics

As GRECO notes in a recent evaluation of corruption and anti-corruption policy in Lithuania, "Although there are some indication[s] and estimations on the size of the [corruption] problem, there is a general lack of research, including data and official statistics…"[1] Table 1 shows prosecutions of corrupt acts and related criminal activities between 1997 and 2001. The only clear trend in the figures is a clear increase in prosecutions for passive bribery.

Table 1: Prosecutions under anti-corruption legislation, 1997–2001

Criminal Act	1997	1998	1999	2000	2001
Acceptance of a bribe (Article 282)	10	27	40	36	73
Bribing (Article 284)	1	6	11	2	9
Abuse of office (Article 285)	2	17	27	9	19
Acceptance of an undue payment (Article 283)	0	2	2	0	0
Total					

Source: Analytical-Methodological Division, Special Investigation Service.

According to statistics provided to GRECO by the General Prosecutor's Office, two-thirds of the 319 people prosecuted for corruption offences between 1995 and 1998 were police officers, 58 were customs officers and 39 local government employees.[2]

Surveys

International surveys of corruption indicate that corruption is a significant problem in Lithuania, but that it ranks among the least affected of EU candidate countries.

---

[1] GRECO, *Evaluation Report on Lithuania,* adopted by GRECO at the 8th Plenary Meeting, Strasbourg, 4-8 March 2002, p. 22.

[2] GRECO, *Evaluation Report on Lithuania,* p. 7.

- Lithuania ranked 38th in the Transparency International CPI in 2001 with a score of 4.8 (0 meaning most corrupt and ten least corrupt), an improvement from 4.1 in 2000 (43rd place) and 3.8 in 1999 (50th place).

- According to the *1999 Business Environment and Enterprise Performance Survey* carried out by the World Bank and the EBRD,[3] Lithuania ranked in the middle of a sample of 20 Central Eastern European countries but worse than any country except Romania in terms of administrative corruption, with an average of 2.8 percent of annual revenues spent on unofficial payments to public officials. Sixteen percent of firms said they pay six to ten percent of annual revenue in unofficial payments to officials, while five percent pay 11-15 percent and four percent pay 16-20 percent. On the other hand, Lithuania ranked favourably in reference to "State capture" (actions to influence the formation of laws and rules) with a rank of 1.7 out of a maximum of seven. Fifteen percent of firms said that sales of parliamentary votes have a significant or very significant impact on their activity, while 13 percent said private contributions to political parties have a significant or very significant impact on them.

According to the first comprehensive survey of corruption in Lithuania, carried out for PHARE in 1999, at least one-third of ordinary citizens and more than one half of businessmen had experienced corruption or bribery. PHARE concluded on the basis of its survey and report that a corruption prevention strategy should be developed.

The most detailed information about corruption to date is the *Map of Corruption in Lithuania: 2001* survey by the Lithuanian Chapter of Transparency International.[4] According to the results of the survey,

- Fifty-two percent of entrepreneurs believed that corruption had increased in the past five years, while 15 percent thought it had decreased. The figures for the general public were 52 percent and six percent respectively.

- Thirty-one percent of respondents spontaneously labelled corruption as the most important obstacle to business development – a dramatic increase from the results of similar questions in previous surveys (12 percent in 1994 and nine percent in 1997[5]). Twenty-four percent of entrepreneurs said that corruption is creating lots of obstacles for their business at the moment, and seven percent said it is creating major obstacles.

---

[3] See World Bank, Anti-corruption in Transition. *A contribution to the Policy Debate,* World Bank, 2000, pp. xvi–xvii.

[4] A. Dobryninas, L. Zilinskiene and R. Alisauskiene, *Map of Corruption in Lithuania: 2001,* Transparency International, Lithuanian Chapter, Vilnius 2001.

[5] Baltic Surveys, *Lithuania Private Enterprise Survey,* November 1994 and July 1997.

- Thirty-seven percent of entrepreneurs said they had had to bribe in the past five years: eight percent once, 18 percent two or three times, five percent four to nine times and six percent ten times or more.

- Sixty-three percent of the general public said they had had to bribe in the past five years: 14 percent once, 17 percent two or three times, four percent four to nine times and two percent ten times or more.

- Fifty-seven percent of entrepreneurs said they had been demanded or expected to give a bribe in the past five years: 12 percent once, nine percent four to nine times, and 12 percent ten times or more.

- Thirty-five percent of the general public said they had been demanded or expected to give a bribe in the past five years: 12 percent once, 15 percent two or three times, four percent four to nine times and four percent ten times or more.

- Thirty-seven percent of entrepreneurs said they had demanded or expected to give a bribe in the last twelve months, while 26 percent said they had had to bribe in the past twelve months.

One worrying result found in surveys by the VILMORUS agency was an increase in the percentage of respondents saying they or their family/friends had bribed, which rose from 23 percent in 1999 to 34 percent in 2002.[6]

1.2 Main loci of corruption

According to surveys conducted in 1999 and 2000 and TI's corruption review, the public regards the customs administration and law enforcement bodies as the most corrupt institutions. These findings are consistent with the results of the 2001 survey, the results of which are summarised in Tables 2, 3 and 4. The survey also reveals high perceptions of political corruption at the levels of Government and Parliament, and also that experiences of corruption are prevalent in contacts with the traffic police and the healthcare system.

---

[6] VILMORUS, Corruption Phenomenon in Lithuania: Inhabitants' Views & Experience, survey data provided by VILMORUS.

Table 2: Which spheres of life in Lithuania are most affected by corruption? (percentage of respondents, spontaneous answers)

Sphere	General public	Entrepeneurs
Justice (law enforcement, courts, prosecutors)	39	33
Governance and public administration	27	21
Healthcare	21	13
Politics (Parliament, political parties, President's Office)	16	6
Customs	14	18
Privatisation	6	10
Education	5	3
Oil, petroleum industries	4	9
Real estate and land ownership	3	2
Tax administration	3	3

Source: Map of Corruption in Lithuania: 2001, Transparency International Lithuania.

Table 3: Which institutions in Lithuania are most affected by corruption? (percentage of respondents, spontaneous answers)

Institution	General public	Entrepreneurs
Courts	20	19
Customs	18	24
Police	13	10
Government	13	9
Parliament	12	10
Healthcare institutions	12	5
Municipalities	4	7
Tax Inspectorate	3	9
Traffic Police	3	4
Universities, schools	3	1
Privatisation institutions	2	5
Ministries	-	4

Source: Map of Corruption in Lithuania: 2001, Transparency International Lithuania.

Table 4: Evaluations of selected institutions as "very corrupt"

Institution	General public	Entrepreneurs
Courts	49	52
Government	40	45
Parliament	39	44
Traffic Police	42	50
Border Police	38	42
Tax Police	37	42
Customs	58	66
Privatisation Agency	47	57
State Tobacco and Alcohol Control Service	30	33
State Medicines Control Service	24	39
Public Procurement Office	21	33
State Land Cadastre and Register	20	26

Source: Map of Corruption in Lithuania: 2001, Transparency International Lithuania.

According to the survey results, the general public had the most experience bribing traffic police (12 percent in the past five years), followed by local hospitals (12 percent), polyclinics (11 percent) and central hospitals (seven percent), with customs at five percent.

Entrepreneurs' responses to questions concerning their own experiences with bribery and knowledge of others' bribery indicated clearly that the worst affected institutions are the traffic police, customs and the tax inspectorate. Thirteen cent of entrepreneurs said their firm had bribed the traffic police in the last five years and 25 percent said their colleagues in other firms had done so. The figures for customs and the tax inspectorate were only slightly lower.

The results of a survey carried out by the VILMORUS survey agency in 2002 confirm these findings, but show a fall in the perception of "widespread corruption" in the health system since 1999 (from 64 percent to 53 percent), despite a large increase in the perception of such corruption among politicians (from 26 percent to 42 percent).[7]

GRECO cites representatives of the Investors' Forum, an organisation of foreign investors and companies, who describe the police, tax and customs authorities and public procurement procedures as "particularly surrounded by corruption."[8]

---

[7] VILMORUS, *Corruption Phenomenon in Lithuania.*

[8] GRECO, *Evaluation Report on Lithuania,* p. 6.

There are few other analyses of the loci of corruption in Lithuania. One exception is the *Annual Report* of the SIS. The European Commission's *2000 Regular Report* stated that corruption occurs mainly in the areas of public procurement and customs.[9] There is little evidence of corruption in privatisation in Lithuania, although charges were recently filed against several MPs who took part in the privatisation of the country's largest company, Mazeikiu Nafta, in 1998–1999.[10]

1.3 Government anti-corruption policy

Since the early 1990s, Lithuania has put in place most of the components of an anti-corruption legislative framework. Examples are the 1996 Act on Declaration of Property and Income of Residents, the 1997 Act on Adjustment of Public and Private Interests in the Public Service, the 1997 Act on Money Laundering, the 1999 Public Procurement Act, the 1997 Act on Control of the Financing of Political Campaigns and the 2000 Amendments to the Criminal Code (see individual sections of this report). Since 1997-98 in particular, there has been intensive progress on the anti-corruption front. The Special Investigation Service was created in 1997 and granted full independence in 2000 (see Section 2.5), while Parliament approved a National Anti-corruption Strategy in January 2002 (see below).

The National Anti-corruption Strategy is divided into three components: prevention, investigation of corruption-related offences, and education of the general public and mass media. The programme is long-term (seven to ten years) with the possibility of modification every two years. It suggests introducing a normative definition of corruption into the Criminal Code that would read,

> … any conduct of a civil servant or an equivalent person, non-conforming with the authority entrusted or standards of conduct established, or promotion of such conduct for the benefit of oneself or third parties, to the detriment of the interests of other people and the state.[11]

---

[9] Cited in: Commission of the European Union, 2001 Regular Report from the Commission on Lithuania´s Progress towards Accession, October 2000, p. 20.

[10] R. Burstein, "Lithuanian Government Questioned on Privatisation Deal", *Transitions Online*, 3-9 September 2002, available at
<http://www.tol.cz/look/TOLnew/article.tpl?ldLanguage=1&ldPublication=4&NrIssue=37&NrSection=6&NrArticle=7068&ST_T1=wir&ST_PS1=8&ST_AS1=0&ST_LS1=0&ST_max=1>, (last accessed 12 September 2002).

[11] *Resolution no. IX-711 of the Seimas of the Republic of Lithuania Concerning the Approval of the National Anti-corruption Programme of the Republic of Lithuania*, 17 January 2002, p. 10.

The most important measures contained in the Strategy, along with deadlines, are listed in Table 5.

The Strategy is very comprehensive, covering:

1   Prevention – political corruption and conflict of interest, administrative corruption, tax and customs authorities, public procurement and privatisation, healthcare, law enforcement and judicial bodies, international cooperation, and public involvement in corruption prevention.

2   Increasing the effectiveness of investigations, ranging from limiting immunity provisions to improving information flows between the various institutions involved in investigation and prosecution.

3   Education, including introducing anti-corruption components into secondary and higher education curricula.

The Strategy is one of the most comprehensive anti-corruption strategies formulated by any EU candidate country, and criticism is more likely to concern problems of implementation than the Strategy itself. GRECO has levelled only one basic concern over the Strategy, namely that the current institutional set-up, under which the Special Investigation Service plays a coordinating role for all three planks of the strategy, appears to have encouraged a repressive bias in anti-corruption efforts to date. GRECO recommends the establishment of a separate body to coordinate the strategy with greater emphasis on prevention.[12]

In addition, GRECO recommended in particular that greater effort be made to carry out detailed research on corruption in particular institutions, so that anti-corruption policy be built on "a reliable assessment of the prevailing situation."[13] On 10 May 2001, the Parliament of the Republic of Lithuania adopted a resolution, "On Corruption Fighting," which, among other tasks, commissioned the Government to arrange research on Lithuania's annual corruption level on the basis of international expertise, and to publish its findings of this research.

---

[12]   GRECO, *Evaluation Report on Lithuania,* p. 28.

[13]   GRECO, *Evaluation Report on Lithuania,* p. 22.

Table 5: The National Anti-corruption Strategy (selected measures)

Measure	Implementation period	Fulfilled?
Draft laws on political party funding, e.g. to prohibit funding by legal entities, establish legal responsibility for indirect/covert sponsorship, personal accountability of party treasurer for party accounts	Q3 2002	under implementation
Draft laws limiting MPs from being local councillors, and councillors/governors from being managers of companies in same district	Q3 2002	not yet
Draft Code of Ethics for lobbying, improve lobbying legislation	Q2 2002	under implementation
Reform to limit possibilities of corruption in legislative process and screen legislation from perspective of corruption	Q2 2002	under implementation
Amending Parliament Resolution to encourage implementation of decisions of Chief Institutional Ethics Commission and ensure publicity of decisions		under implementation
Reduce number of political appointments (positions of trust) in civil service	Q1 2002	fulfilled
Establish motivation-driven system of career development in civil service	Q1 2002	fulfilled
Develop Civil Servants' Code of Conduct	Q4 2002	under implementation
Develop anti-corruption training program for civil servants with legislation regulating attendance	Q2 2003	not yet
Development of sector anti-corruption programmes in all ministries and relevant State institutions	Q4 2002	under implementation
Draft new law on public procurement, *inter alia* to prevent changes in contracts *post hoc*, blacklist corrupt companies	Q1 2002	under implementation
Develop legislation to reduce impact of corruption on judicial and law enforcement bodies, increase openness and transparency.	Q4 2002	not yet
Draft law to ratify Council of Europe Civil Law Convention on Corruption	Q4 2002	not yet
Establish Advisory Council under the Special Investigation Service to represent wider strata of society in anti-corruption strategy	Q3 2002	under implementation
Remove judges' immunity in relation to administrative accountability, develop judges' code of ethics	Q1-3 2002	under implementation

Source: *Resolution no. IX-711 of the Seimas of the Republic of Lithuania concerning the Approval of the National Anti-corruption Program of the Republic of Lithuania,* 17 January 2002, pp. 28–53; Transparency International Lithuania.

Despite the steps achieved in the area of anti-corruption policy, events in July 2002 illustrate some of the problems of achieving political consensus on anti-corruption policy. A cross-party accord on prevention of crime and corruption signed on 17 July by eight political parties was rejected by two of the main opposition parties. The opposition parties denounced the accord as a popularity exercise prior to the Presidential elections, while the ruling coalition parties labelled the rejection as a failure to recognise Lithuania's national interests in its efforts to join the EU and NATO.[14]

1.4 The impact of the EU Accession Process

The concerns of the European Commission about corruption in Lithuania have been very important in the development of Lithuanian anti-corruption policy, and have been coupled with significant assistance. The response of the Government has been reflected in increasingly positive evaluations in the *Regular Reports*.

In its 1997 *Opinion on Lithuania's Application for Membership in the European Union*, the Commission called the fight against corruption an urgent matter. In the *1999 Regular Report* the Commission mentioned the fight against corruption and continued reform of the judiciary as the only two caveats to Lithuania's fulfilment of the Copenhagen criteria.[15] The *2000 Regular Report* identified corruption as a continuing "source of concern," and while applauding measures taken (especially the passage of the Act on the Special Investigation Service), it stressed the need to implement them effectively and approve the National Anti-corruption Strategy. The *2001 Regular Report* was even more positive, stating that, "Although there are still problems, there is evidence that Lithuania has improved its capacity in this domain. Administrative corruption, however, remains a concern."[16]

Reinforcing the fight against corruption in customs, upgrading law enforcement bodies to fight corruption, ratifying relevant conventions, and adopting a national anti-corruption strategy were short-term priorities of the *1999 Accession Partnership* (hereinafter *AP*), while streamlining the inter-agency structure for fighting corruption was a medium-term priority. The *2001 AP* included as priorities adoption and implementation of the National anti-corruption strategy and of a new Act on Corruption Prevention, completion and implementation of the Code of Ethics for Civil Servants and ratification of the relevant international conventions.

---

[14] "Social Democrats called for opposition parties to sign anti-corruption agreement," ELTA, July 22.

[15] Cited in: Commission, *2000 Regular Report*, p. 15.

[16] Commission, *2001 Regular Report*, p. 19.

At the same time, four PHARE projects were implemented or started in 2001. The most important of these was the twinning project "Support to the Lithuanian Government's Anti-corruption Commission," designed to assist the development of the National Anti-corruption Policy and implementation plan. This was considered successfully completed with Parliament's approval of the National Strategy. In 2001, a twinning project for "Establishment of a Group for the Investigation and Analysis of Economic Crime" was implemented with UK experts, focusing on the State Security Department. In December 2001, a twelve-month follow-up project to review the Strategy and its implementation began. At the same time a project on "Building Integrity and Raising Anti-corruption Awareness" was launched, focusing on the public and civil society organisations.[17]

Other actions carried out in 2000-2001 with regard to EU requirements include amendments to the Criminal Code passed in October 2000 (not yet in effect), and Amendments to the Act on State Control passed in April 2000 and December 2001, which gave the State Control the authority to audit the use of EU funds and removed its remaining coercive judicial powers.

Other international activities

Lithuania has also cooperated with the Council of Europe, OECD, World Bank and other international organisations. In particular, in May 2001 Lithuania became a member of GRECO, which completed its first evaluation in early 2002. Lithuania has also taken part in the OCTOPUS programmes organised by the European Commission and the Council of Europe.

2. INSTITUTIONS AND LEGISLATION

2.1 Anti-corruption legislation

Although Lithuanian bribery legislation is not yet fully in line with the requirements of international conventions, legislation has been passed that will fill the remaining gaps – criminalisation of trading in influence, liability of legal entities and coverage of foreign officials – when a new Code of Criminal Procedure comes into effect.

The 1996 Act on Procedure for Drafting Laws and Other Legal Rules stipulates that drafts of regulations governing economic relations should be assessed in terms of their likely effect on corruption. In 2001, the Prime Minister issued an instruction that

---

[17] Information provided by the EC Delegation to Lithuania.

every such draft should be discussed by the Government only after incorporating the comments and recommendations of the Advisor on Corruption and Customs Issues.[18]

In the area of corruption, the Lithuanian Criminal Code criminalises the following acts:

Acceptance of a bribe: applies to public officials or civil servants, punishable by imprisonment for up to five years or a fine and prohibition of certain activities for up to three years. If the bribe is of high value then the sentence can be up to ten years and prohibition of activities up to five years.

Active bribery ("subornation"): punishable by imprisonment of up to three years, correctional work for up to two years or a fine. If the bribe is of high value, the sentence may increase to five years' imprisonment. A person who has been compelled or provoked to give a bribe and informed law enforcement authorities before criminal proceedings were initiated is exempt from liability for active bribery.

Abuse of office: Intentional abuse of office by a public official or civil servant in interests contrary to those of his position, or an act carried out for personal gain or interest or causing substantial damage to the interests of the State and/or other persons is punishable by imprisonment for up to four years and a fine, or a fine and prohibition of certain activities for up to five years. If the act satisfied both criteria (against interests of office and causing substantial damage), the sentence is three to five years' imprisonment and a prohibition for up to five years.

The definition of an official in the Criminal Code is very broad, covering a person working in the civil service as defined by the Civil Service Act, plus any other person who, when working in State or municipal authorities or institutions, judicial law enforcement, State Control or supervisory institutions or institutions equivalent to them, performs functions representing the State or holds administrative powers. In addition, any person working in a State, non-governmental or private institution or engaging in professional activities with similar powers of public administration is considered equivalent to a civil servant or official (with the exception of persons performing menial or technical tasks).[19]

The Criminal Code also provides for active bribery (commercial bribery) and passive bribery (acceptance of an undue advantage) in the private sector. However, there have been a negligible number of prosecutions under these provisions (see Section 1.1).

---

[18] For example, in 2001, an analysis by the Special Investigation Service of the draft Act on Gambling approved by the Parliament revealed corruption-prone elements of the law. The President vetoed the law and sent it back to the Parliament for improvement.

[19] Criminal Code, Article 290.

In October 2000 the Parliament passed a new Criminal Code that will come into force when a new Code of Criminal Procedure, Code of Execution of Punishment and Code of Administrative Offences are adopted, which is expected in 2003. To the existing provisions, the Code adds criminal liability for trading in influence, liability of legal entities for corruption offences and extends the concept of civil servant to include officials of international public organisations and foreign States.

2.2 Conflict of interest legislation and asset monitoring

Lithuania has advanced and comprehensive legislation on conflict of interest in place, and provisions on declaration of assets and income that are so comprehensive that they theoretically apply to the entire population. Enforcement and implementation of the provisions has improved steadily since they were passed in 1997, and have been instrumental in the resignation of several senior politicians.

The Act on Adjustment of Public and Private Interests

Conflict of interest is regulated mainly by the 1997 Act on the Adjustment of Public and Private Interests in the Public Service.[20] The Act applies to politicians, public servants at all levels as defined by the Act on Public Servants, and other persons who perform the functions of a representative of public authority or have administrative powers vested in them when holding public offices in the institutions of central or local administration, or in judicial, law enforcement, State Control and supervision institutions, or in any comparable institution. These officials are duty-bound to avoid situations of conflict of interest, defined as a situation where an official, when discharging his duties or carrying out instructions, is obliged to make a decision or participate in decision-making or carry out instructions relating to his private interests. The Act regulates this issue in some detail, in particular:

- Officials may not participate or influence in any way decisions that could lead to a conflict of interest situation, and must notify their superiors of any such conflict of interest situation in advance and not participate. This provision is not applicable to the President of the Republic, MPs, judges, prosecutors, investigators, persons conducting an inquiry or other officials for whom the conflict of interest issue is dealt with in the specific laws regulating their post.

- Officials may not represent the State, municipality or institutions thereof if this causes a conflict of interest when dealing with natural or legal persons from

---

[20] Act no. VIII-371 On the Adjustment of Public and Private Interests in the Public Service, July 1997.

whom they, close relatives, or other persons related to them receive any kind of income; or when dealing with any undertaking in which their close relatives or persons related to them own over ten percent of the authorised capital or shares.

- Officials may not use their duties, authority or names in order to influence another person to make a decision that would directly or indirectly result in the emergence of a conflict of interest situation; or use or allow information obtained in the course of official duties to be used in a manner and scope other than that specified.

- Persons in central or local public service may not directly or indirectly accept gifts or services the provision of which was directly or indirectly connected with the performance of official duties. Gifts with a value exceeding €29.3 or gifts from one source exceeding a value of €147 in one year must be declared within one month and attached to the official's Declaration of Private Interests (see below).

- After leaving public service, for a period of one year officials may not be employed by any company with which their offices came into direct contact in a supervisory or controlling capacity. Officials must notify their superior of any job offer that might lead to a conflict of interest situation, and notify immediately in writing the acceptance of any job offer.

- For a period of one year after leaving service officials, or an undertaking in which they, close relatives or family members hold a stake of over ten percent or are employed in the management or audit institutions, may not enter into contracts with the institution or seek individual privileges provided by the institution. This does not apply to contracts awarded by public tender whose value does not exceed €2,930 per year.

- For a period of one year officials may not represent any natural or legal person before the institution in which they were employed, except as attorneys.

The 1999 Civil Service Act also lays down a number of incompatibility and conflict of interest provisions for civil servants (see Section 3.3).

Officials violating conflict of interest provisions may be dismissed, reduced in rank or exposed to official penalties defined by the Civil Service Act. Ministers may be impeached by the Parliament.

Declarations

The Act on Adjustment of Public and Private Interests also requires all officials covered by the law to submit annual Declarations of Private Interests and of Property and Income for the previous calendar year by 1 March each year and additional declarations in case their circumstances change. Candidates for public office must make declarations for the period from the beginning of the calendar year to the moment they take office.

These declarations must contain comprehensive information on all income and assets according to the individual's tax return, gifts over €29.3, interests and ownership conditions of the individual or relatives that could cause a conflict of interest situation and travel paid for by other persons.

The declarations of private interests are filed with the head of the institution, while declarations of income and assets are filed with the National Revenue Service (tax authority). The declaration of private interests also includes a copy of the declaration of income and assets. The requirements to present these declarations are reiterated also in the 1999 Act on Public Service and 1996 Act on Declaration of Property and Income of Residents. Under the National Anti-corruption Strategy, the Government plans to extend the latter Act to cover all residents of Lithuania.

The President of the Republic and the heads of central or local administration institutions specified by the Chief Official Ethics Commission must file declarations to the Commission. The declarations may be verified against tax returns, while the Chief Official Ethics Commission may verify the information submitted on external interests.

The declarations of assets and income of the President, ministers, other heads of central institutions and their deputies and a wide range of other senior officials (for example, country governors, senior officials of the State Control and of the Customs and Tax Inspectorate) are published in the *Official Gazette*. The private interest declarations of these officials are also public.

Monitoring

The Chief Official Ethics Commission (COEC), the key institution for monitoring adherence to the conflict of interest provisions and the veracity of declarations of interests, is a legal entity responsible to the Parliament. The Commission is composed of five persons of whom one each is appointed by the President, Speaker of the Parliament, Prime Minister, Chairman of the Supreme Court and President of the Lithuanian Bar Association. The Commission may initiate investigations on the basis of any information and, after analysing data submitted, provides recommendations for action to a court (since conflict of interest is subject to administrative liability) or to the institution concerned. The Commission is not only a controlling body but is also responsible for providing consultation and instruction to MPs, although according to MPs it has not fulfilled this role.[21]

The Act seems to have been applied and enforced with increasing efficiency. In 2000 and 2001, two ministers had to resign partly as the result of the Commission's work,

---

[21] OSI Roundtable Discussion, Vilnius, 8 March 2002. *Explanatory note: OSI held a roundtable meeting to invite critique of the present Report in draft form. Experts present included representatives of the Government, international organisations, and civil society organisations. References to this meeting should not be understood as an endorsement of any particular point of view by any one participant.*

and a number of municipal officials were fined. In late 2001, the Ethics Commission issued warnings to a number of MPs because of conflict of interest situations.

The Act on Lobbyist Activity

The COEC also monitors adherence to the Act on Lobbyist Activity, which was adopted in June 2000 and has been in force since 1 January 2001. The Act describes lobbing activity, lobbyists, and their possible clients and forbids entities from lobbying unless they are officially registered as lobbyists. The Act also contains some conflict of interest provisions concerning those who are lobbied similar to the provisions in the Act on Adjustment of Public and Private Interests.

Under the Code of Administrative Violations, public officials who violate the provisions of the Act may be held administratively liable and fined 500-1,000 Litas (€144-289). Repeated violations are punishable by a fine of 1,000-2,000 Litas (€289-578) or removal from office.

As of May 2002, there were six registered lobbyists (five individuals and one company), and a National Association of Lobbyists. There is no evidence that the Act has been effective in preventing illicit lobbying.[22]

2.3 Control and audit

Reflecting EU requirements, a three-tier system of financial control is being implemented in Lithuania: State Control (reorganised on a new basis in 1990 and most recently reformed in March 2002), municipal control (established in 1994), and internal audit structures of the State sector (established in 2000).

State Control

The State Control (SC) is an independent audit institution under the Constitution and Act on State Control. The Auditor-General is appointed by the President of the Republic on the Parliament's recommendation for a period of five years. Persons who were members of the Government or elected leaders of the central organisation of a national political party within the past three years may not be nominated. The Parliament sets and approves the budget of the SC, which is not in line with best international practice.

The SC audits: State budget implementation; use of State funds; management, use and disposal of State property; the budget of the State Social Insurance Fund; the budget of

---

[22] Information provided by Aleksandras Dobryninas, Chairman of the Board, Transparency International Lithuania.

the Compulsory Health Insurance Fund; and use by recipients of EU funds. It may also audit municipal budgets and management and disposal of municipal property.

The SC reports its findings to the Parliament annually. Although the law does not mandate publication of the reports, most findings are published on the SC's website.

In 1999, the SC started conducting performance audits, and in 2000 began implementing methods of programme auditing. In 2000, SIGMA experts positively evaluated the contribution of the SC, although SIGMA experts continue to regard the concept of financial control (audit) applied in Lithuania as close to an outdated "culture of control." As a result, the new Act on State Control passed in December 2001 removed the SC's powers to fine officials, leaving it with standard powers for a supreme audit institution: the SC may recommend to audited institutions that individuals be held liable, that funds be returned to the budget, or may refer findings to law enforcement authorities. The Prosecutor's office received 30 cases in 2000 and 12 between January and October of 2001.[23]

Since these changes to the Act came into effect in March 2002, it is not yet clear how enforcement of SC recommendations will work once the Parliamentary Budget Committee takes over the SC's previous enforcement role.

In 2000, the Auditor-General approved a new Code of Professional Ethics of State Control Officers.

In 1999-2001, the President of the Republic filed some inquiries to the SC concerning certain privatisation transactions and improper use of budgetary funds. The SC found serious infringements in privatisation of the energy sector, which led to the revision of privatisation procedures by the Government. In particular, the SC objected repeatedly to a deal reached to resolve a €52m debt owed by Belarus to the Lithuanian national electricity company. In April 2001, the Government agreed to sell the debt to a Russian company, Vanguard, which agreed to pay back the debt over ten years. The SC objected partly on the grounds of conflicts of interest concerning individuals who played roles both in the companies that caused the debt problems and in Vanguard.[24]

Internal audit

Following a February 2000 Government resolution, internal audit services have been formed in all ministries, and almost all other State institutions and local authorities.

---

[23] GRECO, *Evaluation Report on Lithuania,* p. 20.

[24] The Government subsequently decided to sell part of the debt to two companies, Vanguard and the Lithuanian agricultural company Dzeirana. See Economist Intelligence Unit, *Lithuania Country Report,* October 2001, p. 22; interview with Romualdas Čepaitis, Senior Auditor, State Control, 7 March 2002.

The *2001 Regular Report* noted progress in this area: in September 2001, the Government aligned internal audit standards with international audit standards, and in October of the same year, a Central Harmonising Department at the Ministry of Finance was formed to develop harmonised control and audit methodology.

On the other hand, the EC noted that,

> [T]he legal basis for the system of Public Internal financial Control has been improved but is far from fully operational. Substantial efforts will have to be made in order to introduce internal audit structures and to strengthen capacity in line with EC requirements...[25]

2.4 Anti-corruption agencies

The Special Investigation Service

The most important specialised institution in the fight against corruption is the Special Investigation Service (hereinafter SIS), established by the Government in February 1997. In May 2000, the Act on the Special Investigation Service was adopted, which made the SIS independent of the executive. As the GRECO evaluation put it, this "paved the way for strengthening anti-corruption efforts in Lithuania."[26] The SIS is the body responsible for coordinating the National Anti-corruption Strategy, detecting and preventing corruption offences and ensuring coordination of anti-corruption measures both among State institutions and between them and society.

The Director of the SIS is appointed for five years by the President upon the Parliament's consent. The SIS is accountable to the President and Parliament, and is required by law to submit reports to the President and Chairperson of the Parliament on the results of its activities and recommendations for improving its activities. These reports are not public. State authorities and institutions, political parties, public organisations and movements are explicitly prohibited from interfering in SIS activities. Moreover, investigation departments of the SIS are responsible in specific investigations to the Prosecution Office, and not even the SIS Director can interfere in their activities.

Statistics on SIS's activities display a lack of clarity that is also apparent in Lithuanian criminal statistics on corruption. Between 1997–2000, SIS detained 337 public officials. According to information submitted to GRECO evaluators, SIS had disclosed 523 corruption-related crimes up to October 2001.[27] It is not clear what relation these statistics have to the statistics presented in Section 1.1. More importantly, it is not clear

---

[25] Commission, *2001 Regular Report,* p. 84.

[26] GRECO, *Evaluation Report on Lithuania,* p. 8.

[27] GRECO, *Evaluation Report on Lithuania,* p. 9.

if information on final convictions is available at all. GRECO noted that SIS has suffered problems because of inadequate means of measuring corruption, shown by the lack of statistics in particular.[28]

The SIS has improved its relations with the public substantially since 1997. Its executive officers regularly hold public meetings in different locations, and individuals may contact the SIS via a 24-hour "hotline." However, its central function is clearly investigative, and GRECO has questioned the wisdom of making SIS additionally responsible for wider aspects of anti-corruption policy, particularly prevention (see Section 1.3).

The EU has been cooperating with the SIS since its establishment, particularly on the development of the National Anti-corruption Strategy (see Section 1.4).

The Police and Prosecution Offices

Corruption cases not submitted to SIS are dealt with by the Organised Crime and Corruption Investigation Department of the Prosecutor General's Office. The Department was formed in 2001 through the reorganisation of the Organised Crime and Corruption Investigation (OCCI) Units at district prosecution offices. A PHARE programme to develop the Department's capacities is described in Section 1.4.

Within the police, corruption cases fall under the responsibility of the Organised Crime Investigation Service of the Criminal Police. Courts complain about the poor quality of police investigations into corruption.[29] Moreover, GRECO noted a lack of clarity in the division of functions between police investigators and prosecutors during pre-trial investigations.[30]

Money laundering

The 1997 Act on Prevention of Money Laundering established money laundering as a specific offence applying to both natural and legal entities. Under the Act, all financial institutions and notaries are obliged to inform the Financial Intelligence Unit of the Tax Police (FIU) of any transaction they suspect may be related to money laundering, within three working days of the transaction being documented. Financial institutions must also report any transaction exceeding Lts 50,000 or the equivalent in a foreign currency (approx. €14,667). All notifications must include the identity of the client.

---

[28] GRECO, *Evaluation Report on Lithuania,* p. 9.

[29] GRECO, *Evaluation Report on Lithuania,* p. 17.

[30] GRECO, *Evaluation Report on Lithuania,* p. 16.

In the *2001 Regular Report*, the European Commission noted that implementation of the anti-money laundering measures should be improved and the independence of the FIU ensured.[31]

In addition to these investigation institutions, the State Security Department (the State intelligence agency) also plays an important role in fighting corruption, in particular by assisting other institutions through its provision of information and data processing capabilities.

In February 2001, all law enforcement agencies signed an Agreement on Cooperation of Subjects of Operational Activities and Coordination of Operational Activities. The Agreement established uniform procedures for cooperating in investigations and exchanging and transmitting information.

The Parliamentary Anti-corruption Commission

The Commission was established in October 2001 as the successor to the previous Commis for the Investigation of Economic Crimes (established in 1993). The Commission analyses crimes involving corruption, hears report of various institutions on their measures against corruption and submits proposals to institutions, the Government and the Parliament.

2.5 Ombudsman

Parliamentary ombudsmen and ombudswomen were first established in 1994; by early 2002 there were five. They are appointed for four-year terms and can be dismissed only by a majority vote of all members of Parliament.

Ombudsmen and ombudswomen review complaints of the public regarding alleged abuse of office and bureaucracy of officials in the executive, control and audit, municipal, military institutions and their equivalents. They may not investigate the activities of the President, MPs, the Government as a collective body, judges, criminal investigation and prosecution proceedings or court decisions.

Having reviewed a complaint, ombudsmen/ombudswomen may:

- refer the matter to investigatory bodies if criminal actions are suspected;
- bring an action before a court to remove officials or pursue compensation for persons who have suffered as a result of official actions;
- recommend that an institution or official change or overturn decisions;

---

[31] Commission, *2001 Regular Report*, p. 46.

- impose disciplinary penalties to officials;

- reimburse moral or material loss incurred by a person due to infringements of officials;

- draw official attention to infringements and problems in official behaviour and recommend corrective measures;

- report to the Parliament or President on infringements of ministers or other officials accountable to them.

The ombudsmen and ombudswomen report annually to the Parliament, publish an annual activity report and quarterly information bulletins, provide information to the media on their activities and cases of abuse of office or mistreatment by officials.

According to a representative of the Lithuania Centre for Human Rights, the ombudsmen play a positive preventative role, but their impact is weakened by the fact that their recommendations are not always enforced.[32]

3. EXECUTIVE BRANCH AND CIVIL SERVICE

The Lithuanian civil service has undergone fundamental reform, partly as a result of the requirements of EU accession. Strengthening the capacity of the public administration has been an accession priority since the EU's *Opinion on Lithuania's Application for Membership in the European Union*, which referred to the insufficient administrative capability of Lithuania to fulfil tasks of governance and public administration.[33] The Commission has mentioned this same problem in every subsequent *Regular Report.*

Reform of the public administration has been strongly influenced by accession requirements, ranging from changes to the legal framework to increased training of civil servants.[34] The most important laws passed to this effect have been the Government Act,

---

[32] Conversations with Elvyra Baltutyte, Lithuanian Centre for Human Rights, 23 July 2002.

[33] Commission, *Opinion on Lithuania's Application for Membership in the European Union,* July 1997, p. 47.

[34] Lithuanian legislation now provides that at least three percent of public budgets assigned for civil servant salaries should be assigned to training. A strategy to train civil servants for EU membership was developed in 1998 with the Finnish Institute of Public Administration, and the Lithuanian Institute of Public Administration (LIPA) was established in 1999. The Institute currently runs five international projects, four of which are directly related to and/or financed by the EU. In the autumn of 2000, the Lithuanian Institute of Public Administration started a two-year "Civil Service Training and Twinning Project" with the Danish Institute of Public Administration and the Finnish Management Institute.

Civil Service Act and Act on Local Governments. Since the passage of the 1999 Civil Service Act, the civil service has been largely de-politicised. Under Lithuanian administrative law citizens may appeal to administrative courts against both the legality and substance of official actions, although citizens are generally not aware of their rights in this area. Civil servants are subject to restrictions on ancillary activities, and a Code of Ethics is under preparation by the Government. There is limited protection for whistleblowers.

3.1 Structure and legislative framework

The civil service is formally de-politicised. Under the 1999 Civil Service Act, which satisfies all EU requirements, almost all civil servants must be recruited by open public competition, and may be dismissed only for violations of law, failures to meet necessary professional qualifications, retirement, disease or temporary transfer to a different position. These provisions do not apply to "civil servants of political (personal confidence)," which in the State administration means ministers, deputy ministers and department directors, who are political appointments without security of tenure.

Under the Act, civil servants are protected from being forced to take any actions or decisions for political interests in excess of their powers.[35] Civil servants may be members of political parties or organisations, but may only engage in political activities when off duty. Public officials and civil servants must be recruited by means of competitive selection.

These provisions appear to function reasonably well in practice: for example, after the change of Government following the 2000 parliamentary elections, there were no widespread personnel changes in the civil service. Despite this, the National Anti-corruption Strategy contains a commitment to decrease the number of "positions of trust" (political appointments) in order to achieve a "reduction of reshuffles in the public service following changes in political power."[36]

The Act is being implemented in phases and will come into full effect in 2005. As the *2001 Regular Report* noted, progress has been made in implementing the new framework, for example through the creation of a new ranking and remuneration system in 2000, although the Commission still regards remuneration rates as unattractive.[37]

---

[35] For example, civil servants may refuse to take such actions and require a written order, and in such situations responsibility for such actions rests with the superior.

[36] Resolution of the Seimas on National Anti-corruption Strategy, p. 29.

[37] Commission, *2001 Regular Report,* p. 17.

Immunity

The Prime Minister and members of the Government enjoy the same degree of immunity as MPs (see Section 4.4). Immunity from criminal prosecution may be lifted by the Parliament.

3.2 Administrative procedure and redress

Under the Act on Administrative Proceedings, individuals may apply with a claim (petition) concerning the legality or reasonableness of an official act first to a higher-ranked officer of the same institution or another superior institution. Appeals may then be lodged with the Commission for Administrative Disputes, which must deal with them within 14 days, and thereafter to an administrative court. Administrative courts began functioning in July 1999, and may judge both the legality and validity of administrative decisions.[38]

However, neither the Commission nor the courts may judge acts by the President, Parliament, MPs, Prime Minister, the Government as a collective body, ombudsmen and ombudswomen, judges, prosecutors, interrogators and investigators related to law enforcement or case investigation.

According to the Head of the Commission for Administrative Disputes, although the legislative framework for resolving administrative disputes is in place, citizens are insufficiently aware of their rights of appeal.[39]

3.3 Conflict of interest and asset monitoring

In addition to the conflict of interest and asset monitoring provisions described in Section 2.2, the Act on Public Service dictates that civil servants may not in particular:

- be members of or receive remuneration from management bodies of enterprises or non-profit organisations unless this is specifically provided for by law;

- enter into contracts on behalf of their institution or an agency with private enterprises of which they are owners or partners;

- represent the interests of their country or foreign enterprises, other institutions or agencies, or travel abroad at the expense of a private company;

---

[38] Act on Jurisdiction of Administrative Cases; Act on the Commission of Administrative Disputes.

[39] Conversation with Adolfas Gilys, Head of Commission for Administrative Disputes, 23 July 2002.

- work in any capacity in a private institution or enterprise or receive a salary other than their official salary.

The Act on Public Service also reiterates the duty to submit declarations of private interests, property and income.

3.4 Internal control mechanisms

In October 2000, the Government adopted Rules of Imposing Disciplinary Sanctions upon Civil Servants, which establish a procedure for imposing disciplinary sanctions on civil servants for misconduct in office.

3.5 Interaction with the public

The Act on Public Service specifies that institutions of public administration should take advice from organisations and persons representing the public interest when making decisions related to the public's common legal interests and important to a significant portion of the population.

Freedom of information provisions are covered in Section 9.2. There appear to be problems with access to information for citizens, due to poor implementation of relevant legal provisions.

In 2000, the Government approved the Regulation for Servicing Visitors in State and Municipal Authorities based on the "one window" principle. According to the regulation, procedures should be designed so that individuals have their affairs handled in one visit to a State authority, and if this is impossible, the authority shall be in charge of the further handling of this issue and appoint staff members to take the necessary action.

As of March 2002, there was no comprehensive code of ethics for civil servants apart from a few partial codes that have not been effective due to lack of implementation. In March 2001, a multi-institutional working group set up by the Parliament drafted a set of principles of ethics for politicians and public officials as a basis for drafting a Code of Ethics of Public Servants. Under the National Anti-corruption Strategy, the Code should be approved by the end of 2002. The concerns of GRECO about the "top-down" approach to preparing codes of ethics in Lithuanian law enforcement agencies might also apply here. GRECO expressed its opinion that, "[C]odes of ethics, focusing on prevention of corruption, should be developed rather by the staff to increase the feeling of "ownership" among public officials over such codes."[40]

---

[40] GRECO, *Evaluation Report on Lithuania,* p. 24.

Complaints

The public may report corrupt actions and infringements of law to the Chief Institutional Ethics Commission, SC, ombudsmen and ombudswomen of local governments and Parliament, and the Commission of Economic Crime Investigation of the Parliament.

There are no special rules to define procedures for encouraging or protecting whistleblowers. Under the Civil Service Act, civil servants are obliged without delay to notify their superiors of tasks or instructions that they deem illegal, and the provision protecting civil servants against illegal instructions by superiors (see above) is also relevant.

3.6 Corruption

Between 1997 and 2001, several ministers, vice-ministers and other senior executive officials were removed or forced to resign as a result of conflicts of interests. For example, in 2001, the former Minister of Economy resigned after travelling to Moscow at the expense of a private local company for a meeting with Gazprom. The local company was interested in buying part of the Lithuanian gas distribution network. After the media exposed the incident, the Chief Institutional Ethics Commission declared that the Minister had violated the Act on Adjustment of Public and Private Interests, leading to his resignation. The Minister of Transportation in the same Government also resigned after revelations concerning the allocation of contracts by the ministry to a company where his wife owned a majority.[41] In 2001, a candidate for the position of the Chairman of the State Social Insurance Fund was charged with abuse of office and forgery of documents.

From 1997 to October 2001, SIS detected 563 public officials suspected of crimes against the public service. In 2000, 98 persons were charged with corruption, and 113 between January and October 2001.[42]

Corruption at the local government level may be a more serious problem than in central government institutions. In November 2001, a major scandal broke in Vilnius surrounding negotiations between the City and the French company Dalkia to manage the Vilnius central heating system. The mayor of Vilnius accused MPs from the Lithuanian National Progress Party of threatening to shut the company out of negotiations with the municipality unless it "supported them financially." Dalkia's representative in Lithuania also said the company was subject to attempted extortion. The Mayor provided tapes of telephone conversations to the State Security Service. The Service subsequently handed

---

[41] Comments at OSI Roundtable Discussion, Vilnius, 8 March 2002; interview with Arturas Račas, Editor-in-Chief, Business Desk, Baltic News Service, 7 March 2002.

[42] GRECO, *Evaluation Report on Lithuania*, p. 9.

over the case to the SIS after claiming that the tapes did not provide sufficient evidence for charges to be brought. At the end of December 2001, the Prosecutor General issued a statement that the contract between Dalkia and the municipality violated the Public Procurement Act, Competition Act and Civil Code. The scandal did not appear to have been investigated any further as of July 2002, and the contract with Dalkia was signed.

Table 6: Perceptions of the public and entrepreneurs of selected ministries as "very corrupt," 2001 (percent of respondents)

Ministry	General public	Entrepreneurs
Justice	30	37
Health	26	33
Interior	26	36
Economy	242	34
Finance	22	25
Agriculture	17	24
Social Security and Labour	17	18
Education and Science	16	15
Transport	15	21
National Defence	13	17
Foreign Affairs	12	15
Environment	7	13
Culture	6	7

Source: *Map of Corruption in Lithuania: 2001,* Transparency International Lithuania.

4. LEGISLATURE

4.1 Elections

Elections in Lithuania are free and fair. Elections are organised and supervised by an independent Supreme Election Commission and local commissions of electoral districts. Voting is also supervised by observers appointed by individual political parties.[43] A few members of local commissions have been prosecuted for procedural

---

[43] In the 2000 parliamentary elections, for example, a very close result in one electoral district was reversed when a liberal candidate appealed a narrow victory by a social democratic candidate. The ballot-papers were recalculated and victory awarded to the appealing candidate. However, the decision of the electoral district was appealed to the Supreme Election Commission, which after recounting established that the social democrat won the election by one vote.

infringements during elections, although investigations concluded that these infringements did not affect the election results.

4.2 Budget and control mechanisms

The State budget is subject to approval by the Parliament. However, a number of State funds are not included in the budget, such as the Social Insurance Fund and the Mandatory Health Insurance Fund and Occupancy Fund, nor are receipts from privatisation. The activities of these funds are non-transparent and lack scrutiny, although the SC can audit the Social Insurance and Health funds.

Budget control mechanisms are discussed in Section 2.4. The main question surrounding State audit is whether the Parliament will effectively take over the SC's role of imposing sanctions for violations of budget rules or other illegal actions.

4.3 Conflict of interest and asset monitoring

In addition to the conflict of interest and asset monitoring provisions covered in Section 2.2, the Statute of the Parliament requires MPs to avoid conflicts of interest and defines rules of conduct for members in case of possible conflicts of interest. These rules prohibit MPs from participation in drafting a decision or consideration of an issue which might involve their private interests, and require that they inform the Parliament and Ethics Procedural Commission and Chairperson of the Parliament of such private interests and abstain from other lobbying activities.

The Ethics and Procedural Commission of the Parliament reviews applications and inquiries concerning MPs' compliance with the Act on Lobbying and the Act on the Adjustment of Public and Private Interests in the Public Service. The Chief Institutional Ethics Commission (CIEC) also monitors adherence of MPs to these laws and may require the Ethics and Procedural Commission to reconsider its decisions. The CIEC informs the Parliament about infringements and has warned a number of MPs about their possible infringement of these acts.

In 1999, an independent audit company inspected the property and income declarations of MPs (including ministers) for 1996, 1997 and 1998. The audit disclosed a number of minor infringements of the Act on Reporting Residents' Property. As a result, the State Tax Inspectorate instructed approximately one third of MPs to correct or supplement their declarations.

After the 2000 elections, nearly one-third of MPs entered politics directly from the business sector. This has resulted in a rapid increase in the activities of the Ethics and

Procedural Commission, which received more applications and complaints in the first three months of its activities than the previous Commission received in an entire year. The Code of Ethics being prepared for public officials will also apply to MPs.

4.4 Immunity

MPs enjoy immunity from criminal prosecution, which may be removed only by impeachment. Initiatives for lifting immunity are the responsibility of the Prosecutor General, after which the Parliament either begins preliminary actions for impeachment proceedings, or forms a commission to consider whether impeachment proceedings should take place. Immunity may be lifted by a vote supported by a simple majority of all MPs, while impeachment requires a three-fifths majority.

Although the immunity provisions are in line with Council of Europe recommendations, GRECO criticised the fact that one person's immunity might have to be lifted several times within a single criminal proceeding. For instance, immunity would have to be lifted not only in order to open criminal proceedings, but also to carry out subsequent coercive measures. [44] According to information provided to GRECO, immunity has been lifted only once since the beginning of the 1990s, for one MP who was convicted in 1998 for attempted fraud.

4.5 Corruption

Public trust in the Parliament is extremely low at around four percent – lower than in any other EU candidate country. However apart from the case mentioned above, there have been no public cases of corruption involving MPs. The only significant scandal involving the Parliament concerned the acquisition by MPs of land for apartments at low prices in a luxurious quarter of Vilnius.

5. JUDICIARY

The Lithuanian judiciary is independent in law and in practice. However, it is ranked in surveys as one of the country's most corrupt institutions, although there are signs that criminal proceedings against corrupt judges may be becoming more effective. An increasing backlog of cases increases the vulnerability of the system to corruption, while

---

[44] GRECO, *Evaluation Report on Lithuania,* p. 22.

there is a lack of public control over both courts and prosecutors and possible concerns stemming from the hierarchical nature of the prosecution system.

5.1 Legislative framework

Courts and judges in Lithuania are independent.[45] Judges enjoy the same immunity provisions as MPs and other functionaries covered by immunity provisions (see Section 4.4). There is significant concern among law enforcement officials and other experts that judges may be excessively shielded from scrutiny.[46]

Judges are subject to the provisions on declaration of assets, income and private interests described in Section 2.2. In addition, under the Act on Courts, judges may not be appointed to courts where their spouses or former spouses, children, parents, siblings or cousins hold office. Persons involved in court proceedings (judges, clerks, specialists, experts and interpreters/translators) may not participate in case hearings if they are or might directly or indirectly have an interest in the outcome of the proceedings, or if there are any other circumstances raising doubts about their impartiality. If a judge is a person appearing before or participating in a court process and the case is within the jurisdiction of the court where the judge or close relatives holds or held office, the case must be heard by a different court.

In 1998, the general meeting of judges approved a Judicial Code of Ethics. This Code specifies that a judge should not yield to influence by other authorities, Government institutions, officials, mass media, the public or individuals. Under the Code, a judge may not accept any gifts or other signs of benevolence or receive credits or other services, if they are provided with the aim of influencing a proceeding.

In its evaluation report, GRECO noted three important reservations about the Lithuanian judiciary. One concerned the serious backlog of cases. This backlog is also a concern of the European Commission, which noted that despite an increase in the number of judges, the number of criminal cases under consideration increased from 5,878 to 6,421 from the end of 1999 to the end of 2000.[47] Their second reservation concerned an apparent lack of public control over the judiciary, specifically the lack of

---

[45] The legal framework for the judiciary is described in detail in an OSI report on judicial independence in Lithuania. EU Accession Monitoring Program, *Monitoring the EU Accession: Judicial Independence,* Open Society Institute, Budapest 2001, pp. 267–306.

[46] Comments at OSI Roundtable Discussion, Vilnius, 8 March 2002.

[47] Commission, *2001 Regular Report,* p. 19.

an institutional system of external control.[48] The third reservation regards not judges, but the Prosecutor General's Office. The Lithuanian prosecution system remains strictly hierarchical; the Prosecutor General retains sweeping powers to influence prosecutors' decisions in individual cases, and could overrule a decision to prosecute, casting doubts on the foundations of prosecutors' independence.[49]

5.2 Corruption

As Section 1.1 shows clearly, the Lithuanian judiciary is regarded as one of the most corrupt institutions in the country. In 1999, the Lithuanian Institute of Philosophy and Sociology surveyed public opinion on trust of courts in Lithuania. Thirty-one percent of respondents cited bribery and corruption as the primary reason for their mistrust in courts.

Between 1997 and 2000, two judges were accused of bribery and subjected to criminal proceedings. One of the cases proved to be a test case for the use of *agent provocateurs*, which was introduced by the Act on Operative Actions. The judge was lured by SIS agents, and the Vilnius District Court applied to the Constitutional Court to decide whether such actions infringed on the Constitution. The Court decided that such techniques do not infringe on the Constitution when they are used to investigate latent crimes or crimes dangerous to the public. The proceedings resulted in the judge's conviction and confiscation of his property.

6. POLITICAL PARTY FINANCE

Lithuania has put in place a relatively advanced legal framework to regulate political party funding, including some State funding. However, State subsidies account for only a very small proportion of total party income. Moreover, supervision of party finances appears to be largely formal, and parties can get around the legal provisions relatively easily. Party expenditures are believed to be significantly higher than officially declared, and there is evidence of strong ties between parties and business groups. The Special Investigation Service views corruption in party financing as a problem requiring further reform.

---

[48] GRECO, *Evaluation Report on Lithuania,* p. 25. According to officials at the General Prosecutor's Office, Department of Organised Crime and Corruption Fighting and Special Investigation Service, Lithuanian courts and judges tend to block effective prosecution of judges or other law enforcement officers for corruption or similar offences.

[49] GRECO, *Evaluation Report on Lithuania,* p. 25.

6.1 Legislative framework

Political party finances are regulated by the Act on Political Parties and Political Organisations, the 1999 Act on the Funding of Political Parties and Political Organisations, and the 1997 Act on the Control of Political Campaign Funding. The latter two acts were drafted after consultation with experts from EU countries. The President of Lithuania submitted amendments to the funding law to the Parliament in 2001, based on documents and recommendations of the EU to reinforce transparency and control of party finance.

Parties are entitled to the following sources of finance:

Party funds: These include membership dues, other voluntary contributions from members, interest from bank deposits, income from publishing, income from property, income from political and cultural events and other non profit-seeking activities.

Donations: Donations are defined broadly as monetary contributions or other contributions to electoral campaign activities with monetary value.

- Parties may receive donations from Lithuanian legal entities where the State or municipality owns no more than 50 percent of capital, permanent residents of the Republic of Lithuania, citizens of the Republic of Lithuania residing in foreign countries and branches of Lithuanian political parties and organisations established in Lithuanian communities.

- Parties may not receive donations from charity or support funds, religious organisations, trade unions, companies owned by foreign capital registered in Lithuania, executive and municipal authorities of foreign countries or legal and natural persons of foreign countries.

- Parties may not establish special funds to support a party or organisation.

- Parties may not receive anonymous donations exceeding €29.3, nor receive funding through third parties; all donations and gifts over €29.3 must be recorded in party financial accounts.

- Funds or gifts donated by one individual or legal entity may not exceed 500 times the official minimal subsistence level in any one year.

- All donations exceeding €293 must be submitted to the party's bank account, not in cash.

- Donations to the party and donations to individual campaigns must be kept in separate accounts, and every donation and gift received during a political campaign must be recorded in donation sheets issued by the Supreme Election Commission.

- Contributions from illegal funding sources are to be returned to the donor or handed over to the State.

Subsidies from the State budget. Parties and organisations that received at least three percent of the vote in elections to the Parliament or local councils are entitled to a State subsidy. The subsidy allocated to each political party or organisation is determined by the Supreme Election Commission each year. Total subsidies may not exceed 0.1 percent of the official State budget. The total amount allocated to subsidies for 2002 is €141,680, distributed among the parties as shown in Table 7. Subsidies are allocated on a six-monthly basis. According to press reports, parties' total declared income was many times higher than the State subsidy. For example, the Homeland Union declared €176,880 in income, the Social Democrats €202,693 and the Union of Liberals €152,533; the Conservatives declared €72,453 in donations from individuals, while the Union of Liberals declared €102,667 donated by businesses.[50]

Table 7: Distribution of State subsidies among Lithuanian parties, 2001

Political party/organisation	Total annual subsidy, 2001 (€)
New Union (Social Liberals)	33,222
Lithuanian Union of Liberals	30,725
Democratic Labour Party of Lithuania	21,434
Lithuanian Social Democratic Party	17,861
Homeland Union (Lithuanian Conservatives)	16,824
Lithuanian Peasants' Party	12,649
Lithuanian Union of the Centre	12,221
Lithuanian Christian Democratic Party	8,772
Total	153,708*

Note: Figures may not round because of summing of six-monthly subsidy.
Source: Supreme Election Committee.

Neither the Act on Political Parties and Political Organisations nor the Act on Funding of Political Parties and Organisations regulate maximum party expenditures.

6.2 Control and supervision

Political parties and organisations must publish financial reports with information on income and sources of income as described above, and expenditures and purposes

---

[50] *Kauno diena,* 4 March 2002.

thereof. Initiators of and participants is a political campaign (parties, nominees, candidates to the nominees, non-registered nominees, initiators of referendums) should submit to the Supreme Election Commission two financial accounts on the donations and other funds and their use: a preliminary account ten days before voting and a final account 25 days after voting or the publishing of referendum results. The final accounts of political campaigns are published in the *Official Gazette*. Any person entitled to donate to political parties or any representative of the media has the right to see the reports at the Supreme Election Commission and to publish data from such accounts in the mass media.

If a party fails to submit financial reports, the Supreme Election Commission first issues a warning, and may then recommend to the Ministry of Finance the suspension of budget funding to the party unless it takes corrective measures within 60 days. Funding may be renewed only after all infringements have been resolved.

The SC monitors how political parties and organisations use funds from the State budget.

6.3 Party finance in practice

There is virtually no direct evidence of corrupt or suspicious funding of political parties, and there have been no major scandals. However, the largely formal nature of party funding regulations means that parties and sponsors can easily get around the law while limited of State funding creates incentives to maximise donations. SIS officials believe that corruption in party funding is a significant problem, and are pushing for new legislation to prohibit funding by legal entities entirely.[51]

Political scientists and other experts believe that several parties spent significantly more in the 2000 parliamentary and local elections than they declared, although the State Tax Inspectorate failed to detect any significant infringements. During the 2000 elections, some parties also took out loans, although this is prohibited by the Act on Control of Political Campaign Funding. The Homeland Union and Union of Liberals still owed money as of March 2002. The Social Democrats allegedly borrowed substantial sums of money from a company owned by the local manager of LUKOIL, towards which the current Prime Minister (a Social Democrat) is thought to be favourably inclined.

A number of local financial groups have had strong ties to one or more parties. A company that supported the Homeland Union (Conservatives) in the 1996 elections subsequently became the subject of media speculation for winning a number of public contracts. The Lithuanian Confederation of Industry is thought to have close ties to the Social Democrats; a fertiliser company owned by the President of the Confederation won

---

[51] Comments at OSI Roundtable Discussion, Vilnius, 8 March 2002.

a tender in the mid-1990's to buy some port facilities from the State and was subsequently allowed to delay payment. The Western Lithuanian Industrial and Financial Corporation, which was implicated in the scandal that led to the resignation of the former Minister of Economy (see Section 3.6), supported the Union of Liberals when it was in power before the 2000 elections, and after the elections supported the New Union (Social Liberals), now part of the governing coalition.[52]

7. PUBLIC PROCUREMENT

7.1 Legislative framework

Although public procurement legislation is relatively advanced, loopholes and problems with review procedures exist, and corruption is considered a significant problem.

The Public Procurement Act provides for five methods of procurement: open tender; restricted tender; competitive negotiations; request for quotations; and single source procurement. The Act applies to all institutions, enterprises and organisations performing public procurement from the budget or equivalent funds, when the value of a contract for goods or services exceeds €22,000, or €88,000 in the case of public works contracts; and all enterprises controlled by the State or local government and affiliated companies included in a Government-approved list, should the value of goods or services procured annually equal €528,000 or more, (€293,333 in the case of works contracts). The Public Procurement Office exists to coordinate and monitor the compliance of public procurement procedures with the Act.

Single source procurement is allowed only in the following circumstances:

- goods, works or services can be supplied (rendered) only by one supplier;

- there is an urgent need for goods, services or works due to unforeseeable extraordinary events;

- goods to be procured are manufactured only for the purpose of testing, experimental, scientific work or technical improvements;

- the procuring entity procured goods or services from a supplier (contractor) under a previous former contract and found that additional procurement is reasonable from the technical point of view of combination with the already

---

[52] Interview with Arturas Račas, Editor-in-Chief, Business Desk, Baltic News Service, 7 March 2002.

procured goods or services; in this case additional procurement should not exceed 30 percent of the value of the original contract;

- due to unexpected circumstances additional work or services are needed that were not included in the original contract, but without such work or services might not be completed;

- an open tender, restricted tender or competitive negotiations failed, because only a single bid was received.

When the value of a procurement exceeds €44,000, single source procurement requires the approval of the Government. However, regulation of single source procurement is insufficiently clear, and the mandatory approvals of the Government often turn out to be merely formal. SIS officials believe the Public Procurement Office should assess the terms and conditions of important procurements in advance, rather than reviewing them only after the fact as is currently the case, and that the names of officials who approve the terms of reference for tenders should be published.[53]

Public procurement regulations *are* public. All terms and conditions for public procurement and individual tenders are public and available. Preliminary announcements of tenders planned in a given year and tender invitations are published in the *Official Gazette*. The Public Procurement Office places information on tenders on the Internet.

Under the Public Procurement Act, tenders must be carried out according to the Methodology for Calculating Procurement Value, established and issued by the Public Procurement Office. If bidders offer unreasonably high or low prices to the procuring entity, the Public Procurement Commission (see below) should disallow all bids and receive consent from the Public Procurement Office to proceed with further negotiations and actions.

Procurement decisions are made by a Public Procurement Committee selected by the procuring entity, consisting of at least three individuals. The Act does not set special criteria for selecting Committee members, but all Committee members must sign a declaration that they will act impartially with regard to different bidders. Committee members and bidders may not provide information on the tender to third parties.

Tender decisions are published in the *Official Gazette* and communicated to other bidders within three days of signing the contract. Notification must include the winning price and rate of discount indicated in the contract. The procuring entity must report on the procedures of every procurement within ten days of signing the contract or completing the procurement procedures.

---

[53] OSI Roundtable Discussion, Vilnius, 8 March 2002.

There is no special code of ethics for public procurement officers nor any system for blacklisting companies who have acted corruptly in procurement.

The Programme of the Government for 2002 to 2004 includes amendments to procurement regulations to tighten procurement procedures, introduce mechanisms and procedures to discourage collusion and increase control of contract fulfilment. In addition, the Government plans to harmonise the Public Procurement Act with EU directives and requirements of the World Trade Organisation, and to establish a public procurement information system meeting EU standards and practice.

7.2 Review and audit

If a bidder believes that a procurement procedure infringed its rights, it may appeal to the procuring entity. If the reply does not satisfy the bidder it can lodge a complaint with the Public Procurement Office. Complaints there are reviewed by an *ad hoc* three-member Commission for the Examination of Complaints: one member is appointed by the bidder, one by the procuring entity and one appointed by the Office from a list of experts nominated by suppliers, procuring entities or the Government. Members of the Commission must sign an impartiality declaration and may not be in any relation with the supplier.

Finally, bidders can appeal to a court against the actions of the Public Procurement Office and decisions of the Independent Commission for Public Procurement Complaint Review. The Public Procurement Office may also appeal against suspicious transactions to the SC or law enforcement institutions for their investigation.

GRECO has criticised two aspects of the appeals system. Firstly, there is no mechanism by which the Office can remove unsuitable persons from the list of experts to sit on complaint commissions. Second, a bidder must pay a fee of €880 to appeal to the Office, and, if the complaint is found groundless, the full cost of the process as well.[54]

7.3 Corruption

According to experts, the media and a number of participants involved in public procurement, corruption in this area is very widespread. For example, SIS officials estimate on the basis of information supplied to them by companies that around ten percent of contract value is required on average in bribes.[55] According to TI's *Map of Corruption in*

---

[54] GRECO, *Evaluation Report on Lithuania,* p. 19.

[55] Comments at OSI Roundtable Discussion, Vilnius, 8 March 2002.

Lithuania: 2001 survey (see Section 1.1), 74 percent of entrepreneurs were of the opinion that the Public Procurement Office is somewhat or very corrupt, although this score is lower than the courts, Government, Parliament and several other State institutions and ministries.

8. PUBLIC SERVICES

8.1 Police

As the surveys detailed in Section 1.1 show, the police are regarded as one of the most corrupted institutions in Lithuania, especially the traffic police, and a large proportion of persons prosecuted for corruption have been police officers.

Internal investigation units have existed within the police since 1998 to supervise officers and combat illegal activities including corruption, while police officers receive more severe sentences for corrupt acts than ordinary citizens. However, one of the key factors contributing to police corruption is the combination of low pay with wide discretionary powers: for example, traffic police officers earn approximately €205, yet are authorised to issue cash fines of up to €1,466.[56]

8.2 Customs

The Customs Department is also perceived by the public as one of the most corrupt institutions in Lithuania (see Section 1.1). Yet the Customs Department has been implementing a number of reforms to combat smuggling and related corruption. PHARE assistance has been provided to help install a modern information system and customs declaration processing system. Customs offices and terminals are being provided with special equipment and facilities allowing for more effective control of customs officers' work, along with more operative and better inspection of customs. In 2000, an Intelligence and Analysis Unit was established, and the Customs Department signed a cooperation agreement with the SIS to fight customs crime. A new structure of the Department came into effect in July 2001, including a Division for Investigations in Office to investigate the illegal activities of customs officials.

---

[56] GRECO, *Evaluation Report on Lithuania*, p. 11.

In 1999, the Director of the Customs Department at the Ministry of Finance approved a Code of Ethics of Customs Officers, which includes explicit instructions to avoid conduct likely to be regarded as a request for a bribe.

8.3 Health

The Lithuanian healthcare system is regarded by the public as one of the most corrupt institutions, and on the basis of responses concerning actual experiences it is considered most corrupt, along with the traffic police (see Section 1). Staff members of healthcare institutions are not regarded as public officials and, thus, not subject to the provisions of the Act on the Adjustment of Public and Private Interests in the Public Service.

Low salaries underpin the persistence of bribery in the health system, along with a surviving tradition of "remuneration in advance" to medical staff, which is based on patients understanding that without a bribe, they will be treated worse or not at all.

One of the priorities under the PHARE 1995 programme was the development of the Primary Health Care Sector. A long-term PHARE Advisor was assigned to the Municipality Boards of Vilnius, Siauliai and Klaipeda regions for two years to assist with the preparation and implementation of a "Primary Health Care Plan" (PHC). The project was expanded under the 1997 PHARE programme.

8.4 Licensing and regulation

Although international organisations like the World Bank regard business conditions in Lithuania as similar to those in other Central and Eastern European countries and organisations have positively registered the country's efforts in the area of business liberalisation,[57] a PHARE-funded study carried out in 1999 to map the corruption situation and outline an anti-corruption strategy stated that, "[The] basic obstacles (causes) impeding business development are identical to the reasons inducing corruption."[58]

Corruption in business registration is not regarded as a problem. However, in certain sectors, barriers to entry may have been deliberately erected in laws regulating those

---

[57] For example, the Heritage Foundation improved Lithuania's ranking in its "Index of Economic Freedom" from 61 in 1999 to 44 in 2000 – the biggest change for any post communist country in that period. After several years of negotiations, on 1 June 2001, the Republic of Lithuania became an equal member of the WTO.

[58] PHARE, *Preliminary Assessment of Corruption in Lithuania and Preparation of Corruption Fighting Strategy Outline,* 1999, p. 41.

sectors, for example pharmaceuticals, [59] private medical practices, and the legal profession.[60]

9. ROLE OF THE MEDIA

The legal framework for the media in Lithuania is regarded by lawyers and journalists as one of the most liberal in Europe. According to various opinion polls, the mass media is the most trusted institution in Lithuanian society,[61] and despite certain attempts by representatives of State institutions to inflict "soft sanctions" on critical publications[62] there is a deeply ingrained cultural bias against interference in freedom of the press. Access to information is guaranteed by law, although the implementation in practice of freedom of information provisions has not yet been adequate. While the press has been relatively active in uncovering corruption, public broadcasting remains subject to strong political influence, and the activities of the media are still restricted by poor access to information and perhaps in some cases by intimidation.

9.1 Press freedom

In Lithuania, the media's freedom is guaranteed by the Constitution and the Act on Provision of Information to the Public. Under these laws, the professional work of journalists may be restricted only because of the need to defend the interests of the State and other individuals.

There are few restrictions on journalistic freedom and none that address coverage of corruption cases specifically. In addition to standard provisions on libel and slander, the Act on Provision of Information to the Public allows damages against journalists who violate the honour or dignity of an individual. In 1999-2000, a proposal by some MPs to raise the limit on compensation for violations of honour or dignity was

---

[59] See, for example, A. Semiene, "Milijardini vaistu versla lydi kysiai" [Bribery is part of a pharmaceutical business worth billions], *Respublika,* 7 March 2002.

[60] Interview with Arturas Račas, Editor-in-Chief, Business Desk, Baltic News Service, 7 March 2002.

[61] *Lietuvos rytas,* 19 May 2001, p. 7.

[62] For example, after anti-corruption articles were published by *Lietuvos Rytas* and *Respublika,* financial audits of the publications took place, along with withdrawal of official State advertisements.

rejected. However, in the Civil Code which came into force on 1 July 2002, there is no limit on compensation for moral damages.

9.2 Access to information

Under the Act on the Right to Obtain Information from Governmental and Municipal Offices, Governmental and municipal offices are obliged to answer written requests for information within 14 days (or one month in certain cases). Information may be withheld only if this is essential to protect a democratic society and is more important than the individual right to obtain information. Official information is free of charge, although institutions may charge a fee to cover service expenses (costs of searching for information, copying).

In cases of refusal to provide information, citizens may appeal to the court. The effectiveness of these norms was shown in 1999 by a journalist's successful lawsuit against the Minister of Health. On the other hand, no systematic and standard procedures by which authorities provide information are yet in place, and GRECO found that,

> There were indications that it is generally difficult for journalists and the public to have access to public documents, and that journalists needed informants to work effectively, due to limited access to public documents provided for in law and disloyal application of the law.[63]

9.3 Broadcasting regulation

Broadcasting activities are licensed and regulated by the Radio and Television Commission, except in the case of public television and radio (see below). Licensing procedures are clear. The Commission is accountable to the Parliament and consists of 12 members representing different public, cultural and scientific institutions. Members are nominated by the Parliament, President and professional journalist and cultural organisations. The composition of the Commission protects commercial radio and television broadcasters from executive interference, and there have been no official complaints about its activities.

National Radio and Television of Lithuania (NRTL) is governed by a Council consisting of 12 members representing various non-governmental cultural, academic and civic institutions and nominated by the President of Lithuania, Parliament, and non-governmental organisations. The Council is under the responsibility of the Parliamentary

---

[63] GRECO, *Evaluation Report on Lithuania,* pp. 5–6.

Committee on Education, Science and Culture. The Council elects the Director General of NRTL, and appoints and approves assistants by means of public tender.

Although the intention of this Act is to make NRTL independent of political forces, in practice all NRTL Councils have been politicised and Governmental institutions have tried either directly (by changing the composition of the Council) or indirectly (through financing policy) to influence NRNL's work. For example, one respected journalist was hired but, after investigating the property deals of some MPs, was effectively dismissed.

9.4 Corruption in the media

There is little evidence of direct bribery of journalists. According to media experts, however, problems exist in general with media and journalist ethics, which result in a number of practices that sometimes constitute corruption. These include influence by companies of editorial content through advertising pressure, extortion of advertising by the media through threats concerning editorial content, as well as some political pressure, especially on public media.[64] But this appears to be a largely uninvestigated area.

9.5 Media and corruption

Media coverage of corruption is dominated by the press, where coverage of corruption has steadily increased. Figure 1 below shows the number of articles on corruption in the main dailies between 1990 and 1997. Between January 1998 and November 2000, the biggest and most influential Lithuanian daily *Lietuvos Rytas* published around 13 articles per month on corruption.

---

[64] Information provided by Aleksandras Dobryninas, Chairman of the Board, Transparency International Lithuania.

Figure 1. Number of publications on crimes against civil service in Lithuania in main national newspapers during 1990–1997[65]

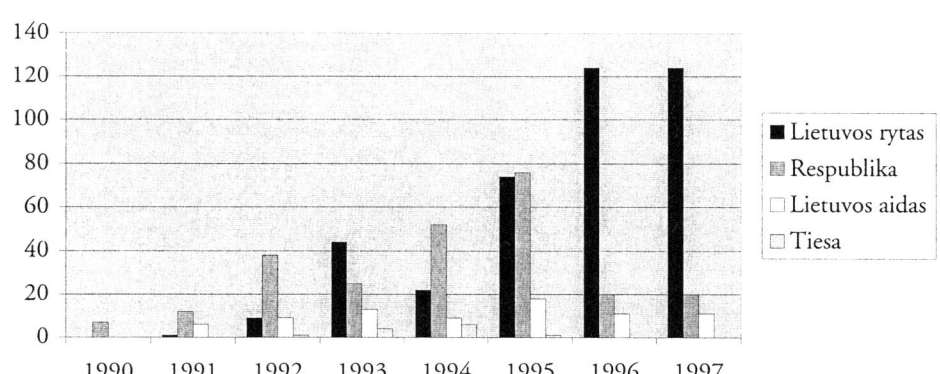

Source: Transparency International, 2001

The media has had a significant impact not only on the public but also on the Government. For example, a media investigation into conflicts of interest at the Governmental level forced the resignation of three members of the present Government, and influenced the creation of the Principles of Governmental Ethics and Code of Conduct for Governmental offices. The SIS cooperates with the media as a systematic part of its anti-corruption strategy.

10. RECOMMENDATIONS

The following recommendations have been highlighted as particularly important to Lithuania. For additional recommendations applicable to candidate States generally, please see Part 5 of the Overview report.

1   Ensure that complete statistics are available on criminal proceedings and convictions for corruption-related acts.

---

[65]   A. Dobryninas, "Corruption as a Public Matter: The Case of Mass Media," in: *Transparency International. The Anti-corruption Agenda in a New Decade: Defining Issues, Identifying Allies,* Transparency International, Berlin 2001, p. 73.

Corruption and Anti-corruption Policy in Poland

Table of Contents

OPEN SOCIETY INSTITUTE 2002

Corruption and Anti-corruption Policy in Poland

EXECUTIVE SUMMARY

Although Poland is not ranked poorly compared to other EU candidate countries in international indices of corruption, the evidence presented in this report suggests that corruption is at best not decreasing, and in a number of areas may be on the increase. There has been a marked increase in the number of corruption-related scandals involving ministers and other politicians in the past two or three years, as well as an increase in discussion of legislation and other measures to curb corruption. Although there have also been marked increases in convictions for corruption since 1998, the increase in scandals and the public profile of corruption has been the result of media activity rather than an increase in the effectiveness of institutions of prosecution and enforcement. Surveys indicate that corruption is most widespread in the healthcare system, judiciary, sub-national governments and central State administration. In addition, corruption appears to have been a more-or-less severe problem in privatisation, the activities of off-budget agencies, political party finance, the tax and customs administrations, while private sector corruption is thought to be growing rapidly.

Poland does not yet have a coordinated anti-corruption strategy, and the will of the Government to create one is doubtful. Since 1997 a number of legislative and other measures have been introduced against corruption, notably an Act on Access to Information, a new Electoral Act to tighten regulation of political party financing, and important changes to bribery legislation. However, none of the initiatives were introduced by the Government, which has failed even to discuss initiatives to formulate a national anti-corruption strategy, while political parties in the previous coalition rejected a proposal to create a central anti-corruption authority. The public debate on corruption is undermined by the prevalence of corruption as a political issue. Moreover, the growing support for the most populist of party leaders indicates that public opinion may be a destabilising factor in the creation of effective anti-corruption policy rather than a force encouraging such policy.

The European Commission has consistently regarded corruption as a serious problem in Poland and criticised the Government's insufficient efforts to tackle it. A number of the more important measures implemented by the Government have been more-or-less the result of EU pressure, notably amendments to public procurement legislation. The Commission has not provided any direct assistance for the creation of anti-corruption policy.

A number of gaps remain to be filled in Polish bribery laws in order to satisfy the requirements of international anti-corruption conventions. As of June 2002 legal entities were not criminally liable for bribery, bribery in the private sector was not criminalised, non-material benefits provided to third parties were not yet classifiable as bribes, and the definition of a public official remained insufficiently clear.

Senior officials are subject to incompatibility provisions to prevent abuse of conflicts of interest. These provisions are commonly violated. Other public officials may not hold ancillary employment without the agreement of superiors, but this agreement appears to be granted in most cases, especially at local government level. Parliamentarians are subject to limited restrictions on ancillary activities, which do not appear to function effectively in practice. Both senior officials and parliamentarians must also submit declarations of income and assets, although the provisions have been ineffective: the declarations cannot be verified effectively, violations are common, and the declarations of officials are not public.

Poland has made major progress towards putting in place a functioning system of State financial control. In particular, the Supreme Audit Chamber (NIK) is the most effective supreme audit institution of any EU candidate country and has contributed extensively to revealing corruption and the legislative and institutional defects facilitating corruption. On the other hand, the implementation of the NIK's findings remains unsatisfactory. Although internal audit is less well developed, new legislation in effect from 2002 represents a very important step towards creating independent internal audit bodies.

There are no specialised anti-corruption agencies, although special units exist within the police for fighting corruption. The ability of prosecution offices to fight corruption appears to be undermined by a lack of specialised capacity, as well as a lack of independence underpinned by the political nature of the office of Prosecutor-General. An office of the ombudsman has existed since 1987, although it does not appear to deal with corruption.

The Polish public administration has undergone several major reforms since 1990, especially through decentralisation and the passage of the Civil Service Act, which represents an important step towards a depoliticised administration. However, patronage remains a significant problem, and the current Government has regressed in this area. Bribery does not appear to be a very serious problem, at least not at the level of central Government, but there are serious problems with uncontrolled outsourcing of public administration activities.

A large proportion of Polish public spending is accounted for by State agencies whose budgets are not approved by the Polish House of Deputies (Sejm). By all accounts, these off-budget funds have been one of the main loci of high-level corruption, are one of the main loci of political party patronage (along with State-owned companies) and may have provided money to political parties. A major source of corruption remains a complete absence of regulation of lobbying, and there are a number of examples of suspicious ancillary activities of, or lobbying by, parliamentarians.

Courts are regarded in surveys as one of the most corrupt institutions in Poland, although direct evidence of corruption is largely anecdotal, and much of what is interpreted as judicial corruption may be only corruption of lawyers. Poor court organisation, burdensome procedures, long delays and (at least until 2002) poorly functioning disciplinary mechanisms have created a system that is vulnerable to corruption, although important changes to disciplinary proceedings came into effect recently. The European Commission has paid particular attention to corruption in the judiciary.

Until amendments to the Electoral Act came into effect in 2001, party funding was very weakly regulated and regarded as highly corrupt. However, new provisions may do a lot to reduce corruption, introducing State funding, setting ceilings on expenditure, banning corporate donations and giving a strong monitoring role to the Elections Commission. The strength of the new system was under test in early 2002 as the Commission found that several parties violated the law during the previous elections. Meanwhile, corruption has been regarded as widespread; in particular, a characteristic that seems specific to Poland among candidate countries has been the tendency of State-owned companies to provide money to parties in a disguised way or illegally.

Polish public procurement legislation is largely compatible with EC requirements, and changes to the law that came into effect in 1997 have done much to end the most flagrant corrupt practices. However, the Public Procurement Office appears unable to check enough procurements, and various sources indicate that corruption remains widespread. The biggest scandal of the present Government resulted from corruption in a public tender at the Ministry of Defence.

Corruption in a number of Polish public services may be very widespread. Corruption in the police is a serious problem, especially in the traffic police. A number of recently-established anti-corruption mechanisms may have helped to improve the situation with regard to corruption in the customs administration, which has long been regarded as a serious problem. The tax administration has been highly vulnerable to corruption due to wide discretion enjoyed by both central and local tax officials to grant tax breaks to companies, although the extent of such favours has fallen greatly since 1998. According to surveys, corruption is most widespread in the healthcare system, with informal payments so pervasive that they are not even hidden. Likewise, corruption in the education system appears to be a big problem. In both healthcare and education, corruption has been facilitated by the failure of the bribery law to cover doctors and teachers adequately. Finally, licensing and regulation in general appear to be subject to widespread corruption, although new legislation in 1999 liberalised licensing procedures significantly. Corruption is firmly established in business registration.

Freedom of speech is threatened to a limited extent by criminal sanctions against insulting public officials, although the impact of this in practice does not appear to be serious. An Act on Access to Public Information came into effect in 2001, although the impact of the law as of March 2002 appeared to have been limited. Broadcasting regulation is highly politicised, and Polish Television appears to lack any capacity to carry out independent investigative journalism as a result of political control. Despite these problems, the press in particular has been very active in uncovering corruption, and has prompted official action in a number of cases.

1. INTRODUCTION

Perceptions of the prevalence of corruption have grown quite rapidly in recent years, as corruption has become a prominent political issue. Surveys indicate that experience of bribery among the population is common. Although Poland is not ranked poorly compared to other EU candidate countries in international indices of corruption, the evidence presented in this report suggests that corruption is at best not decreasing, and in a number of areas may be on the increase.

1.1 The data and perceptions

The number of persons convicted under the relevant anti-corruption acts is shown in Table 1. The main elements of the anti-bribery framework have all been in place only since 1998, and trends are difficult to assess. There appears to have been an increase in convictions for giving bribes. The number of convictions is smaller – notably for acceptance of bribes – than in the Czech Republic or Hungary, relative to country size.

Table 1: Number of final convictions for corruption, 1993-2001[1]

Criminal Act	1993	1994	1995	1996	1997	1998*	1999	2000	2001**
Passive bribery	96	71	68	72	106	28	116	104	99
Active bribery						60	305	395	415
Traffic in influence							16	22	20
Harm to public or private interest by public functionary	34	30	30	46	62	25	57	59	100

Notes: * Statistics for 1998 are for the four months of September to December, as a new Criminal code came into effect in September 1998.
       ** Sentenced without legal validity (i.e. some cases may be appealed).
Source: Ministry of Justice, Poland.

---

[1] Passive bribery was covered by Article 239 of the Criminal Code until 1997, and by Article 228 from 1998. Article 229 sanctions active bribery. Article 230 sanctions traffic in influence in State or territorial self-government institution. Harming the public or private interest through violation of duties of a public official was covered by Article 246 until 1997, and by Article 231 from 1998.

Perceptions

Poland's position in the Transparency International Corruption Perceptions Index has remained stable since 1999 with a score of 4.2[2] in 1998 (44th place), 4.1 in 2000 (43rd place) and 4.1 in 2001 (44th place). According to the World Bank/EBRD 1999 Business Environment and Enterprise Performance Survey administrative corruption is a relatively minor problem in regional comparison, with firms saying they pay an average of 1.2 percent of annual revenues in bribes.[3] According to the World Bank's interpretation of the same survey, Poland does not suffer from a serious problem of "State capture," with a "capture economy index" of 12, similar to the best performing countries in the region.[4]

However, perceptions by the public of corruption among politicians have increased since the mid-1990'. The proportion of respondents in national surveys conducted by theS agency that considers corruption to a "very great problem" has increased steadily: 33 percent in 1991, 49 percent in 1992, 46 percent in 2000 and 68 percent in August 2001.[5] Moreover, according to the last survey 70 percent of respondents agreed that many top officials make improper profits – an increase from 50-60 percent over surveys in the previous five years.

In November 2000 a survey on bribery of 1,055 people was commissioned by the Batory Foundation's "Against Corruption" programme and the Institute of Public Affairs.[6] Fourteen percent of respondents declared they had given a bribe in the past three or four years – a slight reduction from very similar surveys carried out previously by CBOS (19 percent in July 1999, 20 percent in April 1997 and 16 percent in October 1993). Twenty-nine percent declared they know personally someone who takes bribes, while the percentage was higher among more professional and educated

---

[2] Scores range from 0 (highly corrupt) to 10 (least corrupt). Information from <http://www.transparency.org>, (last accessed 23 August 2002).

[3] J. Hellman, G. Jones and D. Kaufmann, "Seize the State, Seize the Day: State Capture, Corruption and Influence in Transition," Policy Research Working Paper 2444, World Bank Institute and EBRD, September 2000, p. 7.

[4] J. Hellman, G. Jones and D. Kaufmann, "Seize the State, Seize the Day: State Capture, Corruption and Influence in Transition," p. 9. The index is the average percentage of firms reporting they are affected by State capture (corruption in the formation of rules and laws) in various spheres.

[5] Twenty-four percent thought it was rare, one percent that it does not happen at all, and 14 percent found it difficult to answer. A. Grudniewicz, "Korupcja i afery korupcyjne w Polsce" [Corruption and Corruption Affairs in Poland], CBOS report no. 2554, 20 August 2001: survey made in August 2001 on a sample of 964 people.

[6] A. Kubiak, *Corruption in Everyday Experience: Report on Survey,* Institute of Public Affairs, Warsaw 2001.

groups and students. Experimental estimates by the same agency of the real number of people giving bribes indicate that the percentage may have been over 50 percent in the group examined. According to responses most bribes were of modest value: 23 percent were under €27 and only 11 percent exceeded €400. However, most of the larger bribes were given to doctors, indicating the seriousness of the corruption problem in that sector and raising concerns about its impact on the poor. Although 80 percent of respondents agreed that bribes are always and everywhere unethical, 42 percent considered giving bribes as justified in certain situations.

In 1998, a random sample of 101 deputies in the House of Deputies completed a questionnaire on their perceptions of corruption.[7] Eighteen percent of deputies answered that corruption is frequent or very frequent among politicians, 40 percent believed it is "medium," while 32 percent thought it is rare or very rare.

Although the surveys suggest strongly that corruption is a significant problem, they also appear to confirm the results of other surveys (for example of civil service clients; see Section 3.6) indicating that perceptions of corruption are significantly worse than citizens' real experience of corruption.[8]

1.2 Main loci of corruption

According to public opinion surveys, corruption is most widespread in the healthcare system, judiciary, sub-national governments and central State administration. Corruption appears to have been a pervasive problem in privatisation, the activities of off-budget agencies, political party finance and the tax and customs administrations, while private sector corruption is thought to be growing rapidly.

According to the 1999 CBOS public opinion survey mentioned above, 67 percent of respondents believed corruption is prevalent in the health service, followed by the judiciary (49 percent), territorial government administration (39 percent), central State administration (25 percent) and the police (23 percent). Parliamentary deputies most often pointed to customs officers (89 percent), followed by local politicians (63 percent), local government administration (53 percent), national public administration (50 percent), the police (46 percent) and national politicians (38 percent).[9]

---

[7] J. Kurczewski, *Poslowie a opinia publiczna* [Deputies and Public Opinion], Warsaw 1999.

[8] Specifically, "Korupcja w życiu publicznym" [Corruption in public life], CBOS report, November 1999.

[9] J. Kurczewski, *Poslowie a opinia publiczna* [Deputies and Public Opinion], Warsaw 1999.

A report on corruption produced by the Ministry of Interior and Administration in 2000 – based mostly on police data – suggested that corruption is most frequent in the following areas:[10]

- Insurance (falsification of policies, issuing policies for fictitious vehicles, registration of fictitious losses in traffic and in agriculture);

- public enterprises, especially in the energy, food and concrete sectors;

- national State and local self-government administration, especially in the course of issuing administrative decisions;

- the banking sector (cooperation of bank employees with organised criminal groups to violate banking regulations);

- the health service (issuing false certificates of sickness and entitlements to other benefits);

- privatisation and restitution;

- control and audit agencies, including in the tax administration, customs control and in commercial courts in cases of bankruptcy;

- public procurement.

The Supreme Audit Chamber (NIK) has uncovered substantial evidence of corruption, or at least malpractice, in the privatisation process in particular. The main findings relate to the absence of clear criteria or objectives of privatisations, (sometimes gross) undervaluation of assets,[11] disadvantageous contracts with privatisation consultants, and the absence of an independent verification system for valuations by advisers. NIK also issued a report in March 2000 on the risk of corruption, based on its own audits.

---

[10] "Działania podejmowane przez rząd w celu przeciwdziałania przestepczosci gospodarczej i korupcji" [Governmental Actions Against Economic Crime and Corruption], <http://www.kprm.gov.pl>, (last accessed 23 August 2002).

[11] See, e.g., NIK 1996 audit of the privatisation of Cementownia Ożarów S.A. [State Cenment Factory Ożarów]: "Zagrożenie korupcją w świetle kontroli NIK" [Danger of Corruption in Light of the NIK Audits], NIK, March 2000, annex 3, pp. 5–6, or NIK 1998 audit of the privatisation of Domy Towarowe Centrum [State Centrum Department Stores]: "Zagrożenie korupcją w świetle kontroli NIK" [Danger of Corruption in Light of the NIK Audits], NIK, March 2000, annex 2, pp. 2–5. In the latter case NIK stated that the Minister of State Treasury "ignored numerous signals, including in particular indications from the Supreme Chamber of Audit, pointing to the need to verify the conditions of the wrongly prepared contract." After its audit of the privatisation of Krajowa Agencja Wydawnicza [State National Publishing Agency] suspicions of corruption led NIK to notify the Prosecutor's Office.

The report identified the following areas as "most seriously threatened... by corruption:" privatisation, management of public property, activities of special purpose funds and agencies (off-budget funds, see Section 5.1), public procurement, quotas and licences, tax administration, customs, inspection bodies, the police, and funding scientific research. NIK also identified the following "corruption fostering mechanisms:" excessive powers of individual officials; excessive discretion enjoyed by civil servants; inadequate documentation and reporting of decision-making processes; weakness of internal controls; unequal access to information; lack of accountability, including the abuse of collegial decision-making structures; and failure to take specific anti-corruption steps, in particular the inadequacies of the regime for monitoring officials' asset declarations.[12]

The 1999 World Bank report, based on qualitative research and interviews, identified "high level corruption" (defined as corruption committed by high and elected officials including parliamentarians, ministers, prosecutors and judges) as the most serious corruption problem facing the country. The report also pinpointed as problem areas conflict of interest, political party finance, judicial and prosecution bodies, sub-national government, public procurement, privatisation, extra-budgetary funds, the customs and tax administrations, concessions and licences, and healthcare.[13]

Off-budget funds, which account for over one-third of both public revenue and spending in Poland, remain a key source of corruption in the political and administrative system. Polish political parties are widely regarded as having engaged in extensive corrupt practices throughout the 1990's, although there has never been a proven case. Parliamentarians alluded to these practices in general when interviewed,[14] and the extent of the problem was one of the main reasons for the passage of a new act on party finances (see Section 6.1). There is widespread agreement that corruption is a major problem in local government, especially after Poland's extensive decentralising reforms. Despite the passage of a law compatible with EU directives, the public procurement process remains prone to widespread corruption.

Regarding trends in corruption, the evidence collected for this report indicates that corruption is at best not increasing, although the trend varies according to location.

---

[12] Summary materials of 2000 report, "Danger of Corruption in Light of the NIK Audits, March 2000," provided to OSI, 19 March 2002.

[13] "Corruption in Poland: Review of Priority Areas and Proposals for Action, World Bank, Warsaw, 1999; for section on main areas of corruption in Poland see <http://www.worldbank.org.pl/ECA/Poland.nsf/ECADocByUnid/85256B560077051E852 56AA400741B32?Opendocument>, (last accessed 27 August 2002).

[14] J. Kurczewski, *Poslowie a opinia publiczna* [Deputies and Public Opinion], Warsaw 1999.

For example, while corruption in political party finance may be starting on a downward trend as a result of the introduction of more effective legislation, NIK officials believe that corruption is spreading rapidly in the private sector.

1.3 Government anti-corruption policy

Since 1997 (and in 1999 in particular), a number of legislative and other measures have been introduced against corruption[15] – notably an Act on Access to Information and a new Electoral Act to tighten regulation of political party financing. However, none of the initiatives were introduced by the Government, but were proposals by MPs. On the other hand, a proposed act to establish a Central Anti-corruption Office that was introduced by deputies from the governing AWS party in the 1997-2001 Parliament was rejected due to opposing votes from another party of the coalition and the then opposition SLD and PSL parties.

Poland does not yet have a coordinated anti-corruption strategy. In May 2000, the then Deputy Minister Leszek Balcerowicz initiated the creation of a working group by the Council of Ministers in order to prepare a report on sources of corruption and plan measures to eliminate them. The working group, chaired by a Deputy Minister of Finance, brought together deputy ministers from all the key ministries and central Government institutions; the group also referred to experts from the Supreme Chamber of Control, the World Bank, the Institute of Public Affairs, and the Stefan Batory Foundation's Anti-corruption Programme. The report suggested a number of amendments to draft legislation and other legislative initiatives that should be undertaken. It also proposed a number of specific measures with regard to the treasury administration, the customs services, the traffic police, healthcare, and the judiciary.

In August 2000, the Economic Committee of the Council of Ministers approved the results presented by the working group. However, the Government never discussed it, mainly as a result of the collapse at that time of the ruling coalition and specifically the departure of the Freedom Union (of which Balcerowicz was a member). While individual ministries, acting of their own accord, did put into practice some of the document's recommendations, the strategy never became an official policy paper, binding on the Government, nor was it fully implemented.

Another initiative that took place around the same time was the establishment, with World Bank support, of an Anti-corruption Working Group, composed of about 30

---

[15] See "Działania podejmowane przez rząd w celu przeciwdziałania przestepczosci gospodarczej i korupcji" [Governmental Actions Against Economic Crime and Corruption], <http://www.kprm.gov.pl>, (last accessed 23 August 2002).

people: politicians, deputies, State officials, researchers, NGO activists, trade union representatives, clergy and journalists. In May 2001, the Group published a document entitled Premises for a Strategy of Combating Corruption in Poland, proposing a number of somewhat general anti-corruption measures. Although four political parties responded formally to the initiative, the Group has not been able to interest any Government authorities in the initiative, even after the September 2001 elections.

The new Government, which came to power in September 2001, has not yet elaborated an anti-corruption programme, despite being elected on an anti-corruption platform. While the Anti-corruption Group coordinates the activities of the various branches and agencies falling under the Minister of Interior, confusion surrounds the creation and coordination of anti-corruption policy in most other State institutions.

Other important legislation passed in recent years includes:

- an Act on Counteracting the Introduction into Economic Circulation of Assets from Illegal or Undeclared Sources (2000);[16]

- amendments to the Public Procurement Act (2001);[17]

- an Act on Access to Public Administration (2001).[18]

Other important steps taken by the 1997-2001 Government were the establishment in 1998 of Interior Services in the police and border guards to prevent and investigate internal corruption, and the establishment in 1999 of a new Civil Service Corps aimed at implementing a fully professional civil service.

Corruption as a political issue

Paradoxically, a major problem facing efforts to tackle corruption in Poland appears to be its very prominence as a political issue. Corruption shot to prominence as an election issue in 2001 after the Government was hit by a series of scandals, and was used not only by the mainstream opposition but also by more radical parties, in particular Samoobrona (a highly populist party that has come close to inciting citizens to civil disobedience) and Prawo i Sprawiedliwość (Law & Justice). Under these circumstances, corruption is such a highly-politicised issue that the prospects of securing cross-party consensus on a systematic and focused anti-corruption strategy are very small.

---

[16] Act on Counteracting of Introduction into Economic Circulation Property Assets Coming from Illegal or Undeclared Sources, passed on 16 November 2000, in: *Law Journal 2000*, no. 116, item 1216.

[17] Act on Amendments to Law on Public Procurement, passed on 26 July 2001, in: *Law Journal 2001*, no. 113, item 1208.

[18] Act on Access to Public Information, passed on 6 September 2001, in: *Law Journal 2001*, no. 112, item 1198.

1.4 The impact of the EU Accession Process

The European Union has regularly cited corruption as an important problem in Poland and criticised the Government's insufficient efforts to tackle it:

- In 1998 it was pointed out that the statement in the EC *1998 Regular Report* – that the fight against corruption needs to be intensified – had not met with an adequate response "and little progress has been made on the establishment of a genuine anti-corruption policy."[19]

- Corruption continued to be "a source of serious concern" in the *1999 Regular Report*, according to which "Poland should address this serious problem. The implementation of the reform to the statutes of civil servants could provide an important element to remedying this problem."[20]

- The *2000 Regular Report* expresses the opinion that the available evidence "point[s] to a... series of deficiencies which create an environment in which corruption can flourish: excessive but poorly managed bureaucracy, insufficient controls, lack of transparency and a general lack of accountability."[21]

- In 2001, the Commission observed, with regard to corruption in Poland, that "there is a general perception that corruption is widespread. This is damaging both domestically and internationally."[22] The *2001 Regular Report* praised recent legislation (for example on money laundering) and the signing of the Council of Europe Civil Law Convention on Corruption, but added that "a sustained effort will be required to step up the fight against corruption both by the police and the border guard service."[23]

Although it is impossible to isolate the extent to which the EU accession process has been the motor behind anti-corruption measures, the attention paid to corruption by the Commission and its perception of corruption as a potential brake on the accession process has clearly been an important influence, shown by the adoption by the Government of many of the anti-corruption measures advocated by the Commission such as civil service reform[24] or legislation on access to public information.[25] One

---

[19] Commission of the European Union, *1998 Regular Report from the Commission on Poland's Progress towards Accession,* p. 11.

[20] Commission, *1999 Regular Report,* p. 15.

[21] Commission, *2000 Regular Report,* p. 18.

[22] Commission, *2001 Regular Report,* p. 21.

[23] Commission, *2001 Regular Report,* p. 21.

[24] Commission, *1998 Regular Report,* p. 11.

[25] Commission, *2000 Regular Report,* p. 18.

deputy of the Polish House of Deputies stated, with regard to the recently passed amendments procurement legislation, that, "The main purpose of the amendment is to make the law compatible with EU legislation, increase competition in the internal market and increase the transparency of proceedings by making access to information easier at each level of bargaining."

There have been no PHARE programmes to assist the development of anti-corruption policy in Poland.

2. INSTITUTIONS AND LEGISLATION

2.1 Anti-corruption legislation

Both giving and accepting a bribe are criminal offences under the Polish Penal Code. The Penal Code fulfils the requirements of international anti-corruption conventions, with the exception of the requirements of the Council of Europe Criminal Law Convention on Corruption to criminalise bribery in the private sector, introduce criminal liability of legal entities and criminalise the provision of non-material benefits to third parties. The definition of a public official remains somewhat unclear, although recent court decisions have somewhat clarified the situation.

- Acceptance of a bribe is punishable by six months to eight years imprisonment, and up to ten years if bribery was to secure an infringement of law. Public servants who accept material gains of considerable value or a promise thereof are subject to 2 to 12 years imprisonment.[26]

- Penalties for giving or offering a bribe are the same as for accepting a bribe.

Both active and passive bribery are limited in scope to acts which are either (respectively) directed towards or perpetrated by a "person who performs a public function." This is wider than the notion of a "public official," and includes any person who performs a function within the public sector and administers, disposes of or participates in decision-making concerning public assets. In June 2001 the Supreme Court extended the scope of passive bribery provisions to cover hospital ward heads,

---

[26] In practice, "material benefit of considerable value" is regarded as the same amount as "property of considerable value," defined as property worth two hundred times the minimum monthly wage. At the time of writing this report, "considerable value" was regarded as more than €40,000.

and a March 2002 decision extended the interpretation to cover presidents of housing cooperatives managing public assets.

In 2000, several legislative amendments modified bribery legislation considerably, including the following:

- The Act on Competition and Consumer Protection was amended to include "bribery of a person performing a public function" in the definition of unfair competition.[27]

- The Public Procurement Act was amended to prohibit persons or companies whose members of statutory organs or managers have been convicted of corruption from bidding for public contracts.

- Procedures were established to facilitate international cooperation and legal assistance in the fight against corruption.[28]

Several gaps remain in anti-corruption legislation. Legal persons are still not criminally liable for corruption; however, in June 2002 Poland ratified the Council of Europe Criminal Law Convention on Corruption, which means the criminal law must be changed to introduce criminal liability for companies. Corruption in the private sector is not yet criminalised, although a proposal was introduced to Parliament in early 2002. Third, non-material benefits provided to a third party cannot yet be classified as a bribe under Polish law. Perhaps more important, the definition of persons performing a "public" function remains unclear, and it remains impossible to prosecute ordinary doctors or teachers for bribery. Finally, a major barrier to reporting of bribery is the fact that even those who bribe and then notify the police immediately risk prosecution, although as of March 2002 a proposal to change this was under preparation.

2.2 Conflict of interest and asset declaration legislation

In Poland, the executive and legislative branches both have separate legal frameworks for regulating conflict of interest and asset monitoring. These are covered in the relevant sections below. As those sections show, the provisions in force have proved largely ineffective.

---

[27] *Law Journal 1993,* no. 47, item 211, amendment 2000, in: *Law Journal 2000,* no. 93, item 1027.

[28] For example, the Banking Act was amended to impose the duty on banks to disclose banking secrets to courts and prosecutors in relation to legal assistance requested by a foreign State.

2.3 Control and audit

Poland has made major progress towards putting in place a functioning system of State financial control. The Supreme Audit Chamber is the most effective supreme audit institution of any EU candidate country and has contributed extensively to revealing corruption and the legislative and institutional defects facilitating corruption, although the implementation of its findings by other institutions remains unsatisfactory. Internal audit is less well developed, but new legislation in effect from 2002 has put in place the legal framework for genuinely independent internal audit bodies.

The Supreme Audit Chamber (NIK)

The chief audit institution for the public sector is the Supreme Audit Chamber (NIK). The President of the NIK is appointed for six years by an absolute majority of MPs upon request of the President of the House of Deputies or a group of at least 35 MPs, and the appointment is subject to approval by the Senate. The President may only be removed under the same procedure under certain legally specified conditions; this has never happened.

The President may not hold any other office with the exception of university professor, may not perform any other professional occupation, be a member of any political party or trade union, or conduct public activities that "cannot be reconciled with the honour of the office."

The NIK may audit the budget, financial and asset management of: central State administrative bodies; the National Bank; other State bodies;[29] local and regional self-government bodies; legal entities established by regional and local governments; legal entities in which the State owns more than a 50 percent stake; and any other organisations in their use of public budget funds or fulfilment of public contracts.[30]

The NIK audits on the basis of initiatives submitted by Parliament or its constituent bodies, the President of the Republic of Poland, the President of the Council of Ministers (Prime Minister) or on its own initiative. It works on the basis of an audit plan submitted to the House of Deputies, but may also carry out immediate inspections without warning. It is not bound by initiatives from external institutions,

---

[29] For example, the Office of the President of Poland, the Parliament and Senate Office, the Constitutional Court, Citizen Rights Spokesmen, the National Radio and Television Board, the General Inspector for Protection of Personal Data, the National Remembrance Institute, the National Elections Office, the Supreme Court, the Chief Administrative Court and the State Labour Inspection.

[30] Constitution of the Republic of Poland, Article 203, p. 3.

with the exception of parliamentary committees, which may commission audits through a special procedure. However, this generally occurs only once or twice a year.

The NIK reports to the House of Deputies on the execution of the State budget and monetary policy, including its decisions on whether or not to accept the accounts of the Government, information on all significant audits including all charges presented as a result of audits, as well as its annual report. Local branches of the NIK provide voivody (governors of local branches of central Government in provinces) and local self-government bodies with the results of important local audits. The NIK's analysis of State budget and monetary policy execution and its annual report are available to the public, and the main findings of all significant audits are available on its website.[31] The President of the NIK participates in the House of Deputies' debates and has the right to participate in Cabinet meetings.

The NIK has published two reports on corruption, the most recent from March 2000 and 2001[32] (see Section 1.2), and has gained a reputation as the most independent and effective supreme audit institution in post-communist countries. The difference between the President of the NIK's term of office and the normal electoral cycle has resulted in a high degree of independence, although this is mainly due to the fact that to date the President generally has been of the same party as the parliamentary opposition.[33]

According to NIK officials, parliamentary committees use its reports quite extensively, often triggering motions, resolutions or initiatives to ministers demanding corrective measures. However, the same officials also say that prosecution offices very often fail to proceed on the basis of initiatives from the NIK. The World Bank 1999 report mentions the need to enquire into the "low response rate to [the NIK] reports, whether by prosecutors, Parliament, or other responsible public bodies."[34] NIK reports have

---

[31] On internet since 1998; see <http://www.nik.gov.pl>, (last accessed 23 August 2002).

[32] Supreme Audit Chamber, *The Danger of Corruption in Light of the Audits Research of the Supreme Audit Chamber,* March 2000.

[33] This does not guarantee objectivity in reporting. For example, an audit of a Polish company importing liquid fuels that was completed in 2001 initially concluded that there were no irregularities; however, when the report was finally released it was much more critical. The company was created on the basis of an intergovernmental Polish-Russian agreement. Forty-eight percent of the stake belongs to a Polish State company, 48 percent to a Russian State company, and 4 percent to a private Polish company which has very close financial relationships with the Russian liquid fuels industry. The owner of the latter company is a Polish businessman who previously provided loans to the Prime Minister and is leader of the Democratic Left Alliance that governs in coalition with the Peasants' Party. The President of the NIK when the audit was originally completed was a member of the Peasants' Party, while the new President is from the opposition AWS (Solidarity).

[34] World Bank, *Corruption in Poland,* p. 27.

resulted in the removal of a number of senior officials, the most prominent case being the recent removal of the President of the State Pension Fund after a NIK audit of its procurement of IT equipment. In 2001, Minister of Telecommunications Tomasz Szyszko was also removed after a NIK report that uncovered "irregularities" involving losses of millions of złoty, although no charges of corruption were made.

Internal audit

According to a report issued by SIGMA in 2001, although each central institution of public administration includes an internal audit unit, these lack a unified structure, common methodology and functional independence. The report noted that the activities of these units lack routine procedures and tend to be reactions to signals of misconduct initiated by superiors.

The European Union has drawn attention to internal audit problems as well. The EU 2000 Regular Report stated the necessity of further efforts to develop internal auditing, including an act on internal auditing and a clear-cut division of duties between the Ministry of Finance, and internal audit units. On the basis of amendments to the Act on Public Finances, passed in July 2001,[35] it became mandatory from 1 January 2002 for State organisations to implement internal audit procedures. The amendments defined the scope of inspections and laid down criteria and procedures for appointing auditors. The Government authority coordinating financial inspections and internal audits is the General Inspectorate of Internal Audit at the Ministry of Finance. Steps towards functional independence include the requirement that audits are carried out on the basis of an annual internal audit plan, and the requirement of an opinion from the Inspector-General before any auditor may be removed.

2.4 Anti-corruption agencies

There are no specialised anti-corruption agencies,[36] and the ordinary police and Prosecutor's Office remain the most important institutions in the fight against corruption. Several special units established to fight against organised and drug-related crime, such as the Central Investigation Department and National Criminal Record Centre, report directly to the Chief of Police. According to police officials, around 80

---

[35] Act on Amendments to Law on Public Finances, passed on 27 July 2001, in: *Law Journal 2002*, no. 1, item 145.

[36] As noted in Section 1.3 the idea of setting up a special Central Anti-corruption Office was debated in the Sejm on 25 April 2001 and was rejected.

policemen deal with corruption, of whom about 20 are based in Katowice, the biggest industrial centre in Poland.[37]

Prosecutors are organised hierarchically under the Minister of Justice, who simultaneously holds the position of Prosecutor-General.[38] The fact that the Prosecutor-General is appointed by the ruling party raises serious doubts about the capacity of the prosecution system to pursue high-level corruption cases. NIK officials believe prosecution offices are insufficiently specialised to fight against corruption and financial crime, while some other respondents suggested that prosecutors are not sufficiently independent and sometimes operate to protect the politically powerful.[39]

Money laundering

Poland did not pass an anti-money laundering act until September 2000 (the Act on Prevention of the Introduction into Financial Circulation of Assets derived from Illegal or Undisclosed Sources).[40] The Act created a Financial Information Unit (hereafter, FIU) headed by a General Inspector of Financial Information as the body responsible for monitoring suspicious financial transactions and established the duty of financial institutions to notify to the Inspectorate transactions exceeding €10,000 or transactions where there is suspicion of a criminal act, and gave the prosecution offices power to suspend a transaction for up to 48 hours. The first Inspector-General was appointed in February 2001.

Although Parliament postponed the duty to register transactions over €10,000 until April 2002 due to the technical unpreparedness of the FIU, 300 notifications of suspect transactions were received during the first nine months the Act was in force.[41] Of these, 28 cases were taken up for further investigation by the Prosecutor's Office; in two cases the proceedings were annulled; and in 210 cases further investigation was in process as of April 2002. As of April 2002, the Inspectorate had suspended transactions for 48 hours on four occasions. From April 2003, financial institutions will have to notify the FIU of all financial transactions.

---

[37] Interview by M. Łajtar with W. Walendzik, Director of Central Investigative Office, 3 March 2002.

[38] Act on Procuracy, passed on 20 June 1985, in: *Law Journal 1985,* no. 31, item 138, with further amendments.

[39] Interview with Anna Marszałek, reporter, *Rzeczpospolita* daily, 19 March 2002.

[40] *Law Journal 2000*, no. 116, item 1216.

[41] Grażyna Leśniak, "Ambitne plany przyczyną kłopotów" [Ambitious plans result in troubles], *Rzecpospolita*, 2 April 2002.

2.5 Ombudsman

The office of the ombudsman was established in 1987, and is largely modelled on the Swedish prototype.[42] The first two ombudsmen were the most popular official figures in Poland after 1989 in most public opinion rankings.

The ombudsman is appointed by an absolute majority of at least half the members of the House of Deputies on proposal of the Marshall (Speaker) or 35 deputies. The appointment is subject to approval by the Senate. The ombudsman's term of appointment is five years and a maximum of two terms. The ombudsmen may be dismissed only by the House of Deputies (with the same voting rules as for appointment) and in cases narrowly defined by law, and enjoys immunity against prosecution unless the House of Deputies decides otherwise.

The ombudsman may not perform any other public function or form of employment except a university professorship; belong to a political party or trade union; or perform any public activity that cannot be reconciled with the dignity of the office.[43]

The office of the ombudsman had 220 staff in 2001. The ombudsman's task is to determine, in response to complaints from citizens and institutions, whether an infringement of human or civic rights and freedoms has occurred, or whether principles of "social coexistence and social justice"[44] have been violated by the actions or inaction of organs of government administration or social organisations and institutions obliged to respect human and civic rights.

Any individual may submit a complaint to the ombudsman, who may also initiate investigations. Anonymous requests are not investigated. Individuals do not need to have exhausted all other legal avenues before turning to the ombudsman, nor does a decision by the ombudsman preclude the individual from pursuing other avenues subsequently. The ombudsman may investigate the activities of any public body, organisation or institution with discretion. Upon reviewing a request, the ombudsman has the right to investigate the case within the institution concerned, to access all files and documents associated with the case, and the right to request all information.

---

[42] See Constitution of the Republic of Poland from 2 April 1997, Dz. U. no. 78, pos. 483, as well as the Legal Act on the Ombudsman of 15 July 1987, Dz. U. from 1991, no. 109, pos. 471 (12 May 2000 amended Dz. U. 00.48.552).

[43] See Constitution of the Republic of Poland, Article 209.

[44] "Principles of co-existence and social justice" mentioned in the Act allow ombudsman to intervene not only when the law had been abused but also when "injustice and wrong had been injured under the Majesty of Law;" see L. Garlicki, *Polskie prawo konstytucyjne* [Polish Constitutional Law], Liber, Warsaw 1998, p. 348.

Upon a determination that the law was violated, the ombudsman may forward the findings to the institution concerned or its superior; request the initiation of disciplinary proceedings; initiate civil or criminal proceedings; initiate and participate in administrative proceedings with the rights of a prosecutor; file a proposal for sanctions or the annulment of a legally binding decision by the institution investigated; file a charge in civil or penal proceedings or an extraordinary appeal to the Supreme Court against the verdicts by the Supreme Administrative Court; or request the House of Deputies to carry out an audit. The institution investigated must inform within 30 days of the corrective measures adopted.

Around 25,000 requests are submitted annually to the ombudsman. However, corruption is a marginal concern: in the past three years only a few isolated investigations have concerned corruption, and the ombudsman has not submitted any motions or proposals to the Government, parliamentarians or the President concerning corruption.

3. EXECUTIVE BRANCH AND CIVIL SERVICE

The Polish public administration has undergone several major reforms since 1990, in particular the decentralisation of many tasks to local and regional governments and the passage of the Civil Service Act in 1996-98, which represents an important step towards a depoliticised administration. However, patronage remains an important phenomenon, and the current Government has regressed in this area, amending the Civil Service Act to increase the scope for political appointments. Bribery in the public administration does not appear to be a very serious problem, at least not at the level of central Government, but there are serious problems with uncontrolled outsourcing of public administration activities.

3.1 Structure and legislative framework

The Polish civil service has undergone fundamental reform since 1990. The 1990 Local Self-government Act devolved extensive powers to local governments, a process completed in 1998 through the creation of counties and regions. The result is a civil service consisting of three parts:

- approximately 178,000 officials in local and regional self-government, to which extensive powers are devolved;

- 130,000 officials in the Government administration (Prime Minister's Office, ministries, central offices and regional branches of central administrative bodies) and 16 regional *voivodships* (regional branches of executive authority).

- 4,000 officials in the parts of public administration subordinated to the President and/ or the Parliament.

Public administration is regulated mainly by three acts: the 1982 Act on Public Officials, the 1990 Act on Self Government Officials, and the 1996 Civil Service Act (amended in 1998).

Anti-corruption policy in the civil service is based primarily on training. A National School of State Administration was established in 1991, modelled on the French ENA and designed to ingrain exemplary ethics within the upper echelons of the civil service. However, according to the 1999 World Bank report on corruption, the number of graduates from the school has been too small so far to create a critical mass or dominate any single unit of public administration.[45] Moreover, despite general agreement on the need for a skilled and honest civil service, successive Governments have succumbed to the temptations of political patronage. European Commission reports have stressed the weakness of the civil service as a major source of corruption.[46]

Under the Civil Service Act, the civil service is divided into political and non-political positions. Ministers, under-secretaries and Cabinet advisers are defined as political positions, while all positions from director-general down are non-political and may only be dismissed on grounds of prolonged illness, refusal to be transferred to another office, disciplinary expulsion, criminal conviction or criminal proceedings lasting more than three months, or "loss of untainted reputation." If it is judged to be in "the special interest of the civil service," an official may be suspended by the Head of the Civil Service for up to 18 months.[47]

The Head of the Civil Service is appointed for five years by the Prime Minister on the advice of the Civil Service Council. Aided by the Council, the Head is responsible for "monitoring adherence to… [civil service] principles," and other activities including organisation of competitive recruitment and examinations for senior positions. The Council is composed of 16 members: half are representatives of all party groupings in

---

[45] The *2001 Regular Report* noted that, "Anti-corruption training has been upgraded and 200 people have benefited from this revamped approach in 2001;" in: Commission, 2001 *Regular Report*, p. 21.

[46] The *2000 Regular Report* noted that, "[T]he rapid implementation of the Civil Service Act will, increasing an independent open civil service, also greatly contribute to developing a corruption inhibiting environment;" in: *2000 Regular Report*, p. 18.

[47] This provision was used to suspend the regional director of the civil service in the Katowice *vojvodina* after a criminal investigation into the activities of local functionaries began.

Parliament and half are appointed by the Prime Minister. The latter serve for six years, the former until the end of each parliamentary term.

The Civil Service Act has done much to limit recruitment to civil service positions on the basis of party patronage and other non merit-based criteria. Since 1999, recruitment has been based on compulsory open public advertisement, and only civil service officials may run for upper level positions. However, the will of the Government to put in place an independent professional civil service has been placed in doubt by an amendment to the Act passed in 2001 that allows persons outside the civil service to be appointed to directorial positions without a selection process. As of March 2002, around 15 of an approximate total of 70 director-generals were recruited without selection and on the basis of political party recommendations.

3.2 Administrative procedure and redress

Under the Polish Code of Administrative Procedure, administrative decisions must be issued immediately, within one month if explanatory proceedings are required, and two months in the most complicated cases. Citizens may appeal against decisions to the authority superior to that which issued the decision, or to the same authority if a minister or territorial self-government board of appeals issued the decision in question. The deadline for deciding appeals is one month. Subsequently, appeals may be lodged at the Supreme Administrative Court or one of its local offices. As of March 2002, a bill was under discussion in Parliament to create district and provincial administrative courts.

Administrative courts may review not only the legality but also the substance of administrative decisions. In practice, however, the Supreme Administrative Court rules only on the formal legality of decisions. Over 50 percent of cases relate to tax matters.[48] According to the Head of the Civil Service and representatives of civil society organisations, this is mainly because ordinary people lack knowledge of the administrative appeals process.

There is no special legal framework either to facilitate whistleblowing by civil service employees or to protect whistleblowers. However, civil servants who are given an order that requires violation of the law or waste of resources may request the order in writing and then refuse to carry it out.

---

[48] Interview with Jan Pastwa, Head of Civil Service, 19 March 2002.

3.3 Conflict of interest and asset monitoring

Conflict of interest

The 1997 Act on Limiting Conduct of Economic Activities by Public Officials[49] regulates conflict of interest for: general directors, department directors and deputies of State institutions; division managers in central administrative bodies; executives in regional government offices[50] and local administrative bodies; Director-General and auditors of the NIK; executives and inspectors at regional tax offices; members of management boards, treasury officials and secretaries in community, poviat and vojvodship offices, executives' companies owned by the State Treasury along with executives in State agencies; and judges of the Constitutional Court.

Persons occupying these positions may not: be members of management boards, supervisory boards or review commissions (internal auditing commissions) of commercial companies subject to or cooperatives (except supervisory boards of housing cooperatives); be employed or perform activities in commercial companies that could provoke allegations of conflict of interest or bias; be members of the management boards of foundations performing economic activities; hold shares or stock exceeding ten percent of the capital in any commercial company; perform economic activities on their own account or with other persons; manage or act in the capacity of representative or attorney of such an undertaking (with the exception of household farming); and for one year after leaving office be employed or perform any other activities for an employer if they acted in any decision-making process concerning that employer.

Violation of any of the above provisions is punishable by termination of employment without notice or recall from office. However, in practice the law has not been enforced and violation is common practice. Many officials have also provided services externally as consultants on official matters of their office. The best-known case of this was a scandal in which the Deputy Minister of Finance was revealed to be advising externally on tax declarations. Moreover, senior officials have been required by law to serve on the supervisory boards of thousands of former State companies undergoing privatisation. Indeed, the 2002 elections have been followed by widespread replacement of representatives of the State on the boards of State-controlled companies, such as the petroleum company PKN Orlen, the copper mining company

---

[49] Act on Limiting Conduct of Economic Activities by Public Officials, passed on 21 August 1997, in: *Law Journal 1998*, no. 106, item 679, amendments from: *Law Journal 1998*, no. 88, item 554; no. 162, item 1126; *Law Journal 1999*, no. 49, item 483; *Law Journal 2000*, no. 26, item 306.

[50] The *vojvode* shall be the representative of the Council of Ministers in a *vojvodeship*; see Constitution of the Republic of Poland, Article 152.

KGHM Polska Miedź, or the State insurance company PZU.[51] These same companies have been the focus of media attention due to their apparent financing of political parties (see Section 6.3). The appointments coincided with efforts by the Government to delay privatisation.

In May 2002, the Ministry of Justice announced that prosecutors had launched an investigation into "incompetent management and corrupt practices" at 14 State-controlled firms, including KGHM Polska Miedź, Totalizator Sportowy, PZU and Poczta Polska (the Post Office). However, no measure to reduce patronage appointments has been announced.[52]

In addition to the provisions applying to senior officials, under the Civil Service Act no civil servant may: be a member of a political party; hold a position in any trade union; be elected to regional or local self-government unless unpaid leave is taken for this purpose; have a relationship of service authority with spouses or other close relatives; or be employed externally, unless authorised by the head of the institution.[53] Finally, officials are "forbidden from actions or activities contravening the legal duties or undermining trust in the civil service."[54]

In practice, senior officials take a liberal attitude to external employment of civil servants, and officials have often been encouraged to take other paid positions and jobs. Conflict of interest appears to be a more severe problem at the local government level where, for example, Government employees (especially in architectural and land surveying departments) are often owners or employees of private companies that prepare documents for applications to the office concerned. A number of officials have argued publicly that the law restricts officials too much given the level of salaries in the public administration.

The effectiveness of incompatibility provisions has been cast in doubt by a detailed study on clientelist networks in the semi State-controlled mining industry, and in particular the established practice of "carouseling" between senior civil service posts and senior positions in the industry.[55]

---

[51] For example, the CEO of PZU was sacked without explanation and replaced with a former political ally of Treasury Minister, Wiesław Kaczmarek; see "Long arm of the Treasury Ministry," *Warsaw Business Journal,* 25 February 2002.

[52] RFE/RL Newsline, vol. 6, no. 86, part II, 9 May 2002.

[53] Civil Service Act, Article 69.

[54] Civil Service Act, Article 72.

[55] K. Gadowska, "Obstacles to Transformation – The Impact of Clientelist Networks on the Process of restructuring of the Coal Mining Industry in Poland," unpublished paper presented at joint LSA-RCSL ISA Conference on Sociology of Law, Budapest 2001.

Asset declarations

The same circle of functionaries covered by the 1997 Act (senior officials) must submit asset declarations on assuming and leaving office and annually in between. Declarations must contain information on: all property including the property of spouses; financial assets, real estate, stocks and shares, and any assets acquired from the State through a tender (including assets acquired in such a way by spouses); all business activities and statutory or other positions in companies or cooperatives.

Statements are submitted to the head of the unit where the functionary works, with the exception of persons holding very high positions – such as the President, speakers of House of Deputies and Senate or Prime Minister, and presidents of the Constitutional Court, who submit declarations to the First President of the Supreme Court.[56] Asset declarations are held for six years and are confidential unless the functionary submitting them agrees otherwise.

Failure to submit declarations entails service liability, and submission of false information is subject to a penalty of up to five years imprisonment. However, according to the NIK, asset declarations are often not submitted, especially by officials in local administration, while superiors tend not to impose any sanctions. A major problem with declarations is that the law does not allow those who receive them to compare them with information from the tax authorities.

The 1997 Act also established a Register of Benefits. Ministers, deputy ministers, secretaries of the Chancellery of the Prime Minister, heads of central State institutions, vojvodes (heads of executive power in provinces), deputy vojvodes and spouses of all these persons must submit information on all benefits, defined as all positions and activities subject to remuneration (both in public administration and private institutions); work carried out on own account, sponsorship of public activities of the functionary, gifts and travel unrelated with the public function, all gifts exceeding in value 50 percent of the monthly minimum wage and all other benefits exceeding the same value. The register is open for the public and is maintained by the State Election Commission.

In 2001, amendments to the 1997 Act were submitted to the House of Deputies that would regulate in more detail the duties of persons performing public functions, tighten the rules on filling in asset declaration, and also facilitate inspection of the sources of assets. The amendments were not passed before the September 2001 elections. In January 2002, the Law & Justice Party submitted the same amendments again, and as of in April 2002, the House of Deputies was working on the proposal.

---

[56] The First President of the Supreme Court submits the statements to the President.

3.4 Internal control mechanisms

The 1982 Act on State Administration lists several disciplinary penalties for civil servants ending with expulsion from the service. Penalties may be applied up to one month after written notice of the misdeed from any superior in charge and up to a year from the misdeed itself. A Higher Disciplinary Commission was established by the Prime Minister on 1 January 2000 to cover the new civil service. Territorial councils elect disciplinary commissions from among their employees, and secondary level (appeal) commissions from among councillors themselves.

Employees of the public finance sector and other persons controlling public funds incur administrative liability for infringing public finance discipline, with penalties ranging from admonition to exclusion from positions associated with controlling public funds for up to five years. This liability is separate from liability under any other law (civil or criminal) and is determined by departmental ministry commissions, the head of the Chancellery of the Chairman of the Council of Ministers, vojvodship commissions and Regional Clearing Chambers.[57] A Sentencing Commission at the Ministry of Finance decides appeals. Subsidies not used for their designated purpose or drawn in excess of needs must be returned to the State budget together with a penalty that is calculated on the same basis as penalties for outstanding taxes.

3.5 Interaction with the public

In 2001, the Head of the Civil Service submitted a draft Code of Ethics to the Prime Minister's Chancellory, which was not accepted after the elections. As of March 2002, it was expected that the draft would be submitted again, and many officials expect that it will be adopted, perhaps in part due to EU pressure. The EU noted continuing work on the Code of Ethics in the 2001 Regular Report.[58]

3.6 Corruption

According to a 1999 Ministry of Interior and Administration Report, 1,563 cases of corruption were registered in 1998, but only 94 public administration officials were

---

[57] Regional Clearing Chambers are State supervisory and inspection authorities responsible for supervising financial management by subnational Government bodies entities using funds allocated by such bodies.

[58] Commission, *2001 Regular Report*, p. 21

accused. The report also described several anti-corruption acts as irrelevant, such as the 1997 Act prohibiting functionaries from involvement in economic activities.

Corruption among senior officials has been discussed extensively in the press, but to our knowledge none has ever been convicted. However, ministerial resignations have taken place following the publication of evidence against their collaborators. The biggest corruption case in recent years broke in 2001 when an advisor to Romuald Szeremetiew, a Deputy Defense

Minister was arrested on charges of illicit possession of secret documents concerning a tender for jackets for pilots, to which bribery charges were later added. The Minister of Defence was sacked as a result, and in August 2002 prosecutors indicted the adviser for attempting to extort $150,000 in bribes.[59]

The Civil Service Office commissioned a survey of 543 clients of the civil service in November 1999.[60] Seventy-five percent of respondents found officials honest, five percent considered them prone to bribery, while the remaining 20 percent reserved judgement. The perception of corruptness increases, however, the higher the position of the target official: 13 percent regarded top officials as prone to bribery. In most surveys[61] a majority of respondents agree that "many top officials gain from public office," but only nine percent reported that officials with whom they had been in contact lately "were willing to earn money."

According to the Head of the Civil Service, corruption is around third or fourth in the list of priority problems for the civil service, while corruption is a less serious problem among rank-and-file civil servants than in local self-government or high-level political positions.[62] Around 200 cases of suspected bribery of officials were handed to the police by the civil service in 2001.

In October 2001, the NIK issued a report sharply criticising the widespread practice of outsourcing functions of public administration (the report covered the largest ministries and a number of other key State bodies) to advisory and expert services. The 1999 World Bank report also drew attention to this practice, which has often been pursued with scant regard for tender procedures and is inherently vulnerable to corruption. For example, agencies often outsource jobs to their own employees.

---

[59] RFE/RL Newsline, vol. 6, no. 160, part II, 26 August 2002.

[60] J. Czapinski, *Urzednik panstwowy w oczcach obywatela* [The State Official in the Eyes of Citizens], Warsaw 1999.

[61] See Section 1.1.

[62] Interview with Jan Pastwa, Head of Civil Service, 19 March 2002.

4. LEGISLATURE

One of the main sources of corruption in Poland is the existence of a number of State agencies set up for special purposes whose budgets are not approved by the House of Deputies. These funds accounts for a large proportion of public spending, and by all accounts have been one of the main loci of high-level corruption, one of the main sources of political party patronage, and may have provided money to political parties. A major source of corruption remains the complete absence of regulation of lobbying. There are a number of examples of parliamentarians carrying on ancillary activities that invite abuse of conflicts of interest, as well as examples of apparently corrupt lobbying.

4.1 Elections

Polish elections are administered by the State Election Commission, and by regional and electoral commissions. The Commission comprises three judges from the Constitutional Court, three Supreme Court judges and three Supreme Administrative Court judges.[63] Regional commissions are composed of judges nominated by the Minister of Justice, while local commissions consist of lay citizens nominated by the parties running in elections plus one local official nominated by the head of the municipality. Neither the fairness of elections nor the integrity of the Commission has ever been called into doubt. In 2001, the State Election Commission was allocated new powers to control party finances (see Section 6.2).

4.2 Budget and control mechanisms

State budget procedure and control mechanisms are laid down in the Polish Constitution and 1998 Public Finance Act (see Section 2.4). Although the budget is subject to parliamentary approval, a number of special funds are excluded from the State budget, which according to the World Bank totalled around 40 percent of expenditure and 30 percent of revenues in 1999. The largest funds are the Social Insurance Fund, Farmers' Social Security Funds and Labour Fund, while the State Fund for the Rehabilitation of the Disabled and the Environmental Protection Fund are also very large. The NIK has repeatedly warned of a lack of control over the operation of these funds, which are not subject to any parliamentary supervision. The most critical findings have related to the Fund for the Rehabilitation of Disabled

---

[63] Judges are nominated by the presidents of the respective courts.

Persons.[64] However, there has also been criticism regarding use of environmental protection funds, and State agencies such as the State Treasury Agricultural Property Agency. One real estate sale at below-market price by the Military Housing Agency resulted in a €800,000 loss to the State budget and an NIK notification of a suspected criminal offence to the Public Prosecutor's Office.

The World Bank report describes these agencies as "States within States: public sector agencies that control and in some cases also lend substantial funds, have important links with the private sector and with political parties."[65] One senior official described off-budget funds as a sinecure of political party patronage and "probably our most important [corruption] danger now."[66]

The House of Deputies is responsible for auditing the implementation of the State budget during the first half of the budget year. The Minister of Finance submits a budget execution report to the House of Deputies' Budget Committee and the NIK by 10 September, while the Council of Ministers submits its budget execution report[67] to the House of Deputies and the NIK by 31 May of the year following the year concerned. After the NIK issues its report, the House of Deputies votes whether to approve or reject the accounts. Responsibility for the supervision of individual budget items lies with budget item administrators.

4.3 Conflict of interest and asset monitoring

Under the Constitution, deputies and senators may not carry on commercial activities for which a source of revenue is public assets or purchase of such assets. Deputies violating the provision may be disciplined, which may result in the withdrawal of their mandate by the Tribunal of the House of Deputies upon a motion of the Speaker of the House of Deputies. However, civil society organisations monitoring corruption do not know of any case where this has happened.

---

[64] See NIK reports on execution of the State budget 1995–1999 and NIK Control no. 123/1998.

[65] World Bank, *Corruption in Poland*, p. 18.

[66] Interview with Jan Pastwa, Head of Civil Service, 19 March 2002.

[67] "The Council of Ministers, within the five-month period following the end of the fiscal year, shall present to the Sejm a report on the implementation of the Budget together with information on the condition of the State debt. Within 90 days following receipt of the report, the Sejm shall consider the report presented to it, and, after seeking the opinion of the Supreme Audit Chamber, shall pass a resolution on whether to grant or refuse to grant approval of the financial accounts submitted by the Council of Ministers." See Constitution of the Republic of Poland, Article 226.

The 1996 Act on Fulfilment of Mandate by Deputies and Senators contains similar provisions in more detail. Deputies and senators may not: run their own or jointly held commercial activities profiting from public assets, nor manage or be an agent or representative for such activities; be members of the managing or supervisory bodies or sales representatives of enterprises in which the State or municipalities hold shares; or hold more than ten percent of the shares of a company in which the State or municipalities own shares. Violation of these provisions may be punished by a fine.

The House of Deputies subsequently approved a set of "Ethical Principles for Deputies" and established an Ethics Committee that may take action against deputies who violate the principles (see below).

In practice, cases of conflict of interest amongst parliamentarians are rarely brought to public attention, and the legal provisions remain largely formal. An exception was the case of the deputy and Chairman of the House of Deputies Finance Committee, Henryk Goryszewski, who was simultaneously joint owner of a law firm.[68] The Ethics Committee found that Goryszewski's conduct "had led to the potential conflict of private and public interests," thereby damaging the reputation of the House of Deputies, and admonished him publicly.[69] He resigned from the chairmanship of the Financial Committee and "partially suspended his work in the law firm." However, the Ethics Committee cannot impose other sanctions against violators. All cases which have been brought to light to date have been uncovered by the press.

Under the 1996 Act, within 30 days of taking up their mandate, by 31 March every year thereafter and two months before elections, deputies and senators must submit a declaration of all financial assets and real estate, including shares and securities of commercial companies and any assets acquired from the State Treasury or other State or commune legal entity; all commercial activities and positions held in commercial companies; and all assets co-owned by spouses. Since January 2002 this information has been published on the House of Deputies website. The declarations are subject to verification by the House of Deputies and the Senate Ethics Commission. Deputies or Senators who supply false information are liable to criminal penalties.

Compliance with asset declaration requirements has steadily improved since the introduction of the Act. Previously, declarations were not checked at all. According to

---

[68] Henryk Goryszewski represented Kredyt Bank in its application for a license to establish a pension fund and advised another company how to deal with VAT arrears.

[69] R. Kasprów, "Dwie role posła. Konflikt interesów Henryka Goryszewskiego" [Two roles of the messenger: Conflict of interests of Henryk Goryszewski], *Rzeczpospolita*, 14 October 1999; <http://arch.rp.pl>, (last accessed 26 August 2002); F. G, K. GR, Sz. K., R. K, M. D. Z., "Goryszewki wynagradzany przez Kredyt Bank" [Goryszewski paid through Kredyt Bank], *Rzeczpospolita*, 27 November 1999, <http://arch.rp.pl>, (last accessed 26 August 2002).

media reports, 35 out of 460 deputies and three out of 100 senators did not submit declarations in 1998, whereas in 1999 only 11 deputies did not submit declarations in time. An amendment now allows analysis of declarations by the Ethics Committee, although they cannot be compared to tax authority information. The Committee has since found several gaps in declarations, mostly of a formal character, and has admonished eight parliamentarians from both ruling and opposition parties.[70]

Under the same Act, any benefits obtained by deputies, senators and their spouses are recorded in a "Benefit Register," including: remuneration for any external positions or activities; donations exceeding 50 percent of the monthly minimal wage; travel expenses for any trips not related to public office and where the cost is not covered by the deputy/senator, spouse, employer, political party, association or foundation of which they are members; and any other benefits not related to work and exceeding 50 percent of the monthly minimum wage. The Register is kept by the Marshall (Speaker) of the relevant chamber and is publicly accessible. Deputies and senators may be punished by reprimand, admonition or rebuke. Compliance with the Benefits Register depends largely on goodwill, and it has had very little effect up to the time of writing. The Ethics Committee has so far admonished only one deputy for not declaring a received benefit.

4.4 Immunity

Parliamentarians may not be prosecuted without a majority vote of all members of the House of Deputies.

4.5 Corruption

Almost no explicit cases of corruption have been revealed in the Polish legislature. The press has reported cases of suspicious business activities carried out by some parliamentarians, such as the purchase of a factory for half its estimated market price, or the business activities of a current deputy and former senator.[71]

A major source of corruption in Parliament remains the complete lack of any regulation of lobbying. The World Bank reported that significant amounts of money

---

[70] J. T. P, PAP, "Posłowie upomnieni. Nierzetelne oświadczenia majątkowe" [Unclear asset declarations], *Rzeczpospolita*, 11 April 2001, <http://arch.rp.pl>, (last accessed 26 August 2002).

[71] Anna Marszałek, "Poseł Kolasiński, Gawronik, Pruszków i Spólka" [MP's Kolasinski, Gawronik, Pruszkow and Company], *Rzeczpospolita*, 27 September 2000. Pruszków is the name of a town near to Warsaw known for its Mafia.

were offered for the passage of certain legislation.[72] In a 1996 survey, 23 percent of deputies said they knew politicians who take into consideration the interests of a particular company in their actions, and ten percent were able to identify individuals who act on behalf of the owners or managers of particular companies.

One of the most effective lobbyists was the owner of the only Polish companies producing gelatine, who from 1995 to 1998 managed to persuade successive Governments to impose high tariffs on imported gelatine and eventually to ban imports altogether.[73] The media subsequently revealed that he had sponsored the election campaigns of the main political parties. No action was taken as a result.

An important lobbying case in 2001 concerned attempts by representatives of Polish breweries to influence a proposed law restricting beer advertising during its debate in the Senate.[74] However, media coverage influenced a number of senators who had been in favour of limiting the restrictions to approve them in the final vote. In another case, an MP introduced a bill mandating the use of "hands-free" sets for mobile phones in cars; after the bill was passed the press discovered he was the only importer of such sets.

5. JUDICIARY

The judiciary is regarded in public opinion surveys as one of the most corrupt institutions in Poland. Direct evidence of corruption is largely anecdotal, and much of what is interpreted as judicial corruption probably reflects corruption of lawyers who may or may not pass on bribes provided in order to influence court decisions. However, poor court organisation, burdensome procedures, long delays and, at least until 2002, poorly functioning disciplinary mechanisms have created a system that is vulnerable to corruption. The European Commission has paid particular attention to corruption in the judiciary.

5.1 Legislative framework

The Polish judiciary does not function effectively to sanction corruption, although this may be to a significant extent a consequence of the problematic functioning of the

---

[72] An Anonymous deputy was quoted claiming that in 1992 assistance in blocking the amendments to the Act on Casinos was worth €541,670, and recently increased up to €800,000; in: World Bank, *Corruption in Poland*.

[73] Information provided by Stefan Batory Foundation.

[74] See, e.g., A. Kocińska, "Senators for sale," *Warsaw Business Journal*, 2 April 2001.

prosecution system (see Section 2.4), judicial delays and burdensome procedures. Moreover, corruption in the judiciary appears to be a serious problem, although its prevalence is difficult to measure.

Judges are appointed for unlimited terms and may be removed only by a disciplinary court decision and under circumstances defined by law. Judges enjoy immunity against criminal prosecution unless a disciplinary court decides to lift immunity, and may not be arrested or taken into custody unless they are caught in the act and custody is necessary for the proper course of criminal proceedings. The President of the respective court may demand a judge's immediate release.[75]

A judge may not be a member of any political party, trade union or conduct public activity that cannot be reconciled with the principle of independence of courts and judges. The law prohibits additional employment except for employment in a scientific or educational position (with the consent of the court president).

Judges are required to submit declarations of assets and interests to the President of the court of appeal of the region.[76] The information is reviewed by the Appeal Court Council.

Presidents of appeals courts submit their own declarations to the National Judiciary Board.

Until January 2002 there were two disciplinary courts: the Disciplinary Court to hear first instance proceedings, and the Higher Disciplinary Court to hear appeals. In 2000, the Disciplinary Court heard around 60 cases. Seventeen judges were found guilty of professional offences: three were expelled from the judiciary, five subject to administrative penalty and eight suspended. Only one of the cases involved corruption.

Until 2002 disciplinary courts met in closed session. As the European Commission's 2001 Regular Report stressed, this raised concerns about the lack of transparency in the system. Moreover, relying on judges to lift immunity from their colleagues is troublesome, particularly if corruption is relatively widespread.

The functioning of disciplinary courts was reformed by amendments in effect from January 2002. Under the new regulations, the disciplinary courts consist of two levels: the ten Courts of Appeal, which are the disciplinary courts of first instance, and the Supreme Court, which hears disciplinary cases if one of the parties – the accused judge, the disciplinary advocate, the Minister of Justice or the National Judiciary Council – appeals the decision of the first instance. In addition, hearings are now public.

---

[75] "The President of the competent local court shall be forthwith notified of any such detention and may order an immediate release of the person detained." See Constitution of the Republic of Poland,, Article 181.

[76] Act on the Common Court System, Article 87.

5.2 Corruption

Evidence on corruption in Polish courts is almost entirely anecdotal. However, a severe backlog of cases and overload of the judiciary has created an environment favourable to corruption, and court procedures remain so complicated that lawyers can and do easily delay cases for years. The most glaring example of never-ending proceedings is the case of the former Foreign Debt Servicing Fund (FOZZ), where trials of former senior managers of the Fund for fraud and theft have not been completed even after more than ten years.[77]

The 2000 Regular Report mentions that,

> [C]orruption among the judiciary has been mentioned in some reports. The very long wait for routine court decisions in commercial matters, including in terms of contract enforcement, constitutes an incentive for bribery and corruption.

The 2001 Regular Report refers to information from the Central Investigation Bureau, according to which three cases of corruption were investigated in 2000, compared to some 20 cases reported.

The World Bank's 1999 Report states: "A number of our respondents noted that sentences can be bought, with members of the legal profession acting as intermediaries; in other cases the lawyer pockets the bribe... while the client is led to believe that the judge is amenable to corruption."[78]

However, judgements about the extent of corruption in the Polish judicial system are very hard to make, partly due to the procedures for lifting immunity, which require judges to turn in their own colleagues in order for criminal proceedings to take place. A highly-respected Polish partner in a large Western law practice referred to several cases where corruption of judges had been a serious problem.[79] The Companies Register is an area where severe problems are reportedly experienced (see Section 9).

The most publicised case of alleged judicial corruption concerns the District Court in Toruń, where the press alleged that the Head Judge of the Criminal Department maintained close contacts with a leader of organised crime, dealt out exceptionally soft sentences and exhibited exceptionally high financial standing. The Judge lost the position of head of the department and was expelled from the judicial service by a Supreme Court decision in October 2001.[80] In another case the Supreme Court also

---

[77] M. Matraszek, "Dirty Tricks?", *Warsaw Business Journal,* 25 June 2002.

[78] World Bank, *Corruption in Poland,* p. 9.

[79] Interview with Polish partner in a highly-respected Western law firm in Warsaw, 19 March 2002.

[80] K. Rak, "Wkracza rzecznik dyscyplinarny" [Disciplinary spokesman enters], *Rzeczpospolita,* 27 February 2002.

confirmed the dismissal of a judge, whose leniency allegedly resulted in the impunity of a local gang boss suspected of murder.[81] In the latter case the Disciplinary Court did not begin proceedings until the media publicised the case, and in September 2001 the Supreme Court issued a judgement dismissing the judge.

6. POLITICAL PARTY FINANCE

Party funding has long been regarded as highly corrupt, a perception supported by the near absence of regulation of party finances. However, party financing rules passed in 1997 and, in particular, amendments from 2001 have put in place a much stricter framework and may do a lot to reduce corruption: the main changes include the introduction of State funding, ceilings on campaign expenditures, a ban on corporate donations and monitoring of party accounts by the Elections Commission. The strength of the new system was under test in early 2002 as the Commission found that several parties violated the law during the previous elections. A particular characteristic of party funding in Poland appears to have been the tendency of State-owned companies to provide money to parties in a disguised way or illegally.

6.1 Legislative framework

The main components of party financing rules were put in place in 1997, and were followed by very important amendments to the Electoral Act in 2001, which were passed in an effort to make party finances more transparent and reduce corruption.[82]

Under the 2001 amendments political parties may receive income from membership dues, donations, legacies, wills, property income and subsidies prescribed by the law.[83] Under the new law parties may no longer hold public collections or accept corporate donations of any kind (prohibitions first introduced in 2000 for Presidential election campaigns). Parties may only use income for the purposes described in their charter or for charitable purposes, and may not carry on business activities (with limited exceptions connected directly to their prime activity).

---

[81] "Odium spada na sedziego" [Odium falls upon the judge], collective interview with Teresa Romer, Supreme Court Judge, *Rzeczpospolita*, 4 April 2001.

[82] Act on Elections to Sejm and Senate of Polish Republic, passed on 12 May 2001, in: *Law Journal 2001*, no. 46, item 499.

[83] Income from property is limited to the sale of property already held. Real estate and offices may be used only for offices of the national or local representatives of the party.

The 2001 Act also introduced State budget subsidies for parties. Parties gaining over three percent of the national vote receive a regressive subsidy per vote: €2.7 for each vote from three to five percent, €2.1 for five to ten percent, €1.9 from ten to 20 percent, €1 from 20 to 30 percent, and €0.4 for votes above 30 percent.[84]

The same Act regulates the financing of election campaigns. Each party must set up a separate Electoral Fund.[85] Donations to electoral committees are allowed only from Polish citizens, and public collections are forbidden. Payments to the Fund must be made by cheque, bank transfer or card only[86] and kept in a separate banking account.[87] The maximum donation from an individual is 15 times the monthly minimum wage (around €2,933). The same rules apply to donations to parties themselves, and donations exceeding the minimum monthly wage may not be provided in cash.

Ceilings for total electoral campaign expenditures are set by the State Election Commission, equal in Polish złoty (PLN) to the number of registered voters in the country divided by the number of seats in Parliament (560) and multiplied by the number of parliamentary seats in an electoral district where candidates have been registered.[88] Of this, not more than 80 percent may be spent on electoral advertisement and press.[89] If a party exceeds its ceiling, the Treasury confiscates an amount equal to the amount of the violation. Parties must transfer any "surplus" difference between money raised and spent to its Electoral Fund or to charity.[90]

6.2 Control and supervision

Under the law parties must submit annual financial statements to the State Election Commission together with statements on their Electoral Funds, while electoral committees must do the same within three months after the elections. Annual statements are published by the SEC within 14 days in the Official Journal. Parties must provide the identity of all donors and sources of income annually, starting from 31 May 2001. The State Election Commission organises an independent audit of the reports.

---

[84] Act on Political Parties, passed on 27 June 1997, with later amendments, Article 29, in: *Law Journal 2002*, no. 79, item 857. The PLN coefficients may be changed if inflation exceeds five percent in a quarter of the year.

[85] Act on Political Parties, passed on 27 June 1997, Article 35.

[86] Act on Political Parties, passed on 27 June 1997, Article 36a, paragraph 3.

[87] Act on Political Parties, passed on 27 June 1997, Article 36a, paragraph 3.

[88] Act on Elections to Sejm and Senate of Polish Republic, passed on 12 May 2001, Article 114.

[89] Act on Elections to Sejm and Senate of Polish Republic, passed on 12 May 2001, Article 115.

[90] Act on Elections, Article 116.

Until amendments passed in 2001 came into effect, the Election Commission could apply no sanctions to parties failing to provide information. Under the new law, parties who fail to submit reports or whose report is rejected by the Commission lose for four years a part of their State subsidy equal to three times the amount of the funds illegally raised or spent, an equal amount of the subsidy for election costs, and in addition must pay to the State budget the amount of funds raised illegally. Individuals responsible for violations are subject to a fine ranging from €266 to €26,660 or up to two years imprisonment.

In February and March 2002, the Election Commission assessed 24 reports from parties on their financing of the 2001 election campaign. Sixteen reports were accepted, including those of the ruling SLD-UP (Democratic Left Alliance-Labor Union), opposition PiS (Law and Justice), and German Minority electoral committees. Eight of these reports were rejected, including those of the coalition PSL (Polish Peasants' Party), and the opposition LPR (League of Polish Families), AWS and Samoobrona.[91] In April the Supreme Court definitely rejected appeals against the decision by the LPR (League of Polish Families) and the PSL (Polish Peasants' Party) parties.

6.3 Party finance in practice

Financing of Polish political parties has been widely regarded as corrupt throughout the 1990's. Parties have tended to be fragmented, unstable, and with low membership, resulting in the extensive use of corrupt or illegal means of obtaining funds.

Until the new law made public membership collections illegal, one of the main methods of securing donations from hidden sources was to attribute such donations to fictitious membership collections.

State enterprises and enterprises where the State owns shares have constituted an important and illegal source of funds for parties across the political spectrum. Enterprises have provided resources indirectly through affiliated media and PR companies, by funding advertising campaigns, concluding fictitious contracts and various other methods.[92] For example, during the 2000 presidential campaign KGHM Polska Miedź (the State copper company) paid approximately €10,833 for a training seminar for its employees; in fact the only person who attended the training session was Marian Krzaklewski (the AWS presidential candidate), and the trainer was a prominent image consultant. The media has also reported that Telekomunikacja Polska S.A.

---

[91] See <http://www.pkw.gov.pl>, (last accessed 26 August 2002).

[92] According to Anna Marszałek, a reporter at *Rzeczpospolita* daily, parties have gained the "bulk" of their financing from State companies.

(State telecommunication company) provided large amounts of money to AWS-Solidarity through contracts with a small advertising agency run by friends of various politicians, although there was no clear evidence for this. For the 2001 election campaign, AWS-Solidarity hired a small, unknown advertising company whose owners were very closely connected to the party.[93]

7. Public procurement

For much of the post-communist period corruption in Polish public procurement has been endemic. However, changes to the law that came into effect in 1997 have done much to end the most flagrant corrupt practices, and procurement rules are now largely compatible with EC directives. However, the Public Procurement Office (hereafter, PPO)appears unable to check enough procurements, and various sources indicate that collusion among bidders and fixed tenders remain widespread. The biggest scandal of the present Government resulted from corruption in a public tender at the Ministry of Defence.

7.1 Legislative framework

Public procurement is regulated by the Public Procurement Act,[94] which has been amended several times since it was first passed in 1994. The most extensive amendments were passed in June 2001[95] in order to make procurement legislation fully compatible with EU directives.[96]

The Procurement Act mandates an open public tender as the main method for allocating public contracts. Contracts between €30,000 and €200,000 may be allocated by restricted tender, request for bids or sole sourcing. Permission of the President of

---

[93] Information provided by Stefan Batory Foundation.

[94] Act on Public Procurement, passed on 10 June 1994, in: *Law Journal 1994*, no. 76, item 344.

[95] Act on Amendments to Law on Public Procurement, passed on 26 July 2001, in: *Law Journal 2001*, no. 113, item 1208.

[96] For example, the amended Act significantly narrows the exceptions from tender requirements, clearly separates price criteria (compulsory for assessing bids) from considerations of the quality of contractors, introduces fully transparent information provision during the tender process, removes provisions for preferring Polish contractors and allows a full two-stage appeal procedure. On the other hand, the thresholds for tender requirements were made less restrictive for certain tenders where required by EU law.

the Public Procurement Office is required to use procedures other than open tender for contracts exceeding €200,000, and to use sole sourcing for tenders exceeding €20,000.

Sole sourcing may be used only if, in addition to the required permission, one of a list of conditions is met. The most important of these are:

- due to unforeseeable circumstances an immediate procurement is required and the time limits for other procurements cannot be met;

- previous tender proceedings failed due to an insufficient number of bids, the original terms have not been changed and the tender can only be satisfied by one supplier or contractor;

- if the contract is a follow-up contract that does not exceed 20 percent of the value of the original contract and where the new contract became necessary as a result of unforeseen factors and the additional contract cannot be separated from the primary contract for technical or economic reasons.

Public procurement regulations are published in the Law Journal and are available to the public. Procurements must be advertised in the Public Procurement Bulletin (published by the Public Procurement Office) and are also placed on website of the PPO.[97]

Contracting parties must communicate the name and address of the winning firm together with the value of the offer to all bidders. The same information must also be placed in a medium accessible to the public. Tender results are also placed in the Bulletin.

Conflict of interest

The law forbids participation for the contract issuer in public procurement proceedings by persons who are married or related to a bidder, its legal agent or the managing members of legal entities soliciting a contract. For three years after a given procurement process, neither persons who have remained in an employment or commissioned work agreement relationship with the bidder, nor persons who remain in a relationship with the supplier or vendor such that their impartiality may be called into suspicion, may participate in the proceeding. There is no information available on whether these provisions are observed or not.

No monitoring of the assets or lifestyles of persons performing public procurement takes place, nor does any code of ethics exist.

---

[97] <http://www.uzp.gov.pl>, (last accessed 26 August 2002).

Blacklisting

The Procurement Act excludes from bidding for public contracts individuals previously convicted of crimes related to public procurement or other crimes committed for material gain, as well as legal entities whose managers have been convicted of such crimes. However, there is no published list of blacklisted persons or companies.

7.2 Review and audit

Public procurement is supervised by the Public Procurement Office (UZP), a separate central office whose President is responsible directly to the premier. The President is required by law to file a yearly report to the Council of Ministers on the functioning of the public procurement system.

Bidders may appeal procurement decisions to the contracting party, and thereafter to the President of the UZP. No contract may be closed until an appeal is finally decided. Appeals are reviewed by a panel of three arbiters: one chosen by the petitioning party, one by the contracting party and one by the President of the Office. Within one week of the panel's decision the parties may appeal further to the Regional Court in Warsaw. The number of appeals has risen steadily. There were 345 appeals in 1995, 837 in 1996, 1,005 in 1997, 1,195 in 1998, 1,327 in 1999, and 1,687 in 2000.

The PPO may also control public procurement proceedings in their course. However, GRECO noted in its May 2002 evaluation of anti-corruption policy in Poland that the Office was only able to control 670 procurements out of a total of 35,794 announced in the Public Procurement Bulletin in 2000.[98] Public procurement audits are performed by various Government departments on two levels: The NIK controls contracts issued by State-wide Government agencies, and Regional Clearing Chambers audit contracts placed by regional and local governments. In the event of violations of procurement law both have the right to petition budgetary discipline commissions in ministries or at voivodship level to impose sanctions against a specific administrator or institution.

Violations of the Public Procurement Act are treated as violations of budget discipline, for which responsibility was largely symbolic until the new Public Finance Act came into effect in 1999.

---

[98] GRECO, *Evaluation Report on Poland*, May 2002, p. 22.

7.3 Corruption

Until 1997, stories of malpractice and suspected corruption in public procurement were continuous.[99] The number of flagrant cases appears to have fallen in recent years, partly due to the tightening of the law in 1997 (which, according to the NIK, has contributed to an improvement in adherence to public procurement procedures). However, impropriety in public procurement is still a serious problem. The World Bank's 1999 Report refers to the responses of bidders saying that bribes are a factor in ensuring early access to vital information, preparation of the offer in such a manner as to advantage a particular bidder. The Report mentions large contracts for information systems and especially construction contracts as problem areas.

Malpractice has also been reported on numerous occasions by the NIK, although it is not known if corruption was involved. Individual cases include the following:

- An NIK audit of a contract to purchase train wagons by Polish National Railways (PKP) carried out in 2000 found that the contract had been issued without securement of financial resources or economic justification. In addition, tender regulations were violated so seriously that PKP cancelled the tender after a motion filed by NIK.[100]

- A 2000 audit of real estate purchases by the City of Lodź Social Insurance Office Department found that the real estate was purchased at a grossly over-inflated price after permission to carry out sole sourcing had been obtained from the PPO. The Director of the Department was earlier employed by the company from which it purchased the land. NIK and criminal proceedings were continuing as of June 2002.[101]

- The NIK has drawn particular attention to the risks of abuse in sole sourcing in other cases. According to the NIK, local governments are particularly vulnerable to such problems, if only because of less intensive control mechanisms at the local level. For example, a 1999 audit of school renovations performed by communes (the

---

[99] One of the more widely reported incidents was awarding of a contract to supply computer technology for the central State administration to an unknown company headed by a friend of the Prime Minister, which subjected the State treasury to large losses; in: Supreme Chamber of Control, *The Danger of Corruption in Light of the Audits Research of the Supreme Audit Chamber*, March 2000, annex 25, pp. 100–108.; M. Łukasiewicz "Było, nie było" [Once upon a time…], *Rzeczpospolita,* 12 October 1996.

[100] Supreme Chamber of Control, *The Danger of Corruption in Light of the Audits Research of the Supreme Audit Chamber,* annex 26, pp. 108–111.

[101] Supreme Chamber of Control, *The Danger of Corruption in Light of the Audits Research of the Supreme Audit Chamber,* annex 28, pp. 116–119.

lowest level of local government in Poland), found that in 16 of the 94 audited the procedures mandated by the procurement law were not applied at all, and in most of the remaining cases numerous improprieties were found.

A report on the Polish mining industry cites interviews with industry managers according to whom bribes of 10-15 percent of contract value were common practice, although the 1997 amendments have made such practices much more difficult. According to one manager,

> X [public official] told me straightway: "It will cost this and this. Y (another competitor) gives 10 percent, you give more, you win. I'm not the only one in the commission." So I could only quit because it was... unprofitable... You could always draw up some annex to the contract..., additional works or unpredicted costs. Now [in the light of the new Act] it's impossible.[102]

Despite this, corruption and rumours of corruption still appear to be widespread. The biggest corruption scandal in the last few years concerned a tender for pilot jackets (see Section 4.1.3). In March 2001 the President of the Totalizator Sportowy State lottery company was removed after the Lodź prosecution office launched an investigation into possible corruption in a tender to supply an online system.[103] According to one respected partner in a large Western law firm in Warsaw, the practice of fixing tenders is endemic.[104]

8. PUBLIC SERVICES

Corruption in a number of Polish public services appears to be widespread. Corruption in the police is a serious problem, especially in the traffic police. The customs administration has long been regarded as corrupt, although a number of recently established anti-corruption mechanisms may have helped to improve the situation. The tax administration has been highly vulnerable to corruption due to wide discretion enjoyed by both central and local tax officials to grant tax breaks to companies, although such exceptions have been restricted greatly since 1998. Corruption in the healthcare system is more widespread than in any other area according to public

---

[102] K. Gadowska, "Obstacles to Transformation – The Impact of Clientelist Networks on the Process of Restructuring the Coal Mining Industry in Poland," unpublished paper presented at joint LSA-RCSL ISA Conference on Sociology of Law, Budapest 2001.

[103] M. Werzchowska, "Kamela-Sowinska sacks lottery chief," *Warsaw Business Journal*, 26 March 2001.

[104] Interview with Polish partner in a highly-respected Western law firm in Warsaw, 19 March 2002.

opinion surveys, and informal payments are so pervasive that they are not even hidden. Likewise, corruption in the education system appears to be very widespread. Corruption in the latter two areas has been facilitated by the fact that – at least until recently – courts have judged doctors and teachers not to be public officials (and therefore not subject to bribery provisions). Licensing and regulation in general appear to be subject to widespread corruption, although new legislation in 1999 liberalised licensing procedures significantly. Corruption appears to be pervasive in business registration.

8.1 Police

Corruption in the police appears to be a serious problem, despite limited evidence from criminal statistics. However, mechanisms for fighting corruption in the police have recently been improved.

According to official police statistics, more than 100 officers were subject to criminal proceedings for corruption in 2001, although other sources say the actual number is at least double.

Table 2: Police statistics of police bribery cases under criminal investigation, 1998-2002

Bribery of police on duty	1998	1999	2000	2001
No. of criminal cases initiated	80	64	81	110
No. of police force under investigation	102	90	131	157

Source: Police HQ 2002.

There is widespread agreement that these figures represent only a tiny proportion of actual cases of corruption within the police. Recent public opinion polls show that the police are considered the second most corrupt institution after the health service.[105]

---

[105] The Batory Foundation survey *Corruption in Everyday Life* gives the figure as 26 percent of reported bribery cases.

Corruption among traffic police is widely regarded as particularly prevalent.[106] Both the EU and the NIK have criticised the traffic police system for its use of on-the-spot discretionary cash fines and lack of supervision.

Possible links between police and organised criminal groups is a potentially far more serious problem, although its extent is unknown. In one recent case seven policemen, including one from the Central Investigative Bureau, were accused of cooperation with a gang selling illegally imported cars and blackmailing.[107] The case is still under judicial investigation.

Corruption among police is encouraged by very low salaries, which begin lower than €267, while a police station chief earns around €671.

Like other public officials, police officers are subject to the bribery provisions of the Criminal Code. In addition, they may be held liable for damages caused by corrupt behaviour. Finally, any police officer committing a criminal offence is also charged with disciplinary liability under the provisions of the Police Act; police officers may also be removed on suspicion of criminal acts.[108] Disciplinary penalties are decided by the officer's superior, and range from admonishment to expulsion from the service. Service liability is an important incentive against corruption as an expelled officer is likely to have acute problems gaining employment elsewhere.

Citizens may notify the Public Prosecutor's Office or any police commander of suspected offences by police officers on a Poland-wide free anonymous infoline or via a special e-mail address.[109] According to police from units in charge of investigating corruption, the effectiveness of these instruments has been minor to date.

The fight against police corruption was long hampered by counterproductive anti-corruption provisions, in particular the lack of protection against prosecution for bribe-givers wishing to notify the police, and a provision that allowed "sting" bribes by undercover officers only in the absurdly high amount of €202,670. Amendments to the Police Act that entered into force in March 2002 allow for more flexibility in sting

---

[106] The press has reported the existence of fixed traffic stopping points where intoxicated drivers have to pay off policemen amounts according to the class of car they drive, in: M. Łajtar, "Corruption in Polish Police," unpublished paper presented at joint meeting of CEEU and Princeton University, Budapest, November 1999. The most publicised case of minor corruption was the operation of a team at one provincial police station that forced money from farmers coming to market, in: Piotr Jastrzębski, "Trzynasty komisariat" [Thirteenth Police Station), *Nie*, 11 January 2000.

[107] Statement by P. Biedziak, Spokesman of Police Headquarters, February 2001.

[108] Act on Police, passed on 6 April 1990, in: *Law Journal 1990*, no. 30, item 179, with later amendments.

[109] <kontakt@kgp.waw.pl>.

operations, have abolished cash tickets for traffic offences and oblige policemen to notify a superior officer of every intervention on duty. In addition, the Internal Affairs Administration (formerly the Police Internal Affairs Board) was created in 1998 to investigate criminal offences committed by police officers. The unit reports directly to the Chief of Police. In addition, special departments at the Chief of Police and Voivodship Police Headquarters are responsible for detecting, monitoring and analysis of criminal offences committed by police. This service includes more than 90 experienced police staff.

The EU has had a direct impact on the Polish police in three respects. First, significant financial and training assistance has been provided under the PHARE programme. Second, the Ministry of Interior and Administration and Police Headquarters teams have been working on integration with EU structures including the accession of Polish police to EUROPOL. Finaly, accession negotiations have encouraged harmonisation of police standards and legislation with EU requirements: for example, reform of traffic policing has taken place in order to satisfy Commission directives.

8.2 Customs

Corruption among Poland's 14,400 customs officers has long been regarded as a serious and widespread problem. Although only 11 officers were expelled from the service for corruption in 1999, this is felt to reflect inadequate control mechanisms rather than real levels of corruption. According to the 1999 World Bank report,

> The existence of *ad hoc* and temporary exemptions and "duty suspensions" aggravates the potential for corruption. There is a hierarchy of corrupt transactions, from... bribes of up to €53 to enable queue jumping, to... more serious activities such as turning a blind eye to falsified documents... or being complicit in smuggling of illegal and dangerous goods or traffic in people.[110]

According to an anonymous survey of the largest importers carried out in 2000 by the Customs Statistics and Analytical, 12.5 percent of respondents judged cooperation with the Customs Office as bad. When asked to assess the integrity of customs inspectors on a scale from Very good to Bad, 12.5 percent chosen "Very good," 27.5 percent "Good," 20 percent "Correct" and 7.5 percent chosen "Bad," while 32.5 percent declined to reply.[111]

---

[110] World Bank, *Corruption in Poland*, pp. 19–20.

[111] Unpublished document provided by former Central Customs Office in March 2002.

Customs officers are liable both under the 1997 Criminal Code, special disciplinary regulations contained in the Act on Customs Service, and customs service work regulations. Under the latter customs officers may not carry on commercial activities, hold shares in commercial entities, hold positions in entities engaging with foreign trade, be on the supervisory board of foundations or employ relatives as subordinates.

A Customs Inspection Department was created under a special act passed in 1997.[112] The unit specialises in fighting customs offences and has similar powers to the police. The Customs Administration also introduced the rotation of officers every three years, and all customs officials must submit asset declarations on taking up and leaving office and annually while employed in between.

In 2001, the former President of the Customs Administration approved an anti-corruption strategy stemming to a large extent from an attempt to recreate an image of customs officers based integrity through a Customs Ethics Code. Citizens may now submit information on malpractice to a special Internet site.

Although the new regulations described above have not yet had a direct influence on levels of corruption, customs officers[113] believe that the new procedures of customs inspection and significant material support from EU resources have improved border crossing procedures and reduced delays, which had been an important factor facilitating corruption. Partly in response to recommendations by the NIK, corruption has also been addressed through the application of the "many eyes" principle (the requirement that more than one officer be present at border inspections) to make bribery of individual officers more difficult.

8.3 Tax collection

A general report submitted by the NIK to the House of Deputies in 1999 – entitled Taxes in Light of Supreme Audit Chamber Findings, 1992-1998 – details the vulnerability of the Polish tax administration due to complex and unclear tax laws and the arbitrary treatment of taxpayers. In particular, the system of tax relief (redemptions, reductions of tax assessment, deferments and so on) has been widely abused, including specific instructions from the Ministry of Finance to the tax offices to grant relief to

---

[112] Act on Customs Inspection, passed on 6 June 1997, in: *Law Journal 1997*, no. 71, item 449.

[113] Interview with K. Urbańska, Director, Customs Statistics and Analytical Office, 7 March 2002.

particular companies.[114] The NIK calculated that the value of income tax breaks in 1996 equalled 22 percent of personal income and 40 percent of corporate tax revenue.

As a result of such criticism, in 1998 the Minister of Finances ceased delivering instructions to tax offices in particular cases, and the level of discretionary relief was reduced by one-half in one year – from €320m to €160m. However, local mayors may still cancel or reduce real estate taxes for a particular entity, and information on such decisions is often concealed from local councillors on the grounds of personal data protection.

The NIK report also highlighted the inadequacy of audit and control within the tax administration, the tendency of tax offices to audit mainly low-income taxpayers (a sign that tax offices have come to "arrangements" with richer taxpayers and companies) and the acceptance of minor gifts by tax officials.

8.4 Health

According to public opinion research the health service is the sector where corruption is most widespread. Surveys indicate that 45-52 percent of those who admitted bribing in general said they had bribed public health employees.[115] The very low salaries of doctors, nurses and other health service employees, combined with a complete lack of ethics training, a non-transparent system of financing by the decentralised National Health Services, and underfunded health clinics provide fertile ground for informal payments and corruption.

According to the World Bank 1999 report,

> Informal payments pervade the Polish medical and health care system, and can range from small gifts ex post facto to poorly paid carers, to "speed money" for faster treatment, to extortion of large bribes on an informally established tariff for surgery and other treatments.[116]

---

[114] According to the Supreme Audit Chamber, "[Ministry of Finance] officers acting upon the Minister's authorization interfered with normal tax proceedings to become advocates of the interests of particular taxpayers. Tax offices to which such instructions were submitted treated them as effective and made decisions… without an appropriate explanatory inquiry, failing to analyse the reasons for granting a relief. Such a situation was undoubtedly corruptive since every relief had a financial impact that could be expressed in hundreds and sometimes million of złoty."

[115] In the Batory Foundation-funded 2000 survey, doctors lead amongst those to whom a bribe was given as declared by the sample – 48 percent of all cases of bribery reported.

[116] World Bank, *Corruption in Poland*, p. 22.

A 1996 audit of clinics by the NIK found that the patient's right to free healthcare was violated in 37 of 50 clinics, and patients' financial participation was so pervasive that there was no attempt to conceal it. Participation included contributions to public collections, decisions to charge for certain services, and appeals by supervisory councils to patients (whose rights they are set up to protect) to contribute to their health clinic. Moreover, the "voluntary" nature of payments was frequently in doubt.

According to anecdotal evidence corruption is widespread in order to gain sick notes for various purposes.[117]

Instances of corruption among health service employees are sometimes reported to Physicians' Chambers and to prosecutors. However, under the Penal Code only ward heads or directors of hospitals can be prosecuted for bribery; regular doctors are not regarded as persons performing a public function. One recent case involved the head of a hospital ward who was convicted of taking money from patients in return for various benefits and sentenced to three and half years in prison, a fine, and a ban from management positions for eight years. As of April 2002 the case was under appeal.

The pharmaceutical industry is also labelled by many as a hot spot for corruption in Poland. The World Bank recently warned of rampant corruption in the industry, affecting all areas from drug registration, drug pricing, Government reimbursements, manipulation of prescriptions and sales, and price controls.[118] Several acts were passed in 2001 to bring Polish legislation fully into line with EU requirements.

8.5 Education

Sociological research indicates that corruption is a serious problem at all levels of the Polish education system. Although a few measures have been introduced to tackle corruption, a major problem remains the fact that teachers appear not to fall under bribery provisions.

Surveys indicate widespread corruption in education:

- A 1999 national survey (CBOS 1999) found that 16 percent of respondents named numerous issues that could be obtained by means of bribery (for example, acceptance to a school or university or passing an exam). Four percent

---

[117] In an extreme case, the media recently reported the case of a defendant prosecuted in an organised crime case who secured a doctor's certificate that he was claustrophobic in order to evade custody.

[118] "World Bank report scolds pharmaceutical industry," *Warsaw Business Journal*, 13 August 2001.

of parents said they had tried to influence their children's results by rewarding teachers, while a full 76 percent said they contributed in collections of gifts for teachers.

- A survey of 203 teachers carried out in 2000[119] found that 25 percent said parents tried to bribe them; although 80 percent said they refused; the same respondents often described instances of corruption around them and 37 percent agreed that, "In schools, as elsewhere, one can buy anything one likes."

A number of reports of corruption have emerged in recent years, for example in the Maritime University and Institute of Physical Education. In 2001, students in Lodź, Białystok and Lublin were caught buying medical school entrance exams.[120] The NIK has identified entrance examinations to secondary schools and higher education as vulnerable to corruption, mainly due to the lack of safeguards on leakage of examination questions. Very low teacher salaries are also a source of corruption. Corruption is not limited to bribery but also includes phenomena such as forced additional tutoring.

The 1982 Teachers' Charter contains a disciplinary code with penalties ranging from reprimand to a lifetime ban. Many schools have introduced much stricter procedures for protecting the integrity of examination materials. However, it remains a problem that while school directors are considered public functionaries under the bribery law, teachers are not. In March 2001, the media reported the case of a high-school teacher who collected €80 from pupils in exchange for a passing grade on mathematics exams. Although the teacher was suspended and a disciplinary investigation started, the Lublin District Court dismissed criminal proceedings on the grounds that the teacher was not performing a public function. Another case similarly dismissed was of a teacher from the Agricultural School Complex who accepted bribes from 14 students. The teacher was barred from the profession for three years. The case was on appeal in early 2002.

8.6 Licensing and regulation

Until 1999, 30 types of economic activities required a licence in Poland, while more than 50 types of activity were regulated by administrative decision. The 1999 Act on Economic Activity liberalised licensing policy considerably, reducing the number of

---

[119] B. Łaciak, "Korupcja w szkolnictwie – formy i zakres zjawiska" [Corruption in Education – Forms and Scope], in: J. Kurczewski and B. Łaciak (eds.), *Korupcja w życiu społecznym* [Corruption in Social Life], ISP, Warsaw 2000, pp. 63–80.

[120] "The myth of the loveable rogue," editorial, *Warsaw Business Journal*, 23 July 2001.

activities requiring licenses to eight.[121] The Act removed 12 types of economic activities entirely from the requirement to obtain a licence or permit. However, corruption remains a serious problem in those areas in which licenses are still required.

The NIK has carried out many audits of licensing and sectors where licensing is still required, with many negative findings. For example:

- The establishment and distribution of customs contingents was subject to arbitrariness, and the manner of distribution at least raised suspicions of corruption.[122]

- Licenses were granted to companies to provide international transport services when they failed to meet statutory requirements, and documentation of the licensing process was full of inaccuracies.[123]

- The process of granting licences for mineral excavation was found to be characterised by imprecise definition of the scope of licences, failure to collect dues, and lack of supervision resulted in many companies performing mining activities without a licence or paying adequate operational fees. The relevant act was amended as a result.

- Serious malpractice was uncovered in the issue of construction permits in 1998, including the issuing of construction permits when applicants did not satisfy basic legal requirements, and approval by construction officials of their own projects.

- A 2001 audit of driving licence procedures found that licences could be obtained with bribes of €19-533. NIK proposed establishing examiner panels to help prevent corruption, but the proposal was rejected by the Infrastructure Minister.[124]

The World Bank noted that its respondents labelled broadcasting licences, telecommunications concessions, transport licences (especially Ministry of

---

[121] These are: prospecting for or finding minerals, mining minerals; manufacturing and trading in explosives, arms and ammunition, and products and technologies for military or police applications; protection of people and property; air transport and other air services; construction and operation of toll highways; railway line management and railway transport; dissemination of radio and television programmes.

[122] Supreme Chamber of Control, *The Danger of Corruption in Light of the Audits Research of the Supreme Audit Chamber,* March 2000, annex 33, pp 130–133.

[123] Supreme Chamber of Control, *The Danger of Corruption in Light of the Audits Research of the Supreme Audit Chamber,* March 2000, annex 34, pp. 134–137.

[124] *Warsaw Business Journal,* 11 February 2002.

Transportation - issued international transportation licences), and permits linked to construction, real estate and commercial activity as the most problematic areas in terms of corruption.[125]

The press has widely discussed a case in Lodź where an officially voluntary Benefit Fund for the City was established and entities that were granted licences had to contribute to the fund. Although corruption was not directly involved, the presence of payments not required by law was regarded as a step in that direction.[126]

Another area of registration that appears to be particularly troublesome is admission to the Polish Bar Association, which both lawyers and NIK officials criticise for its allegedly restrictive practices, whereby a very small proportion of law graduates are admitted each year and where nepotism is widely regarded to play an important role.[127]

Business registration

Business registration is also troubled by corruption. Understaffing, high staff turnover, lack of training and inadequate infrastructure lead to delays, and there is significant anecdotal evidence of bribes being used speed up the process.

Lawyers report that registering a business normally takes around two months, while a wide network of intermediaries can secure registration in two weeks.[128] In addition to a large backlog of cases, a 1998 inspection by the NIK found that courts deal with applications for changes in the real estate register according to unknown criteria.

9. ROLE OF THE MEDIA

Freedom of speech is largely guaranteed. Although criminal sanctions against insulting public officials represent potential threats, the impact of this in practice does not

---

[125] World Bank, *Corruption in Poland*, p. 21.

[126] M. Fuszara, "Obraz korupcji w prasie" [Corruption in the Press], in: J. Kurczewski, B. Łaciak (eds.), *Korupcja w zyciu społecznym* [Corruption in Social Life], pp. 39–62.

[127] Interview with Polish partner in a highly-respected Western law firm in Warsaw, 19 March 2002; OSI Roundtable Discussion, Warsaw, 19 March 2002. *Explanatory note: OSI held a roundtable meeting to invite critique of the present Report in draft form. Experts present included representatives of the Government, international organisations, and civil society organisations. References to this meeting should not be understood as an endorsement of any particular point of view by any one participant.*

[128] Interview with Polish partner in a highly-respected Western law firm in Warsaw, 19 March 2002.

appear to be serious. An Act on Access to Public Information came into effect in 2001, although the impact of the law as of April 2002 appeared to have been limited. Broadcasting regulation is highly politicised, and Polish Television appears to be largely under·the control of party nominees to the broadcasting regulator and to lack the capacity to carry out independent investigative journalism. Despite these problems, the press in particular has been very active in uncovering corruption, and has prompted official action in a number of cases.

9.1 Press freedom

Freedom of speech and the right to obtain information are enshrined in the Polish Constitution. Journalists are subject to standard libel and defamation provisions. However, press freedom is potentially threatened by stringent provisions that make it illegal to insult a public official.[129] Moreover, investigative journalism is not aided by a legal provision that obliges journalists to receive the authorisation of cited sources for their articles. The media may not publish opinions on legal proceedings before the issuance of a verdict by a court of the first instance, or personal data or images of individuals subject to or participating in legal proceedings; or information concerning the private life of any individual unless it is directly relevant to their public activities.[130] Information recorded in audio or video form can be published only with the consent of the person providing the information.[131] Journalists have the right and indeed are obliged to protect the identity of their sources.[132]

9.2 Access to information

In January 2001, a new Act on Access to Public Information came into effect.[133] Under the Act, any individual has the right to public information and access to public documents except for information covered by individual privacy provisions, commercial secrets or any other secrets laid down by law. Public agencies are obliged to provide information inter alia on their staff, budget, programmes, reports, actions,

---

[129] According to the reporter Anna Marszałek , prosecution offices are usually available to their political allies to launch cases against journalists. Interview with the reporter, Warsaw, 20 March 2002.

[130] Press Act, passed on 26 January 1984, Article 13.

[131] Press Act, passed on 26 January 1984, Article 14.

[132] Press Act, passed on 26 January 1984, Article 15.

[133] Act on Access to Public Information, passed on 6 September 2001, in: *Law Journal 2001*, no. 112, item 1198.

rules and decisions to the website Bulletin of Public Information, established by the Minister of Interior and Administration. Other information is to be provided on request within 14 days and without charge unless extra costs are incurred due to the form in which the information is requested.

Refusals to provide information may be challenged before ordinary courts. Legal provisions protecting privacy and commercial secrets do not apply to information on persons performing public functions or related to the performance of such a function. The Act also codifies free access to sessions and reports of all public elected bodies, including local self-government. Failure to provide information is punishable by a fine or up to one years of imprisonment.

Under the Press Act,[134] private businesses and non-profit bodies are obliged to provide information on their activity unless it is defined as confidential under other legal provisions (for example a commercial secret under civil law). The refusal must be delivered in writing within three days, and may be challenged at the Supreme Administrative Court.[135] Information must be provided free of charge unless special costs are involved.

According to journalists, the impact of the Act has been limited. Authorities freely use the exceptions in the Act to withhold information, and as of April 2002 the Government had not yet issued any detailed instructions to authorities on how to apply the Act.[136]

9.3 Broadcasting regulation

Under the Act on Broadcasting and Television,[137] the National Council of Broadcasting and Television is responsible for issuing broadcasting licences and regulating broadcasting. The Council comprises nine members: four appointed by the House of Deputies, two by the Senate and three by the President.

Accusations of unfairness concerning the granting of licenses have often been raised by dissatisfied competitors. For example, Radio Maryja (a far right-wing political/religious radio station) lobbied successfully against the refusal of the Council to grant it nationwide frequencies.

---

[134] Press Act, passed on 26 January 1984, in: *Law Journal 1984* (7 February), with later amendments.

[135] Press Act, passed on 26 January 1984, Article 4.

[136] Interview with Anna Marszałek, journalist, *Rzeczpospolita*, 20 March 2002.

[137] Act on Broadcasting and Television, passed on 29 December 1992, in: *Law Journal 1993*, no. 7, item 34, with later amendments.

The management of Polish Television is appointed and recalled by a Supervisory Board, itself appointed by the National Council, except for one member appointed by the Minister of the State Treasury. Under post-communist Governments from 1993 to 1997, the Board became dominated by appointments of the Social Democratic and Peasant's Party: for example, the President of Polish TV is the former manager of President Aleksander Kwasniewski's 1995 election campaign. In May 2001, the former editor of the SLD daily newspaper revealed that Prime Minister Leszek Miller held weekly meetings with media heads including the management of State television, allegedly laying down the party line. This dominance lasted through four subsequent years of right-wing Government. Public TV does not carry out real investigative journalism, and rather appears to have presented cases for the political ends of the SLD. The most flagrant case of this was the publication in the run-up to the 2001 elections of unfounded allegations that senior politicians associated with Lech Kaczynski's Law and Justice Party (which had been gaining popularity rapidly and represented a real threat to the SLD in the elections) of having received several hundreds of thousands of stolen dollars in the early 1990's.[138] The Polish media condemned the broadcast widely.

9.4 Corruption in the media

Although there is little direct evidence of corruption in the Polish media, the practices of many Polish public relations companies encourage corruption. According to a survey of journalists the SMG/KRC market research company carried out in 2001, one-third of respondents said PR agencies had tried to bribe them.[139] According to Western journalists working in Poland the need to separate editorial policies from advertising remains poorly understood.[140]

Basic principles of media ethics have been accepted by some of the leading media and the Media Ethical Council has been set up as a self-regulatory body that deals sometimes with transgressions by issuing opinions. Recently (5 April 2002) these media (however without the Public Television) accepted the Code of Journalist Ethics.

---

[138] M. Matraszek, "Dirty tricks?", *Warsaw Business Journal*, 25 June 2001.

[139] A. Kocińska, "Firms accused of buying favors from journalists," *Warsaw Business Journal*, 14 January 2002.

[140] Interview with Michael Leville, Editor, *Warsaw Business Journal*, Warsaw, 20 March 2002.

9.5 Media and corruption

The Polish media and the press in particular have devoted much attention to cases of corruption and have been the main reason for the increase in scandals in recent years, and investigative reports on themes related to corruption theme are becoming more and more common.

A number of press reports have prompted official action, such as the previously mentioned reports on a judge's alleged criminal contacts and ostentatious lifestyle, which led to his dismissal, or the exposure of pressure put on senators by the brewing lobby. There are no known cases of reprisals taken against journalists in response to reporting on corruption.

10. Recommendations

The following recommendations have been highlighted as particularly important to Poland. For additional recommendations applicable to candidate States generally, please see Part 5 of the Overview report.

1. Clarify and coordinate anti-corruption policy by creating an independent body at the highest level with explicit Government support.

2. Depoliticise the prosecution system, consider separating the positions of Minister of Justice and Prosecutor General.

3. Limit patronage appointments to State agencies and State companies, and reaffirm commitment to a depoliticised civil service.

4. Carry out budget reform to limit off-budget funds and allow proper scrutiny of their operations.

Corruption and Anti-corruption Policy in Romania

Table of Contents

Corruption and Anti-corruption Policy in Romania

EXECUTIVE SUMMARY

Romania appears to be the EU candidate country most seriously affected by corruption. Corruption is endemic if not systemic in many areas of public life: the customs authorities, judiciary, police, State Property Fund, Parliament and ministers are all perceived as highly corrupt, while "State capture" is also perceived to be a serious problem, particularly through the purchase of parliamentary votes and political party funding. The health service is ranked as the most corrupt institution according to citizens' actual experience.

The Romanian Government has made major progress in developing a national anti-corruption strategy, and some progress in reforming institutions to limit corruption, notably the public procurement system. The Government's National Plan against Corruption contains an impressive list of measures and commitments that constitute a key benchmark for judging the Government's commitment to the fight against corruption.

However, despite the flurry of Government activity in the area of anti-corruption policy, so far the anti-corruption drive has focused on low-level corruption. The political establishment has refrained so far from carrying out reforms that would allow prosecution of corruption at the highest level. In particular, there has so far been no progress towards limiting the immunities enjoyed by members of Parliament, ministers and former ministers, or any progress towards establishing the independence of prosecutors. Likewise, criminal prosecutions and convictions for corruption have touched only lower-level officials and functionaries. This situation justifies the concern that the Government may be as much a source of corruption as a solution to it.

Anti-corruption policy has been to a large extent driven by pressure from the EU, and has recently been given added momentum by the prospect of joining NATO. NATO in particular has labelled corruption as one of the most important barriers to Romania's accession. The EU has provided extensive assistance to the development of an anti-corruption policy, although it has not been able to secure the creation of a truly independent anti-corruption agency. Romania has ratified the Council of Europe Criminal Law Convention on Corruption.

Romanian anti-corruption legislation is fairly comprehensive, although criminal liability of legal entities is not yet recognised. In addition to bribery provisions, the Anti-Corruption Act lays down a number of other anti-corruption provisions. Sentences are severe, which may paradoxically hinder convictions.

Regulation of conflict of interest remained virtually non-existent as of early 2002, with the exception of vague provisions of the Anti-Corruption Act and incompatibility provisions that apply only to local officials. As of June 2002, a draft Act on Conflict of Interest was under discussion in Parliament. Conflicts of interest remain endemic in Romanian politics and the public administration. All public functionaries are subject to the duty to submit asset and income declarations. However, the Act is totally ineffective: the declarations are not public, the framework for investigating violations is not in place and there are draconian sanctions against citizens submitting information on violations that turns out to be false.

State financial control is largely inadequate. The Court of Audit does not enjoy complete operational independence, and its findings are submitted very late and have little impact. The legal basis for internal State financial control has been established, but hardly implemented as of May 2002.

There are several anti-corruption agencies with overlapping agendas, the most important of which (the Anti-Corruption Section of the prosecution service) appears to have been kept weak deliberately. The most important issue for Romanian anti-corruption policy remains the continuing refusal of the Government to give up direct control of prosecution activities. An ombudsman was established in 1997; however, its powers are weak and it is not known to have investigated or initiated any cases of corruption.

Corruption appears to be widespread if not endemic in the executive branch and civil service, ranging from straightforward bribery to widespread traditions of gift giving. This situation is underpinned by executive discretion stemming from the widespread use of ordinances, excessive immunity provisions for both current and former members of the Government, poorly defined civil servant responsibilities, patronage at all levels and the ineffectiveness of procedures for redress against administrative decisions. Although a Civil Service Act was passed in 1999, its implementation requires substantial secondary legislation, for example a Code of Ethics that has yet to be formulated. Provisions to prevent conflict of interest situations or their abuse are inadequate, and are little observed.

Although all public expenditure is included in the official budget, the Government makes extensive use of ordinances to change the budget *post hoc*. There are no specific provisions on conflict of interest for MPs, many of whom are also practising lawyers or carry on other ancillary activities. Generous immunity provisions have proved effective in preventing the prosecution of corruption cases, and may be an important incentive for gaining election to Parliament: according to some estimates as many as half of MPs bribed political parties to be placed in a favourable position on their candidate lists.

Surveys indicate that corruption is widespread in the judiciary, and extremely high levels of distrust contribute to a generalised perception that Romania is governed by vested interests rather than by the rule of law. Interference by the executive branch in the judiciary and corruption within the judiciary itself raise doubts about the will or ability of the Government to pursue an effective anti-corruption policy. The courts are overloaded, resulting in lengthy delays in judicial proceedings, although the backlog of cases has been slowly decreasing.

Political party finance remains non-transparent, uncontrolled and probably highly corrupt. Standard problems of party corruption by business interests are supplemented by a problem of funding by individuals in exchange for places on party candidate lists (see above). Even senior politicians admit that the majority of party funding is illegal or hidden. Party finance yielded the largest corruption affair since 1989.

Corruption appears to be systemic in public procurement, ranging from collusion and strong patron-client networks to standard bribery. However, the most important progress made by the Government in anti-corruption policy so far has been reform of the legal framework for public procurement. However, there is still no independent body for supervising procurement or dealing with appeals. The implementation of the new legislation will be an important test of the State's ability to follow through on anti-corruption policy.

On the available evidence, corruption in Romanian public services appears to be endemic, with the exception of the education system, where unofficial payments appear to be relatively infrequent, small and not required in return for benefits. Corruption in the police is underpinned by widespread collusion between the police and organised crime. There is a long history of corruption in customs, with the involvement of State officials up to the highest level. Corruption of tax authorities is linked in particular to their wide discretion at both local and central level to grant tax breaks to companies. Widespread corruption to gain access to health services (the most seriously affected area according to surveys of experience) deters the poor from visiting doctors. The burden of licensing and regulation authorities is heavy, resulting in widespread corruption to ward off inspections.

The role of the media in exposing corruption is threatened by the continuing existence of draconian defamation provisions in the Criminal Code, which remain on the statute books despite strong criticism from international organisations. A new Act on Free Access to Public Information came into effect in January 2002. Public broadcasting is systematically and politically biased. Corruption of or pressure on media outlets through advertising is common. Despite these problems, the press has been active in exposing corruption.

1. INTRODUCTION

1.1 The data and perceptions

Romania appears to be the EU candidate country most seriously affected by corruption. Corruption is endemic if not systemic in many areas of public life: the customs authorities, judiciary, police, State Property Fund, Parliament and ministers are all perceived as highly corrupt, while "State capture" is also perceived to be a serious problem, particularly through the purchase of parliamentary votes and political party funding. The health service is ranked as the most corrupt institution according to citizens' actual experience.

Figures on criminal convictions alone would indicate that corruption is a very limited phenomenon. Table 1 shows the numbers of convictions under the main anti-corruption paragraphs.

Table 1: Convictions for corruption in Romania, 1995–2001

Criminal Act	1995	1996	1997	1998	1999	2000	2001
Passive bribery (Article 254)	217	281	314	215	168	117	122
Active bribery (Article 255)	92	119	124	107	57	35	89
Receiving undue benefits (Article 256)	34	35	33	22	13	10	4
Trafficking in influence (Article 257)	86	113	165	190	143	136	128
Total	429	548	636	534	381	298	343

Source: Directorate for Coordination of Corruption and Crime Prevention and Control Strategies, Ministry of Justice.

The number of convictions fell steadily on an annual basis from 1997 to 2000, although officials believe the number is now back on an upward trend as a result of the Government's commitment to fighting corruption. Most convictions have been of low-level officials (or their bribers) whose crimes were relatively minor and whose exposure is harmless to the Government, and the complete absence of convictions of high-level officials or politicians is striking. As the Ministry of Justice's *2001 Report on Anti-corruption Activities* notes,

The activity of fighting corruption was directed... [in 2001] towards the achievement of quantity indicators, focusing in minor deeds committed by persons who... did not represent a substantial social danger.[1]

Surveys

Survey evidence paints a very different picture and indicates that corruption is a more severe problem in Romania than in any other EU candidate country. The main data from surveys of public opinion and enterprise behaviour are summarised below:

- Romania ranked 63rd out of 99 countries in the Transparency International CPI in 1999, 68th out of 90 in 2000 and 69th out of 91 countries in 2001. Romania's score ranged between 3.44 (1997) and 2.8 (2001), where a score of ten indicates least corrupt and 0 indicates most corrupt.

According to the results of the EBRD/World Bank *1999 Business Environment and Enterprise Performance Survey,* Romania is the only country of Central and Eastern Europe outside the former Soviet Union that suffers from both high "State capture" and high "administrative corruption."[2]

- The World Bank's *2000 Diagnostic Survey of Corruption in Romania,* commissioned by the Romanian Government in 2000, found that two-thirds of the citizens believed all or most public officials to be corrupt (see Figure 1).[3]

---

[1] Ministry of Justice, *2001 Report on Anti-corruption Activities,* p. 6. According to the official statistics provided by the Ministry of Justice, more than half of the public officials convicted of corruption until 2000 were from the lowest levels of public administration such as guards or train conductors. (*Information Regarding the Evolution of Criminality in 1999,* Directorate for Coordination of Corruption and Crime Prevention and Control Strategies, Ministry of Justice, Bucharest, 2000, pp. 9–13).

[2] World Bank, *Anti-corruption in Transition: A Contribution to the Policy Debate,* 2000, pp. 14–16.

[3] The survey was conducted between April and May 2000 on three samples: 353 Romanian public officials, 417 enterprise managers, and 1,050 ordinary people. World Bank, *Diagnostic Surveys of Corruption in Romania,* an analysis prepared by the World Bank at the request of the Government of Romania, Bucharest, March 2001, p. 4.

Figure 1: Overall corruption: perceptions and experiences

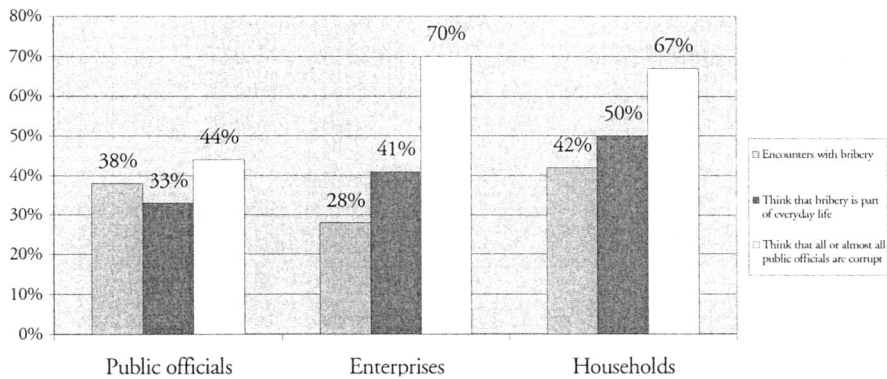

Note: Encounters with bribery means percentage of respondents who encountered bribery in the previous 12 months.

Source: World Bank, Diagnostic Surveys of Corruption in Romania, 2001

- A three-country survey commissioned by the Romanian Academic Society (SAR) found that 26 percent of citizens believed that almost all public officials are involved in corruption (compared to nine percent in Bulgaria and 18 percent in Slovakia) while 44 percent thought most officials are corrupt.[4]

- A *Survey of Official Corruption in Seven Southeast European Countries,* commissioned by the Southeast European Development Initiative (SELDI), showed that the highest perception of overall corruption was in Romania: on an index calculated from 0 (least corrupt) to ten (most corrupt) Romania ranked first (7.3),

BOX A: Leading businessmen's views on Romanian corruption

"Corruption is rife. Crazy people have called my researcher offering bribes in return for a job. Clients have also tried to bribe me by asking for an official lower price, and then offering me a chance to fill my own pockets. The worst case was when an extremely high-level administrator, a person who makes strategic recommendations of national importance, suggested he receive 'a cut' before our consultations went any further. I expressed myself extremely forcibly to him and walked away."

"A major in the Police asked me for €540 before he would instruct his officers to even begin the investigation of the theft of three of our company cars."

"In order to get proper deals even started in, say, the real estate field, officials here don't hint at bribes any more. It's now almost part of the formal conditions."

Source: Tim Johnson, "The Dark Side," *Bucharest Business Weekly,* vol. 4, no. 2, 24 January 2000.

---

[4] A. Mungiu Pippidi (SAR), *For an Institutional Approach to Post-communist Corruption: Analysis and Policy Proposal Based on a Survey of Three Central European States,* Bertelsmann Conference on Accountability, Bucharest, 3-5 May 2001.

followed by Albania (6.8) and Serbia (6.6).[5] Sixty percent of Romanians regarded corruption as the most important problem their country faces.[6] The SELDI survey also indicated that Romania has the lowest level of tolerance in principle toward corruption (1.7), but the highest inclination to engage in corrupt practices (4.4). While this indicates that corruption is more-or-less acceptable to citizens in everyday life, it raises worrying questions about the possible destabilising effect of corruption on overall political legitimacy.[7]

Meanwhile, evaluations of Government anti-corruption policy are generally negative. Since 1995, around 80 percent of the population remained dissatisfied with the anti-corruption policy, with a dramatic but brief improvement in early 1997 probably related to the establishment of the National Council of Action against Corruption and Organised Crime.[8]

1.2 Main loci of corruption

According to surveys of perceptions, corruption is very widespread in most Romanian public institutions. The World Bank's *2000 Diagnostic Survey* found that the customs administration is perceived as the most corrupt institution, followed by the judiciary, State Property Fund and Parliament (see Figure 2, below) The SELDI survey found MPs to be perceived as the most corrupt professional group, followed by police officers, customs officers and ministers (see Figure 3, below). Strong perceptions of high-level corruption are in stark contrast to the complete absence of convictions at that level.

---

[5] SELDI corruption indexes assume values from 0 to ten. Index values closer to 0 indicate approximation to the "corruption-free" ideal. Southeast Legal Development Initiative (SELDI), *Regional Corruption Monitoring* (Albania, Bosnia and Herzegovina, Bulgaria, Macedonia, Romania, the Federal Republic of Yugoslavia, and Croatia), September 2000 – February 2001, p. 12.

[6] For Romanian citizens, the main problems are corruption (59.90 percent), followed by poverty (50.60 percent), and low income (41.3 percent). See SELDI, *Regional Corruption Monitoring*, p. 6.

[7] SELDI, *Regional Corruption Monitoring*, p. 11. SELDI measured citizens' assessments of "the extent to which corruption is becoming an effective means of solving private problems" and it found out that the practical effectiveness of corruption is highest in Romania (7.5), followed by Albania (7.1), and Serbia (7.0). This shows clearly that incentives to engage in corruption are greater than the awareness of its bad effects. In fact, the SELDI survey took also into account citizens' reports of their "involvement in corrupt practices:" Romania ranks third (1.5), after Albania (2.8) and Serbia (1.8).

[8] Surveys since 1995, carried out by Centre for Urban and Regional Sociology, Bucharest; Metro Media Transylvania, Brasov; Universitary Laboratory of Social Analysis, Bucharest; Institute for Research on Quality of Life, Bucharest.

According to President Ion Iliescu,

> In the past four years, we have witnessed a growing complicity between the structures of organised crime and high officers in the Police, Gendarmerie, and secret services, judges, and politicians. This complicity represents a great threat for the national security.[9]

Surveys of citizens' experience with corruption indicate that unofficial payments are most common in the health service (see Figure 3, below). The results must be interpreted with caution, however, since the poor showing of the health service may also be related to the fact that a high percentage of respondents would actually have had contacts with the health system, whereas far fewer would have been involved in other activities, such as obtaining a construction permit.

Both the BEEPS *1999 Survey* and the World Bank's *2000 Diagnostic Survey* measure, among other things, the percentage of firms reporting that they are affected by "State capture" in various spheres (see Table 2). The sale of parliamentary votes figures high in both surveys, although there is a marked difference between the two surveys. The surveys indicate that private contributions to political parties, the National Bank of Romania, and the judiciary are also significant problem areas.

Table 2: Shares of Romanian firms affected by different forms of State capture (percent)

Romania	Parliamentary votes	Central Bank	Political Party Finance	Commercial Courts	Civil Courts	Criminal Courts	Presidential decrees
BEEPS (1999)	22	26	27	17	–	14	20
WB (2000)	42	27	24	13	20	–	–

Sources: World Bank, Anti-corruption in Transition: A Contribution to the Policy Debate, 2000; World Bank, Diagnostic Surveys, 2000 *Diagnostic Survey of Corruption in Romania.*

The evidence presented in this report indicates that corruption is a serious problem in almost all areas, and endemic in several areas, particularly public procurement, the police, political party funding and MPs. The evidence is often not direct: for example, judgements concerning high-level corruption are conditioned to a significant extent by the absurdly indulgent immunity provisions applying to ministers and MPs, and the interference of the Executive in the activities of prosecutors attempting to investigate high-level officials and politicians. Conflict of interest remains a fundamental and largely unsolved problem.

---

[9] President Ion Iliescu, speech at the presentation of the *2001 Activity Report of the Ministry of Interior.*

Figure 2. The perceived level of corruption in various state agencies

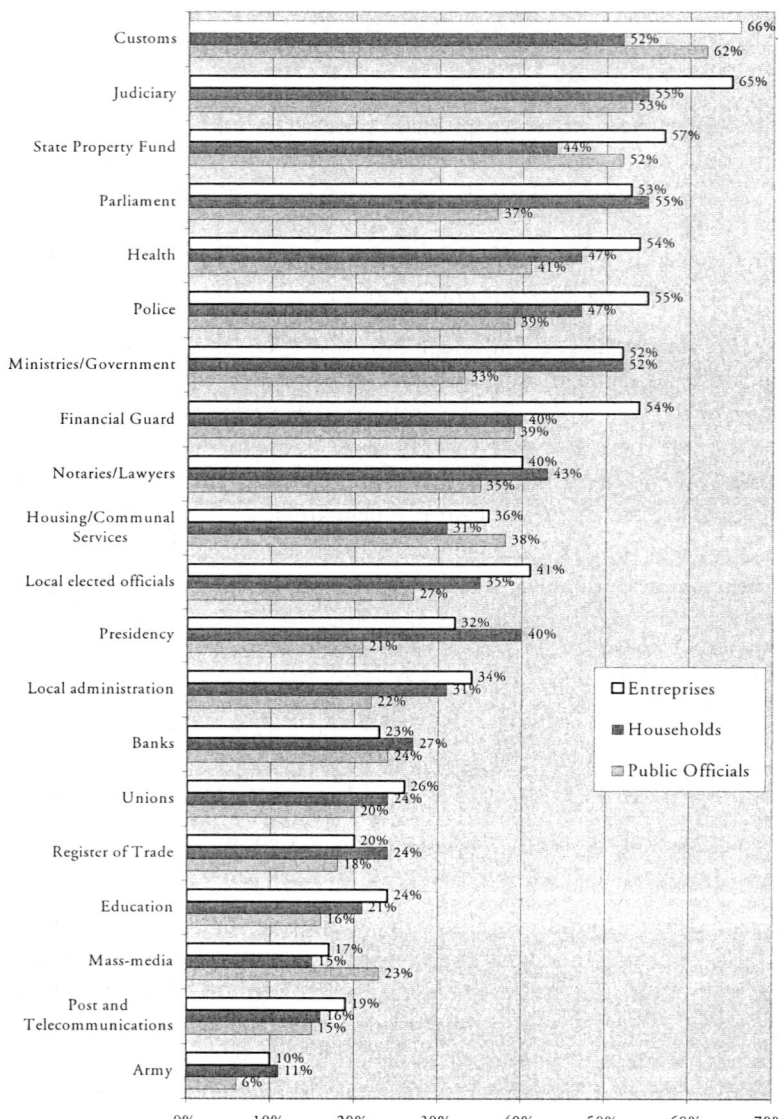

Source: WORLD BANK, Diagnostic Surveys of Corruption in Romania, 2001

Figure 3: Likelihood that Households Would Make Unofficial Payments while Using Service

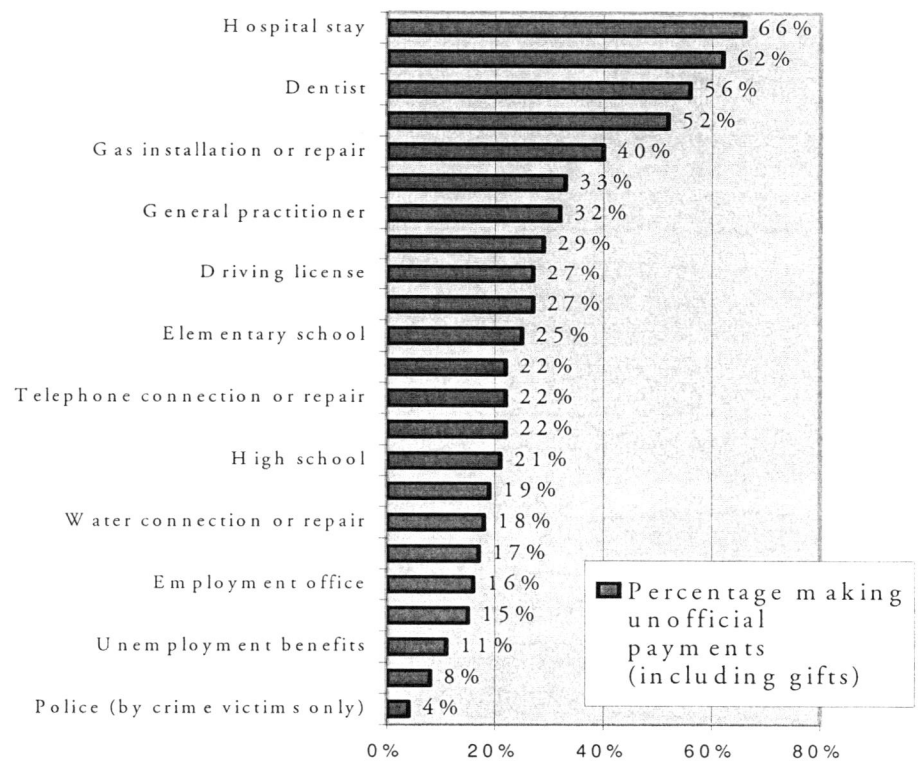

Source: World Bank, Diagnostic Surveys of Corruption in Romania, 2001

1.3 Government anti-corruption policy and the impact of the EU Accession Process

The Romanian Government has made major progress in developing a national anti-corruption strategy, and some progress in reforming institutions to limit corruption, notably the public procurement system. However, so far the anti-corruption drive has focused on low-level corruption and the political establishment has refrained from carrying out reforms that would allow prosecution of corruption at the highest level. Anti-corruption policy has been to a large extent driven by pressure from the EU, and has recently been given added momentum by the prospect of joining NATO, and the EU has provided extensive assistance to the development of anti-corruption policy.

Figure 4: Perceived level of corruption in Romanian State agencies

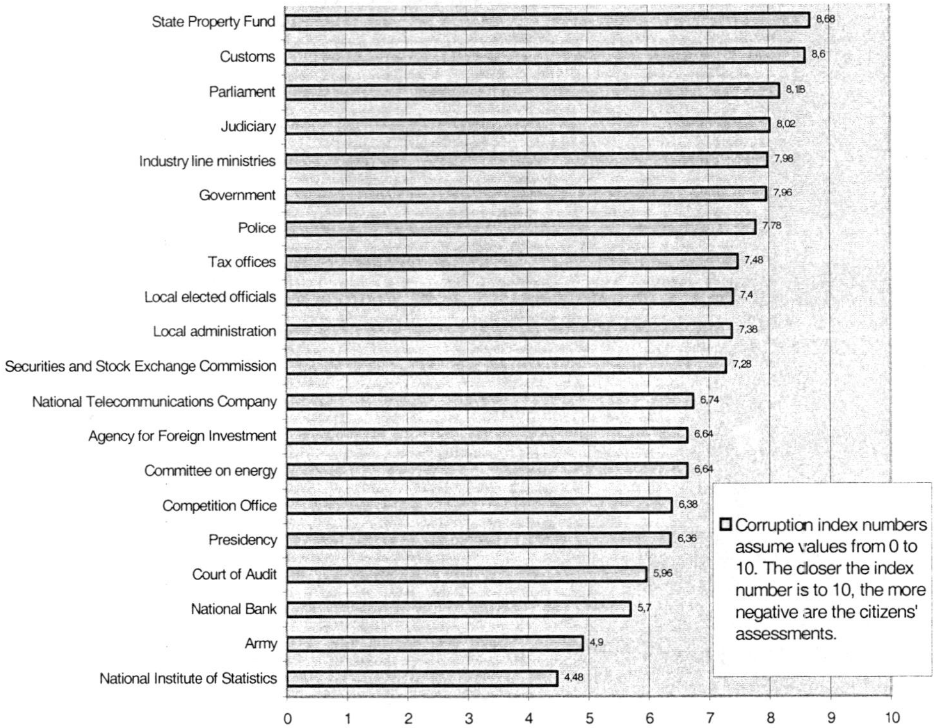

Horizontal bar chart showing perceived corruption index values:

State Property Fund	8,68
Customs	8,6
Parliament	8,18
Judiciary	8,02
Industry line ministries	7,98
Government	7,96
Police	7,78
Tax offices	7,48
Local elected officials	7,4
Local administration	7,38
Securities and Stock Exchange Commission	7,28
National Telecommunications Company	6,74
Agency for Foreign Investment	6,64
Committee on energy	6,64
Competition Office	6,38
Presidency	6,36
Court of Audit	5,96
National Bank	5,7
Army	4,9
National Institute of Statistics	4,48

Corruption index numbers assume values from 0 to 10. The closer the index number is to 10, the more negative are the citizens' assessments.

Source: SELDI, Regional Corruption Monitoring, 2001

Any discussion of Romanian anti-corruption policy must take into account the extent and depth of the corruption problem. As one of the creators of the UK's anti-corruption policy and a participant on an EU expert mission to Romania in September 2000 put it,

> A change in "attitude" and "culture" is necessary. This will inevitably take at least 10 to 15 years to effect, perhaps even two generations... There may well be a will to change but their [the Government's] capacity, in all probability, has been exceeded. Therefore progress must be measured in terms of small steps rather than large leaps.[10]

The European Commission's *Regular Reports on Romania's Progress towards Accession* have all concluded that Romania fulfils the Copenhagen political criteria for accession.[11] However, the reports have placed important caveats on this opinion, and singled out corruption as a "widespread and systemic problem" in 2000.[12] The *2001 Regular Report* reiterated this assessment:

> Last year's *Regular Report* noted that corruption was a widespread and systemic problem that undermined the legal system, the economy and public confidence in Government. Despite a general recognition of the seriousness of this problem by the Government there has been no noticeable reduction in levels of corruption and measures taken to tackle corruption have been limited.[13]

The EU's criticisms led to (and also reflected failure to meet) corresponding commitments in the *1998* and *1999 Accession Partnerships* (hereafter, "AP"). The *1998 AP* includes under "Justice and Home Affairs," a commitment to implement measures to combat corruption and organised crime and improve border management. The *1999 Regular Report* concluded that these priorities had not been addressed, and criticised the absence of a comprehensive anti-corruption strategy.[14] The *1999 AP* included as short-term priorities the adoption of an act on preventing and fighting corruption, the establishment of an independent anti-corruption department;

---

[10] D. Martin, RO98.01 – *A mission report of September 2000, PHARE, 2000,* pp. 4–5.

[11] The Copenhagen European Council in 1993 established the following political criteria: stability of political institutions guaranteeing democracy, the rule of law, human rights, and the protection of minorities. The 1995 Madrid European Council has also emphasized the administrative capacity criterion. See <http://www.europa.eu.int/comm/enlargement/>, (last accessed 20 April 2001).

[12] Commission of the European Union, *1998 Regular Report from the Commission on Romania's Progress towards Accession,* 4 November 1998, p. 13; *2000 Regular Report,* 13 October 2000, p. 18.

[13] Comission, *2001 Regular Report,* p. 21.

[14] "A number of initiatives have been launched to combat corruption, but a comprehensive approach is still lacking... Therefore, this priority has only been partially met." In: Commission, *1999 Regular Report,* 13 October 1999, p. 81.

ratification of the European Convention on Laundering Proceeds of Crime and the Council of Europe Criminal Law Convention on Corruption, and signing the OECD Convention on Bribery.[15]

Although the *2000 Regular Report* acknowledged that acceptance of the anti-corruption law fulfilled one *Accession Partnership* commitment, it not surprisingly concluded that, "[L]ittle progress has been made in reducing the levels of corruption and improved coordination is needed between the various anti-corruption initiatives that have been launched."[16] The *2001 Regular Report* repeated the same opinion, and, in addition, singled out public procurement, access to information and political party finance as areas in need of reform.[17] The *2001 AP* priorities include strengthening all bodies involved in the fight against corruption, improving coordination between them and clarifying their competencies; ratifying relevant international conventions against corruption; and introducing legal liability of legal persons into Criminal Act.[18] The *2001 AP* also contains a number of other commitments relevant to the fight against corruption, for example adopting a comprehensive public administration reform package, guaranteeing the independence of the judiciary and removing provisions of the criminal code that threaten freedom of speech (see individual sections of this report).

Romanian anti-corruption policy

The first example of an articulated anti-corruption policy was the creation in 1997 by President Emil Constantinescu of a National Council for Action against Corruption and Organised Crime following his election victory on an anti-corruption platform. The Council was abolished in September 1999.[19] It had no obvious effect or any public findings, but it initiated a real debate on anti-corruption policy and led to the 2000 Act on the Prevention, Detection and Prosecution of Corruption Offences (hereafter, "Anti-corruption Act").

---

[15] Corruption is also addressed as a short-term priority under the Internal Market chapter, more precisely in what concerns customs: "apply measures to combat fraud and corruption." Commission, *Romania: 1999 Accession Partnership*, 13 October 1999.

[16] Commission, *2000 Regular Report*.

[17] Commission, *2001 Regular Report*, pp. 21–22.

[18] Commission, *2001 Accession Partnership*, p. 6.

[19] This was to deal with "grand corruption" cases threatening to national security, identify sectors controlled by mafia structures and increase cooperation between bodies involved in the fight against corruption.

After two draft acts that would have created a new separate anti-corruption body,[20] Parliament rejected this proposal and opted in February 2000 for an act establishing an Anti-corruption Section within the General Prosecutor's Office and attached to the Supreme Court of Justice.[21] However, the Section has faced problems ever since its establishment due to continuing executive interference, inadequate resources and the lack of political will to grant it sufficient independence to pursue important corruption cases. This model was opted for (chosen) despite the preference of the EU for a body that would enjoy independence from the Executive.[22] The Section was created in October 2000, and has faced problems ever since due to continuing executive influence (see Section 2.5).

In March 2002, the Government approved an Emergency Ordinance transforming the Section into a National Anti-corruption Prosecutor's Office, operating as of September 2002, with 320 staff, including 150 criminal police officers and 75 prosecutors. The Ordinance solves some of the previous problems, for example, establishing a six-year term of office for prosecutors in the Office. However, the key issue – the independence of the Office's chief – was still not solved satisfactorily. It will be headed by a prosecutor appointed by the President of Romania on the recommendation of the Minister of Justice, and will be subordinate to the Prosecutor-General. Moreover, the Minister of Justice may order a reorganisation of the Office.

The National Anti-corruption Policy

Parallel with developments in the Anti-corruption Section, the Government has developed a broader anti-corruption policy. In July 2001, the Government established the National Committee for the Prevention of Criminality (NCPC) led by the Prime Minister and coordinated by the Minister of Justice. Within the NCPC, a Central Group for Analysis and Coordination of Corruption Prevention Activities (CGACCPA) was formed, coordinated by the Prime Minister's Control Department.

---

[20] The original draft of the Anti-corruption Act provided for the establishment of a National Anti-corruption Commission, an inter-departmental body subordinated to the Government and formally led by the Prime Minister. In 1999, this was replaced by a proposal to transform the Government Control Department (GCD) into a new Control and Anti-corruption Department (GCAD) coordinated by the Prime Minister, headed by an apolitical Secretary of State and empowered to control the activity of all governmental organizations.

[21] *Report 133* (supplementary report), Juridical Committee for Discipline and Immunities of the Chamber of Deputies, <http://www.cdep.ro/pls/parlam>, (last accessed 10 May 2001).

[22] This preference has been stated in successive *Regular Reports*, and formulated clearly by twinning partners from the Spanish *Fiscalia Anticorrupcion*. Delegation of the European Commission in Romania, Briefing Note for OSI Roundtable Discussion, Bucharest, 28 March 2002.

The CGACCPA includes representatives of NGOs, while international organisations such as the EC Delegation and the World Bank have permanent observer status.

Based on the activities of the CGACCPA, in October 2001 the Government published a "National Programme for the Prevention of Corruption" and "National Action Plan Against Corruption." The Action Plan sets out specific measures for different areas, and places more emphasis on prevention than previous policies.[23] Programme deadlines and commitments are shown in Table 3. As of May 2002, the Government had failed to meet planned deadlines for a number of the more important measures, namely passing a Lobbying Act, amending asset disclosure legislation and initiating drafts for a new act on political party funding.

While the National Plan contains a large number of measures that are clearly desirable, and, *inter alia*, urged or required by the European Commission, the strategy and focus of Government policy has so far been clearly on low-level corruption. For example, President Ion Iliescu told a meeting of Interior Ministry officials in March 2002 that corruption "must be eradicated from the bottom up,"[24] and there has been a notable absence of even a surface commitment to dealing with corruption at the highest level.

Moreover, a notable absence from the strategy is any specific commitment to change the system of appointing the Prosecutor-General, which this report suggests has been a fundamental obstacle to effective prosecution of important corruption cases (see Sections 2.5 and 5.1). Although the Government has formally fulfilled its commitment to strengthen the role of the Supreme Council of Magistracy and the Anti-corruption Section (see above), it has not addressed the issue of prosecutors' independence, despite the fact that both the EU and the Council of Europe, especially, have highlighted this as a key problem. The Government's inaction on this issue is reflected by its retention of the current system of appointing the chief of the Anti-corruption Section (see Section 2.5).

---

[23] Government of Romania, *National Programme for Prevention of Corruption*, October 2001, p. 17.

[24] "Romanian President says corruption must be eradicated 'from the bottom up," RFE/RL Newsline, 14 March 2002.

Table 3: Selected measures in the October 2001 National Plan Against Corruption.

Measure	Deadline	Fulfilled
Elaboration of Sectoral Anti-corruption Plans (Public Ministry, ministries of Justice, Interior and ministries involved in National Security, Public Administration, Public Finances, Public Information, Forecasting and Development)	2nd quarter 2002	Yes
Prevention measures		
Adoption and implementation of ethics codes for magistrates, police, customs officers and other public officials	3rd quarter 2002	N/A
Amend legislation on asset disclosure establish monitoring mechanism to eliminate non-disclosure	4th quarter 2001	No
Limit immunities to prevent their abuse to hide abuse of power	4th quarter 2002	N/A
Adopt Act on Conflicts of interest	3rd quarter 2002	N/A
Adopt Act on Lobbying	1st quarter 2002	No
Initiate draft act on funding of political parties and campaigns	4th quarter 2001	No
Strengthening capacity		
Strengthen role of Anti-corruption Section, anti-corruption departments in prosecutors' offices and courts	2001–2004	Yes*
Institutional reform		
Increase role of Supreme Council of Magistracy in selection and appointment of magistrates on strict objective professional criteria	1st quarter 2002	Yes*
Reform of public administration		
Set up system for selection, promotion and evaluation of public officials based exclusively on professional skill and performance	2004	N/A
International cooperation		
Introduce criminality for corruption in international business transactions, liability for foreign public officials, liability of legal persons	2002	N/A

Note: * Although these objectives have been formally met, the impact of the changes on judicial and especially prosecutorial independence is doubtful (see above).

The role of NGOs

There is significant activity by Romanian NGOs in the area of anti-corruption. Among the most important is the Pro Democratia Association (PDA), which collaborated with the Ministry of Justice in the implementation of a Public Awareness Campaign (1999–2000).[25] Pro Democratia also carried out an important study on political party funding (see Section 6.3).

EU assistance

This process was accompanied by growing EU assistance for anti-corruption policy. The key project is the 1999 PHARE Inter-institutional Project on Anti-corruption. Due to delays, the cause of which is not clear, the project did not begin until August 2001, with the first component a project twinned with the Spanish *Fiscalia Anticorrupcion*.[26] The remainder of the project envisages support for staff training.

Other anti-corruption-related PHARE projects are assistance for the creation of a case and document management system and legal library documentation system (2000–2002, €3.5m), continuation of assistance to the Ministry of Justice (2001, €4.1m), a twinning project for judicial reform (1999–2001, €1m), and "Prevention and Control of Money Laundering" (started June 2001, €0.5m).

The impact of NATO accession

While EU accession has been a very important influence on the development of anti-corruption policy, from late 2001, a more urgent goal for Romania (as for Bulgaria) has become accession to NATO. In the run-up to the November 2002 NATO Summit in Prague, officials from the alliance and from NATO members have sent clear signals that the most important barrier to NATO accession for Romania is corruption.[27] This has injected visible energy into the Government's efforts to step up

---

[25] The campaign was part of a larger project undertaken by the Ministry of Justice together with UNDP and UNCICP on "Institution Building and Strengthening of Corruption Control Capacity in Romania." The campaign combined advertising, roundtable discussions and press conferences on corruption and a series of local level debates on corruption. In general, the project was a good example of dialogue and cooperation between an NGO and state authorities.

[26] The programme is planned to benefit primarily the Public Prosecutor's Office with three other partners: the ministries of Justice, Interior and Finance (General Customs Administration); see <http://www.europa.eu.int/comm/pas/phare/prog.search>, (last accessed 15 May 2001).

[27] E. Tomiuc, "Balkan neighbours press ahead with NATO bid, vow to tackle corruption," RFE/RL Newsline, 7 February 2002.

its anti-corruption efforts, at least on the surface, and has induced a noticeable change in the public atmosphere.[28]

Other international activities

In addition to EU activities in the area of anti-corruption policy, Romania has participated in a number of international anti-corruption activities and initiatives, including signing up to GRECO in May 1999, participating in the anti-corruption activities of the Stability Pact, establishing a Regional Centre for fighting corruption and organised crime as part of the Southeast European Co-operative Initiative, receiving assistance for institution building from the UNDP and UN Centre for International Crime Prevention in Vienna and judicial assistance from the US Department of Justice as part of a Strategic Partnership between Romania and the USA.

2. INSTITUTIONS AND LEGISLATION

2.1 Anti-corruption legislation

Romanian anti-corruption legislation is fairly comprehensive. The Romanian Criminal Code sanctions both passive and active bribery. Until the passage of the 2000 Anti-corruption Act, the penalties were as follows:

- Passive bribery (bribe taking): imprisonment of 3-12 years;

- Active bribery (offer or provision of a bribe): imprisonment of six months to five years;

- Influence trafficking: imprisonment of two to ten years;

- Receipt of unauthorised benefits: imprisonment of six months to five years.

---

[28] For example, an open letter published in March 2002 to Prime Minister Adrian Nastase from one of the editors of *Evenimentul Zilei*, one of the two Romanian dailies involved in real investigative journalism on corruption, called on the Prime Minister to move radically against corruption as the main condition to take the "historic chance" to be invited into NATO at the November Summit. See C. Nistorescu, Open Letter to Prime Minister Adrian Nastase. For English version of open letter, see front page of *Evenimentul Zilei*, 29 March 2002 (provided by Nicoleta Savin, journalist at *Evenimentul Zilei*).

These paragraphs applied only to public officials [29] until the 2000 Anti-corruption Act extended them to cover managers, persons with control functions, executives, administrators, consultants and internal auditors in private firms, State monopolies, national companies or any other economic structures; leading officials in political parties, trade unions, management bodies and foundations or non-profit associations. Penalties for corruption offences are increased by two to three years if committed by persons with control responsibilities or by persons with investigation, prosecution or judicial powers and by five years if committed for the benefit of a criminal entity or to influence international business transactions.

Bribe givers who notify the police or prosecutors are exempt from punishment. GRECO noted in its *Evaluation Report on Romania* that active bribers could easily abuse this provision, especially as the law provides for the return of assets to the briber.

The extension by the 2000 Act of the Bribery Provisions means that they apply partly to the private sector. However, Romanian legislation does not allow criminal liability of legal entities for corruption. Romania ratified the Council of Europe Civil Law Convention in April 2002, but has not yet ratified the Criminal Law Convention.

The Anti-corruption Act also established a number of other corruption-related offences, including the following:

- Deliberate under-valuation of public assets during privatisation or commercial transactions.

- Violations of law in the provision of loans or subsidies, failure to pursue/collect outstanding loans.

- Using loans or subsidies for purposes other than those for which they have been granted.

If committed in order to obtain money, goods or unauthorised benefits, these three offences are punishable by 5-15 years' imprisonment.

- Persons responsible for supervising, controlling or liquidating a private company who intermediate or facilitate commercial or financial operations by the company in order to obtain, directly or indirectly, undue benefit, are punishable by two to seven years' imprisonment.

---

[29] Under Romanian law, a public official is any person exercising, on a permanent or temporary basis, a mandate within a public authority or institution, regardless of official position or remuneration. An official is any person exercising a mandate in the service of a legal entity other than a public authority or institution.

The Act also applies sanctions to a number of other corruption-related offences. These include hiding benefits obtained through corruption, conspiracy, false declarations and forgery, money laundering, smuggling, fraudulent bankruptcy and drug trafficking.

The sentences laid down in the law for anti-corruption offences are much more severe than is typical in OECD states. This raises questions about the wisdom of punishing corruption so severely, as long sentences may paradoxically deter courts from conviction.

In addition to other anti-corruption provisions, the 1999 Act on Ministerial Responsibility[30] (amended by Government Ordinance 130/1999) defines as criminal offences for members of the Government, "the obstruction, through means of violence or fraudulent methods, of the exercise in good faith of one's rights and liberties; the presentation in bad faith to the Parliament or the President of Romania of inexact or false information regarding the activity of the Government or of a ministry, in order to hide committed deeds of a nature that would cause damage to national interests."[31] This provision is vague and has never been applied.

2.2 Conflict of interest legislation

Conflict of interest legislation remained skeletal in early 2002. A general provision of the Anti-corruption Act forbids

> [T]he undertaking of financial operations, such as commercial acts incompatible with the position, duties, or mandate that a person has, or closing financial transactions by making use of the information received due to one's position, responsibilities, or tasks; using by any means, directly or indirectly, information that is not public, or giving permission for unauthorised persons to have access to this information.[32]

In addition, an Emergency Ordinance passed by the Government in February 2002 introduced incompatibility provisions for officials in local authorities. Neither local government representatives nor their spouses or second-degree relatives, nor employees of local or county councils may conclude services, works or supply contracts with local authorities of which they are members. Representatives who get into such situations

---

[30] Act no. 115/1990.

[31] Act no. 115/1999, as amended by Ordinance no. 130/1999, Article 6. The sanctions provided by the Act consist of a principal punishment, i.e. imprisonment, and a complementary one, i.e. the interdiction to hold a high public office for a period of three to ten years.

[32] When committed in order to obtain, for oneself or for another person, money, goods, or undue benefits, the actions described shall be punished by imprisonment from one to five years. Act no. 78/2000, Article 12.

should resign from their position in the company no later than five days after the ordinance entered into force (2 February 2002) or after signing the contract with the public authority. If these provisions are violated, the representative's mandate is to be revoked by the respective prefect. There are no such restrictions for MPs or other functionaries of the central State administration. Work on incompatibility provisions for a broader range of officials is in progress.

In May 2002, the Government adopted a draft Act on Conflict of Interests. The draft Act would apply only to the following executive branch officials: Prime Minister, ministers, deputy ministers, secretaries of State and other positions equivalent to secretary of State in specialised bodies subordinate to the Government or ministries, prefects and deputy prefects.

The Act would forbid these officials, *inter alia*, from performing other functions, including in commercial entities; performing commercial transactions for their own or others' benefit. Functionaries would have to declare conflicts of interest in specific decision-making processes, whereupon the superior would delegate a different official for that decision. The Prime Minister's Control Department would be responsible for investigating conflict of interest situations and proposing sanctions (including removal).

2.3 Asset declaration and monitoring

The process of financial disclosure for public functionaries is regulated by the 1996 Act on the Obligation of Public Officials to Declare their Personal Wealth and the Procedure for Controlling Wealth Obtained through Illicit Means.[33] The Act applies to: the President of Romania; MPs, ministers; State secretaries and under-secretaries; judges; public prosecutors; county and local councillors; mayors; public officials from the central and local public administration; and directors and other people with controlling responsibilities within self-managed public companies, commercial companies where the State holds the majority of shares, the State Property Fund, National Bank of Romania, and banks in which the State holds a total or the majority of shares.[34]

Such persons are obliged to submit declarations of all personal and joint assets and those of spouses and children living in the same household at the beginning and the end of their term of office. The declarations are not public.

Civil servants submit their declarations to the public authority that employs them, whereas local elected officials (together with the mayor) make their statements to the

---

[33] Act no. 115/1996.

[34] Act no. 115/1996, Article 2.

prefect. A control procedure should take place if officials fail to submit a declaration within 15 days of the deadline or if there is a significant difference between the initial and final declarations and if there is clear evidence that some assets could not have been obtained by legal means.[35] Control procedures are the responsibility of investigation commissions within the Courts of Appeal on receipt of a written and signed petition from any citizen containing evidence of illicit appropriation of wealth.[36] The commission must decide within three months whether to annul the case, send it to the Court of Appeal or transfer it to the Public Prosecutor's Office. The sessions of the investigation commission are not to be public.[37]

Senior officials submit declarations to the Prime Minister, MPs to the President of their respective Chamber of Parliament, the Prime Minister and the Presidents of the two Chambers of Parliament to the President of Romania, the President to the Head of the Constitutional Court, judges to the Minister of Justice and prosecutors to the Prosecutor-General. The control procedure is supposed to be run by an investigative commission in the Supreme Court[38] at the request of the Minister of Justice, the General Prosecutors or the officials concerned, if their wealth is publicly questioned.[39] Officials whose wealth was declared totally or partially unjustified by the court are removed from office, while Members of Parliament are to be stripped of their mandate. Officials who file incomplete or false declarations may be punished by imprisonment from three months to two years or a fine.

In practice, asset monitoring is totally inadequate. In particular, a person who produces false evidence on officials' assets also faces imprisonment from one to five years,[40] and any witness who provides inaccurate information about the illicit nature of a public official's wealth by imprisonment from six months to three years. This makes it highly unlikely that ordinary citizens would ever question public officials' assets. Ministry of

---

[35] Act no. 115/1996, Article 7.

[36] The commission is made up of two judges from the Court of Appeal, a prosecutor from the Public Prosecutor's Office attached to the Court of Appeal, and a secretary (they all serve a three-year term).

[37] The law provides for publicity only cases which have been quashed by the investigation commission or if the competent court decides that wealth was obtained by lawful means. In these cases, decisions shall be published in the Romanian *Official Gazette*.

[38] The investigation commission has a three-year term of service and includes two judges from the Supreme Court, a prosecutor from the General Prosecutor's Office, and a secretary.

[39] However, in these cases the competent court is the Supreme Court of Justice. For the President of Romania, the wealth control procedure may be undertaken at the end of his office or during the mandate only at his request, or upon approval of the Parliament with a simple majority vote.

[40] This sanction does not apply if the petitioner is an institution, e.g. the Public Prosecutor's Office.

Justice officials expect these provisions to be removed by a new conflict of interest act in preparation as of April 2002.

Moreover, investigation commissions for senior officials had not even been established by early 2002, making it pointless to submit a petition.[41] In the four years following the adoption of the 1996 Act, no control procedure was ever initiated. Media reports suggest that it is the norm for officials not to file asset declarations.[42]

As of June 2002 draft amendments to the Act were under discussion in Parliament, although the details of the proposals were not available.

2.4 Control and audit

State financial control is largely ineffective. The Court of Audit does not enjoy complete operational independence, its findings are submitted very late and are not used to impose corrective measures. The legal basis for internal state financial control has been established, but hardly implemented as of May 2002.

The Court of Audit[43]

The Court of Audit (COA) is the supreme audit body for the public sector. The Chairman and members of the Court are appointed by Parliament for six years, and the President of Romania appoints and recalls financial judges and prosecutors on the proposal of the Plenum of the Court. Members of the Court and financial judges are subject to similar conflict of interest provisions as public officials, violation of which may be punished by removal from office.

The COA's main responsibility is to verify the annual accounts of the State budget, social security budget, local government budgets, special funds, the treasury fund, public debt,

---

[41] The spokesman of the Supreme Court of Justice (where the investigation commission for senior officials should have been created) explained to journalists that, "[T]he establishment of the commission was not necessary, because there were no petitions submitted. In addition, the creation of the commission would have entailed supplementary and inefficient expenses." In: "Statesmen, magistrates and civil servants protect their wealth," *Capital,* no. 43, 26 October 2000.

[42] For instance, almost a year after the local elections, Bucharest General-City Councillor Adrian Badila said he had never completed any wealth declaration because nobody asked him to. Statement made at a conference organised by Transparency International Romania and the Foundation for Civil Society Development on Solutions for Combating Corruption in Local Public Administration, Bucharest, 17 May 2001.

[43] The legal framework for the Court is provided by the 1992 Act on the Organization and Functioning of the Court of Audit.

and Government guarantees. It may also audit the budgets of the Presidency, the Government, the Supreme Court of Justice, Constitutional Court and legal entities that administer public resources including companies in which the State holds a majority stake.

The Chamber of Deputies and the Senate can also require the Court to carry out specific audits, and to stop an audit if the Court has exceeded its legal competence. The Court may audit the budgets of the Senate or Chamber of Deputies *only* at the request of each Chamber's Standing Bureau; no such request has ever been submitted.

The Court must report annually to the Parliament. However, reports are not properly debated there – there is no parliamentary committee specifically charged with this task – and are largely ignored by the Government. Under the law, reports are to be published in the *Official Gazette*, but in practice they are too long to be published in ordinary issues of the *Official Gazette* and are published only in its summary or not at all. The full reports can only be viewed at the Court of Audit or Parliament.

The Court sent its *1999 Annual Report* to the Parliament only in March 2001. The Report contained scathing reports on financial irregularities within the banking sector, the Ministry of Finance's allocation of tax relief and illegal reimbursement of VAT,[44] the General Customs Administration (GCA), Ministry of National Defence, and Ministry of External Affairs.[45] However, the report generated little interest as most of the issues had already been covered in the media.

The Court of Audit exercises only *ex-post* financial control, monitoring compliance with legal regulations. It does not yet carry out performance audit, the introduction of which has been urged by the European Commission. A 2001 PHARE project for the Court is intended to support the introduction of performance audit so the Court will be able to audit pre-accession funds.

Internal audit and control

Internal audit and control remains underdeveloped. A 1999 Government Ordinance[46] set out the legal basis for the creation of a financial control system. The act regulating this area is on the public internal audit and the preventive financial control. However, the EU *2001 Regular Report* urged the creation of functionally independent internal audit units, as well as the establishment of a co-ordinating role for the Ministry of Finance in developing a harmonised methodology for financial management, control and audit. As of March 2002,

---

[44] *Evenimentul Zilei*, 17 March 2001.

[45] For further details, see *Romania Libera*, 19 March 2001.

[46] Government Ordinance on Public Internal Audit and Preventative Financial Control, no. 119/1999.

the Office of the Financial Controller was thought to be taking steps to introduce and implement reform of internal financial control.[47]

2.5 Anti-corruption agencies

Romania boasts several anti-corruption agencies with overlapping agendas. However, the common denominator of continuing executive control over and/or interference in the activities of such bodies has fundamentally undermined any real attempt to move against corruption at higher levels.

The Anti-corruption Section

The main specific anti-corruption agency is the Anti-corruption Section, formed in October 2000. The activities of the Section have been directly or implicitly undermined since its creation by the fact that its chief can be removed at any time without justification by the General Prosecutor, who himself is effectively subordinate to the Minister of Justice (see Section 6.1). In March 2001, the first chief of the Section, Ovidiu Budusan, was removed without official justification after moving to investigate a corruption scandal allegedly involving illegal party financing, money laundering and smuggling of fuel to Serbia during the Yugoslav embargo (see the Costea scandal below). The investigation would have resulted in the implication of several former ministers and senior officials.

Second, the Section's staff worked on the basis of secondary secondment from the police and other prosecution offices on an uncertain basis for up to one year, which created insecurity and discontinuity. The Office was not supplied with sufficient resources or even a building for several months.

As of early 2002, the section still did not have enough staff to engage in a twinning project and at the same time fulfil its functions.[48] According to the EU's *2001 Regular*

---

[47] Comments from officials, OSI Roundtable Discussion, Bucharest, 28 March 2002. *Explanatory note: OSI held a roundtable meeting to invite critique of the present Report in draft form. Experts present included representatives of the Government, international organisations, and civil society organisations. References to this meeting should not be understood as an endorsement of any particular point of view by any one participant.*

[48] The Anti-corruption Section and its territorial structures have, according to the law, the following legal responsibilities:

- to undertake criminal proceedings in cases of corruption offences and offences committed in conditions of organized crime;
- to lead and control activities undertaken by other authorities involved in the detection and criminal proceeding of these offences;
- to collect, analyse and evaluate data and information related to the fight against corruption and organized crime.

Report the section only had 17 prosecutors instead of 38 as planned.[49] It was not possible to obtain consistent information on the staffing of the section for this report. Whether the new Anti-corruption Bureau (see Section 1.3) will solve this problem remains to be seen, since the Ordinance establishing the bureau has failed to establish the independence of its chief.

The Costea scandal

The biggest scandal in Romanian politics since 1989 was the Costea Affair, named after Adrian Costae, a French businessman of Romanian descent. Costea had been suspected by French authorities of laundering around €6.5m. In 2001, the Romanian media claimed to have discovered Costea's prior involvement in the illegal smuggling of petroleum over the Yugoslav border during the UN embargo. Numerous MPs and ministers were called in 2000 to testify before a commission of visiting French judges and prosecutors, after Budusan provided the French authorities with documents relating to the case. He was subsequently removed. In addition, Costea claimed to have provided the Party of Social Democracy in Romania (PSDR) with hundreds of tons of posters for Ion Iliescu's 1996 presidential campaign before the 1996 elections.[50] A former Secretary-General of the Alliance for Romania Party (APR) also claimed that Costea financed the PDSR electoral campaign and later the political activities of APR.[51]

The Prime Minister's Control Department

In April 2001, the Prime Minister's Control Department was established under the 2000 Anti-corruption Act. In reality, it was created from the previous Government Control and Anti-corruption Department. The department has around 50 staff and may undertake inspections of any form of legal violation in governmental structures, ministries or other specialised bodies subordinate to the Government or ministers, and also, since May 2001, in financial and banking operations that are related to acts of public officials.[52] Evidence of criminal activity is passed onto the prosecution offices and may be used as evidence. Between April and October 2001, the PMCD carried out around 60 inspections. An inspection by the department into conflict of interest in Bucharest carried out in late 2001 concluded that 38 out of 65 city councillors were involved in firms that gained contracts

---

[49] Commission, *2001 Regular Report*, p. 21.

[50] Interview with Adrian Costea, *Evenimentul Zilei*, 18 May 2000.

[51] *Evenimentul Zilei*, 10 May 2000.

[52] The PMCD is divided in five units: the Direction for control of privatisation, post-privatisation and the application of free market mechanisms; Direction for control of actions of corruption and organised crime; Direction for control of the contracting and utilization of funds and international credits granted to Romania; Direction for control of ministries and other institutions subordinated to the Government; Direction for control of institutions and persons with special jurisdictional regime.

from the City. The inspection resulted in the resignation of the City Council. However, concerns exist that the inspection may have been motivated primarily by the Prime Minister's opposition to the Mayor of Bucharest.[53]

Other anti-corruption agencies

Other agencies with a special role in fighting corruption are listed below.

- Within the General Police Inspectorate[54] two departments play roles in combating corruption: the Directorate of Financial and Economic Police, which includes a central Anti-corruption Service (ten people) and territorial anti-corruption bureaus (five to six people each); and the Criminal Police Directorate, which has a small anti-corruption unit. The Public Prosecutor's Office has to cooperate with these two departments separately when investigating corruption, which appears to burden their activity.

- At the Ministry of Justice, the Directorate for Relations with the Public Prosecutor's Office and for the Prevention of Corruption and Criminality is responsible for communication with the Public Prosecutor's Office in criminal investigations.

Money laundering

To fight money laundering, the Office for the Prevention and Control of Money Laundering was established in 1999,[55] composed of seven representatives from the Ministries of Finance, Interior and Justice, Prosecution Service at the Supreme Court, National Bank, Court of Audit and Association of Romanian Banks. Under the Act, financial institutions, notaries, casinos and other selected entities must notify suspicious transactions or those over a certain threshold to the Office. By early 2002, the General Prosecutor's Office had investigated around 20 cases transferred to it by the Office, but there were no known convictions. A new Ordinance passed by the Government in March 2002 widened the circle of entities with the duty to notify transactions to the Office, and also lowered the threshold for mandatory reporting of transactions from €10,000 to €5,000.

---

[53] As of June 2002, the PMCD's findings were being contested in court by several city councillors, and no elections to the City Council had been scheduled.

[54] The former Squad for Countering Organised Crime and Corruption under the General Police Inspectorate was reorganised in March 2000 as the Directorate for Countering Organised Crime, thus removing its anti-corruption role.

[55] Act no. 21/1999.

2.6 Ombudsman

The ombudsman *(Avocatul Poporului)* was established in 1997[56] to defend citizens' rights and freedoms in their interactions with public authorities. The ombudsman is appointed by the Senate for a four-year term and can be removed from office by a majority vote of the Senate only for violating the Constitution or other laws. The ombudsman reports to Parliament annually.

The office investigates complaints from citizens, press or NGOs concerning infringements of fundamental rights and freedoms by the public administration. Complaints may not be anonymous. The ombudsman does not have authority to investigate complaints concerning the judiciary.

The powers of the ombudsman are weak. Although public authorities are bound to provide the office with all documents and information relating to a specific complaint, public authorities are not sanctioned if they fail to do so. The ombudsman may request that an authority or official undertake corrective measures if an individual's rights were infringed. If this does not happen within 30 days, the ombudsman notifies the superior authority, which in turn must reply within 45 days (20 days in the case of the Government) and specify measures that will be taken. The office has no further powers to enforce corrective measures.

The number of complaints to the ombudsman has grown from 1,168 in 1997 to around 4,500 in 2000. However, most complaints are rejected because they relate to the judiciary[57] – a sign of limited public awareness of the office's role.[58] No cases of corruption have been mentioned in the ombudsman's annual reports.

3. EXECUTIVE BRANCH AND CIVIL SERVICE

Corruption appears to be widespread if not endemic in the Romanian executive branch and civil service. This situation is underpinned by executive discretion stemming from the widespread use of ordinances, excessive immunity provisions for both current and

---

[56] 1997 Act on the Organization and Functioning of the Office of the Ombudsman.

[57] Ninety-one percent of complaints were rejected in 1997, 81 percent in 1998, while in 1999 the number decreased to 61 percent.

[58] Most of the complaints concern land restitution cases and other infringements of property rights. In 1999, 35 percent of the complaints dealt with infringements of individuals' right to private property. In: *Ombudsman's Annual Activity Report*, January 1999-December 1999, <http://www.avp.ro>, (last accessed 20 April 2001).

former members of the Government, poorly defined civil servant responsibilities, patronage at all levels and the ineffectiveness of procedures for redress against administrative decisions. Although a Civil Service Act was passed in 1999, its implementation requires substantial secondary legislation. Provisions to prevent conflict of interest situations or their abuse are inadequate, and are little observed.

3.1 Structure and legislative framework

Public administration reform represents one of the main challenges facing the Romanian Government. Corruption is widespread both in central and local administration, exacerbated by poorly defined responsibilities, a blurred boundary between administrative and political functions and a lack of transparency in administrative procedures.[59] Both central administration – ministries and other central agencies – and local administration suffer from poor organisation and facilities as well as a lack of equipment. In practice, citizens have limited rights of redress against administrative decisions.

For the purposes of this report, a fundamental legal issue is the immunity from investigation or prosecution enjoyed by both current and former members of the Government, against whom criminal proceedings may only be initiated by the Chamber of Deputies, Senate or President. As is similar for MPs, this provides *de facto* complete immunity, and no minister or former minister has ever been stripped of immunity (and therefore never been prosecuted or convicted).

The Romanian Parliament took a major step towards the creation of a modern civil service by passing the Act on the Status of Civil Servants (hereafter Civil Service Act) in November 1999.[60] The adoption of a Civil Service Act was a short-term priority under the *1998 AP*,[61] and pressure from the EC on the Government was a vital factor in

---

[59] The following depressing picture of the civil service was provided by one former local public official: "I have worked for seven years in local public administration, yet I don't know what it means or whether such thing as 'public administration' even exists. The only thing that I know for sure is that public administration is run according to the law of the 'seven Fs': 'Steal from my brother with no fear, just push paper!' *(Fura Frate Fara Frica, Formele Fie Facute!)*." Interview carried out for TI Romania project, "Corruption in Local Public Administration," 9 February 2001.

[60] Act no. 188/1999 on the Status of Civil Servants, adopted 29 November 1999, in: *Official Gazette,* no. 600, 8 December 1999.

[61] According to the General Secretary of the new National Agency for Civil Servants, the Act was delayed because, "[N]o political party wanted a class of professional civil servants, dependent only on the law." Interview with Paul Mitroi, General Secretary of the National Agency for Civil Servants, 9 May 2001.

securing the passage of the Act.[62] However, the implementation of the Act will require substantial secondary legislation. For example, it envisages a Code of Ethics for public officials, but none had been prepared as of summer 2002.

The Act defines a civil servant as a person appointed to a public office, defined as "the totality of competencies and responsibilities established by the public authority or institution, according to the Act, in order to realise its competencies."[63] According to the Act:

- Civil servants must carry out their activities in a prompt, efficient, impartial manner without corruption, abuse of power or political pressure;

- Selection for public office is to be governed by competence as the sole criterion;

- Accession and promotion within the civil service is to be governed by equality of opportunity;

- Civil servants are to enjoy stability in their office.[64]

Among the conditions Romanian citizens must satisfy to be eligible for employment is a record free of convictions for offences that would render them unfit to occupy public office; however, corruption offences are not mentioned explicitly.[65]

The Act stipulates the creation of a National Agency for Civil Servants, the main management body for the Civil Service.[66] As of June 2001, the NACS was understaffed and lacked resources.[67] Moreover, the NACS's tasks are tied to the adoption of several secondary acts that will clarify the provisions of the Statute (for example regarding recruitment and the establishment of disciplinary commissions). As of April 2002 these acts had not been passed. In the meantime, the NACS was subordinated to the

---

[62] The Commission consistently criticised the delays, and regarded the law as the "prerequisite for any meaningful reform of the public administration." See Commission, *1999 Regular Report,* p. 62.

[63] Act no. 188/1999, Article 2, paragraph 1; Article 3, paragraph 1.

[64] Act no. 188/1999, Article 4.

[65] Act no. 188/1999, Article 6.

[66] The Agency is subordinate to the Ministry for Public Administration. It is responsible for: elaborating civil service legislation, policy and strategy; implementing and enforcing the Act on the Status of Civil Servants; setting criteria for evaluating civil servants' activity; keeping records of civil servants' careers; organising a system of professional training; and preparing an annual report for Parliament on the management of the Civil Service.

[67] At the time of writing, the Agency had 85 staff. According to General Secretary Paul Mitroi, Agency employees had to queue for computers.

Ministry of Public Administration by a Government decision,[68] meaning it is no longer an independent agency.

In practice, the Act has not prevented patronage at senior levels. After the 2000 elections, the Romanian Government replaced a large number of civil servants, including a number of state secretaries. The Prime Minister has criticised and cautioned against the hiring of friends and relatives by local government officials.[69] The press recently reported the case of a prefect who appointed his wife as director of his own cabinet. Press exposure and an investigation by the Prime Minister's Control Department resulted in her resignation.[70]

EU assistance

The 1998 PHARE programme for public administration reform includes a €1.7m project focused on "Support for the NACS in Designing and Implementing Civil Service Reform." The project, which was in progress at the time of writing, is aimed at strengthening the operational capacity of the NACS, elaborating on the civil service regulatory framework relating to the Act (including an ethical code), and improving civil service training.

3.2 Administrative procedure and redress

Under Romanian rules of administrative proceedings, administrative decisions must be issued within 30 days. Under the Romanian Constitution, "Any person aggrieved in his legitimate right by an administrative act or failure of a public authority to solve his application within the legal term is entitled to the acknowledgement of his right, annulment of the act, and remedies for the damage."

Appeals against administrative decisions must first be filed to the authority that issued the decision, after which they may be filed to a county court or Court of the City of Bucharest.[71] The Administrative Disputes Section of the Supreme Court of Justice decides appeals. Courts have the power to annul an administrative decision and decide on compensation for damages.

---

[68] Government Decision 8/2001.

[69] *Evenimentul Zilei,* 26 April 2001.

[70] *Adevarul,* 24 April 2001.

[71] Act no. 29/1990 on Administrative Litigation.

However, the Act is limited by the fact that there are certain types of acts of the Executive that may not be appealed by citizens in court.[72] Moreover, public authorities are not required to justify administrative decisions, which means in practice that persons can only make an appeal against the failure of an authority to meet the legal deadline.

In practice, the review of executive actions is much more often pursued by prefects (the county level representatives of the Executive) against the county or local council, and by the Mayor against the Prefect, than by citizens against the public administration. A draft of a new Act on Administrative Litigation that would give citizens the right to appeal the acts of any public authority in court was under discussion in Parliament as of May 2002.

According to GRECO, investigations of corruption in the public administration are hampered by shortcomings in legislation on conserving, filing and archiving official documents. Although destruction of documents is subject to penalties of up to five years' imprisonment, "[I]tems of this sort are destroyed relatively frequently in order to conceal acts of corruption that would entail a more serious penalty."[73]

3.3 Conflict of interest and asset monitoring

In addition to the general provision against conflict of interest in the 2000 Anti-corruption Act (see Section 2.2), the Act on the Organisation and Functioning of the Government[74] forbids members of the Government "from the exercise of any commercial acts, except the selling and buying of shares; the exercise of the office of administrator or auditor of a commercial company or member of the administration council of self-administered companies, state companies and national companies; or the exercise of public office within a foreign organisation, unless otherwise provided by agreements and conventions to which Romania is a party."[75] The Prime Minister is responsible for judging whether situations violate these provisions and taking steps to end such situations, but has never taken actions to enforce the law.

---

[72] Such acts refer, among others, to the relations between Parliament, President and Government; the administrative acts concerning internal and external security of the State; those that relate to the interpretation and enforcement of international acts; emergency measures taken by the Executive in cases of natural calamity or other serious events; commanding acts of a military character; acts of the State regarding the administration of its patrimony; and administrative acts adopted in the exercise of powers of hierarchical control. See Act no. 29/1990, Article 2.

[73] GRECO, *Evaluation Report on Romania,* p. 13.

[74] Act no. 90/2001, Article 4.

[75] Act no. 90/2001, Article 4.

No minister or other senior official has ever been sanctioned for violating incompatibility rules. However, the media have covered widely the ancillary activities of ministers, including the apparently universal practice of state secretaries and other senior officials sitting in on the administrative councils of companies where the State is shareholder.[76]

The occupation of ancillary positions and business activities by civil servants is widespread. The President of one County Chamber of Audit described the reality as follows:

> Very many employees of the Ministry of Finance have supplementary jobs (as auditors, accountants, etc), thereby ensuring the protection of the firms that hired them. In my county, there are cases of high officials of the Finance Department who take as many as 19 salaries from different secondary employments. This means at least 19 days wasted per month – do they still have time for their official jobs? Another effect of this is that officials are put in a situation where they control each other and not the firms themselves.[77]

Although Romanian officials believe this is an extreme example, it is noteworthy that such a situation is not against the current law. Senior officials defend such situations on the grounds that such officials are paid very low wages and must make money from additional sources.[78]

The 1991 Act on Local Public Administration also forbids prefects and sub-prefects from performing professional, paid activities in self-managed public companies, and other companies or profit-seeking organisations.[79] Infringement of these provisions is also widespread. When the media exposed a prefect who was also a member of the administrative council of a trade company,[80] the prefect's superiors took no action.

Under the 1999 Civil Service Act, all public officials are obliged not to solicit gifts during the exercise of their duties.[81] However, Romanian law defines neither gifts nor hospitality, mirroring a reality that is very difficult to regulate given the high social and cultural acceptability of gift giving and receiving. In practice, the provision of gifts to public officials is widespread and goes unsanctioned. In 2000 and 2001, the media covered the practice of giving "Easter Bribes" *(Spagile de Pasti)* – where delegates from country directorates of the Ministry of Agriculture supply various gifts of lamb meat to senior officials in the Ministry,

---

[76] For example, the *Adevarul* daily recently published a series of 12 articles titled "The firms of MPs," analysing the commercial interests and businesses of MPs representing various constituencies. In: *Adevarul*, weekly from 26 April 2001.

[77] Interview within the TI Romania project, "Corruption in local public administration," 22 April 2000.

[78] OSI Roundtable Discussion, Bucharest, 28 March 2002.

[79] Act no. 69/1991, Article 107.

[80] *Adevarul*, 6 April 2001.

[81] Act no. 188/1999, Article 46, paragraph 1. For details, see chapter on Civil Service.

for example to maintain favour in subsidy allocation or keep jobs which depend on the discretion of ministry officials.[82] The director of a local branch of the Ministry of Transport invited the author to come and witness how local ministry officials also load cars with all kinds of presents for their superiors in Bucharest: a necessary ritual by which local officials demonstrate their loyalty towards "Bucharest."

3.4 Internal control mechanisms

Control mechanisms in the executive have been covered under Section 2.4 (Control and audit) and 2.5 (Anti-corruption agencies – the Prime Minister's Control Department).

3.5 Interaction with the public

The Civil Service Act states a number of duties for civil servants, including:

- the obligation to fulfil their responsibilities with professionalism, loyalty, correctness and conscientiousness and to refrain from any act that may prejudice a public authority or institution;

- the obligation to perform their official duties as assigned;

- the obligation not to receive requests or applications whose resolution does not fall under their area of competence or to intervene in favour of such petitions.[83]

Breaking these provisions results in the application of administrative sanctions (warning, reprimand, wage penalty, suspension of promotion for one to three years, transfer to an inferior office for 6-12 months, or removal from office).[84] However, the Act is too vague to provide any real framework for interactions with the public and has not been supplemented by any specific instructions.

There is no legal protection for whistleblowers in Romania.

---

[82] "Easter Bribes," *Evenimentul Zilei,* 24 April 2000. Lambs were also supplied to high officials in the National Health Insurance House, and the General Inspectorate of Police; see "Operation the Lamb," *Evenimentul Zilei,* 13 April 2001.

[83] Act no. 188/1999, Articles 41–48.

[84] Act no. 188/1999, Article 70.

3.6 Corruption

The most straightforward accusation of governmental corruption was issued by the chief of a Parliamentary Commission of Inquiry into the privatisation of RomTelecom, the national telecommunications company. He accused four ministers from the RomTelecom Privatisation Committee of having received several million dollars as a "commission" to favour the winner of the contract, Greek OTE.[85] The report of the Parliamentary Commission of Inquiry also stated that the State lost more than €867m because of the manner in which the privatisation contract was drafted.

The media has also covered evidence from military contracts that indicate widespread corruption in the allocation of defence contracts, resulting *inter alia* in damage to Romania's preparations for NATO membership.[86]

As Section 1 has already made clear, citizens' perceptions of the civil service are, to a large extent, dominated by their views on corruption, with over 70 percent of survey respondents believing that all or most public officials are corrupt.

Ordinances

According to the Romanian Constitution, the Government may *de facto* legislate directly through ordinances in fields that do not require an organic law.[87] Emergency ordinances may be issued "in exceptional cases." Ordinances come into effect immediately and are approved by Parliament retrospectively[88] while emergency ordinances must be approved by Parliament before they come into effect. In practice emergency ordinances come into effect in the same manner as normal ordinances.

In recent years, all Governments have extensively used ordinances and emergency ordinances, officially to compensate for the sluggishness of Parliament. Moreover, emergency ordinances are used not just in exceptional cases but in all areas, even to alter organic laws. For example, an emergency ordinance was used in 2001 to alter the Code of Civil Procedure, specifically the process of appeal against the General

---

[85] *Evenimentul Zilei*, 25 October 2000.

[86] According to Mircea Toma, an investigative journalist and Director of the Media Monitoring Agency, only four of the army's 19 investment projects in early 2002 were useful for NATO preparation; defence contracts are mediated mainly through a network of 30-40 small Romanian arms trading companies that are linked to or corrupt officials at the Ministry of Defence. One of the consequences of the system was a contract for ammunition that is not used by any weapon the army possesses. See M. Toma, "Arma scapa tuma," *Academia Catavencu*, 12 March 2002.

[87] Under the Romanian Constitution, there are three types of laws: constitutional (dealing with constitutional revision), organic (regulating areas of special importance), and ordinary.

[88] Constitution of Romania, Article 114.

Prosecutor's final judgements.[89] In 2001, the Prime Minister at the time of writing has himself admitted that issuing numerous emergency ordinances is a "perverse practice," but has continued using them.[90]

The European Commission has repeatedly criticised the abuse of ordinances. The *2001 Regular Report* notes that, although an increase in the efficiency of Parliament has led to a fall in the number of ordinances,

> [L]egislation by ordinance remains too common and has frequently been used without a clear justification for bypassing parliamentary procedures. This... can result in legislative instability... [and a] further concern is that Parliament's ability to carry out the essential function of scrutinising legislation remains limited.[91]

The extensive use of ordinances opens up wide space for executive discretion – especially in the area of public expenditure – thereby facilitating corruption. For example, several emergency ordinances have been issued over the past three years to reschedule the debts or exempt from taxes both state companies and private firms. SIDEX (the largest state-owned steel plant in Romania) has benefited from more than €226,333 in State subsidies, mainly through tax relief.

4. LEGISLATURE

Although all public expenditure is included in the official budget, the Government makes extensive use of ordinances to change the budget *post hoc*, facilitating the allocation of favours to selected interests in return for bribes or contributions to political parties. There are no specific provisions on conflict of interest for MPs, many of whom are also practising lawyers or carry on other ancillary activities. Generous immunity provisions have proved effective in preventing the prosecution of corruption cases, and may be an important incentive for gaining election to Parliament. Contributions to parties by their own candidates in return for favourable positions on candidate lists may be a widespread phenomenon.

---

[89] Emergency Ordinance no. 59/2001.

[90] Prime Minister's speech, issued at the Presentation of the Annual Activity Report of the Ministry of Justice, 28 February 2001, cited in: *Evenimentul Zilei,* 3 March 2001.

[91] Commission, *2001 Regular Report*, p. 17.

4.1 Elections

Romanian elections are regarded as generally free and fair. A Central Electoral Bureau (CEB), together with constituency bureaus and electoral bureaus of polling stations, is responsible for maintaining the "good conduct" of electoral proceedings. The CEB is established at election time and is composed of seven Supreme Court judges chosen by lot, and 16 representatives of the political groups contesting the elections, represented according to their share of the total number of candidates.[92]

The only area which appears to have been prone to illegalities is the registration of candidates for presidential elections, where candidates must present a list of 100,000 signatures. Before the 1996 and 2000 elections, several media reports drew attention to the CEB's lack of control of signature lists, which contained many signatures that were invalid for various reasons.[93]

4.2 Budget and control mechanisms

Under the 1996 Public Finances Act all public expenditure is subject to parliamentary approval, including the State budget, social security budget, local government budgets and budgets of special funds for other public institutions.

However, during the implementation of the budget, the Government may modify the provisions of the Annual Budgetary Act. In practice, the budget as approved by Parliament only bears limited resemblance to the real pattern of public expenditure and revenue, as the Government makes extensive use of ordinances to alter the budget ex post.

Audit

Although the Court of Audit audits the fulfilment of the national budget and performs numerous audits of specific government activities, it does not function in practice as an effective mechanism for controlling public expenditure (for a full description of the Court, see Section 3). The Court's reports are generally submitted very late to Parliament, which does not debate them properly.

---

[92] No grouping may have more than five representatives on the CEB, and candidates may not be members.

[93] Up to summer 2002, neither the CEB nor any other authorities had investigated this matter further.

4.3 Conflict of interest and asset monitoring

The Standing Orders of the two chambers of Parliament do not constrain MPs' involvement with private firms or require them to disclose their interests (such as public and private appointments, property, shares, or campaign accounts). There are also no legal provisions regulating the acceptance of gifts or hospitality by MPs. The majority of MPs sit on the administrative councils of State enterprises or manage their own companies.[94]

The media recently exposed a senator's position as a consultant in a Romanian bank that itself played a key role in a major investment funds scandal.[95] Following repeated media coverage and criticism from other politicians, he gave up the banking position. The GRECO Evaluation Report on Romania criticised in particular the practice of elected representatives practicing simultaneously as lawyers.[96] Senator Antonie Iorgovan, a member of the governing Party of Social Democracy for several years, defended judges and other senior officials accused of corruption.[97]

Monitoring of assets is covered in Section 2.2.

There is no regulation of lobbying in Romania, although the National Anti-corruption Plan envisaged the passage of a lobbying act by the first quarter of 2002.

4.4 Immunity

Under the Romanian Constitution, deputies and senators enjoy immunity from prosecution not only for opinions expressed during the exercise of their mandate, but also from arrest, detainment, search and prosecution for any criminal offence or transgression unless the Minister of Justice submits an application for removal of immunity and Parliament authorises prosecution by a two-thirds majority in the Chamber of Deputies and a simple majority of the Senate. The case is then heard by the Supreme Court of Justice.[98] Immunity is automatically restored if an MP is re-

---

[94] The *Adevarul* daily recently published a series of 12 articles titled "The firms of MPs," analysing the commercial interests and businesses of MPs representing various constituencies. In: *Adevarul,* weekly from 26 April 2001.

[95] Information provided by Mircea Toma, Director of Press Monitoring Agency.

[96] GRECO, *Evaluation Report on Romania,* p. 20.

[97] He agreed to stop only after the Prime Minister Adrian Nastase requested that he cease in order not to make the anti-corruption efforts of the government look ridiculous.

[98] In cases of *flagrante delicto* (capture in the act of committing the offence), a deputy or senator may be detained and searched but not prosecuted. The respective Chamber must be promptly informed and may order the cancellation of the detainment.

elected,[99] and is not terminated when elections take place. As GRECO noted, "This situation has an undeniable potential for permanent obstruction of the judicial system."[100]

There have been very few cases of MPs being stripped of their immunity, and none concerning corruption cases. For example, in 1997 the Chamber of Deputies refused to cancel Deputy Gabriel Bivolaru's immunity in connection with a €2.425m fraud. The Anti-corruption Section has unsuccessfully requested that the Minister of Justice apply to lift another MP's immunity. According to one prosecutor from the Section,

> We have problems with parliamentary immunity. In my opinion, it is not normal that an MP who plundered a bank or who engages in smuggling benefits from immunity. These are some of the reasons why the judiciary is often powerless.[101]

Indeed, immunity may have itself become a significant source of corruption as persons needing legal protection pay their way onto party election lists in order to enter Parliament. One respected investigative journalist estimates that almost half of all current MPs paid to gain places on party candidate lists.[102]

The Government's National Anti-corruption Plan includes a commitment to limit immunity in general by the end of 2002, although according to senior officials the Government plans to solve the issue by 2004.[103] The EC *Regular Reports* have not mentioned the issue of immunity.

4.5 Corruption

Taken together, the factors described above provide an ideal environment in which corruption can flourish in Parliament. This is exacerbated by the weaknesses of regulation of party financing (see Section 6).

---

[99] This happened in the case of Senator Vadim Tudor, who was stripped of immunity in 1996 in connection with a case of defamation. After being re-elected before the final court judgment, he was stripped of immunity again in 1999 for participating in a miners' march on Bucharest, only to be re-elected again in 2000.

[100] GRECO, *Evaluation Report on Romania*, pp. 24–25.

[101] Interview with Flavius Craznic, prosecutor from the Anti-corruption Section, cited in *Evenimentul Zilei,* 18 August 2000.

[102] Interview with Nicoleta Savin, journalist. A businessman from Hunedoara confessed to having paid €10,833 to the Democratic Convention in order to be given the first place on the county list for the Chamber of Deputies before the 2000 elections. Despite making the payment, was not placed on the list. *Evenimentul Zilei,* 27 June 2001.

[103] OSI Roundtable Discussion, Bucharest, 28 March 2002.

World Bank research indicates that the capture of parliamentary votes by private interests is a major problem for almost half of Romanian firms.[104] More than two-thirds of the public thinks that almost all or most MPs are involved in corruption,[105] while Parliament is regarded as the fourth most corrupt institution[106] and is the least trusted Romanian institution.[107]

5. JUDICIARY

Surveys indicate that corruption is widespread in the judiciary, and extremely high levels of distrust contribute to a generalised perception that Romania is governed by vested interests rather than by the rule of law. Although the main foundations of an independent judiciary have been put in place,[108] interference by the executive branch in the judiciary and corruption within the judiciary itself raise doubts about the will or ability of the Romanian Government to pursue an effective anti-corruption policy. These problems are exacerbated by the overloaded court system and consequent lengthy delays in judicial proceedings; the average length of criminal proceedings is two years,[109] although the backlog of cases has been slowly decreasing.[110]

---

[104] Forty-two percent of Romanian firms think they are significantly affected by the capture of parliamentary votes. See World Bank, *Diagnostic Surveys of Corruption in Romania,* p. 18.

[105] Sixty-six percent of Romanians consider that most MPs are corrupt. This makes MPs the most corrupt professional group. See SELDI, *Regional Corruption Monitoring,* p. 14.

[106] World Bank, *Diagnostic Surveys of Corruption in Romania,* p. 5.

[107] Eighty-eight percent of Romanians have little or very little trust in the Parliament. See Open Society Foundation, *Public Opinion Barometer,* Bucharest, November 2000, pp. 19–20.

[108] See EU Accession Monitoring Program, *Monitoring the EU Accession Process: Judicial Independence,* Open Society Institute, Budapest 2001, p. 352., available at <http://www.eumap.org.>

[109] GRECO, *Evaluation Report on Romania,* p. 12. Sixty-eight percent of Romanian enterprises reported that slow courts are a serious obstacle to doing business; see World Bank, *Diagnostic Surveys of Corruption in Romania,* p. 11.

[110] The Commission's *2000 Regular Report* noted that the number of files pending in courts has been slowly decreasing since 1998 (in 1998 the number of pending files in civil cases was 357,307, in 1999 it was 284,942, while in July 2000 it had been reduced to 173,056). See Commission, *2000 Regular Report,* p. 17.

5.1 Legislative framework

The Romanian judiciary is described in detail in the Open Society Institute's *2001 Report on Judicial Independence in Romania.*[111] The most important aspects of the legal framework for the purposes of this report, drawn from the above-mentioned OSI report, the GRECO *Evaluation Report* and the findings of this report are as following.

Although the Constitution asserts the independence of judges, it places "Courts of Law" and the "Public Ministry" under the same heading of Judicial Authority, blurring the distinction between the Judiciary and the Executive.[112] Both judges and prosecutors have the quality of magistrates, meaning "judicial authority" in the Romanian system.

The President of the Republic appoints judges for life on the nomination of the Superior Council of Magistracy (SCM), which also handles promotions and transfers. Although the SCM consists of ten judges and five prosecutors and is elected for a four-year term by both chambers of Parliament, the operation of the Council gives more room for influence by the Minister of Justice than is compatible with Council of Europe recommendations. The SCM is chaired by the Minister of Justice in a non-voting capacity, the Minister may impose disciplinary sanctions on judges and prosecutors, and may give permission for them to be investigated and prosecuted. Moreover, Supreme Court judges are appointed for a renewable term of only six years, which GRECO noted "with concern" and regarded as unjustified.[113]

More serious concerns relate to the independence of prosecutors. The Prosecutor-General is appointed and recalled by the President on the proposal of the Minister of Justice, and other prosecutors are nominated by the SCM and appointed by the President. The prosecution system is strongly hierarchical: the Prosecutor-General can order any subordinate prosecutor to drop a case, although formally only on the grounds that the subordinate had proceeded illegally. The Minister can give written instructions directly to prosecutors or through the General Prosecutor's Office to initiate criminal proceedings. Moreover, criminal investigation of a magistrate, MP or minister requires the approval of the Minister, which effectively makes prosecutions of politicians dependent on political will.

This situation is exacerbated by the nature of disciplinary proceedings against judges and prosecutors. The SCM is responsible for disciplinary proceedings against judges,

---

[111] Open Society Institute, *Monitoring the EU Accession Process: Judicial Independence,* pp. 349–94.

[112] A 1997 amendment of the Act on Judicial Organization clarifies in part this confusion by stating that, "Judicial Power is separate from other powers and shall be exercised only by courts of law." In: Act no. 92/1992 on the Organization of the Judiciary, as amended by Act no. 142/1997, Article 1.

[113] GRECO, *Evaluation Report on Romania,* p. 23.

but the Minister of Justice decides whether a disciplinary measure will be imposed. Disciplinary proceedings against prosecutors are initiated by the Minister or the Prosecutor-General, but the decision to proceed is made by a Discipline Committee of five prosecutors. In the case of both judges and prosecutors, the Act on the Organisation of the Judiciary allows for two types of proceedings: a standard procedure with the right of appeal, and a similar process with no right of appeal. According to the former Head of the Anti-corruption Section, the former is very rarely used, while the use of the second type of procedure has "promoted political obedience."[114]

Although disciplinary proceedings against judges appear to be have been mainly used weakly rather than as tools of political influence,[115] recent developments confirm that the independence of prosecutors is not guaranteed in practice. The current Government removed the Prosecutor-General, Chief of the Military Prosecutor's Office and the Chief Prosecutor of the Anti-corruption Section – all of whom had investigated important cases involving senior politicians or officials.[116] In March 2001, the Minister of Justice issued a letter to all appellate courts in the country, advising judges to favour the rights of tenants over landlords in restitution cases.[117] In April of the same year, the Government wrote to the Cluj Local Court requesting that bankruptcy procedures against a specific bank be suspended until the Government took a decision "favourable to the interests of the Romanian economy."[118] Although the Government subsequently admitted to the European Commission that this was a mistake,[119] media reports suggest that, "Since the November 2000 elections, interference of the Executive in the Judiciary has reached unprecedented levels."[120] In April 2001, EU Commissioner for Enlargement Guenter Verheugen singled out judicial independence in Romania as an important accession issue and asked the Government to explain recent personnel changes in the judiciary.[121]

In 2001, the SCM adopted the Magistrates' Deontological Code (Code of Conduct), and in early 2000 was negotiating with the International Centre for the Prevention of

---

[114] Interview with Ovidiu Budusan, 27 March 2002.

[115] On leaving office, former Minister of Justice Valeriu Stoica labelled the Council as too indulgent, a fact that in his opinion it "disappointed and discouraged honest magistrates, while encouraging the others to persevere in their erroneous practices."

[116] When leaving office in 1998, Sorin Moisescu, a former General Prosecutor, made a significant declaration. He said he had received "hundreds of interventions from politicians for the appointment or dismissal of prosecutors." Cited in: *Evenimentul Zilei,* 22 June 1998.

[117] *Evenimentul Zilei,* 3 April 2001

[118] *Evenimentul Zilei,* 30 April 2001

[119] Comments from OSI Roundtable Discussion, Bucharest, 28 March 2002.

[120] Interview with Liviu Mihaiu, deputy editor of *Academia Catavencu,* 11 April 2001.

[121] *Adevarul,* 27 April 2001.

International Crime and the United Nations in Vienna for an assistance programme to consolidate the integrity of the judiciary, including a mechanism to monitor adherence to the Code.

The Judiciary and EU accession

Reform of the Romanian judicial system has been identified by the European Commission as one of the important requirements for Romania's accession to the EU. The judiciary is dealt with both in the *Regular Reports* and the *AP*, and has been the main target of PHARE programmes related to corruption (see Section 1.4).

5.2 Corruption

Trust in the judiciary is low. The percentage of citizens expressing little or very little trust in the judiciary rose from 62 percent in November 1998 to 74 percent in November 1990 and 77 percent in November 2000.[122] The judiciary is less trusted than the police, army or church.

According to the World Bank's *2000 Diagnostic Survey,* 65 percent of private businessmen agreed that all or most officials in the judiciary engage in corruption, making the judiciary the second most corrupt agency in their perception. Fifty-five percent of ordinary citizens and 53 percent of public officials shared the same opinion.[123] Twenty-two percent of ordinary citizens reported that they pay bribes while dealing with the judiciary. However, only five percent of companies reported encountering bribery in courts, interpreted by the survey to mean that most bribes in the judiciary are mediated by lawyers.[124] Corrupt practices seem to be most commonly used to speed up court proceedings or secure the assignment of a case to a particular judge.[125]

Ironically, security of tenure has been viewed in this context as an institution encouraging corruption in the judiciary.[126] A number of cases of corrupt judges have recently attracted public attention. The most publicised case is that of the President of

---

[122] Open Society Foundation, *Public Opinion Barometer,* Bucharest, November 2000, p. 19. The poll was performed on a sample of 1,775 persons.

[123] World Bank, *Diagnostic Surveys of Corruption in Romania,* p. 5.

[124] Recently an attorney has been arrested for demanding money (€15,680) from his client in order to bribe the judge. See *Evenimentul Zilei,* 26 January 2001.

[125] World Bank, *Diagnostic Surveys of Corruption in Romania,* p. 15.

[126] Both the former and present Ministers of Justice, as well as the current President and Prime Minister, have expressed concerns that judges invoke lifetime appointment as a shield against accountability.

the Criminal Section of the regional Appellate Court of Cluj, who was recently convicted of influence trafficking and sentenced to four years imprisonment. This was the first ever conviction of a Romanian judge for corruption. The testimony of the local businessman who broke the affair (an important figure of the Cluj underworld, according to witness testimony in court) implicated local police, a local prison commander and two other officials in corruption.

Another case concerns the arrest of a judge and a prosecutor for influence trafficking. Allegedly, the judge served as an intermediary to bribe another judge in Bucharest to facilitate the release of a famous arms dealer from custody. This dealer is already famous for having escaped prosecution for trading with embargoed countries. The case was in court as of June 2002.

6. POLITICAL PARTY FINANCE

Political party funding is non-transparent, uncontrolled and probably highly corrupt. Standard problems of party corruption by business interests are supplemented by a problem of funding by individuals in exchange for places on party candidate lists (see Section 4.4). Even senior politicians admit that the majority of party funding is illegal or hidden. Party finances yielded the largest corruption affair since 1989.

6.1 Legislative framework

Under the 1996 Act on Political Parties, political parties may receive the following sources of income:

Membership fees

There is no limit on total income from membership fees, but the total fees paid by a single person in one year may not exceed fifty times the minimum monthly salary.

Income from own activities

Permitted sources of income include editing and distribution of party publications; entertainment, sporting and cultural activities; internal services; rental of spaces for conferences and social and cultural activities; interest on bank deposits; and sales of assets, excluding those received as donations from abroad.

Donations and legacies

Donations represent the main funding source for Romanian political parties. The 1996 Act prohibits donations from companies, public organisations and foreign organisations or states. Donations received by any single party in a non-election year may not exceed 0.005 percent of GDP (approximately €162,500 in 2000), and 0.01 percent in an election year.

Parties must publish in the Government's *Official Gazette* a list of all persons who donated amounts exceeding ten times the monthly minimum wage in any given year. Anonymous donations may not exceed 20 percent of the state subsidy allocated to the party in that year.

Parties violating provisions on donations are subject to symbolic sanctions: donations received under illegal conditions become "income to the State budget."[127] Although the 1996 Act states that "donations of material goods and money obviously made to obtain a political or an economic advantage are prohibited," no method of determining the intent of donors has been established.

State subsidies

Total State subsidies to political parties may not exceed 0.04 percent of that year's GDP (around €2.6m in 2000). State subsidies to political parties are divided into three shares:

- Political parties, which at the beginning of the legislature are represented by a parliamentary group in at least one Chamber, are entitled to receive a so-called "basic subsidy." Basic subsidies make up one-third of the total budgetary subsidies allocated to political parties.[128]

- All political parties represented in Parliament also receive a subsidy proportional to their number of mandates. The sum allocated for one mandate is calculated by dividing the remaining two-thirds of budgetary subsidies by the total number of MPs.

- Political parties that did not win any parliamentary mandates but obtained at least two percent of votes cast receive equal subsidies calculated by dividing the remaining part of state subsidies by the number of such parties. The total subsidy granted to a non-parliamentary party cannot exceed a basic subsidy.[129]

- Any sum remaining after this redistribution is allocated to parliamentary parties according to their number of mandates.

---

[127] Act no. 27/1996, Article 45.

[128] Act no. 27/1996, Article 39, paragraph 3.

[129] Act no. 27/1996, Article 39, paragraph 6.

- The State subsidises political parties indirectly, as all party income is tax-free and donations from abroad are duty-free.

- The total yearly subsidy granted to one political party cannot exceed five times the basic subsidy (around €433,340).

- Income from subsidies cannot be spent on electoral campaigns.

Reform

Before the November 2000 elections, the former Minister of Justice initiated a draft Act on the Financing of Political Party Activities and Electoral Campaigns.[130] The draft Act would set limits on campaign expenditure, forbids certain categories of expenses, specify clearly the duties of the electoral treasurer, oblige political parties to submit financial reports to the Court of Audit within 15 days of the end of electoral campaigns, and increase sanctions for violations. According to Ministry of Justice officials, three draft acts were under discussion as of March 2002, although none had been submitted to Parliament by June 2002.

6.2 Control and supervision

Apart from the obligation to publish donations in the *Official Gazette*, parties do not publish any other kind of financial documents. The electoral treasurer of each party is responsible for keeping the accounts of the party and making them available on request to the Court of Audit or special Commissions of Inquiry set up by Parliament.[131]

In practice there has been no control of party finances. The Court of Audit began its first audit of party finances in February 2001, based only on financial documents provided by parties. A Parliamentary Commission of Inquiry established in June 2000 was to submit a report to the Parliament by 1 October 2000, but the report had not been submitted by early 2002.

6.3 Party finance in practice

Political party financing is troubled by widespread non-compliance with disclosure provisions, together with extensive evidence of corruption. The real extent of corruption in Romanian political party financing is impossible to measure. However, Valeriu Stoica, former Minister of Justice, summarised the situation in the following statement:

---

[130] The draft Act was designed together with the members of Pro Democratia Association.

[131] Constitution of Romania, Article 61, paragraph 4.

> Political parties should have the courage to admit that, at this moment, the financing of political parties' activities and of their campaigns is carried out 80 percent illegally. And, even though the proportion of illegality is 80 percent, there is no sanction to counter it.[132]

In December 2001, Traian Basescu, president of the Democratic Party and General Mayor of Bucharest, denounced the corruption existent in the financing of political parties, offering examples from his own party. According to his estimations, the Democratic Party officially declared €108,340 as revenue from donations, while the whole cost of the campaign was around €1.625m, adding that,

> We all know that we used money from donations made by businessmen or firms, which hoped that DP would continue to govern and thus pay them, back the services they had made during the campaign... If this is what happened in our party, I wonder what was going on in the others?[133]

A recent study of the Pro Democratia Association shows that political parties have spent much larger amounts than they declared in the *Official Gazette*, based only on media reports (see Table 4).[134]

Table 4: Difference between the amounts declared and actually spent by parties in the 2000 electoral campaign

	Amounts declared in the Official Gazette (€)	Amounts monitored by APD (€)
National Liberal Party	420.567	2,664.846
Party for Social Democracy in Romania	51.502	4,046.877
Democratic Party	354.033	2,767.471
Alliance for Romania	72.158	1,183.243
Union of Rightist Forces	54.167	247.937
Socialist Party of Labour	1.741	215.867
National Alliance (Party of National Unity in Romania – National Romanian Party)	2.851	351.632

---

[132] Valeriu Stoica, cited in: *Dilema*, no. 405, 17-23 November 2000, p. 8. When he made this statement, Stoica was the Minister of Justice. Valeriu Stoica is now the President of the National Liberal Party.

[133] Nicoleta Savin and Ondine Ghergut, "Inviting Adrian Nastase to do the same thing, Basescu admits that DP did not declare all the money from the campaign," *Evenimentul Zilei*, 27 December 2001. The meaning of the last sentence from Traian Basescu's declaration is that bigger parties receive many more illegal donations than the smaller ones.

[134] Pro Democratia Association, *Romanian Political Parties' Funds in the Electoral Year 2000*, Bucharest, May 2001. The study is part of the project "Transparency, Trust, Democracy," financed by Open Society Foundation Romania.

In its *2001 Regular Report*, the EC referred to these discrepancies in calling for "a fully transparent system of party funding."[135] Moreover, the Pro Democratia Association did not monitor several important categories of expenses, such as those for the design and production of electoral materials, street posters, transportation and accommodation expenses, the cost of electoral polls, staff and communication expenses. Pro Democratia estimated that the amounts actually spent by political parties in the 2000 electoral campaign were twice as big as the ones the organisation evaluated.[136] Finally, many firms finance parties indirectly, for example by paying directly for election advertisements.[137]

Numerous media reports have linked the illegal financing of parties with the rescheduling of debts of certain firms, with the privatisation of many state enterprises, with the questionable lending policies of some banks, illegal reimbursement of VAT, tolerance of tax evasion and allocation of public contracts. For example, contributions to parties by alcohol producers in Romania and promotion on party lists of candidates favourable to their cause (they supported financially almost 100 candidates for the 2000 parliamentary elections) provide substantial circumstantial evidence of corruption.[138] Tax evasion is rampant in this field: it is estimated that only ten percent of total alcohol production is officially taxed. In addition to tolerance of tax evasion, after the elections the same companies received huge tax exemptions and debt rescheduling.[139]

The biggest affair to have been publicised concerning Romanian party financing is the so-called Costea Affair (see Section 2.5).

All this helps to explain the fact that according to opinion surveys 86 percent of Romanians have little or very little trust in political parties,[140] while more than half of the public thinks that "nearly all" or "most" political party leaders are involved in corruption.[141]

---

[135] Comission, *2001 Regular Report*, p. 22.

[136] C. Pirvulescu, "Political parties and illegal funding," *22* (weekly), 15-21 May 2001, p. 6.

[137] Interview with Adrian Moraru, coordinator of the APD project "Transparency, Trust, Democracy."

[138] *Capital*, no. 47, 23 November 2000, pp. 8–9.; *Capital*, no. 14, 6 April 2000.

[139] The media has covered extensively the cases of European Drinks, the biggest alcohol producer and recipient of several billion Lei debt relief, and of Moldo Production company, which in June 2000 owed more than €1.94m in taxes. As one small alcohol producer explained, "It is only natural that the Minister of Finance, police and prosecutors tolerate the huge illegal production of alcohol... because there is no political party in this country without a distillery... and... no distillery without political backing." In: *Capital*, no. 47, 23 November 2000, p. 8.

[140] Open Society Foundation, *Public Opinion Barometer*, Bucharest, November 2000, p. 20.

[141] The exact percentage is 53.7. See SELDI, *Regional Corruption Monitoring*, p. 14.

7. PUBLIC PROCUREMENT

Corruption appears to be systemic in public procurement, ranging from collusion and strong patron-client networks to standard bribery. The most important progress made by the Government in anti-corruption policy so far has been reform of the legal framework for public procurement, and the implementation of the new legislation will be an important test of the State's ability to follow through on anti-corruption policy. As of June 2002 there was still no independent body for supervising procurement or dealing with appeals against procurement decisions.

7.1 Legislative framework

Until 1999, the only public procurement legislation in effect was a 1993 Government ordinance, which together with secondary legislation established a rough legal framework for procurement. Under these rules, contracts with a value exceeding a certain threshold had to be procured through an open public tender, a public tender with pre-selection, or through a restricted procedure. The 1993 legislation (changed around 600 times) contained very unclear tender rules, allowed excessive discretion in the use of sole sourcing, did not include provisions on transparency or conflict of interest or any significant sanctions for violation of the law.

The 1999 and 2001 Public Procurement Acts

In 1999, a comprehensive new governmental ordinance was passed to amend the shortcomings of the previous regulations.[142] The ordinance was drafted with the support of the European Commission (SIGMA experts).[143] In 2001, the Government changed the law again through an emergency ordinance, largely as a result of EU pressure.[144] There is widespread agreement that the Government's main goal in postponing the 2001 ordinance was to allow officials to raise funds for the coming electoral campaign and to award many contracts in exchange for the generosity of private firms that had contributed to the electoral campaign of 2000.[145]

Under current legislation, public authorities must submit contracts to open tender if they exceed €40,000 in value for a goods or services contract and €100,000 for a public works contract. Contracts may be allocated by sole sourcing:

---

[142] Government Ordinance no. 118/1999.

[143] Government Ordinance no. 118/1999, regarding Public Procurement, *Official Gazette,* no. 431, 31 August 1999.

[144] Commission, *2000 Regular Report,* p. 39.

[145] See, e.g., *Capital,* no. 39, 28 September 2000.

- if only a single contractor is capable of fulfilling the contract;

- to supplement or replace products already purchased from the supplier (for up to three years after the original contract) or which for unforeseeable reasons have become necessary and can only be purchased from the same supplier;

- if the authority decides to purchase new services or works similar to the subject of a previous contract, which was originally awarded according to an open or restricted tender and which mentioned the possibility of such sole sourcing, provided that the services or works observe the original terms of reference, are valued as they were in the original contract and are purchased within three years of the award of the initial contract;

- when contractors that operate in the utilities sectors purchase goods that are quoted and transacted on the stock exchange, or have an extremely profitable short-term opportunity to purchase goods at a price considerably lower than market price;

- in situations of *force majeure* (for example, a natural disaster).

The 2001 Ordinance is published in the *Official Gazette* and is available on the Internet. Contracting authorities must publish a notice of intent to procure in the *Official Gazette* for all contracts exceeding €750,000. Invitations to bid must be published similarly for all contracts to be allocated by tender. Tender documentation must be prepared containing standard tender information including general and specific contract conditions and the criteria used for assessing bids. The results of tender procedures must be published in the *Official Gazette* within 30 days of the award of the contract.

The following persons may not be members of an assessment commission or jury deciding a tender: spouses or relatives (to the third degree) of one of the bidders or candidates; persons who have in the last three years been members of the statutory, management or administrative organ of a bidder, or had any commercial contract with a bidder. There is no code of ethics or behavioural guidelines for public procurement officials or provisions to monitor the assets of members of commissions assessing bids, with the exception of the (entirely ineffective) provisions applying to all public officials since 1996 (see Section 2.2).

Bidders may be excluded from a tender if they are in bankruptcy or liquidation, have tax arrears, provide false information, or did not fulfil obligations under another public contract. Bidders who can be proven to have been involved in corrupt or fraudulent practices related to the procedure for the contract in question must be excluded.

The European Commission acknowledged the new Procurement Act as an exception to Romania's poor progress in the fight against corruption, and expressed the opinion in 2001 that, "[E]ffective implementation of new legislation on public procurement should play an important role in the fight against corruption…"[146]

In addition, in January 2002 the Government passed an Emergency Ordinance on Public Procurement by Means of Electronic Devices, providing a legal framework for e-procurement and facilitating use of the Public Procurement Electronic System.[147]

7.2 Review and audit

Under the new Act, bidders may appeal procurement decisions first to the contracting entity and thereafter to an administrative court. There are no official statistics concerning the number of administrative or judicial appeals made in public procurement in the last three years. Indeed, there is no official data even on the number of contracts, their size or the winners. Unofficial estimates are that as many as 50 percent of procurement decisions are challenged.[148] However, the widespread practice of collusion between bidders (see below) may make this proportion much lower.

The Ministry of Finance and the Ministry of Public Works are responsible for enforcing the public procurement legislation, while a new Directorate for Public Procurement Regulation at the Ministry of Finance is responsible for producing an annual report on the operation of the public procurement system and building a database of public contracts awarded. GRECO recommended in its March 2002 evaluation report that the Service be strengthened, and preferably that an independent Public Procurement Office be created.[149] The Court of Audit is responsible for *post hoc* audit of public contracts.

7.3 Corruption

According to the available evidence, corruption in public procurement is endemic both at central and local levels although the media has tended to cover scandals in central Government procurement. Factors leading to corruption include the lack of qualified staff running tenders, problems in existing legislation (see above) and the existence of strong clientelistic networks binding officials to business interests.

---

[146] Commission, *2001 Regular Report*, p. 101.

[147] The system can be accessed at <http://www.e-licitatie.ro>, (last accessed 15 August 2002).

[148] Interview with Simona Nanescu, European Commission Delegation, 19 April 2001.

[149] GRECO, *Evaluation Report on Romania,* p. 26.

Collusion and fixing

Local businessmen and even public officials "take it for granted" that small contracts should be fixed by means of an agreement between local bidders. A businessman (and local councillor) from Olt county explained that he had to obtain "bids" from two other firms for a contract to provide bread to a local military unit. These offers were drawn up so that he could win the contract. In return he does the same for other firms in other tenders. According to Court of Auditors officials from three different counties, 99 percent of all public tenders in Romania are "arranged" or "fixed." Officials from the Prime Minister's Control Department identify the preparation of tender documents in order to favour a particular contractor as one of the most important forms of corruption in procurement.[150]

"Commissions"

Another widespread corrupt practice is the "commission" *(comisionul)*, usually estimated as at least ten percent of the contract value. The commission is a bribe that is taken for granted before negotiations on procurement even begin.[151]

Conflict of interest

Large proportions of firms winning public contracts are those with important officials from the local government among their shareholders. Many public officials do not even hide the fact that they work, at the same time, as private managers or consultants of local companies doing business with the municipality.

Clientelism

Entrance into local markets for public procurement (especially construction work) is invariably controlled by a group of firms that are protected by corrupt local officials and/or politicians. The relationships between businessmen and politicians are not transitory, but embedded in powerful networks of reciprocity and solidarity.

The extent of corruption in procurement is so severe that it has resulted in a number of Sicilian-style public contracts that will never be completed.

---

[150] OSI Roundtable Discussion, Bucharest, 28 March 2002.

[151] Public officials sometimes raise the amount demanded as commission: in this case, firms will either adapt to the new bribe thresholds or be forced to withdraw. The latter option is most common for small firms, which usually survive from subcontracting. The owner of a small firm doing road maintenance explained how he prepared for a tender organized by the County Directorate for Roads and Bridges with the ten percent "commission" in mind; however, the officials running the tender asked for 20 percent, forcing him to withdraw, as the revenue remaining would not cover the cost of participation in the contract.

8. PUBLIC SERVICES

Corruption in Romanian public services appears to be endemic, with the exception of the education system. Corruption in the police is underpinned by widespread collusion between the police and organised crime, while corruption in the customs authorities has rich historical roots and has implicated politicians up to the highest level. Corruption in the tax authorities is underpinned by wide discretion of tax authorities to grant tax breaks to companies. Widespread corruption to gain access to health services deters the poor from visiting doctors. The burden of licensing and regulation authorities is heavy in Romania, resulting in widespread corruption to ward off inspections.

8.1 Police

Corruption among Romania's 52,000 police is by all accounts endemic, although there are very few convictions – 21 cases in 1997, 24 in 1998, 26 in 1999 and only 17 in 2000 according to the Minister of Interior.[152] Many media reports suggest that the police and organised crime operate in cooperation, and the Prime Minister stated at the launch of the Ministry of Interior *2000 Activity Report* that,

> The police cannot ensure public order if at the same time it shares the city of Bucharest with fifteen bands of robbers and pretends not to see the tax evasion taking place in the domain of alcohol.[153]

According to the World Bank's *Diagnostic Surveys*, 55 percent of enterprises, 47 percent of households and 39 percent of public officials consider that all or most police officers are corrupt.[154] The same surveys found that although bribery is not frequent during police investigations, it is very common in interactions with the traffic police.[155]

Puiu Latea, board member of Transparency International Romania, commented on police corruption in the following way:

> I myself could give 17 examples of corrupt policemen (never proven) from a single town... [who] coordinate the trade in scrap iron, protect the illegal functioning of the only "exchange office" in town, don't pay a thing for their daily purchases (not even for bread!) and take bribes in order to return driving licenses that they themselves had previously confiscated. In my opinion, the

---

[152] *Curentul,* 27 April 2001.

[153] *Adevarul,* 6 March 2001.

[154] World Bank, *Diagnostic Surveys of Corruption in Romania,* p. 5.

[155] World Bank, *Diagnostic Surveys of Corruption in Romania,* p. 15.

Police of this town are very similar to a firm with a diffuse area of activity, which extracts profit by protecting a vast array of illegal activities.[156]

One investigative journalist cited the example of a number of businesses that have had to close down as a result of police harassment, and according to one EU pre-accession adviser, the situation in the police "could not be worse."[157]

Corruption in the police is underpinned by several fundamental institutional deficiencies. First, the police remain a military organisation. It is deeply hierarchical and is not amenable to any concept of responsiveness to community needs. Police officers are not governed by any civil statute on their role, rights and duties, and are disciplined and tried for offences by military courts that are not public. Demilitarisation remains a fundamental condition for any real reform of the police. Although demilitarisation has been under discussion for a decade, the relevant acts have not yet been adopted.[158]

Second, police salaries are extremely low, at around €130 a month. According to GRECO, "[T]he absence of appropriate remuneration appears as one of the main risks of corruption of police officers in Romania."[159] This is compounded by very poor working conditions. According to research carried out by the Institute for the Research and Prevention of Criminality, only 301 of 2,688 rural police posts have a permanent telephone connection, while rural police posts have 495 cars of which only 58 are effectively functioning. According to the same research, 73 percent of police officers considered their present financial situation as poor, while 1.5 percent was content.[160]

Corruption offences among police officers are investigated by the Minister [of Interior]'s Control Group and the General Directorate for Information and Protection (Military Unit 0962). Both units, and especially MU 0962, are fundamentally non-transparent: for example, although citizens can submit complaints to both units, there

---

[156] Interview with Puiu Latea, Board Member of Transparency International Romania, 3 May 2001.

[157] OSI Roundtable Discussion, Bucharest, 28 March 2002.

[158] Ever since 1998, the Commission has urged in its *Regular Reports* the initiation of a reform of the police. For instance, the *1999 Regular Report* includes the following observations: "In general, a fundamental reform of the Ministry of the Interior is required before the Ministry can become an efficient and 'civil' organisation with sufficient capacity to implement the acquis in this important area… The demilitarisation of the police must also be pursued as a prerequisite for the development of an effective and accountable police force." In: Commission, *1999 Regular Report*, pp. 74–75.

[159] GRECO, *Evaluation Report on Romania*, p. 21.

[160] Institute for the Research and Prevention of Criminality, *Diagnosis of Institutional Abandon. Police Officers' Perception of Professional Satisfaction in the Present Social Context*, Bucharest, 2001.

is no feedback or information available on whether investigations are started as a result.[161] In early 2001, the Control Group carried out a number of investigations in county police inspectorates, some of which resulted in transfers and disciplinary sanctions. One investigation was initiated by the appearance of an Internet site describing corrupt police activities.[162] According to the GRECO *Evaluation Report*, in 2001, 140 cases of corruption in the police were investigated by judicial authorities and around 3,000 dealt with at disciplinary level.[163]

EU assistance

EU assistance for the Romanian police consisted, at the time of writing, of a two-year €2m twinning project with the UK (France and Spain are the other two partners) to aid the fight against organised crime and corruption. The project began in 2000 and has the ambitious objectives of legal approximation, demilitarisation, institutional reform of the Ministry of Interior, and improvement of the police structures countering organised crime.

Although the project has had led to some changes (for example, the transformation of the Organised Crime and Corruption Squad into a Directorate for Countering Organised Crime), the process of providing assistance has been troubled from the beginning by lack of will and cooperation form the Ministry of Interior. For example, in September 2000, a twinning expert from the UK submitted a report on anti-corruption policy: it took the Ministry until March 2002 to respond, and there appears to have been little or no change in police structure or policy in that period.[164]

8.2 Customs

The Romanian customs authority is considered to be one of the sectors most vulnerable to corruption, exacerbated by the fact that, like its neighbours, the country is an important transit route for trafficking in various illegal goods. According to the

---

[161] The President of the Chamber of Deputies Committee for Defence, Public Order and National Security has also complained about the lack of parliamentary oversight over the activities of MU 962. See interview with deputy Razvan Ionescu, President of the Commission for Defence, Public Order and National Security of the Chamber of Deputies, in: *Adevarul*, 2 May 2001.

[162] The site <http://www.politisti-corupti.go.ro/politia> was launched in March 2001, but has since been removed from the Internet. Another Internet site dealing with the corrupt policemen of a different County Inspectorate was launched two weeks after the first one: <http://aradeana.homestead.com/arad-main.html>, but has also been removed from the Internet.

[163] GRECO, *Evaluation Report on Romania*, p. 7.

[164] Comments at OSI Roundtable Discussion, Bucharest, 28 March 2002.

World Bank's *2000 Diagnostic Survey*, the customs authority is regarded as the most corrupt institution in Romania: 66 percent of companies believed that all or almost all customs officials are corrupt (see Section 1.1).

As in Bulgaria, the integrity of Romanian customs and border control was seriously undermined by the Yugoslav embargo, which resulted in extensive smuggling operations involving the Romanian Intelligence Service and Adrian Costea. The investigation of these activities by the Anti-corruption Section appears to have been the reason why the Chief of the Section was removed in 2001 (see Section 2.5).

Direct evidence on corruption among customs officials is patchy, but available indicators are worrying. For example, one investigative journalist was told by an unsuccessful candidate for the post of Head of the Customs Authority that the "price" to secure the post was €1.3m.[165]

In 1995, the Customs Authority introduced asset monitoring for customs officials as an anti-corruption measure, although it is not known whether the provisions have had any effect. The Government also introduced compulsory tax returns for customs officials in January 2001 as a further means of monitoring discrepancies between lifestyle and declared assets. GRECO noted in its *Evaluation Report* the absence of specialised training in preventing and combating corruption among customs staff.[166]

8.3 Tax collection

There is little evidence available on the general prevalence of corruption among the Romanian tax authorities, and they were not investigated by the World Bank's *2000 Diagnostic Survey*. However, it appears that the tax system is used by political parties to return favours to donors (see Section 6.3). According to Mugur Isarescu, former Romanian Prime Minister,

> [T]he situation of the budget is devastating. Practically, there are no budgets anymore. There are only exceptions, facilities, tax exemptions – an overwhelming corruption that originates in the very text of laws. And this is because everything is discretionary, everything is negotiable.[167]

The Government and tax authorities have wide discretion to award companies tax relief in various forms. A report of the Government Control Department issued in November 2000 identified the wide discretion of tax officials to grant tax breaks to

---

[165] Interview with Nicoleta Savin, journalist at *Evenimentul Zilei*, 29 March 2002.

[166] GRECO, *Evaluation Report on Romania,* p. 21.

[167] *Evenimentul Zilei*, 17 January 2000.

private or State-owned companies as a major source of corruption. The report underlined the existence of "a permissive and optional legal framework" (for example, the lack of criteria for determining companies as having liquidity problems) and arbitrary interpretation of the Act by officials.[168]

8.4 Health

According to the World Bank's *2000 Diagnostic Survey*, health services were regarded as the fifth most corrupt institution by families (see Section 1.1). More importantly, the survey indicated that a larger proportion of respondents that used medical services had paid bribes than for any other category of service: 66 percent made unofficial payments for hospital stays, 62 percent for treatment in an emergency, 56 percent for dental treatment and 52 percent to a medical specialist.[169] According to the World Bank one of the worst effects of corruption may be the fact that poor households were twice as likely as rich households to say they had not sought healthcare even when they needed it.[170]

8.5 Education

Compared to other institutions, the Romanian education system is not regarded as particularly corrupt, and was among the least corrupt institutions according to the World Bank's *2000 Diagnostic Survey*. While up to a quarter of respondents reported providing some unofficial payment to education staff in the previous year, these were mostly in the form of small gifts, and more than half those doing so reported that the payments were not required.[171]

8.6 Licensing and regulation

A major source of corruption remains the heavy burden of State controls on businesses. As the *2001 Regular Report* notes:

> A large number of bodies are authorised to conduct inspections and audits of businesses. Businesses can be expected to be investigated several times a year

---

[168] *Adevarul*, 9 December 2000.

[169] World Bank, *Diagnostic Surveys of Corruption in Romania*, p. xi.

[170] World Bank, *Diagnostic Surveys of Corruption in Romania*, p. 15.

[171] World Bank, *Diagnostic Surveys of Corruption in Romania*, p. 16.

and the wide degree of discretion left to inspectors creates opportunities for corruption.[172]

The former head of the Anti-corruption Section expressed the opinion that the fear of being inspected by such bodies is a more serious concern for businesses than organised crime.[173]

9. ROLE OF THE MEDIA

The role of the media in exposing corruption is threatened by the continuing existence of draconian defamation provisions in the Criminal Code, which remain on the statute books despite strong criticism from international organisations. A new Act on Free Access to Public Information came into effect in January 2002. Public broadcasting is systematically and politically biased, and increasingly so since the last elections. Corruption of or pressure on media outlets through advertising is common. Despite these problems, the press has been active in exposing corruption.

9.1 Freedom of speech

Freedom of expression and prohibition of censorship are enshrined in the Romanian Constitution.[174] However, the Constitution allows restriction of this right to prevent a number of actions such as "defamation of country and nation," "instigation to class hatred" or "instigation to territorial separatism."

In addition, the Penal Code contains offences that entail potentially severe threats to freedom of expression, in particular provisions on defamation.[175] Since 1996, over 400 cases under such articles have been brought (mainly against journalists), the vast majority under the provision,[176] and up to July 2001, around 50 journalists had been convicted. Another article forbids "communication or dissemination, by any possible means, of false news, facts or information or forged documents, if this could impair state security or its international relations," with penalties from one to five years

---

[172] Commission, *2001 Regular Report*, p. 74.

[173] Interview with Ovidiu Budusan, 27 March 2002.

[174] Constitution of Romania, Article 30.

[175] Criminal Code, Articles 205 and 206.

[176] Interview with Mircea Toma, Director, Media Monitoring Agency, 21 March 2002

imprisonment. Although this is rarely used against journalists, it was used in a recent case against an anonymous Internet news portal.

According to human rights experts, "[Such] prohibitive grounds… cannot be found in any international document related to the acceptable limitations on freedom of expression."[177] A resolution of the Parliamentary Assembly of the Council of Europe explicitly referred to Romania's failure to reform these Acts, despite the fact that they "seriously imperil the exercise of fundamental freedoms."[178] Repealing the provisions on outrage and insult are priorities of the *2001 AP*, although in March 2002 it was unclear when or if the Government would do so.

The media regulations mentioned above provide potentially serious barriers to corruption reporting. A 1999 Freedom House report noted that in the previous three years the Romanian Committee for the Protection of Journalists documented at least 19 instances of harassment, legal action and threats of violence against journalists.[179] According to the Committee, harassment of journalists creates huge pressure, and has been getting worse as financial claims in court have increased.[180] One of the main Romanian dailies (also one of the two publications that carries out effective investigative journalism) faced defamation charges in March 2002 that could financially threaten its existence.

The legal framework regulating the media contains several other shortcomings. There is no legal limitation of searches of media facilities/premises during criminal investigations. Finally, although the Act on Public Television and Radio gives journalists of public radio and TV the right to conceal sources, they may be forced to reveal their sources by a court order "where the public interest is at risk," and other journalists have no such right.

9.2 Access to information

Although Romanian authorities have been notoriously poor at providing information – most Government agencies hide behind a veil of secrecy and journalists are forced to use clandestine channels of information including paying public officials for

---

[177] Monica Macovei, *Some Aspects of the Media Law*, report prepared for the FreeEx network for the protection of freedom of expression in Southeast Europe, available at <http://www.freeex.org/medialw.htm>, (last accessed 15 August 2002).

[178] Parliamentary Assembly of the Council of Europe, Resolution no. 1123/97.

[179] Freedom House, *Media Reponses to Corruption in the Emerging Democracies: Bulgaria, Hungary, Romania, and Ukraine,* May 1999, p.12.

[180] In one recent case a journalist was fined the equivalent of €32,500 for insulting another journalist. Interview with Mircea Toma, Director of Press Monitoring Agency, 21 March 2002.

information – recent legislative developments and the stated commitments of the Government provide reasons for optimism.

In October 2001, Parliament adopted the Act on Free Access to Public Information. The Act was prepared in close cooperation with NGOs (especially the Media Monitoring Agency), and is regarded by media representatives to be of high quality. Under the Act, verbal requests submitted by the media for public information are to be granted immediately or within 24 hours. Any other person can make oral or written requests for public information – these are to be granted by the public institution in ten or 30 days, depending on the complexity of the request. Information of public interest is defined as "any information regarding the operations or resulting from the operations of a public authority or public institution, irrespective of the information source, form or expression." *Public authority* or *institution* is defined as "any public authority or institution, as well as any autonomous administration *[regie autonomă]*, utilising public financial resources and operating on the territory of Romania, under the Constitution."

Citizens do not have right of access to: information concerning national defence, security and public order, if such information is classified; information on the deliberations of the authorities; information concerning the economic and political interests of Romania if such information is classified; information on commercial or financial operations, if disclosure would violate the principle of fair competition under the law; information on personal data as defined by law; information on criminal or disciplinary investigation procedures if disclosure would endanger the result of the investigation, reveal confidential sources or endanger the life, physical integrity or health of an individual; and information on court proceedings if disclosure might undermine a fair trial or the legitimate interest of any of the parties to a trial.

The Act states explicitly that, "[I]nformation which favours or conceals law-breaking by a public authority or institution cannot be considered classified information, but information of public interest." This might provide the media with explicit legal protection when exposing corruption cases.

If refused access to information, a citizen may complain to the head of the respective public institution; and thereafter to an administrative court, which can force the respective public institution to grant the information requested.

As of early 2002, it was too early to judge the effect of the new Act in practice.

9.3 Broadcasting regulation

Licensing

The regulatory body for the broadcast media is the National Council of Broadcasting (NCB). The NCB is composed of 11 members: two appointed by the President of Romania, six by Parliament and three by the Government.

Broadcasting licenses are granted on a competitive basis for a period of seven years (for television) and five years (for radio), and renewed by a new tender. Criteria for awarding the licenses must be published 45 days before the competition date. The final selection criteria must be defined so that "they ensure pluralism in the opinions expressed, equal treatment of competitors, quality and diversity of programmes, open competition, editorial independence and impartiality." However, the law does not establish precise criteria and procedures to ensure transparency in license allocation. The Government recently took away from the NCB the allocation and administration of radio high frequencies.

Public broadcasting

There are two State-owned broadcast media institutions: the Romanian Broadcasting Company (RBC) and the Romanian Television Company (RTC). RBS and RTS are managed by an Administration Council composed of 13 members elected by Parliament: Parliament nominates members for eight positions, the President of Romania and the Government one each, the employees of the RBS and RTS two positions, and representatives of ethnic minorities in Parliament one position which appoints a Director General and Board of Directors to RBS and RTS.

Although the Committee regards the public media coverage of the 1996 and 2000 elections as relatively unbiased, since then the state news agency Rompres has been put under control of the Ministry of Information and the PSD has received approximately 70 percent of airtime devoted to political parties by main terrestrial TV stations.[181]

9.4 Corruption in the media

Although corruption of individual journalists has not attracted significant attention, advertising is widely used by both State institutions and business interests to influence the printed press in particular. Some public authorities (e.g. the State Property Fund)

---

[181] Economist Intelligence Unit, *Romania Country Report,* January 2002, p. 16. The representative of the Committee for the Protection of Journalists confirmed that this proportion applied also to public television.

have used advertising to channel public funds to complacent media outlets. This has been mentioned in international reports, such as those of Freedom House.[182]

A bigger problem, according to the Media Monitoring Agency, are ties between business interests and/or politicians and the media, especially at the local level; in at least two cases the mayor of a medium-sized town is also the most important local businessman and owner of the local press.

9.5 Media and corruption

Despite the limits on press freedom, the Romanian print media has been active in exposing corruption. Quality investigative journalism is carried out by a few national newspapers, particularly *Evenimentul Zilei* and *Adevarul* and the weekly *Academia Catavencu*. Neither private nor public TV stations play a significant role in reporting corruption.

The Government's National Action Plan Against Corruption includes measures to strengthen investigative journalism, in particular through courses for investigative journalists and the establishment of journalists' unions to provide journalists with a collective voice and protection against employers.

10. RECOMMENDATIONS

The following recommendations have been highlighted as particularly important to Romania. For additional recommendations applicable to candidate States generally, please see Part 5 of the Overview report.

1. Streamline the anti-corruption framework by consolidating the Anti-corruption Bureau and abolishing the Prime Minister's Control Department.

2. Restrict immunity provisions for current and former Government members and MPs.

3. Remove legislative barriers to effective media activity.

---

[182] Conversely, following a series of articles about suspicious privatisation deals, *Adevarul* (the largest circulation Romanian daily) lost advertising from the State Property Fund. See Viorel Salagean, "Presa economica – fata in fata," *Adevarul Economic*, no. 41/18, 24 October 2000: "The freedom of press is still relative… There are 3-4 newspapers literally bought by the State Property Fund. One newspaper *[Adevarul]* which officially won the tender [for advertising] has been ruled out for being too critical."

Corruption and Anti-corruption Policy in Slovakia

Table of Contents

Corruption and Anti-corruption Policy in Slovakia

EXECUTIVE SUMMARY

Corruption is a serious problem in Slovakia in most public institutions, although there is some evidence to suggest levels of corruption have fallen since 1998. Public opinion appears to be more tolerant towards corruption than in any other EU candidate country. According to surveys, corruption is most widespread in the health service, judiciary, National Property Fund, customs, police and ministries.

The Government that came to power in 1998 made anti-corruption one of its highest priorities, and approved a National Programme for the Fight against Corruption in 2000. The Government has taken very important steps in the fight against corruption: apart from presiding over a major reduction in official tolerance towards corruption, the most important specific measures include a Freedom of Information Act, amendments to the Public Procurement Act and party financing rules, a new Judicial Code and the creation of the ombudsman. However, a number of the most important measures have not yet been carried out and have little chance of being implemented before the September 2002 elections – in particular, the failure to implement a new licensing framework, restrict parliamentary immunity, improve provisions on conflict of interest and declarations of assets and income and pass further reforms of party funding. Civil society organisations have played a major role in the formation and implementation of anti-corruption policy.

The European Commission has exercised a very important influence on the development of anti-corruption policy. After acknowledging that Slovakia fulfilled the Copenhagen Criteria in 1998, the Commission has exerted continuous pressure on the Government to fight corruption more effectively. The Commission has acknowledged progress in this area in successive *Regular Reports,* and has provided significant assistance to anti-corruption policy, mainly to improving law enforcement.

Bribery legislation satisfies the requirements of international anti-corruption conventions, with the exception of criminal liability of legal persons for corruption. A new Criminal Code under preparation is expected to fill this remaining gap.

A general Conflict of Interest Act regulates both conflict of interest and declarations of assets and income for senior State functionaries. However, the Act is largely ineffective, covering too narrow a category of official, not allowing publication of declarations, and imposing almost no sanctions for violation. Attempts to amend the Act have been rejected.

Slovakia has recently passed legislation to establish a coordinated system of State financial control. However, the impact of the Supreme Audit Office has been limited for a number of reasons including political interference, gaps in its audit competence, lack of a mechanism for enforcing its findings, and the fact that its reports were not public. In all these areas improvements have been made since 1998. The European Commission has praised Slovakia for its progress in State internal financial control, although it remains to be seen what impact the system will have in practice.

There is no special anti-corruption agency, although the police and General Prosecutor's Office contain special anti-corruption departments. Although the police department has initiated several high-level corruption investigations, none of these had resulted in court proceedings as of May 2002. Slovakia established the office of the ombudsman in January 2002.

Slovakia has passed important reforms to reform its public administration, in particular a new Civil Service Act, in effect since April 2002. Conflict of interest remains a widespread problem, however, and procedures for redress against official decisions remain inadequate. Corruption also remains a serious problem, encouraged by burdensome licensing procedures. The Government has not yet managed to push through proposed fundamental reforms of licensing procedures, although an audit of State administration carried out in 2000 has led to some measures to increase transparency.

Control of the State budget has been improved since 2001 with the inclusion of previously off-budget funds into the budget. Evidence of corruption among MPs is limited. However, there is substantial evidence of undesirably close ties between MPs and business interests. Conflict of interest provisions are ineffective and immunity provisions excessive, and attempts to reform these areas as part of the Government's anti-corruption strategy have been rejected.

The judiciary is ranked as one of the most corrupt institutions in surveys, and there is some direct evidence to suggest that corruption is a problem. Important judicial reforms have been carried out or are in the process of being implemented, which should help to limit corruption in the future.

Corruption is a serious problem in political party funding. Although significant reforms have been passed since 1998, regulation remains weak: unlimited private donations are permitted, supervision of party funding remains ineffective and party financial reports are not public. Proposals to amend funding regulations have been proposed, but are unlikely to be adopted in the near future.

Public procurement has undergone reform since 1998 that put in place a relatively advanced legal framework. These include a new Public Procurement Office that appears to be relatively effective. However, corruption remains widespread in procurement, and proposals that have been prepared to further improve the legal framework are unlikely to be adopted in the near future.

Corruption is a serious problem in several key sectors of public service, particularly health and education, while licensing procedures are severely affected by bribery. Corruption in health and education appears to be encouraged by high levels of tolerance towards bribery among citizens.

The media has played an increasing role in exposing corruption, and an increasing role in calling senior politicians to account. A new Freedom of Information Act in force since 2001 has been a major breakthrough in access to information. Allocation of licenses to private broadcasting companies is subject to suspicions concerning corruption, while regulation of public broadcasting has allowed political interference in the activities of Slovak Television.

1. INTRODUCTION

1.1 The data and perceptions

Despite very few convictions for corruption-related offences, all other evidence indicates that corruption is one of the biggest problems Slovakia faces. There is some limited evidence indicating that the prevalence of corruption has fallen since 1998. However, the general public perceives levels of corruption to be stable or worsening. In particular, the level of tolerance towards corruption shown by citizens in surveys indicates a level of cultural acceptance of corruption that is likely to hinder efforts to fight corruption considerably.

Criminal statistics

According to official criminal statistics, corruption is almost non-existent. Table 1 shows the number of bribery prosecutions and indictments from 1993 to 2001.

Table 1: Officially recorded cases of corruption in Slovakia

Criminal office	1993		1994		1995		1996	
	P	I	P	I	P	I	P	I
§160 Accepting bribes	18	13	24	2	30	12	28	17
§161 Giving/offering bribes	0	0	0	0	0	0	3	0
§162 Indirect corruption	5	3	4	2	5	3	0	2

Criminal offence	1997		1998		1999		2000		2001	
	P	I	P	I	P	I	P	I*	P	I*
§160 Accepting bribes and other inappropriate benefits	23	13	35	16	28	13	44	63	18	27
§161 Giving/ offering bribes	0	0	4	4	21	7	62	52	29	37
§162 Indirect corruption	0	0	1	0	1	1	2	1	5	3

Notes: P = number of people prosecuted,
I = number of people indicted.
*Number of people indicted plus number of people convicted.
Source: *Office of the General Prosecution of the Slovak Republic.*

Other available evidence suggests that these figures provide very little information about the real extent of corruption, but rather indicate the lack of enforcement of the existing provisions.

Perception indicators

The World Bank's *Diagnostic Surveys of Corruption in Slovakia* carried out in 1999–2000 among households, entrepreneurs and civil servants indicate that unofficial payments to public officials are routine. Table 2 provides the main results of the surveys.

Table 2: General experience with corruption (in percent)

Households	Have made an unofficial payment over the past two months	14.4
	Have made an unofficial payment over the past three years	41.3
Entrepreneurs	Have made an unofficial payment over the past two months	17.6
	Have made an unofficial payment over the past two years	41.4
Civil servants	Have been offered a small gift over the past two years	42.3
	Have been offered money or an expensive gift over the past two years	9.7

Source: World Bank, *2000 Diagnostic Survey of Corruption in Slovakia.*

There is some evidence that corruption has decreased in certain areas in recent years (notably in the banking sector and in privatisation). According to surveys by the Slovak Statistics Office, the percentage of respondents saying they had given a bribe in a given year has decreased steadily since 1998 (see Graph 1).

Graph 1: Percentage of respondents who admitted offering money or a gift in the past year

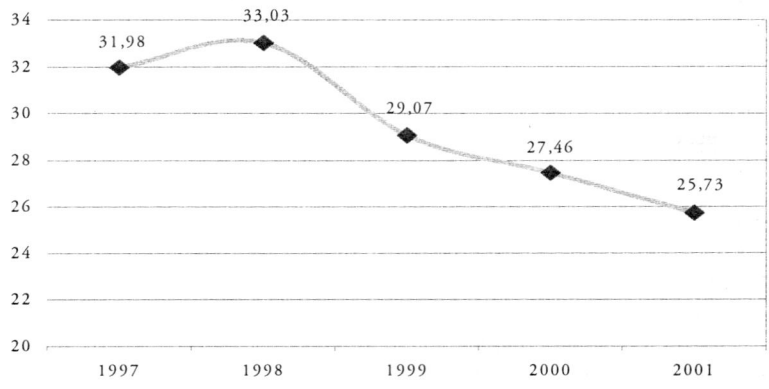

Source: Institute for Public Opinion Research, Slovak Statistical Office.

However, many citizens believe that corruption is equally widespread as it was before and even worse in some areas (see Section 1.2, Table 4). Moreover, only one in nine Slovaks believed in 2001 that corruption would decrease in the following three years, while one in three thought it would increase.[1]

There is considerable evidence that corruption is widely tolerated. Many officials stated that they would not inform on their colleagues if they learned that they had accepted bribes. Moreover, households and entrepreneurs who paid bribes usually claimed that officials did not demand the bribes explicitly but that they expected a bribe to be required (see Table 3).

Table 3: How does corruption work?

"Imagine that someone comes to an institution like yours and asks for something. What would happen if the person is a ... "			
	Citizen[a]	*Local Entrepreneur*[b]	*Foreign Entrepreneur*[b]
The worker of the institution would indicate that a bribe would be very appropriate	3.0	4.4	6.8
The person would unilaterally offer a bribe	6.0	20.2	9.1
The application would be processed in accordance with the law	91.0	75.5	84.2

Note:　a. Includes only the responses of officials that frequently interact with private people;
　　　　　b. includes only the responses of officials that frequently interact with enterprises.
Source: World Bank, *2000 Diagnostic Survey of Corruption in Slovakia.*

Moreover, according to a survey of values conducted in 1999–2000 in 32 European countries, Slovak citizens were the second most tolerant in respect of those accepting bribes.[2] The Slovak score in terms of "strictness" towards bribe giving was 2.94, better only than Belarus (3.09) and compared to a European average of 1.824. This is widely regarded by both Government officials and other anti-corruption experts as one of the most serious problems facing efforts to tackle corruption.[3]

---

[1] For details, see *Korupcia na Slovensku (2000)* ["Corruption in Slovakia (2000)"]. The survey was carried out by GfK Slovakia in March 2000.

[2] Tiburg University/Sociological Institute of Slovak Academy of Sciences, *European Values Study 1999/2000*, 2001; see <http://.nie.savba.sk/sav/inst>, (last accessed 30 August 2002).

[3] Comments from Mário Virčík, Central Coordinating Unit for the Fight against Corruption, Office of the Deputy Prime Minister for Economic Affairs; Comments from OSI Roundtable Discussion, Bratislava, 22 February 2002. Explanatory note: OSI held a roundtable meeting to invite critique of the present Report in draft form. Experts present included representatives of the Government, international organisations, and civil society organisations. References to this meeting should not be understood as an endorsement of any particular point of view by any one participant.

1.2 Main loci of corruption

According to the World Bank surveys cited above, corruption is perceived as most prevalent in the health sector, judiciary, National Property Fund, customs, police and ministries. Detailed information on the share of people who believe that corruption is "very widespread" in a certain field are presented in Graph 2.

Graph 2: Share of people who believe that corruption is "very widespread" in a certain field (percent)

Perceptions of corruption

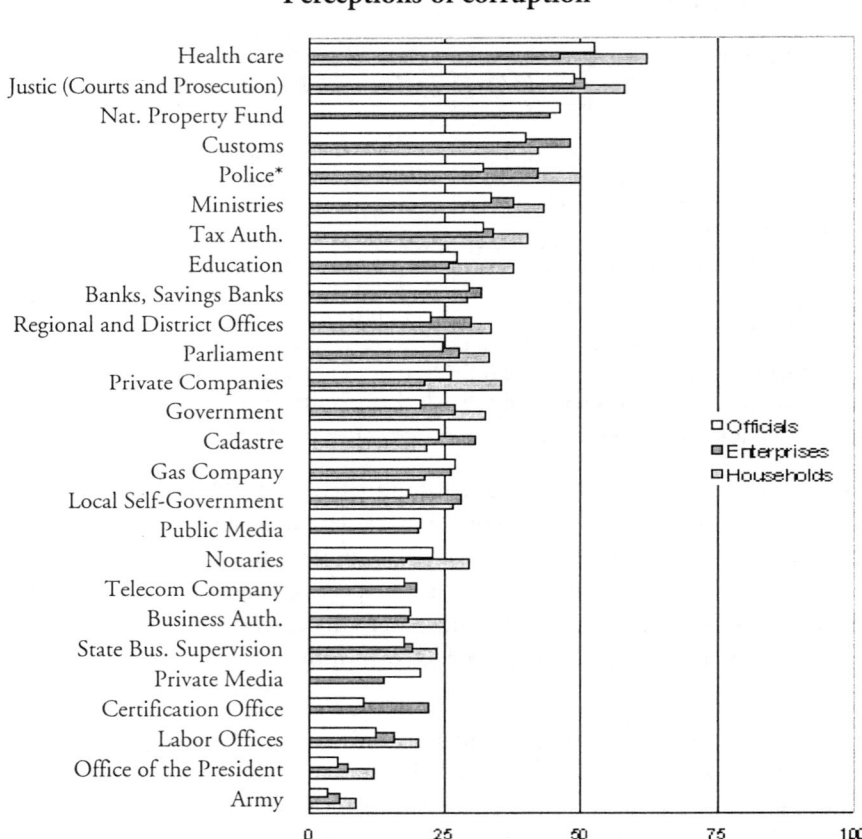

Note: A missing stripe means that data on perception of corruption in a given organisation did not come from households.

*The survey of households and entrepreneurs distinguished between traffic police and other police corps, but the calculation for the police in general uses the average of the two figures.

Source: World Bank, *2000 Diagnostic Survey of Corruption in Slovakia.*

The World Bank survey yielded the following results:

- Both households and entrepreneurs stated that they often encountered corruption in court proceedings.

- All three groups surveyed perceived the health service as beset by widespread corruption; ordinary citizens voluntarily provide "gratuities" much more often than for any other service (see Section 8).

- Gratuities and bribes are common in the education system, and most prevalent at law schools and medical schools (see Section 8).

- Several regulation, certification, and licensing institutions were also identified by respondents as being receptive to bribery: for instance, authorities that issue import and export certificates, building permits and other kinds of licences, the Commercial Register, Certification Office, customs authorities, and the State Commercial Inspectorate.

- Roughly one in nine enterprises said they sponsor political parties, and eight percent that they provide unofficial payments (see Section 6.2).

- Of the 20 percent of companies reporting they receive some form of subsidy, 12 percent said they bribed to get the subsidy, 40 percent admitted using friends or relatives and seven percent admitted using political influence; the three methods were usually combined in some way. The majority of respondents reported that ten percent of the subsidy amount must be paid in bribes.

- Privatisation is regarded as a hotbed of corruption, although the proportion of respondents with this perception has dropped sharply since 1998.

Table 4: Proportion of survey respondents believing bribes are necessary in various institutions (in percent)

	1997	*1998*	*1999*	*2000*
Courts	22.51	23.65	26.37	26.18
Privatisation	22.59	22.17	12.67	12.46
Banks	8.9	8.27	4.78	4.87
Police	14.45	16.71	14.18	17.18
Healthcare	66.62	68.93	66.77	66.89
Education	28.59	33.72	27.89	32.01
Business	17.95	18.3	16.25	15.78
Customs offices	5.1	6.32	6.85	6.12
Tax authorities	6.69	7.03	7.81	6.64
Labour offices	8.29	8.43	6.69	8.48
Certification offices	3.57	2.97	2.63	3.32
Local self-governments	14.37	12.57	13.55	12.83
Others	6.24	2.73	5.42	2.58

Source: Institute for Public Opinion Research, Slovak Statistics Office.

The results of the World Bank survey are confirmed by a more recent survey, conducted in March 2002 by Focus Marketing and Research.[4] The survey produced strikingly similar results both in terms of perceptions and experience, and ranked health, education and the police as the most corrupt institutions.

1.3 Government anti-corruption policy

The first attempt to solve the problem of corruption took place in 1995 when the previous Government adopted a "Clean Hands" (Čisté ruky) anti-corruption programme. Although the programme proposed a number of new laws or amendments, it faded away with few specific results or evidence of genuine commitment by the Government.

The National Programme for the Fight against Corruption

The Government that came to power in 1998 made fighting corruption one of its highest priorities, and since then has made major progress in making anti-corruption

---

[4] Focus Marketing and Research, *Záverečná správa z prieskumu verejnej mienky pre Transparency International* [Final Report on Public Opinion Research for Transparency International], March 2002 (unpublished).

measures an established part of public policy. On 21 June 2000, the Government approved a National Programme for the Fight against Corruption.[5] The Programme was developed by the Office of the Deputy Prime Minister of Economic Policy on the basis of a proposal prepared by the NGO Transparency International Slovakia (TI Slovakia), and submitted in February 2000 as a draft for public discussion.

The Programme is based on the general objectives of increasing transparency, limiting the scope for abuse of discretionary powers, reinforcing control and audit mechanisms, enhancing the quality and impartiality of the civil service and strengthening law enforcement. An anti-corruption steering committee was set up in July 2000 at the Office of Government to implement the National Programme, including representatives from ministries, other State administration, NGOs and international donors. As of June 2002, however, the Committee had not met since March 2001.

In one of the most important planks of the strategy, the June decree charged the Deputy Prime Minister's Office with the task of analysing all licences, concessions and permissions, contributions and grants granted by ministries and their institutions (see Section 8). In August 2000, the Government approved an Audit of Central State Administration,[6] which analysed the sources of corruption in the State administration and contained a set of proposed measures the Government intends to implement (see Section 3.1). In addition, an analysis of the functioning of the cadastral authorities, which according to the World Bank *Diagnostic Surveys* are affected by corruption, was carried out and presented in April 2001.

Ministries and central administrative bodies were charged with the task of drafting Action Plans by September 2000. Based on these, the Government approved an overall Action Plan[7] on 22 November 2000, containing around 1,600 tasks divided between all State authorities and with a significant proportion falling under the Ministry of Economy.

A Central Coordination Unit for the Fight against Corruption was established in December 2000 to draw up and coordinate specific plans for implementing the Programme, and screen complaints and proposals received from citizens. As of March 2002, the Unit had around 15 staff.

The National Programme for the Fight against Corruption has brought about or contributed to several important developments in anti-corruption policy. Indirectly, the National Programme began to be implemented even before the cabinet approved it, when Parliament passed the Freedom of Information Act in May 2000 – the most

---

[5] Government Decree no. 461, 21 June 2000.

[6] For more details, see p. 11.

[7] The Action Plan can be found at <http://www.government.gov.sk/bojprotikorupcii>, (last accessed 30 August 2002).

important step in the fight against corruption so far.[8] The Act, which came into effect on 1 January 2001, was initiated and strongly supported by a strong civic campaign joined by over 120 non-governmental organisations and the media.[9]

According to Government officials, around 600 tasks remained at the end of February 2002.[10]

The more important measures or laws implemented include the following:

- Amendments to the Act on Budgetary Rules[11] entered into force in January 2001, improving the administration and control of resources allocated from the State budget or EU and other international funds.

- The Public Procurement Act has been amended twice and further amendments were in preparation in early 2002 (see Section 6).

- An Act on Prevention of Legalisation of the Proceeds of Crime came into effect in January 2001.

- Slovakia ratified the Council of Europe Criminal Law Convention on Corruption, OECD Convention on Combating Bribery of Foreign Public Officials in International Business Transactions and signed the Council of Europe Civil Law Convention.

- Between October 2000 and April 2001, Parliament approved new rules on political party financing (see Section 6).

- A Civil Service Act and Public Service Act were adopted in June 2001.

- Changes to the Constitution have been carried out to facilitate the establishment of the Office of the Ombudsman. The first ombudsman was appointed in February 2002.

- A new Judicial Code was adopted in 2000, which among other things introduced disciplinary proceedings and asset declarations for judges. A pilot project introducing computer-based assignment of cases was implemented at the Banská Bystrica District Court in 2000 and is being extended to all courts (see Section 5).

---

[8] For example, since January 2001, audit reports of the Supreme Audit Office have been available to the public, which was not the case before. The Government has begun publishing information on public procurement on the Internet, and the Commercial Register has been fully available on the Internet since January 2001.

[9] A similar campaign was held in support of amendments to conflict of interest legislation. See <http://www.konfliktzaujmov.sk>, (last accessed 30 August 2002).

[10] Comments at OSI Roundtable Discussion, Bratislava, 22 February 2002.

[11] Act no. 303/1995 on Budgetary Rules.

Changes in preparation or under discussion include the following:

- The Ministry of Justice prepared a draft act to establish a special prosecution office for detecting corruption and organised crime. The draft was under discussion in March 2002. The objective of the new unit is to break through the personal networks connecting various State institutions and criminal groups at regional and local level, which prevent effective prosecution. However, the proposal is unlikely to be implemented before the September 2002 elections. Meanwhile, the institution of *agent provocateur* has been introduced, and had been used successfully in three cases as of early 2002.

- A Civil Service Act and Public Service Act were adopted in July 2001. The Central Coordination Unit submitted a draft Code of Conduct of Civil Servants for public discussion at the end of 2000. The Code will be enforced through the Civil Service Act (see Section 3).

- On the basis of recommendations of the Audit of Central State Administration Bodies, from November 2001 all legal proposals of ministries have been made available on the Internet for comments from the public. The Central Coordination Unit has prepared a proposal for an Act to regulate organised lobbying at the stage of parliamentary discussion and approval.

A number of the more important changes remained at the stage of preparation or discussion as of May 2002, exposing them to the risk that the reform momentum in this area will be reversed after the September 2002 parliamentary elections. Restrictions of parliamentary immunity, improvements in conflict of interest legislation and enforcement and asset monitoring stand out,[12] as does the failure as of May 2002 to agree or implement the new licensing framework. Important changes in the legislative framework for the judiciary and law enforcement bodies have not yet translated into visible improvements in their ability to proceed corruption cases, especially important high-level cases.[13]

Transparency International Slovakia has voiced several criticisms of Government anti-corruption policy, namely that many of the tasks in the Strategy are only formal, and many do not deal with restricting corruption; that the process has been over bureaucratised; that

---

[12] The rejection of a proposed constitutional law on conflict of interest was rejected in May 2002, ending any chance of further reform in this area (see Section 2.2).

[13] For example, after a scandal broke in Spring 2001 over the misuse of PHARE funds, the official under suspicion was not questioned for a month and then only under media pressure. As of March 2002, it appeared doubtful that charges would be pressed. At the beginning of November 1999, the first trial related to organised crime began, but neither this case nor numerous other investigations into alleged fraud, corruption and abuse of power connected with the previous Government have yielded any convictions.

coordination between various ministries and other central authorities has been poor; that deadlines have not been met; and that the Steering Committee is not functioning.[14]

Although the current Government has broken clearly with the style of the previous Government, and ministers in the current Government have had to resign as a result of more-or-less corruption related scandals (see Section 3.6), there appears to be a perception that the Government itself has not set the right example. This may be the result of the fact that ministers continue to employ advisers with a bad reputation, or the fact that even when officials under suspicion are removed they are not punished or soon appear in a different position.[15] This also reflects the failure of the Government to persuade the public of the need to fight corruption actively and to provide information on the steps it has taken.

Role of civil society

The non-governmental sector has played a very important role in the development of anti-corruption policy, and since the 1998 elections, a major shift towards cooperation between civil society groups and public authorities has taken place. For example:

- NGO campaigns were instrumental in securing the passage of the Freedom of Information Act in 1999, and have played an important part in lobbying for and influencing acts on the ombudsman, public procurement and civil service.

- The Government's anti-corruption strategy itself was formulated on the basis of a proposal written by TI Slovakia, and the draft strategy was opened to comments from civil society organisations.

- The NGO Alliance – Stop Conflict of Interests was created in 2001 to lobby for more effective conflict of interest legislation.[16]

- NGOs have played an active part in implementing the strategy: for example, the Institute for Economic and Social Reforms (INEKO) organised and led the Audit of Central State Administration carried out in 2000 (see Section 3.6). TI Slovakia prepared the Privatisation Information Minimum (PIM) and asked representatives of all political parties to proclaim publicly their resolve to observe it. The PIM has been incorporated into the Action Plan of the Ministry of Privatisation. The American Bar Association – Central and Eastern Europe Legal Initiative (ABA

---

[14] Information provided by TI Slovakia.

[15] One of the more blatant examples of this was the appointment of Jaromír Košín as Director of the State Fund for Market Regulation in 1999, despite the fact that all parties in the governing coalition were aware of indictments against him for embezzlement, fraud and other offences as a previous director of a private company. See *Národná obroda* daily, 17 September 1999.

[16] More on <http://www.konfliktzaujmov.sk>, (last accessed 30 August 2002).

CEELI) has provided translation, analysis, workshops and training on the Freedom of Information Act for judges, journalists and NGOs, financed a project to evaluate the Government's anti-corruption Action Plans, and co-operate with the Ministry of Justice on court reform and with the Slovak Judges Association on a survey on corruption in the judiciary and ethics workshops.

A major gap remaining in terms of civil society and the fight against corruption is the absence of participation by any business organisations.

1.4 The impact of the EU Accession Process

EU assessments of Slovakia

Until 1999, the European Commission did not regard Slovakia as having fulfilled the Copenhagen political criteria. The Commission's *1998* and *1999 Regular Reports* did not make any statements regarding levels of corruption, and were restricted to statements that efforts to fight corruption were so far insufficient.[17] The *2000 Regular Report* acknowledged progress, especially the launching of the Government anti-corruption strategy, but stressed the need to translate the strategy into concrete measures, adding that, "[T]he perception exists, confirmed by various sources, that corruption is widespread in Slovakia and that it is either rising or at best not decreasing."[18] The *2001 Regular Report* was noticeably more positive, acknowledging a number of positive steps.[19]

The crime prevention strategy adopted by the Government in 1999 reflected the recommendations of the joint EU/Council of Europe OCTOPUS programme, and pressure from the EU has been one of the important motors for the development of the National Programme for the Fight against Corruption.

The assessment on corruption in the *Regular Reports* has gradually improved. By 2001, the Commission acknowledged "continued progress" in the fight against corruption, particularly in the translation of the National Programme into specific policies and the transposition of international obligations. However, the report stated that,

> Corruption, however, remains a serious cause for concern. In order to continue improving the fight against corruption. Slovakia should rigorously carry on the implementation of the action plans, strictly enforce existing

---

[17] Commission of the European Union, *1998 Regular Report from the Commission on Slovakia's Progress towards Accession,* p. 10; *Commission, 1999 Regular Report,* p. 15.

[18] Commission, *2000 Regular Report,* p. 18.

[19] Commission, *2001 Regular Report,* p. 18.

legislation and complete planned legislation as well as strengthening administrative capacities and coordination among the bodies involved.[20]

A European Parliament Report on Slovakia's membership application to the EU and the state of negotiations (2001) noted that Slovakia has made progress in the fight against crime and corruption by formulating targeted Government policy and welcomed increased international cooperation.[21]

EU assistance

The EU has assisted the Government in anti-corruption policy through several PHARE programmes (see Table 5).

Table 5: PHARE programs to assist anti-corruption policy in Slovakia

Period	Programme	Beneficiary/funds (€)
1999	The Fight against Corruption and Organised Crime	Ministry of Interior, 2.2m
	Strengthening Police Capacity in the Fight against Corruption and Organised Crime	Ministry of Interior, 5m
	Assistance to Customs Office in the Fight against Organised Crime, Corruption, Money Laundering	Customs Office, 700.000
1999–2001	The Fight against Corruption and Organised Crime	Supreme Audit Office, employees of National Bank and State-owned banks
2000	Support to the Implementation of the National Programme for the Fight against Corruption: Increase in the Capacity of Bodies Responsible for Penal Proceedings to Fight Corruption	Ministries of Justice and Interior, monitoring reports and support for act on fight against corruption
	Reducing corruption in the State administration and society, decreasing possibilities for corruption and strengthening capacity of law enforcement agencies	Office of the Government, 6.5m

Source: Transparency International Slovakia.

Slovakia became a member of GRECO in April 1999, and was evaluated in September 2000. The report acknowledged progress in anti-corruption policy, but expressed

---

[20] Commission, *Regular Report 2001*, p. 24.

[21] Draft Report on Slovakia's Membership Application to the European Union and the State of Negotiations, (COM[2000]711 – C5-0611/2000 – 1997/2173 [COS]), Committee on Foreign Affairs, Human Rights, Common Security and Defence Policy, rapporteur: Jan Marinus Wiersma, draft from 8 May 2001.

concern at the prevalence of corruption, especially in the judiciary, and urged effective implementation of a broad range of measures including more effective control of privatisation, reform of the police and judiciary, tax offices and licensing procedures, and conflict of interest regulation.[22]

2. INSTITUTIONS AND LEGISLATION

2.1 Anti-corruption legislation

The Criminal Code sanctions active and passive bribery in both direct and indirect forms, and also bribery of foreign and domestic officials, bribery of judges, judiciary officials and employees of international or intergovernmental organisations and bodies, and bribery in the private sector.[23] Bribery provisions apply not just to officials but to any action connected with provision of a thing of public interest, as following:

- Penalties for passive bribery are up to three years or a fine, and up to five years if the result is large damages, the perpetrator is a public official or the bribe was in exchange for a violation of a law regulating his/her duties.

- Active bribery is subject to a penalty of up to two years (three years if the perpetrator is a public official), and up to five years in the case of large damages or if the perpetrator bribes as part of an organised group.

- Abuse of power – where a public official, in order to cause damage to another person or secure undue advantage, exercises power in an illegitimate way, exceeds powers or fail to fulfil duties – is subject to six months to three years imprisonment or a fine.

- Article 49 of the Commercial Code includes bribery as a form of unfair competition, and the damaged party may request a civil court to annul the act and claim compensation from the party who caused the damage.

---

[22] GRECO, *Evaluation Report on Slovakia,* adopted by GRECO at the 4th Plenary Meeting, 12-15 December 2000.

[23] Two amendments in 1999 were of key importance: Act no. 10/1999 (effective 27 January 1999), Act no. 183/1999 (effective 1 September 1999).

The Supreme Court has defined the term "socially acceptable gift" as a "very small gift, or gift of very small value."[24] Small gifts (for example flowers or a pen) are not considered a bribe, although no exact threshold is defined.

A new Criminal Code has been prepared that would implement the remaining obligations of international treaties by establishing criminal liability of legal persons for corruption. As of May 2002 the proposal had not been submitted to the National Council.

2.2 Conflict of interest legislation and asset declaration

Until April 2002, the Slovak Labour Code contained some general conflict of interest provisions, including that public officials may not accept external employment or carry on business activities without the permission of their superior. The new Labour Code does not cover public employees, who are now covered by the Civil Service Act (see Section 3.1).

The Conflict of Interest Act

The main regulation of both conflict of interest and asset declarations is the 1995 Act on Prevention of Conflict of Interest in Performance of Tasks of Constitutional Officials and High-Ranking Officials.[25] The Act lays down various duties for the following high-ranking functionaries: President, deputies of the National Council, ministers, Chairman and Vice-Chairman of the Supreme Audit Office, judges of the Constitutional Court, Chairman and Vice-Chairman of the Supreme Court, General Prosecutor and his deputy, Chairman of the President's Office, Chairman of the Office of the National Council, heads of main central State institutions, State secretaries, members of the Banking Council of the National Bank and the Director of the Slovak Statistics Office. The Act applies to around 230 functionaries.

Functionaries may not, *inter alia*:

- accept or offer gifts in connection with performance of their duties;

- use or allow to be used their person, name, voice, picture or signature for advertising purposes;

- mediate a business contact with State or State companies for a profit;

- receive other income exceeding the minimal monthly salary (€114 in 2001);

- perform other paid functions or run private business activities;

---

[24] Supreme Court Decision no. 17/1978.
[25] Constitutional Act no. 119/1995.

- obtain assets from the State except through an open tender, auction or voucher privatisation;

- be a dormant partner in a company.

Under the same Act, functionaries must submit annual declarations of:

- compliance with the above provisions restricting activities, any positions or functions held in addition to their official one, all incomes from such activities, and any changes to these within 30 days of the change;

- assets and property, including any real estate and movable property with a value exceeding €34,850;

- any gift accepted with a value exceeding the minimum monthly salary.

Declarations are submitted to the Chairman of the National Council, and may be checked by the National Council Committee for the Incompatibility of Public Officials' Functions. However, the Committee does not have access to tax returns. According to a report issued by the Slovak National Council on compliance with the Act in 2000, nine functionaries did not state any information including seven MPs and one minister; seven violated the Conflict of Interest Act; 50 functionaries performed functions based on employment relation or similar employment contact (including 34 MPs and seven ministers); 34 performed functions in the bodies of other legal entities (including 20 MPs and two ministers); 35 held functions in local Government (including 29 MPs, one minister and two State secretaries); and 28 functionaries stated interests in commercial companies (including 22 MPs and two ministers).[26]

The Act is not effective in practice. Relatives of the functionaries covered by the law do not have any obligations to declare assets, while State companies and companies with State ownership are not covered. Moreover declarations of assets and interests are not publicly available, which largely rules out public scrutiny, although recently some MPs decided to publish their own declarations. Although the National Council can vote to force a functionary who violates the Act to stop illegal practices, and even punish refusal to do so by removal from office, these proceedings have never been used.

Two proposed amendments to the Act were rejected by the National Council in 2001; the amendments would have made declarations public, increased the powers of the Committee and specified prohibited activities more precisely. A working group established by the National Council submitted a proposal for three new laws governing conflict of interests to the Council in January 2002: a general constitutional act, an act

---

[26] Report of the Slovak National Council Committee for the Incompatibility of Public Officials' Functions on Results of Investigations at Adjustments of Public Officials' Declarations and Asset Declarations, 2000.

regulating MPs and constitutional functionaries, and an act covering local and regional governments. However, in May 2002 Parliament rejected the constitutional bill, and the remaining two bills were not even discussed.

2.3 Control and audit

Slovakia has passed legislation establishing an overall framework for public financial control and audit, notably through a new Act on Financial Control and Internal Audit that came into effect in January 2002.

Supreme Audit Office

External audit of the public sector is carried out by the Supreme Audit Office (SAO), set up in 1993[27] to monitor State finances, budgets and payments, and to manage State property and property rights. The Slovak National Council elects the Chairman and two Vice-Chairmen of the SAO for seven years, and may dismiss them under certain conditions including conviction for a criminal act, failure to perform duties or performing an activity incompatible with the office. However, the Council removed one Chairman and two Vice-Chairmen in 1994 without any such conditions being satisfied. The independence of the Office now appears to be relatively secure.

The SAO may audit management and use of property budget funds approved by the National Council or Government, including management and use by local governments and legal entities; all assets and funds for which the Government has issued a guarantee; and management and disposal of assets and resources from foreign sources (including the EU). Collection of taxes and customs duties is within the SAO's audit competence. Changes to the Constitution that came into effect in January 2001 and amendments to the Act on the SAO that were adopted in October 2001 have broadened the Office's competence explicitly to cover all public funds, including local government (a particular area of weak control previously), the National Property Fund and EU funds.

The Act does not lay down clearly the independence of the SAO in determining its audit plan, and explicitly states that the National Council may mandate the SAO to carry out specific audits. However, in practice this does not occupy a significant proportion of the SAO's work.

The SAO reports on the results of audits at least once a year to the National Council. It may carry out additional controls at the request of the National Council. However, there are no effective mechanisms as yet to ensure compliance with SAO findings, and audited

---

[27] Act on the Supreme Audit Office of the Slovak Republic, no. 39/1993.

bodies do not always take corrective measures.[28] In its *2000 Evaluation Report,* GRECO recommended that the powers of the SAO be extended, in particular to evaluate and make effective suggestions for improving the management of public entities.[29]

Since January 2001, SAO audit reports have been available as a result of the Free Access to Information Act, and the media has used the reports to push for changes.

Although the SAO is often requested by the Government to audit institutions that have been publicly exposed as non-transparent, its audits are focused on formal compliance with the law on performance or efficiency criteria. From 1995 to March 2000, the Office submitted only 11 cases to the General Prosecutor's Office, none of which led to conviction.[30]

Internal control and audit

The new Act on Financial Control and Internal Audit established functionally independent internal audit units in all budget spending centres and gave the Ministry of Finance responsibility for ensuring coordination and supervision of financial control. In October 2001, the Ministry established a Department for Financial Control and Internal Audit Methodology. The EU praised Slovakia for its progress in the area of financial control in the *2001 Regular Report.*[31]

2.4 Anti-corruption agencies

There is no single central anti-corruption agency. However, the following units partly or wholly focus on investigation and prosecution of corruption:

- A Department for the Fight against Corruption was created in 1998 within the Office of Organised Crime of the Criminal and Financial Police Administration. The Department has authority over the entire country, and operates from two sites in Žilina and Košice with a staff of 28 (as of February 2002). The statistics on investigated and solved crimes are fully available and regularly presented at press conferences of the Ministry of Interior. The Department initiated criminal proceedings in 33 cases in 2001, including several high-level ones – for example

---

[28] For example, in 2001, the SAO conducted an audit at the Ministry of Agriculture related to implementation of recommended corrections resulting from an audit in 1999, and discovered that only four out of 15 corrective measures had been adopted. See *Národná obroda,* 20 July 2001.

[29] GRECO, *Evaluation Report on Slovakia,* p. 16.

[30] TI Slovakia, *Control and Its Role in the Fight against Corruption,* Bratislava 2001, p. 30.

[31] Commission, *2001 Regular Report,* pp. 86–87.

the alleged offering of a bribe to the Minister of Transport, a party financing scandal allegedly involving the Christian Democratic Movement (see Section 6.3), and a scandal involving the allocation of EU funds (see Section 3.6). No high-level cases had entered court as of February 2002. A separate department exists to investigate corruption within the police (see Section 8.1).

- In April 2000, a Department for Combating Corruption was established in the General Prosecutor's Office to manage and coordinate the fight against corruption across all prosecution offices. The Department does not have any explicit legal powers or competencies.

2.5 Ombudsman

The Ombudsman Act was approved by the National Council in December 2001 and came into effect in January 2002. The National Council elects the ombudsman for a five-year term on the proposal of at least 15 Members of Parliament. The first election was expected to take place in February 2002, and the activities of the ombudsman are difficult to assess at such an early stage.

The function of the ombudsman is to protect the fundamental rights and liberties of individuals and legal entities where the action, inaction or decisions of bodies of the public administration are contrary to the law or principles of a democratic and legal State. The ombudsman may investigate actions by State agencies, municipalities, as well as legal entities and individuals that have been given the power by law to make decisions on the rights and responsibilities of natural persons or legal entities in the area of public administration. The ombudsman may not investigate the Government, National Council, Constitutional Court, SAO, intelligence bureau, police investigators, prosecutors or courts (except the administration of courts).

The ombudsman is competent to investigate motions and, if the results of an investigation disclose a violation of law, to notify the institution. The institution must report to the ombudsman within 30 days on corrective measures taken. If it fails to do so, the ombudsman notifies the superior office and then the Government. The Office submits a report on its activities to the National Council in the first quarter of every year.

3. EXECUTIVE BRANCH AND CIVIL SERVICE

Slovakia has passed important legislative reforms to put in place a depoliticised and professional civil service, and has implemented other measures to increase transparency.

However, procedures for appealing against administrative decisions remain ineffective. Corruption in the public administration is a serious problem, exacerbated by widespread problems of conflict of interest and burdensome licensing procedures.

3.1 Structure and legislative framework

Until 1 April 2002, the civil service was regulated mainly by the Labour Code (see Section 3.2). A new Civil Service Act came into effect from 1 April 2002. The Act creates the framework for a merit-based and independent career civil service.

Under the Act, civil servants must be recruited by competitive selection, with the exception of ministers and deputy ministers. A Central Civil Service Office is to exercise overall supervision of compliance with the new Act. The Office had not yet been created as of March 2002, and it is too early to judge the effect of the new system.

3.2 Administrative procedure and redress

Under the 1967 Act on Administrative Procedure, an administrative decision must be issued within 30 days. Authorities may prolong this deadline to 60 days in complicated cases, and then further with explanation to parties to the decision. All parties have the right to be informed of the reasons for a decision. The reasoning behind decisions is generally not made public, although the Freedom of Information Act (see Section 9) should grant access to such information.

Under the Act, all participants to administrative proceedings have the right to be informed of the reasons for an administrative decision. However, "participant" is defined very narrowly as the entity whose interests may be dealt with by a decision. A participant can also be anybody who affirms that he may be affected by the decision of this office, if the authority agrees.

Participants may appeal against decisions within 15 days to the authority that issued the decision. The authority may decide only if it complies with the complaint in its entirety, otherwise the superior authority decides. Decisions may be appealed thereafter to the courts, which may cancel but not change decisions.

The current framework is not effective in practice. The ease with which authorities can extend deadlines, the narrow definition of participants and the fact that appeals concern only the formal legality of the decision and not its content mean that there is no effective redress. In early 2002, an amendment to the Act on Administrative Procedure was being prepared that would broaden the definition of a "participant."

In practice, the scope for arbitrary decisions by senior officials is broad. For example, the Act on Administrative Procedure allows officials to decide differently to the recommendations of expert commissions on an arbitrary basis. A recent example in which the Minister of Health decided to what extent health insurance funds particular medicines differently to the Ministry commission advising on the issue is typical.

Compensation

Under the 1969 Act on Damages Caused by an Unlawful State Decision or Unlawful State Action, citizens may claim compensation for damages incurred as a result of unreasonably lengthy proceedings. Citizens have a right to damages on satisfaction of three conditions: that the official procedure was violated, that damages were suffered, and that there is a causal link between the two. The term "wrongful official procedure" is not defined and is left for interpretation by jurisprudence and case law. Damage claims are exempt from court fees. Citizens claiming damages in this way may also file claims in separate civil proceedings.

Complaints mechanisms

Under the 1998 Act on Complaints, any individual may lodge a complaint against the actions of an institution of public administration if his/her rights or interests have been violated or threatened by the actions or inaction of the institution. Generally, the head of the authority in question is competent to handle complaints. The authority is required to investigate every complaint and inform the petitioner of the result within 30 days. Authorities must keep a written record of complaints and a record of the results of the complaint proceedings, measures taken and the time at which they were taken.[32] Investigation of complaints is not limited only to the formal legality of the actions of the authority, but also to the substance of the decision, the reasons for the decision and who was responsible.

Table 6 shows the number of petitions and complaints filed between 1993 and 1999. Since the new Act came into effect, the number of complaints has increased dramatically.

---

[32] In especially complicated cases the deadline may be extended. The new term for an answer is 30 days and the head of office can prolong this term by another 30 days, for which an explanation to the petitioner is required.

Table 6: Petitions, complaints and legal notices, 1993–1999

Year	Complaints and legal notifications
1993	2,325
1994	1,696
1995	2,688
1996	2,827
1997	1,678
1998	2,515
1999	24,400

Source: Government Office of the Slovak Republic, *Reports on Settlement of Petitions and Complaints.*

3.3 Conflict of interest and asset monitoring

In addition to the conflict of interest provisions described in Section 2.2, the Civil Service Act also contains provisions on conflict of interest and monitoring of the assets of State employees. Civil servants must disclose any real or possible conflict of interest to the Civil Service Office, while relatives may not work in a position of subordination to them. The Act also lays down broad prohibitions against carrying out business activities or other gainful activity, although there are no restrictions on post-public service employment.

Up to the time of writing, there have been many cases that indicate abuse of conflict of interest situations. For example, as of early 2002 one of the Prime Minister's advisors on safety and crisis situations was also in the statutory organ of a company that had won a Government contract to build a bridge (with EU support).[33] Surveys indicate, for example, that connections and family are very often used to gain public contracts (see Section 7.3).

3.4 Internal control mechanisms

The Act on Civil Service defines new complaints mechanisms for public servants. Servants who presume that their rights relating to performance of duties were violated, may complain to the Head of the Civil Service Office, which must decide on the complaint.

---

[33] Information provided by TI Slovakia.

The legal system does not provide for protection of whistleblowers, and local culture discourages the practice. Indeed, according to the Criminal Code,

> Any person who lets be known information that may jeopardise the reputation of somebody in their employment, to disturb his/her family relationships or induce any serious damage shall be punishable by imprisonment of two years or by a fine.[34]

A working group established by the Ministry of Justice has been developing on recommendations to establish whistleblowing and whistleblower protection in Slovak legislation. However, there is no chance of any proposal being adopted before the 2002 elections.

3.5 Interaction with the public

In addition to the provisions concerning gifts and hospitality in legislation, the employment rules of many State institutions define what kind of gifts employees may accept. In most cases the formulation is vague; for example, the acceptance of small gifts is prohibited without giving any definition of small gifts.

A Code of Ethics for the Employees of the State Administration, Public Administration and Elected Representatives of Self-administration had been submitted for public discussion by the Civil Service Office as of July 2002. The Code would be binding on civil servants under the Civil Service Act,[35] and would serve as a recommendation for the other groups to which it applies.

3.6 Corruption

According to the World Bank's *2000 Diagnostic Survey of Corruption in Slovakia*, over 35 percent of households and 40 percent of businesses regarded corruption as very widespread in ministries (see Section 1.2). There have been a number of serious indications of corruption in the public administration. According to the SAO *1999 Annual Report*, a total of 10,471 breaches of laws in the State administration were identified in that year alone.[36] The report suggested that "State funds" (extra-budgetary bodies established to promote specific aims, such as road infrastructure or culture, and financed by taxpayer contributions) have become exemplary examples of the non-

---

[34] Criminal Code, Article 206.

[35] Civil Service Act, Article 6, paragraph 2 s).

[36] *Sme* daily, 4 May 2000.

transparent use of public money, and that their activities have provoked many suspicions of corruption. However, most of these funds have not been abolished, and those that remain are included in the State budget approved by Parliament (see Section 4.2).

An audit by the SAO of the Agency for the Administration of Material State Reserves coincided with an investigation by the economic crime unit of the police. The SAO report made insinuations that Agency officials had been involved in criminal activities, while the former chairman of the Agency publicly stated that "certain influential groups were content with the SŠHR's former style of work."[37]

Another inspection by the SAO uncovered widespread irregularities in administration of the Slovak Road Administration's (SSC) liabilities to highway construction companies. The audit revealed, *inter alia,* that certain long-abandoned financial claims had been settled with "mysterious" speed after being purchased by other companies with commissions as high as 20 percent for settling claims paid by the SSC. A number of settlements of liabilities were carried out on the basis of written orders from the SSC business director or general director.[38]

One of the most prominent corruption cases in recent years was the dismissal in 2001 of the Head of Department responsible for PHARE coordination at the Government Office for European Integration amid suspicion that he benefited through private companies from funds allocated to them from PHARE projects. As of March 2002, the police had not found enough evidence to press charges.[39]

An Audit of Central State Administration[40] (see Section 1.3) carried out as part of the Government's efforts to fight corruption revealed widespread overstaffing of the central State administration, a more-or-less corrupt phenomenon that emerged especially under the previous Government.[41] The Audit also identified a number of serious deficiencies creating the potential for corruption, in particular:

- insufficient transparency of the activities of State institutions;

---

[37] *Profit* weekly, 21 July 2000.

[38] *Profit* weekly, 10 April 2000.

[39] OSI Roundtable Discussion, Bratislava, 22 February 2002.

[40] Government Decree no. 985/1999. The audit focused especially on ministries, other central organs of State administration, and budgetary and contributory (partly financed from the State budget) organisations within their competence. In total, 172 institutions with 40,962 employees were inspected. For more details, see <http://www.ineko.sk> (last accessed 30 August 2002).

[41] Colourful examples include a large number of subsidiary organisations established by the Ministry of Agriculture, including an Institute of Grass employing some 130 people. Comments from OSI Roundtable Discussion, Bratislava, 22 February 2002.

- failure of the State administration to calculate costs and prices for the goods and services it provides;[42]

- lack of a clear division of functions and responsibilities;

- widespread avoidance of the Public Procurement Law: many contracts were not subject to any tender requirements as they fell under the financial threshold for compulsory tenders;

- the administration of real estate owned by State organs suffers from an arbitrary system of allotting space to central State administration organs and accommodation to employees based to a significant extent on personal connections.

As a result of the Audit, a number of measures to increase transparency have been implemented, in particular the duty of all State administration bodies to produce annual reports, public hearings on legislative proposals, Internet access for public comments on proposals, and regulation of below-the-threshold procurement (see Section 7.1).

4. LEGISLATURE

Control of the State budget has been improved since 2001 with the abolition or inclusion in the budget of previously off-budget funds that were shielded from scrutiny. However, there is substantial evidence of undesirably close ties between MPs and business interests. Such practices and corruption are encouraged by the absence of effective conflict of interest regulation and excessive provisions on immunity for MPs. Attempts to reform these areas as part of the Government's anti-corruption strategy have been rejected.

4.1 Elections

Slovak elections are free and fair. An Electoral Commission consisting of one representative from every political party putting up candidates supervises elections.

---

[42] For instance, when organisations provide quasi-commercial activities, they may practice unfair competition and waste State funds. The system of providing State subsidies to service providers – generally contributory and budgetary organisations – instead of service purchasers also leads to the provision of quasi-commercial goods and services without a clear calculation of costs and prices.

4.2 Budget and control mechanisms

The State Budget Act is subject to approval by the Parliament. Some categories of public expenditure did not formerly require legislative approval, in particular the State pension budget, healthcare and sickness insurance, municipal budgets and the Central Bank budget. However, nine of the former 12 State funds were abolished in 2001, and starting in 2001 all expenditures have been included in the budget. Control and audit of public expenditure is covered in Section 2.4.

4.3 Conflict of interest and asset monitoring

As outlined in Section 2.2, current provisions on conflict of interest and asset declarations are ineffective, and reform appears to be blocked by opposition from MPs. The Central Coordination Unit for the national anti-corruption strategy has prepared a draft Act on Regulation of the Access of Interest Groups to the Decision-Making and Legislative Process, based on the duty of all State bodies involved in the preparation of laws to publish proposed laws before they are approved. In addition, the Unit has prepared a set of Principles for the Legal Regulation of Lobbying, which would define lobbying, lobbyists and lobbied subjects, define the rights and duties of lobbyists and establish sanctions for violations of these duties. Neither of these proposals is likely to be adopted before the September 2002 elections.

4.4 Immunity

Parliamentary immunity is generally regarded as excessive: MPs are immune from prosecution or pre-trial detention unless the National Council votes to lift immunity on the basis of a proposal of the Mandate and Immunity Committee. According to figures cited in the GRECO evaluation, in the two years prior to September 2000, 20 proposals were filed to lift immunity, and the Committee met the "vast majority" of requests. However, there have been clear cases of abuse of immunity, in particular the refusal of the National Council to remove immunity from Gustáv Krajči, an MP for the former ruling Movement for a Democratic Slovakia (HZDS) and former Interior Minister who was suspected of bribery. On the other hand, Parliament removed immunity from Imrich Sládeček, an MP for the ruling coalition Party of Civil Understanding (SOP), suspected of involvement in a Centrogel company fraud.[43] As

---

[43] Sládeček and four former officials of the Martin District Labour Bureau and Žilina Regional Labour Bureau were indicted in the Centrogel fraud case. See *Národná obroda* daily, 23 February 2000.

part of the amendments to the Constitution passed in 2000, there were proposals to include the narrowing of MPs' immunity, but these were rejected. There has been no apparent progress on this issue as part of the Government's anti-corruption strategy.

4.5 Corruption

There have been no criminal cases of corruption of MPs in the past three years. However, there have been a number of strong indications that MPs are strongly tied to private companies. For example, the use of cars by MPs at the expense of private companies – a technically legal practice – is common. The most publicised case was of Minister of Economy Ľubomír Harach, who used a car owned by a private company named Mecom, Inc. The media published a list of many MPs who use cars provided by private companies.

5. JUDICIARY

Perceptions of corruption in the judiciary are very high, and there is evidence to suggest that they are well-founded. The Government has carried out important reforms to the legal framework for the judiciary, and is in the process of implementing important reforms in court organisation. If implemented, these reforms should to help limit corruption.

5.1 Legislative framework

Although not all aspects of judicial independence have been fully met,[44] the current Government has made major progress in this area. A new Judicial Code[45] was adopted in 2000, and the passage of the Act on the Judicial Council in April 2002 was expected to result in a functioning Judicial Council by the end of 2002. However, clear standards for promotion and selection of judges are still absent, representing risks for judicial independence.[46]

---

[44] For a detailed discussion of the judiciary, see EU Accession Monitoring Program, *Monitoring the EU Accession Process: Judicial Independence,* Open Society Institute, Budapest 2001, pp. 395–430, available at <www.eumap.org>.

[45] Act on Judges and Associate Judges no. 385/2000.

[46] See EU Accession Monitoring Program, *Judicial Capacity in Slovakia* (forthcoming).

Under the Constitution and Judicial Code, judges may not hold any other employment or function with a few exceptions such as educational or scientific activity. In addition, since January 2001 judges have had to submit declarations of interests and asset declarations to the Chairman of the Judicial Council and Minister of Justice within 30 days of taking office and by 31 March of every year.

Disciplinary proceedings may be initiated by the Minister of Justice or chairmen of a regional or district court, and are dealt with by disciplinary courts appointed by the Judicial Council. This is an important change to the system previously in operation, under which disciplinary proceedings were solely in the hands of judges.

In addition, the Ministry of Justice has introduced important reform in the organisation of court work, based on a pilot project in Banská Bystrica in 2000. The new system introduced principles such as automated allocation of judges, deadlines for carrying out certain acts, and the abolishment of judicial offices and their replacement by assistants. According to Government officials the changes have reduced the average time taken to deal with a case file from 124 days to 51, as the average number of actions taken in relation to a file has fallen from six to two. The changes were assisted by extra funds: €2.742m from the Government and €1.859m from EU funds.

Following its *Diagnostic Surveys,* the World Bank has been preparing a project on judicial reform.

5.2 Corruption

According to the surveys that have been carried out, the judiciary is seriously affected by corruption (see Section 1.2). The average size of bribes according to the World Bank's *1999 Diagnostic Survey* was approximately €256.[47] Although concrete evidence on judicial corruption is scarce, certain events indicate that there is worryingly little intolerance towards corruption within the judiciary. For example, in 2001, the Supreme Court requested that a Banská Bystrica judge who had been the subject of criminal proceedings for suspected bribery be seconded to the Supreme Court.[48] Recently, a Supreme Court deputy chief justice was chosen as one of the five judges to decide a dispute over ownership of a famous health spa, despite having been a prominent guest at the spa, which was owned by the former Minister of Health.

---

[47] World Bank, *2000 Diagnostic Survey.*

[48] *Pravda,* 27 November 2001.

The *2001 Regular Report* from the European Commission noted specifically that,

> The judiciary is not united in approaches to combat corruption. For instance, the attempts of some courts to monitor corruption have been criticised by a number of judges, including the President of the Supreme Court.[49]

6. POLITICAL PARTY FINANCE

There is substantial evidence that corruption in political party financing is widespread. The legal framework for party funding has seen significant reform since 1998. However, regulation remains weak: unlimited private donations are permitted, and supervision of party funding remains ineffective. Proposals to amend funding regulations have been proposed, but are unlikely to be adopted.

6.1 Legislative framework

Political party funding is governed by the 1991 Act on Political Parties and Movements, which was amended in October 2000.[50] Since the amendment came in effect in January 2001:

- Parties may receive income from the following sources: membership dues, donations, inheritance, sale or lease of assets, interest on deposits, profit from a limited range of business activities (writing, printing, lotteries, cultural activities etc.) and income from the State budget.

- There are no limits on size of private donations and total donations to a single party, but anonymous donations are prohibited.

- Expenditure by any political party in an election campaign may not exceed €278,800. The Ministry of Finance may impose a fine of up to double the amount by which the party exceeds the limit.

Parties now receive three different annual contributions from the State budget:

- Parties that gain more than three percent of votes receive €1.4 per vote received.

- Parties also receive a contribution towards party activities, equal to one quarter of the contribution for votes.

- Parties receive in addition €11,617 per mandate gained in the National Council.

---

[49] Commission, *2001 Regular Report,* p. 18.

[50] Act no. 424/1991, paragraphs 17–20.

6.2 Control and supervision

Parties must submit an annual financial report to the Ministry of Finance and National Council by 31 March annually, containing information on all donations and the name, address and identification number of all donors. Parties must also make their financial reports public by 30 June, and the Ministry of Finance may impose a fine of €2,323 for failure to do so. Parties must also submit reports on campaign expenditures within 30 days of elections.

Other amendments to the Act on Political Parties and Movements came into effect in May 2001, introducing the obligation of parties to be audited annually by an independent auditor chosen at random from a list of approved auditors. The Supreme Audit Office does not possess powers to audit political party finances.

The Government's Central Coordination Unit has produced further proposals for reforming party finance. Each party would receive a basic State contribution multiplied by the percentage of total votes gained in the previous election, up to a certain limit. The mandate contribution would be retained. Donations exceeding ten times the minimum monthly wage would have to be provided on the basis of a written declaration. Voluntary membership contributions would be forbidden, removing one of the main methods for avoiding declaration of donation, and membership contributions would not be allowed to exceed 15 times the minimum wage per member. Supervision and control of party finance would be performed by an independent body established by the National Council. Sanctions for violation of financing rules would be a fine of up to €23,233. However, there was no formal discussion of the proposal with parties themselves during preparation of the proposal, and as of June 2002 it had little chance of being adopted before the September elections.

6.3 Party finance in practice

In the World Bank's *2000 Diagnostic Survey,* most firms believed that unofficial payments to parties were common practice, although a larger percentage believed it was common practice before the 1998 elections. Eleven percent of firms reported that firms like theirs "sponsor political parties" in 1999, and eight percent that firms like theirs provide unofficial payments to political parties. Larger firms reported unofficial sponsoring at a higher rate: 13 percent of firms with more than 15 employees said they provided unofficial payments to political parties. Sixty-three percent of firms that admitted to unofficially sponsoring political parties reported paying a bribe in the three years before the Survey.

Slovak political parties have been the subjects of a number of financing scandals, *inter alia:*

- In November 1999, the ruling coalition Christian Democratic Movement (KDH) was hit by revelations that TV Com, a company that published *Fakty* magazine, placed a total of 67 KDH officials on its payroll, officially designating regional party secretaries as "heads of promotion teams" and district secretaries as "promotional staff."[51] This case, together with a business relationship between TV Com and a major foreign investor, were investigated by the police Department for the Fight against Corruption in 2001, although as of July 2002 no further proceedings had taken place.

- In February 2000 it emerged that the Party of the Democratic Left (SDL, another party of the ruling coalition) owned a stake in Prima-Print, a private printing company. In 1999, Prima-Print was awarded a four-year contract by Slovenská poisťovňa (SP), a State-run insurance company, to supply printed materials. According to the media, the contract was signed for SP by Rudolf Janáč (President of SP) and Vladimír Hudec (a member of the board), both nominated by the SDL.[52]

More than one-third of Slovak parties (40 out of 107) violated the Act on Political Parties and Movements in 2001. Twenty-five parties did not submit an Annual Financial Report for 2001, and 15 did not reside at their official address. Moreover, the National Council only provided very general information to the public on party financial reports. According to the press, the information provided by parties on their income is generally inaccurate.[53]

7. PUBLIC PROCUREMENT

Important changes to public procurement legislation have put in place a relatively advanced legal framework governing allocation of public contracts. These include a new Public Procurement Office that appears to have teeth, although it cannot cancel tenders on the basis of suspicion of corruption. Corruption remains widespread in procurement, and proposals that have been prepared to further improve the legal framework are unlikely to be adopted in the near future.

---

[51] *Pravda,* 5 November 1999.

[52] *Pravda,* 9 February 2000.

[53] *Národná obroda,* 20 April 2002.

7.1 Legislative framework

Public procurement is regulated by the 1999 Act on Public Procurement. Under the Act, contracts with values over €11,617 (€23,233 for works contracts) are to be allocated by open tender with the following exceptions:

- **Restricted tendering** permits contracting authorities to restrict the number of bidders to no less than five and not more than 20 bidders.

- **Negotiated procedure with Prior Notification** may be used if an open or restricted tender failed and tender conditions remain the same; if precise performance parameters are difficult to define; for tenders for research and development; and if it is not possible to stipulate price requirements because of the nature of works and services and the risk involved.

- **Negotiated procedure without prior notification** can be used in case there is only a single source of supply, copyrighted products, natural disasters, for extension of existing contracts (up to 50 percent of the original contract value), failure of the open or restricted tender, and time pressure.

Contracting authorities are forbidden from splitting tenders, and the Act contains provisions to prevent conflict of interest: a member of a commission may not be a bidder, related to any bidder, employed by a bidder or an interest association of which a bidder is a member, or by the Office of Public Procurement. Neither a member of a commission or relatives may be a statutory representative or a member of a statutory body of a contracting authority, or a partner in a legal entity acting as a bidder. Companies that have been convicted, or their statutory organs or members of statutory organs have been convicted of a crime related to entrepreneurial activities, may not participate in public tenders.

However, the Act remains somewhat vague in defining a number of conditions under which tenders may be restricted, and leaves quite broad discretion for authorities, especially the provision allowing sole sourcing for the extension of an existing contract by up to 50 percent.

Amendments to the Act that came into effect in January 2001 allow all bidders to participate in the processing of opening bids, and allow authorities to invite third parties to monitor tenders. Further amendments from January 2002 regulate procurements that fall below the financial thresholds, establishing some basic rules on competitive procedures.

The Government has issued regulations defining access to information in the procurement process. All major public procurements are widely advertised, and procurement decisions are published in the *Journal of Public Procurement.*

There is no Code of Ethics for public procurement officers or other special provisions in addition to normal rules for civil servants. The assets of public procurement officers are not monitored. There are no provisions to blacklist companies proved to have bribed in a procurement process.

The Government Central Coordination Unit claims to be working on proposals to improve the Public Procurement Law further, *inter alia,* by introducing black-listing, an ethical code for contracting authorities, use of standard form contracts, joint procurement, and also a number of more sophisticated control measures such as preliminary audit, cost-benefit analysis, programme budgeting and so on. However, no such proposals will be adopted before the September elections.

The 1999 Act also created the Office for Public Procurement, which is responsible, *inter alia,* for supervising compliance with procurement legislation, keeping statistics and publishing information on procurement and deciding appeals. The Government appoints the Chairman of the Office for a five-year term.

7.2 Review and audit

Under the 1999 Act, bidders or candidates to bid in tenders may appeal to the Office of Public Procurement against conditions stated in the notice of invitation to tender (within ten days of the advertisement), conditions stipulated in the tender documentation (within seven days of receipt of the documentation), exclusion of a bidder or potential bidder (within ten days of receipt of notice of exclusion), or the ranking of bids (within seven days of receipt of notice of the tender results).

In 2000, the first year of the Office's existence, 508 appeals were submitted (see Table 7 below). Of 185 appeals against tender decisions, the Office recognised 80 as justified, which indicates that the Office is willing to use its powers.

Table 7: Appeals to the Public Procurement Office, 2000

Manner of settlement of appeal	Against tender materials	Against exclusion	Against tender decision	Against conditions stated in the notice or call for tender	Other	Total
Satisfied (appeal successful)	5	55	80		2	142
Rejected	6	207	67			280
Withdrawn		5	2			7
In progress		2	4			6
Resigned	1	4	10			15
Untreated		3		2		5
Other		7	7			55
Total	15	304	185		4	508
percent of total appeals	3	59,8	36,4	0	0,8	100

Source: Office of Public Procurement, <http://www.uvo.gov.sk>, (last accessed 30 August 2002).

Decisions of the Office can be appealed to a court. In 2000, eight petitions against office decisions were lodged at the Supreme Court, five by bidders and three by contracting authorities. In five cases, the petition was subsequently withdrawn. Two initiatives were lodged by contracting authorities at the General Prosecutor's Office, which made protests, that is, a special right of appellation of the General Prosecutor, against two of the Office's decisions. In response, the Office altered the form but not substance of the two decisions.

An example of where the Public Procurement Office (PPO) intervened to reverse apparent corruption was the case of two tenders held by local State-owned bus companies for small buses. The tender contained a required technical requirement that the external width of the buses be over 2.45 metres, which it was alleged meant that only one company (SOR Lichavy) could win. An objection against the tender conditions was filed at the Public Procurement Office by Slovak Automobile Repair Lučenec. The PPO cancelled both tenders.[54]

---

[54] *Národná obroda* daily, 6 January 2001; *Hospodárske noviny* daily, 29 January 2001.

7.3 Corruption

Corruption in public procurement is considered to be widespread. According to the World Bank's *Diagnostic Survey*, 30 percent of enterprises reported that they had participated in at least one public tender in the previous two years before the survey, and nearly all of those firms participated in multiple tenders. Very few of these enterprises believe that public sector tenders can be won entirely without bribes, and many believed that bribery for public sector tenders occurs frequently (see Graph 3).

Graph 3: "How frequently do enterprises have to pay bribes to win public sector tenders?"

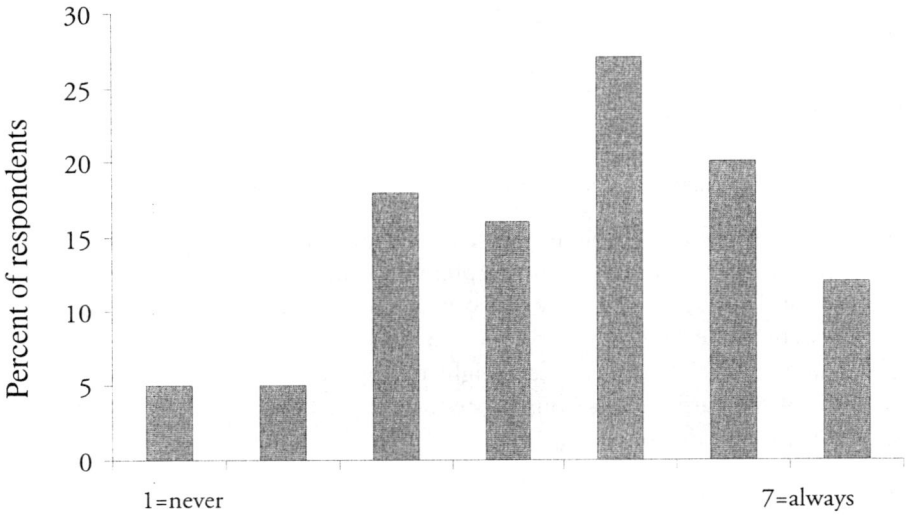

Note: This chart includes only the opinions of respondents that participated in tenders in the previous two years.
Source: World Bank, *2000 Diagnostic Survey of Corruption in Slovakia.*

Moreover, one-third of enterprises that decided not to participate in tenders cited the need for unofficial payments as an important reason (see Table 8 below).

Table 8: Reasons for not participating in public sector tenders

Percent of respondents saying it was an important reason	
The process was too **complex**; there were too many documents to submit	46.2 percent
The process was **too expensive**, or participants were required to make a prepayment to demonstrate earnestness	26.9 percent
Participants must make **too many unofficial payments** (bribes)	34.6 percent
Competition was **unfair**	51.9 percent
No personal connections with organisers	36.5 percent
The conditions of the tender were **not transparent**	44.2 percent

Note: Includes only the experiences of enterprises that said public sector procurement was relevant to the enterprise's business.
Source: World Bank, *2000 Diagnostic Survey of Corruption in Slovakia.*

Unfortunately, the PPO cannot stop a tender on suspicion of corruption alone. For example, in 2001, the Ministry of Finance requested the PPO to halt a public tender for an information system for the State Treasury, on grounds of suspicion of corruption and breach of procedure of public procurement. The press reported that the Chairman of the tender commission accused the Siemens company of attempting to pay him a bribe for €34,850, or €58,083 if he could secure the vote of another commission member. As the PPO did not register any breach of the Public Procurement Act itself, the tender was not stopped. In other words, under current rules on public procurement corruption is tolerated.[55] In this case, the Ministry of Finance cancelled the tender itself and as of May 2002 was preparing a new tender.

8. PUBLIC SERVICES

Corruption is a serious problem in several key sectors of public service, particularly health and education, while licensing procedures are severely affected by bribery. GRECO noted in its evaluation carried out in 2000 that:

---

[55] *Trend,* 15 August 2001; *Profit,* 17 August 2001; *Sme,* 22 August 2001.

> [I]t is a common and widely accepted practice that citizens pay "additional fees" to augment the fees legally due to persons who provide basic public services (such as health care and education).[56]

Corruption is underpinned, *inter alia,* by an apparent high propensity of Slovak citizens to bribe even when this is not explicitly required.

8.1 Police

According to figures from the Ministry of Interior, there were 15 cases of police officers accepting bribes in 2001.[57] However, surveys indicate there is much more corruption than shown by official indicators (see Section 1.2).[58] Surveys of experience suggest that the situation varies greatly: while the traffic police appear to be frequent recipients of bribes, far fewer bribes were reported for criminal investigations and provision of ID cards, passports and driving licenses.

The police is subordinate to the Ministry of Interior. Although the 1998 Act on State Service for Police Corps Members specifies professional criteria required for appointment to various positions in the police force, and the 1993 Police Act forbids police from being members of a political party or movement, senior police officials are replaced after every election. Within the Ministry of Interior, the Bureau of Control and Inspection is authorised to use special operative measures (for example, *agent provocateur*) to detect criminal activity in the police.

A major barrier to fighting corruption in the police is the unwillingness of the public to report cases of corruption. According to a survey conducted by Focus in March 2002, only 17 percent of respondents would report cases of police corruption, and only four percent would definitely do so. Eighteen percent of respondents would not do so for fear of retaliation, while 15 percent believe that doing so would not lead to any result.[59]

8.2 Customs

The customs administration is regarded by both households and firms as one of the most corrupt institutions, with only healthcare, the judicial system and the National

---

[56] GRECO, Evaluation Report on Slovakia, p. 7.

[57] Stav a úroveň policajného vyšetrovania v roku 2001 [Situation and level of police investigation in 2001], <http://www.minv.sk>, (last accessed 22 May 2002).

[58] For example see World Bank, *2000 Diagnostic Survey.*

[59] Focus Marketing and Research, *Záverečná správa* [Final Report], pp. 5–6.

Property Fund evaluated as more corrupt (see Section 1.2). There has been no detailed research carried out on corruption in customs, or surveys of importers and exporters. According to a focus survey carried out in March 2002 for Transparency International, 42 percent of households regard corruption in the customs administration as widespread, nine percent said it existed but was less widespread, while 30 percent judged it to be present but were unable to express an opinion on its prevalence.

8.3 Health

Corruption in the healthcare system is very widespread. According to one analysis the total volume of corruption in healthcare amounts to €278.8m per year, the equivalent of €51.5 for every citizen.[60] Approximately 50 percent of respondents in the World Bank's *1999 Diagnostic Survey*[61] expressed the belief that corruption in healthcare was widespread. Nearly six out of ten respondents paid a gratuity for a hospital stay, with lower figures for other medical services (see Table 9).

Table 9: Percentage of those using various medical services who paid a gratuity

Type of medical service	Percentage of users paying a gratuity
General practitioner	15.8
Medical specialist	29.5
Dentist	18.2
Hospital stay	58.6
Emergency unit	5.4

Source: World Bank, *2000 Diagnostic Survey of Corruption in Slovakia.*

Moreover, 43 percent of those who offered a gratuity said that "nobody asked for it – they simply wanted to offer it" 52 percent said that "nobody asked for it but that is the way it works," and five percent said that it was "required by health care staff." This indicates a very high degree of internalisation of bribery – or at least informal payments and gifts – as normal, and is regarded by Slovak officials as one of the greatest barriers to fighting corruption.[62]

---

[60] P. Pažitný, R. Zajac, *Stratégia reformy zdravotníctva – reálnej reformy pre občana* [Strategy of the Health Care Reform – The Real Reform Aimed at a Citizen], MESA 10, Bratislava 2001.

[61] World Bank, *1999 Diagnostic Survey.*

[62] OSI Roundtable Discussion, Bratislava, 22 February 2002.

The average size of a bribe for medical treatment was €25.8, ranging from an average of €5.3 for visits to a general practitioner to €85 for hospital stays. According to press reports, the "price" for important operations ranges from €233 to €466.[63]

The press has also commented extensively on allegedly widespread corruption of doctors by pharmacies and pharmaceutical companies: typical examples are where doctors sent their patients to a particular pharmacy in return for bribes, or where pharmaceutical companies provided lucrative benefit to doctors (such as exotic foreign trips) in return for prescription of their medicines.[64]

8.4 Education

Corruption also appears to be widespread in the education system, especially at the level of higher education. According to the World Bank's *Diagnostic Survey*,[65] 13 percent of all households with a member enrolled in education reported paying a gratuity in the previous term, while 23 percent reported this for higher education (see Table 10). The trend at the higher education level is particularly striking, with 82 percent of respondents of the opinion that bribery had increased, and almost half believing that it had "increased immensely." On the other hand, the research conducted by Focus Marketing and Research in March 2002 indicated a lower prevalence of corruption: nine percent of respondents said they had provided educational staff with a benefit in return for something during the last two school years, while only two percent provided money.[66]

---

[63] World Bank, *Corruption in Slovakia.*

[64] *Národná obroda,* 21 April 1999; *SME,* 6 May 1999; *Pravda,* 2 May 2001. According to the latter article, "Pharmaceutical companies have developed various strategies in this field, even their own travel agencies – congresses, seminars or straight holidays in exotic countries are then organised. Long gone are the times when a consideration involved a T-shirt bearing the company's logo, a pen or a notebook. Today, they go for computers, sometimes with printers, mobile phones, but even cars or foreign accounts."

[65] World Bank, *2000 Diagnostic Survey.*

[66] Focus Marketing and Research, *Záverečná správa* [Final Report], p. 5.

Table 10: Paying gratuities at educational institutions

	N	*Percent reporting paying a gratuity the previous term*
Overall	701	12.7
Primary schools	366	12.6
Vocational schools	71	9.9
Secondary schools	194	10.3
Universities	70	22.9

Note: Includes only the experiences of households with at least one member at that level school in the previous term.
Source: World Bank, *2000 Diagnostic Survey of Corruption in Slovakia.*

At lower levels of schooling, the most prevalent form of gratuity came in the form of gifts. At university level, cash payments were made more frequently than gifts, and the average size of gratuities was almost €163 (see Table 11).

Again, there appeared to be a striking level of cultural acceptance of bribery in education. One-fifth of households that paid gratuities reported that educational staff required it, while almost half reported paying of their own free will; the remaining 30 percent reported that, "Nobody required it, but I know this is the way it goes."

The most important reason reported for bribing school employees was to gain admittance to a school, with over 80 percent of households claiming this to be "very often a reason." Worryingly, only 14 percent of respondents believed it is possible to gain admittance to medical school without bribes, while only ten percent of respondents believed the same for law school. This indicates that high levels of corruption in both education and health are not just related to shortages but are also encouraged by the very institutions that train and certify professionals.

Table 11: Size of gratuities encountered by households in the health and education sectors (€)

	N	*average*	*min*	*max*
Primary school	27	18.3	0.8	116
Vocational school	4	20.3	2.3	69.7
Secondary school	12	54.8	2.3	348.5
University	10	159	11.6	1.162

Source: World Bank, *2000 Diagnostic Survey of Corruption in Slovakia.*

8.5 Licensing and regulation

The system of licensing appears to be a major source of corruption, and its reform has been one of the main objectives of the Government's anti-corruption strategy. GRECO noted in 2000 that,

> The... way in which... licences, authorisation and state subsidies are granted at the moment is problematic, especially because many of them are not given on the basis of objective criteria... it is of utmost importance, for the business community and the public at large, that such practices be put to an end.[67]

According to the World Bank *Diagnostic Survey*,[68] nearly 15 percent of enterprises surveyed had obtained an export licence in the two years before the survey, and 21 percent had received an import licence. Over half of enterprises that had obtained export or import licences reported that they had used connections, political influence, or outright bribes in order to win the licences. Of those who had tried to get an import or export licence in the previous 12 months (including those who gained licence), one in three reported that they had encountered bribery. Small enterprises were more likely to encounter bribery: 38 percent of small companies encountered bribery in allocating of import/export licences, compared to 27 percent of medium and large ones. The average size of bribes to gain export licences was reported as €325.

In September 1996, the SAO presented to Parliament a report on grain exports which revealed gross violations of various regulations. Two senior officials at the Ministry of Economy dealing with the grain export licences were charged.[69] The SAO also disclosed serious irregularities in the registration of licence applications at the Ministry of Economy, which resulted in criminal proceedings against two officials.

One quarter of firms that received other types of licences (such as retail trade licences) reported paying a bribe, with the average size of bribe reported as €183.[70]

---

[67] GRECO, *Evaluation Report on Slovakia*, p. 8.

[68] World Bank, *Corruption in Slovakia*.

[69] *Pravda* daily, 13 May 1998. The substance of the case was as follows: one official, intending to obtain unlawful material benefits for third parties, illegally entrusted the second official with the power to sign export licences for goods and grain commodities. The second official granted numerous licences for which fees were never paid, which the Licensing Commission never approved, or for which licence requests were not even filed.

[70] World Bank, *Corruption in Slovakia*.

Licensing reform

As part of the National Programme for the Fight against Corruption, the Government charged the Deputy Prime Minister's Office with the task of analysing all licences, concessions and permissions, contributions and grants granted by ministries and their institutions. The Central Coordination Unit prepared a set of proposals for reform of licensing procedures. All licences that are supposed to be granted automatically by law (around 84 percent of all licences) would be abolished, and for restricted licences a new auction-based allocation system would be adopted. Deadlines for decisions on licences would be shortened from 30 days (60 days in complicated cases) to five days, and a taxative list of reasons for licence decisions would have to be provided. As of March 2002, the Deputy Prime Minister for Economy was expected to submit the proposed Licensing Policy to the Government. However, the proposal faced opposition from the Ministry of Economy, which would prefer to maintain the original system for restricted licences. As of May 2002, this issue had not been resolved.

9. ROLE OF THE MEDIA

Slovak law guarantees press freedom, and a new Freedom of Information Act in force since 2001 has been a major breakthrough in access to information. However, allocation of licences to private broadcasting companies is subject to suspicions concerning corruption, while regulation of public broadcasting has allowed political control of Slovak TV. Corruption in the media is regarded as a serious problem, although steps have been taken to encourage professional ethics. The media has played an increasing role in exposing corruption, and an increasing role in calling senior politicians to account.

9.1 Press freedom

Under the Slovak Constitution, freedom of expression may be lawfully curtailed only where it is necessary to protect the rights and freedoms of others, national security, law and order, health or morality. Under the Media Act, journalists have the right to protect the identity of their sources. Journalists are subject to ordinary civil law provisions on libel and protection of reputation.

9.2 Access to information

Government agencies are increasingly coming under pressure from the media and NGOs to be transparent and make information and documents available. Internet websites of Government agencies are becoming more common.

The Act on Free Access to Information,[71] which has been in force since January 2001, has been a major breakthrough in access to information. The Act applies to State agencies, municipalities, legal entities and natural persons that have been given the power by law to make decisions on the rights and responsibilities of natural persons or legal entities in the area of public administration, legal entities established by law or by a State agency or municipality, and legal entities established by any of these entities and that manage public funds or operate with State property or property of municipalities.

The Act states in some detail the types of information that State institutions must make available for mass access: for example, in the case of Parliament draft laws or the voting records of MPs, or for ministries draft laws and any conceptual materials. Citizens may file requests for information orally or by any other technically reasonable method. Requests for information must be dealt with without undue delay, and not less than ten days after the receipt of the request unless there are important reasons. Information is to be provided free of charge, with the (optional) exception of the payments not higher than the cost of material for reproduction, cost of technical carriers and delivery of information to the applicant.

Exceptions to the duty to provide information apply to classified information, personal data, commercial secrets, information that was obtained from a person to whom the freedom of information provisions do not apply.[72] Disclosure of information relating to the use of funds or State or municipal property is not to be regarded as violation of a commercial secret.

Applicants may appeal within 15 days against a refusal to provide information, to the same institution. The appeal is to be decided within 15 days by the superior of the entity that issued or should have issued the decision on provision of information. If no decision is made within this period, it is deemed that the appeal was refused. Applicants may thereafter appeal to the courts.

This Act has proved to be an effective tool for increasing access to information. For example, since the Act came into effect, the SAO has published its audit reports, in

---

[71] Act no. 21/2000.

[72] The authority is obliged to inform the person concerned of the request for information and request permission for disclosure; if the person does not reply within seven days this is to be regarded as consent for disclosure.

contrast to previous practice. The media has also used the Act to monitor the activities of State institutions more effectively, for example the allocation of subsidies by the Ministry of Economy or Agriculture. One indication of the Act's effectiveness is the dissatisfaction voiced by many officials. The Ministry of Education prepared a proposal to amend the Act by introducing longer deadlines for provision of information and widening the exceptions to the duty to provide information. After strong criticism from the media and NGOs, the Minister withdrew the proposal.

9.3 Broadcasting regulation

Licences for private TV and radio stations are allocated by the Council for Broadcasting and Retransmission. The nine-member Council is appointed by the Slovak National Council from candidates nominated by MPs from members of professional media organisations and NGOs in the sphere of media, education, sport and religion.

Although licence applicants must fulfil certain criteria for a broadcasting licence to be allocated, the media have voiced numerous suspicions regarding licence allocation. Moreover, the independence of private stations has been put in doubt on numerous occasions, exacerbated by numerous ties to politicians and/or other business interests. For example, according to MEMO 98, an NGO that monitors the media, the news programmes of TV Markíza showed systematic bias towards one political party between April and September 2001.

Slovak Television (STV) and Slovak Radio are also regulated by the same Council, which appoints their directors. Due to this framework, the management of Slovak TV has been clearly political, and the Director in 2001 was already the 11th director since 1991. The political dependence or bias of STV has frequently been evident, for example when it breached the pre-election moratorium in 1998 by broadcasting live coverage of the Prime Minister's question hour in the National Council.

Under amendments to the Act on Broadcasting and Retransmission passed in September 2000, all voting in the Council is now public.

9.4 Corruption in the media

Corruption in the media is regarded as a serious problem. Although the Slovak Syndicate of Journalists approved a Code of Ethics in 1990, the Code is vague and lacks any enforcement mechanism. Ethical standards remain largely a question of individual integrity, and there are no mechanisms for protecting or promoting journalistic ethics.

As part of the Government's national anti-corruption strategy, and with support from the PHARE programme for Support for the Implementation of the National Programme for the Fight against Corruption (see Section 1.4), in the Autumn of 2001 the Government's Central Coordination Unit initiated a project entitled "Ethics in Journalism." The project, which began with a series of roundtables with the participation of the main representatives of the media industry, aims to establish professional and ethical media values in a new Media Act. A draft Act is under preparation. Two EU experts are assisting with the project.

As of July 2002, no specific changes or proposals had resulted from the project.

In April 2002, the Syndicate of Journalists created a Slovak Press Council, a self-regulatory body that, *inter alia,* will regulate issues of journalistic ethics.

9.5 Media and corruption

The media has played an increasingly important role in uncovering corruption cases and scandals. Graph 4 illustrates the steady increase in coverage of corruption issues by the print media. A key indication of the increasing importance of the media in this area is the fact that several members of the current Government resigned under media pressure, a phenomenon that never occurred under previous Governments.

Graph 4: Number of articles on corruption in Slovak print media

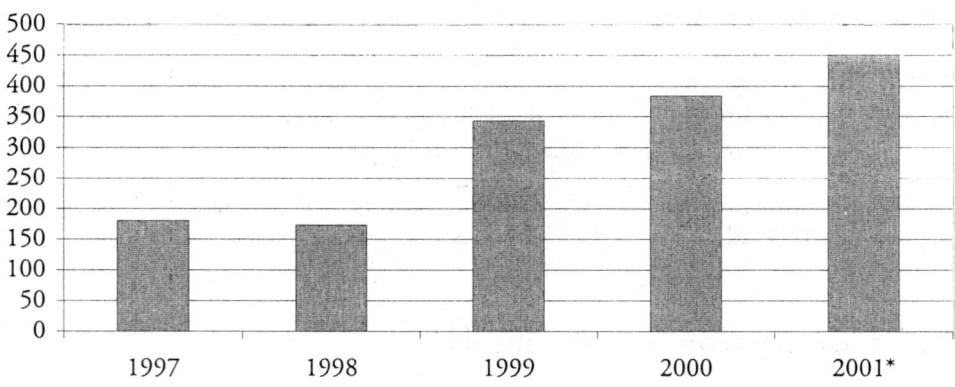

Note: *Estimate, based on data from the 1st half of 2001.
Source: Central Coordination Group, Office of the Slovak Government, *Report on the Fight against Corruption,* October 2001, <http://www.vlada.gov.sk/bojprotikorupcii>, (last accessed 30 August, 2002).

10. RECOMMENDATIONS

The following recommendations have been highlighted as particularly important to Slovakia. For additional recommendations applicable to candidate States generally, please see Part 5 of the Overview report.

1. Carry out an extensive public awareness campaign in cooperation with Slovakia's active NGO sector to build public intolerance to corruption.

2. Implement proposal for fundamental reform of licensing procedures, and implement the recommendations of the Audit of State Administration concerning downsizing of public administration.

Corruption and Anti-corruption Policy in Slovenia

Table of Contents

Corruption and Anti-corruption Policy in Slovenia

EXECUTIVE SUMMARY

Statistics on criminal proceedings and the opinions of analysts and international organisations including the European Union indicate that corruption is not a serious problem in Slovenia. However, Slovenia has slipped downwards somewhat in some international rankings, and citizens' perceptions are that corruption is both widespread and increasing. Certain findings of this report indicate that problems of corruption may be considerably more serious than have been previously acknowledged. While there is little direct evidence that corruption is serious in any particular area of public life, institutions of prosecution and enforcement appear to be weak, the effectiveness of several other institutions of oversight is questionable, and conflicts of interest appear to be a widespread phenomenon. These problems may be exacerbated by the small size of the country, a long history of close interaction between the public and private sectors, and the predominance of personal contacts as the means by which institutions function in practice.

Anti-corruption policy has not been a political priority, at least until 2001 when the Government initiated efforts to respond to a critical report by the Council of Europe, and specifically established a coordinating anti-corruption commission. As of July 2002, the country still lacked a national anti-corruption strategy. The EU accession process has had limited impact on anti-corruption policy until recently, as the Commission has never highlighted corruption as an important problem. However, the EU is assisting in the development of a national strategy. Civil society appears to be weak in the area of anti-corruption, and has played no role in pushing the issue into the public eye or creating anti-corruption policy.

Slovenian anti-corruption legislation is almost fully harmonised with the requirements of international conventions on corruption. Ratification of the last convention not yet in force, the Council of Europe Civil Law Convention, is expected in the near future.

Provisions on conflict of interest and asset and income declarations exist and apply to executive officials, while ordinary officials are not much restricted in their ancillary activities. Asset declarations may be checked by a special Parliamentary (National Assembly) Commission. Neither the conflict of interest nor asset declaration provisions are effective in practice: there are no real sanctions for violation, and the provisions appear to allow clear abuses of conflict of interest situations in practice. Recent exposures of several cases of conflict of interest have resulted in a number of resignations, however.

Legislation on State financial control is relatively advanced. The Court of Audit is independent both formally and financially, although its findings are not generally used effectively. Legislation has been in effect since 1999 to establish an integrated international financial control system in the State administration, although the European Commission has recommended improvements in implementation.

The Office for the Prevention of Corruption was created by the Government in July 2001 and has been preparing an anti-corruption strategy and a proposed Act on the Prevention of Corruption. Until recently the Office did not appear to play an active role in initiation of corruption cases or implementation of specific anti-corruption policies. However, recent developments indicate that the Office may be beginning to play a more active role. Although the police has been restructured significantly to facilitate investigation of corruption, in some cases there are reasons for doubting the independence and effectiveness of both prosecutors and police, especially in the investigation of sensitive and important corruption cases. An office of the ombudsman has been established since 1994, but has not dealt with any major cases of corruption.

There is very little evidence of corruption in the executive branch or civil service, with the exception of a case against one State Secretary still in proceedings. Reform of the public administration has been only limited until recently: although the law has distinguished between political and career appointments, patronage appears to have been common and there have been few restrictions on the political party activities of civil servants. However, a major package of new laws passed in June 2002 will limit political appointments and make competitive selection procedures compulsory. There is evidence that procedures for appealing against administrative decisions are too time-consuming and costly to be effective. A Code of Conduct was adopted in 2001. Conflicts of interest appear to be an important problem, especially at local government level.

All public expenditure is included in the State budget approved by Parliament. Available evidence suggests that corruption is not a serious problem, although Parliament is the least trusted public institution in surveys. However, the inadequacy of conflict of interest and asset declaration provisions, and the absence of any provisions to regulate lobbying hinder assessment in this area.

Although the legal framework for the judicial branch is advanced and reform has been consistently high on the Government's agenda, concerns persist over the extent of judicial independence, as well as the adequacy of provisions to prevent judicial corruption. In particular, proposed reforms of the composition of the Judicial Council may undermine independence. Although there is virtually no evidence of corruption among judges, court delays are still a serious problem.

Political party funding is subject to relatively strict and detailed rules, with restrictions on donations and expenditures, and parties receive significant subsidies from the State budget. However, parties appear to be able to circumvent the rules with relative ease, while supervision of party funding by the Court of Audit has not resulted in any significant sanctions for violations of financing rules. A number of cases of covert financing have come to light, while the increased indebtedness of some parties has increased the incentives for illegal financing.

Public procurement appears to be vulnerable to corruption, despite relatively advanced legislation. A long tradition of overlapping public and private sectors provides the context for a situation in which oversight is weak and collusion both among bidders themselves and between bidders and contracting agencies may be widespread. Moreover, the efficacy of review of procurement procedures and appeal processes is questionable. The European Commission has drawn attention explicitly to problems of conflict of interest in procurement. A few procurement scandals have broken in recent years at ministry level, while there is some evidence that procurement at local government level may suffer serious problems of corruption.

Corruption in public services appears to be a minor problem in most areas, despite comments or indications to the contrary, most frequently in healthcare. A possible exception is tax collection, where officials are regarded as highly exposed to bribery, and the size of the grey economy indicates that corruption may be a more serious problem than official data suggest. Licensing regulation may suffer from some problems of corruption, especially in the allocation of zoning and construction permits.

Freedom of speech is not threatened under Slovenian law. However, provisions on access to information do not appear to be effective. Broadcasting regulation appears to be relatively free from direct political interference, although there is evidence that public television is resistant to broadcasting evidence of corruption. While direct corruption of journalists does not appear to be a serious problem, hidden advertising is common. A more serious barrier to effective media investigation activities may be the close personal connections between media companies, other powerful private companies and Slovenian banks. A recent case of violence against an investigative journalist has raised concerns about the ability of journalists to investigate corruption without risk of reprisal.

1. INTRODUCTION

1.1 The data and perceptions

The European Union (in its *1998, 1999, 2000* and *2001 Regular Reports on Slovenia's Progress towards Accession*),[1] the Council of Europe (in the GRECO *2000 Evaluation Report*),[2] as well as other international organisations and many domestic analysts regard corruption in Slovenia as a problem that does not present an acute or major threat to society or democracy. However, international rankings and public perceptions indicate a negative trend. In addition, the findings of this report indicate that while there is little evidence of serious corruption in any particular area, the weakness of institutions of enforcement and oversight combined with certain aspects of cultural legacy may create an environment vulnerable to corruption.

Statistics on corruption cases and convictions shown in Tables 1 and 2 support these views. However, for reasons presented in this report, these statistics probably measure more accurately the effectiveness of enforcement institutions than levels of corruption.

---

[1] Commission of the European Union, *1998, 1999, 2000* and *2001 Regular Report from the Commission on Slovenia's Progress towards Accession,* <http://europe.eu.int/comm/enlargement/slovenia/index.htm>, (last accessed 27 August 2002).

[2] See <http://www.greco.coe.int>, (last accessed 27 August 2002).

Table 1: Number of criminal complaints filed by the Police for criminal offences of corruption under the Slovenian Penal Code,[3] 1991–2001[4]

Criminal Offence	1991	1992	1993	1994	1995	1996	1997	1998	1999	2000	2001
Private sector passive corruption (Article 247)	28	5	8	9	1	3	0	3	2	1	16
Private sector active corruption (Article 248)	23	6	8	4	1	2	0	3	1	2	1
Passive bribery of public officials (Article 267)	5	11	23	10	2	1	2	5	13	5	16
Active bribery of public officials (Article 268)	16	28	28	32	31	26	17	22	38	17	24
Trafficking in influence (Article 269)	0	0	0	0	1	2	0	3	18	1	1
Active bribery/election or balloting (vote buying) (Article 162)	0	0	0	0	0	0	0	0	0	1	0
Passive bribery/election or ballot (Article 168)	0	0	0	0	0	0	0	0	2	0	0
TOTAL	72	50	67	55	36	34	19	36	74	27	58

Source: *Statistical Office of Republic of Slovenia.*

---

[3] The Penal Code, *Official Gazette,* 63/1994, 70/1994, 23/1999.

[4] See M. Jager, "Raziskanost korupcije v Sloveniji in problemi z definicijo" [Corruption research in Slovenia and Problems of its Definition], paper presented at the Colloquium "Korupcija kot realnost današnjega časa" [Corruption as the Reality of Today], organised by the Ministry of Interior, Gotenica, Slovenia, May 2001, in: *Korupcija kot realnost današnjega časa,* conference proceedings, pp. 37–50. Under the valid Penal Code, the criminal offences of corruption cover the following areas: public office (active and passive bribery of public officials, trafficking in influence), business transactions in the private sector (active and passive bribery in the private sector), and elections or balloting (active and passive bribery at election or balloting). Criminal offences cited in Table 1 do not appear under their official titles. Some of the statistics were provided by the Slovenian Ministry of Internal Affairs.

Table 2: Number of convictions (by final judgement) for criminal offences of corruption, 1995–2000

Criminal Offences (Penal Code, PC)	1995	1996	1997	1998	1999	2000
Article 162	0	0	0	0	0	0
Article 168	0	0	0	0	0	0
Article 247	0	0	0	0	0	0
Article 248	1	1	0	1	0	0
Article 267	0	1	0	2	1	0
Article 268	14	17	13	13	14	9
Article 269	0	0	0	0	0	0
TOTAL	**15**	**19**	**13**	**16**	**15**	**9**

Source: *Statistical Office of Republic of Slovenia.*

Perceptions

Slovenia's ranking in the Transparency International Corruption Perception Index (CPI) indicates that Slovenia is (along with Estonia) among the least corrupt countries in Central and Eastern Europe.[5]

According to the EBRD/World Bank *1999 Business Environment and Enterprise Performance Survey,* Slovenia experiences medium levels of "State capture" – basically the influencing by private firms of the formulation of rules and laws, ranking it with the least affected post-communist countries. Four percent of firms reported that they employ tactics of State capture to influence policy-making.[6]

National public opinion polls measure various indicators that might be indicative of the corruption situation in Slovenia, in particular perceptions of corruption, levels of intolerance of corruption and levels of trust in institutions.[7] In a 1995 national opinion

---

[5] The CPI ranges between 10 (clean) and 0 (highly corrupt). For Slovenia's rankings, see <http://www.transparency.org>, (last accessed 16 August 2002).

[6] See EBRD, *1999 Transition Report,* London 1999, pp. 117–120; J. Hellmann, G. Jones and D. Kaufmann, "Seize the State, Seize the Day: State Capture, Corruption and Influence in Transition Economies", *World Bank policy research working paper* No. 2444, 2000; <http://www.worldbank.org/wbi/governance>, (last accessed, 15 July 2002).

[7] The project "Slovensko javno mnenje" [Slovene Public Opinion] has been for years continuously carried out by Prof Niko Toš and his collaborators at the Center za raziskovanje javnega mnenja in množičnih komunikacij [CJMMK, Public Opinion Research Centre], Faculty of Social Science, University of Ljubljana. "SJM" is the broader longitudinal empirical research project in Slovenia. It is based on a representative sample (n=2100) of adult inhabitants.

poll, respondents ranked corruption in the lower third among the 37 problems listed, and in 1997, corruption was together with crime in general at the bottom of the list.[8] The polls also indicate that tolerance towards corruption is low. The question "Could you find it acceptable that someone in a position of trust accepts bribes?" was answered negatively by 76.8 percent of respondents in 1992, 73 percent in 1995 and 73 percent of respondents in 1999.[9]

However, domestic public opinion and many domestic commentators believe that the situation is now worse than it was before the transition. In one major survey carried out in 1999, 62 percent of respondents believed the level of corruption in Slovenia to be increasing, while 38 percent believed that almost all or the majority of public officials were involved in corruption (49 percent believed that some were).[10] Moreover, levels of trust in some important State institutions, notably Parliament, Government, political parties and the police, have fallen significantly in the last ten years,[11] which might in part reflect increasing perceptions of corruption or falling tolerance for corruption.[12]

Nonetheless, surveys of individual experience indicate that there is a difference between perceptions and actual victimisation. In 1997, only 1.2 percent of respondents reported having been victimised by corruption in the previous year (1.5 percent in Ljubljana).

---

[8] Slovene Public Opinion project, University of Ljubljana.

[9] D. Mesner-Andolšek, *Public Awareness of the Threat that Corruption Represents for Society*, report for GRECO, University of Ljubljana, Faculty of Social Sciences, Ljubljana 2000, p. 2.

[10] Slovenian Institute of Social Sciences, "Awareness of Corruption in Slovene Society – Opinion Poll Survey 1990–1999," cited in: GRECO, *Evaluation Report on Slovenia*, adopted by the GRECO at its 4th Plenary Meeting, 12-15 December 2000, <http://www.greco.coe.int> p. 4.

[11] *Human Development Report Slovenia 2000–2001*, M. Hanžek, M. Gregorčič (eds.), Institute of Macroeconomic Analysis and Development, Ljubljana 2001, pp. 54–55.

[12] D. Mesner-Andolšek, "Sociološki vidiki korupcije" [Sociological Aspects of Corruption], paper presented at the colloquium "Korupcija kot realnost današnjega časa," [Corruption as a Reality of Today], Gotenica, May 2001.

These figures rose in 2000 to 2.1 percent and 1.9 percent respectively.[13] The surveys also revealed that corruption is very seldom reported to the police, which helps to explain the low criminal statistics on corruption. The corruption victimisation rate is higher than in most Western European countries (where it ranges from 0.0 to 0.7 percent) but the lowest among the transitional countries of Central and Eastern Europe.

As this report goes some way to show, the prevalence of corruption in Slovenia is particularly difficult to assess as there are numerous indications that informal networks, connections and acquaintances (*veze in poznanstva*) play a crucial role in Slovenian society. This may give rise to networks of clientelistic or nepotistic social relationships that are corrupt but not characterised by direct exchanges of money or benefits. One example that may apply to Slovenia is the effect many believe personal connections have on criminal proceedings (in particular in the phase of investigation), or the effect that extensive personal connections (for example multiple board membership) across media companies, banks and other companies (many of which are still State-controlled) may have on media independence. As the GRECO *Evaluation Report* notes,

> Slovenia is a small country and this can bring with it some degree of permissiveness, tolerance or even a certain endogamy among officials serving in different institutions. The GET observed that there seemed to be more reliance on personal relationships among State officials and feelings of mutual trust and confidence than on a sound constitutional approach of *"checks and balances"*... which is essential in the fight against... corruption.[14]

---

[13] *International Crime Victim Survey* (ICVS) is an international comparative survey covering 11 main forms of crime victimisation. It is carried out by using two main survey methods: computer-assisted telephone interviewing (CATI) and face-to-face interviewing of a sample from 1,000 to around 2,000 respondents (depending on a country). For methodological details, see Z. Pavlović, "Mednarodna anketa o kriminaliteti oz viktimizaciji – Slovenija (Ljubljana) 1992–1997" [International crime victim survey – Slovenia (Ljubljana 1992–1997], parts 1, 2, 3. and 4, in: *Revija za kriminalistiko in kriminologijo,* Ljubljana, 49/1998/3, pp. 257–265; 50/1999/1, pp. 30–37; 50/1999/2, pp. 122–130; 50/1999/3, pp. 234–239. On results, see M. Jager, *Raziskanost korupcije v Sloveniji,* [Corruption research in Slovenia], *Podjetje in delo* XXVI, 6-7/2000, pp. 1013–1019; Z. Pavlović, *The International Crime Victims Survey in Countries in Transition,* UNICRI, Publication no. 62, Rome 1998, pp. 493–450; U. Zvekić, *Criminal Victimization in Countries in Transition,* UNICRI, Publication no. 61, Rome 1998. The question concerning corruption was the following: "In some areas there is a problem of corruption among government or public officials. During [last year] has any government official, for instance a customs officer, police officer or inspector in your country, asked you or expected you to pay a bribe for his service?" Further on the respondents were asked to identify the category of public official and whether they reported the event to the police or public prosecutor or other public or private agency. Results for the 2000 survey are from Statistical Office of the Republic of Slovenia, *Rapid Reports,* no. 265, p. 3.

[14] GRECO, *Evaluation Report,* p. 11.

1.2 Main loci of corruption

There is no direct evidence that corruption is a serious problem in any one area of Slovenian public life. However, the weakness of a number of institutional anti-corruption mechanisms is a significant concern in a country of Slovenia's size, where personal relations and contacts can – if not subjected to regulation and countervailing forces – integrate a small number of interests in ways that conflict with broader public interests, rather than facilitating social integration in general.

In particular, conflict of interest remains an important corruption threat, and there are indications that it is a serious problem given the size of the country and the weakness of conflict of interest rules in the public administration. Both the EC *2000* and *2001 Regular Report* specifically mention conflict of interest as a problem, with the Commission noting in 2001 that, "[P]reventing conflict of interest situations, including those in public procurement, should be given more attention."[15]

Another theme that is not addressed directly by this report, but which may be of considerable significance in the context of corruption, is the existence of a large number of (directly or indirectly) State-owned corporations. Because of this situation, the winning coalition of political parties that forms the Government does not win only the majority of seats in the Parliament but also extensive influence in State-owned corporations. The Government (representing the owner, i.e. the State) controls the appointment of top managerial positions in these firms and through more-or-less political hiring in these cases extends its influence over the economy and control over substantial assets.

1.3 Government anti-corruption policy

Although Slovenian anti-corruption legislation is relatively advanced and is almost fully harmonised with the EU *acquis,* anti-corruption policy has not been a Government priority at least until 2001. As a result no specific and comprehensive anti-corruption strategy or programme has been designed or implemented so far. One of the main findings of the GRECO *Evaluation Report* cited above was the absence of a national anti-corruption strategy and a central body to formulate and coordinate it.

In reaction to these findings and GRECO recommendations, the Government set up a Coordinating Commission for Combating Corruption in 2001, composed of representatives from various ministries and other executive bodies; representatives from the Supreme Court, State Prosecutor's Office, Court of Audit and the National Review

---

[15] Commission, *2001 Regular Report,* p. 18.

Commission are invited to participate in the Commission's meetings.[16] In July 2001, the Government established an Office for the Prevention of Corruption.[17] Directly responsible to the Prime Minister, the Office has been in charge of preparing a national anti-corruption strategy, drafting new legislation and implementing the recommendations of the first GRECO report. As of June 2002, the Office was preparing a National Anti-corruption Strategy and an Act on Prevention of Corruption with the assistance of Dutch experts (see Section 1.4 below).

The role of civil society

Slovenian civil society appears to be surprisingly weak in the area of anti-corruption. For example, a recent attempt to form a branch of Transparency International failed due to lack of interest. Although the Government has recognised the importance of NGOs in the EU accession process and invited NGOs to co-operate in the preparation of negotiation positions for individual accession chapters, NGOs have not been involved in any specific initiative regarding corruption.

1.4 The impact of the EU Accession Process

Accession negotiations between Slovenia and the European Commission began in 1998, and EU accession is currently the most important foreign policy goal of the Government.

According to the Commission, Slovenia has satisfied the Copenhagen political criteria in every *Regular Report,* and corruption has never been highlighted as problematic.[18] As stated in the *2000 Regular Report,* "According to the available statistics and reports, problems of corruption are relatively limited in Slovenia."[19] Likewise, corruption has either not been mentioned at all under "ability to assume the obligations of membership," or mentioned favourably (in 2000).

However, although the EU has not exerted any substantial pressure on the Slovenian Government regarding corruption, the influence of the EU and the Council of Europe has been the principal reason for those limited initiatives the Government has made.

---

[16] See "Amendments to the Republic of Slovenia's National Programme for the Adoption of the *Acquis* by the End of 2002," May 2001, Government Office for European Affairs, <http://www.gov.si/svez/novosti/npaa_an.htm>, (last accessed 27 August 2002).

[17] Sklep o ustanovitvi, delovnem področju in organizaciji Urada Vlade Republike Slovenije za preprečevanje korupcije, *Official Gazette,* Government Resolution 58/2001.

[18] Commission, *1998, 1999* and *2000 Regular Reports.*

[19] Commission, *2000 Regular Report,* p. 16.

First, Slovenia has entirely harmonised its criminal law with the *acquis*. One motive behind harmonisation was a set of recommendations and guidelines issued after the 1998 evaluations of Slovenia by the European Commission and Council of Europe through the OCTOPUS 1 programme. The main areas highlighted as being in need of reform were: various specific amendments to the Penal Code; modernisation of means of investigating organised crime and corruption; the adoption of certain multilateral instruments in the field of international cooperation and improvement in the quality of analytic assessment of organised crime and corruption (statistics). The Slovenian Government took notice of these recommendations and assigned specific tasks in order to implement them.[20]

In addition, Slovenia has more recently embarked on an effort to construct a more comprehensive anti-corruption strategy, partly in response to the recent GRECO findings (see Section 1.1). The Republic of Slovenia's National Programme for the Adoption of the *Acquis* by the end of 2002 identifies the need for 2002 PHARE assistance of €300,000 for the fight against corruption under the Justice and Home Affairs requirements regarding implementation of the *acquis* and strengthening of institutions. A pre-accession programme managed by Dutch experts is aiding the preparation of the Government anti-corruption strategy. The aim of the programme is to "assist in the development of an anti-corruption policy for Slovenia, with the emphasis on corruption prevention," and the programme places special emphasis on drawing together all relevant governmental and non-governmental organisations.[21]

Slovenia collaborates with the EU Anti-fraud Unit and other EU agencies in the field of Justice and Home Affairs, and has also participated in OCTOPUS I and OCTOPUS II, a two-part joint EU and Council of Europe Programme on the Fight against Corruption and Organised Crime in States in Transition (see above).[22] Slovenia is a founding member of the Council of Europe Group of States against Corruption (GRECO), and was the first country in the region to be evaluated (see above).[23]

Slovenia is also actively involved at the non-governmental level in the preparatory phase of the EU "Corpus Juris" project, which focuses *inter alia* on corruption in the

---

[20] See Republic of Slovenia's National Programme for the Adoption of the *Acquis* by the End of 2002, pp. 18–19, and amendments and supplements to this document from May 2001. On implementation, see also Commission, *2000 Regular Report*. All these documents are posted on <http://www.gov.si/svez/svez1ang.htm>, under "Documents," (last accessed 27 August 2002).

[21] Center International, *Terms of Reference 2001, Fight against Corruption,* Pre-accession programmes, September 2001.

[22] D. Kos, "Delovanje Sveta Evrope in EU na področju preprečevanja in obravnavanja korupcije" [Activities of the Council of Europe and the EU in Preventing and Handling Corruption], in: *Podjetje in Delo,* 6-7/2000, Ljubljana, pp. 1077–1088.

[23] GRECO, *Evaluation Report.*

context of the financial interests of the European Union. According to a recent report on the compatibility of Corpus Juris with the Slovenian legal system,[24] the substantive Criminal Code is harmonised with the *acquis*. However, proposals of the Corpus Juris concerning criminal procedure and international cooperation in criminal matters would require substantial changes in domestic legislation and even amendments to the Slovenian Constitution.

2. INSTITUTIONS AND LEGISLATION

2.1 Anti-corruption legislation

Slovenian bribery legislation is almost fully harmonised with the major international conventions: active and passive bribery are illegal both in the public and private sector, as is traffic in influence and electoral bribery, while recent legislation has established the criminal liability of legal entities for corruption:

- The penalty for requesting or accepting a bribe by a public official is one to five years' imprisonment. If the bribe is accepted in return for performance (or non-performance) of an official act that should (or should not) have been performed anyway, the sentence is up to three years' imprisonment. Passive bribery after the act has been performed (or not performed) is punishable by a fine or imprisonment of up to one year.[25]

- Giving or offering a bribe to a public official is punishable by up to three years' imprisonment. In cases where the bribe is given to perform an official act that an official should or may perform in any case the punishment prescribed is up to one year imprisonment.[26]

- Trafficking in influence by a public official is punishable by a fine or imprisonment of up to one year, but in more serious cases – where improper influence is made for a gift or other benefit and is exercised to induce on official

---

[24] D. Korošec, K. Šugman-Gotvan, M. Jager, "Penal and Administrative Sanctions, Settlement, Whistleblowing and Corpus Juris in the Candiate Countries: Slovenia Report, Corpus Iuris documents," ERA, Trier 2001 (CD-ROM).

[25] Penal Code, Article 267, paragraphs 1, 2, 3.

[26] Penal Code, Article 268.

act which should not have been performed in any case – the prescribed penalty is up to three years imprisonment.[27]

Under the Code of Criminal Procedure,[28] State bodies, public authorities and public officials must report all criminal offences that come to their attention and are subject to a penalty of three years' imprisonment or more. It is a criminal offence for a public official not to do so. However, the three-year threshold means that the only corruption offence to which this duty applies is request or acceptance of a bribe by a public official.

As of July 2002 Slovenia was in the process of ratifying the Council of Europe Civil Law Convention on Corruption, after new legal provisions came into effect in January 2002 that harmonised Slovenian law with the requirements of the Convention. In addition, the Act on the Responsibility of Legal Persons has introduced criminal responsibility of legal persons in cases of corruption crimes.[29]

2.2 Conflict of interest and asset declaration legislation

Provisions on conflict of interest and asset and income declarations exist and apply to executive officials, while ordinary officials are not much restricted in their ancillary activities. Neither the conflict of interest nor asset declaration provisions are effective in practice: although adherence to the provisions may be checked by superiors or a special Parliamentary (National Assembly) Commission, there are no real sanctions in practice for violation and the provisions appear to allow clear abuses of conflict of interest situations in practice. However, the Office for the Prevention of Corruption and the media have publicly exposed a number of cases of conflict of interest recently, resulting in several resignations of senior officials.

For the public sector issues of conflict of interest, monitoring of assets, receiving gifts and/or hospitality is regulated primarily by the Act on Incompatibility of Holding Public Office with a Profit-Making Activity (hereinafter, Incompatibility Act).[30] The Act applies to Members of Government, MPs, all functionaries holding an executive

---

[27] Penal Code, Article 269, paragraph 3.

[28] Code of Criminal Procedure, *Official Gazette* 63/94, 72/98.

[29] Act on the Criminal Liability of Legal Persons, *Official Gazette* 59/1999, 12/2000.

[30] Act on Incompatibilities of Holding Public Office with a Profit-Making Activity (AIHPOPMA), *Official Gazette* 49/1992, 10/1992. In addition, this area is partly regulated also by the Code of Conduct for Public Employees valid also for high officials of the executive, the Act on Government and the Act on Functionaries in State Bodies. For a general overview, see, e.g., K. Stroligo, "Slovenia: Ethics and Good Governance," *Journal of Financial Crime,* vol. 7, no. 2, 1999, pp. 188–190.

position in the State administration or local government, members of municipal councils and judges of the Court of Audit.

Functionaries covered under the Incompatibility Act may not in general hold other offices in State organs, courts, bodies of local administration; hold other public offices; conduct any other profit-making activities incompatible with their function; receive gifts in connection with the performance of their office; nor obtain any advantages that could affect their actions. The prohibition on profit-making activities and receipt of advantages also applies to spouses, children, parents, grandchildren and brothers and sisters living in a joint household.

Officials who do not hold office as a full-time job (i.e. some mayors) may perform a profit-making activity provided the activity does not negatively affect the performance of their functions and the nature of the activity does not create a conflict of interest. Ordinary civil servants are subject to the same rule.

The EU *2001 Regular Report* notes these legislative provisions, but adds that, "[P]reventing conflict of interest situations, including in public procurement, should be given more attention."[31] According to officials from the Office for the Prevention of Corruption, the conflict of interest legislation will be amended to widen the circle of officials governed by incompatibility provisions.[32]

Asset declarations

Functionaries covered by the Incompatibility Act are required to report their financial situation at the beginning and end of their term, every two years and upon specific request one year after the end of their term. The declarations must include gifts; functionaries in general must not receive gifts in connection with performance of their duties. Asset declarations are submitted to a special Commission of the Parliament: the information they contain on assets is not public, although salaries and other income received from the budget are public. The Commission is composed of seven members: the President of the Commission, four deputies of the Parliament and two deputies of the National Council.

If a functionary does not provide a declaration despite a warning made by the Commission, the Commission can only report this fact to the body of which the

---

[31] Commission, *2001 Regular Report,* p. 18.

[32] OSI Roundtable Discussion, Ljubljana, 19 February 2002. *Explanatory note: OSI held a roundtable meeting to invite critique of the present Report in draft form. Experts present included representatives of the Government, international organisations, and civil society organisations. References to this meeting should not be understood as an endorsement of any particular point of view by any one participant.*

official is a member or that elected or appointed him. In local self-government institutions, local commissions are formed to monitor local officials.

If the Commission concludes that a functionary has received gifts or acquired benefits that affected the performance of his functions, it notifies the body of which the official is a member or the body that elected or appointed him. If the body in question establishes that the allegations are grounded, it must initiate a procedure for dismissal.

If the Commission establishes that the financial situation of a certain official has "increased exceptionally," it must notify the same body. The Commission may demand information on the financial situation of an official from the tax authorities, which must provide the information. The same provision applies if the Commission establishes that the assets of family members living in the same household as the official have increased exceptionally. The body of which the official is a member can at any time request a report on his assets. During all these proceedings the Government official must be present to answer the Commission's questions.

In practice, neither the conflict of interest nor asset declaration provisions are effective. The conflict of interest provisions are highly formal, based on a strict "incompatibility" approach aimed (formally) at preventing combinations of functions, rather than focusing attention on conflict of interest problems as they arise in individual situations. In May 2002 it emerged that the Director of the Office for Consumer Protection awarded a contract to a company owned by her husband. No action was taken, as the action was not technically illegal, despite clearly violating the principle of conflict of interest.[33]

As of June 2002, new legislation was under preparation that would impose stricter sanctions for not complying with asset declaration provisions, but had not yet been submitted to Parliament.

2.4 Control and audit

Legislation on State financial control in Slovenia is relatively advanced. The Court of Audit is independent in theory and in practice, and is the only supreme audit institution among candidate States to control its own budget. Legislation has been in effect since 1999 to establish an integrated international financial control system in the State administration. However, the European Commission has recommended improvements in implementation, particularly increases in staff and strengthening the independence of internal auditors.

---

[33] Information provided by Ali Žerdin, Deputy Editor, *Mladina* weekly.

The Court of Audit

The Court of Audit began its work in 1995, and has ultimate responsibility for auditing State finances, the State budget and other public finances (including the budgets of local Governments, public funds, public agencies or services and recipients of EU subsidies). The Court applies the standards of the International Organisation of Supreme Audit Institutions (INTOSAI) and a newly enacted Court of Audit Act (CAA)[34] that is fully harmonised with the EU *acquis*.

The Court of Audit has three members (the President and two Deputy Presidents) and six supreme State auditors who head the audit units. In 2000, the Court employed a total of 56 auditors.[35] The members of the Court are elected by the Parliament upon the nomination of the President of the Republic for a term of nine years. The Parliament can remove a member of the Court of Audit if there are statutory grounds for removal. The president of the Court appoints the supreme State auditors for terms of nine years.

In the framework of CAA provisions, the Court of Audit is independent in choosing subjects to audit. In deciding its yearly plan of audits, the Court has to take into consideration the suggestions of MPs and Parliament's working bodies, the Government, ministries and the local government bodies. Under the CAA the Court must include in its yearly plan five suggestions from the Parliament, at least two suggestions of the opposition and at least two suggestions of the Parliament's working bodies. The CAA also stipulates that the Court is bound every year to audit the execution of the State budget, the Institute of Public Health (in the area of compulsory insurance), the Institute of Public Pension Insurance (in the area of compulsory insurance), a certain number of local governments and municipalities, a certain number of public service providers and a certain number of providers of non-economic public services.[36]

The work of the Court of Audit is public. At least once a year the Court reports to the Parliament about its work. The CAA requires that the particular audit reports be sent to the subject of audit, to the head of the subject of audit, to the Parliament and (optionally) to other State institutions that the President of the Court decides to inform. In case the Court finds severe violations of regulations it issues an appeal to discharge the head of institution and a report to the public. The Court also notifies the Parliament. The relevant Committee of the Parliament discusses such reports and issues a decision on the measures that have to be imposed on the institution in question.

---

[34] Court of Audit Act (CAA), *Official Gazette* 11/2001.

[35] See, Court of Audit website <http://www.sigov.si/racs/druge00.htm>, (last accessed 27 August 2002).

[36] CAA, Article 25.

However, although the Court's audit findings are used by journalists as a valuable source of information, in general its findings do not appear to be used by Parliament in order to impose corrective measures, although recent amendments to the Act on the Court of Audit have provided for more established mechanisms for use by Parliament of the COA's audit reports. In the six years since its existence, the Court of Audit has reported only 15 criminal offences to the police.[37]

If it has "grounded suspicion" that an administrative offence has been committed, the Court of Audit must by law initiate proceedings at the court of administrative offences. Beside the general obligation under the CCP to notify suspected criminal offences to the police, the CAA (Article 30) specifically prescribes that reporting suspected crimes to the competent authorities is obligatory if there is "grounded suspicion" that a criminal offence (for example corruption) has been committed. In case of suspicion of an administrative or criminal offence the CAA also enables the Court of Audit to seize the relevant incriminatory documentation for a period of eight days. As already explained above in case of such severe violations the Court must also issue a report to the public, inform the Parliament and/or demand the dismissal of the responsible person. The institution concerned may or may not remove the person from office, but in either case it has to inform the Court about its decision in writing within 15 days.

In January 2001, a new Act on the Court of Audit came into effect, which further strengthened the independence of the COA by removing its budget from parliamentary control. The amendments reduced the number of members of the Court to three, increased the powers of the President, removed the Court's remaining judicial powers and provided for more systematic use of the Court's reports by Parliament. The Court now audits the use of EC funds all the way to the final recipients, helping to confirm the statement by the Commission in its *2001 Regular Report* that, "External audit in Slovenia is largely satisfactory."[38]

Internal control

Under the 1999 Act on Public Finance (hereinafter APF),[39] all State organisations must have a system of internal control and revision and a system of procedures and responsibilities of employees within each agency receiving budget funds. By early 2002, all ministries had established internal audit units. Responsibility for supervision of internal financial control and establishment of harmonised procedures and rules lies with the Budget Supervisory Service (BSS) at the Ministry of Finance. The BSS

---

[37] B. Habjan, paper presented at the colloquium "Korupcija kot realnost današnjega časa," Gotenica, May 2001.

[38] Commission, *2001 Regular Report*, p. 86.

[39] Act on Public Finance (APF), *Official Gazette* 79/1999.

conducts budgetary inspections and revisions in bodies or agencies that receive budget funds. The budgetary inspector has (among other powers) statutory authority to suspend *ex ante* the use of budgetary funds and to mandate the return of illegally spent funds to the budget.

The effectiveness of the internal control system is difficult to assess, as it is still in the process of being established. However, according to the EU internal financial control, it "should be improved,"[40] and the *2001 Regular Report* recommended a number of measures including increases in staff and strengthening of the functional independence of internal auditors.

2.5 Anti-corruption agencies

The Office for the Prevention of Corruption

As Section outlined in 1.3, the Government Office for the Prevention of Corruption has since July 2001 been preparing a draft national anti-corruption strategy and Act on Prevention of Corruption. The Office is not independent of the Government, and until recently did not appear to have played any active role in initiating corruption cases or implementing any specific anti-corruption policies. However, the Office has recently analysed several cases of privatisation (for example, the privatisation of Triglav insurance company and the management buyout at BTC), along with corruption in the non-profit sector (including humanitarian organisations), and the pharmaceuticals sector. From 15 October 2001 to 23 July 2002 the Office received reports of 112 cases of suspected corruption, and as of the end of July 2002 had forwarded 39 cases to the police. The Office has also played an active role in several recent cases of suspected corruption and conflicts of interest, notably the following:[41]

- The President of a district court hired her husband's company to assist in the relocation of the court (see Section 5.2).

- The Director of the Office for Gaming Supervision allegedly asked for favours from a casino (he resigned).

- A district State prosecutor hired his partner as head of his office (he was discharged).

---

[40] Commission, *2001 Regular Report*, p. 86.

[41] For more information on these cases see: "Najbolj smrdi v zdravstvu" [Health care stinks the worst], *Delo*, 25 July, 2002; "Disciplinski ukrep: Izprašaj si vest!" [Disciplinary measure: examine your conscience!] , *Delo*, 13 June, 2002; "Razlogi so drugje" [The reasons are elsewhere], *Delo*, 19 April, 2002; "Podjetni javni uslužbenci" [Business-motivated public employees], *Dnevnik*, 12 July, 2002.

- A State undersecretary at the Ministry of Defence allegedly maintained his position as director of a private company (the case was under disciplinary proceedings as of July 2002).

- The Director of the Office for Consumer Protection awarded a contract to a company where her husband was a director and shareholder (she was discharged).

The Office also recently financed a large corruption victimisation survey.

The police

Since 2000 the police has been restructured significantly to facilitate investigation of corruption. However, in some cases there are reasons for doubting the independence and effectiveness of both prosecutors and police, and police investigations appear to be vulnerable to political pressure, at least in sensitive high-level cases. An office of the ombudsman has been established since 1994, but has not dealt with any cases of corruption.

In April 2000, the police created special anti-corruption divisions at both central and regional level to investigate corruption crimes.[42] The central Anti-corruption Division is supposed to plan, organise, direct and supervise investigation activities in the following areas: corruption in State authorities; corruption in authorities and organisations with public authorisation; corruption in obtaining and granting public investment works, investment purchases, concessions, financial subsidies and credits; trading in influence; and other corruption offences.[43]

The number of officers serving in the central division has increased since the publication of the GRECO *Evaluation Report*. The number of officers working in regional divisions is planned to be 25, but in early 2002 the units were only 50-60 percent occupied. The GRECO Report also criticised an unclear division of responsibilities between the police, prosecutors and investigating judges: cooperation in criminal proceedings appears to depend mostly on good personal contacts between the police and prosecutors, and the Report pointed out that, "[A] negative atmosphere between the police and the Public Prosecutor… could lead to a complete collapse of criminal investigations."[44] It should be

---

[42] The State-level anti-corruption division is one of five divisions in the Organized Crime section of the Criminal Police Directorate. The Criminal Police Directorate is part of a General Police Directorate headed by the Director-General of the police. On the need to introduce such units, see D. Kos, "The Setting up of Special National Services for the Fight Against Corruption – Slovenia's Point of View," in: *Corruption in Central and Eastern Europe at the Turn of Millennium – A Collection of Essays,* Open Society Institute Slovenia, Ljubljana 1999, pp. 129–135.

[43] Point 2.3.3.4 of the Regulation on Organisation and Systemisation of Working Places at the Ministry of Interior and the Police.

[44] GRECO, *Evaluation Report,* p. 13.

noted that the importance of and reliance on good personal contacts could clearly be dysfunctional in the case of corruption investigations.

Significantly, the Report also noted that the Government appoints prosecutors, and career prospects depend largely on decisions taken by the Ministry of Justice. Most worryingly, the report stated that, "[GRECO] was informed that investigations on high-level cases had been hampered, delayed or brought to an end through pressure put on police officers in charge of the investigation."[45] One possible example of such pressure is provided by an investigation initiated several years ago into the financing of the Slovenian People's Party. Senior officials involved in anti-corruption policy regard the subsequent departure of all the officers involved in the investigation as a sign of likely political pressure.[46]

The European Commission has welcomed the introduction of specialised anti-corruption divisions, and no additional requests or suggestions have been made in this area.

The Office of Money-Laundering Prevention

According to the EC, Slovenian money-laundering legislation is in line with the *acquis.* The Office of Money-Laundering Prevention (OMLP), which began functioning in 1995 as a unit of the Ministry of Finance, receives information from entities required to report specific transactions under the law, and may order postponement of transactions for up to 48 hours. According to the OMLP, the number of money laundering cases has been increasing, and in 2000, the Office investigated 95 suspicious transactions totalling €49.5m. Money laundering was connected in particular to all kinds of illegal trafficking, as well as to different forms of corruption and tax fraud.[47]

2.6 Ombudsman

The Human Rights ombudsman was established in December 1993, and the first ombudsman was elected in September 1994. The ombudsman is elected by a two-thirds majority of votes of both houses of Parliament upon nomination by the President of the Republic, and may be re-elected once. The ombudsman may be removed only at his/her own request, on conviction for a criminal act, permanent loss of ability to perform the office, or by the proposal of one-third of MPs and a two-

---

[45] GRECO, *Evaluation Report,* p. 12.

[46] OSI Roundtable Discussion, Ljubljana, 19 February 2002.

[47] See, e.g., "Primerov pranja denarja je vse več" [The number of cases of money laundering is increasing], *Delo,* 27 March 2001.

thirds vote of all MPs present. At the beginning of 2001, the ombudsman had three deputies and 20 staff.

The ombudsman may not hold any office in the State administration, local government, political parties, and trade unions or perform any other activity incompatible by law with public office. The ombudsman enjoys immunity for both opinions and proposals expressed during the performance of duties, and may not be subject to any criminal proceedings for actions performed during the performance of duty without the prior consent of the Parliament.

On the basis of complaints from citizens or its own initiative, the ombudsman may monitor all State bodies, local authorities and bodies entrusted with public authority apart from judges and courts (except in cases of improper procedural delays or abuse of power).[48] Institutions must provide the office with any information requested regardless of the level of confidentiality, and the ombudsman may call witnesses and experts for questioning.

After an investigation, the ombudsman may: submit an opinion, suggestions and recommendations, to which the institution must respond within the deadline set by the office; propose disciplinary proceedings; file complaints to the Constitutional Court, and request that the Court assess the constitutionality of regulations. The ombudsman reports in detail on all his activities annually to Parliament; the reports are public and available on the Internet.[49]

In 2000, the ombudsman received more than 3,000 complaints, one-third of which related to court and police proceedings.[50] The office has not dealt with any major cases of corruption.[51]

3. EXECUTIVE BRANCH AND CIVIL SERVICE

Until recently, reform of the Slovenian public administration had been limited. Laws in effect have not distinguished between political and career appointments sufficiently

---

[48] The Human Rights Ombudsman Act (HROA), *Official Gazette* 71/1993, 15/1994, Article 1.

[49] See <http://www.varuh-rs.si>, (last accessed 28 August 2002).

[50] See *Human Rights Ombudsman 2000 Annual Report,* Office of the Human Rights Ombudsman, Ljubljana, May 2001.

[51] One case in 1996 aroused suspicions concerning the way in which agricultural subsidies were distributed. The Ministry of Agriculture amended its regulations in response to the Ombudsman's recommendations.

strictly, patronage appears to have been common and there have been no restrictions on political party activities of civil servants. Moreover, there is evidence that procedures for appealing against administrative decisions are too time-consuming and costly to be effective. However, major public administration reform took place in June 2002 with the passage of a comprehensive package of laws. A Code of Conduct for civil servants was adopted in 2001. The new legislation will limit political appointments and make competitive selection procedures compulsory, although the provisions will not start to come into effect until mid-2003. There is very little evidence of corruption in the executive branch or civil service, with the exception of a case against one State secretary, still in proceedings. However, conflicts of interest appear to be an important problem, especially at local government level.

3.1 Structure and Legislative Framework

The public administration (central and local) is regulated by various legal acts. For the purposes of this report, the most important (beside Constitutional provisions) include the Acts on State Administration,[52] on Employees in State Bodies,[53] on General Administrative Procedure[54] and on Administrative Disputes.[55]

At present, the personnel of the State administration of the central Government can be divided into two main categories. The first group is comprised of the political functionaries: the Prime Minister, ministers, State secretaries in various ministries, the Secretary-General of the Prime Minister's Office and the heads of special Government agencies offices (like the Intelligence and Security Agency, Government Office for Legislation, etc.). The second group consists of career civil servants. The status of the first group is regulated by the Act on Government[56] and the Act on Functionaries in State Bodies.[57] It is not illegal for members of the second group to be part of the leadership of a political party, with the exception of the police or armed forces.

---

[52] Act on State Administration, *Official Gazette* 52/02.

[53] Act on Employees in State Bodies (AESB), *Official Gazette* 15/1990, 5/1991, 18/1991, 22/1991, 2/1991-I, 4/1993, 18/94 70/1997, 38/1999.

[54] General Administrative Procedure Act (GAPA), *Official Gazette* 80/1999, 70/00, 52/02.

[55] Act on Administrative Disputes (AAD), *Official Gazette* 50/97, 65/97, 70/00.

[56] Act on Government (AG), *Official Gazette* 4/1993, 23/1996, 47/1997, 119/00.

[57] Act on Functionaries in State Bodies (AFSB), *Official Gazette* 30/1990, 18/1991, 22/1991, 2/1991-I, 4/1993.

Under the Slovenian Constitution, appointments to the civil service must be made via a public selection procedure except in cases defined by law.[58] However, public selection procedures are sometimes avoided, particularly for higher civil service positions, and the media has published information on the practice of "political hiring."[59] After changes of Government, many new people were appointed as State secretaries and directors of various governmental and semi-governmental agencies and other high executive posts, many of which were professional by nature, such as directors of tax or customs administrations, senior civil servants, or directors of public enterprises.[60]

The EC has continuously stressed the need for convincing progress on overall public administration reform.[61] In June 2002, Parliament passed a package of important new laws: the Act on State Administration,[62] Act on Public Agencies,[63] Act on Inspections,[64] Act on Public Employees,[65] and Act on Salaries in the Public Sector.[66] These laws form the bulk of public administration reform. The Act on Public Employees makes public competitive selection procedures mandatory for selection of all civil servants and contains sanctions for not complying with public selection mechanisms including the nullification of the employment contract.[67] Implementation of the provisions of this Act will begin in July 2003, while the provisions of the Act on Salaries will start being implemented in January 2004. Under the new Act on State Administration the only functions that remain political are: the Prime Minister, ministers, the Secretary-General of the Government and (optionally) one State secretary per ministry.[68]

---

[58] Constitution of the Republic of Slovenia, Articles 120, 121, 122.

[59] "Vladno kadrovanje pod lupo" [Government's hiring under scrutiny], *Delo,* 13 July 2001.

[60] See, e.g., Economist Intelligence Unit, *Slovenia Country Profile 2001–2002,* p. 11.

[61] See, e.g., Commission, *2000 Regular Report,* pp. 14–15.

[62] Act on State Administration, *Official Gazette* 52/02.

[63] Act on Public Agencies, *Official Gazette* 52/02.

[64] Act on Inspections, *Official Gazette* 56/02.

[65] Act on Public Employees, *Official Gazette* 56/02

[66] Act on the System of Salaries in the Public Sector, *Official Gazette* 56/02.

[67] Act on Public Employees, Articles 74–77. See also "Kovanje uradniške elite" [Creation of a Civil Service Elite], *Delo,* Saturday enclosure, 10 November 2001.

[68] Act on State Administration, Article 17.

3.2 Administrative procedure and redress

Under the Slovenian Constitution, any person may sue the Government and demand compensation for damages suffered as a result of the wrongful actions by any government body, local government body or other statutory authority.[69]

Under the Act on Administrative Disputes citizens may appeal against administrative decisions first to the body issuing the decision and thereafter to administrative courts, which were established in 1998. The courts may review both the legality and substance of decisions, and the Supreme Court is the final arbiter of such disputes.

Although judicial review of administrative decisions is guaranteed as a constitutional right, in practice the procedure can take a long time and is very costly in some cases.[70]

3.3 Conflict of interest and asset monitoring

As noted in Section 2.2, the Incompatibility Act applies only to Government executive functionaries and other functionaries that hold an executive position on State or local Government level, to MPs and to members of local municipal councils.

Under the Act on Employees in State Bodies, senior civil servants may not accept external employment except in independent scientific, pedagogical, cultural, sport, humanitarian or publicist activities.[71] All other State employees may accept any external employment subject to the written approval of their superior.

However, ordinary civil servants are free to own private companies that do business with the agency for whom they work. According to media reports, the Government intends to widen the sphere of functionaries to whom the Act applies.[72]

---

[69] Constitution of the Republic of Slovenia, *Official Gazette* 333/1991, 42/1997, 66/2000, Article 26.

[70] The media reported a privatisation case where an individual appealed against an allegedly corrupt decision. The case was not completed in mid-2001, seven years after its initiation, and the individual concerned stated that the procedure had so far cost him €27,000. See "Neomajen boj za resnico: V letih, ko se je boril za pravico, si je nabral za več kot šest milijonov tolarjev dolga" [The unlimited fight for justice: in years of fighting for his rights he ran up a debt of six million tolars], *Dnevnik,* 16 May 2001.

[71] AESB, Article 27.

[72] "Krog se sicer širi, a bo obseg še premajhen" [The circle widens but not enough], *Delo,* 9 August 2001.

In January 2001, the Government adopted a Code of Conduct for civil servants,[73] which fully adopts Council of Europe recommendations. The Code establishes guidelines for the interaction of officials with citizens, conflicts of interest, acceptance of gifts and post-public service employment, and is binding for ministers and other functionaries.[74] Breach of the Code of Conduct can trigger disciplinary proceedings, as its provisions form part of the general conditions of employment for civil servants. The Code forbids officials to accept or demand gifts or benefits that could influence or appear to influence the performance of duties, with the exception of conventional hospitality and minor gifts. The Code also regulates in detail the proper reaction to improper offers and prohibits various kinds of conflict of interest, putting oneself in a position of obligation to return a favour and misuse of public office.

Under the Code, a civil servant should also avoid the possibility of a conflict of interest arising from the prospect of future employment outside civil service, and is obliged to report to his superior any such employment offer that could create a conflict of interest. In addition civil servant should not "for an appropriate period of time" act or advise in matters in which they were involved as a civil servant, nor use or disclose confidential information acquired as a civil servant.

Regulations on asset declarations are also covered in Section 2.2. In practice, senior Governmental officials sometimes do not submit reports on their assets to the Parliamentary Commission as required by the Incompatibility Act.

The media has also reported a number of irregularities among local government functionaries. These cases typically involve alleged "soft" improper influences, connections, family ties and political party connections and often involve conflict of interest as defined by the Incompatibility Act. In such cases, the local Commissions in charge of supervising conflict of interest provisions in many cases either do not receive the data or remain passive.[75] One case investigated by a private TV station of irregularities in construction permits involved a situation where the head of an Office for Urban Planning was also a manager of a construction company to whom he awarded permits.[76]

---

[73] Code of Conduct of Public Employees, *Official Gazette* 8/2001.

[74] The Conclusion of the Government, *Official Gazette* 8/2001, 18 January 2001.

[75] See, e.g., "Do kod sežejo obalne korupcijske zgodbe" [Where do the seaside corruption stories end?], *Dnevnik*, 12 December 2000; "Sporna navodila iz županove pisarne" [Questionable guidelines from the Mayor's Office], *Delo*, 4 April 2001.

[76] Interview with Borut Meško, journalist, POP TV, 19 February 2001.

3.4 Internal control mechanisms

Under the Act on Employees of State Bodies, a civil servant convicted of bribery is subject to mandatory termination of employment, may be suspended during criminal proceedings, and may be held liable for damages.

Under the Code of Conduct, a superior is responsible and accountable for the conduct of subordinates if he or she has not taken reasonable steps to prevent them, and must take steps to prevent corruption such as education and training, be alert to signs of financial or other difficulties of subordinates, and set a personal example. The superior is also responsible for initiating disciplinary proceeding against civil servants who fail to comply with the Code.

According to the Code of Conduct, each civil servant is bound to report all illegal, wrongful or non-ethical conduct to the "competent bodies." The Code does not require that such reports about alleged transgressions be made to the superior first. If a civil servant believes that the response of the competent body is inadequate, a written complaint may be submitted to the head of that body. If a criminal offence is suspected, the civil servant is bound to report his suspicions and evidence to the competent body (police/State Prosecutor).

The Code of Conduct obliges the public administration to protect whistleblowers who reported on reasonable grounds and in good faith. In practice, whistle blowing has been rare, although the effect of the new Code of Conduct remains to be seen.

In practice, an important defect of Slovenian public administration appears to be inadequate internal supervision and control. The great majority of cases of corruption are discovered by the media or the police through the initiative of individual citizens, not by the administration itself. Disciplinary proceedings and suspensions tend to take place only after the case has been initiated or made public.

3.5 Interaction with the public

Various provisions on how civil servants must interact with the public are contained in the Acts listed in Section 3.1. However, the Code of Conduct is the most important provision in this respect. In addition to the provisions mentioned above, civil servants are expected to be honest, impartial and to act with courtesy to all with whom they have contact; are forbidden from acting arbitrarily to the detriment of any person, group or body; and must respect both the right of access to official information as well as confidentiality where relevant.[77]

---

[77] Code of Conduct for Civil Servants, Articles 4–11.

3.6 Corruption

Although the Commission's *Regular Reports* continuously stress the need for public administration reform to create "more professional, impartial, efficient and effective civil service,"[78] according to the Commission, the Executive "continues to operate smoothly"[79] and corruption has not been raised as an issue. However, there exists both direct and indirect evidence of corruption in the executive branch and civil service.

The most well-known case was the conviction in early 2002 in the court of first instance of a State secretary in the Ministry of Economic Affairs for bribery in the allocation of a subsidy. The State secretary headed a special commission at the Ministry that allocated subsidies to small and medium-sized companies. According to media reports, one entrepreneur who was to pay a €35,000 kickback reported the case to the police. The official was sentenced to three years' imprisonment, but as of June 2002, the Court of Appeal had overturned the conviction and the outcome of the case was uncertain. The media has suggested that in previous cases bribes were disguised as payments for fictional research projects or in other ways.[80]

No research project exists focusing specifically on corruption in the civil service. At the same time, a number of *ad hoc* surveys by newspapers indicate that citizens perceive corruption to be relatively high in this area.[81]

Areas where corruption is felt to be more widespread include the so-called Decentralised Administrative Units (bodies of the ministries organised in regions with one or more local communities to perform administrative tasks) and local municipalities. An especially vulnerable area appears to be town planning, with regard to which media reports on corruption are continuous.[82] For example, evidence and allegations supplied to the reporter indicate that ties between the construction industry in Ljubljana and town planning officials have reached serious proportions, with officials in the City Planning Department often signing permits for construction companies of which they are owners or directors. In July 2001, a Slovene inhabitant of

---

[78] Commission, *1998, 1999* and *2000 Regular Reports.*

[79] Commission, *1998 Regular Report*, p. 8.

[80] See, e.g., "Korupcija" [Corruption], *Mladina* weekly, 11 November 2000; "Minister ni kriminalist" [The Minister is not a criminal investigator], *Dnevnik,* 22 November 2000.

[81] See, e.g., "Kje se začne korupcija" [Where Corruption Begins], *Dnevnik,* 19 March 1999.

[82] See, e.g., "Sumljiva kuverta" [The Suspicious Envelope], *Dnevnik,* 18 August 2000; "Gradnjo je preprečila korupcija" [The Course of construction obstructed by corruption], *Delo,* 12 April 2001; "Je denar urbanizma vladar?" [Does money rule urbanism?], *Delo,* 24 August 2000; "Rekorderji spornih gradenj" [Record holders of contestable constructions], *Mladina,* 7 May 2001.

Ljubljana filed an application to the European Court of Human Rights concerning "rife corruption" in the city and in particular focusing on ties between ZIL Inženiring construction company and the City Planning Department.[83] The applicant alleges that a clique built around the company and senior city officials not only has perpetuated corruption in city planning and the issue of permits, but also has prevented programmes being run on both public and private television and has influenced the police to intimidate him.

4. LEGISLATURE

All public expenditure in Slovenia is included in the State budget approved by Parliament, although there is room to improve the effectiveness of State audit. Available evidence suggests that corruption is not a serious problem, although Parliament is the least trusted public institution in surveys. On the other hand, the inadequacy of conflict of interest and asset declaration provisions and the absence of any provisions to regulate lobbying makes assessment of this area difficult.

4.1 Elections

Slovenian elections are considered free and fair by all international institutions. The State Electoral Commission (together with local electoral commissions) organises and supervises the conduct of elections. The six-member Commission is appointed by the Parliament, and its President and Vice-President must be judges of the Supreme Court.

4.2 Budget and control mechanisms

All significant categories of public expenditure require parliamentary approval as part of the State budget. Budget control mechanisms are discussed in Section 2.4: as stated in that section, the effectiveness of State audit could be improved.

---

[83] Application by Iztok Šterbenc to the European Court of Human Rights concerning "severe violations of human rights and life endangerment," 18 July 2001. Interview with Iztok Šterbenc, Ljubljana, 19 February 2002. Other journalists support the allegations: Borut Meško, a journalist at private TV station POP TV, was prevented from continuing reporting on a case because of advertising pressure by the construction company concerned (interview with Borut Meško, Ljubljana, 19 February 2002).

4.3 Conflict of interest and asset monitoring

Conflict of interest and monitoring of assets of deputies are regulated by the Incompatibility Act (see Section 2.2) and are largely ineffective as a deterrent sanction.

4.4 Immunity

MPs may not be held criminally liable for opinions or votes cast. Moreover, they may not be investigated or prosecuted for certain criminal acts, including corruption, if the maximum prescribed sentence is up to five years without the authorisation of the Parliament. The Parliament Commission for Mandate and Immunities considers requests from prosecutors for lifting immunity and submits an opinion to the Parliament. Up to the end of 2000, the Commission had dealt with 13 cases, none of which were corruption-related.[84]

4.5 Corruption

The EU has never considered the Slovenian Parliament to be problematic with respect to corruption. However, in public opinion polls it is the least trusted of all institutions surveyed.[85] Nevertheless, in the past two years there have been no explicit cases of corruption, although on several occasions media attention was attracted by MPs switching sides just before important votes.

In the 1999 EBRD/World Bank *Business Environment and Enterprise Performance Survey* (see Section 1.1), only eight percent of Slovenian firms reported that the sale of parliamentary votes or presidential decrees had a significant impact on their business.[86] However, in the absence of any regulation of lobbying and a low degree of party discipline, there is little to prevent such influence, and more detailed research would be required to assess the real extent of external influence on MPs.

---

[84] GRECO, *Evaluation Report,* pp. 10–11.

[85] *Human Development Report Slovenia 2000–2001,* pp. 53–56.

[86] *Human Development Report Slovenia 2000–2001,* p. 119, Chart 6.3.

5. JUDICIARY

Slovenia has gone a long way towards creating an independent judicial branch, and reform has been consistently high on the Government's agenda. However, concerns persist over the extent of judicial independence, and current proposals for changes in the composition of the Judicial Council could undermine its independence. Although there is virtually no evidence of corruption among judges, court delays are a serious problem.

5.1 Legislative framework

Judges are appointed for life by the Parliament upon the proposal of the Judicial Council.[87] The majority of members (i.e., six) of the Judicial Council are judges elected by their peers.

There are a number of areas of concern, including several of relevance to corruption:[88]

- Parliament and the Government display a lack of commitment to full judicial independence. Some officials have advocated abolishing life tenure, and in 2001 a government commission for Constitutional Changes proposed introducing a five-year probation period after which tenure would be subject to approval by the Judicial Council.

- Disciplinary proceedings are confidential, and few judges have been convicted of disciplinary transgressions. Amendments to the Act on Judicial Service passed in July 2002 introduced extensive, more detailed provisions on disciplinary responsibility and disciplinary proceedings for judges.[89]

- Although the amended Act on Judicial Service prohibits judges from receiving gifts or benefits in connection with their work, until recently judges did not have to submit asset or income declarations. The introduction of such declarations has been recommended both by the Open Society Institute and the GRECO *Evaluation Report*.[90]

---

[87] For a detailed description of the legislative framework for the Slovenian judiciary, see EU Accession Monitoring Program, *Monitoring the EU Accession Process: Judicial Independence,* Open Society Institute, Budapest, 2001, pp. 434–472. Available at <http://www.eumap.org>.

[88] Open Society Institute, *Monitoring the EU Accession Process: Judicial Independence,* pp. 434–436.

[89] Amendments to the Act on Judicial Service, *Official Gazette* 67/02.

[90] GRECO, *Evaluation Report,* p. 17.

The GRECO Report also expressed concern that, given the fact that judges are allowed to be members of political parties, the system of election of judges by the Parliament could lead to politically motivated choices and impair judicial independence.[91]

Basic principles concerning independence, impartiality, incompatibility with other offices and conflict of interest are also laid down in a new Code of Judicial Conduct adopted by the Slovenian Association of Judges in June 2001.

Decisions of the Supreme Court, Constitutional Court and European Courts are regularly published in a special publication and online. Domestic case law is also available online. Important decisions of higher courts are expected to be published regularly in the near future. Trials are as a general rule open to the public. In criminal cases anyone with a "legitimate interest" may have access to a case file.[92]

Some of the reforms proposed by the Government during 2001–2002 do not appear likely to improve the situation of the judiciary, and may in fact undermine independence. These include in particular the introduction of a five-year probationary period for judges and an increase in the influence of the Ministry of Justice and Parliament in the Judicial Council.[93]

5.2 Corruption

There have been no publicly exposed cases of corruption in the judiciary in the past three years, and media coverage suggests that such cases are extremely rare.[94] Recently the President of a district court resigned after it was revealed that she had hired her husband's firm to assist in moving the court to another location.

The European Commission has not mentioned corruption in the judiciary. However, a major concern in the Commission's *Regular Reports* and for EC officials is the problem of judicial backlogs. The *2001 Regular Report* acknowledged significant progress in cutting backlogs in civil cases, partly as a result of reforms to the Act on Judicial Service passed in May 2001, which facilitated the "Hercules" project involving rotation of judges to assist overburdened courts.

---

[91] GRECO, *Evaluation Report,* p. 14.

[92] CCP, Article 128, paragraph 1.

[93] See EU Accession Monitoring Program, *Judicial Capacity in Slovenia,* (forthcoming).

[94] In one high profile criminal case covered by the media in the mid-1990's, the judge delayed judgement until a case fell under the statute of limitations. The case received enormous public attention and the judge resigned.

However, the *2001 Regular Report* also noted that there had been no improvement in criminal cases, around 60 percent of which take more than a year. Moreover, queues at the land register have been increasing, although a project to computerise the register is in progress.

6. POLITICAL PARTY FINANCE

Political party funding is regulated by quite strict and detailed rules, with restrictions on donations and expenditures. Parties receive significant subsidies from the State budget. However, parties appear to be able to circumvent the rules with relative ease, while violations of the provisions (revealed by Court of Audit supervision) has not resulted in any sanctions against parties. A number of cases of covert financing have come to light, and the increased indebtedness of some parties may increase the danger that parties turn to illegal sources of funding.

6.1 Legislative framework

Political party financing is subject to rather strict and detailed regulations, although parties appear to be able to get around the provisions with relative ease.

Funding of political parties is regulated by the Act on Political Parties[95] and campaign funding by the Act on Election Campaigns.[96] The main provisions for financing in general are as follows:

- Political parties may receive funds from the State budget, membership fees, donations from individuals or legal persons, property income, inheritances, and profits from a company it owns (which may only be in the area of culture or publishing).

- Annual income from property and a subsidiary company may not exceed 20 percent of total income.

- The following sources of income are prohibited: contributions, donations or legacies from foreign entities; income from property abroad; any other funds or services from abroad; funds from State authorities, public institutions, public companies, authorities of local communities, humanitarian organisations,

---

[95] Act on Political Parties (APP), *Official Gazette* 62/94, 1/99, 70/00.
[96] Electoral Campaign Act (ECA), *Official Gazette* 62/1994, 17/1997.

religious communities and business entities in which the State or public authority owns more than a 50 percent stake.

- Contributions from individuals or legal persons must not exceed ten times the average monthly wage. The party's annual financial report must include data about entities that donated more than three times the monthly wage in any given year, including the total amount donated.

Political parties receive funds from the State budget according to the following rules:

- The total State subsidy is defined as 0.017 percent of GDP in the previous year.

- Parties that won at least one percent of the vote and nominated candidates in at least two-thirds of electoral districts receive funds from the budget receive ten percent of total State funding in equal shares, while the other 90 percent is allocated in proportion to the total number of votes received.[97]

- The result of this system in 2002 is that parties receive the following amounts: Liberal Democracy of Slovenia, €882,000; Social Democratic Party, €396,000; United List of Social Democrats, €306,0000; Slovenian People's Party, €247,500; New Slovenia-Christian People's Party, €234,000; Democratic Party of Slovenian Pensioners, €144,000; Slovenian National Party, €130,500; Slovenian Youth Party, €130,500.[98]

According to parties' official financial reports, the bulk of their funding comes from the State budget. Parties can also receive funding from local municipality budgets in proportion to the votes cast in their favour.[99]

Under the Election Campaign Act

- Expenses for both national and municipal elections may not exceed €0.27 per voter in a given constituency or electoral territory.[100] The penalty for exceeding this amount by more than ten percent is a 50 percent reduction of the funds the party is entitled to receive from the budget for the period from six months to one year. If campaign expenses exceed the limit by 20 percent, the party loses the right to any State funding for a period of six months to one year,[101] as decided by the Court of Audit.

---

[97] APP, Article 23.

[98] "Koliko glasov, toliko denarcev" [As much money as votes], *Delo,* 22 January 2002.

[99] For details, see APP, Article 16.

[100] The ECA defines expenses for the electoral campaign as expenses for printing and hanging posters, advertisements and notices in public media, organization of pre-election rallies and printing materials to be sent directly to voters.

[101] ECA, Article 30a.

- All funding for electoral campaigns must be collected and spent from a single special account established at least 45 days before the elections.

- Parties that won seats in the Parliament are also entitled to a State contribution to election expenses of €0.27 per vote; the total amount of reimbursement however may not exceed actual expenses as reported by the Court of Audit.[102]

6.2 Control and supervision

Every party must submit to Parliament an annual financial report including all income and expenses. The report must include all contributions that exceeded three times the average monthly wage and their source; data on election expenditures; changes in assets including the sources of any increase where the assets provided by one entity exceed five times the average monthly wage. Before submission to Parliament the report is audited by the Court of Audit, whose evaluation and comments are attached.

Parties that in the previous year received any funds from State or local budgets or private contributions in excess of the amount of three average monthly wages are obliged to publish a shorter version of their report in the *Official Gazette* by 30 April. If such a report is not forthcoming, funding from the State or local budget is suspended until submission.

Organisers of election campaigns (usually a political party itself) are obliged to submit an interim report on campaign expenses 11 days before the elections. A final report must be submitted to the Parliament (or local Council in case of local elections) and to the Court of Audit within 30 days following the elections. Within three months, the Court of Audit must carry out a full audit of all campaign organisers who have the right to claim partial reimbursement of expenses. The Court must verify the accuracy of data on campaign finance provided in the reports, the legality of the way these funds were collected and used and the accuracy of the amount claimed for reimbursement. The COA's final report is published in the *Parliamentary Bulletin*.

Under the Election Campaign Act, the COA can impose a fine on campaign organisers for violation of the above rules at a minimum of €4,500, while the minimum fine for responsible individuals is €450. The only other sanction is publicity.

---

[102] ECA, Article 21.

6.3 Party finance in practice

According to the Court of Audit, in the October 2000 parliamentary elections no party obeyed the Financing Act, and a number of parties violated the Act seriously. One party used 36 accounts and another 45 to finance its campaign, despite the explicit provision mandating a single account.[103] No party was seriously fined or otherwise sanctioned for this. Five complaints against responsible individuals were filed for administrative offences.[104]

Another recent affair, in which the media reported that the United List of Social Democrats (now in the governing coalition) received €24,758 from a British foundation for the 2000 electoral campaign, drew attention to the ways in which parties may bypass the financing law.[105] The funding from abroad was provided not to the party directly (which is illegal) but to a little known association run by party members and functionaries. Other political parties remained more-or-less silent on the issue.[106]

Other scandals surrounding donations to parties concern events that happened in the early to mid-1990s. In 2001, POP TV broadcast allegations that slaughter company Koto provided around €1.95m to Liberal Democracy of Slovenia in the 1992 parliamentary elections through a Swiss subsidiary named Costello, and that the Government had paid the company significantly more for slaughter services than in other European countries. In September 2001, *Zeleni Slovenije* (the Green Party) filed a notification to the Public Prosecutor's Office in Ljubljana of criminal offences against the Government and several ministers in connection with the case. The State Prosecutor did not initiate any proceedings.[107]

Another case, which did not involve any violation of the party financing law, was the financing by pharmaceuticals giant LEK of the Slovenian People's Party in 1992. LEK

---

[103] *Poročilo računskega sodišča RS o reviziji poslovanja organizatorjev volilne kampanje,* Poročevalec Državnega zbora R Slovenije [Report of the Court of Audit to Parliament on the financing of Election Campaigns], October 2001.

[104] See Poročevalec Državnega Zbora Republike Slovenije [Report on the Work of the Court of Audit for 2001], March 2002, p. 52.

[105] "Angleški pacient" [The English patient], *Mladina,* 31 August 2001; "Denar za delavnice, ki se jih ne spomni nihče" [Money for the workshops that no-one remembers], *Delo,* 17 August 2001; "Spretno po nezakoniti poti" [Skillfully on the illegal path], *Mladina,* 27 August 2001. The illegal funding was discovered on the Internet; the donor Foundation posted the recipients and the amounts of donations on its homepage.

[106] One commentator described this as a "silence of solidarity"; in: "Molk solidarnosti," *Delo,* 18 August 2001.

[107] "Švicarska zveza" [Swiss connection], POP TV, 19 September 2001; interview with Borut Meško, journalist, POP TV, 19 February 2002.

carried this out by ordering video clips from a sister company of the agency in charge of the SPP's election campaign. LEK paid €107,800 for clips that were never provided and the money was spent on the SPP campaign.[108]

A recent scandal involving not donations but the use of State money to finance a party broke in 2000. Each parliamentary party receives money from the State budget to pay for an adviser and other office costs. In 1999, the People's Party parliamentary caucus paid a consulting company (Ivas) €22,500 from budget funds, and Ivas provided €6,750 for its election campaign.[109]

In general, political parties' annual reports show that many are in deficit, increasing the incentives for illegal financing and corruption.[110] According to the press, a number of companies that gave donations to governing parties were among the recipients of public procurement contracts.[111]

7. PUBLIC PROCUREMENT

The legal framework for public procurement is relatively advanced. However, a long tradition of overlapping public and private sectors provides the context for a situation in which oversight is weak and collusion both between bidders themselves and between bidders and contracting agencies may be widespread. Moreover, the efficacy of review of procurement procedures and appeal processes appears to be inadequate, and the European Commission has drawn attention explicitly to problems of conflict of interest in procurement. A few procurement scandals have broken in recent years at ministry level, while there is some evidence that procurement at local government level suffers from serious problems of corruption.

---

[108] Information provided by Ali Žerdin, deputy editor, *Mladina*.

[109] Information provided by Ali Žerdin, deputy editor, *Mladina*.

[110] "Večina strank v rdečih številkah" [Majority of parties in the red], *Delo*, 30 March 2001.

[111] "Prevladuje princip: ti meni, jaz tebi," [The principle "I to you, you to me" prevails], *Delo*, 11 April 2001; "Evropa brez meja" [A Europe without Frontiers], *Delo*, 18 August 2001.

7.1 Legislative framework

Public procurement is regulated by the Public Procurement Act (hereinafter PPA), which has been in force since April 2000.[112] Contracts with a value of over €36,000 for goods and services and €67,000 for construction works must be awarded by open tender.[113] For contracts with a lower value the procedure must be laid down in the internal regulations of the contracting authority.

The PPA lists a number of circumstances in which authorities may award contracts without a tender:

- when the supplier has an exclusive legal right to provide specific services;

- in cases where the supply is regulated with international agreements or the procedures are regulated by an international organisation;

- pursuant to a particular procedure laid down in an agreement on the stationing of troops;

- in case of natural catastrophes and emergencies;

- in case of a confidential procurement like the purchase of arms, military equipment and the like.[114]

Notices in connection with public procurement (over the values stated earlier) must be published in a standard form in the *Official Gazette*. Any individual that has or has had an interest in a specific public procurement procedure has the right to obtain data on a specific public procurement.[115]

No specific Code of Conduct of public procurement officers exists at the moment and is not under consideration. No official blacklisting of companies proved to have bribed in the public procurement process exists – not a single case has been proven in court so far. The Chamber of Commerce has drawn up a list of companies considered fit to bid for public contracts.

---

[112] Public Procurement Act (PPA), *Official Gazette* 39/2000. The PPA has been criticised as too rigid and even more strict in comparison to the EU recommendations. See e.g., "Urad, ki bo dal vetra birokraciji" [The Office that will put pressure on bureaucracy], *Delo,* 7 March 2001; "Za red, pa za zdravo pamet tudi"[For order, and common sense too], *Delo,* 27 March 2001.

[113] Act on the Execution of the Budget of the Republic of Slovenia for 2002 and 2003 (hereinafter AEBRS), *Official Gazette* 103/01, Article 14.

[114] PPA, Article 2. See also PPA, Articles 109 and 110.

[115] PPA, Article 6, paragraph 2.

The PPA contains only one direct provision on corruption, stating that,

> The contracting authority must reject a tender if the bidder who submitted it gives or is prepared to give to a current or a former employee of the contracting authority a gift in the form of cash or in any non-cash form whatsoever, an offer of employment or any other thing or favour the value of which could be expressed in money, as an attempt to influence an action or a decision or the course of the public procurement procedure.[116]

In such a case, the contracting authority must inform the bidder and the OPP of the rejection of the tender and the reasons for it in writing. Failure to do so is an administrative offence punishable by a fine of up to €4,500, while the "responsible person" on the side of the bidder is subject to a fine of up to €1,350.

The PPA also established the National Review Commission (see below) and the Office for Public Procurement (OPP). The main tasks of the OPP are to propose reforms of public procurement legislation, collect data on public procurement, report to the Government once a year, maintain a public list of legal entities that have used corruption in public procurement (in order to be put on the list corruption must be proven by a final court ruling) and to organise education on public procurement procedures.[117]

The present public procurement legislation does not contain any specific provisions on conflict of interest or asset monitoring for officials involved in procurement. The *2001 Regular Report* mentions public procurement specifically under a recommendation to pay more attention to conflict of interest (see Section 2.2).

7.2 Review and audit

Under the PPA, contracts made contrary to its provisions are legally null and void. Procedures for reviewing procurement decisions are laid down by the Review of Public Procurement Procedures Act of September 1999 (RPPPA).[118] A review claim may be submitted by an individual who has shown an interest in the awarding of a contract and has suffered or could have suffered damage due to the act of the contracting entity. Upon appeal, the contracting body must carry out a primary internal review within 20 days,

---

[116] PPA, Article 14.

[117] PPA, Article 129, and Odlok o ustanovitvi, nalogah in organizaciji Urada za javna naročila, *Official Gazette* 12/2001.

[118] Review of Public Procurement Procedures Act (RPPPA), *Official Gazette* 78/1999, 90/1999. Some EU experts opine that the RPPPA is better than in many countries of the EU. See "Zakon o javnih naročilih čisto zanič" [Public Procurement Act good for nothing], *Delo,* 28 March 2001.

including the participation of a special review expert to ensure impartiality.[119] However, up to July 2002 the participation of such experts had not taken place in practice.[120]

Upon rejection of a first appeal, the participant may appeal to the National Review Commission, which must suspend the procurement process until the appeal is decided. The Commission must decide all complaints within 15 days (or 20 days in justified cases). The Commission may either reject the complaint or partially or entirely annul the procurement procedure. The Commission must justify its decision and also give instructions on how to carry out the annulled part of a procedure. There is no appeal against decisions of the Commission, although damaged parties may sue the contracting authority for damages. Under the PPA, contracts made contrary to its provisions are legally null and void.

Of 900 first-level appeals filed in 2000, only 240 bidders decided to appeal further to the National Review Commission, despite the fact that the initial procurement decision was rarely changed. The reason for this is thought by analysts to be agreement or dealings between tendering authorities and bidders after initial appeals.[121] The National Review Commission received 242 claims for revision; in 114 cases the contract award procedures were partially or entirely annulled.[122] The vast majority of cases involved some other form of discrimination between bidders, while no appeals cited corruption directly.[123] The number of appeals rose to 306 in 2001. In 2001 the National Review Commission reported one important case of suspected corruption to the State Prosecutor.[124]

The Slovenian Chamber of Commerce believes that the authorities often focus on small tenders of little importance, and that the thresholds for procurement rules should be raised in order to focus the regulator on large tenders.[125]

---

[119] RPPPA, Articles 14–15.

[120] OSI Roundtable Discussion, Ljubljana, 19 February 2002.

[121] See I. Šoltes, "Revizijski postopki in javna naročila (zakonodajni okvir)" [Review Procedures and Public Procurement – the Legal Framework], paper presented at the colloquium "Korupcija kot realnost današnjega časa," Gotenica, May 2001, in: *Korupcija kot realnost današnjega časa*, conference proceedings, p. 103.

[122] *Letno poročilo o delu državne revizijske komisije v letu 2000* [2000 Annual Report on the Activities of the National Review Commission], Ljubljana, March 2001.

[123] *Letno poročilo*, p. 19.

[124] *Letno poročilo o delu državne revizijske komisije za leto 2001* [2001 Annual Report on the Activities of the National Review Commission], March 2002, p. 167.

[125] OSI Roundtable Discussion, Ljubljana, 19 February 2002.

The GRECO assessment of Slovenia recommended that the National Review Commission look more thoroughly behind the formal irregularities detected, and levelled significant criticism at the Commission, noting that,

> The members of this Commission did not seem fully aware that irregularities in tendering procedures could sometimes be the visible part of hidden, underlying corrupt practices. The Commission should therefore be prepared to verify irregularities also from this angle and to report to the Police and/or the…Public Prosecutor…any suspicion of corruption.[126]

Proposed amendments to the PPA that were under discussion in mid-2002 would explicitly codify the independence of members of the National Review Commission and explicitly authorise the Office for Public Procurement to review procurements in certain cases where the public interest may be harmed. The proposed changes would also authorise the Commission to require a report from contracting authorities on implementation of its findings and instructions, and the Commission would report non-compliance to the superior body or the Government.

7.3 Corruption

Media reporting on public money being wasted through public procurement procedures is common, although specific accusations of corruption are rarely made due to lack of clear evidence. In 2000, the Ministry of Economy avoided a public tender to purchase computer equipment by splitting the purchase into nine separate contracts, and paid much higher prices than would have emerged from an open tender.[127] An internal review carried out under a new Minister established that the PPA had been violated, the contracts were declared void and in early 2002, the Ministry was attempting to return the equipment and obtain its money back.[128] In another tender in 2001, the Ministry of Education allegedly violated the PPA in signing a contract for computer software at far above market prices.[129] In another case that received considerable attention, the Government purchased a passenger aircraft from a European manufacturer that had been involved in a major corruption scandal in the

---

[126] GRECO, *Evaluation Report,* First round, 15 December 2000, p. 15.

[127] "Kraljestvo za računalnik"[Kingdom for the Computer], *Mladina,* 26 March 2001. For example, the Ministry purchased a lap-top for €14,083.

[128] "Nabava računalniške opreme v nasprotju z zakonom" [Computer equipment purchases against the law], *Delo,* 29 March 2001.

[129] "Davkoplačevalski denar z lopato skozi okno" [Taxpayers' money thrown out the window], *Delo,* 28 March 2001.

1990's; the Government avoided normal tender provisions by classifying the purchase as a confidential procurement.[130]

Anecdotal evidence suggests that the other main problem area in procurement besides contracts for the purchase of computer equipment is construction contracts. According to journalists, malpractice in public procurement has become more sophisticated in recent years: instead of violating tender requirements blatantly (for example by failing to hold tenders), corruption centres on preparation of tender documentation in such a way as to suit a chosen contractor.

8. PUBLIC SERVICES

Corruption in the allocation of public services does not appear to be a major problem, although there have been some indications to the contrary, for example in healthcare. A possible exception is tax collection, where officials are regarded as highly exposed to bribery, and the size of the grey economy indicates that corruption may be a more serious problem than official data suggest. Licensing regulation may suffer from some problems of corruption, especially in the allocation of zoning and construction permits.

8.1 Police

The available evidence indicates that the integrity of Slovenia's 6,500-strong police force is relatively high. A 1999 public opinion survey found levels of trust in the police to be slightly lower than the Western Europe average, but higher than trust in the army, Church, trade unions, or Parliament.[131] In 1999, 72 formal indictments were made against police officers, among them three for bribery and 30 for corruption-related offences (abuse of official data, abuse of powers and rights).[132] An internal analysis carried out in 1999 by the Office for Complaints and Internal Protection found that most police officers investigated for corruption were young and from the border or traffic police.

No specific strategy for preventing corruption exists within the police. However, any police officer found to be responsible for "severe or minor violations of his professional

---

[130] OSI Rountable Discussion, Ljubljana, 19 February 2002. See also "Izjema je lahko skoraj vse" [Almost everything can be an exception], *Delo,* 19 April 2002.

[131] SJM 99/3; cited in: *Human Development Report Slovenia 2000–2001,* p. 55.

[132] GRECO, *Evaluation Report,* 15 December 2000, p. 7.

duties and responsibilities" can be subject to disciplinary measures. Severe violations include accepting presents or other benefits that influence the conduct of policeman's duty, and any action bearing the characteristics of a premeditated criminal offence.[133] Suspicion of such violations may be grounds for temporary suspension, and for termination of employment if the officer is indeed found responsible. Conviction for a criminal offence results in termination of employment. Finally, a police officer is financially liable for any damage he causes to the police or other individuals by committing a corruption offence.[134]

Complaints from citizens relating to police procedure are processed by a special Bureau for Complaints and Internal Protection at the Ministry of Interior. The Bureau is directly responsible to the Director-General of the Police and has regional branches, which, *inter alia,* are responsible for investigating cases of suspected or alleged corruption. In 1998, Bureau inspectors uncovered 80 percent of all irregularities found within the police. The level of independence of the Bureau is hard to estimate, and some experts have suggested reforms to strengthen its organisational independence.[135]

8.2 Customs

According to the available official evidence, the incidence of corruption among Slovenia's 2,300 customs officials is marginal, with only one or two cases a year of disciplinary proceedings for corruption in 1999–2000, of five to eight disciplinary proceedings in total. There is no survey evidence available on corruption among customs officials. Since customs is a highly vulnerable area with respect to corruption, these statistics may be a reflection of a lack of functioning oversight. However, the European Commission has not mentioned corruption specifically in the customs administration.

The customs administration includes internal control units at each of the nine regional directorates (employing around 50-60 officers in total), and a special inspection unit at the General Customs Directorate (120-member staff). Accepting or requesting/extorting bribes is a disciplinary offence, and if grounded suspicion of such an offence arises,

---

[133] Police Act (PA), *Official Gazette* 49/98, 66/98, 93/01, Article 99.

[134] Police Act, Article 100, paragraph 1.

[135] See Anžič, Sotlar, "Internal Policing: Possibilities and Opportunities of a Struggle against Corruption," in: Open Society Institute, *Corruption in Central Eastern Europe at the Turn of the Millenium – A Collection of Essays,* Open Society Institute Slovenia, Ljubljana 1999, pp. 19–22; A. Anžič, "Notranji nadzor v policiji – dileme in perspektive" [Internal policing – Dilemmas and Perspectives], in: *Zbornik strokovno znanstvenih razprav Višje šole za notranje zadeve v Ljubljani,* December 1992, pp. 35–42.

disciplinary proceedings must be initiated. If proven (the disciplinary procedure is independent of the criminal procedure), corruption is a serious violation of working responsibilities leading to obligatory termination of employment. Citizens may file complaints against the customs administration through a telephone hotline.

A Code of Conduct of Customs Officers introduced in 2000 declares that customs officials should avoid accepting gifts, and moral sanctions are decided by a three-member Ethical Arbitration Panel at the General Customs Directorate. In addition, a newly established strategy for the customs service stresses the importance of corruption prevention.

8.3 Tax collection

Although the tax administration includes conflict of interest rules, a Code of Honour in addition to the Code of Conduct of Public Officials, an Internal Control Unit, and a special Investigation Office (since 2001), disciplinary mechanisms appear to be weak and there are reasons for suspecting corruption might be an important problem. From 1998 to 2000, only 14 disciplinary proceedings took place, which in three cases were reported to the police. Although none of the violations were defined as corruption, most of the allegations were defined as abuse of office or similar transgressions.

According to the GRECO *Evaluation Report* of 2000, "[T]ax officials are highly exposed to bribery in Slovenia but there are no particular means in place to prevent or detect acts of corruption in the tax administration."[136] GRECO recommended additional training for tax officials in particular.

In addition, a startling characteristic of the Slovenian economy is the apparent size of the grey economy, which gives further reason to suspect that corruption is more prevalent than official data suggest. According to *The World Competitiveness Yearbook,* Slovenia was ranked 48th out of 49 countries in terms of prevalence of the grey economy (the higher position the smaller the grey economy),[137] and 29th out of 49 states on the indicator "avoidance of taxes."[138] The Government has recently introduced measures to reduce the grey economy, including the introduction of value-added tax and stricter labour inspection control.

---

[136] GRECO, *Evaluation Report,* p. 10.

[137] *The World Competitiveness Yearbook 1999; The World Competitiveness Yearbook 2000; The World Competitiveness Yearbook 2001,* IMD, Lausanne 1999, 2000, 2001.

[138] *The World Competitiveness Yearbook 1999, 2000, 2001.* See also "Konkurencnost držav – Korupcija" [The competitiveness of states – Corruption], *Ekonomsko ogledalo* 1/2000, <http://www.sigov.si/zmar/arhiv/>, (last accessed 28 August 2002).

8.4 Health

According to a recent corruption victimisation survey commissioned by the Office for the Prevention of Corruption, citizens experience corruption most frequently in the healthcare system.[139] The GRECO *Evaluation Report* reported that Slovenian authorities told its evaluation team that medical care was the area most exposed to corruption (along with public procurement).[140]

Cases of corruption have been reported by the media: a doctor was convicted in 2001 for accepting a €1,960 bribe to speed up a surgery (the case was on appeal in early 2002),[141] and another was convicted for demanding a €5,880 bribe to grant a patient disabled status.[142] According to press reports another doctor was recently sentenced to a year's imprisonment and forbidden from practising for two years for demanding a €363 bribe to perform a Caesarean section.[143]

Doctors are subject to passive bribery provisions. The Act on Medicine prohibits certain methods of advertising by pharmaceutical companies, the aim being to prevent more-or-less corrupt "special incentives" being offered by pharmaceutical companies to doctors to purchase their medicine.[144] This provision was introduced shortly after an affair in 1999 in which a large pharmaceutical company organised and financed a trip to Africa for a number of doctors and their spouses.[145] In August 2001, the press reported another similar case.[146]

The medical profession regulates itself. The Medical Chamber of Slovenia imposes a Code of Medical Deontology (i.e., ethics),[147] and the ethical tribunal of the Medical Chamber of Slovenia deals with violations of the Code and other irregularities occurring within the medical service.[148] Cases of corruption are dealt with by the Tribunal only

---

[139] "Najbolj smrdi v zdravstvu" [Health care stinks the worst], *Delo*, 25 July 2002.

[140] GRECO, *Evaluation Report*, p. 3.

[141] "Črna packa na beli zdravniški halji" [Black lap on the white doctor's gown], *Delo*, 8 May 2001.

[142] "Izsiljeval pacienta" [Patient extorted], *Delo*, 24 September 1998; "Namesto mark zapor" [Prison instead of German Marks], *Delo*, 6 July 2001.

[143] "V.Č. leto zapora" [V.Č. sentenced to one year imprisonment], *Delo*, 3 July 2002.

[144] Act on Medicine and Medical Equipment (AMME), *Official Gazette* 101/1999, 70/2000.

[145] "Vroči kenijski spomini" [Hot memories from Kenya], *Dnevnik*, 19 March 1999.

[146] "Kdo je njihov patron?" [Who is their patron?], *Delo*, 23 August 2001.

[147] Kodeks medicinske deontologije Slovenije [Codex of Slovenian Medical Deontology], ISIS, Ljubljana, May 2000, pp. 47–51, *Official Gazette* 64/1996, 22/1998, 113/2000.

[148] The Statute of the Medical Chamber of Slovenia (SMCS), *Official Gazette* 64/1996, 22/1998, 113/2000.

after final conviction by a regular court. Acceptance of a bribe is defined as a major transgression for, which possible sanctions include revocation of a doctor's license.

8.5 Education

The integrity of the public education system is generally high, and evidence of corruption is extremely rare. However, isolated cases have been reported. A high-profile case in 1998 involved a secondary school student whose father (a well-known Slovenian manager) allegedly "arranged" through the intervention of a senior civil servant that he could take the school-leaving exam despite not being legally eligible.[149] The case became one of the grounds for an unsuccessful attempt to initiate a vote of confidence in the Minister of Education. Anecdotal evidence suggests that students and parents sometimes use connections, trading in influence and bribes in order to pass exams, for which oral exams provide especially ample opportunities.[150]

8.6 Licensing and regulation

No research exists on corruption in the area of licensing or inspection activities and the media generally has not reported any corruption. An exception is a recent case involving four private driving school instructors and four members of a driving exam commission, in which bribes of €588–980 were allegedly paid by candidates to pass the written or practical exam (around €1,960 for both exams). Criminal proceedings were in progress in early 2002.[151]

Rules governing licensing procedures depend upon the legislation that regulates the specific area (for example, concessions for fishing, logging, allocation of radio frequencies, and so on). Many inspection bodies complain of being understaffed, and often the laws and regulations they are supposed to supervise contain loopholes or weak sanctions for violation. Many cases arising from inspection findings fall under the statute of limitations due to delays at the Courts of Administrative Offences.

---

[149] See, e.g., "Korupcija v vrhu slovenskega šolstva?" [Corruption at the top of Slovenian education?], *Dnevnik,* 7 July 1998.

[150] But the School Inspectors have not encountered any cases of corruption; see "Največ kršitev pri ocenjevanju – pogovor z glavnim šolskim inšpektorjem" [Most violations found in grading – discussion with main school inspector], *Dnevnik,* 28 May 2001.

[151] "Mimo znakov in čez polno črto do vozniškega izpita" [By-passing the traffic signs and across the full line to a driving licence], *Večer,* 2 February 2001.

As described in Section 3.6, serious concerns are justified by practices in the allocation of zoning and construction permits, with what appears at least in certain cases to be a system of bribery in allocation, encouraged by flagrant conflicts of interest, disinterest from prosecutors and facilitated by pressure on the media not to publicise information on such practices.

9. ROLE OF THE MEDIA

Freedom of speech is not threatened under Slovenian law. However, provisions on access to information do not appear to be effective. Broadcasting regulation appears to be relatively free from direct political interference, although there is evidence that public television is restricted from playing an effective watchdog role. Direct corruption of journalists does not appear to be a serious problem, although phenomena such as hidden advertising are common. A more serious barrier to effective media investigation activities may be the close personal connections between media companies, other powerful private companies and the Slovenian banks. A recent (unsolved) case of violent intimidation against an investigative journalist has raised concerns about the ability of Slovenian journalists to investigate corruption without risk of reprisal.

9.1 Freedom of speech

Freedom of expression and of the press are enshrined in the Constitution. The Constitution also guarantees the right to correction and of reply, and the general right of access to information of a public nature.[152] Freedom of the press may only be restricted if the particular nature of another right requires it or in exceptional cases such as war or a state of emergency. These rights are guaranteed in practice and there are no extraordinary restrictions on the media's freedom.

Journalists are subject to normal legal provisions on offences such as libel, slander, insult and defamation. The number of proceedings of this type against journalists has increased, although there are no known cases connected with corruption. Under the present Media Act, journalists are not obliged to disclose the source of their information, unless it is demanded by specific provisions of the criminal law.

---

[152] Constitution of the Republic of Slovenia, Article 40,39, paragraph 2. On the interesting Slovenian peculiarity of the "right to reply in the public interest," see M. Krivić, S. Zatler, *Freedom of the Press and Personal Rights: Right of Correction and Reply in Slovene Legislation,* Open Society Institute Slovenia, Ljubljana 2000.

9.2 Access to information

Under the Media Act,[153] all State bodies, local government bodies, public enterprises, public institutions (*javni zavodi*) and individuals performing public functions must provide "timely, complete and true" information to the media on issues from their area of work which can be made public through the media.[154] The only exceptions are State, military, official or commercial secrets, information whose disclosure would violate the confidentiality of personal data according to the Act on Protection of Personal Data[155] and information whose disclosure would be detrimental to court or pre-trial criminal proceedings.[156] Information is free of charge, and authorities can only charge for the actual cost of copies. Public bodies that refuse to provide information must give reasons in writing by the end of the following working day.

In practice, Slovenian public authorities are not accustomed to providing information under the provisions of the law. Journalists say that in many cases ministries refuse to provide information by official channels, even though they will often provide information off the record.[157]

In July 2001, the Slovenian Association of Journalists expressed concern about what they perceived as legislative trends in the area of provision of information, and in particular Parliamentary Standing Orders that have reduced the level of required publicity of the work of the State administration and other State institutions.[158]

A proposed new act on access to public information was under discussion in Parliament in mid-2002, aimed at uniformly regulating access to information held by the State and public authorities.

---

[153] Media Act , *Official Gazette* 35/2001.

[154] Media Act, Article 45. Generally on the legislative history and "purpose" of the new law, see S. B. Hrvatin, "Kdo potrebuje medijski zakon?" [Who needs the Media Act?], *Pravna praksa* 19/2001, enclosure, p. I.

[155] Act on the Protection of Personal Data (APPD), *Official Gazette* 59/1999.

[156] Even such information may not be denied if its publication would prevent a severe criminal offence or prevent imminent danger to life or property.

[157] A specific example of this is the Ministry of Economy's refusal to provide information on State subsidies to the weekly *Mladina,* although officials provided the information off the record.

[158] See "Država omejuje dostop do informacij" [State restricts access to information], *Delo,* 6 July 2001.

9.3 Broadcasting regulation

Public radio and television are provided by Radio-Television Slovenia. Under the Act on Radio-Television Slovenia, public broadcasting is regulated by the Council of Radio Television. The Council has 25 members, five of which are appointed by the Parliament, three elected by employees of Radio-Television and the rest distributed among a wide range of civil society groups and organisations. The mandate of the Council's members is four years and they can be re-elected. Their independence from the influence of political parties is hard to assess. The Council elects the director, whose appointment is confirmed only with the consent of the Parliament. There is no direct evidence of political influence on the public media, although journalists say it is very difficult to get a corruption-related programme onto public TV.[159]

The central licensing authority for radio and television programmes in general is the Slovenian Broadcasting Council. The Council consists of seven experts appointed by the Parliament. Candidates can be proposed by the two Slovenian Universities, the Association of Artists, the Slovenian Business Chamber and the Slovenian Association of Journalists. The Council is designed to be completely independent from the Government and private broadcasting companies and so far has maintained its independence.

9.4 Corruption

Corruption among journalists may also be a problem. Although the Code of Ethical Conduct of Slovenian Journalists (adopted in 1991) explicitly prohibits accepting bribes or "publishing information to the benefit of an external client," there are reports that various kinds of bribery do occur.[160] The Court of Honour of the Slovenian Association of Journalists has not dealt with any cases of alleged corruption.

The Code of Conduct also requires that PR statements and advertisements be clearly distinguished from editorial content. In practice, however, "hidden advertising" is a widespread reality.[161] Moreover, the cases mentioned in Section 3.6 indicate that powerful economic interests in a small country are in a relatively strong position to influence the content of articles and programmes through advertising pressure.

---

[159] Interview with Borut Meško, journalist, POP TV, 19 February 2002.

[160] "Podkupljivi novinarji" [Corrupt journalists], *Delo,* 27 December 2000; D. Kos, *Situation in the Field of Corruption in the Republic of Slovenia,* report to the OECD, Ljubljana, Spring 2001, pp. 36–37; "Kupljeni novinarji" [Bought journalists], *Delo,* 31 December 2001.

[161] B. Bizjak, "So novinarji podkupljivi?" [Can journalists be bought?], *Medijska preža,* no. 10, winter 2001, pp. 8–10; "Bodi novinar ali piarovec, ne moreš biti oboje" [Be either a journalist or a PR person – you cannot be both], *Delo,* 22 December 2001.

An equally serious problem may be raised by the network of interconnections between the boards of media companies, banks and other important private companies. For example, the statutory organs of two important dailies, *Delo* and *Večer*, are linked by personal connections to the boards of at least of one major bank and a number of other companies. Although there is no systematic evidence of the impact of this phenomenon on media activity, the case of Miro Petek offers a possible example.

9.5 Media and corruption

In the past three years there have been various reports on corruption in the media. The most significant was the recent case of a State Secretary charged with corruption (see Section 3.6) and a recent case in which a State Prosecutor was accused of bribery. However, these cases were not uncovered by the media, which only disseminated information provided by the police.

There have been no known cases of reprisals or criminal libel prosecutions for media exposés of corruption in the last two years. However, one recent case raises serious concerns about the freedom of journalists to investigate corruption without risk of reprisal. Miro Petek, a local reporter at regional daily *Večer*, was beaten almost to death in 2001 after writing a number of articles on corruption in the region. The articles concerned the purchase by an MP of land from a local company at a fraction of market value, the secret sale under market value to a foreign company of assets in a steelworks being restructured with Government assistance, suspicious loans by a Nova Kreditna banka Maribor (a State-owned bank) to a local businessman on less-than-economic criteria, and suspected money laundering at the same bank.[162] In early 2002, the case was still under police investigation, and a parliamentary commission was also investigating.

---

[162] According to Mr. Petek, after the articles concerning the bank were published, editors at the *Večer* newspaper were removed. The boards of Nova Kredina banka Maribor and *Večer* are personally connected.

10. RECOMMENDATIONS

The following recommendations have been highlighted as particularly important to Slovenia. For additional recommendations applicable to candidate States generally, please see Part 5 of the Overview report.

1. Sponsor detailed research on corruption in Slovenia, with particular emphasis on the role of the State in the economy and the effect of intertwining political, business and personal connections.

2. Promote civil society involvement in anti-corruption efforts as part of a broader public awareness campaign.